HANDBOOK OF PERCEPTION

Volume X

Perceptual Ecology

This is Volume X of

HANDBOOK OF PERCEPTION

EDITORS: *Edward C. Carterette and Morton P. Friedman*

Contents of the other books in this series appear at the end of this volume.

HANDBOOK OF PERCEPTION

VOLUME X

Perceptual Ecology

EDITED BY

Edward C. Carterette and Morton P. Friedman

Department of Psychology
University of California
Los Angeles, California

ACADEMIC PRESS   New York San Francisco London   1978

A Subsidiary of Harcourt Brace Jovanovich, Publishers

ACADEMIC PRESS, INC.
111 Fifth Avenue, New York, New York 10003

United Kingdom Edition published by
ACADEMIC PRESS, INC. (LONDON) LTD.
24/28 Oval Road, London NW1 7DX

Library of Congress Cataloging in Publication Data
Main entry under title:

Perceptual ecology.

(Handbook of perception ; v. 10)
Includes bibliographies and index.
1. Perception. 2. Environmental psychology.
I. Carterette, Edward C. II. Friedman, Morton P.
[DNLM: 1. Perception. 2. Ecology. WL700 H234 v. 10]
BF311.P3625   153.7   78–11805
ISBN 0–12–161910–9 (v. 10)

CONTENTS

PART II.   SENSORY DISORDERS AND
PROSTHETICS

Chapter 3.   Perception by the Deaf

Harry W. Hoemann

Chapter 4.   Perception by the Blind

David H. Warren

Chapter 5.   Prosthetics of Perceptual Systems

*John M. Kennedy, Daniel Klein,
and Lochlan E. Magee*

PART III.   AESTHETICS

Chapter 6.   Aesthetic Theories

Irvin L. Child

Chapter 11. The Perception of Motion Pictures

Julian Hochberg and Virginia Brooks

PART V.   ODOR AND TASTE

Chapter 12. Odors in the Environment: Hedonics, Perfumery, and Odor Abatement

Howard R. Moskowitz

Chapter 13. Food and Food Technology: Food Habits, Gastronomy, Flavors, and Sensory Evaluation

Howard R. Moskowitz

PART VI.   PARAPSYCHOLOGY

Chapter 14. Parapsychology

Edward Girden

CONTENTS

LIST OF CONTRIBUTORS

Numbers in parentheses indicate the pages on which the authors' contributions begin.

VIRGINIA BROOKS (259), Department of Psychology, Columbia University, New York, New York 10027

IRVIN L. CHILD (111), Department of Psychology, Yale University, New Haven, Connecticut 06520

DIANA DEUTSCH (191), Department of Psychology, University of California, San Diego, La Jolla, California 92093

EDWARD GIRDEN (385), Department of Psychology, Florida International University, Miami, Florida 33199

JULIAN HOCHBERG (225, 259), Department of Psychology, Columbia University, New York, New York 10027

HARRY W. HOEMANN (43), Department of Psychology, Bowling Green State University, Bowling Green, Ohio 43403

KRISTINA HOOPER (155), Department of Psychology, University of California, Santa Cruz, Santa Cruz, California 95064

JOHN M. KENNEDY (91), Department of Psychology, Scarborough College, University of Toronto, Ontario, Canada M1C 1A4

DANIEL KLEIN (91), Department of Psychology, Scarborough College, University of Toronto, Ontario, Canada M1C 1A4

LOCHLAN E. MAGEE (91), Department of Psychology, Scarborough College, University of Toronto, Ontario, Canada M1C 1A4

HOWARD R. MOSKOWITZ (307, 349), MPi Sensory Testing Division, MPi Marketing Research, Inc., New York, New York 10021

ANNE D. PICK (19), Institute of Child Development, University of Minnesota, Minneapolis, Minnesota 55455

HERBERT L. PICK, JR. (19), Institute of Child Development, University of Minnesota, Minneapolis, Minnesota 55455

GEORGE STINY (133), Design Discipline, The Open University, Milton Keynes, England

DAVID H. WARREN (65), Department of Psychology, University of California, Riverside, Riverside, California 92521

RIK WARREN (3), Department of Psychology, State University College at Buffalo, Buffalo, New York 14222

FOREWORD

The problem of perception is one of understanding the way in which the organism transforms, organizes, and structures information arising from the world in sense data or memory. With this definition of perception in mind, the aims of this treatise are to bring together essential aspects of the very large, diverse, and widely scattered literature on human perception and to give a précis of the state of knowledge in every area of perception. It is aimed at the psychologist in particular and at the natural scientist in general. A given topic is covered in a comprehensive survey in which fundamental facts and concepts are presented and important leads to journals and monographs of the specialized literature are provided. Perception is considered in its broadest sense. Therefore, the work will treat a wide range of experimental and theoretical work.

This ten-volume treatise is divided into two sections. Section One deals with the fundamentals of perceptual systems. It is comprised of six volumes covering (1) historical and philosophical roots of perception, (2) psychophysical judgment and measurement, (3) the biology of perceptual systems, (4) hearing, (5) seeing, and (6) which is divided into two books (A) tasting and smelling and (B) feeling and hurting.

Section Two, comprising four volumes, covers the perceiving organism, taking up the wider view and generally ignoring specialty boundaries. The major areas include (7) language and speech, (8) perceptual coding of space, time, and objects, including sensory memory systems and the relations between verbal and perceptual codes, (9) perceptual processing mechanisms, such as attention, search, selection, pattern recognition, and perceptual learning, (10) perceptual ecology, which considers the perceiving organism in cultural context, and so includes aesthetics, art, music, architecture, cinema, gastronomy, perfumery, and the special perceptual worlds of the blind and of the deaf.

The "Handbook of Perception" should serve as a basic source and reference work for all in the arts of sciences, indeed for all who are interested in human perception.

EDWARD C. CARTERETTE
MORTON P. FRIEDMAN

PREFACE

Perceptual Ecology means to convey the idea that Volume X deals with perceptual aspects of the study of interaction of persons with their environment. The lead chapter on the ecological nature of perceptual systems takes as an axiom: *We perceive so that we may act.* But getting and using information implies activity. Therefore: *We act so that we may perceive.* With a Gibsonian impetus it is argued by Rik Warren in Chapter 1, *The Ecological Nature of Perceptual Systems*, that an ecological approach to the perceptual systems, one not restricted to the laboratory, broadens the domain of perception and seeks a unified theory of perception and action. That there are nontrivial problems of theory and method in going beyond the laboratory is made clear by Pick and Pick's *Culture and Perception* (Chapter 2). If cultural differences in perception can be attributed to physiological or anatomical differences among people, they may afford insights for studying perceptual mechanisms. Cultural differences arising from experience are "natural experiments demonstrating the flexibility of perception." Perception of color may fit the first category, speech the second. Can the reader categorize the other areas considered: pictures, visual illusions, constancies, and spatial orientation?

Three chapters are devoted to impaired perception and action. Paradoxically, perceptual studies of the deaf are rare, as Hoemann shows in Chapter 3, *Perception by the Deaf*. Deficiency in English contrasts markedly with fluency in ASL (American Sign Language) acquired spontaneously by the deaf, which suggests that studying the acquisition of ASL will illuminate related perceptual systems. But, as for studies of the perceptual abilities of the blind, we are told by D. H. Warren (Chapter 4) that the research literature "is so varied as to almost defy organization and inclusion in a single chapter." The selective review of Chapter 4, *Perception by the Blind*, singles out audition, touch, space perception, and (very briefly) illusions. We are reminded that perceptual research on the blind is hampered by sampling limitations and by problems of method (being blind and being blindfolded are not the same). While offering some basic information about sensory aids, Kennedy, Klein, and Magee in their brief overview (Chapter 5) of *Prosthetics of Perceptual Systems* aim at outlining intellectual principles necessary for understanding these sensory aids.

A set of six chapters on aesthetic forms begins with Irvin L. Child's discussion of the central problem of *Aesthetic Theories* (Chapter 6), namely: *Why do people enjoy or seem to enjoy the perceptual experience itself?* Not perception of art but hedonic value of the perceiver's experience and acts is addressed in a threefold classification of aesthetic theories. A general theory of art must go beyond response to art and also deal with its creation. In *Generating and Measuring Aesthetic Forms* (Chapter 7) Stiny attempts both by means of formal, algorithmic procedures. It is intensely interesting to see how far an algorithmic approach succeeds in generating, describing, evaluating, and criticizing aesthetic objects.

"And, inquiring more deeply, he discovered that in truth it was not simply a matter of form expressing function, but the vital idea was this: That the function *created* or organized its form," said Louis H. Sullivan, in his *Autobiography of an Idea.* Chapter 8, *Perceptual Aspects of Architecture*, by Kristina Hooper takes a line akin to Sullivan's in saying that architecture follows perception and perception follows architecture, thus what is livable comes from their effective interaction.

Musical Acoustics in Volume IV of this *Handbook* is generally complementary to Diana Deutsch's present *The Psychology of Music* (Chapter 9) which deals with the more strictly perceptual aspects of music. A rich area for the study of recognition, attention, memory, and abstract cognition (and an area that is often free of problems of verbal codes), work in musical perception has been enormously enhanced by the confluence of ideas from information processing, psychoacoustics, and computing.

One of the most celebrated fields of visual perception is art in pure and applied form. The task of Hochberg in Chapter 10, *Art and Perception*, is dual: (*a*) to bring up-to-date the nature of perceptual theory as it is important to an understanding of pictorial and nonpictorial art; and (*b*) to consider how perceptual theory is affected by what we learn about art. Of all the art forms the cinema surely has the greatest potential. And cinema uses more of the established principles of perception and sets more challenges to perceptual theory than any other art form. In Chapter 11 it is said that

> An understanding of the processes that initiate and sustain the succession of glimpses by which we sample the world, and the mechanisms by which we integrate the informative content of such sequences, is fundamental to any general theory of perceptual organization and attention.

Julian Hochberg and Virginia Brooks' *The Perception of Motion Pictures*

(Chapter 11) is an important, major attempt to integrate perceptual and cinematic mechanisms.

Olfactory hedonics play an important role in the two primary areas surveyed by Moskowitz in Chapter 12, perfumery and the assessment and abatement of noxious odors. The two are related almost as thesis and antithesis: We blend fragrant chemicals in order to please; we seek to destroy or mask noxious odors. Moskowitz points out in *Food and Food Technology: Food Habits, Gastronomy, Flavors, and Sensory Evaluation* (Chapter 13) that the main role of psychology in the study of food habits, gastronomy, flavors, and sensory evaluation of foods has been as a resource science that offered procedures to other experimenters such as chemists, quartermasters and connoisseurs. But surely it is astonishing that psychologists have been so little involved with indispensable food and its basic ecological, ethnic, economic, dietary, and acceptance problems?

Perceptual psychologists are often asked about psychic research and the validity of its reported findings. Some useful and interesting answers are given by Chapter 14, *Parapsychology*. There Girden reviews the experimental evidence on telepathy, clairvoyance, precognition, and psychokinesis. The aim is to assess the status of parapsychology and show why it is paradoxy, outside of accepted opinion, after some 100 years of psychic research.

Financial support has come, in part, from the National Institute of Mental Health (Grant MH-07809), The Ford Motor Company, and The University of California.

Editors of Academic Press both in New York and in San Francisco have been extremely helpful in smoothing our way.

Part I

Introduction

Chapter 1

THE ECOLOGICAL NATURE OF PERCEPTUAL SYSTEMS*

RIK WARREN

> *We regard the objects that environ us in proportion as they are adapted to benefit or injure our own bodies. . . . And for this end the visive sense seems to have been bestowed on animals, to wit, that . . . they may be able to foresee . . . the damage or benefit which is like to ensue upon the application of their own bodies to this or that body which is at a distance.*
>
> —BERKELEY, 1709, SEC. 59

I. WHY PERCEPTION?

What is the purpose of perceptual ability? Why can some forms of life perceive and others not? Why do perceptual system characteristics and capabilities differ from species to species?

* Preparation of this chapter was supported, in part, by grants to the University of Minnesota, Center for Research in Human Learning, from the National Science Foundation BMS72-02353 A03, The National Institute of Child Health and Human Development (HD-01136), and the Graduate School of the University of Minnesota.

A plant needs no eyes or ears. Because it is rooted, a plant on the edge of a cliff is not in danger. However, because it is rooted, a plant being approached by a hungry cow is very much in danger but can do nothing. Tropisms excluded, plants can neither approach nor avoid.

By contrast, animals are manipulators and exploiters of the environment. They are ever seeking, ever avoiding, ever exploring, ever moving to and from cliffs, succulent plants, prey, predators, and mates. The environment affords both sustenance and danger to all life, but for organisms capable of locomotion, the possibilities and varieties of dangers and comforts increase. These potential damages and benefits of the environment must be foreseen, and it is for this reason that animals are endowed with perceptual ability, or so argued Berkeley (1709). I agree, but, foreseeing damages and benefits, that is, detecting the affordances of the environment, is of little value unless the animal can approach or avoid them. *We perceive so that we may act.*

The task of the perceptual systems, then, is the obtaining of useful information about the environment, as opposed to simply responding to energy (Gibson, 1966). In this sense, the perceptual systems are environmentally or ecologically oriented. Thus, we may gain a better appreciation of the ecological nature of perceptual systems in general by studying those aspects of the environment to which they are adapted and directed. A perceptual system—and the whole animal—takes its definition from the environment. Thus, it is reasonable to start a study of the perceptual systems with an analysis of the environment: What is there to be perceived?

Il. WHAT IS THERE TO BE PERCEIVED?

A. Toward an Ecological Theory of Perceivables

If the purpose of perception is to guide action and enable survival, what must an animal perceive of its environment? To be able to exploit and manipulate the environment, the animal must know where it is in its environment and what it needs to approach and avoid. Successful approach and avoidance depend upon the animal's being able to perceive and guide its own displacements, or *egomotion,* which in turn is dependent upon the animal's being able to perceive the *layout* of the environment. Obstacles must be detected and negotiated, but so also must openings and safe paths. The impending *event* of violent collision with a rival must be differentiated from the event of gentle contact with a mate or offspring. Round red objects must be differentiated from branches. That an apple is red or green is not important, what matters is that the *affordance* of edibility be perceived. To survive, the animal must perceive the ripe from the unripe, the edible from the inedible.

The concepts of environment layout, events, egomotion, and affordances show promise for advancing an ecologically motivated theory of perception. But these concepts still need to be clearly defined and examined. Gibson (1966, in press) offers a first attempt at a detailed theory of the environment and its affordances. Such a theory of what there is to be perceived is not itself a theory of perception, but rather a propaedeutic for a theory of perception and action.

A theory of the environment and its affordances would permit us to make an inventory of "perceivables" based on a consideration of "ecologically valid" relations between the animal and its environment. One value of such an inventory would be that particular perceptual problems could be studied and assessed within a unified and ecologically justified framework.

Historically, the analysis of perceivables has all but been ignored. The classical list of, for example, size, distance, form, color, and motion perception is often presented without analysis or justification. As such, the classical list is a very arbitrary scheme around which to organize perceptual phenomena and problems. How are various perceptual phenomena to be evaluated for significance? What would significance refer to?

Besides arbitrarily partitioning the domain of perception, nonecological theories also tend to arbitrarily restrict the size of the domain of perception. Interesting and ecologically relevant but hard problems such as affordances are sloughed off as being the concern of the so-called higher mental processes. The criteria by which a phenomenon is considered perceptual or cognitive are, however, never made wholly clear.

Closely related to the question of the inclusiveness of perception is the question of the directness–indirectness of perception. Ecologically motivated theorists generally conceive perception as being direct—but see Shaw and Bransford (1977) and Section V for a discussion of the meaning of *direct*.

I would like now to illustrate the ecological orientation of the perceptual systems with a few selected perceivables. The selections are only intended to be a sampler and an introduction, since much theoretical and empirical work still needs to be done. The visual system dominates much of the specific discussion, but the points to be made are meant to apply to the perceptual systems in general.

B. The Layout and Material Composition of the Environment

Gibson's (1966, in press) analysis of the environment starts with the distinction between substance and medium. The medium is important, for it is within the medium that the animal moves about; substances are important for they can support or impede, nourish or poison the animal. The interface between a substance and medium is a surface; these are important because they define the structure, or layout, of the environment.

A very important class of surfaces is that of surfaces of support. The principal surface of support is the ground, the literal foundation upon which all else rests. It is, on the average, flat, and will generally encompass the whole lower hemisphere of the animal's environment (the upper hemisphere being occupied jointly by sky, various degrees of vegetation, and other animals). It is in the lower hemisphere that most of life takes place. When water is the medium, surfaces of support are less important, but while the analysis of the environment for aquatic life must be modified, the principle that perceptual systems are oriented to the environment and are ecologically attuned remains the same.

The distinction between ground and sky would be unimportant except that an animal that could not orient to the *up–down* of the environment would soon die. One source of information about verticality is gravity, and perceptual systems have evolved to pick up this most cardinal information about the environment. But, given the importance of *up–down* information, it would be evolutionarily advantageous to involve other perceptual systems. The main optical boundary between the ground and the sky is the horizon. The horizon is nearly ubiquitous and thus it is not surprising that it is potentially a source of information for *up–down* orientation. But the horizon can also be a powerful source of information for the layout of the environment, including the sizes and distances of objects on an ego-relevant scale. Human beings, at least, are indeed sensitive to horizon information (Sedgwick, 1973). Note that the "basic orienting system [Gibson, 1966]" is *not* simply synonymous with the classical vestibular system.

Only on average is the terrain flat. Even the Great Plains and the oceans have inhomogeneities and, therefore, structure. At the microlevel, grains of sand, grassland, and waves all have a layout structure—however dreary; at the macrolevel of rivers and mountains, the terrain has a more interesting sculpting. What then is the proper level at which to discuss layout? Gibson (1966, in press) answers that there is no one proper unit for structure and that an ecological analysis requires the concept of *nested* structures. There are shapes within shapes, structures within structures. The proper scale depends on our purpose: Sometimes we must concern ourselves with molehills, other times with mountains.

An important consequence of layout structure is that not all parts of the environment are visible at a single point of observation. For an occluded object to come into view, there must be either object motion or egomotion. Thus, the perception of layout entails event perception.

Some events cause an object to disappear from view simply by hiding the object from the viewer. An apple may disappear behind a branch, but the animal can make it reappear by walking around the tree. Other events may cause an object to disappear from view by changing the object's material composition. An apple may rot, and nothing the animal can do will make it visible again. Knowledge of being out of view as opposed to being out of existence is essential for guiding action. When a bird leaves its nest, it needs to know that the nest will continue to exist where it left it. Must an animal come to this knowledge solely on the basis of past experience? Where would the past experience come from? In a case of something being out of existence, an animal would have no way of knowing when to terminate a futile search; in a case of something being out of view, an animal might err and give up the search too soon because it was looking in the wrong places.

Gibson, Kaplan, Reynolds, and Wheeler (1969) have argued that humans can directly perceive going or coming out of view as opposed to going or coming out of existence. The optical bases that physically differentiate these events involve the manner in which optical texture is accreted or deleted in the optic array available to the observer. In a change of material state, such as occurs when paper burns, the accretion or deletion of optical texture is irregular and noncoherent, both spatially and temporarily. Background texture may appear anywhere, suddenly, as the paper burns. When an object simply becomes hidden or unhidden, optical texture belonging to the farther, and hence occluded, object is coherently and systematically deleted or accreted along an optical contour defined by an occluding edge of the nearer object. The object is wiped into or out of view by an occluding–disoccluding edge.

The optical specification of an occluding edge, the depth at that edge, and the concept of accretion–deletion of optical texture have been further studied by Kaplan (1969). However, one object being behind another does not necessarily imply occlusion, as the nearer object may be transparent or translucent, and both objects or surfaces may be seen simultaneously, the farther surface is seen through the nearer also visible surface. Metelli (1974a,b) has presented several interesting examples of this phenomenon and provided an algebraic theory of the optical bases for transparency–translucency. The phenomena of occlusion, transparency, and depth between two surfaces have been brought together by Mace and Shaw (1974). They used displays that appear as single surfaces in a static condition, but then appear as two surfaces separated in depth when particular optical motions are introduced. Metelli's and Kaplan's theories are not sufficient to explain the Mace effect, but they are a good start. An adequate theory of the perception of the layout of the environment must be able to explain the complex problems of transparency and occlusion.

The surfaces of the environment are textured and colored. They have definite material compositions that have survival significance for animals. For instance, hard must be differentiated from soft, rough from smooth. A suggestion as to the nature of the optical basis for the perception of roughness–smoothness is provided by an illustration of Beck's (1972, p. 156). He presented a photograph of a smooth, shiny, glazed clay pitcher alongside one of a rough, dull, unglazed clay pitcher. The second photograph is really just the first with the highlights filled in. Just changing a few small local sectors of an optic array—those involving highlights—results in a profound and global effect on the ensuing perception of surface properties and material composition. Beck (1972) was studying the perception of surface colors of real environmental objects, as opposed to the perception of essentially abstract film colors.

C. Events

The perception of events provides more information about the environment than just its layout. Moreover, event perception is concerned not only with the detection of motions, but also with the detection of any change in the environment of relevance to the animal, regardless of the time scale. Impending rapid changes of weather, such as a fastbreaking summer storm, must be prepared for, as well as the more gradual changes of the seasons. A sudden plunge in temperature requires different activity than the coming of winter. The study of event perception is thus more ecologically directed and more general than the classical study of motion perception.

The rubric *motion perception* underscores the interest in abstract change. Velocity thresholds as such are themselves an object of study; hypothesized motion detectors are designed to signal only the occurrence of *some* motion. Indeed the term *disembodied* motion is sometimes used. But detecting motion by itself is not useful. To act purposely, an animal also needs to know *what* has moved or changed. Thus, in contradistinction to motion perception, event perception is dual and has two componants: detection of the *transformational invariants*, which specify the nature of the change, and the detection of *structural invariants*, which specify the identity or unity of the structure that undergoes the change (Pittenger & Shaw, 1975; Shaw, McIntyre, & Mace, 1974).

An example of this dual character of event perception is provided by the event of aging. Knowing a fellow individual's identity and age is clearly important for harmonious social interaction. A particular individual must be treated differently from all others; while juveniles in general, whether familiar or novel, must be treated differently from seniors. Since age is not a permanent feature like sex, and since an individual's appearance changes with age, how are individual identity and general age level known? How do people recognize someone they have not seen in years? Pittenger and Shaw (1975), using the concepts of structural and transformational invariants, argue that aging is a perceivable event. They further argue that form perception is a special case of event perception: An object's static shape is not the primary information for perceptual identification. The identity of an object depends on the nature of the events in which it is involved and what remains invariant over change.

Aging is a very slow event without any rigid motion. Also important for survival are fast events with rigid motions. The same rigidly moving object will have a radically different significance depending on whether it is moving sideways, away, or toward an animal. Approach events are of particular consequence, and an animal needs to be sensitive to rapidly looming objects in order to be able to duck or flee. The optical specifier of this future event of impending collision is a particular optical expansion of a closed contour in the optic array (Schiff, 1965). But not all optically expanding contours specify violent collision. An animal may want to bring about gentle contact with another animal or food. A moving animal that is slowing down needs to know if its rate of deceleration is appropriate to its goal. When flying an airplane, overshooting or undershooting a runway can be fatal. All these approach events involve an optically expanding contour, but the rate of expansion is specific to the final state and may thus be used to guide action (Lee, 1974, 1976).

Approach may also produce accretion–deletion of optical texture as well as optical contour expansion. Approach to a doorway, for example, will have different consequences depending on whether the door is open or closed. The optically expanding contour is the same in both events, but when the door is open, there is a concommitant disocclusion of next-room texture along the inside edge of the doorframe. Thus, passage is specified. Passage is similarly afforded between tree trunks and branches.

The opposite of approach is recession and the opposite of covering is uncovering, but not all events are physically or perceptually reversible. If an event is run backward, for example, using a motion picture, the phenomenological character of the event may change. The ensuing perceptual experience is not only that the event is unfolding backward, but that it is somehow unnatural in other undefined ways. For example, the burning of paper or the flowing of water downstream are naturally and perceptually irreversible events. The flow of an event must conform to the laws of physics; reversing the time flow would violate some laws—for example, entropy. The differences between physically permissible and nonpermissible flow characteristics are subtle considering the magnitudes involved in a short sequence of events. Yet, informal studies show that observers readily sense the unnaturalness of the reversed ecological events depicted in motion pictures by Gibson (1968) and Gibson and Kaushall (1972). These events include waves on a beach and burning paper. Notice the contrast between these events and those, such as moving dots, used in more classical motion-perception studies.

Another feature of ecologically important events is that they may require an observer for their very definition. The significance of perceptual guidance for *participatory events* is obvious, but perceptual guidance may also be significant for *spectator events*, for they too may require action by the animal. Events such as forest fires and falling rocks must be kept as spectator events—the animal's body must not interfere with and modify the event (for example, by deflecting the path of a rolling boulder).

The task of a football referee may be illuminating: At one level he must remain a pure spectator, he must not, in any way, influence the course of legal action by the players. But to do his job of being a diligent and privileged spectator, he must actively seek illegal events. Only if he finds one may he influence the game event. If he is to avoid becoming a participant in the game, his egomotion must be nimble. But his egomotion is a participatory event in itself, and one that requires acute perceptual guidance through an everchanging environmental layout composed of the moving bodies of the players. Here there is simultaneous spectator and participator perception of events. Notice that perceiving a spectator event is not at all a case of passive perception.

The above examples suggest that events may be classified usefully in several ways. The problem of an inventory of events is a difficult one, although such an inventory would be valuable for research. The case for an inventory of events and more detailed classifications are offered by E. J. Gibson (1975) and J. J. Gibson (in press).

D. Egomotion

Egomotion refers to an animal's own displacement in the environment. Egomotion may be either passive or active and contrasts with locomotion: A bird in a stiff breeze and a fish in a swift stream must move their bodies actively in locomotor action to stay fixed relative to the environment and null their egomotion. A gliding bird and a passenger in a car may displace quickly (a rapid egomotion) without performing any locomotor acts.

What gives rise to the perception of egomotion? Optically, egomotion induces a particular total transformation of the ambient optic array at a moving point of observation (Gibson, 1950; Lee, 1974; Nakayama & Loomis, 1975). Gibson (1950, 1958) has hypothesized that the egomotion optical flow pattern is a psychologically effective optical basis for the perceptual experience of egomotion. Observers who view abstract computer-generated movies describable solely by the egomotion flow pattern equations do report compelling experiences of egomotion and can indicate their direction of heading with a fair degree of accuracy for egomotion toward a wall (Johnston, White, & Cumming, 1973) or for egomotion over an endless, flat terrain (Warren, 1976). In the case of a flat terrain, the focus of expansion need not be explicitly in the view sample for the observer to experience egomotion and to indicate his heading.

Vision and the optical flow pattern are, however, neither necessary nor sufficient for the detection of true egomotion. People experience egomotion in enclosed elevators even though there is no optical flow, and people may experience overwhelming feelings of egomotion when they know they are sitting in a movie theater. Nevertheless, vision seems to be a highly sensitive (and often the only reliable) indicator of real egomotion in natural situations.

In the case of a fish in a swift stream, the fish must use a visual anchor (that is, swim so as to null any optical flow) to remain fixed relative to the stream bed. When there is a conflict between vision and another modality, vision will tend to dominate (Lishman & Lee, 1973). The development of visual sensitivity and dominance of egomotion appears quite early (Lee & Aronson, 1974).

E. Affordances

The mere ability of an animal to move safely without falling off a cliff or crashing into a tree is hardly sufficient to satisfy its commercial needs with its environment. It has specific need of specific aspects of the environment at specific times. A safe but random walk would bring the animal into contact with random nutrients, assorted poisons, and hungry enemies at irregular intervals.

To survive, the animal needs to know what to approach and what to avoid; what will satisfy and what will frustrate its needs. The animal needs to perceive the meaning that particular aspects of the environment hold. Thus, more importantly than detecting the environment and the events, the animal needs to perceive the *affordances* of that environment. Affordances are defined as invariant combinations of properties at the ecological level, taken with reference to the anatomy and action systems of a species or individual and also with reference to its biological and social needs. Gibson (in press) argues that affordances are directly perceived and that, whereas they do not cause behavior, they do constrain or control it.

Affordances focus attention on and help to explicate another of Gibson's points, namely, the *mutuality* of an animal and its environment. The environment must surround a living organism and depends on the particular organism. The environment of a fly is not the same as that of a horse; water affords support to a spider but not to an elephant. Likewise, an animal cannot exist independently of its environment. This mutuality must be remembered in studying the perceptual systems. A perceptual system must be studied in the context of the environment in which it evolved to function, for it is both a product and a reflection of that environment.

III. THE PHYSICAL BASES FOR PERCEPTION

An ecological approach to perception starts with a consideration of the environment and what there is to be perceived in it. The next step is to consider the potential physical bases for perception at a possible point of observation *without* any animal present *and* independently of any particular species' perceptual system. This approach may seem at first counterintuitive and nonecological, so let us examine its rationale.

One approach to studying perception is to start with a consideration of sensory physiology, especially with human visual physiology. However, this approach can detract from and ignore the ecological nature of perceptual systems in general; the questions of why a particular physiology evolved and why that particular physiology is interesting are ignored. Furthermore, the variety and diversity of sensory systems at the level of organs and neural architecture are enormous. Each species and individual presents new problems for study and enables a new theory of sensory organization. What principles can underly and unify this diversity? Are there any invariances under the varieties of perceptual systems?

At one level we may study common anatomical and neural components, such as feature detectors and their principles of organization. Some of these principles may apply over many animals, but each new animal must be studied in turn. While there may be impressive progress in studying one animal's solution to the problem of perception, there is no guarantee that this analysis will generalize to other animals. The concentration of effort on a few species, because of convenience or inherent interest, can lead to a biased view of perception. For example, understanding human eye movements is important for understanding human vision, but a theory based on those eye movements may not apply to species without the same eye movements, such as insects. In fact, such a theory based on eye movement might, in turn, be misleading even about the true nature of human vision, for it is by studying variations over different species that the essential and necessary can be distinguished from the accidental and local.

Another way to start the study of perception is to take a phenomenological approach and, as did Koffka (1935), ask the question: "Why do things look as they do?" This question assumes an answer to the surprisingly difficult question, "How do things look?" From an analytic, introspective view, one answer leads to the concept of the visual field and the problem of how experience can be built up from a patchwork of sense impressions. From a phenomenological, introspective view, another answer leads to the concept of the visual world and the problem of how we perceive features not present in sense impressions. I used to agree with Merleau-Ponty (1945) that a phenomenological analysis was essential and prior to a theory of perception. However, such questions as "How do things look?" and "Why do things look as they do?" lead, or rather, mislead our attention to the peculiarities of human experience rather than to the commonalities of perceptual purpose across species. As with physiologically based theories, phenomenological theories suffer from a lack of generality, but worse than this, from a lack of ecological justification.

Where then do we begin if our goal is a unified, ecologically motivated theory of perception? The first place to begin is in the environment. The environment is the underlying unity for perception. The second place to examine is the potential point of observation. At any place where an animal could be, and before any animal occupies such a potential point of observation, there is an influx of energy to that point. The arrangement of the set of *relative* light energy *differences* in different directions constitutes the ambient optic array.

The ambient optic array has a structure due to the structure of the environment. Gibson (1966) has contended that the environment, in turn, is fully specified by the structure of the ambient optic array. To achieve this mathematical recovery of the environment from light, structural changes over time and displacement of the point of observation must be considered. The main contention is that to every perceivable there exists at least one mathematically definable *optical specifier*. In fact, there may be several structural variables, each of which may be a sufficient, although independent, optical specifier of the same perceivable. Gibson calls the study of the optical bases for perception *ecological optics*.

The chief implication for perceptual systems is that the environment is mathematically "contained" in the ambient optic array. A perceptual system is thus a biological organization for the purpose of extracting physically existing information about the environment. The biological extraction or resonating solutions to a given physical basis need not be unique. Indeed, different species may capitalize on different physical bases for the same perceivable.

This approach of beginning with the physical basis for the environment in ambient energy prior to the placement of an arbitrary animal leads to a number of difficult issues. Given the existence of a physical basis and a healthy perceptual system, there is no guarantee or necessity that perception will ensue. Ecological perception is *not* a function of stimulation in a stimulus–response sense. (Upon adopting an ecological approach to perception in the early 1960s, Gibson abandoned his earlier claim that perception was a function of stimulation. See Gibson, 1959 and Lombardo, 1973.) Thus, if a physical basis is not a sufficient condition for perception, under what conditions will perception arise? This leads to the problems of information pickup (that is, perception), selective attention, and perceptual learning and development.

IV. ADAPTATION OF PERCEPTUAL SYSTEMS
   TO THE ENVIRONMENT

The activity of the perceptual systems, as well as their structure and organization, is adapted to pick up environmental information useful to the animal. The environment enables but does not force perception; the presence of a physical basis for a perceivable is not a sufficient condition for perception. This lack of sufficiency permits species, age, and individual differences in perception. Indeed, what is perceivable at any given time and place in a natural environment is so vast that survival requires the ability to select perceivables on the basis of their importance, but how the environment conditions a perceptual system to pick up, for example, affordances is not yet known; how a perceptual ability develops within an individual, and once developed, how that ability may be selectively utilized, is also not known.

However, the literature on the adaptation of the perceptual systems to the environment is vast. E. J. Gibson (1969) has provided a thorough review of the data and has also offered a comprehensive theory of perceptual learning and development. The following examples are meant to illustrate the breadth of the problems.

The difference between the visual systems of prey and predators provides a striking example of the *phylogenesis* of perceptual systems. The food supply of the rabbit is stationary and ubiquitous. However, the rabbit, as a hunted animal, needs to keep an eye open in all directions. If it is being chased, it needs to keep track of the pursuer's progress without turning its head and breaking stride. Accordingly, the rabbit's eyes are placed laterally, which allows for panoramic vision. A fox, on the other hand, need not fear attack from behind, but must concentrate on seeking out its shy and elusive food. Thus, foxes have frontal eyes with good binocular overlap. Other examples of the adaptive radiation of the eye may be found in Walls (1942) and Polyak (1957).

A desirable feature of the *ontogenesis* of a perceptual system within an individual is that it be ready when needed. It would be maladaptive if an animal could walk before it could perceive danger. A major finding of studies with the visual cliff was that the young of the several species tested did indeed perceive and avoid cliffs as soon as they could walk (E. J. Gibson, 1969). Also, the young of several species perceived impending collision with approaching objects at least as soon as they were able to make appropriate responses. Species tested included fiddler crabs, chicks, frogs, kittens, rhesus monkeys, and humans (Schiff, Caviness, & Gibson, 1962; Schiff, 1965).

The perceptual systems of mature animals, in addition to those of the young or the species as a whole, must be flexible and adaptable to the changing demands of the environment and the changing needs of the animal. This *epigenesis* of a perceptual system is marked by increasing selectivity, specificity, and economy of information pickup. (E. J. Gibson, 1969, has also identified these trends in the phylogenesis and ontogenesis of perception.) So much clamors for attention that the initiated perceiver learns what to attend and what to ignore. The ability to resist distraction does not necessarily mean losing touch with the environment. Rather, successful exploitation and mastery of the environment depend upon the perceiver's ability to concentrate on the task at hand and resist the incessant, but irrelevant, pushes and pulls of the environment. The successful perceiver must, however, keep alert for significant new information.

V. THE ENVIRONMENTAL REACH OF PERCEPTUAL SYSTEMS

The perceptual systems are, by necessity, well adapted to pick up useful information about the environment. The ecological nature of perceptual systems is also evident when we turn to the more difficult problem of perceptual experience. The environment is experienced as being "out there," as indeed it is. Even nonecological or artificial activation of the perceptual systems tends to result in experience localized in the environment. For example, afterimages are experienced as being localized on, and a quality of, environmental surfaces. This is a striking demonstration that perceptual experience is of the environment and not of the state of the nerves. Also, this is one reason why an ecological approach to perception starts with the question: "What is there to be perceived?" and why I have given so much space to the discussion of perceivables.

To be aware of what is out there means not to be aware of the causal basis for perception. I am not normally aware of a spectacle lens between my eyes and the environment. I am not even normally aware of the "blind ring" due to the occlusion of the environment by my spectacle frames. When I wear sunglasses for a while, I am no longer aware of the coloring effect and they become phenomenally transparent. This transparency applies to any extension of a perceptual system, such as a blind person's cane. When I explore my desk top with my pen as a probe, I am aware of the contact between the pen and the desk *at the surface* of the desk. My experience is of the desk—not of the probe, nor of the nerves of my fingers, nor of any neural process further inside my skin.

Austin (1962) asked, "If I touch you with a barge-pole, do I touch you indirectly? [p. 16]." An ecological approach to perception implies that perception is direct, that not only is the barge-pole epistemically transparent, but also the entire perceptual system that is involved. Shaw and Bransford (1977) have presented a clear statement and extensive discussion of the implications of an ecological approach for both theory and research. Central to their argument is the distinction between perception as a causal process and perception as an immediate epistemic act. Considering perception as a time-dependent causal process with physical and physiological support emphasizes the *how* of psychological processing. Considering perception as an immediate epistemic act stresses the functional transparency of the causal support and emphasizes that *what* of psychological processing. An ecological approach to the perceptual systems thus begins with an analysis of the permanent possibilities for perception, with what is "out there."

What is out there, the environment, is unbounded, and perceptual experience should also be unbounded—as opposed merely to reflecting the unboundedness. Koffka (1935, p. 178) claimed that he could see his table *underneath* his book. Merleau-Ponty (1945) stated that:

> Our visual field is not neatly cut out of our objective world, and is not a fragment with sharp edges like the landscape framed by the window. We see as far as our hold on things extends, far beyond the zone of clear vision, and even behind us. When we reach the limits of the visual field, we do not pass from vision to non-vision [p. 277].

Everyday experience with the perceptual world supports this claim, as do studies of the phenomenal persistence of occluded objects (Kaplan, 1969; Gibson *et al.*, 1969) and of perceived direction of one's egomotion heading when the heading point is out of view (Warren, 1976). With the exception of stroboscopic motion, nonecological approaches to perception tend to ignore perceptual experiences for which there is no obvious retinal stimulation, whereas ecological considerations invite a widening of the scope of perceptual research.

VI. THE ENVIRONMENT, PERCEPTION, AND ACTION

Perception in the natural environment is an active process of information seeking and not simply a passive registration of energy. An animal then uses this actively obtained knowledge to preserve and further its well-being. Survival requires action. Thus, both the obtaining and use of environmental knowledge imply activity. We perceive so that we may act, and we act so that we may perceive. Yet, little is known about this linkage between perception and action. As Turvey (1977) notes, action-based theories of perception exist, but these theories, curiously, have been advanced on a virtually nonexistant theory of action. These motor-theoretic accounts of perception have offered only trivial explanations, if any, of how acts are actually produced. Turvey (1975, 1977) has provided a review of the little data and less theory that are extant, as well as a preliminary analysis toward a theory of action with reference to the environment and perception.

VII. CONCLUSION

The extreme variety of ecological niches has led to a large diversity of animal forms, along with a multiplicity of solutions to the problem of maintaining contact with and operating on the environment. The wealth of life on earth testifies to the viablility of these solutions. Must this diversity be a problem for perceptual theory? For instance, would we need a separate theory for human eyes and insect eyes? In science, the search for symmetry principles and the finding of invariance under transformations of phenomena has led to the most satisfying results and the greatest predictive power (Shaw *et al.*, 1974). An ecological approach to the perceptual systems, by freeing itself from considering only humans in laboratory situations, would simultaneously lead us to broaden the domain of perception and to seek a simplified and unified theory of perception and action.

References

Austin, J. L. *Sense and sensibilia.* New York: Oxford Univ. Press, 1962.

Beck, J. *Surface color perception.* Ithaca, New York: Cornell Univ. Press, 1972.

Berkeley, G. An essay towards a new theory of vision. In C. M. Turbayne (Ed.), *Works on vision: Berkeley.* New York: Liberal Arts Press, 1963. (Originally published, 1709.)

Gibson, E. J. *Principles of perceptual learning and development.* New York: Appleton, 1969.

Gibson, E. J. *A classification of events for the study of event perception.* Paper for symposium on "Event Perception" at a meeting of the American Psychological Association, Chicago, September 1975.

Gibson, J. J. *The perception of the visual world.* Boston: Houghton Mifflin, 1950.

Gibson, J. J. Visually controlled locomotion and visual orientation in animals. *British Journal of Psychology,* 1958, **49,** 182–194.

Gibson, J. J. Perception as a function of stimulation. In S. Koch (Ed.), *Psychology: A study of a science* (Vol. 1). New York: McGraw-Hill, 1959.

Gibson, J. J. *The senses considered as perceptual systems.* Boston: Houghton Mifflin, 1966.

Gibson, J. J. *The change from visible to invisible: A study of optical transitions.* State College, Pennsylvania: Psychological Cinema Register, 1968. (Film)

Gibson, J. J. *An ecological approach to visual perception.* Boston: Houghton Mifflin, forthcoming.

Gibson, J. J., Kaplan, G. A., Reynolds, H. N., & Wheeler, K. The change from visible to invisible: A study of optical transitions. *Perception & Psychophysics,* 1969, **5,** 113–116.

Gibson, J. J., & Kaushall, P. *Reversible and irreversible events.* University Park, Pennsylvania: Pennsylvania State Cinema Register, 1972. (Film)

Johnston, I. R., White, G. R., & Cumming, R. W. The role of optical expansion patterns in locomotor control. *American Journal of Psychology,* 1973, **86,** 311–324.

Kaplan, G. Kinetic disruption of optical texture: The perception of depth at an edge. *Perception & Psychophysics,* 1969, **6,** 193–198.

Koffka, K. *Principles of gestalt psychology.* New York: Harcourt, 1935.

Lee, D. N. Visual information during locomotion. In R. B. Macleod & H. L. Pick (Eds.), *Perception: Essays in honor of J. J. Gibson.* Ithaca, New York: Cornell Univ. Press, 1974.

Lee, D. N. A theory of visual control of braking based on information about time to collision. *Perception,* 1976, **5,** 437–459.

Lee, D. N., & Aronson, E. Visual proprioceptive control of standing in human infants. *Perception & Psychophysics,* 1974, **15,** 529–532.

Lishman, J. R., & Lee, D. N. The autonomy of visual kinaesthesis. *Perception,* 1973, **2,** 287–294.

Lombardo, T. J. *J. J. Gibson's ecological approach to visual perception: Its historical context and development.* Unpublished doctoral dissertation, Univ. of Minnesota, 1973.

Mace, W. M., & Shaw, R. Simple kinetic information for transparent depth. *Perception & Psychophysics*, 1974, **15**, 201–209.

Merleau-Ponty, M. *Phenomenology of perception*. New York: Humanities Press, 1962. (Originally published, 1945.)

Metelli, F. Achromatic color conditions in the perception of transparency. In R. B. MacLeod & H. L. Pick (Eds.), *Perception: Essays in honor of J. J. Gibson*. Ithaca, New York: Cornell Univ. Press, 1974. (a)

Metelli, F. The perception of transparency. *Scientific American*, **230**(4), 1974, 90–98. (b)

Nakayama, K., & Loomis, J. M. Optical velocity patterns, velocity-sensitive neurons, and space perception: A hypothesis. *Perception*, 1974, **3**, 63–80.

Pittenger, J. B., & Shaw, R. E. Aging faces as viscal-elastic events: Implications for a theory of nonrigid shape perception. *Journal of Experimental Psychology: Human Perception and Performance*, 1975, **1**, 374–382.

Polyak, S. L. *The vertebrate visual system*. Chicago: Univ. of Chicago Press, 1957.

Schiff, W. Perception of impending collision: A study of visually directed avoidance behavior. *Psychological Monographs: General & Applied*, 1965, **79**, (Whole No. 604).

Schiff, W., Caviness, J. A., & Gibson, J. J. Persistent fear responses in rhesus monkeys to the optical stimulus of "looming." *Science*, 1962, **136**, 982–983.

Sedgwick, H. A. *The visible horizon: A potential source of visual information for the perception of size and distance*. Unpublished doctoral dissertation, Cornell Univ., 1973.

Shaw, R., & Bransford, J. Introduction: Psychological approaches to the problem of knowledge. In R. Shaw & J. Bransford (Eds.), *Perceiving, acting, and knowing: Towards an ecological psychology*. Hillsdale, New Jersey: Erlbaum, 1977.

Shaw, R., McIntyre, M. & Mace, W. The role of symmetry in event perception. In R. B. MacLeod & H. L. Pick (Eds.), *Perception: Essays in honor of J. J. Gibson*. Ithaca, New York: Cornell Univ. Press, 1974.

Turvey, M. T. Perspectives in vision: Conception or Perception? In D. Duane & M. Rawson (Eds.), *Reading, Perception and Language*. Baltimore, Maryland: York, 1975.

Turvey, M. T. Preliminaries to a theory of action with reference to vision. In R. Shaw & J. Bransford (Eds.), *Perceiving, acting, and knowing: Towards an ecological psychology*. Hillsdale, New Jersey: Erlbaum, 1977.

Walls, G. L. *The vertebrate eye*. Bloomfield Hills, Michigan: Crainbrook Institute of Science, 1942.

Warren, R. The perception of egomotion. *Journal of Experimental Psychology: Human Perception & Performance*, 1976, **2**, 448–456.

Chapter 2

CULTURE AND PERCEPTION*

ANNE D. PICK AND HERBERT L. PICK, JR.

I. INTRODUCTION

Psychologists interested in perception have always been intrigued by cultural differences. Cultural differences in perception, when attributable to experience, seem to be the result of natural experiments demonstrating the flexibility of perception. The engaging theoretical problem in such cases lies in understanding the essential nature of the relevant experience and the mechanism of its operation. When perceptual differences can be attributed to physiological or anatomical differences among people, they provide clues for investigating the mechanisms of perception, especially of the visual system.

The perception of colors provides an example of cultural differences that may be attributable to physiological differences. Bornstein (1973a,b) has integrated the evidence supporting the hypothesis that cultural differences in color naming reflect physiologically based differences in color vision. Bornstein's argument begins with the observation that in the color-naming systems of some languages, categories at the blue end of the spectrum are

* Preparation of this chapter was supported by Special Fellowship No. 1F03HD54324 from the National Institute of Child Health and Human Development to the first author, and also by Program Project Grants No. 2P01HD0502706 and No. HD01136 from the National Institute of Child Health and Human Development to the University of Minnesota.

collapsed—for example, green and blue, or blue and black, or green, blue, and black are not distinguished by different names. Such collapsing of name categories is more prevalent the nearer the language group is to the equator. Differences in color-naming systems might occur because of differences in sensitivity at the blue end of the spectrum. A decrease in sensitivity at the blue end of the spectrum could be produced by increased interocular yellow pigmentation, the geographic distribution of which is associated "strongly with the geographical patterning of appropriately collapsed color-naming systems [Bornstein, 1973a, p. 276]." Additional evidence in support of this argument is that groups differing in amount of pigmentation do show differences in sensitivity; also, blue-blind and blue-weak persons from language groups that do differentiate at the blue end of the spectrum do collapse color names. On the other hand, some of the details of the geographical distribution of color-naming differences are not incorporated by the argument—for example, the collapsing of red and yellow under the same name, and the reason for the geographical distribution of blue–green identification as compared with blue–black identification. Also, monkeys from tropical areas, that presumably would be subject to the same type of environmental influences as humans, do not show a corresponding decrease in responsivity to any of the hue categories.

The perception of speech provides an example of cultural differences in perception attributable to ontogenetic experience. The effect of the experience may be to bias detectors in the perceptual system. The phonemes of languages are distinguished by certain acoustic and articulatory features. The phonemes *pa* and *ba*, for example, are distinguished by voice onset time. For articulation, voice onset time is the time between the start of the vibration of vocal cords and the release of air from the mouth. For *pa*, in English, the vocal cords start to vibrate after air is emitted from the mouth, whereas for *ba* the vocal cords start to vibrate before or at about the same time air is released. Sounds with various delays in the onset of voicing are all heard as unvoiced—for example, as *pa*, so long as the voicing starts 40–70 msec after air is released from the mouth. Within wide limits, sounds with shorter delays will all be heard as voiced, as *ba*. In fact, within the *ba* category itself or within the *pa* category itself, it is very difficult for English speakers to distinguish sounds, even though voice onset times may differ greatly. This phenomenon is known as *categorical perception* (Liberman, Cooper, Shankweiler, & Studdert-Kennedy, 1967). Thai listeners, on the other hand, are able to distinguish between two types of *ba*—one in which voicing starts very early in relation to the release of air and one in which the vocal cords start about the same time as the release of air (Abramson & Lisker, 1967; Lisker & Abramson, 1967). That is, in the speech perception of the Thais there are three categories along the *ba–pa* dimension, whereas for native English speakers there are only two. There is evidence that a feature detector or detector-like mechanism underlies these kinds of discrimination (Cooper, 1974; Diehl, 1975).

As intriguing as cultural comparisons are for identifying the roles of experience and of physiological differences in perception, there are important difficulties in interpreting such comparisons. A major difficulty is that cultures vary in so many ways that identifying the critical dimension is often logically or practically impossible. In general, in addressing substantive questions about cultural differences in perception, one especially must be aware of and sensitive to issues of methodology. The traditional problems of research design are further complicated in cross-cultural research by issues of comparability of samples of subjects, language and communication ambiguities, and cultural biases in research materials and tasks. All of these issues are inherent—either explicitly or implicitly—in any comparisons of cultures. In addition to color perception and speech perception, several aspects of perception have been studied extensively in members of different cultures: pictorial perception, visual illusions, perceptual constancy, and space perception. In research, each of these topics also illustrates one of the issues of methodology that pervades cross-cultural research. Thus, the literature about each of these topics will be reviewed in the context of the issue that must especially be considered in interpreting that literature.

II. PICTORIAL PERCEPTION

Do members of different cultures perceive pictures differently? The question has intrigued anthropologists and psychologists for years and has been the subject of extensive investigation for at least 15 years (Deregowski, 1968a,b,c, 1972a; Deregowski & Byth, 1970; Dutoit, 1966; Hudson, 1960, 1962a,b, 1967; Mundy-Castle, 1966; Mundy-Castle & Nelson, 1962; Omari & Cook, 1972; Waldron & Gallimore, 1973). The reason the question is intriguing is because cultural differences in pictorial perception may imply that a special type of experience is necessary in order accurately to perceive representations in two dimensions of objects or scenes ordinarily encountered in three dimensions. Also, cultural differences or similarities in pictorial perception bear on the question of whether the rules for representing three dimensions in two dimensions are arbitrary conventions, or whether they have a natural relation to the three-dimensional world being represented (Goodman, 1968; Kennedy, 1974). The specific question asked by most investigators of pictorial perception is whether South Africans or East Africans perceive pictures in the same way that Europeans or North Americans do. An example of the answer consistently given is that "The results from African tribal subjects were unequivocal: Both children and adults found it difficult to perceive depth in the pictorial material. The difficulty varied in extent but appeared to persist through most educational and social levels [Deregowski, 1972a, pp. 84–85]." To evaluate this answer requires evaluation of the experimental procedures used to study pictorial perception, and specifically introduces the issue of communication (especially *ambiguous* communication) in the study of culture and perception.

The procedure typically used since the first systematic investigation (Hudson, 1960) includes outline drawings of hunting scenes, some of which are reproduced in Fig. 1. The scenes include a hunter, an antelope, and an elephant, and they contain the pictorial cues to distance of familiar size, overlap, and perspective. The cue of familiar size indicates that the elephant is farther away than the antelope; the cue of superposition indicates that one object is in front of another; and the cue of perspective—the parallel lines drawn to converge—indicates increasing distance away from the viewer.

The questions respondents typically are asked about the pictures are: What do you see? What is the man doing? Which is nearer to the man, the antelope or the elephant? A reply that the man is hunting the elephant or that the elephant is nearer to the man is taken to indicate an inability to perceive the represented distance relations. Conversely, a reply that the man is hunting the antelope or that the antelope is nearer the man is taken to indicate accurate perception of the distance relations represented in the picture.

Typically, illiterate respondents give few answers indicating perception of the distance relations, and the frequency of such answers is correlated with the number of years of the respondents' schooling (Kilbride, Robbins, & Freeman, 1968; Mundy-Castle & Nelson, 1962). In addition, whites in Africa give more such answers than do blacks with the same number of years of schooling (Hudson, 1960, 1962a,b).

In order for these findings to be interpreted meaningfully, communication between the tester and his respondents must be unambiguous. In the proce-

FIG. 1. Drawings used for studying recognition of portrayed distance. [Reproduced from W. Hudson, Pictorial depth perception in subcultural groups in Africa, *Journal of Social Psychology*, 1960, **52**, 183–208.]

dure for studying pictorial perception, there is, first, ambiguity in the draw-ings themselves, specifically in the information provided by the cues for distance. The familiar-size information depends on elephants being larger than antelopes, but in Africa there are hundreds of species of antelope, and their adult height ranges from 13 in. at the shoulder to 6 ft. (Williams, 1967, pp. 210, 219). Elephants also come in a wide range of sizes depending on their age, and hunters can be young boys or grown men. The information about distance provided by the perspective cues also is ambiguous, since some respondents do not recognize the objects that are drawn in perspective (Hudson, 1960; Mundy-Castle, 1966).

A second, intended ambiguity is in the question: Which is nearer to the man, the antelope or the elephant? (See Miller, 1973, for additional discus-sion of this ambiguity.) A reply that makes reference to distance on paper is interpreted as demonstrating the respondent's inability to perceive the rep-resented distance relations, but respondents who reply with reference to the picture plane are not further interrogated to determine whether they can interpret the question in another way.

A third ambiguity in communication has to do with whether the meaning of the respondent's answer is sufficiently obvious to interpret it as indicating how the picture is perceived. Language interpreters are frequently required and used for testing, but even when the translation is as accurate as possible, there is still the question of whether the tester and respondent share common meaning when they communicate. For the question: What is the man doing? the reply that he is hunting the antelope is taken to indicate accurate perception of the distance relations, but that interpretation implies that only nearby animals would be hunted and assumes that there are no important cultural differences in the frequency of hunting elephants as compared to antelope.

Interpreting the cultural differences in pictorial perception is difficult since cultural differences may be confounded with educational differences. That is, blacks and whites who have had the same number of years of (segregated) schooling in Africa may not have achieved the same level of education. That there are educational differences in these tasks is clear. Possibly the educa-tional differences and the related cultural differences have to do with how respondents interpret the task they are asked to perform. Besides the repre-sentational information in pictures, there is also information specifying that it is a two-dimensional object (Hagen, 1974). One effect of schooling and of using pictures as pedagogical devices may be to learn to attend routinely to the representational information in a picture and to ignore the two-dimensional information. Schoolchildren and educated adults may simply assume that questions about which animals are nearer in pictures, or what animal is being hunted, refer to the representational aspect of the picture. On the other hand, children and adults who have little schooling may interpret questions about represented objects literally, in terms of the two-dimensional relations. This assumption may be made not because they cannot perceive the represented depth relations, but rather because they have no reason to assume that the question refers to anything other than the object, the piece of paper, that they are shown. The effect of the ambiguities in communication may be to introduce discrepant rather than shared meaning between the respondents and the investigator—discrepancies about what the task means and how it should be performed. Such discrepancies may be related to observed differences in performing the task.

In spite of difficulties in interpretation, cross-cultural observations can be informative, especially about aspects of pictures that are perceived similarly by different groups of people. Accurate perception of pictorial perception has several components. The depicted objects, as well as the depicted relations (both spatial and dynamic) among those objects must be correctly identified. The dynamic relations include both objects depicted in motion (e.g., people walking or running) and interpersonal or motivational relations among objects (e.g., one individual depicted as being angry at another).

Perception of depicted objects has been studied using recognition tasks. The simplest recognition task is one in which objects and their representations (e.g., photographs) are simultaneously present and the respondent is asked to match the two. Schoolchildren in Zambia, as well as unschooled Zambian adults, can perform such a task with a high accuracy (Deregowski, 1968a,b,c, 1971a,b).

The typical task for picture perception requires identification of depicted objects when the object itself is not simultaneously present. Very young children in the United States (Hochberg & Brooks, 1962) and in South Africa (Liddicoat & Koza, 1963) can perform such a task with high accuracy—as can unschooled adults in Rhodesia (Brimble, 1963, p. 28) and children and adults in a Papua New Guinea culture in which there is no indigenous pictorial art (Kennedy & Ross, 1975). There is a report indicating that 5-month-old infants can recognize facial photographs of persons whom they have seen previously (Dirks & Gibson, 1976). Thus, recognition of depicted objects seem to depend neither on specific experience with pictures nor on formal schooling. There is one apparently contradictory set of observations by Duncan, Gourlay, and Hudson (1973), but Kennedy and Ross (1975) have pointed out extreme problems of interpretation of those observations.

The cases just cited included photographs, realistic representations, and line drawings. When representations were ambiguous or unrealistic, accuracy of their recognition was related to the number of years of schooling for Africans (Hector, Dlodlo, & DuPlessis, 1961; Hudson, 1962a,b, 1967; Kilbride & Robbins, 1968). Some rules for representation (e.g., dominant figures being large, converging lines indicating distance, foreshortening to indicate activity) may be more culture-specific than others. To the extent that pictures are drawn according to rules that are culture-specific, then correct recognition and interpretation of those pictures may require explicit instruction, or at least exposure within the culture (Omari & MacGinitie, 1974). Little is known about how people recognize dynamic relations in pictures; it is an obvious problem for further study.

Some investigators have used peoples' own drawings as an index of how they interpret pictured information (Bradley, 1960; Deregowski, 1969a; Hudson, 1962a; Morgan, 1959b). Preference for one or another type of drawing has also been used as an index of accuracy of pictorial recognition of objects (Deregowski, 1969b,c, 1970a,b). Occasionally people are asked to construct models from drawings as an index of how the drawing is perceived (Deregowski, 1968a,b,c; Jahoda & McGurk, 1974a). All three procedures reflect recognition accuracy only indirectly, and for all three, schooling is related to accuracy. The validity of using one's own drawings or constructed models to assess recognition assumes (a) that people have no difficulty performing the construction task; and (b) that identical processes are required to recognize representations and to draw representations or construct objects.

III. VISUAL ILLUSIONS

Cultural differences in susceptibility to visual illusions has been the most extensively observed phenomenon in the cross-cultural study of perception. The purpose of studying such phenomena is to try to identify specific conditions that affect perceptual development. If, for example, it is thought that susceptibility to a particular illusion depends on seeing the illusion figure as a line-drawing representation of an object, then it can be predicted that individuals who have not seen such an object may not be susceptible to the illusion, whereas individuals who have seen the object will be. If the prediction is confirmed, there is new knowledge both about the basis for the illusion and about the effect of a particular kind of experience on perception. In short, hypotheses are tested simultaneously (a) about why the illusion occurs; and (b) about why there are cultural differences in its magnitude. The methodological issue illustrated by this strategy has to do with identifying the source of cultural differences in perception. Specifically, since there are many potentially relevant differences among a set of cultures, how can the important one(s) be identified if there is not prior knowledge about why the illusion occurs—that is, what is the important perceptual mechanism? The difficulty of providing an answer to this question will be apparent as evidence about cultural differences in each of three illusions is summarized.

A. The Müller–Lyer Illusion

The Müller–Lyer illusion is shown in Fig. 2. The illusion occurs when the length of segment a is overestimated relative to the length of segment b. This familiar illusion has been the object of more cross-cultural study than any

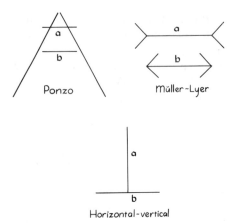

FIG. 2. Three illusion figures. For each figure, segments a and b are equal in length; the illusion is the overestimation of segment a.

other illusion. The magnitude of this illusion has been found by many investigators to decrease with age (cf. Pick & Pick, 1970, p. 804), and susceptibility to the illusion is thought to vary with cultural variables.

The first reported cross-cultural study of the Müller–Lyer illusion was that of Rivers (1901) in which a comparison was made of the magnitude of the illusion in residents of Papua and of Great Britian. Using a method of adjustment, Rivers found the illusion to be present in both groups, but its magnitude was somewhat greater among the British. The meaning of this difference is hard to assess, since Rivers discarded judgments of some Papuans that were in a direction opposite to that of the illusion (Rivers, 1901, p. 118) and also those of at least one Papuan whose judgments were "almost exactly right every time [p. 119]." In addition, there were variations in the procedure used, especially with the Papuans (p. 118).

The most systematic investigation of susceptibility to the Müller–Lyer illusion in members of different cultures was made by Segall, Campbell, and Herskovits (1963, 1966). They tested the hypothesis that visual illusions occur because habits of perceptual inference are transferred from the spatial environment to line drawings. These habits of inference are acquired in the environments in which one lives and moves from childhood onward. Of specific relevance to the Müller–Lyer illusion is the presence in the environment of many rectangular objects: rectangular buildings with doors, windows, etc. Individuals who live in such a "carpentered world" may perceive drawings containing obtuse and acute angles as representations in perspective of three-dimensional rectangular objects. Such perception would be enhanced by the presence in the culture of pictures that are representations of three-dimensional objects and scenes.

Segall *et al.* tested members of more than a dozen different cultural groups in eastern, western, and southern Africa, the Philippines, and the United States. They found that the magnitude of the Müller–Lyer illusion was generally greater for children than for adults from the same culture (a fact somewhat discrepant with the hypothesis being tested, though consistent with the findings of other investigators) and that it also was greater for people in environments containing more rectangular objects—that is, in the American (Evanston) and South African European (Johannesburg) samples—than for people in the non-Western environments.

These findings stimulated many subsequent studies, most of which were restricted to comparisons among groups from only one or two cultures. The general pattern of results was congruent with the hypothesis of Segall et al. (Gregor & McPherson, 1965; Morgan, 1959b). However, the form of the Müller–Lyer figure (Davis, 1970; Davis & Carlson, 1970; Segall et al., 1966) and the method of presentation (Bonte, 1962; Jahoda, 1966; Jahoda & Stacy, 1970) affected the magnitude of the illusion, and even whether cultural differences in the magnitude of the illusion were observed at all. Why such procedural differences should affect perceptual inferences has not been explained, and some investigators have suggested alternative hypotheses to account for cultural differences.

One alternative to the carpentered-environment hypothesis is that anatomical characteristics of the retina, specifically interocular pigmentation, are responsible for cultural differences in the susceptibility to the Müller–Lyer illusion (Bornstein, 1973b; Pollack, 1969). One form of the hypothesis is that increased pigmentation produces decreased image contrast on the retina; which, in turn, produces more veridical perception of the illusion-eliciting figure. This hypothesis is supported by the finding that decreased figural contrast reduces the Müller–Lyer illusion and that subjects with intraocular pigmentation exhibit less illusion than subjects without such pigmentation (Ebert & Pollack, 1972). Bornstein (1973b) has hypothesized that the decreased susceptibility to the illusion occurs because of increased acuity, which is associated with the decreased chromatic aberration resulting from pigmentation. What is in dispute is whether the improved acuity and its effects on the illusion are greater than the decrease in contrast (due to light scattering of the pigment) and its effects.

The retinal-anatomy hypothesis has been studied cross-culturally by Berry (1971) and by Jahoda (1971). Berry ranked a number of cultures in terms of their "carpenteredness" and in terms of the skin pigmentation (which was assumed to be related to retinal pigmentation) of the people in the culture. He reported a higher correlation between skin pigmentation and magnitude of the Müller–Lyer illusion than between carpentering and magnitude of the illusion. However, the relevance of this observation for the hypothesis is unclear, since "both sets of ranking suffer from a lack of checks on reliability [p. 194]," and the basis for the rankings is unspecified.

Jahoda (1971) tested Malawi and Scottish university students on red and on blue illusion figures and predicted, from Pollack's argument, that the

Malawi students (but not the Scottish students) ought to be more susceptible to the illusion with the red than with the blue figures. That prediction was confirmed (the difference in magnitude of illusion for the two figures was 1.2%), but there was no overall difference in illusion magnitude between the two groups—a difference one would expect from the findings of Segall *et al.*. However, the form of the illusion used by Jahoda (1971, p. 202) and also by Pollack (Pollack & Silvar, 1967, p. 83) is quite different from that used by Segall *et al.*

That there are differences in magnitude of the Müller–Lyer illusion among the groups tested in these studies is clear. Whether the differences are a function of an environmental variable (such as "carpenteredness"), an anatomical variable (such as retinal pigmentation), or some other cultural variable has not been resolved. Cultural differences in magnitude of the illusion are small compared to differences in magnitude of the illusion observed with different forms of the illusion. The fact that there is not clear support for one or another hypothesis illustrates the problem of trying to identify features of the milieu that are relevant for perception when the perceptual phenomenon being investigated is itself not well understood.

B. The Horizontal–Vertical Illusion

Another illusion studied by Segall *et al.* is the horizontal–vertical illusion illustrated in Fig. 2. The illusion is an overestimation of the vertical line, segment a, relative to the horizontal line, segment b. Segall *et al.* hypothesized that the illusion occurs because the vertical line is perceived as a perspective representation of a line extending away from the viewer. The presence of open vistas, rather than rectangularity, is the environmental characteristic hypothesized as relevant for this illusion. Thus, the predicted ordering of cultures in terms of the magnitude of this illusion might differ from that for the Müller–Lyer illusion, and, indeed, the ordering is different for the two illusions (Jahoda, 1966; Jahoda & Stacy, 1970; Morgan, 1959b; Rivers, 1901; Segall *et al.*, 1966). The magnitude of the horizontal–vertical illusion, like that of the Müller–Lyer, also varies with the particular form of the illusion figure (Deregowski, 1967).

Segall *et al.* have pointed out that the type of environmental hypotheses they have advanced about the basis of illusions become increasingly compelling as they predict different orderings among cultures for different illusions. Thus, it is unlikely that any single one of the other variables considered, such as retinal pigmentation, will account for cultural differences in the magnitude of illusions in general.

One other illusion, the trapezoidal window illusion, has been studied in relation to an environmental hypothesis. The illusion occurs when a rotating trapezoid is perceived as an oscillating window. Allport and Pettigrew (1957) tested rural and urban groups of Zulu children in Natal with the illusion and predicted that rural Zulu children, whose environment contains few rectangular objects, would report the illusion less frequently than would urban Zulu children. Actually, most children in all groups reported the illusion in all except the first condition presented. In that condition most rural children did not report the illusion, whereas 60% of the urban children did (Allport & Pettigrew, 1957, p. 108). Since the group differences only occurred in the first condition, and since verbal communication may have been constrained by the absence of words for *window, square,* or *rectangle* in the Zulu language (pp. 106–107), the relation between environmental "carpentering" and illusion magnitude seems less obvious for this illusion than for those used by Segall *et al.*, whose procedure assured unambiguous communication.

C. The Ponzo Illusion

The Ponzo illusion is illustrated in Fig. 2. The illusion occurs when the length of the upper horizontal line (segment *a*) is overestimated relative to the lower horizontal line (segment *b*). The magnitude of the illusion increases with age (Leibowitz & Judisch, 1967), and, for American and Ugandan college students (and to a lesser degree for Guamanian students), the magnitude increases when the figure is viewed on a background containing information for distance—for example, when it is superimposed on a photograph of a field (Leibowitz, Brislin, Perlmutter, & Hennessy, 1969; Leibowitz & Pick, 1972). However, a context containing distance information does not affect the magnitude of the illusion for uneducated Ugandan village residents, who show virtually no illusion at all.

The illusion may occur because the figure is perceived as perspective information for represented distance away from the viewer, since accurate judgment of the line lengths is more difficult for educated respondents when the figure is seen with depth information. One hypothesis about the difference between the Ugandan groups argues that using books and viewing pictures enables one to learn to disregard the flatness of such material—a skill not acquired by the rural villagers (Kilbride & Leibowitz, 1975). However, since the respondents were explicitly directed to compare the actual lengths of the lines, a plausible rival hypothesis is that extensive use of the representational information in pictures hampers one's ability to use the two-dimensional information provided in pictures.

In summary, cultural differences in susceptibility to several visual illusions have been observed. Milieu characteristics, anatomical characteristics, and education have all been hypothesized as important determinants of these differences. Since the illusions themselves are not well understood, and since they may occur for different reasons, the source of the cultural differences cannot be identified. This is so because cultures vary, simultaneously, in a multitude of ways. This fact deeply affects the interpretation of many cultural differences in perception.

IV. PERCEPTUAL CONSTANCY

One of the classical topics of experimental psychology is the perception of the constancy of objects in spite of changes in certain aspects of the objects. Size constancy (perceiving the size of objects as invariant in spite of changes in the object's distance) and shape constancy (perceiving the shapes of objects as invariant in spite of changes in their slant or orientation) have been assessed cross-culturally. The purpose of making cultural comparisons is to assess the degree of constancy typically achieved by members of different cultural groups. The difficulty in interpreting cultural comparisons of perceptual constancy is that measurements of constancy vary greatly with differences in the particular conditions in which they are obtained (cf. Gibson, 1969, pp. 333–339, 363–368). This dependence of the apparent degree of constancy on the procedures by which it is assessed is a striking example of the general problem of determining the validity of tasks used to study cultural influences on perception. If one wants to make cultural comparisons of perceptual constancy, should one select a task in which subjects generally show a high degree of constancy, or one in which they do not? The answer is not only unapparent, but is an issue that has not even been considered in interpreting cultural differences in perceptual constancy. Yet, the meaning of cultural differences in constancy is constrained by the extent to which the experimental procedures determine the degree of measured constancy.

Early cross-cultural comparisons (Beveridge, 1935, 1940) were interpreted as demonstrating a greater constancy of shape and size among West African adults than among British adults. More recently, shape constancy was assessed in children and adults, both educated and uneducated, in Malawi (Myambo, 1972). In a first experiment, the degree of constancy shown by adult Malawi university students, European members of a university teaching staff, and uneducated Malawi adults was compared. The task was to view a disk that was inclined at various angles and to select an ellipse most like it in shape from among a set of comparison ellipses. The uneducated adults, who were tested in their local language, showed almost perfect constancy, whereas the educated Africans and Europeans, who were tested in English, did not. The purpose of a second experiment was to study developmental trends in shape constancy. Malawians from 5 to 20 years of age, most with little education, were tested; all showed nearly perfect shape constancy, and there was no apparent developmental change.

The differences in degree of constancy observed in educated and uneducated groups were interpreted as reflecting cultural and linguistic differences that were diminished by education. For example, it was said that the culture of the Africans provided few opportunities to learn about geometric forms and that, unlike English, the local Bantu language did not have words allowing clear shape distinctions. Consequently, the uneducated Africans were said not to have adopted an analytic approach to the shape constancy task (Myambo, 1972, p. 230). Since education and language were covariants in this study, it is difficult to evaluate this interpretation. What is clear is that it was the uneducated groups who performed the task most accurately (i.e., who showed the highest degree of constancy). The implication that education in the English language should lead people to perceive inaccurately the true shapes of objects around them is puzzling, and it illustrates the necessity for determining the validity of tasks used to assess constancy.

V. SPATIAL ORIENTATION

The methodological issue to be considered in reviewing cultural influences on the perception of spatial relations is that of the selection of subject samples. An obvious but often neglected requirement for identifying relations between perception and culture is that the samples of subjects must be representative of their cultures. Many investigators working in "foreign" cultures have used as subjects people who are most easily available, with the result that the representativeness of the group is simply unknown (Brislin & Baumgardner, 1971). This problem is not unique to the study of cultural influences on perception of spatial orientation, but it is especially apparent in the study of this topic.

An hypothesis guiding a number of cross-cultural investigations is that people who live in different environments—social and physical—develop different systems of spatial reference. Aspects such as left and right, up and down, assume more significance in some cultures than in others. Geographic features such as mountains and shores affect the terms of local reference systems, and differences in reference systems may, in turn, be related to differences in perception of spatial orientation.

The most comprehensive study of a spatial reference system is that by Gladwin (1970), who described the system used by Puluwat sailors to navigate among clusters of islands in the Western Pacific. The journeys of these people often last many days, and there are long periods during the day and night when no obvious landmarks are in sight. Yet charts, radios, and other aids to navigation are not used, and even compasses have begun to be used only recently.

Gladwin's method of studying this navigation system sets a high standard for investigators desiring to study systematic but unfamiliar behavior patterns in other groups. Gladwin acquired the information on which the navi-

gation system was based and the rules for using that information. He en-
gaged a master navigator to teach him the system, and by discussing the
rules of the system with his teacher, Gladwin constructed what seemed to
him an accurate description of the conceptual basis for the system. Then he
asked questions of his teacher; in effect, he made predictions about some as
yet undiscussed or inexplicit aspect of the system, and thus checked the
accuracy of his own model.

Many features of the sea and sky comprise the information on which the
Puluwat system is based. Knowledge of the habits of local sea birds provides
cues for one's location. Likewise, the sailors learn to detect the coral reefs
around the islands by changes in the color of the water and in the wave
formations—changes that, of course, differ depending on the conditions of
weather, sea, and sky. Ability to detect change in the "feel" of the boat
moving through the waves on a particular course is a skill used to maintain a
course. There is a complex reference system based on the positions and
patterns of stars in the night sky, and the rules for navigating between
specific islands are described in terms of the star patterns and reference and
islands. Parallax information is also explicitly included in the system as
descriptions of the way in which the islands "move" as a boat passes on one
or the other side of them.

The spatial reference system of the Temne in West Africa has been
described by Littlejohn (1963). (However, this is a less involved work than
Gladwin's detailed description of the Puluwat system.) Littlejohn's observations, together with the concepts of field dependence and field independence, have generated a good deal of empirical study. Concepts of field
dependence refer to how an individual relies on visual and other information
in making perceptual judgments—especially judgments about subjective
spatial orientation or the orientation of objects. Since personality characteristics are thought to underlie the extent of one's field dependence, the focus
of cross-cultural studies has been on child-rearing practices as predictors of
personality and degree of field dependence (Pick & Pick, 1970; Witkin, 1967;
Witkin & Berry, 1975; Witkin, Dyk, Faterson, Goodenough, & Karp, 1962;
Witkin, Lewis, Hertzman, Machover, Meissner, & Wapner, 1954). Dawson
(1967) studied the relation between strictness, or punitiveness, of upbringing
and degree of field dependence among young men in Sierra Leone. The men
rated the strictness of their own upbringing and their reported severity of
upbringing was related to their degree of field dependence. This finding was
interpreted as evidence that development is limited by severe upbringing. A
question that must be asked in evaluating this interpretation is whether the
men rating the severity of their own upbringing understood the scale of
severity that the experimenter intended. Interpreters were used for some of
the men, but not for others; also, both educated and uneducated men were
included in the samples. A plausible alternative interpretation is that educa-

tion or familiarity with rating scales accounts for the common variance among the ratings of severity of upbringing and of field dependence.

Berry (1966) thought that the type of task typically learned by members of a culture, as well as severity of upbringing, should be related to the degree to which perceptual skills will be developed. He predicted that Canadian Eskimos, who treat children kindly, who by trade are hunters, and who thus must attend to the slightest variation in an otherwise uniform visual environment, should be more field independent than should the Temne, who punish children severely and who are farmers who "rarely have to leave the numerous paths through the bush [Berry, 1966, p. 211]." Berry also predicted that more "Westernized" groups within each culture should be more field independent. Accordingly, he sampled four groups: one traditional and one transitional Eskimo group, and one traditional and one transitional Temne group. He used tests of discrimination and spatial skill and other measures of field dependence. The results were as predicted. Within each culture, the transitional group generally scored higher than did the traditional group, and there were striking differences between the two cultures, with the Eskimos performing better than the Temne. The meaning of this pattern possibly is obscured by the fact that the groups varied in the proportion of people who could perform the tasks at all. For instance, one task required drawing, and the proportion of subjects in the groups who were able to make any drawing at all varied in the order of the reported results (i.e., nearly all of the transitional Eskimo group were able to draw, whereas less than half of the traditional Temne sample were able to draw). The results for the other tests of spatial skills followed the same pattern. The Eskimos performed better than the Temne, and many of the Temne could not do some tests at all. For example, nearly 90% of one Temne group could not perform one of the tests, and 50% could not do another (p. 219). Berry concluded that "perceptual skills vary predictably as the demands of the land and the cultural characteristics vary [Berry, 1966, p. 228]." This idea that socialization practices are related to the development of field dependence remains influential (Lloyd, 1972, pp. 142ff; MacArthur, 1969; Witkin & Berry, 1975; Wober, 1967). However, the confounding of task familiarity (i.e., the ability to perform the tasks with assessed spatial skills) makes the idea problematic as well as interesting (Okonji, 1969; Siann, 1972).

The samples tested by Berry illustrate the issue identified at the beginning of this section—that of the relation of the representativeness of samples to the interpretation of cultural influences on their behavior.

For instance, the transitional Temne group consisted of 32 people from a town whose total population was 4000 and in which there had been European-run mission schools for many years. The 32 people were "contacted through a local bar owner [Berry, 1966, p. 209]."

The traditional Temne group was made up of 90 people from a farming

village with a population of 200. Europeans infrequently visited the village
and there were no Western schools. The subjects were selected in an
unspecified way from among those coming to the test center to play the
games (Berry, 1966, pp. 209–210).

The transitional Eskimo group consisted of 31 people from a community of
1000. Many non-Eskimos lived in the town and English was widely spoken.
The method of subject recruitment was not specified (Berry, 1966, p. 210).

The traditional Eskimo group was made up of 90 people from an area of
hunting camps with a total population of 300 and in which contact with
non-Eskimos was said to be limited. Subject recruitment occurred when
"the more populous camps were visited by dog team and all available people
were tested; word was left for those out hunting to visit the test centre when
they were next in to trade [Berry, 1966, p. 210]."

The problem posed by these samples for interpreting the findings of the
study is that the extent to which the people in the same group are representative of their respective groups simply is unknown. Likewise, the degree to
which the groups are "transitional" or "traditional" is unknown.

In one study, an environmental experience thought to be related to spatial
ability (i.e., exploring one's environment) was assessed directly (Munroe &
Munroe, 1971). Pairs of children (matched for age) from a village in Kenya
were observed on several occasions to determine how far from their homes
the children wandered. Two tests of spatial ability were then administered to
the children in their local language. On one test, the child who had been
found farther from home was also the member of the pair who performed
better. In a follow-up study (Nerlove, Munroe, & Munroe, 1971), additional
pairs of children (matched for age and ranging in age from 5 to 13 years) from
another village in Kenya were observed to determine the distance away from
home they wandered during free time. Three tests of spatial ability were then
administered, and on all three, in a significant number of pairs, the child
found farther from home was also the child who performed better. Thus,
there is evidence of a relation between spatial experience in the environment
and skill at performing a spatial task.

Many tasks used to assess spatial skills require a production such as
building a model or copying a form (Deregowski, 1968a,b,c, 1971a,b, 1972a;
Tekane, 1963). Unfortunately, such tasks are not appropriate if the people
being tested have varying experience at drawing or copying. In one instance
many of the people whose spatial skills were assessed in this way had never
before even held pencils (Shapiro, 1960). The usual criterion for scoring the
copies people make is whether they are oriented in the same way as a model;
however, the instructions are usually not explicit about whether one should
take orientation into account. There is evidence from studies in Ghana
(Jahoda, 1956) and Zambia (Serpell, 1971a,b) that when instructions are
explicit about the relevance of orientation for a task, orientations of shapes
can be noticed and used by young children.

In sum, members of different cultures operate in terms of complex spatial reference systems. The environmental and socialization experiences influencing the development of spatial perception have been difficult to identify clearly. One basis for the difficulty has been that the samples of subjects observed from different cultures have not been selected for their representativeness with regard to their respective cultures.

In conclusion, it might be recalled that psychologists have been interested in cultural differences in perception mainly for theoretical reasons. However, there are also practical reasons for such interest. For instance, the construction of graphic educational materials should be based on an understanding of perception. In general, little is known about the perception of educational materials, and many of these are simply translated from one culture to another. Esthetics is another area in which cultural differences in perception may be important. Music and art from one culture often are unappreciated by members of another culture. What aspects of music and art are perceived? Can such perception be modified, and by what types of experience and training? Finally, communication between members of different cultures (aside from language translation itself) may be aided or inhibited by the perception of the individuals. Anthropologists have pointed out occasional instances of differences in responsivity to such factors as personal proximity, facial expression, etc., but there is little information about the perceptual processes underlying these differences. Psychologists could fruitfully turn their attention to these differences that make a difference.

Acknowledgments

The chapter is based partly on a paper prepared by the first author at the Center for Advanced Study in the Behavioral Sciences, Stanford, California, and the support from that institution is acknowledged with pleasure. The authors are also grateful to Judith Allen and to Marsha Unze for their assistance.

References

Abramson, A. S., & Lisker, L. Discriminability along the voicing continuum: Cross-language tests. *Status report in speech research*. Haskins Laboratories, SR 11, 1967.

Allport, G. W., & Pettigrew, T. F. Cultural influence on the perception of movement: The trapezoidal illusion among Zulus. *Journal of Abnormal and Social Psychology*, 1957, **55**, 104–113.

Berry, J. W. Temne and Eskimo perceptual skills. *International Journal of Psychology*, 1966, **1**, 207–229.

Berry, J. W. Müller–Lyer susceptibility: Culture, ecology or race? *International Journal of Psychology*, 1971, **6**, 193–197.

Beveridge, W. M. Racial differences in phenomenal regression. *British Journal of Psychology*, 1935, **26**, 59–62.

Beveridge, W. M. Some racial differences in perception. *British Journal of Psychology*, 1939–1940, **30**, 57–64.

Bonte, M. The reaction of two African societies to the Müller–Lyer illusion. *Journal of Social Psychology,* 1962, **58,** 265–268.

Bornstein, M. H. Color vision and color naming: A psychophysiological hypothesis of cultural difference. *Psychological Bulletin,* 1973, **80,** 257–285. (a)

Bornstein, M. H. The psychophysiological component of cultural difference in color naming and illusion susceptibility. *Behavior Science Notes,* 1973, **8,** 41–101. (b)

Bradley, D. J. The ability to black groups to produce recognisable patterns on the 7-squares test. *Journal of the National Institute of Personnel Research,* 1960, **8,** 142–144.

Brimble, A. R. The construction of a non-verbal intelligence test in Northern Rhodesia. *Rhodes-Livingstone Journal,* 1963, **34,** 23–35.

Brislin, R. W., & Baumgardner, S. R. Non-random sampling of individuals in cross-cultural research. *Journal of Cross-Cultural Psychology,* 1971, **2,** 397–400.

Cooper, W. E. Adaptation of phonetic feature analyzers for place of articulation. *Journal of the Acoustical Society of America,* 1974, **56,** 617–627.

Davis, C. M. Education and susceptibility to the Müller–Lyer illusion among the Banyankole. *Journal of Social Psychology,* 1970, **82,** 25–34.

Davis, C. M., & Carlson, J. A. A cross-cultural study of the strength of the Müller–Lyer illusion as a function of attentional factors. *Journal of Personality and Social Psychology,* 1970, **16,** 403–410.

Dawson, J. L. M. Cultural and physiological influences upon spatial-perceptual processes in West Africa. *International Journal of Psychology*, 1967, **2,** 115–128 (Part I), 171–185 (Part II).

Deregowski, J. B. The horizontal–vertical illusion and the ecological hypothesis. *International Journal of Psychology,* 1967, **2,** 269–273.

Deregowski, J. B. Pictorial recognition in subjects from a relatively pictureless environment. *African Social Research,* 1968, **5,** 356–364. (a)

Deregowski, J. B. Difficulties in pictorial depth perception in Africa. *British Journal of Psychology,* 1968, **59,** 195–204. (b)

Deregowski, J. B. On perception of depicted orientation. *International Journal of Psychology,* 1968, **3,** 149–156. (c)

Deregowski, J. B. Perception of the two-pronged trident by two- and three-dimensional perceivers. *Journal of Experimental Psychology,* 1969, **82,** 9–13. (a)

Deregowski, J. B. A pictorial perception paradox. *Acta Psychologica,* 1969, **31,** 365–374. (b)

Deregowski, J. B. Preference for chain-type drawings in Zambian domestic servants and primary schoolchildren. *Psychologia Africana,* 1969, **12,** 172–180. (c)

Deregowski, J. B. Chain-type drawings: A further note. *Perceptual and Motor Skills,* 1970, **30,** 102. (a)

Deregowski, J. B. A note on the possible determinant of "split representation" as an artistic style. *International Journal of Psychology,* 1970, **5,** 21–26. (b)

Deregowski, J. B. Responses mediating pictorial recognition. *Journal of Social Psychology,* 1971, **84,** 27–33. (a)

Deregowski, J. B. Orientation and perception of pictorial depth. *International Journal of Psychology,* 1971, **6,** 111–114. (b)

Deregowski, J. B. Pictorial perception and culture. *Scientific American,* 1972 (November), **227,** 82–88. (a)

Deregowski, J. B. Reproduction of orientation of Kohs-type figures: A cross-cultural study. *British Journal of Psychology,* 1972, **63,** 283–296. (b)

Deregowski, J. B. The role of symmetry in pattern reproduction by Zambian children. *Journal of Cross-Cultural Psychology,* 1972, **3,** 303–307. (c)

Deregowski, J. B. & Byth, W. Hudson's pictures in Pandora's box. *Journal of Cross-Cultural Psychology,* 1970, **1,** 315–323.

Diehl, R. L. The effect of selective adaptation on the identification of speech sounds. *Perception and Psychophysics*, 1975, **17**, 48–52.

Dirks, J., & Gibson, E. *Infants' perception of similarity between live people and their photographs.* Unpublished manuscript, Cornell Univ., 1976.

Duncan, H. F., Gourlay, N., & Hudson, W. *A study of pictorial perception among Bantu and white primary school children in South Africa.* Johannesburg, South Africa: Witwatersrand Univ. Press, 1973.

Dutoit, B. M. Pictorial depth perception and linguistic relativity. *Psychologia Africana*, 1966, **11**, 51–63.

Ebert, P. C., & Pollack, R. H. Magnitude of the Müller–Lyer illusion as a function of lightness contrast, viewing time, and fundus pigmentation. *Psychonomic Science*, 1972, **26**, 347–348.

Gibson, E. J. *Principles of perceptual learning and development.* New York: Appleton, 1969.

Gladwin, T. *East is a big bird: Navigation and logic on Puluwatatoll.* Cambridge, Massachusetts: Harvard Univ. Press, 1970.

Goodman, N. *Languages of art: An approach to a theory of symbols.* Indianapolis, Indiana: Bobbs-Merrill, 1968.

Gregor, A. J., & McPherson, D. A. A study of susceptibility to geometric illusions among cultural subgroups of Australian aborigines. *Psychologia Africana*, 1965, **11**, 1–13.

Hagen, M. A. Picture preception: Toward a theoretical model. *Psychological Bulletin*, 1974, **81**, 471–497.

Hector, H., Dlodlo, M. S., & DuPlessis, C. F. An experiment on silhouette recognition and projection with Bantu children of different ages. *Journal of the National Institute of Personnel Research*, 1961, **8**, 195–198.

Hochberg, J., & Brooks, V. Pictorial recognition as an unlearned ability: A study of one child's performance. *American Journal of Psychology*, 1962, **75**, 624–628.

Hudson, W. Pictorial depth perception in sub-cultural groups in Africa. *Journal of Social Psychology*, 1960, **52**, 183–208.

Hudson, W. Pictorial perception and educational adaptation in Africa. *Psychologia Africana*, 1962, **9**, 226–239. (a)

Hudson, W. Cultural problems in pictorial perception. *South African Journal of Science*, 1962, **58**, 189–196. (b)

Hudson, W. The study of the problem of pictorial perception among unacculturated groups. *International Journal of Psychology*, 1967, **2**, 89–107.

Jahoda, G. Assessment of abstract behavior in a non-Western culture. *Journal of Abnormal and Social Psychology*, 1956, **53**, 237–243.

Jahoda, G. Geometric illusions and environment: A study in Ghana. *British Journal of Psychology*, 1966, **57**, 193–199.

Jahoda, G. Retinal pigmentation, illusion susceptibility and space perception. *International Journal of Psychology*, 1971, **6**, 199–208.

Jahoda, G., & McGurk, H. Development of pictorial depth perception: Cross-cultural replications. *Child Development*, 1974, **45**, 1042–1047. (a)

Jahoda, G., & McGurk, H. Pictorial depth perception: A developmental study. *British Journal of Psychology*, 1974, **65**, 141–149. (b)

Jahoda, G., & Stacey, B. Susceptibility to geometrical illusions according to culture and professional training. *Perception & Psychophysics*, 1970, **7**, 179–184.

Kennedy, J. M. *A psychology of picture perception.* San Francisco: Jossey-Bass, 1974.

Kennedy, J. M. African peoples abilities with outline drawings. *Journal of Aesthetics and Art Criticism*, 1977, **35**, 293–300.

Kennedy, J. M., & Ross, A. S. Outline picture perception by the Songe of Papua. *Perception*, 1975, **4**, 391–406.

Kilbride, P. L., & Leibowitz, H. W. Factors affecting the magnitude of the Ponzo perspective illusion among the Baganda. *Perception & Psychophysics*, 1975, **17**, 543–548.

Kilbride, P. L., & Robbins, M. C. Linear perspective, pictorial depth perception and education among the Baganda. *Perceptual and Motor Skills*, 1968, **27**, 601–602.

Kilbride, P. L., Robbins, M. C., & Freeman, R. B., Jr. Pictorial depth perception and education among Baganda school children. *Perceptual and Motor Skills*, 1968, **26**, 1116–1118.

Leibowitz, H. W., Brislin, R., Perlmutter, L., & Hennessy, R. Ponzo perspective illusion as a manifestation of space perception. *Science*, 1969, **166**, 1174–1176.

Leibowitz, H. W., & Judisch, J. M. The relation between age and the magnitude of the Ponzo illusion. *American Journal of Psychology*, 1967, **80**, 105–109.

Leibowitz, H. W., & Pick, H. L., Jr. Cross-cultural and educational aspects of the Ponzo perspective illusion. *Perception and Psychophysics*, 1972, **12**, 430–432.

Liberman, A. M., Cooper, F. S., Shankweiler, D. P., & Studdert-Kennedy, M. Perception of the speech code. *Psychological Review*, 1967, **74**, 431–461.

Liddicoat, R., & Koza, C. Language development in African infants. *Psychologia Africana*, 1963, **10**, 108–116.

Lisker, L., & Abramson, A. S. The voicing dimension: Some experiments in comparative phonetics. *Status report in speech research.* Haskins Laboratory, SR 11, 1967.

Littlejohn, J. Temne space. *Anthropological Quarterly*, 1963, **36**, 1–17.

Lloyd, B. B. *Perception and cognition: A cross-cultural perspective.* Middlesex, England: Penguin, 1972.

MacArthur, R. Sex differences in field dependence for the Eskimo. Replication of Berry's findings. *International Journal of Psychology*, 1967, **2**, 139–140.

Miller, R. J. Cross-cultural research in the perception of pictorial materials. *Psychological Bulletin*, 1973, **80**, 135–150.

Morgan, P. Observations and findings on the 7-squares test with literate and illiterate Black groups in Southern Africa. *Journal of the National Institute of Personnel Research*, 1959, **8**, 44–47. (a)

Morgan, P. A study in perceptual differences among cultural groups in Southern Africa, using tests of geometric illusion. *Journal of the National Institute for Personnel Research*, 1959, **8**, 39–43. (b)

Mundy-Castle, A. C. Pictorial depth perception in Ghanaian children. *International Journal of Psychology*, 1966, **1**, 289–300.

Mundy-Castle, A. C., & Nelson, G. K. A neuropsychological study of the Knysna forest workers. *Psychologia Africana*, 1962, **9**, 240–272.

Munroe, R. L., & Munroe, R. H. Effect of environmental experience on spatial ability in an East African society. *Journal of Social Psychology*, 1971, **83**, 15–22.

Myambo, K. Shape constancy as influenced by culture, Western education, and age. *Journal of Cross-Cultural Psychology*, 1972, **3**, 221–232.

Nerlove, S. B., Munroe, R. H., & Munroe, R. L. Effect of environmental experience on spatial ability: A replication. *Journal of Social Psychology*, 1971, **84**, 3–10.

Okonji, M. O. The differential effects of rural and urban upbringing on the development of cognitive styles. *International Journal of Psychology*, 1969, **4**, 293–305.

Omari, I. M., & Cook, H. Differential cognitive cues in pictorial depth perception. *Journal of Cross-Cultural Psychology*, 1972, **3**, 321–325.

Omari, I. M., & MacGinitie, W. H. Some pictorial artifacts in studies of African children's pictorial depth perception. *Child Development*, 1974, **45**, 535–539.

Pick, H. L., Jr., & Pick, A. D. Sensory and perceptual development. In P. H. Mussen (Ed.), *Carmichael's manual of child psychology* (Vol. 1). New York: Wiley, 1970.

Pollack, R. H. Some implications of ontogenetic changes in perception. In D. Elkind & J. H. Flavell (Eds.), *Studies in cognitive development: Essays in honor of Jean Piaget.* New York: Oxford Univ. Press, 1969.

Pollack, R. H., & Silvar, S. D. Magnitude of the Müller–Lyer illusion in children as a function of pigmentation of the Fundus oculi. *Psychonomic Science*, 1967, **8**, 83–84.

Rivers, W. H. R. Introduction and vision. In A. C. Haddon (Ed.), *Reports of the Cambridge anthropological expedition to the Torres straits* (Vol. 2, Part I). New York: Cambridge Univ. Press, 1901.

Segall, M. H., Campbell, D. T., & Herskovits, M. J. Cultural differences in the perception of geometric illusions. *Science,* 1963, **139,** 769–771.

Segall, M. H., Campbell, D. T., & Herskovits, M. J. *The influence of culture on visual perception.* Indianapolis, Indiana: Bobbs-Merrill, 1966.

Serpell, R. Discrimination of orientation by Zambian children. *Journal of Comparative and Physiological Psychology,* 1971, **75,** 312–316. (a)

Serpell, R. Preference for specific orientation of abstract shapes among Zambian children. *Journal of Cross-Cultural Psychology,* 1971, **2,** 225–239. (b)

Shapiro, M. B. The rotation of drawings by illiterate Africans. *Journal of Social Psychology,* 1960, **52,** 17–30.

Siann, G. Measuring field dependence in Zambia: A cross-cultural study. *International Journal of Psychology,* 1972, **7,** 87–96.

Tekane, I. Symmetrical pattern completions by illiterate and literate Bantu. *Psychologia Africana,* 1963, **10,** 63–68.

Waldron, L. A., & Gallimore, A. J. Pictorial depth perception in Papua New Guinea, Torres Strait, and Australia. *Australian Journal of Psychology,* 1973, **25**(1), 89–92.

Williams, J. G. *A field guide to the national parks of East Africa.* London: Collins, 1967.

Witkin, H. A. A cognitive-style approach to cross-cultural research. *International Journal of Psychology,* 1967, **2,** 233–250.

Witkin, H. A., & Berry, J. W. Psychological differentiation in cross-cultural perspective. *Journal of Cross-Cultural Psychology,* 1975, **6,** 4–87.

Witkin, H. A., Dyk, R. B., Faterson, H. F., Goodenough, D. R., & Karp, S. A. *Psychological differentiation: Studies of development.* New York: Wiley, 1962.

Witkin, H. A., Lewis, H. B., Hertzman, M., Machover, K., Meissner, P. B., & Wapner, S. *Personality through perception: An experimental and clinical study.* New York: Harper, 1954.

Wober, M. Adapting Witkin's field independence theory to accomodate new information from Africa. *British Journal of Psychology,* 1967, **58,** 29–38.

Part II

Sensory Disorders and Prosthetics

Chapter 3

PERCEPTION BY THE DEAF*

HARRY W. HOEMANN

I. INTRODUCTION

Since deaf persons lack a major sensory channel, it is natural to wonder whether such persons perceive the world or specific aspects of worldly phenomena differently than people with normal hearing. *Differently* in this case is likely to imply a deficiency, since everyone able to hear can surely think of numerous benefits that would be lost if he or she were to become deaf. Moreover, since hearing seems to play a central role in language

* The preparation of this manuscript was supported by N.I.H. Research Grant NS-09590-05 from the National Institute of Neurological Diseases and Stroke. The assistance of Jennie Bridges and Judi Zink is sincerely appreciated.

acquisition, formal education, and cultural transmission, speculation about deaf people's perceptual abilities is typically colored by the suspicion that the visual channel, without auditory support, may produce an inferior outcome with regard to adaptive awareness of the environment.

Meanwhile, there is the intriguing possibility that, for deaf persons, there might be some kind of compensation by which their visual channel could take on some or all of the functions ordinarily played by the auditory channel.

One would think that researchers would be quick to exploit the opportunity furnished them by nature to study the perceptual abilities and perceptual activities of persons born profoundly deaf. Contrary to expectation, there have been very few studies of deaf persons' perceptual behavior. *DSH Abstracts* (Moncada, 1960–1976), the major index of literature in the field of deafness, speech, and hearing, does not generally list perception in its annual index of contents, since there are too few perception studies involving hearing-impaired subjects to warrant a separate listing. The few studies that have been conducted, some of which are reviewed in what follows, have yielded inconclusive answers to the more crucial questions, and their results have often been overinterpreted.

Why conclusions have frequently gone beyond the data and why so few studies have been conducted in the area of perception by the deaf are recurring questions in Sections II and III of this chapter. Section IV deals with the perception of language, oral and manual, and describes proposals designed to make the rules of English more accessible to deaf persons either through visual or tactile cues or through modified systems of sign language. Section V ventures some comments on future directions for research.

II. RESEARCH FINDINGS

A. Visuo-Motor Coordination and the Generalized-Perceptual-Deficiency Hypothesis

The hypothesis has been advanced that an auditory deficit may affect the neurological development and organization of other perceptual systems and, therefore, the total reactivity of an organism (Myklebust & Brutten, 1953). Evidence in support of this hypothesis has been derived primarily from the results of administrations of batteries of perceptual tests to age samples of deaf and hearing subjects. Comparisons are typically made between the group performances of the deaf and the hearing samples, between age groups within deaf and hearing samples, or between performances on individual tests within the battery.

Myklebust and Brutten administered the Keystone Visual Survey (Myklebust, 1950), the Goodenough Draw-A-Man Test (Goodenough & Harris,

1950), the Marble Board Test (Werner & Strauss, 1941), some figure–ground tests (Werner & Strauss, 1941), some tachistoscopically presented materials, a perseveration test (Werner & Strauss, 1942), and a pattern-reproduction test (Yacorzysnki & Davis, 1945) to deaf pupils enrolled in a residential school. They reported numerous deficiencies in the deaf subjects' performances in visual perception and in the reproduction of spatial figures.

Larr (1956) administered a battery of tests that included two versions of the Marble Board Test (Werner & Strauss, 1941), a Picture Test (Werner & Strauss, 1940) that assessed subjects' inclination to make "background responses," and two versions of a Tactual Motor Test (Werner & Strauss, 1940). Larr found no evidence of visuo-motor disturbance in the Marble Board protocols, but his subjects gave more background responses on the figure–ground test than the hearing controls.

Binnie, Elkind, and Stewart (1966) administered a picture integration test, a diamond illusion test, and a picture ambiguity test to 80 hearing-impaired children 6–13 years of age, and compared their performances with hearing norms. The hearing-impaired children's performances were inferior to the norms on all three tests. Oral subjects performed better than nonoral subjects, but there was no significant relation between the degree of hearing loss and visual perceptual ability.

Sterritt, Camp, and Lipman (1966) required deaf and hearing subjects to reproduce patterns of dots and dashes presented visually and above threshold auditorially. They reported that the deaf subjects reproduced the auditory patterns less accurately than the visual patterns and that they scored below the hearing subjects on the visual patterns.

Inferior performances by deaf subjects in any or all of the comparisons made during such investigations have sometimes been taken as evidence that auditory impairment also affects other perceptual reactivity, including vision and visuo-motor coordination. Myklebust and Brutten (1953) concluded on the basis of deaf subjects' relatively greater difficulty with geometric figure–ground stimuli that abstraction is a special problem for deaf children and that deafness restricts the child functionally to a world of concrete objects and concrete situations. Such conclusions clearly go beyond the data.

Meanwhile, other studies have reported perceptual abilities in deaf persons equal or superior to that in hearing persons. Gates and Chase (1926) cited deaf subjects' competent performances in a perceptual task as supportive evidence for their claim that superior perceptual abilities in deaf persons contribute to their remarkable spelling ability. Rosenstein (1957, 1959) and Thompson (1964) found no evidence of inferiority in deaf children's perceptual behavior. Studies using tachistoscopic presentation of materials to deaf and hearing subjects have also reported adequate performances on the part of the deaf subjects (Mandes, Allen, & Swisher, 1971; McKeever, Hoemann, Florian, & VanDeventer, 1976).

Some investigators have been appropriately cautious in their interpretations of lower performances by deaf subjects in perception tasks. For example, Rileigh and Odom (1972) observed age-related differences between deaf and hearing subjects in rhythm perception, but they considered the result to reflect a developmental lag attributable to an experiential deficit, rather than to a qualitative difference in the deaf children's perceptual development.

B. Tactual Perception and the
Compensation Hypothesis

Batteries of tactual perception tasks have typically yielded results that show deaf persons to be equal or superior to hearing controls in the accuracy of their perceptions (Blank & Bridger, 1966; Larr, 1956; Rosenstein, 1957; Schiff & Dytell, 1972). Generalizations about deaf persons' tactual sensitivity, however, cannot be made with confidence on the basis of their performances on tactual perception tasks, since factor analyses of the component tests of a battery have not yielded high enough correlations among the tests within the battery to justify confidence in their validity (Schiff & Dytell, 1972).

Deaf children's superior sensitivity to vibrotactile stimulation has been cited as support for the compensation hypothesis. According to this view, deprivation in one sensory system may lead to heightened ability to use the cues processed by one or more alternative channels. Thus, a hearing loss may lead to a compensatory use of the visual or tactual sensory systems. However, there is no evidence that such compensation is automatic. Given an opportunity through experience to develop other sensory channels, compensatory sensitivity may be acquired. However, it does not seem to be the case that greater visual or tactual acuity is an inevitable effect of deafness. Deaf children receive a great deal of training in the use of tactile cues in speech training, and they are frequently asked to hold their hands on a piano while it is being played so as to experience the rhythm of music through vibrations. Some evidence for the role of experience in the development of sensory awareness can be found in research on oral sensory perception. Bishop, Ringel, and House (1973) found that deaf children trained orally were equal to hearing children in the orosensory discrimination of changes in size, changes in shape, and changes in both size and shape. Manually trained deaf children, however, made significantly more errors in discriminating changes in shape and changes in size and shape. Although poorer performances by the manually trained children may merely reflect less efficient strategies for remembering shapes, integration of oral sensory activity with oral motor activity may require the kind of practice that is optimally provided by the articulation of speech.

If compensatory sensitivity in another sensory channel is acquired only by appropriate training or experience, a battery of tests not matched to the subjects' life circumstances may not show any evidence of it. A well-designed training study is called for. Training can be a powerful technique for uncovering latent capacity in target populations, since they should generate more rapid improvement than either deficient or normal controls. One training study of preschool deaf children's perceptual skills has been conducted (Fitch, Sachs, & Marshall, 1973) in which there were significant gains on a number of tasks, including figure–ground, spatial position, and spatial relations.

C. Summary

Mixed results such as have been obtained in studies of deaf subjects' perceptual abilities warrant the same conclusions that have been drawn in the case of deaf subjects' performances in cognitive tasks (Furth, 1966, 1971)—namely, that no single, simplistic explanation is able to account for both their successes and their shortcomings. Age-related differences between deaf and hearing groups may merely reflect a developmental lag stemming from an experiential deficiency. The generalized-deficiency hypothesis advanced by Myklebust and Brutten (1953) must be considered as unconfirmed, since it fails to account for the many instances in which deaf persons' perceptual behaviors and abilities have been observed to function at least as well as those of hearing controls. The compensation hypothesis has yet to be tested adequately, since compensation for a sensory deficiency by refining an alternative channel may require training or experience specific to life's circumstances.

III. METHODOLOGICAL PROBLEMS

A problem associated with deafness research in general, including perception by the deaf, is that too little attention has been given to variables that might be implicated in explanations of obtained results and that determine the population or populations of deaf persons to which results may be generalized. Among these variables are age of onset, etiology, type and degree of loss, and educational treatment. In addition, hearing subjects have often been tested on the same tasks and used for comparison purposes, even though they have not been appropriately matched on such important variables as educational background, socioeconomic status, or linguistic competence in English.

A. Age at Onset

If the ages at which tested subjects lost their hearing remain unspecified, one cannot be sure whether the results are supposed to be typical of persons born deaf or whether they are also supposed to apply to persons who became deaf in middle childhood or in old age. Especially in perception research it clearly makes a difference whether there has been prior sensory experience in the affected channel, or whether the condition has been present in the subject from birth.

Unfortunately for researchers, the age of deafness onset is often unknown. Even when it is listed among the data on school records, the source of the information may be only parents' memories, and these are known to be very unreliable. This places the researcher in an uncomfortable position. Either noise is added to the data by including children whose age at onset of deafness cannot be documented with certainty, or the size of some age samples is reduced to the point where statistical tests may lack the power to reject the null hypothesis. If the size of age groups is augmented by including additional institutions, there will be additional variance from this source. Moreover, the need to consider this additional variable may offset any advantage gained by adding a few more subjects to the study.

Age at onset is especially important for considering the possible role of linguistic factors. Adventitiously deaf persons can be presumed to have some level of linguistic competence in spoken language, especially if deafness occurred during middle childhood. In contrast, an early onset of deafness precludes spontaneous acquisition of linguistic competence in a spoken language. This is a matter of considerable importance, since reduced competence in English may affect the subjects' comprehension of test instructions, their rapport with the experimenter, and their ability to make the required response. Among populations of deaf people for whom English may have the status of a second language, poorer performances may be expected in any task that presents the instructions orally or in writing, uses English-language stimuli, or requires an oral or written English response.

B. Etiology

Etiology would appear to have considerable relevance for perception research, since the cause of deafness might also be the cause of other neurological deficits (Vernon, 1968) that could affect performance in perception tasks. This is a reasonable hypothesis, since the incidence of visual defects is known to be considerably higher in deaf populations of schoolchildren than in the general population of the same age (Lawson & Myklebust, 1970; Pollard & Neumaier, 1974). Moreover, some etiologies, such as rubella, are known to cause a wide variety of additional handicaps (Vernon, 1967; Zwirecki, Stansbery, Porter, & Hayes, 1976). One direct comparison of 30 rubella-deaf young adults with 30 deaf persons with other etiologies yielded significantly lower performances by the rubella-deaf group in language, reading, reasoning, computation, lipreading, and digit-symbol (coding) tasks, even though the samples scored similarly in performance I.Q., visual retention, manual dexterity, and degree of hearing loss (Lehman & Simmons, 1972). Of the 30 rubella-deaf subjects, 25 had more than one handicap, such as heart trouble, small body size, slow learning, impaired vision, or suspected aphasia.

Gilbert and Levee (1967) applied the Pascal and Suttell (1951) scoring system to Bender Gestalt protocols obtained from 50 deaf pupils of a Newark, New Jersey day school and 50 hearing controls enrolled in a Newark parochial school. They also administered the Archimedes Spiral Test, which is reported to indicate brain damage in persons who fail to see its spiral aftereffect when the spiral is rotated and then stopped (Price & Deabler, 1955). Gilbert and Levee obtained significantly lower Bender Gestalt scores and significantly fewer reports of a spiral aftereffect in the deaf subjects. Confidence in their results is shaken somewhat by the relatively low correlations obtained between the two tests ($\rho = .35$ for the hearing and .37 for the deaf samples) and by an undiscussed significant difference between the variances of the deaf and the hearing groups on the Bender Gestalt scores. The authors considered the poorer performances of the deaf children to be suggestive of a higher incidence of brain damage among deaf subjects than is found in the general population. The burden of the diagnosis, however, was on the two tests, since none of the deaf subjects was suspected of having brain damage prior to testing.

Keogh, Vernon, and Smith (1970) scored 160 Bender Gestalt protocols by means of the Koppitz (1964) method and compared the results with the etiologies of deafness known to be present in the sample. Five types of etiology were identified: meningitis, maternal rubella, premature birth, Rh incompatibility, and genetic causes. No relation could be discerned between etiology and the Koppitz scores. Moreover, the usefulness of the Bender Gestalt for diagnosing minimal brain damage was left open to serious question. Three clinical psychologists working independently were unable to agree in their diagnoses of the protocols in more than 50% of the cases, even though the age, sex, and I.Q. of each subject were supplied.

Although the deaf subjects scored significantly lower than the hearing subjects, this result must also be interpreted with caution, since the age-related trend among the deaf subjects was in the appropriate direction. Their performance was a developmental lag, rather than a qualitative, irrevocable deficiency. It is one thing to describe a deaf protocol as immature, and quite another to say that it is indicative of an organic lesion. Koegh et al. (1970) were reluctant to rule out the possibility that their results might constitute evidence of the pervasive effect of extreme auditory deprivation. But this conclusion is no more obvious than the one drawn by Gilbert and Levee (1967) that poorer performances by deaf children on the Bender Gestalt suggested a greater incidence of brain damage among the deaf. If a certain amount of brain damage sometimes accompanies deafness, it appears that it cannot be diagnosed reliably by means of the Bender Gestalt Test. Bolton (1972, 1973) has also reported disappointing results from an attempt to quantify Bender Gestalt protocols so as to relate them to the personality assessment of deaf rehabilitation clients.

The crucial question is whether auditory deprivation itself causes a neurological deficit in other sensory systems, or whether the factors that sometimes cause deafness may also cause other organic impairments as well. If additional handicapping conditions are prevalent among deaf populations, lower performances are more likely to be found in groups of casually screened deaf subjects than in any control group. Wilson, Rapin, Wilson, and VanDenburg (1975) have provided a tentative answer to this question. They used school records to select 34 pupils from a private deaf school and gave them medical, pediatric neurological, otological, and audiological examinations. The more thorough examination disclosed evidence of organic dysfunction in eight pupils whose status had not been suspected from the information contained in their school records. There was also a relatively high incidence of exogenous causes of deafness in their sample (16 out of the 34) owing to liberal admission policies of the cooperating school, which did not systematically exclude multiply handicapped children. The authors administered an extensive battery of tests to the children over a 2-year period. After comparing the brain-damaged and the other deaf subjects, they concluded that the intact deaf subjects were not deficient in their perceptual abilities.

Although the Wilson et al. (1975) study sets an appropriately rigorous standard for subject evaluation in deafness research, it offers few consolations to the investigator who plans to test deaf subjects. The etiology of 6 of their 34 subjects was unknown, and the investigators have warned readers that samples selected on the basis of chart review are likely to include a motley assortment of cases.

C. Type and Degree of Loss

A third variable of interest in perception research is the type and degree of loss. Three types of hearing loss can be distinguished based on the site of lesion: conductive losses, sensorineural losses, and retrocochlear losses. The anatomical structures associated with these sites of lesion are described in some detail by Webster (1973).

A conductive loss, whose site of lesion is the eardrum, ear canal, or middle ear, is not as severe a handicap as a sensorineural loss. Conductive losses typically yield a flat audiogram, that is, the loss is about the same at all frequencies. A hearing aid, which amplifies the signal, can be of great benefit to a person with a conductive loss, although the ability to localize the source of sounds will often be impaired.

A sensorineural loss generally produces a sloping audiogram, with more severe losses in the higher frequencies. Such losses cause considerable distortion. Since the consonants, which embody many of the distinctive features of spoken languages, are associated with higher frequencies, a sensorineural loss affects discrimination. Even with amplification, there may be poor speech comprehension. This explains why a hearing aid does not correct defective hearing as successfully as eyeglasses correct many forms of defective vision. A sensorineural loss is more like a scarred or detached retina than myopia, and a hearing aid is no more able to compensate for a defective cochlea than glasses can replace a damaged retina.

A retrocochlear loss may leave sensitivity relatively unaffected but diminish a person's ability to comprehend the meaning of speech or to interpret the significance of other auditory stimuli. Retrocochlear lesions also tend to affect performance adversely when there is a low signal-to-noise ratio or when the perceptual task becomes more complex, involving some kind of information processing along with the perceptual activity.

When hearing loss is profound, a hearing aid is less adequate as a prosthesis than when the loss is moderate to severe. A comfortable listening level for speech requires that the signal be presented at about 50–60 dB above threshold for a normal environment (Kopra & Blosser, 1968) or at even higher levels for a noisy environment (Richards, 1975). If hearing loss is as great as 90–100 dB, the amplification needed to reach a comfortable listening level would exceed the threshold for tickle or pain. A good hearing aid will suppress the volume of the signal to avoid further damage to the cochlea, but this, of course, introduces additional distortion.

Meanwhile, it must be emphasized that there is no clear one-to-one correspondence between the degree of loss as measured by a pure-tone audiogram and the behavioral consequences of deafness. The handicapping effects of any physical disability are mediated by a number of personal and social variables that interact with the disability in complex ways. Although the average pure-tone loss through the speech range of 500–2000 Hz can be taken as a rough approximation of speech reception thresholds for individuals, the prediction is best for extreme values. Similar better-ear averages are often associated with a considerable difference in speech and speechreading ability, and there are individual exceptions that are extreme.

If auditory deprivation is to be used in perception research as an independent variable, it would appear to be important to specify with some precision the nature of the impairment and its severity. There are very few people who are totally deaf. If a hearing loss is typically a matter of degree, then the amount and kind of residual hearing available will have important consequences for conclusions relating to the use of other sensory systems when hearing loss is present.

D. Educational Intervention

A fourth variable of considerable importance for perception research not usually taken into account is the type of educational intervention that has been applied to the persons used as subjects. Deaf children are subjected to a wide variety of educational treatments, ranging from purely oral approaches, which refrain from using any manual method of communication under any circumstances, to programs that openly endorse the use of any and all channels of communication that are available, including colloquial sign language, fingerspelling, and natural gestures, along with amplified speech and speechreading. In between these extremes can be found a wide variety of emphases or combinations of approaches that can be expected to make quite a difference in the manner in which deaf children develop specific perceptual abilities. Clearly, any study of perception that draws subjects from only one educational institution will generate results that may be generalizable only to other institutions that implement a similar educational philosophy by similar means. Researchers should describe in some detail the admissions criteria of their cooperating schools, the prevailing educational philosophy of these schools, and the characteristic educational treatment that was afforded the children included in the study (Barker, Wright, Meyerson, & Gonick, 1953). This requirement is especially important in research with preschool-age children, since the use of children enrolled in preschool programs prohibits generalization of the results to children who have not received such educational intervention. Older children, however, are also affected by different educational treatments, since institutionalized deaf children may constitute a different subject population than children enrolled in day-school programs, and deaf children who are segregated in schools or classes for the deaf may differ from children who have been mainstreamed in public-school classes. Differences due to educational treatment have less to do with the nature of deafness as a handicap than with society's treatment of deaf children on account of their disability.

One of the effects of educational treatment that has obvious importance for "laboratory" research is a general lack of motivation or incentive among many deaf subjects to perform at maximum capacity in any task that has no obvious utility to them. Such children also seem to be unconcerned about an error rate that would not be acceptable to hearing children enrolled in the typical suburban public school. Factors like these are especially likely to affect performances adversely in timed tasks, and it is a matter of record that deaf children whose accuracy in a perception task may be equal to the hearing may, nevertheless, require more time to take note of the stimuli or to execute the required response (Doehring & Rosenstein, 1969; Mandes *et al.*, 1971; Schiff & Dytell, 1972). Deaf children who are taught in highly structured educational settings are also likely to perseverate in a response that an experimenter records without comment, since acceptance of the response may be interpreted as tacit approval. Factors such as these raise doubts about the comparability of data gathered from deaf subjects and so-called hearing controls.

E. Hearing Controls

The proper selection of appropriate hearing control subjects is necessary if deaf–hearing comparisons are to be made with some confidence, yet the problems associated with this are rarely taken as seriously as they ought to be. Research reports abound in which such comparisons were made, even though the only matching variables were age and sex. Sometimes mean I.Q. scores and standard deviations have been reported for each group, so as to assure the reader that the tested samples were within the normal limits of intelligence. Careful researchers may also attempt to control for English-language ability or school achievement. But the latter controls yield a very select group of deaf subjects, since only a small minority of deaf children keep pace with their hearing age peers in school achievement and English-language proficiency. More commonly, matching for English-language proficiency requires that deaf subjects be compared with younger hearing subjects. Meanwhile, factors such as motivation or incentive to perform well in formal tasks, and experiential deficits arising from societal views and treatments of children with disabilities are impossible to eliminate or control.

Careful researchers admit this, using deaf–hearing comparisons either not at all or only for crude approximations of typical performance levels. There is, however, a way to make use of hearing subjects tested concurrently. Instead of making absolute comparisons between the performance levels of the deaf and hearing groups, the relative improvement with age (Doehring & Rosenstein, 1969) or with training (Freides, 1974) can be noted for both groups. If the hearing subjects show an improvement either with training or with age that deaf subjects do not manifest, such an outcome would merit further study. Meanwhile, perceptual deficiencies in deaf subjects compared to hearing subjects should be interpreted relative to age, education, manual and English-language development, reading achievement, and general intellectual functioning.

F. Summary

In deprivation research, one study in which a target population does well is sufficient evidence to conclude that none of the attributes that define the population can be considered to be a cause of the poor performances that are sometimes observed. Failure to recognize this principle will lead to the overinterpretation of research results, since shortcomings will be noted without any attempt to reconcile them with the successes that are sometimes achieved. Clearly, the results of previous studies of deaf persons' perception must be interpreted with considerable caution. It is especially important that deaf deficiencies be evaluated carefully. Unless factors other than deafness can be ruled out as probable causes, the results are uninterpretable. Even replication is not reassuring unless greater control is exercised over such variables as age of onset, etiology, type and degree of loss, and educational history.

IV. PERCEPTION OF LANGUAGE

A. Decoding Speech

Although the relation between the acoustic signal and the speech code is not well understood, it is apparent that the speech code is embedded in the phonetic features of the acoustic signal in a complex manner (Liberman, 1974; Liberman, Cooper, Shankweiler, & Studdert-Kennedy, 1967, 1968). Complex processing is required to decode the speech signal. The absence of a one-to-one relation between the physical properties of the speech signal and its semantic content explains why visual or tactile cues do not readily substitute for auditory cues in speechreading or language learning.

B. Speechreading

It is widely believed by the general public that speechreading, or lipreading, is ordinarily developed by deaf children and by deafened adults to a high level of proficiency, so that their speech reception in social situations is not necessarily seriously impaired. This is an overly optimistic view. As Vernon (1969) has pointedly remarked, college sophomores with no lipreading training score better on lipreading tests than deaf persons, since the college sophomores have a better command of the English language. Berger (1972) has discussed the many variables associated with the speechreader, the speaker, and the environment that are likely to affect speechreading performance.

Early work in the area of speechreading research was devoted to the development of tests of lipreading ability and to a search for variables that might correlate well with lipreading ability. Berger (1972) and O'Neill and Oyer (1961) have reviewed this literature. Information is lacking regarding the predictive validity of such tests for performance in a natural environment and regarding the relative speechreading proficiency that one can take for granted in specific deaf populations as they function in a variety of circumstances. The expectation that speechreading ability would correlate highly with intelligence has not been confirmed, although mentally retarded persons with deficient linguistic skills are not likely to perform well. The search for personality variables that might correlate highly with speechreading skills has also been unsuccessful. There is some consensus that synthetic skills are required (Simmons, 1959) with which the speechreader can assimilate a wide range of information from a number of sources in addition to lip movements. Sharp (1972) concluded on the basis of the results of tests administered to good and poor speechreaders that good speechreaders have the capacity for visual closure, movement closure, and short-term memory, whereas poor speechreaders do not. The ability to perceive rapid movement or to recognize forms quickly may be implicated not only in speechreading skills but in other aspects of language acquisition as well (Olson, 1967).

A review of the state of the art in lipreading (Erber, 1974) enumerated several reasons for the difficulty of learning speech and language through lipreading. There is no self-monitoring feedback system for speech during infancy; different channels (tactile–kinesthetic and visual) rather than the same channel (auditory) must be used to monitor speech in one's self and in others; teachers of the deaf may be unaware of ambiguities in the speech that they model for deaf children; and many visible features of the speech signal are ambiguous.

C. Aids to Speechreading

Profoundly deaf persons seem to derive relatively little benefit from any residual hearing they might have (Erber, 1971, 1972). Unlike severely deaf persons, whose lipreading performance improves when auditory input is added, profoundly deaf persons do almost as well with vision alone as they do with vision and audition combined. Even reaction time in deaf children is not improved by adding an auditory stimulus (Costa, Rapin, & Mandel, 1964). Multisensory approaches to teaching the English language to profoundly deaf children are not supported by these findings.

Since the residual hearing of profoundly deaf persons is generally at the lower end of the frequency spectrum, below the range normally encompassed by most speech sounds, it has been conjectured that profoundly deaf persons might be aided by a frequency transposition from the 500–4000-Hz frequency range down to the 100–250-Hz frequency range, but actual results have been disappointing (Ling & Doehring, 1969; Ling & Maretic, 1971).

Other aids to speechreading that have been explored include visual and vibrotactile cues corresponding to physical properties of the speech signal (Levitt, 1973; Pickett, 1968; Risberg, 1969; Upton, 1968) and manual hand signals designed to disambiguate the information available through speechreading (Heneger & Cornett, 1971; Holm, 1972). Although none of these methods has achieved general acceptance as a superior approach to auditory training or to the enhancement of English-language skills, it has been claimed that well-trained deaf persons may benefit from vibrotactile cues (Engelmann & Rosov, 1975). Moreover, some of the methods have become identified with particular educational programs, such as cued speech (Heneger & Cornett, 1971) and the verbotonal method (Guberina, Skaric, & Zaja, 1972). It is plausible that methods like these have achieved some measure of success because they supplement rather than bypass the auditory system, because they provide information regarding prosodic features of speech, such as rhythm and stress, and because they present this information at a slower rate than is associated with the acoustic speech signal.

As an alternative to providing models of English through frequency transposition or through transduction to a visual or tactual medium, manual language systems have been developed either from the prevailing sign language in use among deaf persons (Anthony, 1971; Bornstein, 1973, 1974; De l'Épee, 1776; Gustason, Pfetzing, & Zawolkow, 1972) or as an entirely new artificial manual language (Gorman & Paget, 1969). Although the originators of these alternative systems have reported clinical evidence that the method achieves the objective of improving deaf children's language competence, hard data to this effect are lacking. Meanwhile, some school programs have adopted one or another of these systems as a method of providing exposure to English to deaf children.

In the same context, the Rochester method (Scouten, 1942) ought to be mentioned as another strategy for making the English language more visible, as it were. Developed as a supplement to oral methods of deaf education, the Rochester method stipulates that everything be fingerspelled manually as it is spoken, using the 26 letters of the manual alphabet. Deaf children who use fingerspelling to communicate socially become adept at spelling English (Hoemann, Andrews, Florian, Hoemann, & Jensema, 1976).

These systems have in common the viewpoint that the deaf child is capable of achieving linguistic competence in English spontaneously, provided a model of the English language can be made available without using sound. If this viewpoint is correct, deaf children's problems with English are primarily perceptual, and the linguistic deficiency proverbially associated with deafness ought to be attributed to the environment, and not to the child.

D. Perception and Acquisition
of American Sign Language

The spontaneous acquisition of American Sign Language (ASL) by young deaf children from available models clearly reflects an adaptive, functional perceptual system in deaf children. Descriptions of young deaf children's acquisition of ASL reveals a complex interaction between the deaf child's sensory capabilities and his linguistic environment (Schlesinger & Meadow, 1972). Meanwhile, the transcription and analysis of ASL productions offer unique and unresolved problems (Hoffmeister, Moores & Ellenberger, 1975).

Structural features of ASL ought to be related to functional properties of the human visual perceptual system. Stokoe (1960) first identified some of the structural aspects of signs from ASL that may function as distinctive features of the language. The first aspects described by Stokoe were the movements, the locations, and the hand configurations of signs. More recent descriptions (Friedman, 1977a; Stokoe, 1972) include the orientation of the hands as a structural feature. These analyses of ASL share the point of view that signs are comprised of a finite number of relatively meaningless aspects that can be combined in a very large number of ways so as to generate a lexicon. Evidence for the psychological reality of these formational aspects of signs has been adduced from slips of the hand in casual conversation and from intrusion errors in short-term memory (Bellugi & Klima, 1975). Stokoe (1975) has reported that hand configurations are perceived categorically in fingerspelled productions, whereas amorphous transitional hand shapes are ignored.

Information gathered from informants for ASL instructional materials (Hoemann, 1976) indicates that semantic content is often coded in facial expressions. Pinched or pursed lips, puffed cheeks, a cocked head, a frown, or a squint may qualify the meaning of manual gestures in systematic ways. The meaning extracted from these facial expressions by native signers may be quite different from the meaning inferred by the uninstructed observer who relied solely on the meanings associated with natural gestures and facial expressions. Nonmanual signals in ASL have begun to receive considerable attention from linguists (Baker & Padden, 1978; Liddell, 1977).

Siple (1978b) has examined ASL for evidence that its reliance on a visual channel has had systematic effects on its structure. She has noted that signs executed on or near the face are likely to make use of small differences in movement, whereas signs executed in locations peripheral to the viewer's visual field make use of larger movements. Also, more symmetry and more repetition are found in signs executed farther from the face. A lawful relation between the visibility of distinctive features and their location of execution suggests that ASL has evolved in such a way as to fit the perceptual capabilities of human vision.

Finally, since ASL relies on a visual channel, spatial organization of ASL utterances is likely to constitute an important source of their linguistic structure (Bellugi & Klima, 1975; Friedman, 1977b; Wilbur, in press). Informants' translations of English prose into ASL (Hoemann, 1976) reveal that spatial organization provides strategies for establishing temporal frames of reference, for linking pronouns to their antecedents, for establishing noun–verb–object agreement, for identifying speaker and receiver in a dramatized discourse, for distinguishing direct and indirect objects, for subordinating clauses, and for marking boundaries between phrases and clauses. The direction of the gaze of senders and receivers also plays

important roles in conversations in ASL, roles that differ in important ways
from the use of eye contact between persons conversing in a spoken language (Baker, 1977).

E. Summary

The perception of language offers a challenging domain in which to study
deaf people's adaptive functioning. The deficiency in English that typically
accompanies deafness stands in marked contrast to the fluency in ASL that
is acquired spontaneously by deaf people when models of ASL usage are
available in their linguistic environments. Although some deaf people become remarkable lipreaders, speechreading is generally an elusive skill. It
seems also to be true that no simple alternative can replace the ear as the
biologically appropriate organ for recognizing and understanding speech.
New methods for studying ASL are likely to shed light not only on manual
languages but also on the perceptual systems that are functionally related to
them (Siple, 1978a).

V. TRENDS AND DIRECTIONS FOR FUTURE RESEARCH

Oral communication skills are very important for deaf persons both for
vocational attainment and for life adjustment. Consequently, a great deal of
research on perception in the deaf has to do with their processing of spoken
English. Although neither visual nor tactual systems seem to be well suited
for representing the complex code embodied in the speech signal, there is
still considerable interest in such prostheses both for more-or-less spontaneous language development and for auditory training programs (Stark, 1974).
Meanwhile, the use of any residual hearing that deaf persons may have and
the development of hearing aids that are smaller in size but better in overall
quality are also matters of interest. Studies of the effects of temporal masking of speech sounds in persons with severe hearing impairments are likely
to lead not only to better hearing aids and better auditory training equipment, but also to a better understanding of the processes underlying the
discrimination of speech by persons with sensorineural losses (Danaher &
Picket, 1975).

How much benefit profoundly deaf persons may derive from auditory
input is unclear at this time. It is a fact that speech comprehension through
lipreading is not always enhanced by adding an auditory signal. It sometimes
happens that a profoundly deaf child will score better on a speechreading test
with vision alone than with vision supplemented by audition (Erber, 1974).
Tasks requiring close visual concentration may lead to a suppression of the
acoustic signal. This might explain the absence of any improvement in

speech comprehension with cued speech when sound was added (Clarke & Ling, 1976). Previous research in bimodal processing has tested normal subjects under poor acoustic conditions in order to simulate deafness. Erber (1974) has reviewed this research and has judged it to be of questionable value. Varying the ease with which the visual signal can be perceived would appear to be a more productive course, since the use that can be made of an acoustic signal may depend on the ease with which the visual signal can be recognized.

Evaluative research on educational procedures such as cued speech (Clarke & Ling, 1976; Ling & Clarke, 1975) and the verbotonal method (Craig, Craig, & DiJohnson, 1973) may also shed new light on the manner in which information about a speech signal may be processed when it is presented in the form of additional visual or tactual cues.

Cochlear implants, although no substitute for an intact cochlea, are reported by patients who have received them to be a satisfying source of stimulation (House, 1974). Experimentation with such devices is a necessary first step toward developing more sophisticated apparatus and perfecting surgical implantation techniques.

Studies of the linguistic properties of ASL call for comparable attention to the perceptual systems by which deaf persons acquire and make use of manual systems of communication. Such research has been conducted (Siple, 1978b) and is still in progress (Siple, Hatfield, & Caccamise, 1978).

The relation between structural features of ASL and human perceptual abilities lends special interest to studies of the acquisition and use of ASL by primates (Gardner & Gardner, 1975). Systematic differences ought to be found in the execution of signs by different species by virtue of physiological differences in the muscles and skeletal structure. Moreover, the need to maintain a sustained gaze at the sender's face may interfere with communication in a visual mode in primates that perceive such behavior as threatening. Perceptual factors in visual communication among primates are likely to be given increased attention in future research.

Investigators interested in the linguistic and psycholinguistic properties of manual languages have made productive use of methods applied previously with some success to spoken languages. These include temporal interruption (Heiman, 1975; Tweney, Heiman, & Hoemann, 1977), time compressed sign language (Heiman, 1976), short–term memory experiments (Bellugi & Klima, 1975; Hoemann, 1978), cluster analyses and multidimensional scaling (Hawes, 1976; Lane, Boyes-Braem, & Bellugi, 1976), computer simulation (Hoemann, Florian, & Hoemann, 1976) and cerebral assymetries (McKeever et al., 1976).

The competencies manifested by deaf persons as they master their many and varied strategies for communicating and manage their public and private lives constitute ecologically valid evidence of their ability to use perceptual resources to adapt successfully to life in a complex society.

References

Anthony, D. A. *Seeing essential English*. Books 1 and 2. Anaheim, California: Anaheim Union High School District, 1971.

Baker, C. Regulators and turn taking in American Sign Language discourse. In L. A. Friedman (Ed.), *On the other hand: New perspectives on American Sign Language*. New York: Academic Press, 1977. Pp. 215–236.

Baker, C., & Padden, C. A. Focusing on the non-manual components of ASL discourse. In P. Siple (Ed.), *Understanding language through sign language research*. New York: Academic Press, 1978. Pp. 27–57.

Barker, R. G., Wright, B. A., Meyerson, L., & Gonick, M. R. *Adjustment to physical handicap and illness: A survey of the social psychology of physique and disability*. Bulletin 55, revised. New York: Social Science Research Council, 1953.

Bellugi, U., & Klima, E. S. Aspects of Sign Language and its structure. In J. F. Kavanagh & J. E. Cutting (Eds.), *The role of speech in language*. Cambridge, Massachusetts: MIT Press, 1975. Pp. 171–203.

Berger, K. W. *Speechreading: Principles and methods*. Baltimore: National Education Press, 1972.

Binnie, G., Elkind, D., & Steward, J. A comparison of visual perceptual ability of acoustically-impaired and hearing children. *International Audiology,* 1966, **5,** 238–241.

Bishop, M. E., Ringel, R. L., & House, A. S. Orosensory perception, speech production and deafness. *Journal of Speech and Hearing Research,* 1973, **16,** 257–266.

Blank, M., & Bridger, W. H. Conceptual cross modal transfer in deaf and hearing children. *Child Development,* 1966, **37,** 29–38.

Bolton, B. Quantification of two projective tests for deaf clients. *Clinical Psychology,* 1972, **28,** 554–556.

Bolton, B. Quantification of two projective tests for deaf clients: A large sample validation study. *Journal of Clinical Psychology,* 1973, **29,** 249–250.

Bornstein, H. A description of some current sign systems designed to represent English. *American Annals of the Deaf,* 1973, **118,** 454–463.

Bornstein, H. Signed English: A manual approach to English language development. *Journal of Speech and Hearing Disorders,* 1974, **39,** 330–343.

Clarke, B. R., & Ling, D. The effects of using cued speech: A follow-up study. *The Volta Review,* 1976, **78,** 23–34.

Costa, L. D., Rapin, I., & Mandel, I. J. Two experiments in visual and auditory reaction time in children at a school for the deaf. *Perceptual and Motor Skills,* 1964, **19,** 971–981.

Craig, H. B., Craig, W. N., & DiJohnson, A. *Verbotonal instruction for deaf children: Interim report*. Pittsburgh: Western Pennsylvania School for the Deaf, 1973.

Danaher, E. M., & Pickett, J. M. Some masking effects produced by low-frequency vowel formants in persons with sensorineural hearing loss. *Journal of Speech and Hearing Research,* 1975, **18,** 261–271.

De l'Épée, M. *Institution des sourds et muets, par la voie des signes méthodiques*. Paris: Chez Nyon l'aîné, Libraire, 1776.

Doehring, D. G., & Rosenstein, J. Speed of visual perception in deaf children. *Journal of Speech and Hearing Research,* 1969, **12,** 118–125.

Engelman, S., & Rosov, R. Tactual hearing experiment with deaf and hearing subjects. *Exceptional Children,* 1975, **41,** 243–253.

Erber, N. P. Auditory and audiovisual reception of words in low-frequency noise by children with normal hearing and by children with impaired hearing. *Journal of Speech and Hearing Research,* 1971, **14,** 496–512.

Erber, N. P. Auditory, visual, and auditory–visual recognition of consonants by children with normal and impaired hearing. *Journal of Speech and Hearing Research,* 1972, **15,** 413–422.

Erber, N. P. Visual perception of speech by deaf children: Recent developments and continuing needs. *Journal of Speech and Hearing Disorders,* 1974, **39,** 178–185.

Fitch, J. L., Sachs, D. A., & Marshall, H. R. A program to improve visual perception skills of preschool deaf children. *American Annals of the Deaf,* 1973, **118,** 429–432.

Freides, D. Human information processing and sensory modality: Cross modal functions, information complexity, memory, and deficit. *Psychological Bulletin,* 1974, **81,** 284–310.

Friedman, L. A. Formational properties of American Sign Language. In L. A. Friedman (Ed.), *On the other hand: New perspectives on American Sign Language.* New York: Academic Press, 1977. Pp. 13–56. (a)

Friedman, L. A. (Ed.), *On the other hand: New perspectives on American Sign Language.* New York: Academic Press, 1977. (b)

Furth, H. G. *Thinking without language.* New York: Free Press, 1966.

Furth, H. G. Linguistic deficiency and thinking: Research with deaf subjects. *Psychological Bulletin,* 1971, **76,** 58–72.

Gardner, R. A., & Gardner, B. T. Early signs of language in child and chimpanzee. *Science,* 1975, **187,** 752–753.

Gates, A. I., & Chase, E. H. Methods and theories of learning to spell tested by studies of deaf children. *Journal of Educational Psychology,* 1926, **17,** 289–300.

Gilbert, J. G., & Levee, R. F. Performance of deaf and normally-hearing children on the Bender–Gestalt and the Archimedes Spiral Tests. *Perceptual and Motor Skills,* 1967, **24,** 1059–1066.

Goodenough, F. L., & Harris, D. B. Studies in the psychology of children's drawings: II 1928–1949. *Psychological Bulletin,* 1950, **47,** 369–433.

Gorman, P., & Paget, G. *A systematic sign language.* (4th ed.) London: mimeographed paper, 1969.

Guberina, P., Skaric, I., & Zaja, B. *Case studies in the use of restricted bands of frequencies in auditory rehabilitation of the deaf.* Zagreb: Institute of Phonetics, Faculty of Arts, Univ. of Zagreb, 1972.

Gustason, G., Pfetzing, D., & Zawolkow, E. *Signing exact English.* Rosmoor, Calif.: Modern Signs Press, 1972.

Hawes, D. *Perceptual features of the manual alphabet.* Unpublished masters thesis, Bowling Green State Univ., 1976.

Heiman, G. W. *The effect of temporal interruption on the intelligibility of American Sign Language.* Unpublished masters thesis. Bowling Green State Univ., Bowling Green, Ohio, 1975.

Heiman, G. W. *The intelligibility and comprehension of time compressed American Sign Language.* Unpublished doctoral dissertation, Bowling Green State Univ., 1976.

Heneger, M. E., & Cornett, R. O. *Cued speech: Handbook for parents.* Washington, D.C.: Cued Speech Program, Gallaudet College, 1971.

Hoemann, H. W. *The American Sign Language: Lexical and grammatical notes with translation exercises.* Silver Spring, Maryland: The National Association of the Deaf, 1976.

Hoemann, H. W. Categorical coding of Sign and English in short-term memory by deaf and hearing subjects. In P. Siple (Ed.), *Understanding language through sign language research.* New York: Academic Press, 1978. Pp. 289–305.

Hoemann, H. W., Andrews, C. E., Florian, V. A., Hoemann, S. A., & Jensema, C. J. The spelling proficiency of deaf children. *American Annals of the Deaf,* 1976, **121,** 489–493.

Hoemann, H. W., Florian, V. A., & Hoemann, S. A. A computer simulation of American Sign Language. *American Journal of Computational Linguistics,* 1976, **13,** AJCL Microfiche 37.

Hoffmeister, R. J., Moores, D. F., & Ellenberger, R. L. Some procedural guidelines for the study of the acquisition of sign language. *Sign Language Studies,* 1975, **7,** 121–137.

Holm, A. The Danish mouth–hand system. *Teacher of the Deaf,* 1972, **70,** 486–490.

House, W. F. The cochlear stimulator. *Oto Review* (special ed.), 1974, **1,** 3–5.

Keough, B. K., Vernon, M., & Smith, C. E. Deafness and visuomotor function. *Journal of Special Education*, 1970, **4**, 41–47.

Koppitz, E. M. *The Bender Gestalt Test for children*. New York: Grune & Stratton, 1964.

Kopra, I. L., & Blosser, D. Effects of measurement on most comfortable loudness level for speech. *Journal of Speech and Hearing Research*, 1968, **11**, 497–508.

Lane, H., Boyes-Braem, P., & Bellugi, U. Preliminaries to a distinctive feature analysis of American Sign Language. *Cognitive Psychology*, 1976, **8**, 263–289.

Larr, A. L. Perceptual and conceptual ability of residential school deaf children. *Exceptional Children*, 1956, **23**, 63–66, 88.

Lawson, L. J., & Myklebust, H. R. Ophthalmological deficiencies in deaf children. *Exceptional Children*, 1970, **37**, 17–20.

Lehman, J. U., & Simmons, M. P. Comparison of rubella and nonrubella young deaf adults: Implications for learning. *Journal of Speech and Hearing Research*, 1972, **15**, 734–742.

Levitt, H. Speech processing aids for the deaf: An overview. *IEEE Transactions on Audio and Electroacoustics*, 1973, **AU-21**, 269–273.

Liberman, A. M. Language processing: State-of-the-art report. In R. E. Stark (Ed.), *Sensory capabilities of hearing-impaired children*. Baltimore: University Park Press, 1974. Pp. 129–141.

Liberman, A. M., Cooper, F. S., Shankweiler, D. P., & Studdert-Kennedy, M. Perception of the speech code. *Psychological Review*, 1967, **74**, 431–461.

Liberman, A. M., Cooper, F. S., Shankweiler, D. P., & Studdert-Kennedy, M. Why are spectograms hard to read? *American Annals of the Deaf*, 1968, **113**, 127–133.

Liddell, S. K. *An investigation into the syntactic structure of American Sign Language*. Unpublished doctoral dissertation, University of Calif. at San Diego, 1977.

Ling, D., & Clarke, B. R. Cued speech: An evaluative study. *American Annals of the Deaf*, 1975, **120**, 480–488.

Ling, D., & Doehring, D. D. Learning limits of deaf children for coded speech. *Journal of Speech and Hearing Research*, 1969, **12**, 83–94.

Ling, D., & Maretic, H. Frequency transposition in the teaching of speech to deaf children. *Journal of Speech and Hearing Research*, 1971, **14**, 37–46.

Mandes, E., Allen, P. R., & Swisher, C. W. Comparative study of tachistoscopic perception of binary figures in deaf children and normally hearing children. *Perceptual and Motor Skills*, 1971, **33**, 195–200.

McKeever, W. F., Hoemann, H. W., Florian, V. A., & VanDeventer, A. D. Evidence of minimal cerebral asymmetries for the processing of English words and American Sign Language in the congenitally deaf. *Neuropsychologia*, 1976, **14**, 413–423.

Moncada, E. J. (Ed.) *DSH Abstracts*. Washington, D.C.: Deafness, Speech and Hearing Publications, Inc., 1960–1976.

Mykelbust, H. R. *Keystone non-language charts*. Meadville, Pennsylvania: Keystone View Co., 1950.

Myklebust, H. R., & Brutten, M. A study of the visual perception of deaf children. *Acta Otolaryngologica*, Supplement **105**, 1953.

Olson, J. R. A factor analytic study of the relation between the speed of visual perception and the language abilities of deaf adolescents. *Journal of Speech and Hearing Research*, 1967, **10**, 354–360.

O'Neill, J. J., & Oyer, H. J. *Visual communication for the hard of hearing*. Englewood Cliffs, New Jersey: Prentice-Hall, 1961.

Pascal, G. R., & Suttell, B. J. *The Bender Gestalt Test*. New York: Grune & Stratton, 1951.

Pickett, J. M. Recent research on speech analyzing aids for the deaf. *IEEE Transactions on Audio and Electroacoustics*, 1968, **AU-16**, 227–234.

Pollard, G., & Neumaier, R. Vision characteristics of deaf students. *American Journal of Optometry and Physiological Optics*, 1974, **51**, 839–846.

Price, A. C., & Deabler, H. L. Diagnosis of organicity by means of spiral after effect. *Journal of Consulting Psychology*, 1955, **19**, 299–302.

Richards, A. M. Most comfortable loudness for pure tones and speech in the presence of masking noise. *Journal of Speech and Hearing Research*, 1975, **18**, 498–505.

Rileigh, K., & Odom, P. Perception of rhythm by subjects with normal and deficient hearing. *Developmental Psychology*, 1972, **7**, 54–61.

Risberg, A. A critical review of work on speech analyzing hearing aids. *IEEE Transactions on Audio and Electroacoustics (Special issue on communication aids for the handicapped)*, 1969, **AU-17**, 290–297.

Rosenstein, J. Tactile perception of rhythmic patterns by normal, blind, deaf and aphasic children. *American Annals of the Deaf*, 1957, **102**, 63–66.

Rosenstein, J. Perception and cognition in deaf children. Unpublished doctoral dissertation, Washington Univ., 1959.

Schiff, W., & Dytell, R. S. Deaf and hearing children's performance on a tactual perception battery. *Perceptual and Motor Skills*, 1972, **35**, 683–706.

Schlesinger, H., & Meadow, K. *Sound and sign: Childhood deafness and mental health.* Berkeley: Univ. of California Press, 1972.

Scouten, E. L. *A reevaluation of the Rochester Method.* Rochester, New York: The Alumni Association, Rochester School for the Deaf, 1942.

Sharp, E. Y. The relationship of visual closure to speechreading. *Exceptional Children*, 1972, **38**, 729–734.

Simmons, A. A. Factors relating to lipreading. *Journal of Speech and Hearing Research*, 1959, **2**, 340–352.

Siple, P. *Understanding language through sign language research.* New York: Academic Press, 1978. (a)

Siple, P. Visual constraints for sign language communication. *Sign Language Studies*, 1978, **19**, 95–110. (b)

Siple, P., Hatfield, N., & Caccamise, F. *The role of visual perceptual abilities in the acquisition and comprehension of sign language.* Paper presented at the American Educational Research Association, Toronto, 1978.

Stark, R. E. Looking to the future: Overview and preview. In R. E. Stark (Ed.), *Sensory capabilities of hearing-impaired children.* Baltimore: University Park Press, 1974. Pp. 209–233.

Sterritt, G. M., Camp, W., & Lipman, B. S. Effects of early auditory deprivation upon auditory and visual information processing. *Perceptual and Motor Skills*, 1966, **23**, 123–130.

Stokoe, W. C., Jr. *Sign language structure: An outline of the visual communication systems of the American deaf. Studies in Linguistics, Occasional Papers:* 8. Buffalo, N.Y.: Univ. of Buffalo Press, 1960.

Stokoe, W. C., Jr. *Semiotics and human sign languages.* The Hague: Mouton, 1972.

Stokoe, W. C., Jr. The shape of a soundless language. In J. F. Kavanagh & J. E. Cutting (Eds.), *The role of speech in language.* Cambridge, Massachusetts: MIT Press, 1975, Pp. 171–203.

Thompson, R. E. *The development of visual perception in deaf children.* Unpublished doctoral dissertation, Boston Univ., 1964.

Tweney, R. D., Heiman, G. W., & Hoemann, H. W. Psychological processing of sign language: Effects of visual disruption on sign intelligibility, *Journal of Experimental Psychology: General*, 1977, **106**, 255–268.

Upton, H. Wearable eyeglass speech reading aid. *American Annals of the Deaf*, 1968, **113**, 222–229.

Vernon, M. Characteristics associated with post-rubella children: Psychological, educational, and physical. *The Volta Review*, 1967, **69**, 176–185.

Vernon, M. Current etiological factors in deafness. *American Annals of the Deaf*, 1968, **113**, 1–12.

Vernon, M. Sociological and psychological factors associated with hearing loss. *Journal of Speech and Hearing Research,* 1969, **12,** 542–563.

Webster, D. B. Audition. In E. C. Carterette & M. P. Friedman (Eds.), *Handbook of perception.* Vol. III. *Biology of perceptual systems.* New York: Academic Press, 1973. Pp. 449–482.

Werner, H., & Strauss, A. A. Causal factors in low performance. *American Journal of Mental Deficiency,* 1940, **45,** 213–218.

Werner, H., & Strauss, A. A. Pathology of figure-background relation in the child. *Journal of Abnormal and Social Psychology,* 1941, **36,** 236–248.

Werner, H., & Strauss, A. A. Experimental analysis of the clinical symptom 'Perseveration' in mentally retarded children. *American Journal of Mental Deficiency,* 1942, **47,** 185–188.

Wilbur, R. B. *American Sign Language and sign systems.* Baltimore: University Park Press, in press.

Wilson, J. J., Rapin, I., Wilson, B. C., & VanDenburg, F. V. Neuropsychologic function of children with severe hearing impairment. *Journal of Speech and Hearing Research,* 1975, **18,** 634–652.

Yacorzynski, G. K., & Davis, L. An experimental study of the functions of the frontal lobe in man. *Psychosomatic Medicine,* 1945, **7,** 97–107.

Zwirecki, R. J., Stansbery, D. A., Porter, G. G., & Hayes, P. The incidence of neurological problems in a deaf school age population. *American Annals of the Deaf,* 1976, **121,** 405–408.

Chapter 4

PERCEPTION BY THE BLIND

DAVID H. WARREN

I. INTRODUCTION

The research literature on the perceptual abilities and characteristics of the blind is so varied as to almost defy organization and inclusion in a single chapter. This variation takes several forms. First, the research has been done by different types of investigators with different sets of goals. One such goal is the relatively applied one, where the work is oriented to the solution of immediate problems, such as the kinds of tactile symbols that may be used on mobility maps. There is a small central core of work that has as its primary goal the construction of a system of knowledge about the perception of the blind. There is a larger group of studies that have viewed blind subjects as a natural experimental control against which hypotheses about perceptual processes in sighted people might be tested. There is valuable information in each of these types of research.

Second, blindness is not a simple condition. The legal definition of blindness is simplistic, but it embraces a group of people who have widely different etiologies, acuities, and extents of visual field, not to mention drastic variations in their tendencies to make functional use of their visual and other perceptual abilities. In fact, many writers prefer to restrict the use of the term *blindness* only to those individuals who have at most only light perception (LP); the term *visual impairment* is often used to refer to the wider population of individuals who are legally blind. In this chapter, though, the term *blindness* will be used in the more inclusive sense.

Third, the research literature is varied in quality and degree of scientific rigor. A discussion of relevant methodological issues will be included in the last section of this chapter.

This chapter is not designed to present an exhaustive compilation of the perceptual research with the blind. Rather, it is a selective review, treating the most important topics and using representative examples of research to illustrate each topic.

II. AUDITION

The auditory abilities of the blind have received far less research attention than have their tactual abilities. At the same time, though, the importance of auditory function for the blind can hardly be overestimated, particularly for verbal communication, mobility in the environment, and identification of environmental events.

A. Sound Discrimination

Numerous studies have been made of basic auditory discriminative abilities. Topics have included loudness discrimination (Yates, Johnson, & Starz, 1972), phoneme discrimination (Hare, Hammill, & Crandell, 1970), sound discrimination and identification (Gibbs & Rice, 1974; Izumiyama, 1956), and musical ability (Pitman, 1965). Most of these studies have not found general differences between sighted and blind subjects. Where marked deficits on the part of the blind occur, they may typically be attributed to specific experiential deprivations rather than to visual loss itself.

Some advantages on the part of the blind occur in tasks that involve a strong attentional component. Witkin, Oltman, Chase, and Friedman (1971) compared the ability of blind and sighted adolescents to identify simple auditory patterns in a complex auditory stimulus. The congenitally blind subjects were better than the sighted. Witkin *et al.* have argued that the result is attributable to better auditory attention by the blind, rather than to superior abstraction abilities, since the same blind subjects showed worse performance than the sighted on a tactile abstraction test. Benedetti and Loeb (1972) have reported results that may be similarly interpreted. Blind adults were better at vigilance and signal-detection tasks than sighted controls. Various threshold measures were also taken and, in general, showed no differences. It is reasonable to propose that the blind have, through need, learned to attend better to auditory stimuli and therefore can make more use of the available auditory information than can sighted people.

Auditory discrimination is important in the mobility of the blind. Riley, Luterman, and Cohen (1964) found significant correlations between mobility scores and pure-tone thresholds over a frequency range of 250–14,000 Hz. The correlations tended to be higher for the higher frequencies, thus lending support to research that has found the higher frequencies to be especially involved in obstacle detection. Curtis and Winer (1969) found that travelers made finer intensity discriminations than nontravelers, Curtis and Winer suggested that the greater sensitivity of the blind travelers was a result of their mobility, rather than a cause of it. That is, through increased contact with the auditory environment, the travelers learned to pay more attention to variations in intensity.

B. Localization and Obstacle Detection

Localization of auditory stimuli is a critical ability for the blind person. Many laboratory localization studies, however, have found the blindfolded sighted subject to be equal to or better than the blind subject. Fisher (1964), for example, found equivalent performance for blind and sighted adults in judging the relative positions of two successively presented auditory (or tactual) targets. Spiegelman (1972) compared the auditory localization abilities of children who were blind early in life, those who became blind later in life, and sighted children. In both fixed-head and free-head conditions, the early blind performed with the same proficiency as the sighted, whereas the late blind performed better. Spiegelman discussed the early–late blind differences in terms of a visual framework, formed during the early years, that continues to facilitate auditory localization after the onset of blindness. Spiegelman also suggested that the sighted subjects performed poorly because they were under the disadvantage of being newly blind and had not learned to pay close attention to auditory cues.

McFadden (1974) has presented interesting data on the use of the various auditory localization cues. Previous work had shown that about 75% of sighted adults tend to use interaural intensity cues, whereas 25% use interaural time cues when time and intensity cues are arranged to produce conflicting information about target location. McFadden tested four blind subjects in a similar conflict situation. Three subjects, who were blind from birth, used predominantly the time cue. The fourth subject, who had become gradually blind since age 8 and who retained peripheral function, was about evenly divided in his reliance on time and intensity cues. McFadden's suggestion that there may be a developmental period during which a cue-use tendency is established has important implications for blind and sighted people and deserves research attention.

There has been a great deal of attention paid to the phenomenon usually called the *obstacle sense*, or *facial vision*. The phenomenon is simple enough: many blind people feel that they can somehow detect the presence of obstacles, and behavioral tests show that they can indeed do so. The history of speculation about the nature and basis of the obstacle sense abounds with claims that it depends on auditory, air-pressure, or olfactory cues, not to mention more mystical notions. The basic issue was resolved during the 1940s and 1950s by an impressive set of studies. Supa, Cotzin, and Dallenbach (1944) were able to rule out the skin as the critical receptor surface and therefore prove the pressure theories untenable. They found auditory information to be both necessary and sufficient. Although blind subjects initially performed better than sighted, the differences quickly disappeared with practice. Worchel, Mauney, and Andrew (1950) conducted a training study with blind children over a wide age range. Substantial individual differences were found, but most subjects were judged to have the obstacle sense. It is interesting that the subject need not himself be moving in order to use auditory cues successfully. Cotzin and Dallenbach (1950), for example, had the subject seated and wearing earphones through which the subject received auditory information that was generated by the experimenter's movements. The subject could successfully instruct the blindfolded experimenter to avoid obstacles. Cotzin and Dallenbach ascertained that the frequencies of 10,000 Hz and above were especially important to the obstacle sense.

Interest in the echodetection aspects of the obstacle sense has led to a number of laboratory studies. Kellogg (1962) studied the ability of two highly mobile blind and two sighted adults to identify differences in distance, size, and texture of objects on the basis of reflected sound. The subjects were free to generate noises, and all used some kind of vocal signal. Kellogg found reasonable performance by the blind subjects, but the sighted subjects performed at a level close to chance in all the tasks. These results are contradictory to those from other work that shows sighted subjects performing well above chance on such tasks, and there would seem to be no ready explanation for the conflict.

Rice has reported some impressive work on echodetection that bears on the question of the role of early vision. Rice, Feinstein, and Schusterman (1965) conducted a training study with five highly mobile blind adults who had had various periods of early vision. The mean threshold size for successful object detection improved with training to about 4 or 5° of visual angle. Rice (1970) reported comparative echolocation results from sighted and early and late blind subjects. When the targets were within 15° of the midline, all subjects performed comparably, but at greater lateral distances, the early blind were better. Rice concluded that the early blind were better at both echodetection and echolocation. It should be noted that Rice's blind subjects were highly mobile and perhaps not representative of the blind population. The apparent contradictions between the studies of Rice and those of Speigelman (1972) and others make it imperative to study the experiential determinants of the obstacle sense, as well as those of auditory localization and other mobility-related skills.

There have been various attempts to provide blind people with sound-producing devices to aid their obstacle detection. Kohler (1964) attached a sound-emitting device to the chests of blind and sighted subjects and found both groups to benefit from practice. In a laboratory training study, Juurmaa (1970) found marked improvements in target detection and localization with the use of a sound-producing device. Perhaps the logical culmination of such devices is the expensive and elaborate Sonic Aid, developed by Leslie Kay. An ultrasonic source, mounted in spectacle frames, produces a signal that, when reflected from objects, provides a complex binaural input. Surface nature, distance, and location of objects are specified by regular variations in the signal. The device requires a great deal of training, and while it is clear that users can learn to interpret the feedback quite well, there is some controversy about the overall usefulness of the device. Some users claim, for example, that monitoring the input decreases the attention that can be devoted to other environmental information that is normally available to the auditory, tactual, and olfactory modes. Nevertheless, several surveys of trained users (e.g., Airasian, 1973) have indicated a high degree of satisfaction with the device. Work is in progress to explore the feasibility of providing blind infants with a similar device. The possibility that very early experience might produce qualitative improvements in the capacity for use of the available information is an exciting one.

C. Compressed Speech

Intensive programs are available to provide blind persons with records and tape recordings (e.g., Talking Books). The rate of such material is about 175 wpm, or about twice the speed of reading by Braille. This speed, which is restricted by the speaking rate of the speaker, apparently does not tap the potential comprehension rate of listeners. Playing the recording at a faster speed than its recorded speed increases word rate, but the increased speed is accompanied by changes in pitch and voice quality that are unpleasant to most listeners. An alternative procedure is speech *compression*. Speech is tape recorded, and very short, randomly selected segments are then excised from the recording. The usefulness of compressed speech depends on the comprehensibility of the material so delivered. Foulke, Amster, Nolan, and Bixler (1962) tested blind sixth- to eighth-grade Braille readers, who had no previous experience with compressed speech, at 175, 225, 275, and 325 wpm. Comprehension for the 175 and 225 wpm rates did not differ from that for Braille, but comprehension began to drop off at 275 wpm for some material. The Braille reading rates for these subjects ranged from 57 to 70 wpm. Gore (1969) compared the comprehension and 1-week recall for material presented at 175 wpm (the normal recording rate) with that for 270 wpm accelerated and 270 wpm compressed speech. Comprehension and recall did not differ for normal and compressed speech, but the accelerated speech produced worse performance on both measures.

Thus, it is evident that moderate degrees of compression allow adequate comprehension and retention of auditory information. The acquisition rate for recorded information need not be restricted to the normal rate of speech.

III. TOUCH

The term *touch* is used here in a very broad sense, perhaps too inclusively, to refer to perceptual abilities that depend on the skin, muscles, or joints as mediators of information. Topics of research have ranged from simple discriminative abilities through pattern and form perception to perception of temporal and spatial patterns and the translation of visual images to the skin via vibrotactile stimulation. The common goal of this work, however, is to evaluate and explore the potential of these senses as channels for the acquisition of information about the world.

A. Discrimination of Simple Properties

Comparisons of tactual discrimination in blind and sighted subjects have been made in weight discrimination (Ahmad, 1971; Block, 1972), force judgments (Nelson & Haney, 1968), two-point and light-touch thresholds (Axelrod, 1959; Heinrichs & Moorhouse, 1969), cutaneous localization (Jones, 1972; Renshaw, Wherry, & Newlin, 1930), texture discrimination (Stellwagen & Culbert, 1963), and size discrimination (Block, 1972; Duran & Tufenkjian, 1970). In general, few differences are found in these studies, although the blind show some areas of advantage.

Davidson (1972) compared congenitally blind with sighted adults in judgments of curvature and found the blind to perform better. Analysis of videotaped scanning behavior revealed that the blind subjects tended to use scanning methods that encompassed the whole stimulus, whereas the sighted subjects tended to scan more locally. Subsequent attempts to restrict sighted subjects to the more holistic strategies produced performance comparable to that of the blind.

Other studies of size and texture discrimination by the blind have centered around applied questions such as Braille reading and the technology of map construction. Nolan and Morris (1965) found a positive correlation between roughness-discrimination ability in the first grade and Braille reading scores at the end of the first-grade year. Berlá and Murr (1975) studied the discriminability of line width in an attempt to generate performance data on which to base the design of maps and other tactual educational materials. The subjects were blind Braille readers drawn from the fourth through the twelfth grades. Variations from wider lines (up to ½ in.) were relatively more discriminable than variations from narrower lines. The fact that sensitivity improved across the set of test trials suggests that attempts to train line-width discrimination might prove rewarding. Berlá (1972) studied the effects of physical size and complexity on the ability of first-and second-grade blind children to discriminate forms. Both increasing complexity and increasing size led to increases in the time needed for response. Stimulus size, however, did not have an effect on the accuracy of response.

As in the auditory area, the evidence on tactual discrimination is mixed with respect to the issue of the comparative abilities of blind and sighted people. More importantly, though, there is an accumulating body of information about tactual discrimination in the blind, and as the acceptance of tactual maps for the blind becomes greater, this information will find important uses. In the meanwhile, though, it would seem valuable to study functional questions such as map use in the same subjects for whom discrimination data are gathered, in order to determine the nature of the relationships between discriminative abilities and functional behaviors.

B. Pattern and Form Perception

There is mixed evidence about the relative abilities of blind and sighted subjects in pattern- and form-perception tasks. Not surprisingly, experience plays a part in the ability to identify forms. Ayres (1966) compared the ability of early blind and sighted adolescents to identify familiar objects from tactual information. The sighted subjects performed significantly better. A larger body of research has used nonfamiliar stimuli. Foulke and Warm (1967) used raised dot patterns of varying degrees of complexity. The subject scanned one pattern and then judged which, if either, of a pair of comparison patterns was identical to the stimulus. Blind adults were better than the sighted at judging the simpler patterns, but there were no differences on the more complex figures. Davidson, Barnes, and Mullen (1974) had subjects explore one three-dimensional solid free-form and then choose a match from among either three or five comparisons. The congenitally blind adults were equal to the sighted on the three-choice task but the blind were better on the five-choice task. The scanning strategies of the blind were apparently more effective in isolating the distinctive features of the forms, and Davidson *et al.* argued that the distinctive-features approach was more critical for success on the more difficult task.

Berlá has produced important information about individual differences among children in the various skills and strategies involved in map reading. Berlá and Murr (1974) examined the effectiveness of various scanning strategies and found that a vertical scan using two hands is more effective than various horizontal strategies. Blind children in the early grades bene-fited from training in the vertical-scan strategy, whereas junior and senior high-school students were disadvantaged by the training. In another ap-proach, Berlá, Butterfield, and Murr (1976) found that children who were relatively good at finding tactual shapes on a map tended to be those who scanned in a regular way and attended to distinctive features of the shapes. Their data also indicated that map searching is improved by training that emphasizes regular scanning and attention to distinctive features.

Some information related to the role of experience in tactual discrimina-tion appears in work on the comparative abilities of Braille and non-Braille readers. For example, Foulke and Warm's (1967) subjects were Braille readers, and there is the interesting possibility that their advantage over the sighted subjects with the simpler patterns but not with the more complex ones was related to the greater similarity of the simpler patterns to the Braille format. Weiner (1963) has described a study of the simple and complex tactual abilities of good and poor Braille readers, matched for school grade. On all tests, the good readers performed better than the poor readers. The question of causality in these studies is complex, since tactual sensitivity may be either a cause or a result of good Braille reading.

The question of the ''educability'' of tactual functions, as well as of many other abilities, is an important one that has received too little attention. It is important to know about the possible effects of practice on discriminative functions, and how practice might interact with naturally occurring differ-ences in sensitivity. The orientation in the work of Berlá and of Davidson is valuable. It is unsatisfying to evaluate an ability and simply conclude the existence of an age trend or a difference between blind and sighted subjects. Both Berlá and Davidson have gone on to isolate behavioral (e.g., scanning strategy) or experiential sources of individual differences in performance, and both have taken the additional step of exploring methods of training strategies or component abilities. It should be encouraging to educators and others concerned with the blind that performance is sensitive to training and experience. These demonstrations are only first steps, though, and it is extremely important for progress in this area to pursue a science of causal-ity, rather than to remain satisfied with a descriptive system.

C. Braille

The invention, by Louis Braille in 1829, and subsequent elaboration of a system for reading by touch marked a most significant breakthrough for the blind in the acquisition of textual information. The Braille system uses raised dots arranged in a matrix of two columns by three rows. Various combinations of dots represent numbers, letters, and several common contractions.

Braille symbols are arranged to be read in rows from left to right on the page. The majority of Braille readers use only one fingertip at a time for the primary input. Thus the Braille reader engages in a linear process, with less chunking of input than the print reader. Because of the linearity of Braille reading, a major problem is reading speed: A good adult Braille reader is not likely to read more than about 100 wpm. The limitation on Braille speed is primarily a function of the linearity of the input process, rather than of the tactual (as compared to the visual) system. Foulke (1970), for example, has cited evidence that when visual material is presented one letter at a time, visual reading speed corresponds roughly to Braille reading speed. Substantially greater rates may be obtained by moving the Braille symbols under a stationary fingertip, and some researchers have suggested that a kind of chunking of symbols emerges with some practice. However, there is also some evidence that the comprehension and retention characteristics of such reading are inferior to those of regular Braille reading (Foulke, 1971).

Lappin and Foulke (1973) explored the possibility of having subjects use both hands, as well as multiple fingers on one or both hands. Performance was best when both index fingers were used. Using multiple fingers on the same hand did not produce an advantage; in fact, the worst performance occurred when two fingers on the same hand were used. There does not seem to be any disadvantage of using the nonpreferred hand: Foulke (1964) found no difference between the two hands, and Hermelin and O'Connor (1971b) found an advantage by the left hand in Braille-reading children, most of whom were right handed. Finally, there has been some work with matrices larger than the two-column, three-row Braille matrix, and the results suggest that the fingertips are capable of obtaining accurate information from the larger matrices. The use of such matrices would, of course, vastly increase the number of patterns that could be used and would therefore allow the use of many more word and syllable symbols.

D. Tactile–Visual Substitution

There have been several interesting lines of research on the capability of the skin to mediate temporal or spatial information, or both, as a substitute for the visual system. Diespecker (1967) and Geldard (1957, 1968) have studied the ability of adults to learn to interpret patterns of vibrotactile stimulation as letters or other symbols of communication. Both projects have reported substantial success, and there is apparently little difference in the potential of blind and sighted subjects. Thurlow (1974) has proposed the possibility of presenting an analog of the spatial Braille code in a temporal–spatial manner and cites preliminary evidence in support of the workability of such a system. Hill and Bliss (1968) have explored the capability of the hand to receive more complex patterns of spatial information, using air jets to stimulate various combinations of the finger joints. One late-blind subject performed similarly to three sighted subjects, whereas an early-blind subject was substantially better. Hill and Bliss (1968) presented an analysis of the results in terms of the information-processing capacity of the tactile hand system.

The most intensive research program on the ability of the skin to substitute for visual function involves the tactile–visual substitution system (TVSS), developed at the Smith–Kettlewell Institute of Visual Sciences. The system involves the translation of visual stimulation, received through a television camera, into a pattern of vibrotactile stimulation that can be applied to the skin. Thus, the skin receives a pattern of stimulation that is spatially correspondent to intensity variations in the visual array. There have been numerous reports of the use of the TVSS (e.g., White, Saunders, Scadden, Bach-y-Rita, & Collins, 1970), and a detailed review is not feasible here. It is clear, however, that blind and sighted subjects can, with considerable practice, learn to identify objects, orientations, and directions of movement. It is reported, furthermore, that the image comes to be perceived in external space rather than on the body surface, particularly when the observer can engage in scanning movements with the camera. Reports of the perceived three-dimensionality of the array (including size constancy and the perception of movement in depth) are also provocative.

A similar and very promising project has been the development of the Optacon (optical-to-tactile converter). Using the Optacon, the blind reader scans inkprint with a small device attached to the finger. The pattern of print is converted to a tactile configuration that can effectively be read at speeds averaging, for accomplished users, from 30 to 60 wpm. As such, the reading speed is only about half that of a skilled Braille reader, but the Optacon provides the inestimable advantage of allowing normal inkprint to be read, so that the blind reader need not rely on sources of recorded or Brailled material.

IV. SPACE PERCEPTION

The literature on the space perception of the blind is exceedingly complex. Tasks have ranged from those that involve *near-space* abilities, such as form perception and finger mazes, to those involving orientation and activity of the body in extended space and those involving the conception or perception of the relationships of objects and directions in extended space. Crosscutting these levels to some extent is the issue of *body image*. Since space perception involves three important modalities, one of which is dysfunctional in the blind, the question of intermodality organization also arises. In the absence of vision, to what extent can the remaining modalities mediate the perception of space and substitute for functions that vision normally serves?

A. Near Space

There has been some research on the ability to produce and reproduce hand and arm movements and positions (Hermelin & O'Connor, 1975; Hunter, 1964; Jones, 1972; Juurmaa, 1967; Lindley, 1973). The pattern of results from these studies is complex. There seem to be two distinct abilities that are tapped by the various tasks: proprioceptive discrimination and some aspect of the perception of external spatial relations. It makes sense of much of the data to propose that the blind may be superior on the tasks that demand primarily proprioceptive performance, such as reproducing a movement extent, but that this advantage is lost when the task requires a response to specific external spatial locations and relations.

Several versions of the formboard have been used to study aspects of space perception. Sylvester (1913) compared congenitally blind children with those blinded before and after 3 years of age and found that the differences between groups were predictable by the duration of visual experience before blindness. The congenitally blind performed worst, whereas those who became blind after the age of 3 performed best. Eaves and Klonoff (1970), testing congenitally blind children from 6 to 16 years, and Koestline, Dent, and Giambra (1972), using congenitally blind high-school students, both failed to find differences between blind and sighted samples on formboard tests. Studies using tactual embedded-figures tests have generally found the blind to perform better than the sighted (Kimura, 1972; Witkin *et al.*, 1971; for an exception, see Packard, 1971).

Worchel (1951), Ewart and Carp (1962), and Gottesman (1971) found no differences between groups of blind and sighted children on simple form-matching tasks. In a second task, Worchel had the subject feel two parts of a form, one part with each hand, and then choose one form from a set of four to correspond to the combination of the two separate forms. The sighted and later-blind subjects performed significantly better than the early blind. O'Connor and Hermelin (1975) also used a form combination task with congenitally blind subjects and two groups of sighted subjects, one performing with vision available and the other performing blindfolded. The subjects who performed with vision were best, but when the matching required a rotation of the form, their performance suffered. Rotation did not affect the performance of the other two groups. In a second experiment, O'Connor and

Hermelin attempted to decrease the salience of form and thereby increase the salience of orientation. The stimuli were plaster casts of right and left hands. Subjects were required to judge whether a stimulus hand was right or left when it was presented in a variety of orientations. The blind group made significantly more errors than the blindfolded group, which in turn made more errors than the visual group. O'Connor and Hermelin suggested that the blindfolded, sighted subjects in this task interpreted the orientation information within a visual reference system, whereas the blind subjects had no such reference system to aid their judgments.

The adventitiously blind perform better on tactual tests of maze learning (e.g., Berg & Worchel, 1956; Koch & Ufkess, 1926). These results are typically discussed in terms of a residual visual imagery ability of the late blind. Cleaves (1975) approached the imagery question in a more direct way. After learning a finger maze to criterion, the subject was required to point to several maze locations, imagining the maze to be in its original orientation or rotated about its vertical or horizontal axis. In each condition, the congenitally blind performed worst; sighted and later blind (after 8 years) groups did not differ significantly from one another. In the late-blind group, the correlations of age at onset of blindness with performance were significant, and indicated that longer periods of early vision produced better performance. This result has repeatedly been found in other studies of spatial behavior. Cleaves also found that, in general, the longer a subject had been blind, the worse his performance was. This result has also been found in previous work, and it is not, of course, totally independent of the relationship between duration of early vision and performance. In fact, Cleaves found the variable "percent of life spent blind" to be a better predictor of performance in the late-blind group than any other variable.

Although the various near-space tasks present a confused picture of the relative abilities of blind and sighted subjects, some sense may be made of much of the data by taking task demands and visualization into account. The tasks on which blindfolded, sighted subjects perform better than the blind tend to be those that involve abilities regarding relatively complex spatial relations. The visualization notion suggests that blindfolded, sighted subjects and blind subjects with histories of early vision have the advantage of being able to evoke visual images of the stimulus materials. This issue will be discussed more extensively in a later section.

Several other status variables have been examined in relation to performance on near-space tasks. In all of the maze-learning studies in which IQ is reported, performance has been better for the higher-IQ subjects. Merry and Merry (1934) even considered the possibility of using a maze test as a supplementary test of intelligence for blind children. Studies that have investigated the relation of IQ or mental age to performance on form-discrimination tasks have also sometimes found stronger correlations for blind subjects than for sighted subjects. It is interesting that, almost without exception, stronger correlations between IQ and maze-learning performance have been reported for blind groups than for sighted groups. Warren, Anooshian, and Bollinger (1973) have suggested that tasks that are facilitated by a visual frame of reference may be relatively easy for the sighted and thus may not be differentiated by IQ, whereas the blind may depend more on verbal or other cognitive interventions for successful performance. Finally, studies that have included a substantial chronological age range have not found a strong correlation between performance and chronological age, although there is some indication that form-perception performance may reach asymptote by the mid-elementary years. Few studies have differentiated among subjects younger than 8 years.

B. Body Image

There has been considerable discussion of the importance of an adequate body image as a basis for successful mobility and orientation in space. In order to maintain orientation in space, it is necessary to perceive adequately the orientation and position of the body; and in order to locomote in space, it is important to be able to get the body to do what you want it to do. To the extent that the perception and control of body position and movements depend on visual function, the blind should be at a disadvantage. There is some evidence to support this formulation. Witkin *et al.* (1971) speak of the role of vision in producing an articulation not only of external space but also of the body concept. They argue that the congenitally blind child is at a substantial disadvantage in this respect. Evidence from the psychoanalytic literature on blind infants suggests that these differences have a very early onset. Several papers (e.g., Wills, 1970) report that blind infants show developmental lags in reaching to objects and in the onset of crawling and walking. The lags are attributed to the lack of vision as a verifier of the existence and identity of objects in space. Without vision, the integration of tactual, auditory, and motor experience is more difficult, and a major stimulus for the infant to reach outward and contact the external world is absent.

C. Mobility

There have been several studies of component motor behaviors that are important to effective mobility in the environment. Cratty (1967) studied the tendency to veer in an open-field situation in which the subject was asked simply to walk in a straight line. Comparisons of performance among various blind and sighted groups suggested that the duration of experience without vision was a more critical variable than the history of early vision: Subjects who had been blind longer performed better. Sensitivity to incline and decline in paths was also evaluated, and the pattern of results was similar to the pattern for veering. Cratty, Peterson, Harris, and Schoner (1968) compared the performances of early- and late-blind children in walking through curved pathways with varying radii of curvature. The late-blind subjects performed better. Leonard (1969) assessed static and mobile balancing in teen-agers who varied widely in residual vision. The mobile balancing test required subjects to walk along a narrow beam, using whatever residual vision might be available. Good static balance was necessary but not sufficient for good mobile balance. Residual vision was also related to mobile balance: Subjects with very little residual vision performed poorly on mobile balancing, but those with a large degree of residual vision did not necessarily perform well. Worchel (1951) used a task in which the subject was led over two sides of a large right triangle and was then asked to return to the starting point via the hypotenuse. A blindfolded, sighted group performed significantly better than a blind group, but there was no significant relation between performance and age at onset of blindness in the blind group.

It is not possible to treat the mobility issue fully in this chapter. Warren and Kocon (1974) provide a review of the factors, both perceptual and nonperceptual, that have been found to bear on mobility success. Briefly, the impact of their review is that mobility is a vastly complicated process that depends heavily on perceptual abilities, but by no means exclusively on them. Furthermore, many of the abilities and characteristics involved in successful mobility are ones that have developmentally early formative periods. This point holds for perceptual and motor abilities, but also for certain nonperceptual areas such as independence and verbal mediation. It is almost beyond question that substantial attention should be paid to such factors in mobility well before the early teens, when blind children are typically enrolled in formal mobility training programs.

An important aspect of the mobility question that has received far too little attention relates to the kinds of information that the blind person is able to receive from a novel environment and the process of integrating the information into an organized and useful format that can serve as a basis for mobility in that environment. Some information is being generated on the relative effectiveness of various kinds of maps, but such efforts will be more successful when they can be based on an understanding of the nature of spatial learning.

D. Intermodality Organization

Although the topic of intermodality organization extends beyond the area of space perception, it is appropriate to consider it here because of its implications for spatial behavior. Vision plays a major role in the spatial behavior of sighted people. It not only provides the most consistent, reliable, and precise source of spatial information, but it also may serve an important organizational and interpretive function with respect to spatial cues received via the other modalities. Thus the nature of intermodality organization in the congenitally and later blind may be qualitatively different. The question then arises whether those organizational functions that vision normally serves can be replaced in the congenitally blind or enhanced in the late blind by functions residing in the other spatial modalities or their interaction.

Warren and Pick (1970) examined the resolution of a spatial conflict created by the presentation of discrepant auditory and proprioceptive information. For the sighted groups, auditory information became more important with age, both in being less influenced by proprioception and in exerting more influence on proprioception. There were no significant age trends within the total blind sample. A further analysis of the blind group included only those subjects who had been blind from birth. The subjects with at least light-perception capability showed age trends similar to those of the sighted subjects. The results were discussed with respect to the possibility that even a small visual capability may allow an organization of the remaining modalities that is similar to that of sighted people.

Fisher (1964) found no significant differences between blind and sighted adults in the precision of judging the azimuth locations of auditory or tactual targets. However, when the task involved comparing auditory with tactual locations, some of the blind subjects performed much worse than the sighted (some of the blind subjects also performed relatively well). One interpretation of these results is that the sighted subjects performed better in this task because of their use of a visual framework to which they could refer the auditory and tactile locations.

O'Connor and Hermelin have reported several experiments designed to compare the encoding of spatial and temporal information in blind and sighted children. In an experiment on spatial coding (Hermelin & O'Connor, 1971a), they studied a group of congenitally blind and two groups of sighted subjects, one that performed with vision and one that was blindfolded. During a training session, the subject learned four words, one corresponding to each of his fingers in a spatial location. The subject was not instructed as to whether the word was to be associated with the finger or with the spatial location, and the testing session was designed to evaluate which association had in fact been made. The blindfolded, sighted children and the blind children made about 75% of their responses to finger location, whereas the unblindfolded, sighted children made about 60% of their responses to external spatial location. In a study similar in rationale to the one previously discussed, O'Connor and Hermelin (1972) studied the situational use of temporal and spatial aspects of auditory information. They presented sequences of three spoken digits via an array of three spatially separated speakers in such a way that when asked for the "middle" digit, the child would have to choose either the spatially middle digit or the temporally middle one. Blind and sighted subjects showed a strong preference for the temporally middle digit. Another group of sighted children was tested on a similar task that involved visual, rather than auditory signals. In this case, there was an overwhelming choice of the spatially middle digit. O'Connor and Hermelin concluded that for the sighted children there was a close relation between the nature of the stimulus material and the mode of processing. The auditory modality is more suited to temporally presented material, whereas the visual modality is more appropriate for spatially presented information. The input modality triggers either a temporal or a spatial organization of the stimulus material. This formulation carries the implication that totally blind children are at a disadvantage in dealing with spatial information because the spatial mode of organization cannot be triggered appropriately.

O'Connor and Hermelin (1971) studied cross-modal transfer performance in blind, sighted, and deaf children. The children learned to discriminate between tactual stimuli of long and short durations. This discrimination was then tested at other positions in the same dimension, on other dimensions within the same (tactual) modality, and in another (auditory) modality. The blind group learned the initial discrimination with fewer errors than the sighted, but the blind were worse on the intermodal transfer task. The relatively poor intermodal transfer performance of the blind group was discussed in the context of the need for visual experience to be concurrent with experience in other modalities in order for effective intermodality organization to occur.

Two lines of attack on these issues should be actively pursued. First, training studies should be used to study the degree to which information can be encoded in formats other than the most spontaneous one. Second, an attempt should be made to identify the variables of early experience that may produce differences in the processing of spatial and temporal information in blind children. The retrospective search for experiential factors is a difficult task, but the ever-increasing evidence that experience and environment are important in shaping future abilities makes such a pursuit a potentially valuable one.

Although it has been discussed in an earlier section, the research on intermodality substitution systems should again be mentioned here, since it involves the processing of spatial information that is normally available to the visual system but that is transduced into formats suitable for other modalities. In addition to the tactile–visual substitution systems and the mobility aids based on auditory information, mention should be made of the demonstration by Fish and Beschle (1973) that a two-dimensional spatial array may be represented aurally in such a way that elevation is represented by frequency and azimuth position is represented by the normal auditory localization parameters. With short periods of training, blind and sighted subjects can learn to discriminate objects and geometric figures. With general regard to such sensory substitution, it should be noted that there may be different ways of representing a parameter from one modality as a parameter in another. It seems likely that when relatively correspondent intermodal parameters are available, their use would generate a more suitable system than would parameters that are not correspondent, since the cognitive load on the subject in learning the correspondences should be less serious.

E. Visualization

Many writers, noting the superior spatial performance of blind persons who have had a period of early vision before becoming blind, have attributed a visualization, or visual imagery ability, to the late blind. The duration of early vision thought to be required for such visual imagery to operate is variously estimated, but many researchers use a rule of thumb in selecting early- and late-blind subjects of 3–5 years. Warren *et al.* (1973) argue that the issue has been conceptually oversimplified and suggest that there may be several developmental eras during which it is particularly advantageous to have vision available. The middle months of the first year may be important in establishing an integration of vision and manual behaviors, whereas the latter part of the first year and the early second year may be important in the integration of vision with locomotor behavior. Still another important period may occur when children are normally acquiring vocabulary and concepts of spatial relations. Thus any attempt to specify an age of effective visual experience should also specify the nature of the performance involved.

A distinction should be drawn between the intermodality-development hypotheses of Warren *et al.* (1973) and O'Connor and Hermelin, on the one hand, and a very different use of the visualization notion on the other. As the term is typically used, *visualization* means the ability to evoke a visual image of the stimulus and to perform a task by using that visual image rather than the original cues. A good example of this usage is shown in the study by McKinney (1964) on finger localization. By contrast, Warren *et al.* suggest that having vision during a particular developmental period may allow the establishment of a spatial perceptual system that is more effectively integrated than would be the case without vision. Having vision available, the infant or young child can see just where a touched or sound-producing object is, and he can thus refine his ability to interpret auditory and tactual cues. Furthermore, he can effectively compare auditory with tactual cues via the integrating bridge of vision. It is the ability to make this more effective interpretation and integration of information that Warren *et al.* suggest is acquired via early vision and is not lost when vision is lost.

An alternative to the hypothesis that places special emphasis on vision is proposed by Jones (1975). Jones suggests that motor behavior serves as the integrating link among the spatial modalities. Vision is, for the sighted, "only one element in a mutually supportive system rather than the primary spatial reference [p. 466]." Differences between the spatial abilities of the early and late blind may then be attributed to the curtailed motor activity of the early-blind child. At present there seems to be insufficient evidence to force rejection of either hypothesis. The issues are important from a theoretical point of view, and they deserve research attention. From a practical point of view, both formulations imply that attempts should be made to identify aspects of experience and training that might, for the congenitally or very early-blind child, effectively substitute for the missing integrative function, whether it be visual or motor.

F. Discussion

As noted at the outset of this section, the issue of space perception is an extremely complex one, and it is correspondingly difficult to make summary statements about the literature. However, several general points do emerge.

First, given the importance of vision in the space perception of sighted people, it is not surprising to find evidence of qualitative differences between the sighted and the congenitally blind. In a wide variety of tasks, the late blind have also been found to perform better than the congenitally or very early blind. The performance differences generally seem to be greater in more complex tasks, suggesting that the spatial conceptions of the congenitally blind are adequate for some behaviors but less adequate for others. The precise nature of the role of early vision is not at all clear, however, and the issue awaits more refined hypotheses and research approaches.

Second, there are a number of other variables besides visual history that apparently contribute to performance on space-perception tasks. Although there are deficits in spatial behaviors found in groups of blind subjects, there are also many blind people who are effectively mobile. Careful evaluation of their experiential histories and ability structures from a multivariate approach might lead to useful guidelines for the structuring of the environment and experience of the blind infant and young child.

Third, the notion that the different modalities are variously suited to various kinds of information appears in the blindness literature as well as in other areas. There is some agreement, although the issue is very complex, that audition is primarily suited to the processing of temporally presented information and is not well suited to the processing of detailed, distal, spatial information. The potential of the auditory sense for processing detailed spatial information has not been thoroughly explored, though, and imaginative attempts at training studies will provide a valuable contribution to the literature.

Finally, much of the research on space perception in the blind has undoubtedly taken a far too simplistic approach to the issue. Studies that have examined the maze-learning or form-combination abilities of the blind, for example, have generally not considered the possibility that variations in performance may be caused by basic differences in tactual discrimination. Similarly, they have not considered the possibility that variations in conceptual abilities may contribute to performance differences. It seems clear that substantial progress in the understanding of the space perception of the blind will only be made by research that takes a sufficiently comprehensive approach to the multiplicity of levels that are involved in space perception.

V. ILLUSIONS

Geometric illusions have been studied extensively with sighted subjects. Tactual analogs of many of these illusions have been studied in the blind. Most studies have found the blind to experience tactual illusions in the same direction, although often not as strongly, as sighted subjects performing visually (Bean, 1938; Patterson & Deffenbacker, 1972; Tsai, 1967; Zemtzova, Kulagin, & Novikova, 1962). Some authors have argued that the precision of tactual abilities and the amount of tactual experience affect illusion strength. Zemtzova et al. reported that the subjects who showed the Ponzo illusion were those with the most developed tactile perception. Other evidence does not support this line of argument, however. Axelrod (1961) compared blind and sighted adolescents on a test of kinesthetic aftereffect and found that the blind group showed consistently less aftereffect. Axelrod concluded that the blind attend better to tactile–kinesthetic events and therefore are better able to withstand the illusory tendency. Thus, Zemtzova et al. concluded that individuals with better tactual abilities show greater illusory effects, while Axelrod reached the opposite conclusion. Tactual abilities undoubtedly affect the strength of illusions, but it may be too simplistic to expect the effect to be the same in all the illusions.

If two objects are equal in weight but different in size, the smaller of the two tends to be judged as heavier. This phenomenon is known as the size–weight illusion. Kanno and Ohwaki (1958) found strong evidence for the illusion in blind subjects when size information was available tactually. Developmental studies of the size–weight illusion have found age-related increases (Menaker, 1966; Zemtzova et al., 1962), although the age curves for the blind were delayed by several years compared to those of the sighted. The developmental evidence supports the notion that blind children, perhaps because of more limited experience, are slower to integrate size and weight information than sighted children.

The goal of many studies of illusions in the blind has been the elucidation of the illusion itself, rather than the understanding of the perceptual processes involved. The research does not seem to have been particularly useful in understanding the illusions, however. It may be that the experimental rationale behind such comparisons is inadequate, since it seems risky to conclude that the process that produces the illusion is the same in the tactual and visual versions, even if the magnitudes of the illusions are equal. As a case in point, Crall (1973) studied the Ponzo illusion developmentally in blind and sighted groups. In the sighted groups, the visual illusion increased over age and reached the adult-like level at age 11, whereas tactually, the illusion decreased from a high at age 9 to zero at age 12. (The blind subjects showed a strong tactual illusion that did not decrease with age.) Thus, even within the sighted group, the tactual and visual versions of the illusion showed opposite developmental trends. Tactual analogs of visual illusions may be interesting in their own right, particularly for blind subjects, but their study may not contribute to the understanding of visual illusions.

VI. DISCUSSION AND SUMMARY

A. Sensory Compensation

One of the oldest and most durable ideas about the perceptual abilities of the blind is sometimes referred to as the notion of *sensory compensation.* Briefly, this idea holds that because of the lack of vision, the blind obtain more practice in the use of the remaining modalities, depend on them more, and therefore develop better nonvisual perceptual abilities. Although there have been several detailed reviews that have in general failed to find supporting evidence for the idea (e.g., Hayes, 1933; Rice, 1970), the compensation belief persists in both the scientific and the lay communities. The issue is by no means a simple one. Some clarification may be gained by separating the question of discriminative abilities from that of effective attention to, or functional use of, information. On the question of discriminative abilities, the available evidence runs heavily against the compensation hypothesis. The vast majority of studies that have isolated sensory discrimination abilities have failed to find differences between blind and sighted groups or among various blind groups. There is, however, good evidence that in some areas of performance the blind have better attentive habits and can make more effective functional use of information. Such results appear in both the auditory (e.g., the obstacle sense) and in the tactual (e.g., scanning strategies) literatures.

B. Methodological Issues

There are several serious methodological difficulties that have plagued past researchers and will continue to plague future ones. These problems do not, in general, have ready solutions: they must simply be regarded as inherent in the area of research.

It is not typically feasible to select a sample of blind subjects at random from a large pool of potential subjects. This fact, when added to the extreme heterogeneity of the blind population, increases the chance that the sample used in any given study is not truly representative of the blind population.

Some areas of disagreement in the literature are undoubtedly attributable to such sampling difficulties. The problem is a difficult one, as is the problem of how to approach the heterogeneity itself. Potential subjects may vary widely in etiology of blindness, age at onset of blindness, degree of impairment, and other important variables. To the extent that any of these variables is related to the dependent measure under study, heterogeneity of the sample increases variability in the dependent measure. Curtailing the acceptable distribution of subjects on the basis of these variables may not be economically feasible, and in any case would reduce the generality of the obtained results.

A related problem occurs in research in which samples of blind and sighted subjects are compared. Often a matching procedure is used, in which sighted subjects are chosen to match the blind subjects on such status variables as age, sex, IQ, and educational level. However, as the list of such variables grows, the technical aspects of matching become more involved, and the astute researcher always has the nagging feeling that despite his efforts at matching samples, he has unwittingly neglected a variable that is critically important.

Sampling difficulties aside, there is serious question about the appropriateness of using a blindfolded, sighted sample as a control group against which to compare the abilities of blind subjects. The possibility that sighted subjects may be able to visualize the stimulus materials in some situations suggests that it is not simply the case that blindfolding produces a test of strictly nonvisual abilities. On the other hand, the blindfolded subject is at the disadvantage of having just lost his sight and of not having had a chance to practice using sources of information that he may, in his sighted existence, typically ignore. In most studies, little practice is allowed, and the performance of the blindfolded, sighted subject may not represent a reliable ability level but rather an arbitrary point taken from a curve of improving performance. In such cases, the blind sample used as a "natural control group" cannot provide an adequate basis against which to evaluate the performance of sighted groups, and comparisons are not meaningful. At another level, the rationale of comparing blind with sighted groups suffers from the fact that it is risky to attribute any perceptual deficit shown by the blind directly to the lack of vision. There is abundant evidence, particularly for the congenitally blind, that nonperceptual factors such as parental overprotection during infancy and early childhood can affect the adequacy of a variety of functions, including perceptual ones. Such effects cannot be directly attributed to the lack of vision. In fact, the evidence suggests that many such deficits need not occur if the interpersonal environment is a suitable one. More than from studies that compare blind with sighted people, the blindness literature will benefit from studies that evaluate variations in abilities as functions of dimensions that are relevant to the blindness itself, such as duration of early vision, amount of remaining vision, and environmental characteristics.

These matters are but aspects of a larger issue that may be the most important of all in conducting research with the blind. The issue has to do with the nature of the tasks that are used to assess abilities and characteristics. It may often be the case, when a task is designed to produce information about a particular characteristic of blind or sighted perceivers, that the same task does not tap the comparable characteristic of the other group. One approach is to somehow ensure that the task is a parallel, or equivalent, one for the various groups involved. Unfortunately, it is not clear on what basis this equivalence should be judged. From one point of view, the experimenter can simply design a task and use it as a criterion task in its own right, testing blind and sighted subjects under exactly the same procedures and conditions. This is probably too naïve an approach, however. Experimental tasks rarely require behaviors that may legitimately be considered criterion behaviors in their own right, in the sense that they need not be referenced to behaviors that take place in the real world. More often, an experimental task is merely one of a number of possible ways of operationalizing a behavior. Thus, it is necessary to consider whether the task is an equally adequate operationalization for all groups involved. In doing so, some attention should be paid to the ecological role of a given ability or characteristic with respect to the total behavioral repertoire of the sample being considered. In this respect, the same experimental task may tap a behavior that serves a very different ecological function for blind and sighted people. Comparison of blind and sighted samples on the behavior would generate conclusions that might misrepresent, for one group or the other, the real adequacy or importance of that behavior.

In short, it may be argued that research that compares blind and blindfolded sighted subjects is generally unsatisfying. The blind rarely form an appropriate control group for sighted subjects, and the perceptual performance of sighted subjects is not typically an appropriate yardstick against which to evaluate the abilities of the blind. The understanding of the perception of the blind will be most effectively advanced by research that concentrates on variables related to visual history and to nonvisual perceptual–motor experience.

References

Ahmad, S. The difference between the haptic perception of sighted and blind persons. *Research Bulletin, American Foundation for the Blind,* 1971, **23,** 103–104.

Airasian, P. W. Evaluation of the binaural sensory aid. *Research Bulletin, American Foundation for the Blind,* 1973, **26,** 51–72.

Axelrod, S. *Effects of early blindness.* New York: American Foundation for the Blind, No. 7, 1959.

Axelrod, S. Severe visual handicap and kinesthetic figural aftereffects. *Perceptual and Motor Skills,* 1961, **13,** 151–154.

Ayres, A. F. *A comparison of selected perception among early blinded and sighted adolescents.* Unpublished doctoral dissertation, Rutgers Univ., 1966.

Bean, C. H. The blind have "optical illusions." *Journal of Experimental Psychology*, 1938, **22**, 283–289.

Benedetti, L. H., & Loeb, M. A comparison of auditory monitoring performance in blind subjects with that of sighted subjects in light and dark. *Perception & Psychophysics*, 1972, **11**, 19–16.

Berg, J., & Worchel, P. Sensory contributions to human maze learning: A comparison of matched blind, deaf, and normals. *Journal of General Psychology*, 1956, **54**, 81–93.

Berlá, E. P. Effects of physical size and complexity on tactual discrimination of blind children. *Exceptional Children*, 1972, **39**, 120–124.

Berlá, E. P., Butterfield, L. H., Jr., & Murr, M. J. Tactual reading of political maps by blind students: A videomatic behavioral analysis. *Journal of Special Education*, 1976, **10**, 265–276.

Berlá, E. P., & Murr, M. J. Tactual scanning and memory for a spatial display by blind students. Unpublished grant report, 1974.

Berlá, E. P., & Murr, M. J. Psychophysical functions for active tactual discrimination of line width by blind children. *Perception & Psychophysics*, 1975, **17**, 607–612.

Block, C. A. B. *Developmental study of tactile–kinesthetic discrimination in blind, deaf, and normal children.* Unpublished doctoral dissertation, Boston Univ., 1972.

Cleaves, W. T. Untitled manuscript, 1975.

Cotzin, M., & Dallenbach, K. M. Facial vision: The role of pitch and loudness in the perception of obstacles by the blind. *American Journal of Psychology*, 1950, **62**, 483–515.

Crall, A. M. The magnitude of the haptic Ponzo illusion in congenitally blind and sighted subjects as a function of age. *Dissertation Abstracts International*, 1973, **33**, 9-B, 5010.

Cratty, B. J. The perception of gradient and the veering tendency while walking without vision. *Research Bulletin, American Foundation for the Blind*, 1967, **14**, 31–51.

Cratty, B. J., Peterson, C., Harris, J., & Schoner, R. The development of perceptual-motor abilities in blind children and adolescents. *New Outlook for the Blind*, 1968, **62**, 111–117.

Curtis, J. F., & Winer, D. M. The auditory abilities of the blind as compared with the sighted. *Journal of Auditory Research*, 1969, **9**, 57–59.

Davidson, P. W. Haptic judgments of curvature by blind and sighted humans. *Journal of Experimental Psychology*, 1972, **93**, 43–55.

Davidson, P. W., Barnes, J. K., & Mullen, G. Differential effects of task memory demand on haptic matching of shape by blind and sighted humans. *Neuropsychologia*, 1974, **12**, 395–397.

Diespecker, D. D. Vibrotactile learning. *Psychonomic Science*, 1967, **9**, 107–108.

Duran, P., & Tufenkjian, S. The measurement of length by congenitally blind children and a quasiformal approach for spatial concepts. *Research Bulletin, American Foundation for the Blind*, 1970, **22**, 47–70.

Eaves, L., & Klonoff, H. A comparison of blind and sighted children on a tactual and performance test. *Exceptional Children*, 1970, **37**, 269–273.

Ewart, A. G., & Carp, F. M. Recognition of tactual form by sighted and blind subjects. *American Journal of Psychology*, 1962, **76**, 488–491.

Fish, R. M., & Beschle, R. G. An auditory display capable of presenting two-dimensional shapes to the blind. *Research Bulletin, American Foundation for the Blind*, 1973, **26**, 5–18.

Fisher, G. H. Spatial localization by the blind. *American Journal of Psychology*, 1964, **77**, 2–14.

Foulke, E. Transfer of a complex motor skill. *Perceptual and Motor Skills*, 1964, **18**, 733–740.

Foulke, E. Non-visual communication: IX. Reading by touch. *Education of the Visually Handicapped*, 1970, **2**, 122–125.

Foulke, E. Non-visual communication: X. Reading by touch. *Education of the Visually Handicapped*, 1971, **3**, 25–28.

Foulke, E., Amster, C. H., Nolan, C. Y., & Bixler, R. H. The comprehension of rapid speech by the blind. *Exceptional Children*, 1962, **29**, 134–141.

Foulke, E., & Warm, J. Effects of complexity and redundancy on the tactual recognition of metric figures. *Perceptual and Motor Skills*, 1967, **25**, 177–187.

Geldard, F. A. Adventures in tactile literacy. *American Psychologist*, 1957, **12**, 115–124.

Geldard, F. A. Body English. *Psychology Today*, 1968, **2**, 43–48.

Gibbs, S. H., & Rice, J. A. The psycholinguistic characteristics of visually impaired children: An ITPA pattern analysis. *Education of the Visually Handicapped*, 1974, **6**, 80–87.

Gore, G. V., III. A comparison of two methods of speeded speech. *Education of the Visually Handicapped*, 1969, **1**, 69–76.

Gottesman, M. A comparative study of Piaget's developmental schema of sighted children with that of a group of blind children. *Child Development*, 1971, **42**, 573–580.

Hare, B. A., Hammill, D. D., & Crandell, J. M. Auditory discrimination ability of visually limited children. *New Outlook for the Blind*, 1970, **64**, 287–292.

Hayes, S. P. New experimental data on the old problem of sensory compensation. *Teachers Forum*, 1933, **5**, 22–26.

Heinrichs, R. W., & Moorhouse, J. A. Touch-perception thresholds in blind diabetic subjects in relation to the reading of Braille type. *New England Journal of Medicine*, 1969, **280**, 72–75.

Hermelin, B. M., & O'Connor, N. Spatial coding in normal, autistic and blind children. *Perceptual and Motor Skills*, 1971, **33**, 127–132.(a)

Hermelin, B. M., & O'Connor, N. Functional assymetry in the reading of Braille. *Neuropsychologia*, 1971, **9**, 431–435.(b)

Hermelin, B. M., & O'Connor, N. Location and distance estimates by blind and sighted children. *Quarterly Journal of Experimental Psychology*, 1975, **27**, 295–301.

Hill, J. W., & Bliss, J. C. Perception of sequentially presented tactile point stimuli. *Perception & Psychophysics*, 1968, **4**, 289–295.

Hunter, W. F. An analysis of space perception in congenitally blind and in sighted individuals. *Journal of General Psychology*, 1964, **70**, 325–329.

Izumiyama, M. The auditory perception of blind children. *Tohoku Folia Psychologia*, 1956, **15**, 13–21.

Jones, B. Development of cutaneous and kinesthetic localization by blind and sighted children. *Developmental Psychology*, 1972, **6**, 349–352.

Jones, B. Spatial perception in the blind. *British Journal of Psychology*, 1975, **66**, 461–472.

Juurmaa, J. *Ability structure and loss of vision.* New York: American Foundation for the Blind, No. 18, 1967.

Juurmaa, J. On the accuracy of obstacle detection by the blind. *New Outlook for the Blind*, 1970, **64**, 65–72, 104–118.

Kanno, Y., & Ohwaki, Y. Formation of the Charpentier illusion of weight in the blind. *Tohoku Folia Psychologia*, 1958, **17**, 21–46.

Kellogg, W. N. Sonar system of the blind. *Science*, 1962, **137**, 399–404.

Kimura, M. Perception of the compound figures by tactile motor scanning. *Japanese Journal of Psychology*, 1972, **43**, 1–12.

Koch, H. L., & Ufkess, J. A comparative study of stylus maze learning by blind and seeing subjects. *Journal of Experimental Psychology*, 1926, **9**, 118–131.

Koestline, W. C., Dent, O. B., & Giambra, L. M. Verbal mediation on a nonvisual formboard task with blind, partially sighted, and sighted subjects. *Journal of Consulting and Clinical Psychology*, 1972, **38**, 169–173.

Kohler, I. Orientation by aural clues. *Research Bulletin, American Foundation for the Blind*, 1964, **4**, 14–53.

Lappin, J. S., & Foulke, E. Expanding the tactual field of view. *Perception & Psychophysics*, 1973, **14**, 237–241.

Leonard, J. A. Static and mobile balancing performance of blind adolescent grammar school children. *New Outlook for the Blind*, 1969, **63**, 65–72.

Lindley, S. P. Kinesthetic perception in blind adults. *Research Bulletin, American Foundation for the Blind*, 1973, **25**, 175–192.

McFadden, D. Detection and lateralization of interaural differences of time and level by the blind. *Perceptual and Motor Skills*, 1974, **38**, 211–215.

McKinney, J. P. Hand schema in children. *Psychonomic Science*, 1964, **1**, 99–100.

Menaker, S. L. Perceptual development in blind children. Unpublished doctoral dissertation, Boston Univ., 1966.

Merry, R. V., & Merry, F. K. The finger maze as a supplementary test of intelligence for blind children. *Journal of Genetic Psychology*, 1934, **44**, 227–230.

Nelson, T. M., & Haney, R. R. Force perception by blind and blindfolded subjects. *International Journal for the Education of the Blind*, 1968, **18**, 116–119.

Nolan, C. Y., & Morris, J. E. Development and validation of the Roughness Discrimination Test. *International Journal for the Education of the Blind*, 1965, **15**, 1–6.

O'Connor, N., & Hermelin, B. M. Inter- and intra-modal transfer in children with modality specific and general handicaps. *British Journal of Social and Clinical Psychology*, 1971, **10**, 346–354.

O'Connor, N., & Hermelin, B. M. Seeing and hearing in space and time. *Perception & Psychophysics*, 1972, **11**, 46–48.

O'Connor, N., & Hermelin, B. M. Modality-specific spatial correlates. *Perception & Psychophysics*, 1975, **17**, 213–216.

Packard, B. L. Performance of blind and sighted on tactual-kinesthetic perceptual tasks. *Dissertation Abstracts International*, 1971, **31**, 12-A, 6443.

Patterson, J., & Deffenbacher, K. Haptic perception of the Mueller-Lyer illusion by the blind. *Perceptual and Motor Skills*, 1972, **35**, 819–824.

Pitman, D. J. The musical ability of blind children. *Research Bulletin, American Foundation for the Blind*, 1965, **11**, 63–80.

Renshaw, S., Wherry, R. J., & Newlin, J. C. Cutaneous localization in congenitally blind versus seeing children and adults. *Journal of Genetic Psychology*, 1930, **38**, 239–248.

Rice, C. E. Early blindness, early experience, and perceptual enhancement. *Research Bulletin, American Foundation for the Blind*, 1970, **22**, 1–22.

Rice, C. E., Feinstein, S. H., & Schusterman, R. J. Echo-detection ability of the blind: Size and distance factors. *Journal of Experimental Psychology*, 1965, **70**, 246–251.

Riley, L. H., Luterman, D. M., & Cohen, M. F. Relationship between hearing ability and mobility in a blinded adult population. *New Outlook for the Blind*, 1964, **58**, 139–141.

Spiegelman, M. N. *A comparative study of the effects of early blindness on the development of auditory–spatial learning*. Paper delivered at the Conference on the Effects of Blindness and Other Impairments on Early Development, American Foundation for the Blind, 1972.

Stellwagen, W. T., & Culbert, S. S. Comparisons of blind and sighted subjects in the discrimination of texture. *Perceptual and Motor Skills*, 1963, **17**, 61–62.

Supa, M., Cotzin, M., & Dallenbach, K. M. "Facial vision": The perception of obstacles by the blind. *American Journal of Psychology*, 1944, **57**, 133–183.

Sylvester, R. H. The mental imagery of the blind. *Psychological Bulletin*, 1913, **10**, 210–211.

Thurlow, W. R. Auditory and visual sequential Braille communication. *Perceptual and Motor Skills*, 1974, **38**, 1000.

Tsai, L. S. Mueller-Lyer illusion by the blind. *Perceptual and Motor Skills*, 1967, **25**, 641–644.

Warren, D. H., Anooshian, L. J., & Bollinger, J. G. Early vs. late blindness: The role of early vision in spatial behavior. *Research Bulletin, American Foundation for the Blind*, 1973, **26**, 151–170.

Warren, D. H., & Kocon, J. A. Factors in the successful mobility of the blind: A review. *Research Bulletin, American Foundation for the Blind*, 1974, **28**, 191–218.

Warren, D. H., & Pick, H. L., Jr. Intermodality relations in localization in blind and sighted people. *Perception & Psychophysics,* 1970, **8,** 430–432.

Weiner, L. H. The performance of good and poor Braille readers on certain tests involving tactual perception. *International Journal for the Education of the Blind,* 1963, **12,** 73–77.

White, B. W., Saunders, F. A., Scadden, L., Bach-y-Rita, P., & Collins, C. C. Seeing with the skin. *Perception & Psychophysics,* 1970, **7,** 23–27.

Wills, D. M. Vulnerable periods in the early development of blind children. *Psychoanalytic Study of the Child,* 1970, **25,** 461–480.

Witkin, H. A., Oltman, P. K., Chase, J. B., & Friedman, F. Cognitive patterning in the blind. In J. Hellmuth (Ed.), *Cognitive Studies.* New York: Brunner-Mazel, 1971.

Worchel, P. Space perception and orientation in the blind. *Psychological Monographs,* 1951, **65,** 1–28.

Worchel, P., Mauney, J., & Andrew, J. G. The perception of obstacles by the blind. *Journal of Experimental Psychology,* 1950, **40,** 747–751.

Yates, J. T., Johnson, R. M., & Starz, W. J. Loudness perception of the blind. *Audiology,* 1972, **11,** 368–376.

Zemtzova, M. I., Kulagin, J. A., & Novikova, L. A. The use of the remaining sensory channels (safe analyzers) in compensation of visual function in blindness. *Research Bulletin, American Foundation for the Blind,* 1962, **2,** 72–87.

Chapter 5

PROSTHETICS OF PERCEPTUAL SYSTEMS

JOHN M. KENNEDY, DANIEL KLEIN, AND LOCHLAN E. MAGEE

1. INTRODUCTION

In prosthetics, we find ways to assist a failing or missing body function with various devices or aids, and, at times, special training too. In this short overview of prosthetics of perceptual systems, we aim (*a*) to outline intellectual principles necessary to understand sensory aids (*b*) to offer some basic information about standard sensory aids and (*c*) to allow a brief (and we hope, tantalizing) glimpse of research on remarkable perceptual prosthetic devices.

The concept of a sensory aid deserves careful thought. Consider the fact that a sensory aid is a tool for a perceptual system. Now tools serve several kinds of functions (perception, manipulation, communication, and transportation in the main—some tools having multiple functions). A noteworthy fact is that psychology has studied tool use only in terms of manipulation, failing to recognize that this is only one kind of function for a tool. Even Kohler

HANDBOOK OF PERCEPTION, VOL. X

(1925), Piaget, and ethologists like Goodall (1971) restrict themselves to manipulative tools like the rake. The occasional research that has noted perceptual functions has been quite revealing, as in Gallup's (1968) study, in which a monkey recognized that a mirror image tells about its own body, or Howard and Templeton's (1966) work with children who readily adapted to vision through a prism.

These examples show that issues in prosthetics are not tied to handicaps, and as we shall see later, keys to the development and evolution of intellect may be researched with prosthetic devices. Accordingly, we need to shift our attention from hardware, like spectacles and amplifiers, to the general principles that lie behind perceptual aids. What is distinctive about perceptual tools?

The function of a perceptual prosthesis is to provide *information* about a world existing independently of the device by capitalizing on information that was present before the device was introduced. The device is supposed to allow perception to occur; in Gibsonian (1966) terms, the device enables the perceiver to pick up information—whether or not it restores or generates new sensations is irrelevant. The device does not create information about its target (the distal source), nor does it make it possible for a preexisting sensory capacity to become sensitive (unlike an operation). It helps the perceiver make the best use of his current range of sensitivities.

The function of an aid is awareness of an environment, to be achieved by fitting preexisting information via a modified signal to a preexisting capacity. The modified signal can be created in various ways. Some procedures amplify energy to above-threshold levels; others simply diminish events like noise (Gordon & Cooper, 1975).

Some procedures bypass or replace weak links in otherwise normal perceptual systems, as bone-conduction hearing aids do. Others compensate for inflexibility in a perceptual system by changing patterns of energy coherently to make them manageable by the perceptual system, as do spectacle lenses in forcing light to converge or diverge. (In some cases, the pattern of energy is simply redirected, as by a mirror). Still others take the energy and patterns in one medium and offer the results to a perceptual system normally blind to the original source, as in devices of sensory substitution that convert light or sound to tactile patterns. One part of the body can act as a prosthesis for another—a sensory system may try to respond to information that normally is the prerogative of another sense, as in lipreading or the so-called facial vision of the blind.

Note that prosthetics raises issues of appearance and reality. The observer has to be able to perceive the original source despite changes in the signal enforced by the aid. The signal may or may not contain both information about the original source and information about the modification placed on the signal by the device. Thus, even with ordinary colored spectacles, young children have trouble answering questions about how things look or how things are. The intellectual structure involved in such questions of perception is evident in the fact that if the child and the experimenter both wear glasses the child's difficulty increases (Liben, 1976)! If the signal does not present information about the modifications, the user is likely to be mislead; he or she may have to screen out permanent additions to the original signal or make a conscious correction of his impressions. Thus, in some fashion, the aid must add to the preexisting information in a manner that will at least *provide information about itself at key times*. One common example is that the hearing-aid wearer needs to be able to pick up signs that the aid is malfunctioning in order to discriminate an echo, say, from the special way reverberation may be created by the instrument.

In its purest form, a sensory aid leaves the environmental source unchanged while it delivers a message about the source to the perceiver, who is aware that the message has come via a special channel. What special channels and messages are readily understood? Which require little training? What is the best system of messages and channels? Stated in these terms, the discipline of prosthetics is seen to bear on the classic questions of the nature of the modalities, sensory equivalence (Bower, 1974), and the idea that information is not tied to sensations (Gibson, 1966). The relationship to epistemology becomes evident when we put the question in Bohr's way: How can we partition the observer, the instrument, and the target (Lenzen, 1938)?

Prosthetics as a *discipline*, rather than a catalog of odd apparatus, encompasses everyday events like testing food with a fork, but is also a key part of intellectual history, for astronomy relied on the telescope and biology on the microscope. To put it dramatically, there is something unusual about sensory prosthesis, for though many animals make and use manipulative tools, human beings are the only animals known to have invented a perceptual prosthetic device.

One likely reason for this inventive achievement is that people have a special capacity to make Bohr's partitions between themselves, the observed, and the tool of observation flexibly, systematically and perceptually. That is, people readily distinguish the perceptual means and the perceptual end, and the distinctions of one moment are readily revised the next moment to suit a new task. This idea has been one of our guides in selecting some issues and devices to describe in this chapter. In what follows, we concentrate on procedures that seem to engage human sensory capacities in this flexible and perceptual way and thus do not, like mere meters and gauges, only act to give a conventional or coded reflection of the distal object. The devices we consider are usually claimed to give a phenomenological impression of a distal object and do not inevitably require explicit coaching or training in a code for the requisite information to be received.

II. ALLEVIATING DEAFNESS

Hearing entails physical conduction being transformed into nerve impulses, so deafness can have many origins. The most common forms of deafness are usually curable by fluid drainage and surgery, but prior to medical intervention, a hearing aid is often required. Also, those older people who lose hearing through presbycusis, the inexplicable "aging" of the hearing nerve, have little recourse except artificial aids (although some say that acupuncture can be helpful in such cases.)

Consider the infant and the aged, especially, and their psychological problems (Ewing & Ewing, 1961; Hartbauer, 1975). Extreme difficulty arises with the child who has total sensory loss. Such a child must learn to talk, using some unusual sensory channel for reception and monitoring of his own speech, and being taught by methods that are more optimistic than established. In the older person, there is also the danger of isolation and despair during the difficult process of learning lipreading, for example, as a poor substitute for what once was effortless.

Direct assistance to the hard-of-hearing can take various forms that seem to relate closely to the normal functioning of audition and vibration sensitivity (in contrast to conventions like sign language or Geldard's (1966) alphabetic skin code). One can amplify signals, employ neighboring structures to reach the ear with bone-conduction devices, or supplement the ear with lipreading (and encourage the hard-of-hearing to *attend* and *guess* to their best advantage) or even bypass the ear, as some research indicates, through vibration reception by the skin.

A. Hearing Aids

Hearing aids call on long-established principles: straightforward amplification (as in ear trumpets and tubes of earlier days, stethoscopes, or the simple cupping of a hand behind the ear), and bone conduction (which was employed in the seventeenth century in a fan-shaped device designed to be held against the teeth). To go consistently beyond the equivalent of 20 dB of amplification, generally requires an electric device—the "miniature telephone" type of hearing aid, developed in the nineteenth century. Our century's contribution (Taylor, 1973) has been to improve the hearing aid's performance (with no major advances since the 1940s) and to make the aid much smaller.

Like any man–machine system, hearing aids have psychological factors to parallel the engineering aspects. In our sampling of the issues we will discuss amplification, binaural–monaural alternatives, restriction on volume, and output distortions.

Amplification is a sine qua non of a hearing aid. Yet we know little of the impression it gives to the perceiver; the impression might be as distinct as the shock we get on hearing our recorded voice for the first time. Imagine the young child wearing a hearing aid for the first time. Does the child's world seem noisier, stranger, closer? Or did the child's ears seem to change, perhaps? Subtleties of a voice are heard for the first time—are these recognizable or frighteningly unfamiliar? What do the changes *mean*? The "acceptability" of the device is a constant problem for clinicians working with adults as well as children, especially in the initial adjustment, a time when the aid is often rejected for short or long periods, or even permanently.

Victoreen (1960) suggests that for the aid to be comfortable it must normally amplify to a level that is midway in the particular user's dynamic range—that is, the interval between threshold and discomfort. It is not easy to measure the discomfort level, and midway varies according to one's measuring scale, but Wallenfels (1971) feels there is very strong clinical support for the idea. At least it suggests one way to think about acceptability.

The binaural aid is generally more acceptable than the monaural (Dirks & Carhart, 1962). It is somewhat surprising then that studies on binaural or monaural aids and sensitivity have been inconclusive or contradictory (Harris & Miller, 1966; Oyer & Frankmann, 1975). Binaural amplification produces "little or no improvement in speech reception in quiet or in noise [Jerger, Carhart, & Dirks, 1961, p. 146]." So-called subjective reports, however, invariably contend that binaural aids are much clearer. If there is an advantage in the normal use of the device, it may be because (*a*) the head mounting of the device dovetails with everyday deployment of attention and head orientation; or (*b*) in switching attention between ears (Broadbent, 1958) we always reach an assisted signal; or (*c*) in everyday use with two aids, high and distorting amplification is not needed as often as with one aid.

We should note, too, that lab tests of aids, using naïve subjects, are not always fair indicators of daily use; "ecological" studies would be useful.

The possible importance of binaural versus monaural practice is shown by Fisher (1963). Children who had no language at 5 years of age on admission to a school for the deaf were fitted with binaural aids, although there was no apparent difference in binaural or monaural tests. After 2 years, their binaural level was markedly better than their monaural scores.

How can we prevent unpleasant volume from nearby loud sounds? One way is peak clipping, but this entails distortion. This result could hinder a child who is trying to achieve clear speech, though it may offer an adult an intelligible signal. An alternative is automatic volume control. Consider the following: *Attack time* is how long it takes to reduce output to tolerable levels given a sustained long noise. *Release time* is required to increase amplification when the noise ceases. Lynn and Carhart (1963) found that an aid with slow attack and release times (about 400 msec) significantly impaired speech reception, indicating an important parameter of echoic memory.

Distortions in output are of several kinds (Miller, 1972). First, aids are selective. High frequencies are often ignored, for example, and many if not most aids are designed to boost frequencies below 3000 Hz. Subtleties of *s*, *v*, and *c* sounds are easily missed. Second, when one frequency arrives, several may be produced, as in harmonic distortion. Third, at the onset and decay of a sound, output may persist in temporal distortion (e.g., a ringing noise). Fourth, in turning the control knobs, extra sounds may be generated (e.g., hums and whistles). The aid is not a Moog synthesizer, but we should add that the distortions are more than additive at times!

How does the user recognize artifacts for what they are? The single most important answer is obvious. Adults should be forewarned and shown examples. The danger of ignoring a genuine warning whistle or bell is too great; the user needs to check reflexively when a potentially ambiguous signal occurs. His community should recognize his needs too, with supplementary visual signals to accompany warning sounds, and more widespread dissemination of information on the problems of the deaf (e.g., that *s*, *v*, and *c* may be confusable).

"Deliberately manipulated distortions" have been attempted in order to bring the essentials of some signals into the deaf person's range of sensitivity. For example, the signal can be transposed in frequencies, much as one could play a melody in different keys. Studies on transposition are difficult to evaluate for several reasons. If the person being tested is totally deaf to high frequencies, then any device that enables signals at those pitches to become partially effective is, on the face of it, contributing something that could otherwise be completely missed. But the essential questions are, how often would those frequencies be of value, and, what is being done with frequencies that would normally occupy the space that is now filled with the transposed message? Bennett and Byers (1967) found that a consistent frequency shift of all of an incoming speech signal lowered speech intelligibility considerably. More encouraging (though not conclusive) were Johannson's findings (discussed in Oyer & Frankmann, 1975, p. 150) with two-channel systems. One channel simply amplified speech, the other transposed high frequencies downwards. Case histories of children indicated considerable improvements in speech discrimination after some months of training with this device.

B. Speechreading (Lipreading)

Our own senses act in a prosthetic way when they take on special discriminations, usually ignored, to assist a failing sense. The ear can locate sound to aid visual–spatial perception, and the eye can watch the speaker to supplement the hearing of speech.

The view that lipreading is possible and teachable is about 100 years old. Today, there are many schools of thought on how it should be taught, some expecting students to learn physiology of the mouth, and others stressing the passage of ideas from speaker to audience. No firm evidence favors one school over the others. However, very definite grounds set restrictions on lipreading (Jeffers & Barley, 1971; O'Neill & Oyer, 1961). First, some speech sounds are homophenous—that is, uttered in ways that look alike. Second, some sounds can be made with essentially *no movement,* whereas some movements are made by simply returning to rest and make *no sounds.* Third, some potentially useful movements are especially small, subtle, or quick, or are unnecessary in some speech contexts; thus, they are only seen in the most favorable conditions. Fourth, the rank order of visibility and the rank order of frequency of occurrence are quite uncorrelated.

Estimates of the amount of speech available via lipreading fall to the 15% mark when the above restrictions are noted.

Fortunately however, the amount can be doubled if the speaker will help by enunciating clearly, which will make his movements more distinct, and by speaking slightly more slowly than normal, which will ensure that a *more complete* set of movements is undertaken. One should note that a slow-motion film of normal and fast speech (Byers & Lieberman, 1959) will simply repeat the *abbreviated* movements of speedy discourse. Also, the speaker should never shout, for shouting distorts the normal mouth movements; it is far better to speak slightly slowly, quite clearly, and to repeat the message two or three times.

C. Speech via the Skin

Since the 1930s, there have been attempts to use the vibration sensitivity of the skin as a substitute for that of the ear. To make this sensory substitution possible, an electromechanical device is necessary to amplify the energy of the speech. Since speech covers a bandwidth of more than 250–4000 Hz and the vibrotactile sense has a ceiling of only about 450 Hz, frequency transposition is useful. Furthermore, differences in location on the skin can be employed as an analogue for differences in frequency, as in the cochlear models of Békésy (1955), Finzenkeller (reported in Keidel, 1974).

Kirman (1973) has argued cogently that the skin channel is potentially suitable for the discrimination of speech. In his opinion, it is not inevitable that only the ear should be able to discriminate phonemes, or even that phonemes are necessary for speech reception. His later work (Kirman, 1974) has employed apparent movements of patterns on the skin to produce fine discriminations of speech events. In contrast, Keidel and his coworkers Biber, Kirsch and Finzenkeller have slowed down speech to one quarter of its normal speed and *sampled* the speech before applying the signal to the listener's skin. It is interesting that both Kirman and Keidel report an apparently significant level of recognition of selected phonemes, at about 35–40% in untrained observers. This level of initial recognition suggests that the skin system is a suitable basis for genuine perception of speech. Furthermore, with less than 20 hr of training, both unknown words and phonemes can be identified by some observers with essentially 100% accuracy (Keidel, 1974, Fig. 4, p. 29). The fact that new words can be identified after merely a few hours of training strongly supports the contention that a genuinely perceptual skill is being reached via the skin.

Cutaneous sensitivities may be able to substitute for a large range of auditory functions. For example, by stimulating two points on the skin with vibrators, an analogue of sound localization can be produced (Gescheider, 1974). For recent brief reviews and an extensive bibliography of auditory aids and substitution devices, see Strong (1975) and Sherrick (1975).

III. ALLEVIATING BLINDNESS

After passing through the tissues and fluids of the eye, light is focused on the retina and transformed into nerve impulses. Obviously, visual difficulties have many causes both in the periphery and in our most central and psychological recesses (Heaton, 1972). Sometimes help can come from medicine, psychotherapy, or training in the deployment of attention (Hanninen, 1975), which can even bypass losses due to lesions (Bach-y-rita, 1972, p. 142). Also, there are many practical devices, some of which, like the guide dog and the cane (Sherrick, 1974; U.K. Survey, 1967), are as old as history. Technology gave us spectacles and magnifying glasses; today it offers embossed maps, Braille and Moon scripts, "talking" typewriters and books, and raised-line drawings (Kennedy & Fox, 1977). As a sample, paralleling Section II, consider optical rearrangement, facial vision, and a television aid applied to the skin.

A. Optical Rearrangement

Whereas a hearing aid increases the intensity of stimuli, most optical devices only redirect stimuli (rays of light), often converging or diverging them. The results of redirection provide both information and puzzles for vision. We will mention aspects of clarity, magnification, movement, orientation, and color.

First, let us review some basic ophthalmology. The eye's lens becomes more spherical in focusing near objects. In presbyopia the ability to focus near objects is lost, and this is a problem that worsens with age. To read a hand-held newspaper, a convex lens before the eye is required to converge the light slightly. In myopia (short sightedness) distant objects are focused on a plane in front of the retina. A concave lens, diverging the light, corrects this condition. In hypermetropia (long sightedness) distant objects tend to focus behind the retina, and the convex lens is a useful corrective, though the subject can correct his condition momentarily, without using a lens, with some effort.

In astigmatism different axes through the eye—say, horizontal and vertical—cannot be focused at the same time. A cylindrical lens brings the axes into conformity.

Eyeglasses were first recorded by Bacon in 1268. Franklin invented bifocals in 1784, and Airy corrected astigmatism in 1827. The development of one-piece bifocals is due to Bentzon and Emerson in this century. Now we have contact lenses of both glass and soft-plastic varieties. Curiously, the psychological research on rearranged vision is mostly from just the past 25 years, yet it is already so voluminous that we can only skim it.

An unfocused image can have its blur reduced by either changing the shape of the lens or by reducing the size of the pupil. The shape of the lens is related to the distance of the object to be focused, at one level of analysis, and to the amount of blur, at another level of analysis. (Interestingly, the eye corrects for blur by *correctly* increasing or decreasing its power, without using a system of estimation and feedback.) Of course, some objects in any complex scene will be out-of-focus when others are in focus. Thus, acceptable and unacceptable blur is a matter of attention. Furthermore, blur is related to both distance (via the lens) and to ambient light levels (via the pupil). When an aid is introduced, not only is blur altered, but the viewed environment may appear shifted in distance and brighter. To complicate matters more, (*a*) apparent brightness is a function of sharp, unblurred contours and (*b*) relative blur is a depth cue, for astigmatics especially (Campbell & Westheimer, 1959)!

Blur, brightness, and distance changes can be evident when one dons spectacles for the first time. Eventually, the changes are at least unsurprising and may even be adapted out, so the world looks the same with and without the aid. But most spectacles are weak, and accordingly we must turn to research on more striking rearrangements with effects that are easier to measure (e.g., magnification of more than 10%).

Sensitivity to magnification and minification is often acute (Smith, 1958), but adaptation can be swift and considerable—for example, 23% after 30 min (Rock, 1966). However, these adaptations occurred with seated subjects viewing a scene through a curved mirror. In contrast, Foley (1965) found that subjects wearing binoculars for 3 weeks showed very little adaptation. Foley's subjects wore the devices intermittently, just as many spectacle wearers do. The results suggest that spectacle wearers may simply become accustomed to magnification (rather than actually *adapting* perceptually) and mentally correct for it (cf. Walls, 1951).

Perceptual adaptation may be possible for stability and movement. Some spectacle devices create vivid impressions of waxy elastic or swinging motions of the environment when the observer moves his head or eyes. Many spectacle wearers notice an unstable visual world with new spectacles, but the scene usually becomes stable within a few days.

Bifocals are two optical systems with a phenomenal "break" dividing them, so that a pole might be seen as two detached sections slightly displaced from one another. In normal use, this *vernier shift* becomes unnoticed. But if one inspects the break, it will be obvious even after prolonged use of a bifocal system (Kohler, 1955, 1962).

Underlying the apparent instability with spectacles is the fact that objects are displaced slightly, by a few degrees, and *inconsistently* (e.g., more near the visual periphery). This kind of slight shift of orientation has been extensively researched (Hochberg, 1971; see *Perception,* 1974, Vol. 3). The results suggest that (*a*) subjects' movements are not necessary for adaptation (Howard, Craske & Templeton, 1965); (*b*) curvature can adapt (Held & Rekosh, 1963); (*c*) somesthesis may adapt rather than the eye (Harris, 1965); and (*d*) previous learning of orientations may be unaffected by new adaptation (Kennedy, 1969). Whether vision changes or somesthesis changes depends on many factors, and piecemeal adaptation of somesthesis seems a well-established fact. Piecemeal adaptation of vision seems unlikely (note the vernier-shift condition), but Taylor (1962) reported that apparent *slant* could adapt in a piecemeal fashion. See Dolezal (1976) for an extensive review.

Eye movements participate in most spatial percepts, and being malleable might be crucial to adaptation (cf. Festinger, Burnham, Ono, & Bamber, 1967). Their role in color perception is slight, so it was interesting when Kohler (1962) argued for gaze—contingent color aftereffects, which could be useful in eliminating color fringes induced by strong lenses. McCollough (1965) found these effects to be low-order aftereffects, rather than conditioned and contingent upon gaze. McCollough's version is accepted today, though there is still some evidence for conditioning color effects (Skowdo, Timney, Gentry, & Morant, 1975).

B. Echolocation (Facial Vision of the Blind)

The eye substitutes for the ear in lipreading, and the ear reciprocates in echolocation, a skill that is, as we shall see, a poor exchange for vision.

That the blind could sense distant obstacles has been known for centuries (Griffin, 1959). It was thought that the sense was based on pressures felt by the facial skin, for those were the sensations reported by the subject (a good demonstration that a prosthesis should replace information, not sensations!). Dressler (1893) found that ear plugs eliminated the sense; and Dallenbach, in a series of studies, demonstrated that echolocation was the necessary and sufficient basis for the sense and that facial skin was irrelevant (Supa, Cotzin, & Dallenbach, 1944).

Kellogg (1962) showed that subjects could detect both moving and static objects, and discriminate the two. Hard surfaces could also be discriminated from soft surfaces. For instance, metal was discriminated from velvet with 99% accuracy, but of course, this is an extreme, and many visibly discriminable textures are echoically indistinguishable. The lower limit of size (about 2 in. at 2 ft, say Rice and Feinstein, 1965) is of course much cruder than vision.

Facial vision depends on tones of 8000 Hz or more, Dallenbach found, which is reasonable, since low frequencies would "wash over" small objects.

Problems can arise with the sound emission masking the (fainter) sound reception. Also, a *tilted* object gives a fainter echo (and little return at all at an inclination of 20% or more). Thus a tilted metal disk could easily be confused with a vertical velvet disk, if amplitude is the normal basis for discriminating textures. If the wind is in the wrong direction, that too can affect amplitude and introduce ambiguity. If the emitted pulses are regular, a temporal ambiguity arises: To which pulse is an incoming echo related? Sound absorption (no echo) is ambiguous in many ways: Is the distal thing a hole, a grassy plain, an ivy-covered wall? Finally, there are extraneous noises—these "mock" echoes sometimes, mask echoes at other times, and can simply distract at the best of times.

Thus, echolocation is useful to the blind, but in principle and in practice it suffers from ambiguity and unreliability in any variegated, noisy environment. For discussions of recent research and engineering, see the Leonard Conference (1972), Cratty (1971), and Strelow and Hodgson (1976).

C. Vision Substitution via the Skin

Objects pushed against the skin make imprints akin to silhouettes, and these are recognizable to a limited degree. Motion, including apparent motion, across the skin can improve recognition, and often results in an impression of an object somewhat detached from the skin (see Kennedy, this volume). Using these effects, an electromechanical device can project a television image onto the skin in the form of regions of small, vibrating rods.

Thus, in the Smith–Kettlewell TVSS (television substitution system— White, Saunders, Scadden, Bach-y-rita, & Collins, 1970; see Geldard, 1974 for related devices) a 20 × 20 array of vibrators makes contact with the skin on the subject's back. If the television camera is confronted with a line, a row of the vibrators becomes active. Naïve subjects can usually detect the orientation of the line, whether it is curved or not, stationary or not, and, if it is moving, in which direction it is going. Blind and blindfolded, sighted subjects are equally adept.

Line perception with the TVSS is moderately interesting, as it supports Gestalt principles, but the importance of the device is in allowing access to standard ecological forms (people, chairs, tables, etc.), rather than elementary geometry alone. When closed forms with internal detail, depth, and foreground–background relations are made available, impressive individual differences among subjects emerge. Some subjects, *in their first session,* were able to detect an internal hole in an object, with a shape they could describe accurately. Eventually, most subjects were able to recognize objects like a telephone or cup within a few moments of exposure and the subjects reported perceiving spatial depth relations, although the locus of the distal object was something of a puzzle (Guarniero, 1974).

Presumably, if the object's locus with respect to the perceiver (and his general surroundings) is varied through all the possible quadrants, above and below, in front and behind, and to the left and right of the TVSS user, then the perceiver will come to apprehend the distal locus quite unequivocally. Other kinds of training conditions that can be helpful are suggested by this report on form discrimination:

> When asked to identify a circle, square or triangle, subjects' performance remained near chance levels after 60 trials when no correction was given and no camera movement was allowed. With correction [alone] accuracy reached 60% after 54 trials. . . . When the subjects were allowed to pan the camera over the forms and given correction, they achieved 100% accuracy in the third block of 18 trials with a mean latency of 1 sec or less . . . . The discrimination was even more rapidly established when the subjects were initially presented in pairs for the subject to inspect after telling him "The square is on the right and the circle is on the left." After as little as 10 min of such training, some subjects could achieve 100% accuracy [White *et al.,* 1970, p. 24].

IV. DISCUSSION

The close parallels in our sections on vision and audition indicate that prosthetics entails general principles as well as idiosyncratic hardware. In this light, we should consider two questions—one on information, the other on output complexity.

A. How Is Information Preserved?

Information is present if distinct *sources* and *effects* are in correspondence, such that a given effect only results from a particular source. Then the effect "informs us about" that source. With a prosthesis, a device or procedure is introduced into the medium transmitting the effects. The source is unchanged, but a new set of effects is generated. To be informative, the new set must be in correspondence with the original set, and for every old effect, there should be a new effect. A one-to-one correspondence is an ideal, and in practice the aim of the prosthesis is to preserve the preexisting heterogeneity, not to add to it: If the input is the same, but the output varies (e.g., if a spectacle glass changes with temperature) that is a needless variation. Devices are not preserving information if there are two inputs but only one output (lack of sensitivity) or if two inputs are repeatedly reassigned at random to either of two outputs (lack of reliability). If there are outputs for which there are no inputs, then information is being added (information about the device itself, most notably).

A hearing aid might indicate it is switched on by adding a hum, for which there is no input; if the hum were to be too like an external event, then information would be lost.

Given correspondence of sources and the new set of effects, information is *available*. The perceiver deploys his sensitivities and employs his prosthesis to reach for the information. However, the new set of effects may be ineffective for any of three reasons. The perceiver might not know what to attend to (e.g., lipreading may be unknown to him), the effects might be unavailable to his sensitivities (as is polarization of light), or the patterns of the output might be abstruse.

The patterning of effects deserves a special mention. As has already been noted, tactual signals can act in place of visual or auditory signals. The modality is entirely changed, but, nevertheless, perception of the source is often above chance with little or no training. Presumably, the perceptual systems recognize some forms of correspondence between the original and the prosthetic signals if the patterning of the signals is closely related. We might say that if the intervals between effects, in space or time or intensity, are preserved, then the potential information is likely to be readily understood. That is, correspondence ensures that information will be present, and if the intervals between effects are also preserved, perceptual intelligibility is more probable.

One should note that even with correspondence and preserved intervals, any change will likely cause *some* confusion, for merely transposing auditory frequencies makes speech somewhat less clear.

Questions of patterning also arise in training with a new aid, as will be shown in what follows.

B. Optimal Conditions and Optimal Outputs for Learning

There are many factors influencing the experimenter or trainer's choice of training conditions, and the factors vary as widely as the devices and procedure employed. For example, many subjects have some initial skills at the outset of controlled formal training—for example, in lipreading and echolocation, or, as noted, in speech and form reception by the skin. An evaluation of the individual subject's skills must precede training. Also, the adult can understand the task he is expected to undertake, and make conscious corrections of misleading impressions or learn to deploy his remaining sensitivities to best advantage. Simply knowing the set of relevant alternatives can speed up his discrimination performance, as was noted above in discussing the TVSS. Furthermore, the adult can be told whether he is correct or incorrect, and can be asked to remain passive while the experimenter instructs him or takes him through the range of displays made possible by the device, or points out the key ambiguities to be wary about.

One issue that is raised time and again is whether the subject should be flooded with information, from which he should learn to select, like a child does in everyday perception, or whether training should concentrate on the maximally discriminable inputs? Perhaps this issue is best answered by closely relating the training procedure to the displays and tasks that the perceiver will have to cope with at the end of training. That is, once the relevant units to be discriminated (be they punctate stimuli, or forms, or forms of forms, or objects in a scene, or phonemes, or words) have been defined, the training should consist initially of practice with items the observer can deal with *part* of the time. The observer's tolerance for low or high levels of accuracy should determine the initial difficulty of the tasks set for him. Progress would consist of mastering new items, becoming more tolerant of low levels of accuracy, making finer discriminations and achieving perception of the structured relations between items (Gibson, 1969). Also, the normal background distractions *and* the normal degree of redundancy between items should be introduced as soon as possible. The subject's abilities and motives should be allowed to guide training, rather than the hardware's sensitivities and potentials.

C. Summary Note

We have sampled a broad spectrum of information in this chapter, we have also tried to indicate how information and ambiguity are interrelated in any prosthetic device and in the perceiver's tasks. To some extent, the research surveyed points to the future, to sources of difficulty that might be overcome, and to sensory-substitution devices that might someday be miniaturized and worn just like a small hearing aid. In principle, any sensory system could be bypassed by a sensory aid, and there are hopes that with clever diagnostic procedures and ingenious machinery, young children need not suffer losses of mobility or cognitive growth through sensory handicaps. Ultimately, some think, these devices could play directly onto the sensory cortex, avoiding the sensory transducers altogether (Leonard Conference, 1972). Such advances will be instructive and important, but let us realize, to repeat our theme, that precisely the same problems will arise: Can we be sure that these devices are providing proper information, and how can the perceiver be helped to avoid ambiguity and arrive at veridical perception?

References

Bach-y-rita, P. *Brain mechanisms in sensory substitution*, New York: Academic Press, 1972.

Békésy, G. von. Human skin perception of travelling waves similar to those on the cochlea. *Journal of the Acoustical Society of America*, 1955, **27**, 830–841.

Bennett, D. N., & Byers, V. W. Increased intelligibility in the hypacusic by slow-play frequency transposition. *Journal of Audition Research*, 1967, **7**, 107–118.

Bower, T. G. R. The evolution of sensory systems. In R. B. MacLeod & H. Pick (Eds), *Perception*. Ithaca, New York: Cornell Univ. Press, 1974. Pp. 141–152.

Broadbent, D. E. *Perception and communication*. London: Oxford: Pergamon, 1958.

Byers, V. W., & Lieberman, L. Lipreading performance and the rate of the speakers. *Journal of Speech and Hearing Research*, 1959, **2**, 272–276.

Campbell, F. W., & Westheimer, G. Factors involving accommodation responses of the human eye. *Journal of the Optometry Society of America*, 1959, **49**, 568–571.

Cratty, B. J. *Movement and spatial awareness in blind children and youth*, Springfield, Illinois: Thomas, 1971.

Dirks, D., & Carhart, R. Reactions from users of binaural and monaural hearing aids. *Journal of Speech and Hearing Disorders*, 1962, **27**, 311–322.

Dolezal, H. *Perceptual adaptation*. Unpublished doctoral dissertation, Cornell Univ., 1976.

Dressler, F. B. On the pressure sense of the drum of the ear and "facial vision." *American Journal of Psychology*, 1893, **5**, 344–350.

Ewing, I. R., & Ewing, A. W. G. *New opportunities for deaf children*. London: Univ. of London Press, 1961.

Festinger, L., Burnham, C. A., Ono, H., & Bamber, D. Efference and the conscious experience of perception. *Journal of Experimental Psychology*, 1967, **74**(4, Whole No. 637).

Fisher, B. An investigation of binaural aids. *Teaching the Deaf*, 1963, **61**, 73–83.

Foley, J. E. *Adaptation to magnifying and minifying spectacles*. Unpublished paper, Univ. of Toronto, 1965.

Gallup, G. G. Mirror-image stimulation. *Psychological Bulletin*, 1968, **70**, 782–793.

Geldard, F. A. Cutaneous coding of optical signals: The optohapt. *Perception & Psychophysics*, 1966, **1**, 377–381.

Geldard, F. A. (Ed.) *Cutaneous communication systems and devices*. Austin, Texas: Psychonomic Society, 1974.

Gescheider, G. A. Temporal relations in cutaneous stimulation. In F. A. Geldard (Ed.), *Cutaneous communication systems and devices*. Austin, Texas: Psychonomic Society, 1974.

Gibson, E. J. *Principles of perceptual learning and development*. New York: Appleton, 1969.

Gibson, J. J. *The senses considered as perceptual systems*. Boston: Houghton Mifflin, 1966.

Goodall, J. van L. *In the shadow of man*. Boston: Houghton, Mifflin, 1971.

Gordon, I. E., & Cooper, C. Improving one's touch. *Nature*, 1975, **256**, 203–204.

Griffin, D. R. *Echoes of bats and men*. New York: Doubleday, 1959.

Gaurniero, G. Experience of tactile vision. *Perception*, 1974, **3**, 101–104.

Harris, C. S. Perceptual adaptation to displaced vision. *Psychological Review*, 1965, **72**, 419–444.

Harris, J. D., & Miller, M. H. Monaural vs. binaural: Are two hearing aids better than one? *Current Medical Practice*, 1966, **3**, 7–8.

Hartbauer, R. E. *Aural rehabilitation*. Springfield, Illinois: Thomas, 1975.

Hanninen, K. A. *Teaching the visually handicapped*. Columbus, Ohio: Merrill, 1975.

Heaton, J. M. *The eye: Function & disorder*. New York: Barnes & Noble, 1972.

Held, R., & Rekosh, J. Motor–sensory feedback and the geometry of visual space. *Science*, 1963, **141**, 722–723.

Hochberg, J. E. Perception II. Space and movement. In J. W. Kling & L. A. Riggs (Eds.), *Experimental psychology*. New York: Holt, 1971.

Howard, I. P., Craske, B., & Templeton, W. B. Visuomoter adaptation to discordant exafferent stimulation. *Journal of Experimental Psychology*, 1965, **70**, 189–191.

Howard, O. P., & Templeton, W. B. *Human spatial orientation*. New York: Wiley, 1966.

Jeffers, J., & Barley, M. *Speechreading*. Springfield, Illinois: Thomas, 1971.

Jerger, J., Carhart, R., & Dirks, D. Binaural hearing aids and speech intelligibility. *Journal of Speech and Hearing Research*, 1961, **41**, 137–148.

Keidel, W. D. The cochlear model in skin stimulation. In F. A. Geldard (Ed.), *Cutaneous communication systems and devices*. Austin, Texas: Psychonomic Society, 1974.

Kellogg, W. N. Sonar system of the blind. *Science*, 1962, **137**, 399–404.

Kennedy, J. M. Prismatic displacement and the remembered location of targets. *Perception & Psychophysics*, 1969, **5**, 218–220.

Kennedy, J. M., & Fox, N. Pictures to see and pictures to touch. In D. Perkins & B. Leondar (Eds.), *Art and cognition*. Baltimore: John Hopkins Univ. Press, 1977.

Kirman, J. H. Tactile communication of speech. *Psychological Bulletin*, 1973, **80**, 54–74.

Kirman, J. H. Tactile apparent movement: The effects of number of stimulators. *Journal of Experimental Psychology*, 1974, **103**, 1175–1180.

Kohler, I. Prolonged optical distortion. *Acta Psychologica*, 1955, **11**, 176–178.

Kohler, I. Experiments with goggles. *Scientific American*, 1962, **206**, 62–72.

Kohler, I. Formation and transformation of the perceptual world. *Psychological Issues*, 1964, 3(4), 1–173.

Kohler, W. *The mentality of apes*. New York: Harcourt Brace, 1925.

Lenzen, V. F. *Procedures of empirical science*. Chicago: Chicago Univ. Press, 1938.

Leonard Conference London: Southern Regional Association for the Blind, 1972.

Liben, L. *Perspective taking skills in young children: Seeing the world through rose-colored glasses*. Unpublished paper, Univ. of Rochester, 1976.

Lynn, G., & Carhart, R. Attack and release in comparison: Amplification and understanding of hyperacusics. *Journal of speech and learning disorders*, 1963, **20**, 124–140.

McCullough, C. The conditioning of color perception. *American Journal of Psychology*, 1965, **78**, 362–378.

Miller, M. H. *Hearing aids*. New York: Bobbs-Merrill, 1972.

O'Neill, J. J., & Oyer, H. J. *Visual communication for the hard of hearing*. Englewood Cliffs, New Jersey: Prentice-Hall, 1961.

Oyer, H. J., & Frankmann, J. P. *The aural rehabilitation process*. New York: Holt, 1975.

Rice, C. E., & Feinstein, S. H. Sonar system in the blind. Size discrimination. *Science*, 1965, **148**, 1107–1108.

Rock, I. *The nature of perceptual adaptation*. New York: Basic Books, 1966.

Sherrick, C. E. Sensory processes. In J. Swets & L. Elliot (Eds.), *Psychology and the handicapped child*. Washington, D.C.: Dept. of Health, Education and Welfare, 1974.

Sherrick, C. E. The art of tactile communication. *American Psychologist*, 1975, **30**, 353–360.

Skowdo, D., Timney, B. N., Gentry, T. A., & Morant, R. B. McCullough effects: Experimental findings and theoretical accounts. *Psychological Bulletin*, 1975, **82**, 497–510.

Smith, O. W. Depth in a photograph viewed from 2 distances. *Perceptual and Motor Skills*, 1958, **8**, 79–81.

Strelow, E. R., & Hodgson, R. M. A spatial sensing system for blind children. *New Outlook for the Blind*, 1976, **70**, 22–24.

Strong, V. Speech aids for the profoundly/severely hearing impaired: Requirements, overview and projections. *Volta Review*, 1975, **80**, 536–556.

Supa, M., Cotzin, M., & Dallenbach, K. M. Facial vision: The perception of obstacles by the blind. *American Journal of Psychology*, 1944, **57**, 133–183.

Taylor, J. G. *The behavioural basis of perception*. New Haven, Connecticut: Yale Univ. Press, 1962.

Taylor, W. (Ed.) *Disorders of auditory function*. London: Academic Press, 1973.

United Kingdom Survey of mobility and reading habits of the blind. London: Ministry of Health, 1967.

Victoreen, J. *Hearing enhancement*. Springfield, Illinois: Thomas, 1960.

Wallenfels, H. G. *Hearing aids for nerve deafness*. Springfield, Illinois: Thomas, 1971.

Walls, G. L. The problem of visual direction. *American Journal of Optometry*, 1951, **28**, 55–83, 115–146, 173–212.

White, B. W., Saunders, F. A., Scadden, L., Bach-y-rita, P., & Collins, C. C. Seeing with the skin. *Perception & Psychophysics*, 1970, **7**, 23–27.

Part III

Aesthetics

Chapter 6

AESTHETIC THEORIES

IRVIN L. CHILD

I. WHAT IS AESTHETIC THEORY?

The central question of aesthetic theory can be posed as follows: "Why do people enjoy or seem to enjoy perceptual experience itself?" Much perceptual experience is obviously sought after because it is instrumental to the attainment of basic goals—whatever those may be in a particular system of thought—but always some perceptual experience appears to be enjoyed for its own sake. Why is this so?

This question is posed most conspicuously by the existence of the arts, and aesthetic theory seems to have been started, and to have been repeatedly invigorated, by an effort to understand why people act and experience in the capacity of appreciators or consumers of the arts. This is a role that seems to be present in all complex literate societies, and in many other societies as well, and is the behavioral basis for such seemingly physical categories as *art* and *works of art*.* Although psychological aesthetics begins with a consideration of the arts, it very naturally broadens its enquiry, seeking through the study of simpler stimuli to arrive at principles that are possibly useful in the psychology of the arts, but in any event significant for general psychology. Theory and research relevant to aesthetics, moreover, is often done in the context of other problems; though aesthetics was one of the earliest specialties in psychology (Fechner, 1876), it has been pursued in recent decades by many who do not think of themselves as aestheticians, along with a few who do.

In view of my definition of the central question, I will concentrate on the experience of and response to art and other stimuli, rather than on their creation, though a general psychology of art must be concerned with both. Theories about each aspect should, of course, help in understanding the other.

I will not be concerned with the *perception* of art, a topic treated in several other chapters in this and earlier volumes. I am addressing myself instead to events beyond the stage of perception, especially the *hedonic value* of the perceiver's experience and acts, or, as often put, the hedonic value that the perceived object or event may be said to have by virtue of its consequences for the perceiver.

In psychological research, a general construct, such as enjoyment or hedonic value, gives rise to various specific measures, and the exploration of these leads to a recognition that the several measures are by no means identical (Berlyne, 1974, pp. 12–17, 321–329; Francès, 1976). For a general survey, a broad construct is useful, but it must not be thought to point to any simple entity. There seems to be little danger of that, for no single term is widely used. I have adopted the term *hedonic value* from Berlyne (1971, 1974). An earlier synthesizer, Beebe-Center (1932), spoke of *hedonic tone*, Guilford (1939) of *affective value*, and Helson (1964) of *affective response*. The behavioristic tradition has led many psychologists to avoid all these terms and use only narrower terms such as *preference* or *choice:* In specific contexts, these, as well as experiential terms such as *enjoyment* and *liking*, are suitable alternatives for *hedonic value*.

Aesthetic theories may be usefully classified into three types: (*a*) extrinsic theories, which view hedonic value as depending on variables extraneous to the stimulus itself; (*b*) intrinsic theories, which view hedonic value as depending on characteristics of the stimulus; and (*c*) interactive theories. Theories in the first two categories, when offered in isolation, might all be said to be oversimplified; yet they may, in common with many other simplifications, be very useful, and their usefulness may be increased if their limitations are clearly recognized.

* I am indebted to Peckham (1965) for his observation that social role is crucial to the definition of art. I speak of *capacity* in addition to *role* to avoid attributing too much to social regulation.

II. EXTRINSIC THEORIES

The first answer to why people seem to enjoy perceiving such things as works of art is that they only *seem* to; the enjoyment is to be ascribed to something else, not to the perception itself. Theories that give this answer are likely to draw upon contiguity or instrumentality in explaining the enjoyment. Some theories, however, are stated in a way that suggests both sources, or at least does not discriminate between them, and I will consider these after looking at theories of contiguity and instrumentality.

A. Contiguity Theories

Contiguity theories are often appealed to in casual discussions of personal preference. The efforts of theaters, concert halls, and museums to provide an environment of luxury, comfort, and prestige suggest that the directors may perhaps be taking such theories seriously. Two separate principles may be involved: hedonic value provided by the present context and hedonic value produced by associative conditioning.

1. CONTEXT EFFECT

The seeming enjoyment of a work of art may result from perceiving the work while enjoying something else. An unmusical couple, if attending a concert together while falling in love, might think the music surprisingly beautiful. This kind of context effect has even been produced (though small in degree) by seemingly slight manipulations in social-psychological experiments. Fisher (1974) found that aesthetic evaluation of the physical setting varied with the degree of harmony in expressed opinion on other matters between the subject and another person working in the same room. To be adequate in detail, a theory would need to distinguish between the conditions for this positive spread of hedonic value and the conditions for contrast effects (cf. Lindauer & Dintruff, 1975), or for independence of attitudes toward the several components of a total experience.

2. ASSOCIATIVE LEARNING

Principles of classical conditioning would suggest that the couple mentioned earlier, when hearing the same music on later occasions, would be especially fond of it. These principles may even be used to explain the immediate context effects, as Fisher (1974, p. 179) does, following Byrne and Clore's (1970) "reinforcement model of evaluative responses." A valuable review of associative principles especially relevant to aesthetics is included in an article by Silverstein (1973). Though art stimuli generally enter his discussion in the role of unconditioned rather than conditioned stimuli, they can easily be imagined in the reverse role.

One experiment that tested implications of the classical conditioning model (among others) for response to pictures would suggest caution in assuming its general applicability. In this experiment Konečni and Sargent-Pollock (1976a) found that pleasingness ratings of paintings increased after pairing the pictures with an enjoyable activity, but also increased after pairing the pictures with an aversive noise. The effect also varied greatly with the type of picture presented. While partly confirming predictions from associative-learning theory, then, their findings cast doubt on its adequacy and suggest that more complicated processes must be considered.

B. Instrumentality Theories

1. INSTRUMENTAL LEARNING

B. F. Skinner (1970) has extended to aesthetics his general argument for the pervasive importance of instrumental learning. Although Skinner gives more attention to the creation than to the appreciation of art, I refer here only to his discussion of the latter. Like any other behavior, he says, looking at art is controlled by its consequences. Skinner believes that people could be shaped into compulsive viewers of art, for example, by creating conditions parallel to those he holds responsible for compulsive gambling (i.e., reinforcement of behavior on a variable-ratio schedule). He does not have much to say about what reinforcements might be provided, but they would presumably be generally extraneous to the work of art itself, such as praise, expressions of agreement, monetary rewards, or scholastic privileges. The scheduling of such rewards as a spontaneous phenomenon seems assumed by Skinner to be largely responsible for a person's response to works of art and to be the appropriate main target for attempts to alter the response.

2. KNOWLEDGE OF INSTRUMENTALITY

When Skinner writes of art, he slips over from a theory of learning (about the automatic effect the consequences of one action are said to have on later response tendencies) to a theory of cognition and decision making (how one now estimates consequences and makes decisions in the light of those estimates). It is this latter theory of instrumentality that seems more obviously relevant to aesthetics. Yet, even in its simplest form, rephrased in explicitly experiential terms, this theory does not seem to have guided research in aesthetics. Despite this, many of us appeal to it in explaining reactions to art—those of other people, at least, and perhaps some of our own. Attention to the arts, knowledgeable discussion of the arts, and appropriate evaluative statements all have clear instrumental value in some groups; they serve in attracting attention to a person not previously noticed by the group, in gaining acceptance, in facilitating lively interaction. Some theorists might claim that hedonic values derive entirely from such instrumentality.

In its more complicated forms, instrumentality theory has guided research in which works of art were used as stimuli, although the context was not aesthetic inquiry. The theory of *reactance* was developed by Brehm (1966) in a series of studies of hedonic value, and in several of those studies musical recordings were the objects whose hedonic value was assessed. In research by Grabitz-Gniech and Grabitz (1973), reproductions of paintings played this part. In these experiments it was shown that the paintings or records gained desirability if a person saw successful choice of them as instrumental to his sense of freedom or control of the situation, much as a person might especially value books he had managed to obtain in the face of difficulties.

C. Other Extrinsic Theories

Extrinsic theories of aesthetic preference include several that might conceivably have been phrased in terms of contiguity and instrumentality, but have more often been stated as isolated principles.

One of these isolated principles is the "mere-exposure" effect proposed by Zajonc (1968) as a general principle of attitude change. As Zajonc pointed out, the notion that repeated exposure leads to a more favorable evaluation of a work of art or other stimulus is now a century old in experimental aesthetics. His broadening of the notion has led to renewed experimentation, some of it with stimuli drawn from the arts, but no consistent confirmation has resulted. This outcome might have been predicted from the history of aesthetic theory, where another principle that is apparently contradictory in its implication has also been long established.

This seemingly contradictory principle is that novelty tends to produce preference. As novelty disappears through repeated exposure, preference tends to decrease, and to this decrease the term *habituation* is often applied. (See Berlyne, 1971, pp. 142–143, 186–196, for the history of novelty in aesthetic theory and research.) Although theoretical efforts might successfully resolve this apparent contradiction through further considerations purely extraneous to the stimuli, it seems likely that the key is rather to be sought in some form of interaction. This interaction may be with stimulus characteristics, as in the notion that relatively simple works of art lose interest, and relatively complex works gain interest, through repeated exploration (Berlyne, 1971, pp. 191–192; Heyduk, 1975); or the interaction may be with the person's response, as in a person's being led by habituation to explore successively different aspects of the stimulus, so that a series of different perceptions that have differing hedonic values are experienced (Helson, 1964, p. 371).

Another isolated principle, often offered both by psychologists and by scholars in the arts as a general explanation of preferences, is what might be called the indoctrination principle. This, in its extreme form, is the notion that a person's aesthetic preferences are based solely on conformity to a cultural tradition or other group-imposed standards. The preferences may be developed in the individual as an explicit part of his socialization, or, having been socialized into general conformity, the individual may be supposed to spontaneously adopt each group evaluation he subsequently encounters. A close approximation to this extreme is found in Farnsworth's discussion (1958, pp. 152–153) of musical taste. Today, discussion of the apparent role of sheer conformity in producing art preferences could take its departure from modern social psychology: From a simple picture of the person's passively taking over attitudes from the group or from prestigious communicators, social psychology has progressed to the recognition of very complex intervening processes, and to the possibility of understanding and possibly predicting various outcomes other than conformity.

D. Conclusions

Do these various extrinsic theories have anything in common? Not necessarily. They represent a number of specific assumptions that might be separately true or false. All these theories, however, seem especially congenial to an emphasis on universal, inborn mechanisms of change or adjustment. Associative and instrumental learning are often considered to be two basic processes of learning. The attractiveness of novelty might be seen to result from an inborn mechanism of habituation. The other theories could well be seen as indirect implications of associative and instrumental learning, or of their parallels in a theory of cognition. All these extrinsic theories, then, view aesthetic enjoyment as a derivative of basic human or mammalian processes of adaptation. Given a physical environment that includes works of art, for example, and a social environment that determines which art will be experienced in which situations, and what consequences will follow from various responses to the art, these theories aim to predict a person's enjoyments and aversions without any reference to characteristics of the art itself. When used crudely for informal predictions or explanations, the principles are obviously useful. Some pertinent research, however, cautions that such predictions may not be as valid as is often supposed, and a glance at the rest of aesthetic theory and research suggests that most knowledge about aesthetics may lie outside the limited range of the effects to which purely extrinsic theories are adequate.

III. INTRINSIC THEORIES

Many a theory relating hedonic value directly to characteristics of the stimulus is little more than an empirical law—a statement that hedonic value is found to vary systematically with a particular stimulus dimension. Even the most empirically phrased of these laws, however, are thus far not broadly established, and to that extent they remain largely theoretical.

A. Laws of Hedonic Value

1. SINGLE DIMENSIONS

Attempts to formulate empirical laws of hedonic value may be illustrated by Guilford's (1939) work on colors. Holding two of the three dimensions of color experience constant, he determined the shape of the curve relating the third dimension to hedonic value. The whole system of curves (portrayed more fully by Guilford & Smith, 1959) was then considered the basis for formulating a more abstract pattern, a set of "natural laws" that might eventually lead to understanding the neural process underlying the dependence of hedonic value upon the dimensions of color.

Another instance (originally stated in an interactive framework with attention to individual differences, but still a useful example here) is Vitz's hypothesis (1964) that people "are motivated to obtain perceived information and they have a preferred and sought for rate of processing or obtaining this information." From this he predicts that hedonic value of tone sequences would vary systematically with a measure of information or uncertainty, maximum preference always lying at an intermediate point, not at extreme values. The prediction was not completely confirmed, and in a subsequent study Vitz (1966) reformulated the stimulus variable as "amount of variation," including spread as well as uncertainty, and obtained better confirmation.

2. SUMMED HEDONIC VALUE

An extremely atomistic theory might hold that the aesthetic value of a work of art can be determined by summing or averaging the hedonic value of all its component aspects and features. For a simpler kind of stimulus (a pair of color patches), Granger (1955) found that hedonic value could be well predicted from the hedonic value of the two components and the distance by which they were separated on the color circle. Encouraged by this result, both he and Eysenck (1957, p. 318) suggested that this approach would probably be of some use in application to actual works of art. It was indeed used in that way (though without a completely independent assessment of components) in an unpublished study summarized by Helson (1964), who concluded that "the complex dimensions of art objects pool to yield overall affective responses [pp. 363–366]."

3. RELATIONS AMONG DIMENSIONS

Several proposed laws of hedonic value pertain to relations among two or more simple dimensions.

a. THE "GOLDEN" PROPORTION. What is the most pleasing division of a line into two parts? What is the most pleasing ratio of length to breadth of a rectangle? A theoretical answer to both these questions is provided by the notion of the "golden" section, or proportion, which holds that the ratio of shorter segment to longer should equal the ratio of longer segment to the sum of the two. Fechner (1876, Vol. 1, pp. 134–202) initiated empirical testing of this simple quantitative model, and it has continued sporadically ever since. Berlyne's review of the evidence (1971, pp. 222–232, 1976) shows that the model has at best only a very limited application.

b. "AESTHETIC MEASURE." Birkhoff (1933) proposed that the hedonic value of a stimulus would be in direct proportion to its orderliness and in inverse proportion to its complexity. He proposed specific ways of measuring orderliness and complexity for polygons, simple ornaments and tile patterns, profiles of vases, metric features of verse, and several aspects of music; the resulting theoretical predictions could be checked against ratings of hedonic value. As Eysenck (1942) pointed out, experimental data suggest that hedonic value should be positively related to complexity as well as to order. Many discussions in the arts would support the same point, and would suggest that Eysenck's substitute formula might be worth testing. A number of studies, however, have been directed at testing Birkhoff's formulation; Eysenck's review of these studies (1941) and his continuing research (e.g., 1968) with Birkhoff's polygons suggest that Birkhoff's formula is not satisfactory, but that revised formulations provide a better fit to some surprising regularities in average polygon preferences.

c. OTHER MATHEMATICAL MODELS FOR HEDONIC VALUE. Another general model for hedonic value of works of art was proposed by Rashevsky (1938), but it has not been widely explored empirically. A new model is proposed in Chapter 7 by Stiny in the present volume; it is based upon more complex and subtle dimensions than earlier quantitative models and therefore seems more likely to be fruitful.

B. Attempts at More Penetrating Theory

Laws of hedonic value have often been stated without any serious effort to delineate the psychological processes that might be involved. When this effort is made, the laws are likely to be reduced to special cases within interactive theories such as those to be described in Section IV. Occasionally, however, an attempt to derive a more penetrating theory from one of these laws has left it as a general law, while setting it in some broader theoretical framework.

This has been done most commonly by viewing such a law as due to an inborn response tendency presumed to have survival value (or to be a by-product of a tendency with survival value) and thus to have been established through biological evolution. This theory seems most plausible for the aesthetics of perfumes and foods, but could also be advanced for some aspects of vision and hearing.

Other connections with general theory can be made. Berlyne (1971, pp. 227–232), for instance, finds six separate ways in which the presumed preference for rectangles of the "golden" proportion might reasonably be connected with general psychological theories.

C. Difficulties with Laws of Hedonic Value

Theories that consist of isolated laws of hedonic value have repeatedly encountered severe difficulties, which will be illustrated in the text that follows.

1. Lack of Replication of Original Findings on Which the Laws Were Based

As has been indicated, reviews of empirical studies relevant to Birkhoff's aesthetic measure and to the golden proportion indicate poor general confirmation of those mathematical models. It seems reasonable to doubt the many other "laws" that have not been extensively tested. Some so-called laws, on the other hand, might well survive an adequate variety of studies testing them under diverse conditions with typical laboratory populations in the United States and Europe; a likely example is the frequently reported preference for cool over warm hues.

2. Variation with Adaptation Level

Laws of hedonic value have generally been stated in a way that predicts hedonic value for any single stimulus; that is, to each possible position along a stimulus dimension is ascribed a particular hedonic value. Helson (1964, pp. 368–373, 1973) has drawn upon adaptation-level theory to put this whole approach in great doubt, and has presented experimental evidence that hedonic value is dependent instead upon the relative position of a stimulus within the series a person is experiencing. A very impressive instance of such dependence has been provided by Steck and Machotka (1975). Various experimenters have used information theory to measure complexity of stimuli and have studied hedonic value as a function of complexity so measured. Steck and Machotka selected tone sequences as stimuli (as had some of the earlier experimenters). Exposing subjects at different times to sets of melodies spanning different ranges of complexity, they found the hedonic value of a stimulus to depend not at all upon its absolute complexity but, rather, solely upon its relative complexity within the set. Some experimenters have used the method of paired comparisons in an effort to reduce the significance of adaptation level, but this device cannot be depended upon (Kennedy, 1961).

This difficulty need not invalidate the quantitative aspect of the laws for which it is relevant; it may only disprove any simple account of the processes by which a particular stimulus comes to have a particular hedonic value. On the other hand, it raises the possibility that findings, especially curves of U or inverted U shapes, are entirely artifactual (Kennedy, 1961).

3. VARIATION WITH GROUP STUDIED

Simple laws of intrinsic hedonic value first arose within an ethnocentric professional tradition in which it was assumed that people of the narrow category readily available for study adequately represented all of competent humanity. When such laws have been tested under widely varying conditions, their validity as generalizations about humanity has sometimes come into doubt. For example, color preferences observed in two Asiatic countries differ in important respects, especially on the dimension of brightness, from those found in the United States (Kastl & Child, 1968; Child & Iwao, 1969), and even some differences between the sexes are found to vary greatly with cultural setting. Yet, some consistencies do emerge. In studies of polygon preferences, consistency seems to predominate. Preferences obtained in England predicted very accurately preferences later obtained in Japan (Eysenck & Iwawaki, 1971) and in Egypt (Soueif & Eysenck, 1971). There clearly seem to be some widespread tendencies toward agreement. Which of these tendencies, if any, will have the genuine universality assumed in the simple laws of hedonic value cannot confidently be judged until more extensive sampling of groups has been done (for a general review of evidence, see Berlyne, 1976); variation with cultural group may vary, moreover, with the particular measure used (Francès, 1976).

4. VARIATION FROM ONE PERSON TO ANOTHER

Laws of intrinsic hedonic value have often been stated as though they applied to a universal human nature from which there would be only random variation. The facts previously mentioned indicate that some group variation is systematic. In addition, systematic individual differences may be found within any group studied. An instance is provided by hue preferences. In a study of American and Japanese college students, individual variation was not random; within a single group, many persons preferred cool colors, but some systematically preferred warm ones (unpublished data of Child & Iwao, 1969). Another instance is provided by the great dispersion of scores on the Barron–Welsh Art Scale (Barron, 1952), indicating that some individuals prefer the complex member of most pairs of designs used, whereas some prefer the simple member.

5. EXPERIMENTAL MODIFICATION

A few experiments on situational influences suggest further limitations of the evidence upon which intrinsic hedonic laws have been based. One experiment on modification of hue preferences by changes in temperature (Kearney, 1966) reported large effects, hue preferences actually being reversed according to whether they were measured in an uncomfortably hot or an uncomfortably cold room. (It seems possible to me, however, that the subjects' expectations may have contributed to the effect.) An experiment by Konečni and Sargent-Pollock (1976) on the complexity of melodies showed that marked changes in complexity preference were induced by aversive stimulation and by difficulty of concomitant task. An experiment by Leahy (1975) with infants under 18 months noted a large decrease (though not reversal) in preference for visual complexity when arousal level is high. These beginnings of experimentation cast serious doubt on the generality of any simple models of hedonic value, and suggest that the data need to be handled by an interactive theory that takes into account crucially relevant aspects of the context, history, and current state of the organism.

IV. INTERACTIVE THEORIES

A. Introduction

Interactive theories are those that view hedonic value as emerging from the interaction between the work of art (or other stimulus) and the characteristics of the person and situation. Many varieties of interactive theory in general psychology could be applied to aesthetic problems. Presented in the following text are some brief illustrations that deserve mention before I turn to the lengthier consideration of theories that have been especially influential, to date, in the study of hedonic value.

1. DEVELOPMENTAL THEORIES

Theories of cognitive development have been applied in understanding age-associated changes in color preference (Child, Hansen, & Hornbeck, 1968) and art preference (Francès, 1968; Machotka, 1966), and have also been applied to problems of art education (Machotka, 1970, pp. 128–129). These same theories have been very extensively applied in research by Gardner (1973) on age-associated changes in artistic understanding, creativity, and performance. Many of his findings and interpretations are at least indirectly pertinent to hedonic value, too.

2. THEORY OF GENETICS

Theory of genetics, and its accompanying techniques, have been little used in aesthetics as yet. But Barron (1970) has shown their potential applicability and reported evidence of substantial heritability for one widely used measure of aesthetic preference, in twin studies both in Italy and in the United States. The finding of a genetic influence implies an interaction between external stimulus and personal characteristics. Generalizing, moreover, from research on heritability of intelligence, I would confidently predict that an interactive theory of development will be needed to understand how genetic influence is exerted.

3. Neurophysiological Theories

In case studies of neurological patients active in the various arts, Gardner (1975, pp. 291–349) has shown the direct relevance of neurophysiological knowledge for any adequate account of their defects in artistic understanding and production (and, by implication, of normal artistic functioning). Relative hemispheric dominance is an instance of the possible application of neurophysiological theory to normal individual differences in aesthetic response. Berlyne (1971) and others have also drawn on neurophysiological knowledge in formulating the arousal theories described in Section IV,B.

4. Social–Psychological Theories

Much theory in social psychology has been concerned with attitudes toward persons and with cognitive influences on those attitudes. Moffett (1975) has pointed out that this body of theory can be tentatively extended to art through the metaphor of art objects as people. The metaphor has some direct justification, and it has the advantage of omitting unrealistic aspects of the older applications to art of the communications paradigm. Instead of the artist's continually reappearing as a communicator, the autonomy of the art object is recognized in this new metaphor. Moffett has illustrated how various aspects of theory from social psychology can then be used to integrate findings in aesthetics research. In social-psychological experiments, these theories often appear as extrinsic theories. In actual application to social attitudes, however, they are likely to be used interactively, with veridical knowledge about the object contributing to what happens. Moffett is obviously proposing this sort of interactive application to art.

B. Theories about Immediate Effects on Arousal

Much theorizing about hedonic value in recent years has centered around the concept of arousal (see, e.g., Berlyne, 1971, pp. 64–95 and throughout). Some theoretical statements simply postulate that the internal event constituting the hedonic effect of a stimulus is a change in arousal. Such statements can be seen as instances of intrinsic theory, but most theoretical statements using the concept of arousal are more interactive, viewing arousal as being modified in a relevant way only if the stimulated person has particular background characteristics or a certain prior degree of arousal, or only if he makes comparisons between the present stimulus and earlier stimuli.

Several relations between arousal and hedonic value have been suggested:

1. Moderate increases of arousal are supposed to produce increases of

hedonic value because, as Berlyne (1971) hypothesizes, the primary reward system in the brain is activated.

2. Increases of arousal beyond a certain point begin to activate the aversion system in the brain, as well, and this creates a negative hedonic value; a rapid enough decrease in arousal will then have positive hedonic value (Berlyne, 1971).

3. Small changes of arousal in either direction from the current adaptation level may have increasingly positive hedonic value; beyond a maximum point, larger changes in either direction produce smaller positive hedonic values, and eventually negative ones. This relationship was suggested by McClelland, Atkinson, Clark, and Lowell (1953, pp. 42–44) in a motivational theory centered on the concept of affective arousal. Helson (1964, pp. 382–388) used it in his aesthetic theory in a manner for which *arousal* might be an appropriate label. Experimental support for it with artlike stimuli has been provided by Terwilliger (1963).

4. Fiske and Maddi (1961, pp. 37–49) proposed a view of positive hedonic value as especially associated with movement toward the level of arousal that is normal for the particular person at the given stage of his daily cycle. A similar position has been included in Kreitler and Kreitler's homeostatic model (1972, pp. 12–22).

If all these hypotheses were adopted simultaneously, positive hedonic value would come very near to being associated with any change in arousal level. Thus far, the hypotheses most used in recent aesthetics have been the first two, which have provided a conceptual background for varied experimentation by Berlyne and others influenced by him (see, e.g., Berlyne, 1974). This work has tended to view arousal reduction as a frequent result of uniformity, simplicity, or order in the work of art (or experimental stimulus), and to view arousal increase as a result of diversity, complexity, or disorder. Explicitness about an internal effect of these collative variables (Berlyne's term for variables that imply comparison) facilitates the recognition of other simultaneous influences on the same internal processes. The concept of arousal thus provides a framework for rethinking intrinsic theories of aesthetics in a way that makes them interactive—that is, in a way that recognizes the dependence of stimulus effects upon situation, history, and the present state of the subject.

The research done in this conceptual setting has largely been the experimental study of collative variables in designs or tone sequences that have been especially prepared as laboratory stimuli (in order to permit greater control over single variables than would be feasible if works of art were the stimuli). This restriction is not necessary, however. Martindale (1975), for instance, has drawn upon these concepts (as well as others) in planning and interpreting psychohistorical research on poetry. Berlyne (1971, pp. 248–

276) used principles of arousal in interpreting personality and culture variables in responses to art. Kreitler and Kreitler (1972) also included them repeatedly as part of the theoretical equipment used in interpreting a variety of experimental results and artistic phenomena, seeming to apply them not only to collative variables of form, but also to the meaningful content of art. Francès (1976) has supplied an experimental instance of testing the effects of collative variables, both with simple stimuli and with photographs, and obtaining very similar results. He shows the equal relevance to both, too, of a theoretical distinction among collative variables according to whether the comparison is within the stimulus object or between it and prior experiences.

C. Theories about Cognition or States of Consciousness

1. INFORMATION PROCESSING

Theories relating hedonic value to the processing of information, in the sense of information theory (i.e., the amount of unpredictability) are closely related to arousal theories. Cognitive theories assume a person's preferences among possible perceptual inputs to be predictable from characteristics of his ongoing processing of information, whereas the arousal theories introduce a motivation-like process as an intermediary. The two have led to very similar kinds of research, and identical research is often cited for equivalent relevance to both kinds of theory, but efforts have begun (e.g., Konečni & Sargent-Pollock, 1977) to distinguish between them experimentally.

A representative information-processing theory of aesthetics is that offered by Munsinger and Kessen (1964, pp. 2–3). According to this theory, people vary in the coding rules and skills with which they process any particular kind of stimulus variability. For a given kind of stimulus, a person will prefer a degree of variability that is near the limit of his processing ability. From this theory, Munsinger and Kessen predict that the dependence of preference upon stimulus variability (e.g., polygon preference as a function of complexity) will follow an inverted U curve, and that the maximum preference will move toward higher levels of complexity as people gain greater skill at processing the relevant kind of information. They point out that their basic assumption of preference for cognitive challenge is consistent with White's (1959) theory of competence, or *effectance*.

A similar theory, developed at about the same time in a somewhat different conceptual setting, has been advanced by Walker (1973). He applies the term *complexity* to the total psychological event at any moment, rather than to stimulus, response, or conscious experience. There is an optimal complexity level for a person at a given time, and preference is for interaction with those stimuli that lead to that level of complexity. Walker seems to define the optimum level more loosely than do Munsinger and Kessen, allowing for its being merely related to information-processing capacity rather than fixed in relation to it. He regards an inverted U as the basic shape of the dependence of preference on stimulus variability, but he also attempts to show how some of the other relationships (outlined, in arousal terms, in Section IV,B) should arise as special cases, and how conflicting theories about effects of repetition (Section II,C) can be resolved within the framework of his theory. This theory has been applied specifically to the arts by Heyduk (1975), using stimuli of conventional music sequences especially composed with experimental alterations. His research confirms Walker's theoretical predictions about the effects of repeated exposure.

Another theory of aesthetic choice based on information processing has been advanced by Konečni and Sargent-Pollock (1976). They propose to regard aesthetic choice as "a decision to allocate more or less processing capacity to the subsequent stimulation [p. 348]." Choices will be a joint outcome of the person's estimate of the processing capacity he will have available and the processing demands of the potential aesthetic objects. Confirmation of predictions made directly from this theory have encourged Konečni and Sargent-Pollock to argue that limits in processing capacity may be an essential intermediary in the effects that arousal has on aesthetic choice.

2. AESTHETIC ORIENTATION

Whereas most aesthetic theories and associated research have started from simple principles tested with simple stimuli, some of my own work (Child, 1965) has started from normal human interaction with visual art. Noting that people who choose to interact a great deal with an art make judgments about the aesthetic value of particular works, I assumed these to be assessments of the adequacy of each work in satisfying the person seeking to interact with it aesthetically. In other words, they are judgments of typical hedonic value of the work for anyone who seeks to obtain pleasure from exploration of it in ways typical of artists and art devotees. This may be expressed in terms of instrumentality, but with recognition of the work of art itself—rather than the surrounding circumstances alone—as one source of the effects to which it is instrumental.

Measurement of the degree to which any person's preferences in art agree with expert judgments of aesthetic value might indicate the degree to which that person shares an aesthetic orientation toward visual art. A study of the differences between people who score high and those who score low on such a measure could then identify the distinguishing characteristics of an aesthetic orientation.

Research prompted by this theoretical approach (briefly summarized in Child, 1973, pp. 60–68) confirms the relevance to art of the general findings of the simpler experimental research prompted by the other interactive theories that have been reviewed here. A liking for cognitive challenge and an interest in cognitive independence tend to appear in people with an aesthetic orientation. Pressing the limits of one's information-processing capacity in response to the total work of art is characteristic of this orientation and distinguishes it from the other possible orientations. The average person's preference, when confronted with the total potential structure and meaning of a work of art, may be to avoid challenge and enjoy the happy reassurance of sentimentality. This research on response to art also involves itself with questions (such as the significance of interest in unrealistic experience) that have not yet been considered by the simpler experimental approach. In finding the correlates of aesthetic appreciation to resemble very strikingly the correlates of aesthetic creativity established, for example, by Barron (1968) and MacKinnon (1965), this research further confirms the active character of aesthetic response.

3. COGNITIVE ORIENTATION

Most of the psychological theories of aesthetics, even those stressing cognition, have developed out of a behavioral approach. Kreitler and Kreitler (1972) have brought to bear on aesthetics, along with a behavioral approach, a cognitive approach that explicitly regards cognition as an end in itself, as well as an influence on behavior. "To our mind," they say, "the major motive underlying the tendency toward voluntary exposure to dissonant views and information in art and elsewhere is the motive to expand, elaborate, and deepen cognitive orientation and to test its range and various implications [p. 331]." The arts are a culturally developed resource that "provide particularly favorable conditions for the evocation and satisfaction of the motive to expand and elaborate cognitive orientation [p. 332]." Rather than using this theory as a heuristic device in the development of specific research, they use it (along with their homeostatic approach) in a major effort to bring together a broad personal understanding of the arts and a synthesis of a wide variety of relevant psychological research.

It is particularly impressive that this theory of the Kreitlers is in very close harmony with a theory developed in a very different context by Peckham (1965). Peckham raises the question: What is the biological function of the arts? He finds a hint in the constant tendency toward change in art styles, and a consideration of art history leads him to conclude that participation in the arts brings the benefits of practice and preparation for change, and of resistance to the stultifying effect of excess stability in the individual and society. The view of the arts' significance in the life of the individual that leads him to this conclusion is almost identical with what the Kreitlers express in speaking of cognitive orientation, except that Peckham places more stress upon *change* of orientation.

These theories are both oriented toward the long-range effects of art that sustain its continual interest to the individual and its support by society, but are compatible with many other theories about immediate effects. They both strongly suggest, however, that even the momentary satisfactions in art grow especially out of novelty or change.

4. FLOW

A theory relating enjoyment to general states of consciousness has been developed by Csikszentmihalyi (1975) through his studies of self-rewarding aspects of several occupational and recreational activities. At times of maximum enjoyment, the chess player or musical composer, for example, is in a state that Csikszentmihalyi terms *flow* and relates to other instances of seeming merger or identity with the environment. His account of the features of activity that give rise to flow shows marked similarity to the account I have given of aesthetic orientation in the activity of seeing or hearing works of art. Perhaps his theory of flow may provide a crucial link between aesthetic appreciation and the enjoyment of skilled participation, not only in artistic creation, but also in a variety of other self-rewarding activities.

D. Theories about Specific Motivational Appeal

Psychoanalysis has provided the most influential theory about the relation of artistic enjoyment to the motives of the individual. Whereas the other intrinsic and interactive theories have been directed mostly at form or structure, psychoanalytic theory has been mostly directed at content. It has regarded art, with respect to both its creators and appreciators, as fantasy that by compromise achieves partial symbolic fulfillment both of unconscious wishes and of the restraining and restitutive forces that conflict with those wishes. One of the best statements of this theory has been provided by Fairbairn (1938a,b). Holland (1968) has applied a diversified modern psychoanalytic approach to the scholarly interpretation of specific works of literary and cinematic art. Holland (1973, 1975) has also used the case-study method, observing the interpretation of specific poems and stories by several readers serving as his research subjects. Holland's work is especially notable for his effort to bring form as well as content into the scope of a motivational theory of artistic enjoyment.

The psychoanalytic theory of aesthetics has not guided psychological research often or steadily enough to have been reshaped by the outcome of this research. In the experiments of Wallach and Greenberg (1960) and Wallach (1960), however, psychoanalytic theory was used to predict personality correlates of symbolic response to music and of liking for music. How well would the psychoanalytic theory hold up, and what aspects would have to be changed, if this or a similar line of research were pursued further? In the absence of such research, advances can nonetheless be made toward clarification of the theory and its modification through integration with the rest of psychology. Major steps in that direction have been made by Machotka (in press) in the general theoretical sections of his work on the nude in art and in a theoretical article (1976).

V. CONCLUSIONS

Aesthetic theories are diverse. Many are specific applications of theories developed in other branches of psychology. Some have arisen in psychological aesthetics and may have an important influence when applied to other branches of psychology. The attempt at psychological study of the arts may pose a special challenge and have an important broadening effect on general psychology—a point that has been expressed with great cogency by Lindauer (1973, 1974, pp. 64–83). Psychological aesthetics has progressed from exclusive preoccupation with the simplified theories of extrinsic or intrinsic sources of the enjoyment of perceptual experience, toward more marked success in formulating and applying the more adequate interactive theories. Perhaps a major development in the future will be the extension of aesthetic theory to deal comprehensively with influences of both content and form.

References

Barron, F. Personality style and perceptual choice. *Journal of Personality,* 1952, **20,** 385–401.
Barron, F. *Creativity and personal freedom.* Princeton, New Jersey: Van Nostrand, 1968.
Barron, F. Heritability of factors in creative thinking and esthetic judgment. *Acta Geneticae Medicae et Gemellologiae,* 1970, **19,** 294–298.
Beebe-Center, J. G., *The psychology of pleasantness and unpleasantness.* Princeton, New Jersey: Van Nostrand, 1932.
Berlyne, D. E. *Aesthetics and psychobiology.* New York: Appleton, 1971.
Berlyne, D. E. (Ed.) *Studies in the new experimental aesthetics: Steps toward an objective psychology of aesthetic appreciation.* Washington: Hemisphere, 1974.
Berlyne, D. E. Psychological aesthetics. In H. C. Triandis (Ed.), *Handbook of cross-cultural psychology.* Boston: Allyn & Bacon, 1976.
Birkhoff, G. D. *Aesthetic measure.* Cambridge, Massachusetts: Harvard Univ. Press, 1933.
Brehm, J. W. *A theory of psychological reactance.* New York: Academic Press, 1966.
Byrne, D., & Clore, G. L. A reinforcement model of evaluative responses. *Personality,* 1970, **1,** 103–128.
Child, I. L. Personality correlates of esthetic judgment in college students. *Journal of Personality,* 1965, **33,** 476–511.
Child, I. L. *Humanistic psychology and the research tradition.* New York: Wiley, 1973.
Child, I. L., Hansen, J. A., & Hornbeck, F. W. Age and sex differences in children's color preferences. *Child Development,* 1968, **39,** 237–247.
Child, I. L., & Iwao, S. A comparison of color preferences in college students of Japan and the United States. *Proceedings, 77th Annual Convention, American Psychological Association,* 1969, 469–470.

Csikszentmihalyi, M. *Beyond boredom and anxiety*. San Francisco: Jossey-Bass, 1975.

Eysenck, H. J. The empirical determination of an aesthetic formula. *Psychological Review*, 1941, **48**, 83–92.

Eysenck, H. J. The experimental study of the "good Gestalt"—a new approach. *Psychological Review*, 1942, **49**, 344–364.

Eysenck, H. J. *Sense and nonsense in psychology*. Baltimore: Penguin, 1957.

Eysenck, H. J., An experimental study of aesthetic preference for polygonal figures. *Journal of General Psychology*, 1968, **79**, 3–17.

Eysenck, H. J., & Iwawaki, S. Cultural relativity in aesthetic judgments: An empirical study. *Perceptual and Motor Skills*, 1971, **32**, 817–818.

Fairbairn, W. R. D. Prolegomena to a psychology of art. *British Journal of Psychology*, 1938, **28**, 288–303. (a)

Fairbairn, W. R. D. The ultimate basis of aesthetic experience. *British Journal of Psychology*, 1938, **29**, 167–181. (b)

Farnsworth, P. R. *The social psychology of music*. New York: Dryden, 1958.

Fechner, G. T. *Vorschule der Aesthetik* (Vol. 1). Leipzig: von Bretkopf & Härtel, 1876. pp. 184–202.

Fisher, J. D. Situation-specific variables as determinants of perceived environmental aesthetic quality and perceived crowdedness. *Journal of Research in Personality*, 1974, **8**, 177–188.

Fiske, D. W., & Maddi, S. R. *Functions of varied experience*. Homewood, Illinois: Dorsey, 1961.

Francès, R. *Psychologie de l'esthétique*. Paris: Presses Universitaires de France, 1968.

Francès, R. Comparative effects of six collative variables on interest and preference in adults of different educational levels. *Journal of Personality and Social Psychology*, 1976, **33**, 62–79.

Gardner, H. *The arts and human development*. New York: Wiley, 1973.

Gardner, H. *The shattered mind: The person after brain damage*. New York: Knopf, 1975.

Grabitz-Gniech, G., & Grabitz, H.-J. Der Einfluss von Freiheitseinengung und Freiheitswiederherstellung auf den Reaktanz-Effekt. *Zeitschrift für Sozialpsychologie*, 1973, **4**, 361–365.

Granger, G. W., The prediction of preference for color combinations. *Journal of General Psychology*, 1955, **52**, 213–222.

Guilford, J. P. A study in psychodynamics. *Psychometrika*, 1939, **4**, 1–23.

Guilford, J. P., & Smith, P. C. A system of color-preferences. *American Journal of Psychology*, 1959, **52**, 487–502.

Helson, H. *Adaptation-level theory*. New York: Harper & Row, 1964.

Helson, H. A common model for affectivity and perception: An adaptation-level approach. In D. E. Berlyne & K. B. Madsen (Eds.), *Pleasure, reward, preference*. New York: Academic Press, 1973. Pp. 189–216.

Heyduk, R. G. Rated preference for musical compositions as it relates to complexity and exposure frequency. *Perception & Psychophysics*, 1975, **17**, 84–90.

Holland, N. N. *The dynamics of literary response*. New York: Oxford Univ. Press, 1968.

Holland, N. N. *Poems in persons*. New York: Norton, 1973.

Holland, N. N. *Five readers reading*. New Haven, Connecticut: Yale Univ. Press, 1975.

Kastl, A. J., & Child, I. L. Comparison of color preferences in Vietnam and the United States. *Proceedings, 76th Annual Convention, American Psychological Association*, 1968, 437–438.

Kearney, G. E. Hue preferences as a function of ambient temperatures. *Australian Journal of Psychology*, 1966, **18**, 271–275.

Kennedy, J. E. The paired-comparison method and central tendency effect in esthetic judgments. *Journal of Applied Psychology*, 1961, **45**, 128–129.

Konečni, V. J., & Sargent-Pollock, D. Choice between melodies differing in complexity under divided-attention conditions. *Journal of Experimental Psychology: Human Perception and Performance*, 1976, **2**, 347–356.

Konečni, V. J., & Sargent-Pollock, D. Arousal, positive and negative affect, and preference for Renaissance and 20th-century paintings. *Motivation and Emotion*, 1977, **1**, 75–93.

Kreitler, H., & Kreitler, S. *Psychology of the arts*. Durham, North Carolina: Duke Univ. Press, 1972.

Leahy, R. L. Arousal and preferences for complexity in infants. *Perceptual and Motor Skills*, 1975, **40**, 179–182.

Lindauer, M. S. Toward a liberalization of experimental aesthetics. *Journal of Aesthetics and Art Criticism*, 1973, **31**, 459–465.

Lindauer, M. S. *The psychological study of literature*. Chicago: Nelson-Hall, 1974.

Lindauer, M. S., & Dintruff, D. D. Contrast effects in the response to art. *Perceptual and Motor Skills*, 1975, **40**, 155–164.

Machotka, P. Aesthetic criteria in childhood: Justifications of preference. *Child Development*, 1966, **37**, 877–885.

Machotka, P. Visual aesthetics and learning. *Journal of Aesthetic Education*, 1970, **4**, 117–130.

Machotka, P. The functions of taste: Toward a workable theory. *Scientific Aesthetics*, 1976, **1**, 107–119.

Machotka, P. *The nude: A psychology of aesthetic attachment*. New York: Irvington (in press).

MacKinnon, D. W. Personality and the realization of creative potential. *American Psychologist*, 1965, **20**, 273–281.

Martindale, C. *Romantic progression: The psychology of literary history*. Washington: Hemisphere, 1975.

McClelland, D. C., Atkinson, J. W., Clark, R. A., & Lowell, E. L. *The achievement motive*. New York: Appleton, 1953.

Moffett, L. A. Art objects as people: A new paradigm for the psychology of art. *Journal for the Theory of Social Behavior*, 1975, **5**, 215–223.

Munsinger, H., & Kessen, W. Uncertainty, structure, and preference. *Psychological Monographs*, 1964, **78** (9, Whole No. 586).

Peckham, M. *Man's rage for chaos*. Philadelphia: Chilton, 1965.

Rashevsky, N. Contribution to the mathematical biophysics of visual perception with special reference to the theory of aesthetic values of geometrical patterns. *Psychometrika*, 1938, **3**, 253–271.

Silverstein, A. Acquired pleasantness and conditioned incentives in verbal learning. In D. E. Berlyne & K. B. Madsen (Eds.), *Pleasure, reward, preference*. New York: Academic Press, 1973. Pp. 189–216.

Skinner, B. F. Creating the creative artist. In A. J. Toynbee, L. I. Kahn, A. Michelson, B. F. Skinner, J. Seawright, J. W. Burnham, & H. Marcuse, *On the future of art*. New York: Viking, 1970. Pp. 61–75.

Soueif, M. I., & Eysenck, H. J. Cultural differences in aesthetic preferences. *International Journal of Psychology*, 1971, **6**, 293–298.

Steck, L., & Machotka, P. Preference for musical complexity: Effects of context. *Journal of Experimental Psychology: Human Perception and Performance*, 1975, **1**, 170–174.

Terwilliger, R. F. Pattern complexity and affective arousal. *Perceptual and Motor Skills*, 1963, **17**, 387–395.

Vitz, P. C. Preferences for rates of information presented by sequences of tones. *Journal of Experimental Psychology*, 1964, **68**, 176–183.

Vitz, P. C. Affect as a function of stimulus variation. *Journal of Experimental Psychology*, 1966, **71**, 74–79.

Walker, E. L. Psychological complexity and preference: A hedgehog theory of behavior. In D. E. Berlyne & K. B. Madsen (Eds.), *Pleasure, reward, preference*. New York: Academic Press, 1973. Pp. 65–97.

Wallach, M. A. Two correlates of symbolic sexual arousal: Level of anxiety and liking for esthetic material. *Journal of Abnormal and Social Psychology*, 1960, **61**, 396–401.

Wallach, M. A., & Greenberg, C. Personality functions of symbolic sexual arousal to music. *Psychological Monographs*, 1960, **74** (7, Whole No. 494).

White, R. W. Motivation reconsidered: The concept of competence. *Psychological Review*, 1959, **66**, 297–333.

Zajonc, R. B. Attitudinal effects of mere exposure. *Journal of Personality and Social Psychology Monograph Supplement*, 1968, **9**(2), 1–27.

Chapter 7

GENERATING AND MEASURING AESTHETIC FORMS

GEORGE STINY

Visual forms are often perceived to have, in addition to compositional and symbolic aspects, aesthetic value. Nonrepresentational primitive art (Boas, 1955), ornament (Jones, 1972; Sullivan, 1967), algebraic and transcendental curves (Lockwood, 1961), symmetrical patterns and configurations (Loeb, 1971; Shubnikov & Koptsik, 1974; Weyl, 1952), and recursively defined geometrical objects (Schrandt & Ulam, 1967; Ulam, 1962), and pictures (Stiny & Gips, 1972) are a few of these forms. An aesthetic measure for forms is suggested in this chapter. This measure is based on a relation between the way forms are generated and the way forms are described.

I. GENERATING FORMS

A. Forms Generated by a Moving Point

Any form may be thought of as a path traced by a moving point. This simple idea is common in both mathematics (for example, an ellipse is the locus of a point in a plane the sum of whose distances from two fixed points is constant) and in the visual arts (see Klee, 1953).

A form can be generated by moving a point in a certain, deterministic way.

HANDBOOK OF PERCEPTION, VOL. X

For example, a rectilinear spiral with n edges and right-angle corners is generated by the simple procedure

1. Let $i = 1$.
2. Move i units and turn left 90°.
3. If $i = n$, halt; otherwise, increase i by 1 and return to Step 2.

The spiral generated when $n = 6$ is shown in Fig. 1a.

An interesting class of forms called *spirolaterals* (Odds, 1973) is defined by the procedure

1. Let $i = 1$.
2. Move i units and turn counterclockwise θ degrees.
3. If $i = n$, return to Step 1; otherwise, increase i by 1 and return to Step 2.

In order to generate a given spirolateral, it is necessary to specify the integer n and the angle of turn θ. Of course, in order for this procedure to terminate, it is necessary to specify how many times the sequence of instructions is to be applied.

The five different spirolaterals produced for $1 \leq n \leq 5$ with counterclockwise turns of 60° are given in Figs. 1b–f. Notice that some spirolaterals are closed, whereas others can be extended indefinitely. Other spirolaterals can be generated by varying the integer n and the angle of turn θ.

Of course, the procedures just given are not the only ones that can guide the path of a point. Other procedures defining interesting classes of forms have been examined (Beeler, 1973; Gardner, 1973; Papert & Solomon, 1971). This work develops the theme that forms can be looked at procedurally as well as descriptively. For example, the form shown in Fig. 1a is not only a "rectilinear, counterclockwise spiral with right-angle corners and six edges

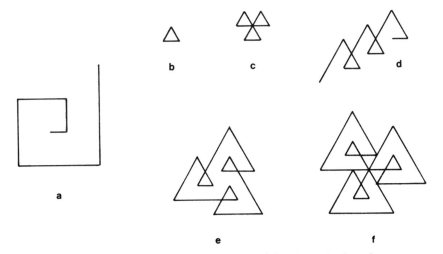

b   c   d

a

e   f

FIG. 1. Forms generated by procedures guiding the path of a point.

of lengths 1, 2, 3, 4, 5, and 6 units,'' but is also the result of applying a simple procedure. Alternative methods for generating forms are discussed in the text that follows.

B. Forms Generated by Rules of Growth

A form may be considered a collection of elements resulting from some fixed subdivision of the plane into identical figures. For example, the plane may be subdivided into equilateral triangles or squares; a form would consist of a finite number of specific elements (e.g., equilateral triangles or squares) in such a subdivision.

A form can be generated in a given subdivision of the plane by recursive application of rules of growth to a given initial form. Consider the subdivision of the plane into squares shown in Fig. 2a. Forms can be generated in this subdivision in the following way:

> We start, in the first generation, with a finite number of squares and define now a rule of growth as follows: Given a number of squares in the nth generation, the squares of the $(n + 1)$th generation will be all those squares which are adjacent to the existing ones but with the following proviso: the squares which are adjacent to more than one square of the nth generation will *not* be taken [Ulam, 1962].

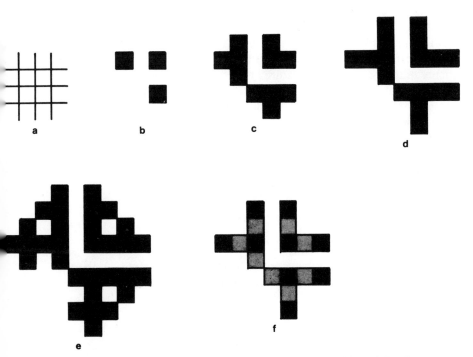

FIG. 2. Forms generated by rules of growth defined in a subdivision of the plane.

If the first generation is the form shown in Fig. 2b, then the forms shown in Figs. 2c–e result in the second, third, and fourth generations by the application of the rule to the first, second, and third generations. Additional applications of the rule would produce more forms. Different forms can be generated in this subdivision of the plane by beginning with a different form in the first generation ȯr by using different rules of growth. Clearly, different subdivisions of the plane would give rise to different forms.

More complicated rules of growth can be given that result in the generation of forms consisting of colored elements. The color of an element in the $(n + 1)$th generation is determined by the colors of the elements in previous generations that are adjacent to it. For example, the rule of growth just given can be modified by the additional proviso:

> *Squares added in the $(n + 1)$th generation are gray if they are adjacent to a black square of the nth generation and are black otherwise.*

If the first generation is the form shown in Fig. 2b, then the form shown in Fig. 2f results in the third generation by the recursive application of the new rule of growth.

Three-dimensional forms can be generated by rules of growth defined by subdividing three-dimensional space into identical three-dimensional fiqures, for example, cubes. Interesting examples of such forms are given in Schrandt and Ulam (1967).

An enormous variety of seemingly elaborate forms can be generated using simple rules of growth similar to those given above. Rules of growth for generating organic-like structures (Schrandt & Ulam, 1967; Ulam, 1962) as well as polygons (Dacey, 1970, 1971) and crystallographic patterns (Sirmoney, Sirmoney, & Krithivasan, 1973) have been given. Methods for generating forms by rules of growth defined by subdividing the plane or three-dimensional space are investigated generally in terms of array grammars and cellular automata. Important formal results in these areas have been discussed in the work of Codd (1968) and Milgram and Rosenfeld (1972).

C. Forms Generated by Shape Grammars

1. Shapes and Shape Relations

Forms may also be considered to be made up of shapes. A shape is taken to be a finite arrangement of lines in the plane. (All shapes are assumed to be associated with a common two-dimensional cartesian-coordinate system.) A shape can be drawn in a finite area in a finite amount of time (for example, on a piece of paper with a finite number of pencil strokes). A shape can contain occurrences of straight or curved lines, connected or disconnected lines, or open or closed lines. The forms shown in Figs. 1 and 2 are shapes.

Shapes may be considered in terms of their possible relations to other shapes. (Treating shapes in this way is common in the visual arts—for example, see Klee, 1953, pp. 16–17; Sullivan, 1967.) For example, the straight line drawn in Fig. 3a is related to the "N" drawn in Fig. 3b as shown in Fig. 3c. That is, the end points of the straight line are the two most distant vertices of the "N." Any two shapes can be seen to be related by simply looking at them together. Three possible relations between two polygons are given pictorially in Figs. 3d–f. Relations between shapes are given very naturally and precisely when given pictorially.

Relations between shapes provide the basis for the definition of rules for generating shapes. In the case where two shapes are related (as in Fig. 3c) and one (the straight line of Fig. 3a) is geometrically similar to some part of the other (any edge of the "N" of Fig. 3b), rules can be defined that apply recursively. Consider the following rule based on the relation between a straight line and an "N", shown in Fig. 3c:

If a straight line occurs in a shape in any location, orientation, scale, or reflection, then an "N" may be superimposed on it so that the straight line and the "N" are related as shown in Fig. 3c.

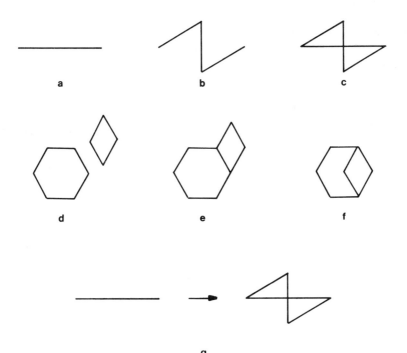

FIG. 3. Some relations between shapes and a rule defined in terms of one of these relations.

This rule is represented pictorially in Fig. 3g. The rule is understood to mean that if the shape on the left side of the arrow occurs in a shape in any location, orientation, scale, or reflection, then the shape on the left side of the arrow can be replaced by the shape on the right side of the arrow in the same location, orientation, scale, or reflection. Possible applications of the rule are made clear by the following example.

Beginning with the straight line of Fig. 4a, Figs. 4b–t show several applications of the rule. The rule can apply to the straight line in two ways: either as drawn in Fig. 3g or as a reflection of Fig. 3g. In both cases, the relation of the straight line to the "N" is the relation given in Fig. 3c. Shapes resulting from the two possible applications of the rule are shown in Figs. 4b 4c. Now, the rule can apply to the "N" in the shapes given in Figs. 4b 4c at three different places (i.e., once for each occurrence of a straight line in the "N," and in two different ways at each place where it applies as already indicated). Some shapes resulting from applications of the rule to one edge, two edges, and three edges of the "N" in the shape given in Fig. 4b are shown in Figs. 4d–g, 4h–n, and 4o–t, respectively. A rule of the kind considered here will apply to the shape resulting from a previous application of the rule to another shape because the shape in the left side of the rule occurs in some other location, orientation, scale, or reflection in the shape in the right side of the rule. When a rule applies in this way, it is said to apply *recursively*. Clearly, the rule given above can be applied to any of the shapes given in Figs. 4d–t to generate new shapes.

This method of generating shapes is made precise by the definition of shape grammars.

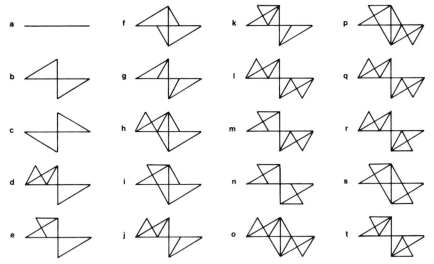

FIG. 4. Shapes generated by a rule defined in terms of a relation between shapes.

2. SHAPE GRAMMARS

In the discussion of shape grammars, the following simple definitions are used.

The *Euclidean transformations* are translation, rotation, scale, and mirror image, or finite compositions of these. A Euclidean transformation G of a shape s is a shape denoted by $G(s)$. The shapes s and $G(s)$ are geometrically similar; that is, they may differ only in location, orientation, scale, or reflection.

A shape produced by combining shapes or Euclidean transformations of shapes in a set of shapes S is said to be *made up* of shapes in S. For example, all rectilinear shapes are made up of the shape consisting of a single straight line.

One shape is a *subshape* of a second shape if and only if every part of the first shape is also a part of the second shape; that is, if the first shape is congruent and coincident with some part of the second shape.

Shape grammars are similar to phrase-structure grammars (Hopcroft & Ullman, 1969), but, whereas a phrase-structure grammar is defined over an alphabet of symbols and generates a language of strings of symbols, a shape grammar is defined over a set of shapes and generates a language of shapes.

A *shape grammar* (Stiny & Gips, 1972) has four parts:

1. V_T is a finite set of shapes.
2. V_M is a finite set of shapes.
3. R is a finite set of shape rules of the form $u \rightarrow v$, where u and v are shapes made up of shapes in V_T or shapes in V_M. The shape u must have a subshape made up of shapes in V_M.
4. I is a shape made up of shapes in V_T or shapes in V_M. The shape I must have a subshape made up of shapes in V_M.

A shape grammar (SG) is given by the 4-tuple: SG = $\langle V_T, V_M, R, I \rangle$. Shapes made up of shapes in V_T are called *terminals*. Shapes made up of shapes in V_M are called *markers*. No subshape of a terminal is a subshape of a marker. This condition ensures that terminals and markers in shapes can be distinguished uniquely. For a shape rule $u \rightarrow v$ in the set R, u is called the *left side* of the shape rule; v is called the *right side* of the shape rule. The correspondence between the left side and the right side of a shape rule is determined by the coincidence of the origins and axes of the coordinate systems implicitly associated with the sides of the shape rule. The shape I is called the *initial shape*.

A shape is generated by a shape grammar SG = $\langle V_T, V_M, R, I \rangle$ by beginning with the initial shape I and recursively applying shape rules in the set R until no shape rule can be applied. A shape rule $u \rightarrow v$ applies to a shape s if and only if there is a Euclidean transformation G such that $G(u)$ is a subshape of s. The result of applying the shape rule $u \to v$ to the shape s under the Euclidean transformation G is the shape produced by replacing the occurrence of $G(u)$ in s with $G(v)$. The shape-generation process terminates when no shape rule in the set R can be applied. The *language* defined by a shape grammar is the set of shapes generated by the shape grammar that are made up of terminals or parts of terminals only.

Figure 5a shows a shape grammar that incorporates the rule given in Fig. 3g. The set V_T contains a straight line. All shapes in the language defined by the shape grammar will be made up of straight lines. The set V_M contains a circle. Shapes made up of shapes in V_T (terminals) are distinguishable from shapes made up of shapes in V_M (markers). The set R contains two shape rules. The first shape rule was formed by adding markers to the rule given in Fig. 3g. Markers are used to restrict the possible applications of a shape rule and to guide the shape-generation process. The second shape rule is required to terminate the generation of a shape. The initial shape is made up of a terminal and a marker.

The generation of a shape using the shape grammar given in Fig. 5a is shown in Fig. 5b. Because the two shape rules of the shape grammar have identical left sides, both shape rules are applicable to a given shape under identical circumstances (i.e., whenever there is a Euclidean transformation

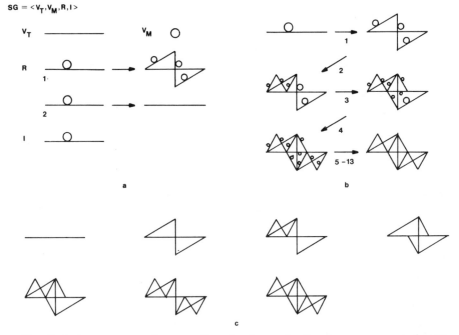

FIG. 5. A shape grammar, the generation of a shape using the shape grammar, and some shapes in the language defined by the shape grammar.

of the left side of either shape rule that is a subshape of the given shape). The shape rules apply to a given shape if that shape contains a straight line with a tangential circle. Because of the asymmetry of the left sides of the shape rules, they can apply in only one way. Application of the first shape rule to a straight line having a tangential circle occurring in a shape results in the superimposition of an ''N'' with tangential circles on each of its edges on the straight line and the removal of the circle tangent to the straight line. The first shape rule provides for the continuation of the shape-generation process by adding markers. The left side of the first shape rule is geometrically similar to each straight line with a tangential circle in the right side of the shape rule. Hence, under the conditions for shape-rule application, this shape rule can be applied recursively. Application of the second shape rule to a straight line with a tangential circle occurring in a shape results in the removal of the circle. The second shape rule provides for the termination of the shape-generation process by erasing markers. A shape in the language defined by a shape grammar contains no occurrence of a marker. In the shape generation shown in Fig. 5b, the shape-generation process begins with the initial shape. The first shape rule is applied to the initial shape in Step 1. In Step 2, the first shape rule is applied to the left edge of the ''N'' added in Step 1; in Step 3, the middle edge; and in Step 4, the right edge. The second shape rule is applied in Steps 5–13 to erase tangential circles. The shape-generation process terminates with the shape produced in Step 13, as no shape rules can apply to this shape. The shape produced in Step 13 is made up of terminals only and, hence, is a shape in the language defined by the shape grammar.

Several of the shapes in the language defined by the shape grammar given in Fig. 5a are shown in Fig. 5c. Because of the location of the markers in the initial shape and the first shape rule of the shape grammar, many of the shapes shown in Fig. 4 are not in the language. Notice that the terminals in each step of the shape generation given in Fig. 5b are shapes in the language. That is, the second shape rule of the shape grammar could have been applied iteratively at any time during the shape-generation process to produce a shape in the language.

Other shape grammars incorporating the rule given in Fig. 3g can be defined. There are 64 of these shape grammars, all of which are identical to the shape grammar given in Fig. 5a except for the location of the circles in the right side of the first shape rule. Each of these shape grammars would generate only certain of the shapes shown in Fig. 4 because of the asymmetry of each straight line and tangential circle in their shape rules. Of course, a shape grammar can be defined that generates all of the shapes given in Fig. 4 by symmetrically arranging each straight line and corresponding circle in its shape rules.

Shape grammars can be defined to generate curved as well as rectilinear shapes, and three-dimensional as well as two-dimensional shapes. Classes of shape grammars defined in terms of shape relations are considered by Stiny (1975, 1976). Parametric generalizations of shape grammars have been used to generate traditional Chinese lattice designs (Stiny, 1977) and the plans for Palladian villas (Stiny & Mitchell, 1978). Other uses of shape grammars are discussed by Gips (1975). The mathematical theory of shape grammars is developed by Stiny (1975).

3. GENERATIVE SPECIFICATIONS

A generative specification provides for the pictorial representation or display of a shape generated by a shape grammar. For example, the pictures, Bridgework I–VI, shown in Fig. 6 are specified by generative specifications. A *generative specification* (Stiny & Gips, 1972) consists of four parts: (*a*) a shape grammar; (*b*) a selection rule; (*c*) coloring rules; and (*d*) a limiting shape. The selection rule determines the exact shape in the language defined by the shape grammar that is to be displayed. The coloring rules determine how the areas in that shape are to be colored. The limiting shape determines the location, orientation, scale, and reflection of the shape in a display of given size and shape. The generative specification for Bridgework I is given in Fig. 7.

The shape grammar used for Bridgework I was obtained from the shape grammar shown in Fig. 5a by replacing each occurrence of a straight line in the shape rules of that shape grammar with an elongated hexagon and positioning circles accordingly. Informally, the shape grammar of Fig. 7 generates shapes by superimposing an "N" made up of elongated hexagons on a larger elongated hexagon in the same way that the shape grammar of Fig. 5a generates shapes by superimposing an "N" made up of straight lines on a longer straight line. The initial shape of the new shape grammar is made up of an elongated hexagon and a circle tangent to one of its sides.

The selection rule used for Bridgework I is given by the integer 2, which indicates that the shape to be displayed is one that, in the language defined by the shape grammar, has two complete levels or superimpositions of "Ns." The level of a terminal in a shape generated by the shape grammar is analogous to the depth of a node in a tree. Level assignments are made during the shape-generation process. The terminal in the initial shape is assigned Level 0. The terminals superimposed on a terminal assigned highest level n are assigned level $(n + 1)$. A level is complete when no terminal assigned level n can be added. Hence, Level 0 consists of the elongated hexagon in the initial shape, Level 1 consists of the "N" superimposed on that elongated hexagon, and Level 2 consists of the three additional "Ns" superimposed on that "N."

The coloring rules used for Bridgework I specify the color of the areas in the shape determined by the selection rule. Areas in the shape are indicated by treating it as a Venn diagram. The terminals of each level in the shape define the boundary of a set. Levels 0, 1, and 2 define sets $L0, L1$, and $L2$. A

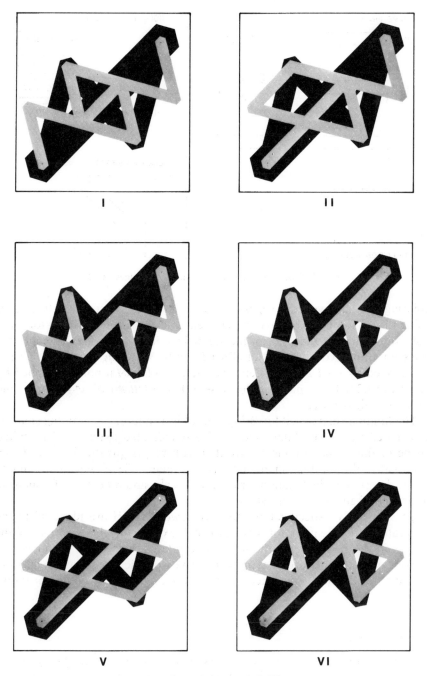

FIG. 6. Bridgework I–VI.

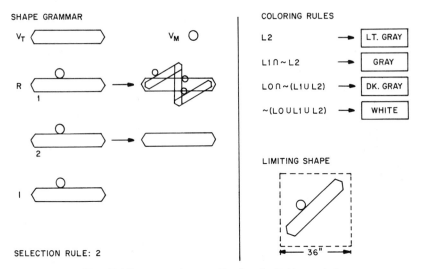

FIG. 7. The generative specification for Bridgework I.

coloring rule has two sides separated by an arrow. The left side defines a set using the sets defined by level assignment and the usual set operators; the right side indicates the color of the set defined in the left side. The coloring rules for Bridgework I allow all of set $L2$ to be seen, the part of set $L1$ not overlapped by set $L2$ to be seen, and the part of set $L0$ not overlapped by sets $L1$ or $L2$ to be seen. The color of set $L0$ is dark gray; of set $L1$, gray; and of set $L2$, light gray.

The limiting shape used for Bridgework I is a square. The limiting shape is designated by broken lines, and its size is indicated explicitly. The initial shape of the shape grammar is located with respect to the limiting shape. Informally, the limiting shape acts like a camera viewfinder. The limiting shape determines the location, orientation, scale, and reflection of a shape in a display of given size and shape.

The generative specifications for Bridgework II–VI are identical to the generative specification for Bridgework I except for the location of the circles in the right side of the first shape rule of their shape grammars.

Well over 100 pictures having generative specifications have been produced by traditional artistic techniques (Stiny, 1975) or by computer (Gips, 1975).

D. Describing Forms

The description of a form specifies its features or properties one by one. In general, a form is described in terms of some canonical and minimal representation of the lines, elements, or shapes in it. For example, the description of a rectilinear form might specify all the lines in the form that are not parts of longer lines by giving their end points. The description of a form made up of a finite number of elements in a subdivision of the plane might enumerate those elements by their coordinates. Given the description of a form, the form can be reproduced in all of its relevant aspects.

In Section II, a method for describing pictures such as Bridgework I–VI, shown in Fig. 6, is required. The following method is used. A picture is described by shape, color, and occurrence tables with the general format indicated in Fig. 8. Each entry in the occurrence table corresponds uniquely to a distinct colored area occurring in the picture. Each entry has seven parts: i_s is the index of a shape entry in the shape table and specifies the shape of the area; i_c is the index of a color entry in the color table and specifies the color of the area; x, y, θ, c, and m are Euclidean transformations that map the shape indexed by i_s from the coordinate system associated with the shape table to the coordinate system associated with the picture, where x and y determine translation, θ determines rotation, c determines scale, and m determines reflection. Entries in the shape table correspond to

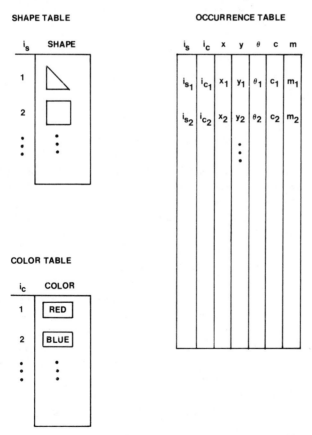

FIG. 8. General format for shape, color, and occurrence tables.

the different shapes of the areas occurring in the picture. Two shapes are different if and only if they are not geometrically similar. Entries in the color table correspond to the different colors of the areas occurring in the picture. Intuitively, the tables of shape, color, and occurrence for a picture list the distinct areas in it by shape, color, and occurrence. Methods similar to this one are commonly suggested in aesthetics (Beardsley, 1958; Goodman, 1968, p. 42) for describing pictures.

II. MEASURING AESTHETIC VALUE

A. Background

In traditional aesthetics, the standard canon for aesthetic value is "unity in variety." As applied to pictures,

> "Variety" . . . would thus primarily imply diversity of colour, differences in appearance and attitude of shapes, variations in direction and qualities of lines. On this interpretation of "variety", "unity" would suggest that those factors are in no way at cross-purposes within the field: they work together towards a single over-all impression; the formal elements balance one another, there is order among them, harmony, coherence [Emond, 1964, p. 54].

The relation between unity and variety is given by a general rule formulated by Hutcheson:

> Where the Uniformity of Bodies is equal, the Beauty is as the Variety; and where the Variety is equal, the Beauty is as the Uniformity [Quoted from Emond, 1964, p. 55].

The canon of "unity in variety" is intuitively appealing, but lacks the precision needed for rigorous application or testing. In particular, measuring unity is often problematical.

A more precise measure of aesthetic value is given by Birkhoff's formula $M = O/C$, where M is the aesthetic measure, O is the order, and C is the complexity of a form (Birkhoff, 1933). Birkhoff applies this formula to polygonal forms by giving explicit criteria to determine the order and complexity of any polygon. The order O of a polygon is given by the expression $O = V + E + R + HV - F$, where V is a measure of vertical symmetry, E is a measure of optical equilibrium, R is a measure of rotational symmetry, HV is a measure of the relation of the polygon to a horizontal–vertical network, and F is a general negative factor that takes into account such features as angles too near $0°$ or $180°$ or vertices too close together. The complexity C of a polygon is defined as the number of indefinitely extended straight lines that contain all the sides of the polygon. The aesthetic measure M of a polygonal form is the ratio of its order to its complexity. Of two polygons, the one with the higher aesthetic measure is considered aesthetically superior.

The main problems with Birkhoff's aesthetic measure are the absence of convincing arguments for the inverse relation between order and complexity, the apparent arbitrariness of the definitions of order and complexity, and the rather narrow applicability of these definitions to polygonal forms only. Furthermore, the formula can be questioned on empirical grounds (Eysenck, 1941). Nevertheless, Birkhoff's formula is a model of clarity and rigor that is all too uncommon in traditional aesthetics.

B. An Aesthetic Measure

The following measure of aesthetic value is suggested for forms:

The aesthetic value of a form is the ratio of the length of the description of the form to the length of the procedure (rules) given to generate the form.

In general, the description of a form and the procedure given to generate it can be represented in a uniform way by finite sequences of symbols over some finite alphabet. The lengths of the description of a form and the procedure given to generate it are determined by counting the number of occurrences of symbols in the sequences representing them.

If the aesthetic value of two forms is determined based on the same descriptive and generative conventions (for example, if they are both described by enumerating the elements in them and generated by rules of growth, or they are both described by shape, color, and occurrence tables and generated by generative specifications), then their aesthetic values can be compared, otherwise, their aesthetic values are incomparable. Of two forms with comparable aesthetic values, the one with the greater aesthetic value is considered aesthetically superior. When two forms have comparable aesthetic values and are generated by procedures of equal lengths, the one with the longer description is preferred aesthetically; when they have descriptions of equal lengths, the one generated by the shorter procedure is preferred aesthetically. In general, the aesthetic measure assigns high aesthetic values to forms that have relatively long descriptions and are generated by relatively short procedures.

This aesthetic measure for forms has an obvious interpretation based on the canon of "unity in variety." Under this interpretation, the variety of a form is given by the length of its description. The longer the description of the form, the greater is its variety. In the case where a picture is described by shape, color, and occurrence tables, the correspondence between its description and its variety as defined in Section II,A is exact. That is, the more shapes, colors, and distinct areas in a picture, the longer its shape, color, and occurrence tables will be, and the greater its variety will be. The unity of a form is given by the length of the procedure given to generate it. The shorter the procedure given to generate a form, the greater will be its unity. This measure of unity assumes that a form perceived to have coherence, organization, or regularity can be generated by a more economical procedure than a form for which no underlying pattern is seen. That is, finding a pattern in a form provides the basis for giving an economical procedure with which to generate it. Clearly, when the lengths of the procedures given to generate two forms and the lengths of their descriptions correspond to unity and variety in this way, their aesthetic values as assigned by the aesthetic measure vary as indicated in Hutcheson's general rule.

The aesthetic measure suggested in this section can also be interpreted in terms of an algorithmic or procedural formulation of information theory. But first, some background is useful.

It has been suggested (for example, in Attneave, 1959; Hiller & Isaacson, 1959; Pinkerton, 1956), that the aesthetic value of objects (typically, musical pieces) depends on their complexity or entropy. This suggestion meets with considerable difficulties when we try to apply the standard statistical definition of entropy (Shannon & Weaver, 1949) to individual objects. Under the standard definition, the entropy of an object of a certain type is given in terms of its probability of occurrence in the universe of all possible objects of that type. For an individual object, such as a form, it is generally infeasible to determine this probability (Greene & Courtis, 1966). If the standard definition of entropy is used, then the suggestion that the aesthetic value of objects depends on their entropy is unproductive, as the entropy of individual objects cannot, in general, be determined. For this suggestion to be productive, a definition of entropy that pertains to individual objects is needed.

Information theory has been reformulated independently by Chaitin (1970), Kolmogorov (1968), and Solomonoff (1964) in terms of algorithms or procedures. The new definition of entropy pertains to individual objects.

Formally, the entropy of a sequence of symbols is given by the length of the shortest procedure (encoded as a sequence of symbols) that generates the sequence. Any sequence of symbols $a_1 a_2 \cdots a_n$ can be generated by the procedure: "Write out $a_1 a_2 \cdots a_n$." That is, the sequence is generated by describing it, by giving it item by item. For some sequences of symbols, there are no procedures for generating them that are much shorter than describing them. The entropy of a sequence of this type is approximately equal to the length of the sequence itself. A sequence of symbols with entropy approximately equal to its length is random (Chaitin, 1975; Martin-Lof, 1966); that is, each symbol in the sequence occurs independently of other symbols in the sequence and, hence, must be given one by one. There are procedures for generating other sequences of symbols that are much shorter than describing them. The entropy of a sequence of this type is substantially shorter than the sequence intself. A sequence of symbols with entropy much smaller than its length is nonrandom; that is, the symbols in the sequence occur with some pattern or regularity that can be used to formulate a relatively short procedure to generate the sequence.

This new definition of entropy can be applied to forms. The length of the shortest procedure that can be given to generate a form can be considered the entropy of the form. If the entropy of a form is approximately equal to the length of its description, then the form can be regarded as random; that is, the most economical way to generate the form is to describe it line by line, element by element, or shape by shape. If the entropy of a form is substantially shorter than its description, then the form can be regarded as nonrandom; that is, some pattern or regularity is discovered in the lines, elements, or shapes of the form that provides the basis for the formulation of an economical procedure to generate the form.

In these terms, the aesthetic value assigned to a form by the aesthetic measure suggested in this section is (when the procedure given to generate the form is the shortest such procedure) the entropy of a random form with a description of the same length as the given form divided by the actual entropy of the form. This expression can be considered the reciprocal of the relative entropy (Shannon & Weaver, 1949) of the form. It follows that any form assigned high aesthetic value (i.e., value greater than 1) is not random.

C. Measuring the Aesthetic Value of Pictures with Generative Specifications

The aesthetic measure defined in Section II,B can be used to assign aesthetic values to pictures such as Bridgework I–VI shown in Fig. 6 when they are described by tables of shape, color, and occurrence and generated by generative specifications. The aesthetic values of Bridgework I–VI are computed in Table I.

The length of a description is taken to be the sum of the lengths of the shape, color, and occurrence tables of which the description is composed. The length of a shape table, a color table, or an occurrence table is given by the number of words of computer memory used to represent it using the program described in (Gips, 1975). The length of a generative specification is given by the number of words of computer memory used to represent it using

TABLE I
COMPUTATION OF AESTHETIC VALUES OF BRIDGEWORK I–VI

Bridgework	Length of shape table	Length of color table	Length of occurrence table	Length of description	Length of generative specification	Aesthetic value
I	177	13	169	359	50	7.18
II	226	13	162	401	50	8.02
III	168	13	127	308	50	6.16
IV	211	13	141	365	50	7.30
V	183	13	155	351	50	7.02
VI	181	13	155	349	50	6.98

the same program. The generative specifications for Bridgework I–VI have the same lengths because they differ only in the location of the markers in the right side of the first shape rule in their shape grammars (see Section I,C,3). The asethetic value of a picture is the ratio of the length of its description to the length of its generative specification. Those pictures with relatively long tables of shape, color, and occurrence and relatively short generative specifications are assigned high aesthetic values.

Because Bridgework I–VI are described and generated using the same conventions, and are assigned aesthetic values by the same aesthetic measure, their aesthetic values can be compared. The aesthetic ordering of these pictures, in order of decreasing aesthetic value, is Bridgework II, IV, I, V, VI, and III.

Informally, the aesthetic values assigned to Bridgework I–VI reflect the variety and occurrence of the shapes in them and the way those shapes are generated by the shape grammars in their generative specifications. Here, aesthetic value is independent of the actual colors used. If two pictures differ only in their colors, then their aesthetic values are identical. Furthermore, the aesthetic values assigned to Bridgework I–VI are biased against symmetry. This bias results from the fact that asymmetric pictures have, in general, a larger variety and more occurrences of shapes than symmetric ones.

Of course, neither the aesthetic values assigned to Bridgework I–VI nor their aesthetic ordering are, in any sense, absolute. These values and this ordering depend on the conventions used to describe and generate Bridgework I–VI as well as on the aesthetic measure applied. Different descriptive methods, generative methods, or aesthetic measures could result in different aesthetic values and aesthetic orderings. It seems reasonable to assume that if the aesthetic values and aesthetic ordering of Bridgework I–VI are to reflect the aesthetc preferences of some person or community, then the methods and measures employed to obtain those values and that ordering should be based on the conventions used by the person or community. Certainly, no claim of this kind is made here. Nevertheless, combining descriptive and generative techniques seems to be a profitable way of looking at the aesthetic value of forms.

A more complete discussion of the ideas presented in this chapter is given in Stiny and Gips (1978).

References

Attneave, R. Stochantic composition processes. *Journal of Aesthetics and Art Criticism,* 1959, **17,** 503–510.
Beardsley, M. C. *Aesthetics.* New York: Harcourt, 1958.
Beeler, M. Patterson's worm. *Massachusetts Institute of Technology AI Memo,* 1973, No. 290.
Birkhoff, G. D. *Aesthetic measure.* Cambridge, Massachusetts: Harvard Univ. Press, 1933.
Boas, F. *Primitive art.* New York: Dover, 1955.

Chaitin, G. On the difficulty of computations. *IEEE Transactions on Information Theory*, 1970, **IT-16**(2), 5–9.

Chaitin, G. Randomness and mathematical proof. *Scientific American*, 1975, **232**(5), 47–52.

Codd, E. F. *Cellular automata*. New York: Academic Press, 1968.

Dacey, M. The syntax of a triangle and some other figures. *Pattern Recognition*, 1970, **2**, 11–31.

Dacey, M. Poly: A two-dimensional language for a class of polygons. *Pattern Recognition*, 1971, **3**, 197–208.

Emond, T. *On art and unity*. Lund, Sweden: Gleerups, 1964.

Eysenck, H. J. The empirical determination of an aesthetic formula. *Psychological Review*, 1941, **48**, 83–92.

Gardner, M. Fantastic patterns traced by programmed "worms." *Scientific American*, 1973, **229**(5), 116–123.

Gips, J. *Shape grammars and their uses*. Basel, Switzerland: Birkhauser Verlag, 1975.

Goodman, N. *Languages of art*. Indianapolis, Indiana: Bobbs-Merrill, 1968.

Greene, R. T., & Courtis, M. C. Information theory and figure perception: The metaphor that failed. *Acta Psychologica*, 1966, **25**, 12–36.

Hiller, L., & Isaacson, L. *Experimental music*. New York: McGraw-Hill, 1959.

Hopcroft, J. E., & Ullman, J. D. *Formal languages and their relation to automata*. Reading, Massachusetts: Addison-Wesley, 1969.

Jones, O. *The grammar of ornament*. New York: Van Nostrand Reinhold, 1972.

Klee, P. *Pedagogical sketchbook*. New York: Praeger, 1953.

Kolmogorov, A. N. Logical basis for information theory and probability theory. *IEEE Transactions on Information Theory*, 1968, **IT-14**(5), 662–664.

Lockwood, E. H. *A book of curves*. New York: Cambridge Univ. Press, 1961.

Loeb, A. *Color and symmetry*. New York: Wiley, 1971.

Martin-Lof, P. The definition of random sequences. *Information and Control*, 1966, **9**, 602–619.

Milgram, D., & Rosenfeld, A. Array grammars and array automata. In C. V. Freiman (Ed.), *Information processing 71*. Amsterdam: North Holland, 1972.

Odds, F. C. Spirolaterals. *Mathematics Teacher*, 1973, **66**(2), 121–124.

Papert, S., & Solomon, C. Twenty things to do with a computer. *Massachusetts Institute of Technology AI Memo*, 1971, No. 248.

Pinkerton, R. Information theory and melody. *Scientific American*, 1956, **194**(2), 77–86.

Schrandt, R. G., & Ulam, S. M. On recursively defined geometrical objects and patterns of growth. *Los Alamos Scientific Laboratory Report*, 1967, **LA-3762.**

Shannon, C., & Weaver, W. *The mathematical theory of communication*. Urbana, Illinois: Illinois Univ. Press, 1949.

Shubnikov, A. V., & Koptsik, V. A. *Symmetry in science and art*. New York: Plenum Press, 1974.

Sirmoney, G., Sirmoney, R., & Krithivasan, K. Picture languages and array rewriting rules. *Information and Control*, 1973, **22**, 447–470.

Solomonoff, R. A formal theory of inductive inference. *Information and Control*, 1964, **7**, 1–22.

Stiny, G. *Pictorial and formal aspects of shapes and shape grammars*. Basel, Switzerland: Birkhauser Verlag, 1975.

Stiny, G. Two exercises in formal composition. *Environment and Planning B*, 1976, **3**(2), 187–210.

Stiny, G. Ice-ray: A note on the generation of Chinese lattice designs. *Environment and Planning B*, 1977, **4**(1), 89–98.

Stiny, G., & Gips, J. Shape grammars and the generative specification of painting and sculpture. In C. V. Freiman (Ed.), *Information processing 71*. Amsterdam: North Holland, 1972. Pp. 1460–1465.

Stiny, G., & Gips, J. *Algorithmic aesthetics: Computer models for criticism and design in the arts*. Los Angeles: Univ. of California Press, 1978.

Stiny, G., & Mitchell, W. J. The Palladian grammar. *Environment and Planning B*, 1978, **5**(1), 5–18.

Sullivan, L. H. *A system of architectural ornament*. New York: Eakins Press, 1967.

Ulam, S. M. Patterns of growth of figures: Mathematical aspects. In *Proceedings of Symposia in Applied Mathematics, XIV: Mathematical Problems in the Biological Sciences*. Providence, Rhode Island: American Mathematical Society, 1962.

Weyl, H. *Symmetry*. Princeton, New Jersey: Princeton Univ. Press, 1952.

Part IV

Architecture, Music, Art, and Cinema

Chapter 8

PERCEPTUAL ASPECTS OF ARCHITECTURE

KRISTINA HOOPER

I. INTRODUCTION

Architecture consists largely of human perceptions. Although architecture is buildings, it is also the lives that go within these buildings; though it is distant vistas, it is also intimate contact. It is hard and solid, yet represents dreams and fantasies. It exists today, yet it reminds us of yesterday and makes us think of designing our tomorrows. Architecture is very public, as it is built and shared by many individuals, but is private in the sense that responses to architectural environments are very personal.

By its very complexity, architecture defies simple analysis. Yet, because architecture affects so many of us so directly and so closely, and because it is continually being created, it is important to consider systematically the architectural environment. It is important to understand how we perceive

HANDBOOK OF PERCEPTION, VOL. X

our environments and how we respond to these perceptions. It is important to note that which we consider to be good environments, functional environments, and beautiful environments, so that we can recreate such environments to house our futures. It is also important to approach this investigation within an explicitly perceptual framework, for although there is no perfect piece of architecture, no ultimate beauty in architecture, and no absolute dictum for functionality, there are perceptions of beauty, of functionality, and of perfection.

Forms follow perceptions, and perceptions follow forms. The reality of architecture exists in the relation between these two elements, their tension and their coexistence. Form must be honored, and it must be systematized, but so must the complexity of human perceptions that make these forms live. It is this precept that provides the thesis for this chapter.

A. Architectural Views of Perception

Architects are consistently involved in the perceptual aspects of the environment, as they are students of applied perception and masters of visual illusions (Lang, 1974; Isaac, 1968). They continually manipulate forms, the relations between these forms, and the relations between forms and human observers. They do this in order to accomplish a wide range of visual illusions. For example, architects attempt to make small spaces appear large and flat surfaces appear curved; the columns of Greek temples appear straight because they are carefully tapered; and church towers appear very tall by contrast with small adjacent elements. Architectural forms appear important and impressive by the nature of the viewing routes that proceed from small enclosed spaces into large expansive areas.

The language of architecture used in formulating these illusions is highly perceptual, as explicitly spatial and visual metaphors are used to communicate the attributes of forms. Buildings are evaluated by how well they capture the attention of viewers and how carefully views are unfolded to provide for aesthetic climaxes. The viewer's perceptions of architectural forms is primary. Physical forms are studied in the context of manipulating these perceptions.

Techniques for these manipulations are described straightforwardly, as deterministic relationships are set up between elements of architectural forms and the perceptions of these forms:

> Thus, as we have seen, high forms command the attention more quickly than low ones; in addition curved elements are more compelling than straight ones; and elements that suggest motion, like doorways, gates, steps, and stairs, are more interesting than those which imply only static attitudes [From T. F. Hamlin (Ed.), *Forms and functions of twentieth-century architecture*, Vol. 2, p. 32. New York: Columbia Univ. Press, 1952, by permission of the publisher.]

Relationships such as these are elaborated within architectural theories to describe the many varied aspects of architectural form. The scale of buildings is amenable to this sort of direct analysis, as is proportion, balance, unification, lighting, and style. Even the rhythm of a building, its sequence of elements and the relations between these elements, can be analyzed in these simple ways.

> Rhythm can be closed by changing the shape of the units at the ends, by changing the size of the units at the ends, or by combinations of both types of change; it can also be closed by adding to each end a strongly marked opposing rhythm [From T. F. Hamlin (Ed.), *Forms and functions of twentieth-century architecture*, Vol. 2, p. 129, New York: Columbia Univ. Press, 1952, by permission of the publisher.]

The assumptions implicit in these rules for design are that there exist deterministic relations between elements of form and that these are generalizable. These assumptions are widespread, as architects actively seek the syntax of visual form that will consistently generate good buildings. Yet, in general, the concepts garnered in these searches are not as straightforward as might be liked by naïve realists, and it becomes obvious that there is no cookbook available for good architectural design.

> We come to the truth that our reactions to architecture are governed not necessarily by what is actually there as conceived in terms of feet and inches and physical properties of materials, but by what appears to be there. Each of us creates his own visual sensations from a building and each of us brings his own unique visual history to the situation. We do not all necessarily have the same visual experience when looking at the building. In spite of this, good architectural form and space is capable of imposing its own articulation upon different observers owing to its high degree of preciseness [Danby, 1963, p. 175].

Great tensions exist between existential design strategies, such as those set forth in the first part of Danby's statement and the deterministic strategies asserted in the last sentence. Tensions exist between the symbolic, illusory qualities of architectural form and its definiteness and simplicity. Langer (1953) speaks well for the illusory qualities of architecture. "Architecture is a plastic art, and its first achievement is always, unconsciously and inevitably, an illusion; something purely imaginary or conceptual translated into visual impressions [p. 93]." Indeed, like the other visual arts, the intent of architecture resides in the illusions that are created. However unlike these other arts, architecture is neither primarily visual nor representational. It is an object in the world designed to serve a function, and it is straightforward and touchable in this regard.

B. Perceptual Psychological Views of Architecture

A critical approach to issues within the domain of architecture is that of perceptual psychology, an approach that makes explicit the relationship between objects in the world and the representations and interpretations of these within the human mind. It provides a framework in which to center the study of architecture upon human responses to these forms, to the perceivers whom Danby alludes to, and to the interpreter of the illusions stressed by Langer. As stated earlier, the issues of architecture become explicitly directed to the relationship between *forms* and *perceptions*.

What are the human perceptions of architectural forms? How do people judge the perceptual aspects of architecture? How do they respond to an architectural environment if they live in it? These issues are discussed in Section III.

What is the nature of the human perceptions that precede architectural forms? What is the nature of the design process? What limits does the structure of the perceiving human mind place upon newly built environments? How do the specific graphic images used in the human designing process influence the form of architectural environments? These issues are discussed in Section IV.

This chapter addresses these questions within the general paradigms of perceptual psychology, paradigms that are directed toward the explication of the relationships between elements of physical form and human responses to these forms. In contrast to the more basic perceptual approaches, which relate human responses to physical elements at the level of lines and angles, or which treat movement within a referent-free system, this chapter tries to explicate the relationships between higher-level elements that are referent bound. Section II sets forth these elements in some detail, as architectural form is defined in terms of space, surface, movement, and function, all of which are user-centered attributes.

As stated at the beginning of this chapter, "architecture consists largely of human perceptions." The intent of this chapter is to explicate this within the domain of perceptual psychology and to explore the complex relationships between human perceptions and architectural form as they follow each other again and again in time.

II. THE PHYSICAL FORM OF ARCHITECTURE

Architectural form can be specified by its structural elements, its materials, and the measurements of its surfaces and angles. These specifications allow a contractor to concretize a plan. However, very different dimensions are relevant in describing the perceptual experiences of architecture. *Spaces* and *surfaces* provide the basic data for perceptual experiences, not the measurements of volumes and surface areas. Similarly, it is the *movement* of an observer through space and the juxtaposition of many egocentric reference systems that describe the perceptual experience of architecture, rather than a reference-free Euclidean system. Finally, the architectural experience must be evaluated in terms of its *function* as well as its perceived form.

A. Architecture as Space

Architects generally describe their plans in terms of spaces: spaces that move in and out of one another, spaces that enclose, spaces that invite, spaces that provide potential for activities. Louis Kahn (1960) described architecture as "the thoughtful making of spaces . . . the creating of spaces that evoke a feeling of appropriate use [p. 118]." Frank Lloyd Wright (1941) said of buildings that "the enclosed space within them is the *reality*" and that architecture was "spiritually (virtually) conceived as appropriate enclosure of interior space to be lived in [p. 189]." Bruno Zevi (1957) suggested that architecture "does not consist in the sum of the width, length and height of the structural elements which enclose space, but in the void itself, the enclosed space in which man lives and moves [pp. 22–23]."

The spaces created by architects are not simple. They cannot be considered as volumes, nor can they be specified independently of a referent framework. Architecture is not simply a container, nor is it sculpture. It is a three-dimensional object within space, that encloses space and that itself consists of the juxtaposition of spaces (see Fig. 1).

In contrast to containers, the dimensions of the solid form of architecture are different from one another. They are nonorthogonal, their scales are different, and they are weighted differently when they are combined in perception. Consider, for example, how gravity prevents individuals from exploring the height, width, and length dimensions of architectural form in the same manner. Also consider what the purposes are of each of these dimensions; consider the differences among floors, ceilings, and walls. The spaces created by these three dimensions are considered differently from one another, and the resultant spaces are not measurable as mere simple volumes. They are much more. This is particularly true when the level of analysis concerns multiple spaces. Though rooms are clearly three-dimensional, buildings generally consist of simple stacks of these rooms, rather than spaces that are integrated within all dimensions. Floor plans in buildings are generally isolated entities, as only limited access is provided to the observer by stairs and elevators. There is no perceptual integration of these levels.

The concept of volume is noted as ineffective in capturing the sense of architectural spaces within the conceptualization of modern architecture. Moholy-Nagy (1946) stated that

FIG. 1. Frank Lloyd Wright uses planar elements in the Kaufman House to define and unite perceptions of several distinct exterior and interior spaces. [Photo by Wayne Andrews.]

> Formerly the architect constructed his buildings from visible, measurable, and well-proportioned volumes, calling them "space creations." But real spatial experience rests on simultaneous penetration of inside and outside, above and beneath, on the communication of the in and the out, on the often invisible play of forces present in the materials and their relationships in space [p. 62].

Architectural space provides for the relationships between enclosed spaces, not simply for their enclosure. There is a distinct top and bottom to good architectural form, and also a front and a back, yet all are integrated into something more.

The modern architecture as represented by Moholy-Nagy gave little credence to the idea of the human observer as a focus point for architecture, as it focused instead upon "free-flowing" and "organic" spaces. More current architectural theory explicitly stresses the interior domain of the human observer in its conception of architectural space, according to Norberg-Schultz (1971), thus differentiating it completely from sculptural conceptions of space (see Fig. 2).

Fig. 2. Charles Moore creates a comfortable human scale interior in this Sea Ranch residence, setting the wooden buildings carefully into the environment to provide a transition between outside and inside. [Photo by Wayne Andrews.]

Architects wanted to liberate the static spaces of conventional buildings, to express positively the new "open" world. Recently, however, the need for defined places and interior spaces has again been felt. As Robert Venturi says: the essential purpose of the interiors of buildings is to enclose rather than direct space, and to separate the inside from the outside [Norberg-Schultz, 1971, p. 66].

The addition of the place of the human observer to architectural space is an important one, as expansiveness and enclosure in spaces depend on the perceptions of observers, not on some absolute, referent-free conception. A long corridor will appear small and enclosed if an observer is provided a viewing position near its end, though it will appear extensive if viewed from its origin. This was demonstrated experimentally by Hayward and Franklin (1971), who showed that the perception of open and enclosed spaces was not a function of the relative sizes of the dimensions of these spaces, as had been suggested by Garling (1969), but was rather a function of the relation of boundary height and viewing distance.

The treatment of spaces in the Hyatt Regency Hotel in San Francisco is instructive in the context of general spatial characteristics, as the boundaries between typical internal and external spaces are blurred in this structure (see Fig. 3). By this blurring, human spaces are created that give the hotel a sense of place, an *ethnic domain,* to use the term of Susanne Langer (1953). It is a structure that is hollow, where empty space is "wasted" for the visitor's pleasure of expanse, rather than organized into compartmental rooms. It is a

FIG. 3. The Hyatt Regency Hotel by John Portman in San Francisco encloses the human observer in a lively interior space. [Photograph courtesy of Hyatt Regency, San Francisco.]

building that truly has interior spaces, which are articulated so as to proclaim human potential rather than human limitation. It is space designed to house human observers; it is not simply a sculpture or a container.

B. Architecture as Surface

The spaces of architecture are created by its surfaces and its illusions of surfaces: by its floors, its exterior facade, its walls, its windows, its ceilings, and its roofs. For example, the balance of the elements on a facade, their rhythm, and their unification, all contribute to the sense of coherence of an architectural space and to the description of its character. Such elements provide information that will separate a building from its surround or, alternatively, integrate it into this surround. For example, the texture of a surface greatly affects perception of architectural form, as it determines the light-reflectance characteristics of a building and the perceptual relationships between surface elements. Surface materials—wood, glass, and steel—create very different perceptions of forms, as do different color schemes. Some will cause a building to appear warm and approachable, whereas others will cause the same building to seem austere. Some will provide cues as to the details of a surface, whereas others will hide certain variances in the surfaces.

Many individuals never interact with a building except from a distance, and it is for this reason that the facade is important in the perceptual definition of a building. The two-dimensional characteristics of this surface can become a painting for distant onlookers, and its three-dimensional aspects can act as a piece of sculpture. This natural ambiguity allows the observer to judge architectural objects according to the criteria of both the plastic and the visual arts.

Facades may become the main element of a design, as the surfaces are predominant and possess an identity that is independent of the space that they create, as the creation of space can be thought to move from the outside to the inside. However, some theorists suggest that this is not the order of architectural creation, nor is it the appropriate way to consider architectural elements.

> Architecture proceeds from the inside to the outside of a building, so that the facade is never a thing separately conceived, but like the skin or carapace of a living creature is the outer limit of a vital system, its protection against the world and at the same time its point of contact and interaction with the world [Langer, 1953, p. 100].

Yet both these approaches miss the essence of the surface in architecture. They either stress the facade or attempt to ignore it as a element in its own right. Facades define the relationship of exterior and interior spaces, and they are critical in this role. They cannot be treated as two-dimensional, but instead must be viewed as boundary conditions.

> Designing from the outside in, as well as the inside out, creates necessary tensions, which help make architecture. Since the inside is different from the outside, the wall—the point of change—becomes an architectural event. Architecture occurs at the meeting of interior and exterior forces of use and space. [From Robert Venturi, *Complexity and contradiction in architecture*, p. 88. Copyright © The Museum of Modern Art, New York, 1966. Reprinted by permission.]

The surface of a space is a place of perceptual and symbolic expression. It is the area that provides observers with their first cues as to the purpose of an architectural form and their first exposure to the integrity of the form. It also is the definition of shelter, as it delineates the differences between the harshness of the environmental elements and the warmth and personalization of lived-in spaces. It is the boundary between the "them" and the "us," between the known and the unknown.

C. Architecture as Movement

Observers move within architectural spaces, and their views can change greatly with each movement. From one position an architectural object will appear angular, though from another it will appear flat and uniform. An architectural space may appear enclosing from one perspective, whereas the same space will appear expansive from another (see Fig. 4).

It is the implicit task of the observer to organize all of these separate images into one coherent whole, in order to ascertain the sense of an entire architectural space from the juxtaposition of multiple exterior and interior views. This sense of architecture is very different from perceptions of single

FIG. 4. Louis Kahn created a complex human viewing context in his library at Exeter Academy, juxtaposing a diverse array of surfaces that unveil changing spaces to the moving observer. [Photo by Wayne Andrews.]

views. It is not like the photograph of a building, but is rather like a schemata (Bartlett, 1932), a schema (Piaget, 1936), or a prototype (Posner, 1970). It is the conceptual representation of the architectural object, which is actively constructed from multisensory impressions. It is the reflection of the imaginary space that Langer speaks of, rendered into concrete form by architects.

Cullen (1961) has suggested that the experience of architecture is the architectural environment in which one is standing (the "here") and the architectural environment that one can view from this position (the "there"). This suggests that the schema of an architectural form is not independent of viewing position; rather, it is directly related to this position. Such a contention is supported by the use of positional restrictions by individuals in the retrieval of memories for architectural form, and also by the nature of people's abilities in identifying the position of view in photographs of architecture (Hooper, 1973). An observer's representation of a building is not limited by single views, yet it does contain information concerning the variants of architecture that result from the different viewing positions.

It is the task of architects to create spaces that can be effectively integrated. They must provide cues to observers so that a general sense of a building from discrete views may be had. One way architects can accomplish this is to sequence views by the movement of observers through space. The

FIG. 5. Moshe Safdie created a unique exterior space by the functional conglomeration of individualized modular units in Habitat. ["Habitat '67, Montreal, Canada." Photograph courtesy of Safdie & Associates.]

movement of the observer can be carefully controlled by the architect by the articulation of walkways and the relations between spaces. The appearance of an area can be unfolded in a specific, controlled manner (Appleyard, 1965). Series of enclosures and open spaces can be used to provide excitement in an area. Overviews can be interspersed with isolated views to add coherence to the general architectural concepts. Long entranceways can create expectations.

> The tendency in every mass and line and detail is to lead the observer from the rear to the front; his eye is directed consistently toward the more interesting details at the entrance end, and he naturally walks toward them and around the corner, where he sights the strong facade, a suitable and sufficient climax to the whole experience [From T. F. Hamlin (Ed.), *Forms and functions of twentieth-century architecture*, Vol. 2, p. 58. New York: Columbia Univ. Press, 1952, by permission of the publisher.]

Similarly, movement can be included in architectural spaces to manipulate the view of the stationary observer. This can be accomplished with angular transitions, moving lights, changes in natural light during each day, or exterior elevators. In addition, moving observers can be used to define spaces. Spaces can be created to provide for the movement of observers and, at the same time, use this movement in the definition of these spaces. The movement of people in an architectural space can be used to bring life and a sense of place to what may be otherwise considered a void.

D. Architecture as Function

As I have been suggesting, architectural forms are not designed to satisfy only visual criteria (see Fig. 5). A primary intent of architectural design is to provide shelter for humans: to effectively provide a place within which human lives can survive, develop, and interrelate. This differentiates architecture from the other plastic arts.

The relationship between the form and the function of architecture is one that has been the subject of ongoing debate in architectural circles since Sullivan stated that form followed function. Moholy-Nagy asserts, for example, that

> In all fields of creation, workers are striving today to find purely functional solutions of a technical–biological kind; that is, to build up each piece of work solely from the elements which are required for its function [Moholy-Nagy, 1946, p. 61].

Others assert that function follows form, and still others argue that the two are mutually dependent and inseparable in architectural concerns: "'Form follows function' is but a statement of fact. When we say 'form and function are one,' only then do we take mere fact into the realm of creative thought [Wright, 1941, p. 236]." A unified stance allows for the systematic investigation of the role of function in architecture. If we examine the two-way relationship between form and function in terms of a specific space, we find a large void between functional requirements and the final form of a building, a void that is the very home of the human beings who will inhabit these spaces. Functional characteristics can determine the skeleton of architecture, the minima that must be satisfied to cover basic needs. Yet other criteria are necessary to create spaces that are beautiful and involving.

There are many problems to which pure physical functionalism can give no certain answer—questions like "How big is a room?" "How tall should a door be?" "How wide must this corridor be made?" To questions like these, functional analysis can answer only with the minima; it can say "Such a room, for such a purpose, *cannot* be smaller than so and so"; "A door must be *at least* so wide"; "This corridor must not be *narrower* than so and so." And an architecture—a world—built only on minima is unthinkable; the human spirit has its demands, too, and among them is its demand for space in which to stretch itself, to enlarge itself, to enjoy [From T. F. Hamlin (Ed.), *Forms and functions of twentieth-century architecture*, Vol. 2, p. 10. New York: Columbia Univ. Press, 1952, by permission of the publisher.]

Human perceptions follow form. These are the realities of an architecture after it meets the minima of functional characteristics (see Fig. 6).

The forms that perceptions follow are more than visual, as are the perceptions that follow these forms. Although the language of design often conceals this, nonvisual perceptual characteristics—audition, temperature sensitivity, kinesthetic orientation, smell—are critical in the evaluation of architecture, and they are critical beyond the level of minima. Surely a building should be insulated so that it is *not* cold. It should be soundproofed so that it is *not* noisy. Yet these criteria can be applied in a constructive manner: Auditoriums can be designed that convey sounds with true fidelity; courtyards can be created that capture a sense of stillness; rooms can be placed along a hall in a way to enhance interaction, to provide a hustle and bustle that creates a sense of place. Forms can—and should be—created to fit specific multisensory human objectives of a place.

FIG. 6. Le Corbusier combines diverse perceptual elements in achieving the symbolic elegance of Notre Dame du Haut at Ronchard. [Photo by Wayne Andrews.]

The considerations of these kinds of criteria affect the physical structuring of spaces. For example, the consideration of the movement of air within a space can directly affect the shapes of the rooms and hallways and the placement of windows and doors. Smells from kitchens can be important in determining the placement of other rooms in a single-family dwelling. The shape of an auditorium space is dictated by the characteristics of sound waves, as the number of surfaces and the relationships of these surface are critical in the transmission of sound.

As with visual characteristics, nonvisual attributes of architecture are primary within the realm of perception. Auditory, olfactory, and kinesthetic sensory inputs combine with visual information to give an individual a sense of space and a feeling of the adequacy of the space. Though these nonvisual attributes may not be consciously included in architectural judgments (except in extreme cases, where they become primary), they actively contribute to architectural perceptions and are important retrieval cues for later memories for spaces. Certain smells, for example, bring forth memories of favorite old houses, and specific sounds recall comfortable home environments. Southworth (1969) demonstrated the importance of nonvisual characteristics experimentally by showing that the sonic attributes of cities were critical in their evaluation. Neutra (1954) consistently asserted that the sensory aspects of environments were critical in the creation of humane environments.

Nonvisual perceptions provide important creative constraints in the design of architecture, and nonvisual responses to architecture contribute greatly to the development of conceptual representations of space. These perceptions must accompany function and visual criteria in the design of architectural form.

III. EVALUATIVE RESPONSES: HUMAN PERCEPTIONS THAT FOLLOW ARCHITECTURAL FORMS

Beautiful and functional buildings should be built to house human lives. Such is the aim of most architects and the desire of most individuals. Yet, this is a difficult task, as concepts of beauty and functionality are forever changing, and the characteristics of the people who will inhabit buildings, their needs, and their values in particular situations, are diverse. Though it seems evident that human responses to environments are important in their development, it is difficult to ascertain how to assess human values in built environments and how to interpret these in the context of an architecture that must be built for a present, pluralistic society as well as an unknown, future society.

Many architects and planners have concluded that the assessment of human responses to architecture is impossible, if not useless. Yet this view is too simple. Perceptions follow forms and make them live. The responses made by humans to architecture are critical in its description.

In order to assess human responses to architectural form in this section, cognitive, affective, and symbolic responses to architectural form are considered (see Table I). These are selected to provide a skeleton for the range of human responses to architecture, to structure the variety of responses that can be made in different exposure contexts, and to provide a language for the description of architectural form in explicitly human terms.

These three kinds of responses are based on different levels of information and are expressed differently by individuals. *Cognitive responses* are based directly on perceptual information (that is, information that is integrated by an individual in comprehending the basic form of an area). Lines, angles, and texture gradients are combined so as to allow judgments of attributes such as largeness, relative spatial positions, and brightness. Cognitive responses are primarily descriptive of architectural forms: The basic vocabulary communicates perceptual characteristics of an area and indicates a basic level of interpretability and comprehension for an area. *Affective responses* generally describe the state of the observer who is making a judgment. They are derived from cognitive responses and reflect how these responses have been combined in the individual's personal assessment of an area. Cognitive attributes, such as clearness and complexity of an area, are combined at this level to yield affective responses, such as comfortableness and friendliness. Subjects explicitly report observer-centered responses at this level, though they are often unable to explicitly identify the attributes of the forms that are responsible for these responses. Most affective responses are clearly evaluative, as in cases where observers indicate their judgments of beauty and attractiveness. Though these responses are not as explicit in their description of the state of the observer, they do evaluate observer states in terms of preferential assessments. It is assumed, for example, that the attractiveness of an architectural form results in a positive observer reaction.

Symbolic responses reflect the meaning and intent of architecture. These responses are quite different from the more informational cognitive and

TABLE I

RESPONSES TO ARCHITECTURE

	Responses		
	Cognitive	Affective	Symbolic
Domain	perceptual	evaluative	inferential
Descriptors	angular	comfortable	spiritual
	imagible	exciting	powerful
	complex	beautiful	important
Form of description	"I hear. . ."	"I feel. . ."	"I think that. . ."
	"I see. . ."	"I like. . ."	"I know that. . ."

affective responses, in that they relate more to an individual's past history and cultural milieu than to the attributes of a form. The judgments and aesthetics at this level relate to the adequacy of the ideal expressed within a form, or the successfulness of the expression of a concept through a physical medium. These responses are the semantics of an architectural environment, whereas cognitive and affective responses relate to the syntax that provides the structure within which the meaning is conveyed.

A. Informational Responses to Architectural Forms

1. COGNITIVE LEGIBILITY IN ARCHITECTURE

An important characteristic of any architectural environment is its coherence and identifiability of form. It needs to be categorizable and memorable to the individuals who interact with it, and it needs to provide cues for this organization and interpretation.

Kevin Lynch (1960) considered this legibility of form in his studies of imagibility on the scale of urban design. In his analysis he addressed himself to cities as compositions of individual buildings and proclaimed that intelligible subjective orderings of cities was critical for effective levels of human existence. In *The Image of the City*, a book that established the base for much of the present perceptual work in the field of environmental psychology, Lynch ascertained a set of attributes of a space that were responsible for imagibility of this space and evaluated these attributes in terms of subject responses to these spaces.

The areas that Lynch chose to examine were the three cities of Los Angeles, Boston, and Jersey City. The attributes that he identified in each of these cities were

1. Paths (the channels containing the movement of human observers)
2. Edges (boundaries between areas)
3. Districts (living areas defined as distinct regions)
4. Nodes (strategic points of activity)
5. Landmarks (important locations used by residents in orientation)

By examining maps drawn to represent these cities, verbal reports used to describe these cities, and performances in identification tasks, Lynch was able to show differences in the visual structuring of these cities. Using this information, he suggested how the visual integrity of the cities might be enhanced and how paths might be used to increase the apparent visual order of a city. He described how edges can be accentuated to add clarity to a city and suggested how landmarks might be systematically used to improve the unity of a city's image. He used visual metaphors to describe the relationships between people and buildings and asserted that the subjective visual and spatial attributes of environments were important.

Lynch's work gave rise to an extensive amount of research. Cities throughout the world were examined in terms of landmarks, edges, etc. These cities were compared and contrasted based on these elements, and new elements were defined (Clay, 1973). Other investigators examined imagibility on an architectural scale. For example, Appleyard (1969) described how certain buildings were known whereas others were not. In addition, the study of residents' concepts of their spatial environments (their cognitive maps) became an important area of investigation (Downs & Stea, 1973). Researchers studied the perceived distances between locations in space and the memories for specific locations. They discussed how cognitive maps were developed as a function of isolated exposures to areas, and they investigated how children developed spatial representations of their environments (Hart & Moore, 1973).

Unfortunately for the direct study of perception, many of the investigations of cognitive mapping became focused on how people draw maps of their environments, rather than how they perceive their environments. Lynch's initial queries concerning the imagibility of cities and the spatial organization of perceptually identifiable aspects of cities were not always evident in the research.

Maps of areas are very conceptual representations. They omit the identifying perceptual features of the architectural environment—for example, color, size, texture, and three-dimensional shape. They represent only the location and basic floor plan of each building and the spatial relationships between the locations of sets of buildings. They do not represent the feelings of the voids of architectural spaces, nor the articulation of the surfaces. They provide us with only a hint of what individuals perceive in their environments and how they put this information together.

The investigation of the specific aspects of environments that are used in orientation has been pursued (Hooper & Cuff, 1976). Pictures of the individual colleges of the University of California, Santa Cruz (UCSC) campus were presented to students for familiarity, recognition, and representativeness ratings. Perceptual features used in the discrimination of different campus buildings were identified by the analysis of these data, and were used in the generation of representative drawings of each of the areas of the university. These drawings represented the "superfeatures" of the environments, rather than any specific view (see Fig. 7). The drawings have been placed onto a map for the use of newcomers to the campus, so that they might orient themselves effectively to this confusing campus by the use of perceptual as well as spatial cues. Though the drawings have yet to be tested with campus newcomers, evidence set forth by Ryan and Schwartz (1956) suggests that the conceptual drawings will be very effective in communicating the areas.

Though much of the research based on Lynch's original study has departed from the study of perceptual elements, Lynch's work has greatly

FIG. 7. This conglomerate drawing combines key elements of several different buildings to display concisely the human perceptions of a large area. The photographs show examples of buildings in the represented area. [Drawing by Dana Cuff.]

influenced the considerations of perceptual attributes in the planning of cities (Lozano, 1974). Urban planning has become urban design, and the overall visual form of a city has become an important criteria in urban development. Perceptual and cognitive characteristics of architecture, insofar as they relate to the individuals who live within these spaces, have been given the same credence as building codes, economics, and politics in the public domain of architectural design.

2. AFFECTIVE DESCRIPTIONS OF ARCHITECTURE

Architecture can be thought of as a composition consisting of perceptual and cognitive attributes, both in the architectural form and in the minds of its observers. It also can be considered evaluatively, as basic perceptual attributes can be combined by observers to produce judgments of attributes such as beauty, excitement, and cheerfulness.

Investigations of affective subject responses to architectural forms have been numerous, as researchers have applied varied sets of evaluative dimensions and techniques to the understanding of architectural forms. Kasmar (1970), for example, systematically derived a large set of environmental descriptors to be used in the discrimination and description of architectural forms. Subject judgments of the appropriateness of different dimensions to architectural forms provided the criteria for the selection of descriptors. The descriptors chosen included aesthetic descriptors such as elegant–unadorned, pleasant–unpleasant, and sparkling–dingy, as well as perceptual descriptors such as comfortable–uncomfortable temperature and good–poor ventilation.

Canter (1969) approached the description of architectural forms within the general approach of person perception, presenting his subjects with bipolar adjective pairs that they used to describe different architectural spaces. Canter identified four important factors in affective judgments of architecture by performing a factor analysis on his data. Character was identified as the main factor, and coherence, friendliness, and activity were identified as other relevant factors.

Other researchers have used factor-analysis procedures based on semantic differentials or adjective checklists in the evaluation of architecture (Sanoff, 1969, 1974), whereas still others have used personal-construct analysis (Hudson, 1974). Dimensions often identified by these procedures include intensity, comfortableness, and harmony.

Most affective responses to architectural forms can be summarized within the evaluative factor described by Osgood et al. (1957). People consistently rate architecture on the dimensions of good–bad and beautiful–ugly. Other evaluations are made, but only after individuals indicate whether or not the architectural form makes them feel good by the way it looks or by the way it functions.

It is difficult to determine whether or not any affective responses made to architecture are independent of this evaluative factor, or if they are all dependent upon stereotypes of evaluative responses that individuals have stored in their memories. It is not clear, for example, that single evaluative judgments can not be expanded into other affective descriptors that are predicted by this initial evaluation. Neither is it clear that all affective responses do not have positive or negative values attached, and that these are not the primary considerations in overall evaluations. Lowenthal (1972), for example, showed that descriptions of imagined environments are very similar to those of real environments, and he suggested that this was a function of the similar linguistic structures used in both sorts of judgments. If a place is described as beautiful, then it is judged as inviting, comfortable, pleasant, and well-articulated. If it is described as ugly, it is then judged as uninviting, uncomfortable, unpleasant, and poorly organized. Yet, though this may be the logical structure of individual memory spaces, it may not be the structure of good architecture, particularly when goodness is judged in terms of living, rather than thinking. It is not clear that these ratings describe (or even include) the complexities of affective response to humans who live in these spaces, even if they do describe initial responses to these areas. Although it is important to consider initial impressions, since many individuals experience architecture in only these ways, it is important to input evaluations of experienced observers to the architectural design process; then new environments can be created that provide for the wide range of affective responses to architecture that are inherent in the complexity of resident–architecture interactions, which encompass the entire life experience.

The use of general affective responses in the architectural design process is difficult, however, because evaluations of architectural forms are typically made in the context of the forms as wholes. Affective responses are then generated independently of specific aspects of the architectural forms and are not directly definable in terms of certain features of these forms. Also, when experienced observers are used in judgments, social, personal, and political variables become important criteria in judgments. This makes specific delineation of the rules of architectural evaluation in terms of physical forms difficult. This delineation is further complicated by the apparent inaccessibility of information related to the specification of individual features by the observers providing affective responses. General observers can rarely describe what it is in a form that makes it beautiful, or comfortable, or exciting. It seems that a large and complex set of elements, some of which are unconscious, are responsible for these judgments. Yet, of course, until these elements are identified, affective judgments of architecture are not generalizable to other architectural forms.

3. The Relationship between Cognitive and Affective Responses

The investigation of the physical determinants of human responses to form has been a major issue within aesthetic theories, as well as being a subject of concern among architects and other artisans. The assumption explicit within these investigations is that there exist identifiable formal structures that are responsible for human responses.

Le Corbusier approached architecture in this context, as he described architecture in terms of directing lines (diagonals and perpendiculars) that dictated proportions and detailing on facades, which resulted in beautiful architectural forms if appropriately configured. In another system, he described a complex formal system of design based on the proportions of the human body (1954). He asserted that humans related effectively to an architecture that related directly to them. Other architects have attempted similar formalizations: "The secret of beauty in buildings is sought in triangles, circles, five-pointed stars, the Golden Section (extreme and mean ratio), root-five rectangles, modules, arithmetic ratios, and so on [Hamlin, p. 11]."

The general approach expressed within these attempts centers around the determination of a psychophysics of architectural form, much like that proposed by J. J. Gibson (1966) for general environmental features. However, as asserted in Section II, the physical features of architecture do not adequately describe the complexities of these forms, except perhaps for the contractor. The experience of an architectural space is dependent not upon directly measurable physical features, but upon human perceptions of these features. It is not a psychophysics that is sought, but rather a "psychoperception" of architectural form.

Human perceptions of physical variables such as those discussed by designers can be related to the evaluative responses of general observers, or cognitive responses of one group of subjects can be related to the affective responses of another.

> Psychologists have made use of variables that physicists have provided, for example, temperature, luminance, chromaticity, and amplitude, but have not attempted to explore the physical variables that geographers and environmental designers provide, or that might be developed through collaboration with these environmental experts [Craik, 1970, p. 14].

Cognitive attributes, such as angularity, rhythm, and texture, can be considered as the basic perceptual dimensions. Affective attributes, such as visual interest, beauty, and friendliness, can be used to represent psychological responses. These responses can then be compared within subjects or between subjects. Information is then provided that considers both cognitive and affective response. In addition, affective judgments are related to specific attributes of forms, and the forms are described, as well as the individuals making the judgments. Of course, these relationships do not explicitly identify physical attributes of form that affect individuals. However, the results can be used as input to new design processes without this explicitness, as designers can use their own perceptual responses to translate cognitive attributes into the physical dimensions of the contractors and the buildings within the design process (Hooper, 1975). The information added is the evaluative perceptions of general human observers.

Complexity is a cognitive attribute of architectural space that has been investigated in terms of its relationship to affective responses. Kaplan *et al.* (1972), for example, demonstrated that preferences for environmental displays were directly related to the complexity of these displays. Pyron (1970) demonstrated that the amount of eye scanning of a visual field increased with increases in the diversity of housing environments.

Rappoport and Kantor (1967) have interpreted results such as these to infer that people need complexity in their environments, that they search for novelty and variety, that they choose complex environments over simple environments, and that they avoid monotonous environments. Such assertions are consistent with Berlyne's (1971) theory of general aesthetics, in which he claims that complex forms evoke curiosity and involvement, and hence preferential responses. It is also consistent with many current architectural theories that are reacting against the formality, starkness, and self-consciousness of the modern architecture of this century, and proclaiming complexity and contradiction in architecture (Venturi, 1966). However, it is apparently inconsistent with Wohlwill's (1975) conclusion that individuals prefer harmonious and simple environments, and with basic tenets of architectural theory that stress the need for unity and coherence in architectural forms. Yet, if one considers the essential difference between complexity and *confusion*, these discrepancies resolve themselves, and the points of view complement one another. Individuals do indeed prefer interesting and varied environments, yet the complexity within these environments can be highly structured and directly accessible to individuals for judgments.

B. Symbolic Aspects of Architecture

Some aesthetic theorists suggest that human evaluations are not directly derivable from the physical attributes of architecture and that they are instead reflective of the meanings that are generated by the architectural forms. They assert that an important attribute of the architectural spaces is the expression of symbolic significance and that an important response to architecture is the interpretation of these symbolic meanings. In this context, architectures can be considered a symbolic representation that can be read by observers within a particular cultural milieu for the purpose of inferring the purpose of a place, understanding the intent of its creation, and identifying that for which it stands outside itself (Levi, 1974; Saarinen, 1969).

> A building may indicate wealth, power, modernity, tradition, ambition or repose. It may suggest withdrawal from society or stand as an invitation to visit and share the hospitality of the owners. It may stand apart from the land, a man-made object suggesting the scientific technology that has resulted from the use of the human mind and the industry or contemporary society, or it may stay close to the earth, rising from the soil and rocks, a part of nature, tying man to all other forms of life, like the great rambling Arizona home and studio of Frank Lloyd Wright [Knobler, 1966, p. 263].

Symbolic aspects are critically important, as it is ultimately the symbolism of a building that is responsible for individual assessment of architecture. Symbolic representations provide the conceptual formulation which is beyond simple spaces and surfaces. They provide for the illusions that Langer (1953) speaks of that make architecture real, the void which Levi (1957) alludes to in which lives pass, and the dreams that Neutra (1954) discusses that allow transcendence beyond physicality and subsistence, through perception, to humane form. For, in terms of human observers, it is the symbolism conveyed by all attributes of an architectural form that is real. It can be the primary basis upon which individuals interpret architectural forms and upon which they judge them evaluatively. A beautiful and successful architectural form is then the church that represents holiness, the sports arena that represents excitement, the house that represents a home, and ultimately the surround that represents oneself (see Fig. 8).

Yet, this communication is not simple, as an important criteria for good architectural communication is the provision of multiple messages that can be read by different individuals in different ways, and by the same individual in different ways at different times. Cues must be provided in the forms that interact effectively with experiential histories of observers, and with purposes of viewing. Spaces should not be so confusing so as to be ineffectual,

FIG. 8. The Long Range Development Plan (1963) for the University of California, Santa Cruz, stated that "there must be a differentiation between the informality of the residential college groupings and the more formal and even sometimes monumental character of the central campus (academic) buildings." The buildings shown here demonstrate the interpretation of these symbolic guidelines.[Photographs courtesy of the Office of Campus Facilities, University of California, Santa Cruz.]

for each reading should be clear. Yet, the complexity introduced by the different meanings of the architectural form will provide liveliness to the form. Venturi (1966) expressed this well in his descriptions of new standards for architectural form.

> Architects can no longer afford to be intimidated by the puritanically moral language of orthodox Modern architecture. I like elements which are hybrid rather than "pure," compromising rather than clean, distorted rather than "straightforward," ambiguous rather than "articulated," perverse as well as impersonal, boring as well as "interesting," conventional rather than "designed," accommodating rather than excluding, redundant rather than simple, vestigial as well as innovating, inconsistent and equivocal rather than direct and clear. I am for messy vitality over obvious unity. I include the non sequitur and proclaim duality. . . . A valid architecture evokes many levels of meaning and combinations of focus: its space and its elements become readable and workable in several ways at once [Venturi, pp. 21–22].

Architecture must evoke contradictory images and descriptions, which provide it with a sense of place, a liveliness, and a realness. It must reflect the complexity of human nature. It must be more than large or small, angular or curved. It must be more than simply good or bad. It must convey symbolic messages beyond its physical form. It must elecit spiritual and cultural symbolic responses as well as cognitive and affective informational responses.

IV. THE ARCHITECTURAL DESIGN PROCESS: HUMAN PERCEPTIONS THAT PRECEDE ARCHITECTURAL FORMS

Architectural forms are created by human minds. Because of this they are tied tightly to the perceptual concepts of designers. It is often asserted, for example, that buildings are built by architects, for architects, that they are based on very particular perceptual experiences, and that they are unsuitable as general human living environments. In a more general comment, Alexander (1965) suggests that the conscious structuring of cities is unsuccessful because the human mind cannot effectively represent the complexity that is necessary to create livable cities. Others suggest that modern societies, and the designers within these, are not at all sensitive to human environments and are therefore unable to generate appropriate criteria for architecture. So, although architecture may meet criteria effectively, human limits in the generation of these criteria limit the success of architecture and the specific abilities and perspectives of architects, which are different in many regards from other individuals (Hall & McKinnon, 1969), may greatly affect the form of architectural environments.

In the past, architectural environments were generally built slowly by the people who planned to live in these environments. The hill towns of Italy and

Spain are examples of such areas, organic environments that reflect the creativity of generations of individual people. The towns of the Sind district in West Pakistan, or Apulia, or Sudan are other examples (Rudofsky, 1964). They are all instances of environments on a human scale designed exclusively for living, rather than for appearances, showing off, or selling. They are environments that have been built within a comprehensible perceptual domain. Individual designers could consider one element of a form at a time, change it, and then stand off and plan another change. They could view the results of their plans and modify them so as to achieve their intentions. They could generate designs and evaluate them simultaneously. Actors in the modern architectural design process do not have these luxuries, as the scale of buildings, the number of experts involved, and the timing sequences make the present process far more complex.

This section considers human perceptions that precede architectural form. It considers both the perceptions of designers who generate forms and the perceptions of evaluators whose task it is to recognize good forms once designs are proposed. Perceptions are considered here in regard to experiential imagery, and in terms of extensions of perceptions made by the use of architectural graphic media.

A. Conceptual Representations of Designs

It is the designer's task to communicate perceptions of life through the media of physical form, to provide the shell in which human activities will exist, to design the physical features of space that provide for human perceptions, and to provide the features that allow for cognitive, affective, and symbolic inferences. Moreover, it is the designer's task to use the language of architecture in such a way as to communicate to observers an understanding of the spaces he has created.

To accomplish this, architects must proceed from ideas to concrete instances. They are given a set of criteria for a building, a program, and they must combine these effectively to provide a design solution. The main tasks for the architect, then, are choosing features that satisfy design problems. To do these things, designers often recognize appropriate features in other designs and combine these in design solutions. In this sense, they view the design process much like a concept-formation task. The designer does not define the set of features that identify a solution, but instead the relations between them (Moore, 1970). New relations and new combinations of features are therefore responsible for effective and creative design solutions.

An important tool of designers in the generation of design proposals is mental imagery. The perceptual imagery of architects, developed by exposure to existing architectural forms and by experience in the manipulation of these forms, is important in providing the basic outlines of design solutions. It provides the initial representation of architectural form and allows the conceptions of multiple designs, before these are limited to a few alternatives. Visual thinking strategies such as those described by Arnheim (1969) and McKim (1972) can be used to process these mental images. They can be used to consider the spatial characteristics systematically and thoroughly and to provide divergent approaches to design problems, approaches that creatively integrate old and new concepts. In this initial processing stage, these visual and spatial images are important by reason of the manner in which they prevent designers from moving too quickly to concrete graphic representations and becoming locked into certain solutions too early in the design process.

The conceptual power of mental imagery and the visual thinking of designers is extended by Christopher Alexander (1964) in his proposal of a language that designers can use to systematically specify their design problems conceptually, so as to avoid the necessity of concretizing a solution prematurely. The basic assertion underlying Alexander's concepts on the synthesis of forms is that there is "underlying structural correspondence between the pattern of a problem and the process of designing a physical form which answers that problem [p. 132]." He utilizes this correspondence to express mathematical criteria for design solutions, to explicate relationships between these criteria and aspects of alternative design solutions, and to thereby provide designers with systematic ways of dealing with conceptual aspects of design.

Other sets of abstract languages developed for use in the architectural design process include the notational systems of Halprin (1965, 1970), Thiel (1962), Litton (1968), and Appleyard, Lynch, and Meyer (1964), systems that have been developed to represent perceptions of architectural environments, rather than perceptions of the design problem. These notation schemes are designed specifically to represent movement and changing views form different locations, and to represent changes of design during the design process.

B. Graphic Representations of Designs

The translation of conceptual representations into concrete forms is one of the main tasks of designers. Important mechanisms in this translation are the graphic media of the designer, such as sections, schematic drawings, and elevations. These allow designers to move beyond many human memory-processing limitations to consider effectively alternative design possibilities.

For example, an important process in design is the continual evaluation of design solutions and their modifications. The use of computer graphics in architecture greatly facilitates this modification process (Negroponte, 1970; Milne, 1968). These graphics allow for systematic changes of potential solutions in very short times. Whereas mental imagery and conceptual visual languages can represent design issues in an abstract form for consideration, the graphic media of the computer can provide concrete visual simulations of buildings that can be directly manipulated.

However, a problem with all graphic media is their two dimensionality. Using these media, the designer must match conceptions of three-dimensional spaces with two-dimensional representations in evaluating and modifying specific design solutions. And though some architectural solutions may look good on paper, they may appear as something quite different when constructed. More devastatingly, the representation of the forms on paper may correspond closely to the final built form, so that architectural spaces look like beautiful drawings or paintings that have been propped up into three dimensions.

Designer evaluation and modifications based on two-dimensional representations are ineffective in the creation of three-dimensional environments, unless designers do have available the perceptual mechanisms to mentally convert these drawings into concepts of three-dimensional environments. Although it is suggested that designers have very well-developed imagery systems, it is not clear that this can be done very effectively, given the nature of human memory limitations. Surely the two-dimensional appearance of buildings existing in our environment suggests failures in this area.

Architectural models are used by designers to represent three-dimensional spaces explicitly. The models provide a symbolic medium for consideration of spatial attributes, as they demonstrate the spatial relationships between and within buildings, and as they provide a medium for manipulations of these relationships. However, models do not allow for the direct perception of an area, for models are viewed from above, whereas real architectural environments will be seen at eye level. Again the designer must rely upon perceptual abilities to translate representational media into their referent objects in order to make effective judgments.

The Environmental Simulation Project at the University of California, Berkeley, was designed by Donald Appleyard and Kenneth Craik to provide realistic representations of architectural environments (Appleyard, Craik, Klapp, & Kreimer, 1973). Its basic assumption is that increases in realism and apparent three dimensionality will enhance environmental decision making, as individuals will have a good sense of how new environments will appear.

The project centers around a simulator that was built to photograph architectural models and to produce movies and videotapes of these models that realistically simulated travel through them. The cinematic results of this system are incredibly realistic (Fig. 9), surely more realistic than computer graphic displays, such as those of Greenberg (1974), produced for the same purpose. In fact, subjects viewing the movies are often unable to distinguish between the simulation movies and movies of actual areas. In addition, their responses to the environments shown in these movies are very similar to those of subjects who tour the same environment in an automobile. Craik

FIG. 9a. The Environmental Simulation Laboratory at the University of California, Berkeley, is used to generate realistic movies of architectural models.

FIG. 9b. This is an example of output from the system.

(1975), for example, demonstrated consistent similarities among cognitive, affective, and symbolic responses made to environments that were toured directly and to these same environments when modeled and viewed through the simulation system.

Of course, realistic media do not completely tame the wicked problem of good architectural design. For, as stressed earlier, the design process exists as an interaction of conceptual representations and alternative solutions. Realistic representations provide designers with techniques for evaluating their designs, techniques to judge whether or not the designs are as intended. However, designers must still rely upon conceptual language and mental imagery in the generation of these alternative design solutions. They are still constrained by perceptual and cognitive abilities in this generation. It is not feasible to generate all possible design solutions, and therefore the structure of human perceptions, the structure of the mind of the designer, becomes critical in the definition of architectural form.

C. Presentations of Designs

Perceptual aspects of the environment are highly valued in our present society. Legislation regarding the perceptual aspects of the environment is prevalent, and local planning agencies are continually attempting to control perceptions of their areas. For example, the policies for San Francisco set forth in the Urban Design Plan of 1971 stress the visual aspects of the city. Policies made explicit in this plan state that new developments should be designed to "promote harmony in visual relationships [p. 91]," that these new developments should "avoid contrasts in color, shape and other characteristics that will cause new buildings to stand out [p. 91]," and that "street spaces import a unifying rhythm to the pattern and image of the city [p. 25]." These kinds of policies require that media be systematically developed that can adequately represent unbuilt environments, in order that policymakers can judge the adequacy of designs in fulfilling these requirements. Similarly, media are necessary for evaluations of nonperceptual aspects of architecture, so that evaluators can determine how an area will function as a living environment.

A principal medium used in the presentation of architecture is the perspective rendering—see Fig. 10. These drawings present detailed three-dimensional space from a particular viewing position. Unfortunately, however, drawings are often designers' concepts rather than their specific proposals. They are, therefore, sometimes misleading. Similarly, the finely executed coloring and edge differentiation of the drawings often creates a sense of spaces that will not exist in the three-dimensionality of the built environments.

Another medium used to present designs is the photograph. Photographs of sites are often presented to decision makers, with and without a proposed development. (The development is simulated and added to the site photograph, as in Fig. 11.) This allows the proposal to be considered in a realistic context. However, there are limits on the viewpoints chosen and the concreteness of the design additions. The movies prepared by the Environmental Simulation Project provide another alternative presentation medium. These movies are not limited to single viewpoints, and they very effectively convey the appearance of three-dimensionality by their movement. They also provide extremely effective presentation media, as they are realistic media that are easily interpretable by general human observers.

Of course, presentation media should be used to convey symbolic aspects of form just as the general design media do. Pictures like Fig. 10c provide the person voting for or against a certain architectural form with a sense of a space and function that realistic representations, such as Figs. 10d,

(a)

FIG. 10. Renderings provide decision makers and designers with "a sense" of a building before it is built. The examples on the left represent a number of different visions of a single proposed building; the photographs on the right display the building as it was constructed.

(b)

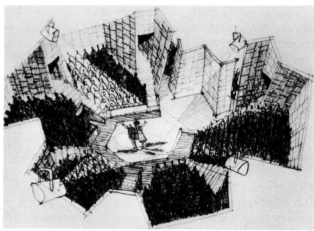

(c)

(d)

(e)

(f)

FIG. 11. Photo-simulation was used to demonstrate the visual impact of the University of California, Santa Cruz Coastal Marine Laboratory.

10e, and 10f do not allow. Of course, both are critical in conveying the sense of architecture to individuals who must make decisions. A building is not only a physical form; it has a functional identity and intention. It is not only an appearance, but a shell for human activities. Presentation media have to provide for these different communications. They must be designed so that they are interpretable by general human observers, and so that they extend perceptions of architectural forms rather than limit them. For again, the human perceptions of the media will greatly influence the physical form of the architecture created.

V. CONCLUSIONS

It would be extremely satisfying to state assuredly that people like round edges and high ceilings in their architectural environments; or that buildings should never be higher than three stories, and that they should be directly related to human proportions; or that the modern architectural forms of Mies Van der Rohe or Le Corbusier create livability by their simplicity and functionality; or that yellow walls calm inhabitants and make them feel comfortable.

Yet the complexities of architectural environments make these and similar statements impossible and somewhat irrelevant. Architecture is very complex and diverse. Therefore, perceptions of architectural forms are also complex and diverse. Architecture follows perception, and perception follows architecture, and the combination is livable because of the effective interaction of these two elements.

Given this relationship between architectural form and perception, the primary role of architecture is illusion, the representation in a physical medium of elements that convey certain conceptual messages. Yet architecture, unlike other arts, exists in everyday reality. It is an object in this world that often is treated as a physical form by passers-by, and even by contractors (Section II). Architecture is a physical space that provides a place for human activities. It is touchable surfaces that provide enclosures for observers and create tensions between human interior space and natural exterior space. Architecture is a physical structure that provides for the movement of individuals through space, whose main function is to provide a shelter for the whole of multisensory human existence.

Yet even in its physical form, architecture exists in relation to human observers. It exists because of uniquely human responses to architectural forms (Section III), responses that vary from cognitive and affective responses to symbolic inferences. Architectural forms are created to adequately explain themselves, to affect the humans who inhabit them, and to represent values of the societies in which they exist. Of course, architectural forms also exist because of the human imagination and perceptions that generated them (Section IV). The conceptual capabilities of the designers greatly influence the form of existing architecture, as do the graphics used to expand these conceptions in the creation and presentation of architectural forms.

In these senses architecture is illusory, despite its concrete physical form. It is the physical reality that generates fantasies and dreams; the physical form that results from human fantasies and dreams; the concrete reality and the symbolic reality. It is hard and soft; touchable, yet illusory. It is inanimate, yet it is the shell for human lives. Ultimately, it exists by these tensions. It is the interaction of physical form and perceptions.

References

Alexander, C. *Notes on the synthesis of form*. Cambridge, Massachusetts: Harvard Univ. Press, 1964.

Alexander, C. A city is not a tree. *Architectural Forum*, 1965, **122**(1), 58–62 and (2), 58–61.

Appleyard, D. Motion, sequence, and the city. In G. Kepes (Ed.), *The nature of art and motion*. New York: George Braziller, 1965.

Appleyard, D. Why buildings are known. *Environment and Behavior*, 1969, **1**, 131–156.

Appleyard, D., Craik, K., Klapp, M., & Kreimer, A. The Berkeley Environmental Simulation Laboratory: Its use in environmental impact assessment. The Institute of Urban and Regional Development, Working Paper No. 206, February 1973.

Appleyard, D., Lynch, K., & Meyer, J. *The view from the road*. Cambridge, Massachusetts: The MIT Press, 1964.

Arnheim, R. *Visual thinking*. Berkeley: Univ. of California Press, 1969.

Bartlett, F. C. *Remembering*. Cambridge, England: Cambridge Univ. Press, 1932.

Berlyne, D. E. *Aesthetics and Psychobiology*. New York: Appleton (The Century Psychology Series), 1971.

Canter, D. An intergroup comparison of connotative dimensions in architecture. *Environment and Behavior*, 1969, **1**, 37–48.

Clay, G. *Close up: How to read the American city.* New York: Praeger, 1973.

Craik, K. Environmental psychology. In *New directions in psychology* (Vol 4). New York: Holt, 1970.

Cullen, G. *Townscape.* New York: Reinhold, 1961.

Danby, M. *Grammar of architectural design.* London: Oxford Univ. Press, 1963.

Downs, R. M., & Stea, D. *Image and environment.* Chicago: Aldine, 1973.

ESP Staff. Environmental Simulation Project. Preliminary Report. Berkeley, California: Institute of Personality Assessment and Research. Univ. of California. June 1975.

Garling, T., II. Judgment of open and closed space by category rating and magnitude estimation. *Scandinavian Journal of Psychology*, 1969, **10**, 257–268.

Gibson, J. J. *The senses considered as perceptual systems.* Boston: Houghton Mifflin, 1966.

Greenberg, Donald. Computer graphics in architecture. *Scientific American*, May 1974, 98–106.

Hall, W., & McKinnon, W. Personality inventory correlates of creativity among architects. *Journal of Applied Psychology*, 1969, **54**, 322–326.

Halprin, L. Motion. *Progressive Architecture*, 1965, **46**, 7.

Halprin, L. *RSVP Cycles.* New York: Reinhold, 1970.

Hamlin, T. F. *Forms and functions of twentieth century architecture.* New York: Columbia Univ. Press, 1952.

Hart, R., & Moore, G. The development of spatial cognition: A review. In R. M. Downs and D. Stea (Eds.), *Image and environment.* Chicago: Aldine, 1973.

Hayward, S., & Franklin, S. Perceived openness–enclosure of architectural space. *Environment and Behavior*, 1971, **6**, 37.

Hooper, K. *The identification of mirror images of real world scenes.* Unpublished doctoral dissertation, 1973.

Hooper, K. On the analysis of the visual characteristics of a new project: How we might effectively use our visual information processing skills in evaluating our future environments. *Design Methods Groups Newsletter*, Spring 1975.

Hooper, K., & Cuff, D. *Superfeatures of the UCSC environment.* Unpublished paper, 1976.

Hudson, R. Images of the retailing environment. *Environment and Behavior*, 1974, **6**, 470–494.

Isaac, A. Perception and Design—I. *The Architecture and Building News*, 1968, **233**(21) 776–779.

Kahn, L. Structure and Form (Forum Lectures, Architecture Series 6), 1960.

Kaplan, S. Kaplan, R., & Wendt, J. S. Rated performance and complexity for natural and urban visual material. *Perception & Psychophysics*, 1972, **12**, 354–356.

Kasmar, J. V. The development of a usable lexicon of environmental descriptors. *Environment and Behavior*, 1970, **2**, 153–169.

Knobler, N. *The visual dialogue.* New York: Holt, 1966.

Lang, J. Theories of perception and "formal" design. In J. Lang, C. Burnette, W. Moleski, & D. Vachon (Eds.), *Designing for human behavior.* Stroudsburg, Pennsylvania: Dowden, Hutchinson and Ross, 1974.

Langer, S. *Feeling and form.* New York: Scribner, 1953.

Le Corbusier. *The modular* (Translated by P. de Franca and A. Bostock.). Cambridge: The MIT Press, 1954.

Levi, D. "The Gestalt Psychology of Expression in Architecture," In J. Lang, C. Burnette, W. Moleski, & D. Vachon (Eds.), *Designing for human behavior.* Stroudsburg, Pennsylvania: Dowden, Hutchinson and Ross, 1974.

Litton, B. Forest Landscape Descriptions and Inventories—A Basis for Land Planning and Design. U.S.D.A. Forest Service Research Paper PSW-49. Pacific Southwest Forest and Range Experimental Station, Berkeley, California, 1968.

Lowenthal, D., & Riel, M. The nature of perceived and imagined environments. *Environment and Behavior*, 1972, **4**, 189–208.

Lozano, E. Visual needs in the urban environment. *Town Planning Review*, 1974, **45**(4), 351–374.

Lynch, K. *The image of the city*. Cambridge, Massachusetts: The MIT Press, 1960.

Mckim, R. H. *Experiences in visual thinking*. Monterey, California: Brooks/Cole, 1972.

Milne, M. (Ed.). *Yale Conference on Computer Graphics in Architecture*. New Haven, Connecticut: 1968.

Moholy-Nagy, L. *The new vision*. New York: Wittenborn, 1946. (Originally published, 1928.)

Moore, G. (Ed.). *Emerging methods in environmental design and planning*. Cambridge, Massachusetts: The MIT Press, 1970.

Negroponte, N. *The architecture machine*. Cambridge, Massachusetts: The MIT Press, 1970.

Neutra, R. J. *Survival through design*. New York: Oxford Univ. Press, 1954.

Norberg-Schultz, C. *Existence, space and architecture*. New York: Praeger, 1971. P. 66.

Osgood, C. E., Suci, George J., & Tannenbaum, P. H. *The measurement of meaning*. Urbana: Univ. of Illinois Press, 1957.

Piaget, J. *The origins of intelligence in children*. New York: International Univ. Press, 1952. (Originally published, 1936.)

Posner, M. Abstraction and the process of recognition. In G. H. Bower & J. T. Spence (Eds.), *The psychology of learning and motivation: Advances in research and theory* (Vol. 3). New York: Academic Press, 1970.

Pyron, B. Form and space diversity in human habitats: Perceptual responses. *Environment and Behavior*, 1970, **3**, 382–391.

Rapoport, A., & Kanter, R. E. Complexity and ambiguity in environmental design. *Journal of the American Institute of Planners*, 1967, **33**(4), 210–221.

Rudofsky, B. *Architecture without architects*. New York: Museum of Modern Art (Distributed by Doubleday, Garden City, New York), 1964.

Ryan, T. A., & Schwartz, C. B. Speed of perception as a function of mode of representation. *American Journal of Psychology*, 1956, **69**, 60–67.

Saarinen, T. *Perception of environment*. Association of American Geographers, Resource Paper, No. 5, 1969.

San Francisco Department of City Planning. The Urban Design Plan, May 1971.

Sanoff, H. Visual Attributes of the Physical Environment. Student Publication of the School of Design, Response to Environment. Raleigh: North Carolina State Univ., 1969.

Sanoff, H. Measuring attributes of visual environment. In J. Lang, C. Bunnette, W. Moleski, & D. Vachon (Eds.), *Designing for human behavior*. Stroudsburg, Pennsylvania: Dowden, Hutchinson and Ross, 1974.

Southworth, M. The sonic environment of cities. *Environment and Behavior*, 1969, **1**, 49–70.

Thiel, P. Experiment in space notation. *Architectural Review*, 1962, **13**, 783.

Venturi, R. *Complexity and contradiction in architecture*. New York: The Museum of Modern Art, 1966.

Wohlwill, J. Environmental aesthetics: The environment as a source of affect. In I. Altman & J. Wohlwill, J. (Eds), *Human behavior and environment* (Vol 1). New York: Plenum, 1976.

Wright, F. L. *Frank Lloyd Wright on architecture; selected writings*. New York: Duell, Sloan and Pearce, 1941. Pp. 189, 236.

Zevi, B. *Architecture as space*. New York: Horizon P, 1957.

Chapter 9

THE PSYCHOLOGY OF MUSIC*

DIANA DEUTSCH

I. INTRODUCTION

The perceptual psychologist will find in music a rich and rewarding area for investigation. Here he can explore many problems, such as shape recognition, attention, memory, and even abstract cognitive activity, generally without the complication of verbal labeling by the subject. Furthermore, he can employ complex stimuli derived from music such as sequences of tones, or complex sounds of varying timbre, to broaden our understanding of the human auditory system beyond that which can be derived from classical psychophysical stimuli.

* This work was supported by United States Public Health Service Grant MH-21001-03.

In the past, the study of musical information processing has been hampered by technical difficulties involved in generating complex auditory stimuli with precisely controlled parameters. However, the technological advances of recent years have completely changed this picture; as a result, experimental interest in this field has developed rapidly. Given the intrinsic interest of the subject, and the fact that it is still largely unexplored, we may expect to see considerable advances in our understanding of musical psychology over the next decade.

Due to lack of space, this chapter omits certain topics that should be included in a comprehensive account of the psychology of music. Questions involving the origins and functions of music are not discussed, since these are not fundamentally problems in perception. For accounts of basic psychoacoustical phenomena and the physiology of the auditory pathway, the reader is referred to Volume IV of this *Handbook*. A comprehensive discussion of tuning systems, and of consonance and dissonance, is to be found in Ward (1970).

II. RECOGNITION OF TONAL SHAPE

The abstraction of tonal information occurs in several stages. The initial stages of abstraction involve the detection of both specific features (such as intervals, chords, and tone chroma) and global features (such as contour). Such features are then combined to form tonal sequences, which are themselves abstracted and combined in systematic ways. These stages of abstraction will be discussed in what follows.

A. Tonal Features

1. TONE CHROMA

The term *tone chroma* refers to the position of a tone within the octave. Tones that are separated by octaves are given the same name in traditional Western music, and are treated as perceptually similar. Indeed, people with absolute pitch sometimes place a note in the wrong octave even though they name it correctly (Baird, 1917; Bachem, 1954). Octave duplications in scales are also found in other cultures (Nettl, 1956a). Further evidence for the perceptual equivalence of tones separated by octaves comes from conditioning studies. Generalization of response to tones placed an octave apart occurs both in man (Humphreys, 1939) and in animals (Blackwell & Schlosberg, 1943). Such octave generalization has been used to produce a compelling illusion. Shepard (1964) generated a set of complex tones, each of which consisted of several tones separated by octaves. When these tones were presented in ascending semitonal steps at a rate of about 1 sec^{-1}, listeners perceived a set of tones that constantly increased in pitch and never returned to the beginning. These tones therefore appeared to be endlessly climbing up an abstracted octave.

The physical octave represents a frequency ratio of 2:1. However, as first noted by Stumpf and Meyer (1898), the subjective octave is slightly larger than this. Ward (1954) made a systematic investigation of this phenomenon. He presented subjects with two pure tones in repetitive succession, and required them to adjust the frequency of one to be exactly an octave above the other. It was found that subjects made adjustments that were reliably larger than a 2:1 ratio and, further, that the amount of deviation from the physical octave increased in the higher frequency ranges. Sundberg and Lindquist (1973) obtained similar findings with complex tones. Furthermore, Burns (1974a) repeated Ward's experiment with professional Indian musicians as subjects, and obtained remarkably similar results; so it would appear that the phenomenon of octave stretch is not dependent on culture. This conclusion is reinforced by the finding that tuning practices in several non-Western cultures agree very well with these laboratory measurements (Dowling, 1973a). Terhardt (1971) proposed that the phenomenon of octave stretch is acquired early in life as a result of exposure to complex sounds. In such sounds, the pitches of neighboring partials move slightly away from each other, as a result of a mutual masking effect, and Terhardt assumed that we generalize from this to harmonically related tones that are presented in succession. On the other hand, the phenomenon may simply reflect innate properties of the auditory system—an explanation favored by Dowling (1973a).

Because of the perceptual similarity of tones separated by octaves, it makes most sense to regard pitch as a bidimensional attribute: one dimension being a monotonic function of frequency, or tone height (at least in the case of pure tones), and the other defining the position of a tone within the octave, or tone chroma. Various representations of pitch have been proposed that accommodate these two dimensions. Drobisch (1846) suggested that pitch be represented as a line spiraling around a helix, with tones separated by an octave lying most proximal within each turn of the helix. Ruckmick (1929) made an essentially similar proposal involving a bell-shaped spiral instead. However, such suggestions do not make plausible neurophysiological models. It would seem more in line with our knowledge of brain function to suggest that neural units underlying tones that are separated by octaves converge onto the same higher-order units (Deutsch, 1969). Indeed, units with two or more "best" frequencies that are octave multiples of each other have been found in the auditory system (Evans, 1974), and such units are very likely to receive multiple projections from units with single best frequencies.

2. Intervals and Chords

The simultaneous or successive presentation of two tones results in the perception of a musical interval; and intervals whose components are separated by the same frequency ratio are perceived as being the same size. That is, tone pairs F_1 and F_2 and pairs F_3 and F_4 are perceived as equivalent when $\log F_1 - \log F_2 = \log F_3 - \log F_4$. This principle forms an important basis for the traditional musical scale. The smallest unit of this scale is the semitone, which represents a frequency ratio of approximately $18:17$; tone pairs that are separated by the same number of semitones are given the same name. Furthermore, although music in other cultures may involve intervals of different sizes, the perceptual equivalence of tone pairs that stand in the same frequency ratio appears to hold cross-culturally (Nettl, 1956a). Attneave and Olson (1971) made a careful study of transposition in a laboratory situation. They presented subjects with a simple melodic pattern, and then required them to reproduce this pattern in a different frequency range. It was found that when the subjects were able to draw on information that was well embedded in long-term memory, they clearly transposed on a log-frequency medium.

Chords of three or more tones are also classified on the basis of the frequency ratios of their components; those standing in the same frequency relationship are given the same name. However, this perceptual equivalence is not based simply on an identity in the set of the component intervals. For instance, a major triad and a minor triad sound quite different, yet both are composed of a major third, a minor third, and a fifth. However, these occur in a different order. In the major triad the major third lies below the minor third; in the minor triad the minor third lies below the major third. Deutsch (1969) proposed a model for interval and chord abstraction that accommodates this feature. This model assumes that such abstractions take place in two stages. At the first stage, units that respond to tones of specific pitch converge in groups of two or three onto the same second-order unit. Such second-order units then converge onto third-order units in such a way that all those activated by tonal combinations standing in the same pitch relationship are linked together. These third-order units therefore respond to intervals and chords irrespective of the pitches of their components.

Another shape-recognition operation is also performed in the case of simultaneous intervals and chords. When the components of such combinations are placed in different octaves, the combinations retain a perceptual similarity. This phenomenon is known in music as inversion. Thus, a simultaneous interval of n semitones is perceptually similar to a simultaneous interval of $12 - n$ semitones. Plomp, Wagenaar, and Mimpen (1973) provided evidence for this perceptual similarity in a laboratory situation. Subjects were required to identify intervals formed by simultaneous tone pairs, and it was found that confusions occurred between intervals that were inversions of each other. In another experiment by Deutsch and Roll (1974), subjects made pitch-comparison judgments when the tones to be compared were accompanied by tones of lower pitch. Misrecognition errors were quite pronounced when the standard and comparison tones differed, but the standard and comparison combinations formed identical intervals. Misrecognition errors were also found to increase significantly when the interval formed by the standard combination was an inversion of the interval formed by the comparison combination. It was concluded that the subjects were basing their false recognition judgments on the perceptual equivalence of the identical or inverted intervals.

3. Categorical Perception of Musical Intervals

As pointed out by Francès (1972), the perceptual elements of music in actual practice are not tones, but rather notes, which are generally very imprecisely emitted. In singing, and also in playing many musical instruments, notes are produced with a vibrato involving substantial frequency modulation. In one experiment, Francès (1972) found that the average range of vibrato for three professional singers was over a semitone. Furthermore, the average pitch of a note generated by voice or by natural instruments often changes during its presentation, and in passing from one note to another, glides through intervening frequencies are common. However, when we listen to music, we generally ignore these irregularities and instead form abstractions out of the tonal elements and the relationships between them. In one study, Burns and Ward (1973) required musicians to make identification and discrimination judgments involving musical intervals and found the same type of categorical perception as has been found for speech stimuli (Liberman, Cooper, Shankweiler, & Studdert-Kennedy, 1967). Similar results were obtained by Siegel and Sopo (1975).

There are various reasons why we should form relatively broad categories in perceiving tonal sequences. First, although the difference limen for pitch, as measured by comparing two pitches in isolation, is well below a semitone, this is drastically raised when the tones to be compared are separated by a sequence of intervening tones (Deutsch, 1970a). The formation of relatively broad categories may therefore be necessary in order for the listener to recognize repeated elements. Second, gross inaccuracies occur in emitting notes by voice and by many natural instruments, and such inaccuracies must be ignored if the listener is to identify repetitions. If this line of reasoning is correct, we should expect to find a certain minimum of interval size to occur cross-culturally. This is in fact the case. Nettl (1956a) concluded upon reviewing scales in primitive cultures that intervals smaller than a semitone are very rare. When such intervals do occur, this is almost always under specialized conditions, such as in ornamentation. For instance, the scale in Hindustani music is theoretically divided into 22 intervals (*shrutis*) to the octave. However, in actual practice, two tones separated by one *shruti* occur only under special circumstances (Bake, 1957). It is particularly interesting in this regard to find that professional Indian musicians, trained in Hindustani music, were unable to identify musical intervals with any more precision than Western musicians (Burns, 1974b), and indeed did not identify *shruti*s with any consistency in the laboratory.

Despite such broad categorization, there do appear to be preferred tunings in at least some musical situations. For a detailed discussion of tuning preferences, the reader is referred to Boomsliter and Creel (1963) and Ward (1970).

4. CONTOUR

The tonal information in a piece of music can also be described in global fashion; for instance, in terms of its range, the proportion and average size of ascending compared with descending intervals, the sequence of directions of pitch change, and so on. There is evidence that such global cues are used in recognizing music. Early psychologists, such as Werner (1925), showed that people could recognize familiar melodies when these were transformed onto very small scales, so that the actual intervals were grossly distorted in size. More recently, White (1960) required subjects to identify well-known melodies that were distorted in various ways. Some recognition was still obtained when all the intervals were set to one semitone, showing that we can recognize a melody on the basis of the sequence of directions of pitch change alone. However, performance was substantially improved when the relative sizes of the intervals were left unchanged, even though their absolute sizes were altered.

The importance of contour in short-term melody recognition is shown by the fact that in actual music, phrases are often repeated under transposition with distortions in the interval sizes but with contour intact (see Fig. 1). In an experiment by Dowling and Fujitani (1971), subjects made short-term recognition judgments involving transposed melodies. The subjects were very proficient at recognizing melodies that were either transposed, but identical, or where the contour alone was preserved. However, they appeared incapable of discriminating between exact transpositions and those that were merely preserved contour. Yet, when long-term memory for familiar tunes was tested instead, recognition on the basis of contour alone was quite unimpressive, so it appears that consolidation of memory for melodies acts on specific interval information, rather than on contour. This may be related to the finding by Attneave and Olson (1971) that some subjects showed considerable variability in transposing tonal sequences in a short-term memory situation, yet clearly transposed on a log-frequency continuum when they were given a highly overlearned sequence as the standard.

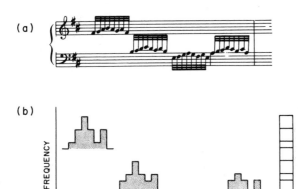

FIG. 1.   Transposition along the scalar alphabet. The same melodic configuration is presented four times in succession, at different positions along the scale. In consequence, there is a variation in the set of intervals involved. The sequence in musical notation is shown in (a). The sequence plotted as log frequency versus time is shown in (b). The ladder at the right shows the scale. [(a) From J. S. Bach, *The well-tempered clavier, Book I, Fugue V*. (b) From D. Deutsch, *Memory and attention in music*. In M. Critchley & R. A. Henson (Eds.). *Music and the Brain*. London: Heinemann Medical Books, Ltd., 1977. Reprinted by permission.]

B. Scales

In all cultures, tonal sequences are formed out of small, fairly well-defined sets of pitch relationships, which constitute their scale. For any given scale, one can also determine a mode (i.e., a set of a priori probabilities of occurrence for notes standing in different positions along the scale) and a set of *transitional* probabilities between the different notes. This is true both for linear successions of tones and also for harmonic sequences. In traditional Western harmony there are very strong *transitional* probabilities governing the root progressions of chords (Piston, 1948). As pointed out by Meyer (1956), the use of scales with strong a priori and transitional probabilities contributes substantially to the ease of musical processing, since it enables us to draw on highly overlearned information in listening to unfamiliar sequences.

C. Recognition of Tonal Sequences
under Various Transformations

The question of how well we recognize a tonal sequence when it has undergone a given transformation is analogous to asking how well a visual shape is recognized when it has been transformed in some way, such as changing its size or position in the visual field or converting it into its mirror image. Various types of transformation are used in actual music. Some of these are spontaneous, others are an intellectual exercise, and musicologists disagree widely on the perceptual equivalence of sequences transformed in various ways.

The case of transposition, where a sequence is presented in a different pitch range, is clear. Transposition occurs so readily in long-term recall that it is rare to be able to sing a melody in the same key after a certain amount of time has elapsed. Furthermore, the same sequence is often presented in transposed form within a given piece of music. This is true not only in Western cultivated music, but also in primitive music of other cultures (Nettl, 1956b). However, in this context transposition often takes place along the scalar alphabet, so that the relative positions of the elements along the scale are preserved, but the pitch relationships are in consequence distorted. Figure 1, for example, shows four presentations of a melodic sequence at different points along the scale, involving three different sets of pitch relationships.

Other transformations performed on linear tonal sequences are known as *inversion* and *retrogression*. In inversion (not to be confused with the harmonic use of the term), the directions of the melodic intervals are systematically reversed. That is, all ascending intervals become descending intervals, and vice versa. In traditional music, inversion generally leads to a change in the set of intervals, in order to preserve the set of elements along the scale. In retrogression, the sequence is played backward. This operation is used only rarely in traditional music (Piston, 1949; Tovey, 1957), and then generally with a change in the set of intervals.

Dowling (1972) has raised the possibility that sequences transformed by the operations of retrogression or inversion are recognized on the basis of their contour, rather than by abstracting their actual melodic intervals. He presented listeners first with a standard five-tone melody and then a comparison melody. The second melody was either unrelated to the first, an exact transposition of the first, or was transformed by the operation of inversion, retrogression, or retrograde inversion (a combination of the two). In a further set of conditions, the comparison sequence under these various transformations was further distorted so that its contour was preserved but the exact intervals were destroyed. Dowling found that although subjects could recognize a transformed sequence with better than chance accuracy, there was no evidence that they distinguished between transformations that preserved the intervals and those that preserved contour alone.

In another study, White (1960) investigated long-term recognition of melodies played in retrogression. He found that although subjects showed some recognition of such melodies, performance was at about the same level as when the melody was played in a monotone with the rhythmic information alone remaining. Even more interestingly, recognition was better for sequences where the intervals within the melody were randomly permuted than for straight temporal reversal. It would appear, therefore, that the subjects were identifying the reversed sequences on the basis of their component intervals alone, rather than on the ordering of these intervals.

A further transformation to consider involves an extension of the principle of octave equivalence to tonal sequences. One might assume that, because of the perceptual similarity of tones separated by octaves, a sequence would also remain perceptually equivalent if its components were placed in different octaves. This question has been experimentally investigated in a long-term memory situation. Deutsch (1972a) presented subjects with the first half of the tune "Yankee Doodle" under various conditions. This tune was universally recognized when presented in any one of three octaves. However, when the notes of the tune were chosen randomly from these same three octaves with the restriction that no two successive notes occurred as in the untransformed version, recognition was no better than when the sequence was played as a series of clicks with the pitch information removed but the rhythm retained. Dowling and Hollombe (1977) obtained similar results using several different tunes. They also found that leaving the melodic contour intact improved performance for subjects informed of the preservation of contour, though performance was still substantially worse than for the untransformed versions. This is in accordance with the evidence described above that contour alone can form a basis for melody recognition.

Deutsch (1972a) also found that when the listeners were informed of the indentity of the tune, they had no trouble in following the randomized-octaves version and confirming that each note was correctly placed within its octave. One can suppose that this was achieved by the subjects imagining the tune to themselves as they heard the randomized-octaves version and matching each note as it arrived with its octave equivalent. Thus, we would expect that recognition of a note when it is displaced to another octave would depend on the strength of expectation for this note. The operation could therefore be meaningfully performed, even using a new sequence, if the cognitive structure of the sequence was such that the displaced note was highly probable. Meyer (1973) has also argued that melodic processes are generally specific to a given octave, and that octave jumps should only be made under special conditions.

D. Hierarchical Organization

Human serially patterned behavior is characteristically organized in hierarchical fashion. In language, for instance, words are combined to form phrases, which in turn combine to form sentences, and so on. Similarly in music, notes are combined to form motives, which in turn form phrases, and these are themselves hierarchically structured.

Restle and Brown (1970) provide convincing evidence that such hierarchical organization of sequential elements is a general cognitive phenomenon. They presented subjects with a row of lights that turned on and off in repetitive succession. The subjects' task was to predict at each point which light would come on next. It was concluded from the speed with which different types of sequences were learned and also from the patterns of error at different points in a sequence that subjects approach this task by grouping the sequence into a series of chunks (in this case, runs and trills). Restle and Brown then constructed sequences in which such basic chunks were operated on by various rules such as repetition, transposition, and mirror-image reversal, so as to form higher-order chunks. These were in turn transformed by the same types of operations at several levels in such a way as to form structural trees. It was found that sequences structured in this fashion were learned substantially more easily than comparable sequences composed of the same subsequences but lacking this higher-level organization. Furthermore, most errors were found to occur at the highest-order transformations, with the probability of error decreasing as the level of transformation along the tree decreased.

As Restle and Brown (1970) point out, such trees in actual music would have to be substantially more complex than those used in these experiments. For one thing, music involves more than one basic theme. Also, various other operations occur in music, such as interspersing of sequences, and Restle (1973) has demonstrated that subjects can indeed process interspersed sequences in the light-switching task. Furthermore, transposition in a tonal system can involve either shifting the sequence along the scale, or shifting the entire range of the scale, which entails a flexibility of alphabet. In modulating from major to minor there is also a change in alphabet, as is also the case with deviations from the diatonic scale (for instance, to the chromatic scale, or to an alphabet based on an arpeggio). Indeed, different alphabets are often used at different levels of transformation.

An additional complexity lies in the fact that cultivated music involves the presentation of more than one sequence of tones at a time, so that more than one tree structure must be operating simultaneously in processing such music. Furthermore, the harmonic sequences produced by simultaneous tonal combinations are also hierarchically structured, so the choice of notes in each linear row must be such as to satisfy these harmonic requirements as well. Listening to cultivated music must therefore involve parallel processing along several such structural trees (see also Winograd, 1968; Deutsch, 1977).

III. THE FORMATION OF PERCEPTUAL CONFIGURATIONS

When we listen to music, we do not simply process each element as it arrives; rather, we form sequential groupings out of combinations of elements. Once such groupings are formed, there is further a tendency for one to come to the foreground of our attention, while others are relegated to the background. The stability of such figure–ground organization depends on the type of music presented. Thus in some music, such as accompanied songs, one voice tends strongly to be heard as the figure and the other as the ground. In contrast, in contrapuntal music, such as canons and fugues, we attempt as much as possible to attend to all voices, which results in our fluctuating between alternative modes of figure–ground organization.

A. Groupings Based on Pitch Range

The principles governing the formation of perceptual configurations in music may be compared with those in vision (Wertheimer, 1923). One important factor is the law of proximity, especially as applied to frequency range. Thus, when a solo instrument plays a melody and an accompaniment, these are generally in different frequency ranges. Similarly, in contrapuntal music, each voice has its own range. An interesting musical technique that takes advantage of this perceptual tendency is known as *pseudopolyphony*. Here a sequence of notes drawn from two different ranges is played in rapid succession, with the result that the listener perceives two melodic lines in parallel. Examples of such music are shown in Fig. 2.

A number of investigators have studied the perception of rapid sequences of tones as a function of their frequency disparity. Miller and Heise (1950) presented sequences of two alternating tones at a rate of 10 sec^{-1}. They found that when the frequencies of these tones differed by less than 15%, listeners perceived a single string of related tones (i.e., a trill). However, with an increase in the frequency disparity between the alternating tones the sequence was heard as two interrupted and unrelated tones. Heise and Miller (1951) explored this phenomenon in sequences consisting of several tonal frequencies and found that if one of the tones was sufficiently different from the others it was heard in isolation, as though emanating from a different sound source. Van Noorden (1975) studied the effect of different rates of presentation on this phenomenon. He found that when subjects were trying to hear the sequence as coherent, decreasing the presentation rate from 50 to 150 msec for each tone enabled coherence to be heard at substantially larger values of frequency separation. However, when subjects were trying to hear two separate streams, changing the presentation rate had very little effect on performance.

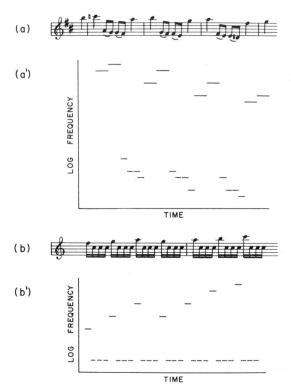

FIG. 2. The grouping of melodic stimuli by frequency proximity. In Sequence (a) we hear two parallel melodies, each in a different frequency range. In Sequence (b) a single pitch is repetitively presented in the lower range, and this forms a ground against which the melody in the upper range is heard. Parts (a) and (b) illustrate the sequences in musical notation. The same sequences plotted as log frequency versus time are shown in (a') and (b'). [(a) From G. P. Telemann, *Capriccio for recorder and basso continuo*. (b) From G. P. Telemann, *Sonata in C major for recorder and basso continuo*. (a') and (b') From Musical illusions, D. Deutsch. Copyright © 1975 by *Scientific American*, Inc. All rights reserved.]

Dowling (1973b) performed an experiment to investigate the effect of frequency disparity on the perception of interleaved melodies. He presented the notes of two well-known melodies alternately at a rate of 8 sec^{-1}, and found that recognition of these melodies was very difficult when their pitch ranges overlapped. Recognition became increasingly easy as one of the melodies was transposed, so that the ranges of the two melodies gradually diverged.

Bregman and Campbell (1971) investigated this question from another point of view. They presented sequences of tones at a rate of 10 sec^{-1} that alternated between two widely different pitch ranges. They found that listeners had considerable difficulty in perceiving the order of tones in such sequences, though this problem did not arise when the tones were close in pitch. They concluded that the higher and lower tones formed separate perceptual streams, and that at rapid presentation rates order relationships cannot be formed across the two streams.

The principle of grouping tonal stimuli by frequency range is also apparent in a dichotic listening situation. Deutsch (1975a,d) presented subjects with a major scale that was played simultaneously in both ascending and descending form, switching from ear to ear in such a way that when a note from the ascending scale was in one ear, a note from the descending scale was in the other, and vice versa. Most subjects perceived this sequence as two separate melodic lines, a higher one and a lower one, moving in contrary motion. Furthermore, there was a strong tendency to hear all the higher tones as emanating from one earphone, and all the lower tones as emanating from the other. The remaining subjects perceived the higher melodic line, but heard little or nothing of the lower. So for all subjects this dichotic sequence was grouped perceptually by frequency range.

As a further manifestation of the law of proximity as applied to frequency range, there is a strong tendency for the frequency of occurrence of a melodic interval to be inversely correlated with its size. This has been found true in very different types of music, including Western cultivated music (Fucks, 1962; Ortmann, 1926), current popular music (Jeffries, 1974), and the music of various primitive cultures (Merriam, 1964). Figure 3 shows the relative occurrence of melodic intervals as a function of their size in these different types of music, and it can be seen that the plots exhibit a striking similarity.

B. Groupings Based on Timbre

Timbre is often used as a marker or carrier of sequential configurations (Erickson, 1975). In the music of composers such as Haydn, Mozart, and Beethoven, adjacent phrases are often played by different instruments, which helps to delimit the structure of the composition. Furthermore, over-

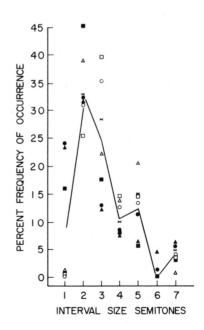

FIG. 3.   Relative frequencies of occurrence of melodic intervals in the music of various cultures. Open circles represent Gêge (Dahomean-derived music of Brazil); open triangles represent Ketu (Yoruba-derived music of Brazil); open squares represent Rada (Dahomean-derived music of Trinidad); crosses represent Cheyenne Indian music; filled circles represent Romantic lieder; filled triangles represent a J. S. Bach orchestral part; and filled squares represent current popular songs. [Adapted in large part from Dowling (1967); data from Merriam (1964), Ortmann (1926), Fucks (1962), and Jeffries (1974).]

PERCENT FREQUENCY OF OCCURRENCE

INTERVAL SIZE SEMITONES

laps in pitch range between figure and ground are far more common when more than one instrument is involved. The formation of separate perceptual streams out of sounds of different timbre is also manifest in the finding that listeners have extreme difficulty in identifying the order of repetitive sequences of unrelated sounds (Warren, 1974; Warren & Obusek, 1972; Warren, Obusek, Farmer, & Warren, 1969).

C. Good Continuation

Divenyi and Hirsh (1974, 1975) provide evidence for the law of good continuation in the perception of rapid sequences of tones. They found that when subjects were required to identify the temporal order of three tones presented in rapid succession, identification was easier for sequences where the frequency change was unidirectional. The addition of a fourth tone generally had the effect of decreasing identifiability; however, performance was best when the fourth tone represented a continuation of a unidirectional frequency range. A related finding was obtained by Van Noorden (1975), who studied the minimum interval between successive components of three-tone sequences necessary to observe temporal coherence between the tones at various presentation rates. He found that for unidirectional three-tone sequences, temporal coherence was observed at rates of pitch change that were either equal to or higher than those necessary for two-tone sequences. However, for bidirectional three-tone sequences, the rate of pitch change had to be set considerably lower before coherence was perceived.

IV. RHYTHM AND TEMPO

A. Rhythmic Organization

When presented with a regular sequence of identical sounds, the listener will spontaneously organize these into subsequences, each consisting of an accented element followed by one or more unaccented elements. Such subjective organization occurs at presentation rates ranging from about 10 sec^{-1} to .5 sec^{-1}, and appears to be optimal at rates of 2 or 3 sec^{-1} (Fraisse, 1956; Vos, 1973). As Fraisse points out, this correlates well with the distribution of melodic tempos in the cultivated music of our tradition. Indeed, tempo, as measured by the number of consecutive notes per unit time, appears to be distributed within this range in widely divergent cultures (Kolinski, 1959). The distributions of tempos in two cultures that are held to differ markedly on this measure are shown in Fig. 4.

Spontaneous rhythmic groupings are often formed simultaneously at more than one structural level (Woodrow, 1951; Vos, 1973). Thus, we may hear groups of four elements with the major accent on the first and a minor accent

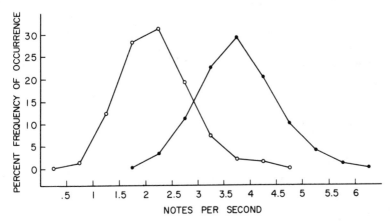

FIG. 4. Relative frequencies of occurrence of tempos in the songs of two cultures that diverge extremely in their average tempos. Open circles represent Dahomean songs, and filled circles represent North American Indian songs. Note that the shapes of the two distributions are remarkably similar and that the total range covered coincides with the range over which spontaneous rhythmic groupings are formed (see text). [Adapted from Kolinski (1959).]

on the third, or groups of eight elements with the major accent on the first and a minor accent on the fifth. This indicates that the mechanism underlying rhythmic grouping is hierarchical in nature. Further evidence has been provided in an experiment by Perkins (1974). He asked subjects to estimate the number of taps in sequences where the first of every 4 taps was stressed and the first of every 16 was doubly stressed. He found that errors differed from the correct responses more frequently by multiples of 4 and 16 than by adjacent numbers and concluded that the subjects were organizing the sequences hierarchically in accordance with the imposed accents. In another experiment, Sturges and Martin (1974) presented subjects with continuous sequences of 14 or 16 binary elements. These were either seven- or eight-element patterns repeated once, or patterns that were changed slightly on repetition; the subjects' task was to recognize sequences containing exact repetitions. They found that patterns that exhibited a simple hierarchical structure were better recognized than others and that eight-element patterns so structured were better recognized than seven-element patterns, even though they contained more items.

In actual music, it is clear that rhythm is hierarchically structured (Cooper & Meyer, 1960). However, such organization may be very complex. For instance, groupings at different levels often consist of different numbers of elements, and even at the same level groupings containing different numbers of elements may be presented in succession. Simultaneous polyrhythms also occur; however, these are very difficult for a single individual to generate. (The reader may try tapping a repetitive pattern consisting of three equally spaced beats with one hand and, simultaneously, four equally spaced beats with the other.) The precise reason for this difficulty is unclear, but the problem seems to lie in dividing a time period simultaneously into overlapping segments. In actual practice, the individual components of simultaneous polyrhythms are most often produced by different people, who need listen to each other only intermittently. It may well be that such music is perceived in a fashion analogous to ambiguous figures in vision, where only one of two alternative organizations is perceived at a time, and the viewer alternates between the two alternatives.

A number of factors are involved in perceiving rhythmic structure. Temporal separation plays a very powerful role (Handel, 1973; Restle, 1972). A second factor is accent. An element that is marked for attention in some way, such as by differing from its neighbors in pitch, loudness, duration, or timbre is heard as accented and combines with adjacent elements to form a group. (However, if an element differs too strongly from its neighbors, it dissociates itself instead [Miller & Heise, 1950].) Furthermore, a set of elements standing in a particular relationship will be grouped together, such as a run of identical elements (Garner, 1974) or similar elements. Groupings will also be formed depending on the abstract structure of the sequence (Simon & Sumner, 1968).

Rhythmic patterning has a powerful influence on perception of the tonal structure of a sequence. First, the formation of subsequences divides the information in manageable chunks, and so facilitates the perception of relationships within each chunk. In one experiment, Dowling (1973c) presented subjects with four five-note phrases that were separated by pauses. Subjects were then required to recognize a five-note test item that corresponded either to one of the phrases or to the last three notes of one phrase and the first two notes of the next. Recognition was better for items that corresponded to separate phrases than for items that crossed phrase boundaries, showing that the information was organized in accordance with the temporally determined phrase structure.

Second, such patterning is important in perceiving higher-order tonal relationships between subsequences. In music, a phrase is often repeated under some transformation with the rhythm intact. Here the corresponding elements of the two phrases stand in identical rhythmic relationship to their neighboring elements. This one-to-one correspondence of the rhythmic position of each element serves to enhance perception of the tonal correspondence. An example of such rhythmic "tagging" is shown in Fig. 5.

Accent provides another important function. Restle and Brown (1970) have shown that when a sequence of unaccented elements forms a structural tree, errors in learning increase monotonically with the level of transformation on the tree. Thus, in the absence of accent, higher-order relationships are perceived with difficulty. However, if the first element of each group is accented, perceptual relationships between these elements is enhanced, and this results in better perception of the higher-order structure. Indeed, a

FIG. 5. In rhythmic tagging, the same (a)
melodic configuration is presented twice
at different positions along the scale, with
the same sequence of durations. Thus,
each element is tagged by its rhythmic
position in the sequence, and the corresponding elements of the two phrases are
tagged identically. (a) The sequence in (b)
musical notation. (b) The sequence plotted as log frequency versus time. [From
W. A. Mozart, *Sonata XVI in A major*.]

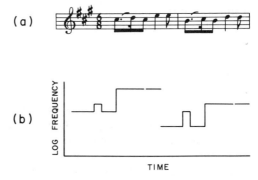

common musical technique is to present a sequence consisting of accented
elements interspersed with unaccented elements. In this way the accented
elements provide the figure and the unaccented elements provide the
ground, yet unitary subgroups are still formed out of accented combined with
unaccented elements.

B. Psychophysical Measurements

When listeners are required to make discrimination judgments involving
time intervals between sound pairs, varying results are obtained depending
on the stimulus conditions. Thus, with a standard interval that varied randomly between .63 and 640 msec, a just noticeable difference (jnd) of 40
msec was obtained at a standard of 100 msec (Abel, 1972). However, with
the standard interval fixed at 100 msec, a jnd of 5 msec was obtained instead
(Van Noorden, 1975). Michon (1964) required subjects to discriminate the
tempos of sequences of regularly presented clicks. Plotting the results as
Weber fractions, he found two maxima of sensitivity; one at an interval of
110 msec with $\Delta t/t$ of about .01, and the other at an interval of about 600
msec with $\Delta t/t$ of about .02.

A further interesting question concerns the detection of rhythmic irregularity in a sound sequence. Lunney (1974) asked subjects to adjust the
temporal position of every fourth in a sequence of metronome pulses that
were otherwise isochronous, so that a rhythmic irregularity was just detected. Repetition rates ranging from 30 to 3200 msec were explored, and
sensitivity was found to decrease exponentially with the duration of the
interval between repetitions. At a repetition rate of 100 msec, a jnd of 3–4
msec was obtained. Van Noorden (1975) studied the effect of frequency
disparity on detection of rhythmic irregularity in a sequence of alternating
tones. He found that sensitivity at high repetition rates was markedly reduced as the alternating tones diverged in frequency. This study may be
related to an earlier finding by Divenyi and Hirsh (1972) that discrimination

of the size of the temporal gap between a tone pair deteriorates with increasing pitch separation between members of the pair.

V. MEMORY

It is clear that memory for music must involve a large set of parallel systems that differ widely in their characteristics. Such systems include those retaining values along unidimensional acoustic continua, those retaining features formed from combinations of such values, and those involved in abstract cognitive activity. These systems must differ widely in the persistence with which they retain information. We know from general considerations that memory for certain relationships between values of an acoustic attribute persists much longer than memory for the absolute values themselves. Thus we can recognize a melody or a harmonic sequence when it is transposed to a different key, and, provided sufficient time has elapsed, we generally have difficulty in determining whether a key change has occurred. Here the absolute pitch information is lost, and recognition can be based only on the abstracted relationships (Attneave & Olson, 1971; Deutsch, 1969). Similarly, durational relationships are abstracted to produce rhythmic patterns, and these are easily recognized when played in a different tempo. However, certain complex acoustic stimuli deteriorate rapidly in memory (Guttman & Julesz, 1963; Pollack, 1972).

One question of importance concerns the nature of the influences acting on musical information in storage. This has been studied in detail in the case of tonal pitch. Deutsch (1970a) has shown that memory for pitch is not subject simply to general factors, such as attention distraction or capacity limitation, in a system that is either indifferent to the kind of information it holds or that retains any type of acoustic information. Subjects compared two tones for pitch when these were separated by a retention interval during which certain other acoustic stimuli were presented. It was found that a severe impairment of performance resulted from interpolating a sequence of six tones, even though the subjects were asked to ignore them. However, only a minimal impairment occurred when six spoken numbers were interpolated instead, even when the subjects were asked to recall the numbers in addition to making the pitch-comparison judgment.

Further studies have shown that the system retaining pitch information is precisely and systematically organized. Deutsch (1972b) required subjects to compare the pitch of two test tones that were separated by a sequence of six interpolated tones. In the second serial position of the intervening sequence was placed a tone whose pitch bore a critical relationship to the first test tone. This relationship varied in equal steps of one-sixth of a tone between identity and a whole-tone separation. It was found that when the critical interpolated tone was identical in pitch to the first test tone, memory facilitation occurred. Errors rose progressively as the pitch difference between these tones increased, peaked at a separation of two-thirds of a tone, and then returned to baseline. Thus, a specific disruptive effect was demonstrated, which varied as a function of the log-frequency difference between the first test tone and the critical interpolated tone.

This specific disruptive effect was further explored using critical interpolated tones that were a semitone removed from the first test tone. It was found that the inclusion in the intervening sequence of two critical tones, one a semitone higher than the first test tone and the other a semitone lower, produced a significantly greater increase in errors than the inclusion of only one critical tone. (Deutsch, 1973a). Furthermore, the size of this disruptive effect was found to be constant whether the critical intervening tone was placed in the second or in the fifth serial position of a sequence of six intervening tones (Deutsch, 1975b).

Given these findings, Deutsch and Feroe (1975) have put forward a specific model of the organization of pitch memory. They propose the existence of a memory array whose elements are activated by tones of specific pitch. These elements are spaced along the array so that elements activated by tones separated by the same distance in log-frequency units are separated by the same distance along the array. It was further assumed that these elements are linked as a recurrent lateral inhibitory network, analogous to those investigated in systems processing incoming sensory information. Evidence for lateral inhibitory interactions in the auditory system has been obtained at the psychophysical level by Carterette, Friedman, Lovell (1969) and Houtgast (1972). At the neurophysiological level, evidence for both peripherally and centrally acting lateral inhibition has also been found (Klinke, Boerger, & Gruber, 1969; Sachs & Kiang, 1968). Indeed, the relative frequency range over which centrally acting lateral inhibition has been plotted corresponds well with that for the present interactive effect.

This hypothesis was given further strong support from an experiment demonstrating disinhibition in pitch memory (Deutsch & Feroe, 1975). In this experiment, subjects were required to compare two tones for pitch when these were separated by a sequence of six intervening tones. In the second serial position of the intervening sequence was placed a tone that was two-thirds of a tone removed from the first test tone. Errors were then plotted as a function of the pitch of a further tone, placed in the fourth serial position, whose relationship to the tone in the second serial position varied in steps of one-sixth of a tone from identity to a whole-tone separation. As shown in Fig. 6, the curve produced was roughly the inverse of the curve plotting the original disruptive effect. Furthermore, in cases where the tone in the fourth serial position was two-thirds of a tone removed from the tone in the second serial position, errors were significantly lower than in the baseline condition, where the tone in the fourth serial position was outside the critical range. As a further test of the disinhibition hypothesis, a baseline

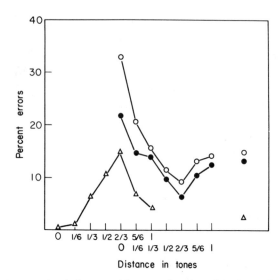

FIG. 6. Percent errors in pitch recognition as a function of various relationships within a tonal sequence. Subjects made pitch-comparison judgments between two tones that were separated by a sequence of interpolated tones. Open triangles display percent errors as a function of the pitch relationship between the first test tone and a critical interpolated tone. (Open triangle at right shows percent errors where no tones were interpolated within the critical range under study.) Filled circles display percent errors in the experiment where a tone that was two-thirds of a tone removed from the first test tone was always interpolated. Errors are plotted as a function of the pitch relationship between this tone and a second critical interpolated tone, which was farther removed along the pitch continuum. Open circles display percent errors for the same experimental conditions predicted theoretically. (Filled and open circles at right show percent errors obtained experimentally and assumed theoretically where no further critical tone was interpolated.) [From D. Deutsch & J. Feroe, Disinhibition in pitch memory, *Perception & Psychophysics*, **17**, 320–324. Copyright 1975 by the Psychonomic Society, Inc. Reprinted by permission.]

curve for the first-order inhibitory effect was obtained using subjects selected on the same criterion as for the disinhibition experiment. These parameters were then used to plot the theoretical disinhibition function. As is also shown in Fig. 6, there was a very good correspondence between the theoretical function and that produced experimentally.

In sequences where the test tones differed in pitch, a further disruptive effect could also be demonstrated. If a tone of the same pitch as the second test tone was included in the intervening sequence, there resulted a substantial increase in errors of misrecognition (Deutsch, 1970b, 1972c). The error rate for such sequences was substantially higher than for sequences including a tone that was also a semitone removed from the first test tone but on the opposite side of the pitch continuum (Deutsch, 1973a). This misrecognition effect was also highly sensitive to the serial position of the repeated tone, being substantially more pronounced when this tone was placed in the second serial position of a sequence of six interpolated tones than when it was placed in the fifth serial position. It has been argued on these and other grounds that this disruptive effect is due to deterioration of information along a temporal, or order, continuum (Deutsch, 1972c, 1975b).

In a further study, specific disruptive effects in pitch memory were found to generalize from one octave to another (Deutsch, 1973b). The amount of generalization varied depending on the octave in which the critical interpolated tones were placed. The disruptive effects from tones that were displaced to a higher octave were greater than from tones displaced to a lower octave. From an analysis of the pattern of errors it was concluded that these disruptive effects took place along both a tone-height and a tone-chroma array.

Memory for pitch in a sequential setting is also subject to consolidation effects (Deutsch, 1975c). When the first test tone is repeated among the interpolated tones, there results a reduction in errors, even when compared with sequences containing a smaller number of interpolated tones. This improvement in performance is highly sensitive to the serial position of the repeated tone, being substantial and highly significant when this tone occurs early in the intervening sequence, but small and insignificant when it occurs late in the sequence.

When we consider absolute levels of performance, pitch memory in a sequential setting is found to be remarkably poor (Deutsch, 1970a; Pollack, 1952, 1964). This emphasizes the involvement of additional memory systems in processing tonal information. For instance, memory for abstracted tonal relationships plays an important role, and this has not been systematically studied as yet. Furthermore, the use of scales with strong a priori and transitional probabilities enables us to draw on information embedded in long-term memory in a short-term context also. Francès (1972) and Zenatti (1969) have shown that short-term recognition of melodies is superior for melodies that are in our tonal system than for those that violate this system. Furthermore, Miller and Cuddy (1972) have demonstrated that recognition of a tonal sequence that is preceded and followed by other tones is improved when the context tones establish a tonality. In music involving harmonic sequences, the strong transitional probabilities between root progressions further reduce the processing load. In addition, if music has a strong abstract structure (Restle, 1970; Simon & Sumner, 1968), the information can be retrieved by reference to this structure.

VI. TIMBRE PERCEPTION

The perception of timbre is a highly complex phenomenon that is, at present, little understood. Timbre is generally defined as that attribute by which two tones can be distinguished from each other when they are equal in pitch, loudness, and duration. Clearly, this definition is consistent with an enormous range of phenomena.

A. Steady-State Tones

Classically, investigations into timbre have been concerned with tones in the steady state. Helmholtz (1954) proposed that differences in the timbre of complex tones depended on the strength of their various harmonics. He concluded that simple tones sounded pleasant though dull at low frequencies, complex tones with moderately loud lower harmonics sounded richer but still pleasant, complex tones with strong upper harmonics sounded rough and sharp, and complex tones consisting only of odd harmonics sounded hollow. Helmholtz further asserted that the timbre of complex tones was affected little if at all by differences in phase relations between the partials. Plomp and Steeneken (1969) investigated this question and concluded that the maximum effect of phase on timbre was indeed very small; in fact, quantitatively smaller than the effect of changing the slope of the amplitude pattern by 2 dB per octave.

Other experiments by Plomp and his collaborators have demonstrated the importance of the critical band in timbre perception. Plomp (1964) and Plomp and Mimpen (1968) found that the number of partials that could be distinguished was limited to the lower five to seven harmonics, depending on the frequency of the fundamental. The higher harmonics, falling within the same critical band, could not be distinguished from each other. Furthermore, Plomp (1970) examined perceptual similarities between pairs of complex tones. For each tone the amplitude pattern of the waveform was quantified by taking the intensity levels for 18 consecutive one-third octave filters, corresponding to critical bands. Differences between the tone pairs were then computed by summing the differences in intensity levels for the 18 consecutive filters, so that the tones were placed as points in an 18-dimensional space. Using the multidimensional scaling technique, he found a good correlation between the perceptual similarities taken from subjects' ratings and the physical differences as determined by this method.

One issue of importance concerns whether timbral quality is based on the relationship between the frequency region of a formant and its fundamental or on the absolute level of the formant, irrespective of the fundamental frequency. Some musical instruments, such as the violin and the bassoon, have spectrum envelopes that are fixed in frequency (Fransson, 1966; Jansson, 1966). On the other hand, the spectral maxima of the flute change in proportion to changes in the frequency of the fundamental (Miller, 1916). Examination of the spectra of musical instruments therefore produces ambiguous expectations. Slawson (1968) asked subjects to make similarity judgments between pairs of complex tones whose fundamental frequencies, two lower formant frequencies, and higher formant frequencies were independently varied. With the fundamental frequency of the second tone of each pair an octave above the first, Slawson found timbral quality to be best preserved when the two lower formants were transposed by about 10% of the transposition of the fundamental. This result therefore supports a modified fixed-formant model of timbre perception. Furthermore, Plomp and Steeneken (1971) presented pulse trains through filters having different center frequencies. They found that tones filtered at fixed frequencies were judged as substantially more similar than tones filtered at frequencies relative to their pulse rates. These authors concluded that timbre was derived from the absolute position of the envelope of the frequency spectrum.

B. Tones Generated by Natural Instruments

With tones generated by natural instruments, temporal characteristics have been found to be very important determinants of timbre (Risset & Matthews, 1969). Traditionally, such tones have been held to consist of three temporal segments: (a) the attack, which includes the initial transient; (b) the steady state; and (c) the decay. Various studies have demonstrated that the attack segment is of particular importance (Berger, 1964; Goude, 1972; Grey, 1975; Saldanha & Corso, 1964; Wessel, 1974). Identification of the steady-state portion has been found to be superior for tones with vibrato (Saldanha & Corso, 1964). The decay portion appears to be of little importance (Saldanha & Corso, 1964). Risset (1966) made a careful study of the perceptual properties of trumpet tones, and concluded that three features were particularly significant: (a) the relationships between the attack times of the different harmonics, with successively higher harmonics taking longer to appear; (b) the low-amplitude, fast-frequency fluctuations; and (c) the harmonic content, including stronger high-frequency components with increases in overall intensity.

Interest has developed in plotting perceptual similarities between different instruments in a multidimensional timbral space. Carterette and Miller (1974) and Miller and Carterette (1975) have shown that such timbral spaces are related to musical training in a complex fashion. In an experiment where fundamental frequency was one of the dimensions varied, no differences were found between musical and nonmusical subjects, due to the overwhelming salience of this dimension. However, when fundamental frequency was held constant so that harmonic and envelope structure were used in judgments, differences between musical and nonmusical subjects emerged. Wessel (1973), studying tones of the same fundamental frequency and duration which were taken from nine orchestral instruments, concluded that these could be arranged along two perceptual dimensions. The first dimension related to the distribution of energy in the steady-state region of the spectrum. Tones with more high-frequency energy appeared at one end of the scale, and those with energy concentrated in the lower harmonics at the other end. The second dimension related to the onset patterns of the tones. Tones whose low-order harmonics entered more rapidly appeared at one end of the scale, and those whose high-order harmonics entered more rapidly appeared at the other. Grey (1975) studied 16 instrumental tones that were resynthesized by computer, and equated for pitch, loudness, and duration. He concluded that subjects' similarity ratings were consistent with a three-dimensional solution. The first dimension related to the spectral energy distribution of the tones: At one extreme, the tones had narrow bandwidths and a concentration of low-frequency energy; at the other extreme the tones had a wide bandwidth and less concentration of energy in the lower harmonics. The second dimension related to the distribution of energy in the attack segment: At one extreme, tones displayed high-frequency, low-amplitude energy (most often, inharmonic energy) in this segment. At the other extreme, there was no high-frequency precedent energy in the attack. The third dimension was given two alternative interpretations: It was considered either to relate to the form of onset–offset patterns of the tones, especially to the amount of synchronicity in the attacks and decays of the upper harmonics, or, alternatively, to represent a cognitive dimension along which stimuli were grouped according to instrumental family (strings, brass, and woodwinds).

In a recent set of experiments, Cutting and Rosner (1974) and Cutting, Rosner, and Foard (1976) have found that timbre based on rise time differences is categorically perceived. Sawtooth sounds of rapid onset sound as though coming from a plucked string, and those of slower onset from a bowed one. Discrimination of such sounds as "pluck" or "bow" was good across categorical boundaries, but poor within a category. Further, prolonged exposure to one such stimulus caused a shift in the rise time boundary between categories, analogous to shifts found in perception of speech sounds.

VII. MUSICAL PREFERENCES

A comprehensive discussion of musical preferences is outside the scope of the present chapter, and the reader is referred to Meyer (1956), Farnsworth (1958), Pratt (1968), and Berlyne (1971) for reviews of the question. Considerable discussion has centered on whether such preferences are innate or culturally determined, and it would appear that a position at either extreme is untenable. Farnsworth (1958) pointed out that many differences in the musical styles of different cultures. On the other hand, certain universal tendencies, such as a general range of tempo (see Fig. 4), a spectrum of probability of occurrence for different melodic intervals (see Fig. 3), octave duplications in harmony, and so on, have also been demonstrated. So it would seem that music is subject to universal laws, but is also subject to cultural variation within the framework imposed by these laws.

Interest has developed in the relationship of various stimulus parameters to aesthetic preference. Such studies have shown, as might be expected, that people tend to prefer intermediate values along a given stimulus dimension and reject the extremes. Vitz (1972) observed that preference for pure tones varied as a U-shaped function of frequency, with the most preferred tones ranging from 400 to 750 Hz. A similar function was obtained for tonal intensity, with the most preferred intensity at around 50 dB. We would also expect, as argued by Attneave (1959), that aesthetic preferences for tonal sequences differing in amount of uncertainty or complexity would be optimal at some level intermediate between homogeneity and chaos. Indeed, such U-shaped functions have been obtained (Berlyne, 1971). Interestingly, such preferences have also been shown to interact with the emotional state of the listener. In an experiment by Konecni, Crozier, and Doob (1976) subjects were made angry by a confederate, and then were given either a chance to administer what they thought to be electric shocks to this person, or were given no such opportunity. A control group of subjects received neither treatment. All subjects then listened to tonal sequences and chose between sequences of differing complexity. It was found that the angered subjects who had no opportunity to retaliate chose the simple sequences more often than either the controls or the angered subjects who had been seemingly able to hurt their annoyer. There was no significant difference in preference between the latter two groups. In a further experiment, Konecni (1975) demonstrated that listening to such sequences when emotionally aroused had specific effects on subsequent social behavior. Subjects were either angered by a confederate or were treated neutrally. Some subjects then listened to tonal sequences that varied in loudness and complexity, and a control group of subjects listened to no sequences. All subjects were then given an opportunity to administer apparent electric shocks to a confederate. It was found that the behavior of the angered subjects was affected by the nature of the sequences they had heard. Those exposed to loud or complex sequences administered considerably more shocks than those exposed to no sequences; however, those exposed to simple and soft sequences administered fewer shocks than the controls. In contrast, there was no effect of the sequences on the behavior of subjects who had not been angered. These two experiments demonstrate an important link between aesthetic preference and social interaction.

VIII. NEUROLOGICAL SUBSTRATES

The neurological substrates of music are, at present, poorly defined. We know, however, that they are not identical with those of speech. In Broca's aphasia, verbal output is grossly impaired, yet the patient can generally sing without difficulty (Geschwind, 1969). Indeed, there are several reports of professional musicians whose work remained outstanding in spite of severe aphasia. Critchley (1953) mentioned the case of a severely aphasic patient who conducted his own orchestra. Luria, Tsvetkova, and Futer (1965) described a distinguished composer who, after being struck with severe aphasia, continued to produce compositions that won him the highest acclaim. If we also consider that singing ability may be lost without concomitant aphasia (Brain, 1965), we must conclude that speech and music involve specialized brain regions. This does not, however, imply a total dissociation between the substrates for these two functions, which are both highly complex and may well share common elements. The evidence simply demonstrates that there are unique regions essential to each.

Most authors agree that the temporal lobes are involved in music perception. Lesions of the temporal lobe, particularly of the anterior temporal region, have been found to produce sensory amusia (Henschen, 1926; Luria, 1966; Milner, 1962; Wertheim, 1963). Furthermore, reports of sounds such as buzzing, humming, and even complex music are evoked by temporal-lobe stimulation (Penfield & Rasmussen, 1968). In contrast to music perception, musical expression involves the motor system, and expressive amusia has been found to result from damage to a variety of brain regions (Luria, 1966; Wertheim, 1963).

Considerable interest has focused on the question of hemispheric specialization and musical function, and here again it is necessary to distinguish between musical expression and musical perception.

Musical expression, as opposed to speech, does not require the presence of the dominant hemisphere. After dominant hemispherectomy, patients have been found to retain their singing ability (Gott, 1973; Smith, 1966). However, musical expression does not require the presence of the nondominant hemisphere, either, as patients with their nondominant hemisphere removed can also sing without difficulty (Smith, personal communication). In one study, Gorden and Bogen (1974) compared the relative roles of the two hemispheres in singing, using the technique of intracarotid injection of sodium amylobarbitone (which produces a transient inactivation of the hemisphere on the side of the injection). Injection in the right carotid artery produced marked deficits in singing, although speech remained relatively intact. After injection in the left carotid, singing was less disturbed than speech. The authors argue from these findings that whereas speech production is overwhelmingly a function of the dominant hemisphere, the nondominant hemisphere plays a more prominent role in singing. It was noted, however, that after injection in the right carotid the patients recognized their own singing efforts as poor and were able to recognize songs sung by the examiner. Inactivation of the nondominant hemisphere did not, therefore, appear to produce deficits in music perception. The relationship of these findings to the findings resulting from hemispherectomy still needs to be explored.

The evidence on hemispheric specialization in music perception is quite complex. From observations on patients with sensory amusia, the dominant hemisphere has generally been implicated to a larger extent than the nondominant (Henschen, 1926; Kleist, 1962; Wertheim, 1963), though lesions of the nondominant hemisphere have also been found to produce impairment (Bogen, 1969; Luria, 1966). Studies involving specific musical attributes have also produced varying results. Thus Milner (1962) administered the Seashore Tests of Musical Talents to patients before and after unilateral temporal lobectomy. Removal of the anterior temporal region of the nondominant side produced significant deficits in the ability to discriminate tonal quality and in the ability to identify which member of a tonal sequence was altered on second presentation. These deficits were not found with lesions of the dominant side. Furthermore, Shankweiler (1966) found that the ability to recognize 4-sec excerpts from instrumental chamber music was selectively impaired by lesions of the right temporal lobe, but not of the left temporal lobe. Vignolo (1969) has reported that patients with lesions of the nondominant hemisphere showed deficits in discriminating sound quality. On the other hand, lesions of the dominant hemisphere (rather than the nondominant) have been found to produce deficits in tasks involving judgments of temporal order (Carmon & Nachshon, 1971; Efron, 1963; Swisher & Hirsh, 1972) and rhythm (Luria, 1966; Subzinski, 1969).

These findings indicate that different musical attributes might be handled predominantly in different hemispheres. In particular, it seems that the nondominant hemisphere predominates in processing the quality of musical sounds, whereas the dominant hemisphere predominates in processing sequential relationships. This conclusion receives further support from dichotic listening studies. A left-ear advantage has been noted in right-handed persons with respect to recognizing auditory materials of complex sound quality, such as melodies generated by musical instruments (Kimura, 1964) or by humming (King & Kimura, 1972), sonar signals (Chaney & Webster, 1966), and environmental sounds (Curry, 1967; Knox & Kimura, 1970). Gordon (1970) failed to obtain evidence of a left-ear advantage in recognizing dichotically presented melodies played on a recorder, but did find a left-ear advantage in recognizing dichotically presented chords that were generated by an electronic organ. In the chords test, two simultaneous tone pairs were presented, one to each ear; therefore, the auditory information present at any one time was rich in timbral and simultaneous interval information.

Other dichotic listening studies have detected a right-ear advantage in processing sound sequences in which evaluation of tonal quality or simultaneous relationships was not involved. Halperin, Nachshon, and Carmon (1973) presented subjects with dichotic sequences varying in frequency or duration. They found that as the number of frequency or duration transitions increased from zero to two, superiority of performance shifted from the left to the right ear. Also, Deutsch (1974, 1975d) presented subjects with a dichotic sequence of sine wave tones, which alternated in pitch from one octave to another such that when the right ear received the high tone the left ear received the low tone, and vice versa. Righthanders here tended to perceive the pitch information presented to the right ear rather than to the left. Furthermore, Robinson and Solomon (1974) presented subjects with dichotic rhythmic stimuli, produced by pure tones of invariant pitch. They also obtained results indicating a right-ear advantage in recognizing these sequences. Also, Papçun, Krashen, Terbeek, Remington, and Harshman (1974) explored the effect of dichotic presentation on Morse code signals. They found that experienced Morse code operators showed a right-ear superiority in perceiving these sequences. Naive subjects also showed a right-ear superiority, provided that the patterns were restricted to seven or fewer elements. With patterns of more than seven elements, ear superiority shifted from right to left. Papçun et al. hypothesized that when the subjects were able to deal with the individual elements and their sequential relationships, then processing took place in the dominant hemisphere. However, when the stimuli became too complex, subjects were forced to adopt a holistic strategy instead, shifting the processing from the dominant hemisphere to the nondominant. A similar line of reasoning was advanced by Bever and Chiarello (1974), who found a right-ear advantage among trained musicians in the recognition of monaurally presented tonal sequences. However, nonmusicians, who showed inferior performance, were found to have a left-ear advantage. The authors concluded that the musicians were processing the sequences analytically—the nonmusicians, holistically. Although the nature of the holistic processing underlying the left-ear advantage in the naive subjects of the experiments conducted by Papçun et al. (1974) and Bever and Chiarello (1974) remains to be clarified, these findings emphasize the specialization of each hemisphere in different aspects of musical processing.

References

Abel, S. M. Discrimination of temporal gaps. *Journal of the Acoustical Society of America*, 1972, **52**, 519–524.

Attneave, F. Stochastic compositional processes. *Journal of Aesthetics and Art Criticism*, 1959, **17**, 503–510.

Attneave, F., & Olson, R. K. Pitch as a medium: A new approach to psychophysical scaling. *American Journal of Psychology*, 1971, **84**, 147–165.

Bachem, A. Time factors in relative and absolute pitch determination. *Journal of the Acoustical Society of America*, 1954, **26**, 751–753.

Baird, J. W. Memory for absolute pitch; Studies in psychology. In *Titchener commemorative volume*. Worcester, 1917. P. 69.

Bake, A. *The music of India.* In E. Wellez (Ed.), *Ancient and oriental music.* London: Oxford Univ. Press, 1957. Pp. 195–227.

Berger, K. W. Some factors in the recognition of timbre. *Journal of the Acoustical Society of America,* 1964, **36,** 1888–1891.

Berlyne, D. E. *Aesthetics and psychobiology.* New York: Appleton, 1971.

Bever, T. G., & Chiarello, R. J. Cerebral dominance in musicians and nonmusicians. *Science,* 1974, **185,** 537–539.

Blackwell, H. R., & Schlosberg, H. Octave generalization, pitch discrimination, and loudness thresholds in the white rat. *Journal of Experimental Psychology,* 1943, **33,** 407–419.

Bogen, J. E. The other side of the brain II: An appositional mind. *Bulletin of the Los Angeles Neurological Society,* 1969, **34,** 135–162.

Boomsliter, P., & Creel, W. Extended reference: An unrecognized dynamic in melody. *Journal of Music Theory,* 1963, **7,** 2–22.

Brain, W. R. *Speech disorders* (2nd ed.). London: Butterworth, 1965.

Bregman, A. S., & Campbell, J. Primary auditory stream segregation and perception of order in rapid sequence of tones. *Journal of Experimental Psychology,* 1971, **89,** 244–249.

Burns, E. M. Octave adjustment by non-western musicians. *Journal of the Acoustical Society of America,* 1974, **56,** S25–S26. (a)

Burns, E. M. In search of the shruti. *Journal of the Acoustical Society of America,* 1974, **56,** S26. (b)

Burns, E. M., & Ward, W. D. Categorical perception of musical intervals. *Journal of the Acoustical Society of America,* 1973, **54,** S96.

Carmon, A., & Nachshon, I. Effect of unilateral brain damage on perception of temporal order. *Cortex,* 1971, **7,** 410–418.

Carterette, E. C., Friedman, M. P., & Lovell, J. D. Mach bands in hearing. *Journal of the Acoustical Society of America,* 1969, **45,** 986–998.

Chaney, R. B., & Webster, J. C. Information in certain multidimensional sounds. *Journal of the Acoustical Society of America,* 1966, **40,** 455–477.

Cooper, G. W., & Meyer, L. B. *The rhythmic structure of music.* Chicago: Univ. of Chicago Press, 1960.

Critchley, M. *The parietal lobes.* London: Arnold, 1953.

Curry, F. K. W. A comparison of left-handed and right-handed subjects in verbal and nonverbal dichotic listening tasks. *Cortex,* 1967, **3,** 343–352.

Cutting, J. E., & Rosner, B. S. Categories and boundaries in speech and music. *Perception & Psychophysics,* 1974, **16,** 564–570.

Cutting, J. E., Rosner, B. S., & Foard, C. F. Perceptual categories for musiclike sounds: Implications for theories of speech perception. *Quarterly Journal of Experimental Psychology,* 1976, **28,** 361–378.

Deutsch, D. Music recognition. *Psychological Review,* 1969, **76,** 300–307.

Deutsch, D. Tones and numbers: Specificity of interference in short-term memory. *Science,* 1970, **168,** 1604–1605. (a)

Deutsch, D. Dislocation of tones in a musical sequence: A memory illusion. *Nature,* 1970, **5242,** 226. (b)

Deutsch, D. Octave generalization and tune recognition. *Perception & Psychophysics,* 1972, **11,** 411–412. (a)

Deutsch, D. Mapping of interactions in the pitch memory store. *Science,* 1972, **175,** 1020–1022. (b)

Deutsch, D. Effect of repetition of standard and comparison tones on recognition memory for pitch. *Journal of Experimental Psychology,* 1972, **93,** 156–162. (c)

Deutsch, D. Interference in memory between tones adjacent in the musical scale. *Journal of Experimental Psychology,* 1973, **100,** 228–231. (a)

Deutsch, D. Octave generalization of specific interference effects in memory for tonal pitch. *Perception & Psychophysics,* 1973, **13,** 271–275. (b)

Deutsch, D. An auditory illusion. *Nature,* 1974, **251,** 307–309.

Deutsch, D. Two-channel listening to musical scales. *Journal of the Acoustical Society of America,* 1975, **57,** 1156–1160. (a)

Deutsch, D. The organization of short-term memory for a single acoustic attribute. In D. Deutsch & J. A. Deutsch (Eds.), *Short Term Memory.* New York: Academic Press, 1975. Pp. 107–151. (b)

Deutsch, D. Facilitation by repetition in recognition memory for tonal pitch. *Memory & Cognition,* 1975, **3,** 263–266. (c)

Deutsch, D. Musical Illusions. *Scientific American,* 1975, **233,** 92–104. (d)

Deutsch, D. Memory and attention in music. In M. Critchley & R. A. Henson (Eds.), *Music and the brain.* London: Heinemann, 1977.

Deutsch, D., & Feroe, J. Disinhibition in pitch memory. *Perception & Psychophysics,* 1975, **17,** 320–324.

Deutsch, D., & Roll, P. L. Error patterns in delayed pitch comparison as a function of relational context. *Journal of Experimental Psychology,* 1974, **103,** 1027–1034.

Divenyi, P. L., & Hirsh, I. J. Discrimination of the silent gap in two-tone sequences of different frequencies. *Journal of the Acoustical Society of America,* 1972, **52,** 166 (Appendix).

Divenyi, P. L., & Hirsh, I. J. Identification of temporal order in three-tone sequences. *Journal of the Acoustical Society of America,* 1974, **56,** 144–151.

Divenyi, P. L., & Hirsh, I. J. The effect of blanking on the identification of temporal order in three-tone sequences. *Perception & Psychophysics,* 1975, **17,** 246–252.

Dowling, W. J. Rhythmic Fission and the Perceptual Organization of Tone Sequences. Unpublished doctoral dissertation. Harvard Univ., 1967.

Dowling, W. J. Recognition of melodic transformations: Inversion, retrograde, and retrograde-inversion. *Perception & Psychophysics,* 1972, **12,** 417–421.

Dowling, W. J. The 1215-cent octave: Convergence of Western and Nonwestern data on pitch scaling. *Journal of the Acoustical Society of America,* 1973, **53,** 373. (a)

Dowling, W. J. The preception of interleaved melodies. *Cognitive Psychology,* 1973, **5,** 322–337. (b)

Dowling, W. J. Rhythmic groups and subjective chunks in memory for melodies. *Perception & Psychophysics,* 1973, **14,** 37–40. (c)

Dowling, W. J., & Fujitani, D. S. Contour, interval and pitch recognition in memory for melodies. *Journal of the Acoustical Society of America,* 1971, **49,** 524–531.

Dowling, W. J., & Hollombe, A. W. The perception of melodies distorted by splitting into several octaves: Effects of increasing proximity and melodic contour. *Perception & Psychophysics,* 1977, **21,** 60–64.

Drobisch, M. W. *Uber die mathematische Bestimmung der musikalischen Intervalle.* 1846. Also, Abh. d. kgl. sachs. Ges. d. Wiss. math.-phys. Cl.b.II. 1855, 35.

Efron, R. Temporal perception, aphasia, and deja vu. *Brain,* 1963, **86,** 403–424.

Erickson, R. *Sound structure in music.* Berkeley: Univ. of California Press, 1975.

Evans, E. F. Neural processes for the detection of acoustic patterns and for sound localization. In F. O. Schmitt & F. T. Worden (Eds.), *The neurosciences: Third study program.* Cambridge, Massachusetts: M.I.T. Press, 1974. Pp. 131–147.

Farnsworth, P. R. *The social psychology of music.* New York: Holt, 1958.

Fraisse, P. *Les structures rhythmiques.* Paris: Erasme, 1956.

Francès, R. *La perception de la musique.* Paris: Vrin, 1972.

Fransson, F. The source spectrum of double-reed woodwind instruments. *Royal Institute of Technology, Stockholm, Speech Transmission Lab, QPSR,* 1966, **4,** 35.

Fucks, W. Mathematical analysis of the formal structure of music. *IRE Trans. Information Theory,* 1962, **8,** 225–228.

Garner, W. R. *The processing of information and structure.* New York: Wiley, 1974.

Geschwind, N. Problems in the anatomical understanding of the aphasias. In A. L. Benton (Ed.), *Contributions to clinical neuropsychology.* Chicago: Aldine, 1969.

Gordon, H. W. Hemispheric asymmetrics in the perception of musical chords. *Cortex,* 1970, **6,** 387–398.

Gordon, H. W., & Bogen, J. E. Hemispheric lateralization of singing after intracarotid sodium amylobarbitone. *Journal of Neurology, Neurosurgery, and Psychiatry,* 1974, **37,** 27–738.

Gott, P. Language after dominant hemispherectomy. *Journal of Neurology, Neurosurgery, and Psychiatry,* 1973, **36,** 1082–1088.

Grey, J. M. *An exploration of musical timbre.* Unpublished doctoral dissertation, Stanford Univ., 1975.

Guttman, N., & Julesz, B. Lower limits of auditory periodicity analysis. *Journal of the Acoustical Society of America,* 1963, **35,** 610.

Halperin, Y., Nachshon, I., & Carmon, A. Shift of ear superiority in dichotic listening to temporally patterned nonverbal stimuli. *Journal of the Acoustical Society of America,* 1973, **53,** 46–50.

Handel, S. Temporal segmentation of repeating auditory patterns. *Journal of Experimental Psychology,* 1973, **101,** 46–54.

Heise, G. A., & Miller, G. A. An experimental study of auditory patterns. *American Journal of Psychology,* 1951, **64,** 68–77.

Helmholtz, H. L. F. *On the sensations of tone, as a physiological basis of music.* New York: Dover, 1954. (Originally published 1862.)

Henschen, S. E. On the function of the right hemisphere of the brain in relation to the left in speech, music and calculation. *Brain,* 1926, **49,** 110–123.

Houtgast, T. Psychophysical evidence for lateral inhibition in hearing. *Journal of the Acoustical Society of America,* 1972, **51,** 1885–1894.

Humphreys, L. F. Generalization as a function of method of reinforcement. *Journal of Experimental Psychology,* 1939, **25,** 361–372.

Jansson, E. Analogies between bowed string instruments and the human voice, source-filter models. *Royal Institute of Technology, Stockholm, Speech Transmission Lab, QPSR,* 1966, **3,** 4.

Jeffries, T. B. Relationship of interval frequency count to ratings of melodic intervals. *Journal of Experimental Psychology,* 1974, **102,** 903–905.

Kimura, D. Left-right differences in the perception of melodies. *Quarterly Journal of Experimental Psychology,* 1964, **16,** 355–358.

King, F. L., & Kimura, D. Left-ear superiority in dichotic perception of vocal nonverbal sounds. *Canadian Journal of Psychology,* 1972, **26,** 111–116.

Kleist, K. *Sensory aphasia and amusia.* The Myelo-Architectomic basis. Oxford: Pergamon Press, 1962.

Klinke, R., Boerger, G., & Gruber, J. Alteration of afferent, tone-evoked activity of neurons of the cochlear nucleus following acoustic stimulation of the contralateral ear. *Journal of the Acoustical Society of America,* 1969, **45,** 788–789.

Knox, C., & Kimura, D. Cerebral processing of nonverbal sounds in boys and girls. *Neuropsychologia,* 1970, **8,** 117–137.

Kolinski, M. The evaluation of tempo. *Ethnomusicology,* 1959, **3,** 45–57.

Konecni, V. J. The mediation of aggressive behavior: Arousal level vs. anger and cognitive labeling. *Journal of Personality and Social Psychology,* 1975, **32,** 706–712.

Konecni, V. J., Crozier, J. B., & Doob, A. N. Anger and expression of aggression: Effects on aesthetic preference. *Scientific Aesthetics,* 1976, **1,** 47–55.

Liberman, A. M., Cooper, F. S., Shankweiler, D. P., & Studdert-Kennedy, M. Perception of the Speech Code. *Psychological Review,* 1967, **74,** 431–461.

Lunney, H. W. M. Time as heard in speech and music. *Nature,* 1974, **249,** 592.

Luria, A. R. *Higher cortical functions in man.* New York: Basic Books, 1966.

Luria, A. R., Tsvetkova, L. S., & Futer, D. S. Aphasia in a composer. *Journal of the Neurological Sciences,* 1965, **2,** 288–292.

Merriam, A. P. *The anthropology of music*. Evanston, Illinois: Northwestern Univ. Press, 1964.

Meyer, L. B. *Emotion and meaning in music*. Chicago: Univ. of Chicago Press, 1956.

Meyer, L. B. *Explaining music: Essays and explorations*. Berkeley: Univ. of California Press, 1973.

Michon, J. A. Studies on subjective duration 1. Differential sensitivity on the perception of repeated temporal intervals. *Acta Psychologica*, 1964, **22**, 441–450.

Miller, D. C. *The science of musical sounds*. New York: Macmillan, 1916.

Miller, G. A., & Heise, G. A. The trill threshold. *Journal of the Acoustical Society of America*, 1950, **22**, 637–638.

Miller, J., & Cuddy, L. L. Tonality as a cue for melody recognition. *Experimental Report 72-1*, Queen's University, Kingston, Ontario, 1972.

Miller, J. R., & Carterette, E. C. Perceptual space for musical structures. *Journal of the Acoustical Society of America*, 1975, **58**, 711–720.

Milner, B. Laterality effects in audition. In V. B. Mountcatle (Ed.), *Interhemisphoric relations and cerebral dominance*. Baltimore: Johns Hopkins Univ. Press, 1962. Pp. 177–195.

Nettl, B. *Music in primitive culture*. Cambridge, Massachusetts: Harvard Univ. Press, 1956. (a)

Nettl, B. Unifying factors in folk and primitive music. *Journal of the American Musicological Society*, 1956, **9**, 196–201. (b)

Ortmann, O. On the melodic relativity of tones. *Psychological Monographs*, 1926, **35** (Whole No. 162).

Papçun, G., Krashen, S., Terbeek, D., Remington, R., & Harshman, R. Is the left hemisphere specialized for speech, language and/or something else? *Journal of the Acoustical Society of America*, 1974, **55**, 319–327.

Penfield, W., & Rasmussen, T. *The cerebral cortex of man*. New York: Hafner, 1968.

Perkins, D. N. Coding position in a sequence by rhythmic grouping. *Memory & Cognition*, 1974, **2**, 219–223.

Piston, W. *Harmony* (2nd ed.). London: Norton, 1948.

Piston, W. *Counterpoint*. London: Gollancz, 1949.

Plomp, R. The ear as frequency analyzer. *Journal of the Acoustical Society of America*, 1964, **36**, 1628–1636.

Plomp, R. Timbre as a multidimensional attribute of complex tones. In R. Plomp & G. F. Smoorenburg (Eds.), *Frequency analysis and periodicity detection in hearing*. Sijthoff: Leiden, 1970.

Plomp, R., & Mimpen, A. M. The ear as frequency analyzer II. *Journal of the Acoustical Society of Amerlca*, 1968, **43**, 764–767.

Plomp, R., & Steeneken, H. J. M. Effects of phase on the timbre of complex tones. *Journal of the Acoustical Society of America*, 1969, **46**, 409–421.

Plomp, R., & Steeneken, H. J. M. Pitch versus timbre. Paper presented at the Seventh International Congress on Acoustics, Budapest, 1971.

Plomp, R., Wagenaar, W. A., & Mimpen, A. M. Musical interval recognition with simultaneous tones. *Acustica*, 1973, **29**, 101–109.

Pollack, I. The information of elementary auditory displays. *Journal of the Acoustical Society of America*, 1952, **24**, 745–749.

Pollack, I. Ohm's acoustical law and short term auditory memory. *Journal of the Acoustical Society of America*, 1964, **36**, 2340–2345.

Pollack, I. Memory for auditory waveform. *Journal of the Acoustical Society of America*, 1972, **51**, 1209–1215.

Pratt, C. C. *The meaning of music*. New York: Johnson Reprint Corp., 1968.

Restle, F. Theory of serial pattern learning: Structural trees. *Psychological Review*, 1970, **77**, 481–495.

Restle, F. Serial patterns: The role of phrasing. *Journal of Experimental Psychology*, 1972, **92**, 385–390.

Restle, F. Serial pattern learning: Higher order transitions. *Journal of Experimental Psychology*, 1973, **99**, 61–69.

Restle, F., & Brown, E. Organization of serial pattern learning. In G. H. Bower (Ed.), *The psychology of learning and motivation* (Vol. 4). New York: Academic Press, 1970. Pp. 249–331.

Revesz, G. *Zur Grundleguncy der Tonpsychologie*. Leipzig: Feit, 1913.

Risset, J. C. *Computer study of trumpet tones*. Murray Hill, New Jersey: Bell Telephone Laboratories, 1966.

Risset, J. C., & Matthews, M. V. Analysis of musical instrument tones. *Physics Today*, 1969, **22**, 23–30.

Robinson, G. M., & Solomon, D. J. Rhythm is processed by the speech hemisphere. *Journal of Experimental Psychology*, 1974, **102**, 508–511.

Ruckmick, C. A. A new classification of tonal qualities. *Psychological Review*, 1929, **36**, 172–180.

Sachs, M. B., & Kiang, N. Y-S Two-tone inhibition in auditory nerve fibers. *Journal of the Acoustical Society of America*, 1968, **43**, 1120–1128.

Saldanha, E. L., & Corso, J. F. Timbre cues for the recognition of musical instruments. *Journal of the Acoustical Society of America*, 1964, **36**, 2021–2026.

Shankweiler, D. Effects of temporal-lobe damage in perception of dichotically presented melodies. *Journal of Comparative and Physiological Psychology*, 1966, **62**, 115–119.

Shepard, R. N. Circularity in judgments of relative pitch. *Journal of the Acoustical Society of America*, 1964, **36**, 2345–2353.

Siegel, W., & Sopo, R. Tonal intervals are perceived categorically by musicians with relative pitch. *Journal of the Acoustical Society of America*, 1975, **57**, S11.

Simon, H. A., & Sumner, R. K. Pattern in music. In B. Kleinmuntz (Ed.), *Formal representation of human judgment*. New York: Wiley, 1968.

Slawson, A. W. Vowel quality and musical timbre as functions of spectrum envelope and fundamental frequency. *Journal of the Acoustical Society of America*, 1968, **43**, 87–101.

Smith, A. Speech and other functions after left (dominant) hemispherectomy. *Journal of Neurology, Neurosurgery, and Psychiatry*, 1966, **29**, 467–471.

Stumpf, C., & Meyer, M. Maassbestimmungen uber die Reinheit consonanter Intervalle. *Beitr Akust. Musikwiss*, 1898, **2**, 84–167.

Sturges, P. T., & Martin, J. G. Rhythmic structure in auditory temporal pattern perception and immediate memory. *Journal of Experimental Psychology*, 1974, **102**, 377–383.

Subczinski, J. Described in R. Masland, "Brain Mechanisms Underlying the Language Function." In *Human communication and its disorders*. Bethesda, Maryland: National Institute of Neurological Diseases and Stroke, 1969.

Sundberg, J. E. F., & Lindquist, J. Musical octaves and pitch. *Journal of the Acoustical Society of America*, 1973, **54**, 922–929.

Swisher, L., & Hirsh, I. J. Brain damage and the ordering of two temporally successive stimuli. *Neuropsychologia*, 1972, **10**, 137–152.

Terhardt, E. Pitch shifts of harmonics, an explanation of the octave enlargement phenomenon. *Proceedings of the Seventh International Congress on Acoustics*, Budapest, 1971, 621–624.

Tovey, D. F. *The forms of music*. London: Oxford Univ. Press, 1957.

Van Noorden, L. P. A. S. *Temporal coherence in the perception of tone sequences*. Unpublished doctoral thesis, 1975. Technische Hogeschool, Eundhoven, Holland.

Vignolo, L. A. Auditory agnosia: A review and report of recent evidence. In A. L. Benton (Ed.), *Contributions to clinical neuropsychology*. Chicago: Aldine, 1969. Pp. 172–231.

Vitz, P. C. Preference for tones as a function of frequency (hertz) and intensity (decibels). *Perception & Psychophysics*, 1972, **11**, 84–88.

Vos, P. G. *Perception of metrical tone sequences*. Unpublished doctoral dissertation, University of Nijmegen, 1973. The Netherlands.

Ward, W. L. Subjective musical pitch. *Journal of the Acoustical Society of America*, 1954, **26**, 369–380.

Ward, W. D. Musical perception. In J. V. Tobias (Ed.), *Foundations of modern auditory theory* (Vol. I). New York: Academic Press, 1970. Pp. 407–447.

Warren, R. M. Auditory temporal discrimination by trained listeners. *Cognitive Psychology*, 1974, **6**, 237–256.

Warren, R. M., & Obusek, C. J. Identification of temporal order within auditory sequences. *Perception & Psychophysics*, 1972, **12**, 86–90.

Warren, R. M., Obusek, C. J., Farmer, R. M., & Warren, R. P. Auditory sequence: Confusions of patterns other than speech or music. *Science*, 1969, **164**, 586–587.

Wedin, L., & Goude, G. Dimension analysis of the perception of instrumental timbre. *Scandinavian Journal of Psychology*, 1972, **13**, 228–240.

Werner, H. Uber Mikromelodik und Mikroharmonik. *Zeitschrift fur Psychologie*, 1925, **98**, 74–89.

Wertheim, N. Disturbances of the musical functions. In L. Halpern (Ed.), *Problems of dynamic neurology*. New York: Grune & Stratton, 1963.

Wertheimer, M. Untersuchungen sur Lehre von der Gestalt, II, *Psychologische Forschung*, 1923, **4**, 301–350.

Wessel, D. L. Psychoacoustics and music. *Bulletin of the Computer Arts Society*, 1973, **1**, 30–31.

White, B. Recognition of distorted melodies. *American Journal of Psychology*, 1960, **73**, 100–107.

Winograd, T. Linguistics and the computer analysis of tonal harmony. *Journal of Music Theory*. 1968, **12**, 2–49.

Woodrow, H. Time perception. In S. S. Stevens (Ed.), *Handbook of experimental psychology*. New York: Wiley, 1951. Pp. 1224–1236.

Zenatti, A. Le developpement genetique de la perception musicale. *Monographies Francaises de Psychologie*, 1969, **17**, 1–110.

Chapter 10

ART AND PERCEPTION*

JULIAN HOCHBERG

I. INTRODUCTION

In this chapter, I will try to bring up-to-date the nature of perceptual theory as it is important to an understanding of pictorial and nonpictorial art and to consider how perceptual theory is affected by what we learn about art.

The importance of perceptual psychology to the applied arts is reasonably clear. The industries in which perceptual decisions must be made most often are probably the communications enterprises—the news media, advertising and packaging, entertainment—in which the primary task is the preparation and presentation of perceptual displays. These are, of course, fields that depend very heavily on applied perceptual knowledge, such as how to specify and produce a given set of colors, the sizes of details that are needed to present pictures and text, and the legibilities of different typefaces and formats. These examples, taken only from the arena of visual psychophysics, involve a great many questions; yet there are similar questions in the sphere of auditory psychophysics that also need be answered, as well

* The preparation of this chapter was carried out in connection with NIH-5RO1-HD-06768.

as more cognitive questions about the factors that determine how people direct their attention to visual and auditory presentations, and about what is needed to make them comprehensible.

These are all straightforward areas in which perceptual knowledge must be sought and applied and about which we already have a fair amount of knowledge. There are two areas of communications research that are by no means so straightforward. The first is the nature of the interaction of message and medium (that is, the interaction of the expressive features of the medium and its substantive content). There is very little knowledge relating directly to these questions, although we will see that such knowledge can probably be obtained. The second area of research concerns the nature of the presentation as an intentional interpersonal act: Even the most seemingly transparent and potentially automatic process, like the making of a photograph, entails a selection and a preparation—a directed effort—that testifies to the existence of a presenter with some purpose and that makes every member of the audience a participant in an implicit dyadic communicative act (e.g., "why is he showing me that in such unexpected detail?") This is probably an extremely important aspect of every artistic presentation, and particularly those in which the close control of the artist is assumed by the nature of the medium, but we have barely begun to assemble an analytic logic for communicative acts (Grice, 1968; Schmidt, 1975; Searle, 1969).

Both of these points bring us to the verge of the distinction between fine and applied art, which is a matter of *aesthetics*, or evaluation. In cases where there is only one way to prepare a communicative presentation, the issue is simply one of sensory engineering. In cases where options are available, where there is a tradition to provide the background against which one displays one's own mark and originality, and, above all, where there is a great deal of Veblenesque prestige and simple financial investment at stake in assessing a given artistic presentation as good or bad (and thereby establishing an artist as worthy of investment), simple issues and unequivocal criteria do not exist. In the applied arts, there are usually more or less assessible criteria to be drawn on. There the study of consumer preference (using the measurement techniques of traditional experimental aesthetics) can at least in principle be subject to validation procedures. In the case of objects that are produced "for their own sakes," the assessment must rely on cultivated taste. A great deal of the appreciation of the work then depends on the education that enables one to place it in its tradition, to see it in terms of its line of development, and to enjoy the object as a piece of history in which one can be evidently expert.

I will not maintain a distinction between pure and applied art here, except where it is natural to our discussion.*

---

* Surely a distinction can be made, if only in the matter of the relative permanence of the

Art history, and the establishment of artistic provenance and tradition, are potentially susceptible to rigorous pursuit. At least some of the functions that artistic presentations are made to serve are similarly assessible. No work of art need fill all functions; each function has been announced, at one time or another, to be *the* basis for evaluating artistic merit. It is no wonder that philosophers and theorists of art have disagreed, and some even deny the possibility of an acceptable definition of either art or aesthetics (Kennick, 1958; Weitz, 1956). Thoughtful artists themselves have maintained that the only judges whose opinions are worth considering are other comparable artists—a case of special pleading that may, nevertheless, be valid to the extent that it reflects the artist's actual goal: to achieve original solutions to the problems posed by the history and demands of his art form as constrained by the options open to him in attempting to make his mark on it.

My own belief is that there is no single realm of art. We lump together a great many different activities having a fair number of different purposes and highly diverse criteria, and what is presently called *art* is more a matter of historical and sociological accident (and vested interest) than anything else. This is compounded by the fact that people really are not able to provide, by introspection alone, effective analyses of why they seek exposure to what we will call artistic presentations (paintings, dance, motion pictures, music, architecture, etc.) any more than they can dissect the bases of their choices in more trivial areas, such as fashion design, popular music, automobile styling, etc., all of which fall within the undisputed domain of applied art.

There are three natural ways in which to divide the functions and criteria of the perceptual study of artistic presentations, which I will describe briefly and then consider in detail.

1. *Art as representation and communication about the world.*

Many perceptual treatments of art deal solely with the representational function of pictures. There are, of course, art forms, like music and dance, that may have no representational or programmatic content, even if the forms from which they are descended did. Other art forms, like architecture, only rarely attempt to represent something. Yet pictorial art, some acting, and descriptive prose *do* have functions of objective communication. In the case of pictorial art, we would surely use pictures for their representational functions regardless of their artistic and other values, as we would continue to use clothes and buildings even if we did not care about their appearances. As we will see, however, there is not a single automatic way of achieving a representation of the world (photographs are not necessarily better than

---

canons. The teenager immersed in assessing practitioners of country rock is acquiring a culture and an appreciation of an art form that probably draws on all of the mechanisms that contribute to a more classical cultural education; but the latter provides a continuity that is of value both to the society (witness the alacrity with which new regimes usually attempt to discard the traditional culture) and to the individual's potential for enjoyment.

drawings!). Even if there were such a way, the means for its achievement would not be immediately evident to the untutored viewer. The methods for preparing pictures were trade secrets among artists, and it was not long ago that it was a legitimate cause for wonder, among the educated as well as among the unlettered, that some artists could render the likenesses of portrait sitters and their household goods in such lifelike detail.

The last century has witnessed a move away from the idea of the artist as a transcriber, or human camera obscura, in the course of development from painting, through photographs, to holograms. That aspect of art which consists in preparing a surrogate that faithfully mimics to the eye the light-waves sent by the represented scene or event has lost its aesthetic interest per se, but there are ways of producing or even enhancing likeness (of making a portrait that is more like the sitter than the sitter is) that remain a matter of interest. We can expect that innovation in the manner or style of representation will continue, which brings us to the two nonrepresentational functions, expression and aesthetic value.

2. *Art as expression: The communication of the artist's state, feelings, or identity.*

The function of art to move the audience emotionally or to express how the artist feels is taken, much more often than representation, as the sole touchstone of artistic merit. It is clear, however, that presentations can be expressive, yet not regarded as good art (remember that the aim of even the most crude forms of advertising, propaganda, and entertainment is to move the audience), and that much art has neither representational nor emotional content other than what is needed for the so-called aesthetic emotion, which is the third function.

3. *The aesthetic function: Art as pleasurable, interesting, or engaging.*

There is a long history of seeking to measure and explicate the beautiful by means of preference judgments tied to specifiable characteristics of the stimulus pattern. Defining the beautiful and pleasurable in terms of physically measurable canons or prescriptions is an enterprise that has been pursued since antiquity. The reward value of the pleasurable has more recently been measured by the tendency to keep looking or listening (the opposite of boredom or habituation). This is an evaluative method that is more interesting than the traditional preference judgments to those theorists concerned with understanding perception as a motivated process, which is what makes the question of aesthetics of immediate concern to a constructivist psychologists of perception.

These three headings are, of course, not completely hard and fast, nor can they really be exhaustive. What makes an artisitc presentation more or less successful, more or less sophisticated and deep, most writers agree, is the extent to which these diverse functions (and yet others) can be met in mutually reinforcing ways, using the expressive features of the medium in concert with the content being dealt with (a traditional desire that has been often expressed in particular connection with poetry). However, a walk through a balanced museum will attest, I believe, to the fact that all functions need not be embodied in any one work of art, or even in one body of work.

We take up, in turn, a survey of perceptual problems and research in each of these three areas.

II. REPRESENTATION AND COMMUNICATION ABOUT THE WORLD

A. Representational Pictures and Perceptual Theories

By far the most familiar topic in perception textbooks is the preparation of a representational picture as a surrogate object, which acts as a likeness because it presents to the eye of the viewer much the same pattern of light as would the scene itself. This is what most perceptual treatments of art are concerned with and, as we will see, it draws unequally on all of the major perceptual theories.

The briefest survey of the most important perceptual theories will suffice to distinguish the different kinds of data and analyses that they can bring to art. Associationism–Empiricism, the oldest theory, assumes all conscious experience to consist of sensations, memory images of sensations, and the arbitrary linkages between them that have been forged by the individual's mind in the course of its encounters with the structure of the world. *Gestalt* theory rejected these mechanistic and atomistic premises, explaining that what we perceive reflects the characteristics of underlying brain fields. Gibson's theory, which is a reanalysis of the variables of stimulation that are to be found in light reaching the eye, has revealed a richness of information that is potentially capable of accounting completely for the veridical perceptions of the world without the mediating processes of associationism or the organizational processes of Gestalt theory. Finally, there is the new–old attempt, which starts with Hebb and Piaget, but in fact reaches back to Helmholtz, to view perception as an active process of fitting mental structure (hypothesized objects, scenes, and events) to selected sensory tests, thus building selective attention and schematization, or abstraction, directly into the heart of the perceptual process.

If we break down the classical empiricist approach into two components—a sensory psychophysical analysis and a cognitive associationist one represented most fully by Helmholtz's doctrine of unconscious inference (i.e., that we perceive those objects and events that are most likely, on the basis of our past experiences, to fit our present pattern of sensory stimulation)—we can see that there are two purely psychophysical approaches (the classical and the Gibsonian varieties) and two approaches that invoke additional mental structure (those deriving from Gestalt theory and those deriving from Helmholtz's conceptions). All of these have been drawn upon by aestheticians and art theorists, with varying degrees of face validity, in the service of all three of the functions (representation, expression, and aesthetic value) that we are to consider. We first consider representation in these terms, and then the other two functions.

B. The Psychophysics of Surrogates

To Leonardo, the painter's task was to present a likeness of the world, which he could learn to do by tracing the outlines of objects in a scene on a pane of glass interposed between him and the scene of interest. By studying the ways in which the shapes and objects in the picture plane are changed by their different dispositions in space, the artist would be able to build his vocabulary of what we now call the pictorial, or monocular, *depth cues*.

These gave the artist a vocabulary for representation and, with the further explication of the geometry of pictorial perspective, it was possible in principle to present to the eye of the stationary monocular observer substantially the same spatial distribution of light as would be given by the represented scene. Leonardo knew the limitations of this technique: The viewer must stand in one location and use only one eye, or the flatness of the picture will be betrayed; therefore, in general, the viewer cannot be fooled. To varying degrees, and for special purposes, these limitations can be overcome: For example, the cues to the flatness and texture of the surface may largely be overcome by restricting the position of the viewer and by painting the scene on some surface that is not in the projective picture plane [e.g., using the ceiling of the nave of a church as the surface on which to paint the continuation of the walls produced the convincing illusion of an additional story (Pirenne, 1971)], or by drastically restricting the depth being portrayed in a trompe-l'oeil painting.

The rationale behind such perspective technique is this: The task of the artist, from this standpoint, is to represent a scene by producing an object that, when viewed from the correct position, produces the same pattern of light that the scene does. Given *what* is to be portrayed, the decision of what the *arrangement* of lines and patches of color on the canvas should be becomes merely a task for the geometer.

With the pattern on the canvas established, we can match the view, point by point, if we have pigments that will look like each patch in the scene when viewed in isolation. Classifying and achieving the possible colors involve rules that, like the other secrets of the trade, could formerly only be learned by the apprentice from his master. Fully developed, they can now be found, with the minimum palettes for additive and subtractive mixtures, in most introductory perception texts. They will not by themselves suffice: The range of reflectances of pigments is exceedingly restricted compared to the luminances in the scenes to be represented; moreover, and partly in consequence of this, contrast effects that are characteristic of the scene (e.g., the induced hue of shadows in the open air) are not automatically achieved simply by matching *hues* on canvas to those in the scene, point by point. The principles of simultaneous contrast may be used to remedy this limitation, and were first exploited in chiaroscuro, of which Rembrandt was a master: by the juxtaposition of shadows, apparent lightnesses can be enhanced. The growing attention to induced colors, like those in shadows, that carries forward through Corot to the Impressionists, made the laws of contrast pictorially important.

With the laws of color mixing and color contrast, and with a very few pigments, the painter or printer can approximate the colors of a wide variety of objects and a much larger range of lighting conditions and brightnesses than the range of reflectances offered by the pigments themselves. In addition, the patterns of color and the afterimages that they produce can be used to generate effects of *vibrancy* and movement, which can be used to overcome some of the inherent limitations of the canvas. These effects can be used for nonrepresentational ends, producing apparent movement on the stationary canvas or printed page. This expressive, active element is exploited by optical art, in which the moiré effects of regular high-contrast patterns, superimposed on their displaced afterimages, amplify and make visible the slight tremors and unnoticed movements of the eye that are responsible for the displacements. The effects of vibrancy and movement were most directly exploited by the Impressionists, for the following purposes.

Pigments can be mixed in various ways (such as physical intermixing, superposition by glazing, etc.) that result in subtractive mixtures by successively interposed filters of pigment; alternatively, colors can be mixed additively by placing small patches next to each other. If these patches fall below the limits of acuity, an additive optical mixture results, This, in effect, is what the pointillist painters hoped to achieve in their attempts to present the light from the scene scientifically, preserving a range of reflectances and saturations that would otherwise be lost in the process of subtractive mixture. The patches used in most Impressionist paintings, however, are much too large to be below the resolving power of foveal vision at practical distances (e.g., perhaps 70 ft. for a Monet, 300 ft. for a Van Gogh). Why then does color mixture occur? Partly, because assimilation rather than contrast occurs when two patches fall within the larger receptive field associated with the individual retinal cell that is also serving to detect the individual patches (Jameson & Hurvich, 1975). Interacting with this is the factor of the much lower resolving power of parafoveal and peripheral vision as compared to foveal vision. From the appropriate viewing distances, the mixture occurs peripherally when the individual patches are visible foveally, producing a vibrancy suggestive of daylight illumination (Jameson & Hurvich, 1975), and introducing us to another line of development that we can trace from Rembrandt to Monet and eventually to the Expressionists.

If the viewer were to keep his fovea fixed on a particular part of the canvas, and the artist were to paint that region in full detail, but use less and less detail in parts of the picture that are progressively farther from the part that falls within foveal vision, the viewer would have no way of knowing that the picture is not painted in full detail everywhere. Conversely, if the artist wished the viewer to look particularly at one place, he could lead him to do so by making only that place detailed. Thus, the way in which detail is distributed is a potential compositional factor. Both Rembrandt and Eakins have left particularly clear examples of such usage, so we may infer that Western painters were aware of this phenomenon. The broadly painted and blurred regions of the canvas that are being prepared for peripheral vision are easily rendered by actually doing the painting in peripheral vision, or by stepping back after each brush stroke to decide the next one. In paintings like those of Rembrandt and Eakins that use this device, when the correct viewing distance is used and the gaze is directed properly at the detailed focal region, the picture looks complete and veridical.

Now, consider an Impressionist painting, in which the fovea meets patches wherever it is directed, and the eye receives normal-appearing forms only in peripheral vision. The viewer soon discovers that the pattern of dots that meets his direct gaze is not random, as it appears when his eye is held stationary; rather it is precisely that pattern which, when the gaze moves elsewhere, snaps into clear vision as the depicted landscape and people. This introduces a feeling of the *rightness* of the artist's work and its inalterability, that in my opinion is a great deal of what we mean by aesthetic quality in real paintings (as opposed to taste, which can be applied to nonproduced or accidental events, and to random-dot patterns or polygons, as well). Furthermore, the viewer is made aware of the necessity for active participation in constructing the picture. I know of no research showing that such specific effects actually contribute to the response to, and evaluation of, such paintings. We will return to the more general issues to which these two points are addressed in other contexts. Let us see where we now stand with regard to representation.

With a working palette, a knowledge of colors and their interactions, and a knowledge of projective geometry (or a mastery of a vocabulary of depth cues), the artist can produce patterns on canvas or paper that can act as surrogates of three-dimensional spaces and volumes. So far, psychology has contributed only the raw materials given by the psychophysics of acuity and color mixing. Geometry contributes the patterns in which the colors are to be distributed, and we have a technology for making representational pictures. After Daguerre replaced the artist's canvas with light-sensitive plates in 1839 (Szarkowski, 1973), the surrogate, *as we have been considering it,* does not need the artist.

C. The Perceptual Issues in Spatial Representation

The trompe-l'oeil picture and the scene it represents both act on the eye in the same way. And there are, of course, an infinite number of arrangements that will do the same, an argument that is surely familiar since Bishop Berkeley. It is also true, therefore, that there are an infinite number of different scenes that would fit a given picture, and that a picture is by necessity ambiguous—we cannot specify three dimensions with only two.

Of that infinity of scenes, why do we perceive only *that* scene which the artist intended to represent? Also (and this is what made pictures and depth cues so interesting to philosphers and psychologists alike), why do we see the world when all we are given is a necessarily ambiguous retinal image?

The classical answer was that, with no specific nerve energies for distance, the only way it can be seen is through our having learned to associate visual depth cues with the tactual–motor experiences we have received in the course of our dealings with the three dimensional arrangements of the world. In the line of thought that evolves from Berkeley through Helmholtz to Brunswik, we conclude that the observer supplies necessary *mental structure:* He perceives this object as being farther away *because* the perspective in the retinal image is perceived as converging, and he sees it as larger *because* (with a given visual angle) it appears farther away. The physical rules of the visual ecology have been incorporated in the perceptual habits of the viewer; all depth cues are symbols, and what makes each effective is its prior association with other depth cues, and with the movements and touching that the history of the viewer has furnished. Although there may be occasional errors in the perceptual structure fitted to such sensory patterns, probablistically they will be right more often than wrong.

Where pictures reflect light to the eye that is in fact identical to that reflected by some scene, they present no new problem: They are perceived in the same way and by the same machinery that we use to perceive the world itself. Where they do not, the empiricist has two options: Either the picture will share *enough* cues so that, in balance, no new problems are introduced; or, considering that the actual picture, as an object, may be very different from the scene it represents (e.g., pen lines on paper), the picture perception will itself have to be learned. This conception is part of the tradition of art theoreticians and philosophers, namely, that all artistic conventions are arbitrary and learned, or invented (cf. Goodman, 1968; Wollheim, 1963), so that it is meaningful to talk about a language of vision that is continually being created and revised at will by the artistic community (cf. Kepes, 1964). We will return to this point shortly.

To the Gestalt psychologists, with their theory of underlying brain-field organization, the determinants of perception are the laws of organization, not those of ecological probability (except as the latter provide the evolutionary matrix for selecting brains organized as they are). According to Gestalt theory, we see the simplest or most homogeneous image that will fit the pattern of stimulation. In fact, most of the classical pictorial depth cues can as readily be treated as examples of simplicity as of familiarity (Hochberg, 1974b). Because the Gestalt theory sees representation as a result of organization, not of perceptual habit, both the main features of space perception, and of the picture perception that follows the same laws of organization, should be expected to hold for any viewer, regardless of his experience with pictures.

To the *Gestaltists,* the basic phenomenon of visual perception was that of figure–ground differentiation: In general, the figure is the area whose shape is recognized, whereas the ground is shapeless and usually farther back, extending beyond the figure. What will be perceived as figure (and consequently, what will be perceived in a picture) depends on the so-called laws of organization. Manipulating drawings so as to discover what makes a particular area's shape be seen as figure, and what causes it to become unrecognizable ground, is therefore a convenient and rapid way to discover what the laws of organization are. It is also a way of prescribing for the artist how to make the object that he is drawing be perceived as figure, and be perceived as he wants it to be (e.g., as solid rather than flat).

This highlights an important limitation to the theory of representation as we have considered it up to this point: Merely producing the same light effect at the eye as does the scene itself is not sufficient to assure that the viewer will see the scene as the artist intended. Anyone who has taken a snapshot that shows a flowerpot growing out of his subject's head knows that violations of the Gestalt laws (in this case, good continuation) can make even the most perfect surrogate become unveridical or unintelligible. For these reasons, the Gestalt laws have seemed immediately relevant to the artist, and their theoretical and graphic concern with the mechanisms of making things be seen one way or another are easy to find (e.g., Tchelitcheff's *Hide and Seek*; Arp's reversible amebas; and the figure–ground exercises of Escher and Albers). Arnheim's essays and books on the psychology of art that were written from the standpoint of a Gestalt psychologist had more to do with what artists were concerned with than had the theoretical treatments that art had previously received (cf. Arnheim, 1966, for a collection of essays; 1954, for a summing up of that viewpoint).

In recent years, more objective formulations of the laws of organization which generally have been closely related to information theory, have proved moderately successful in predicting and prescribing how to make figures seem less dimensionally ambiguous, that is, solid versus flat (cf.

Attneave & Frost, 1969; Hochberg & Brooks, 1960).* We will see later that both the Gestalt approach and its decendants may be useful as a very rough approximation, but it would be a mistake to take it seriously today, either as a theoretical explanation of picture perception or as a viable perceptual approach.

James J. Gibson has argued that neither Helmholtzian mental structure nor Gestalt organization need be invoked to explain perception in general and depth perception in particular: The information in the proximal stimulation is sufficient to account for the direct, correct perception of the surfaces and objects of the world. Higher-order variables of stimulation, like texture–density gradients, directly specify the perception of such components of the layout as surfaces, edges, corners, etc. A picture is a surrogate for a scene precisely because it presents the eye with information that specifies those aspects of the world; to the degree that it does (i.e., that it has fidelity) it should be perceived in the same ways (Gibson, 1950, 1951, 1954, 1966, 1971).

What about the vast class of pictures that lack such features (e.g., outline drawings on a piece of paper), and whose own slants and distances as planes of paper on canvas are specified by the information that they furnish the eye, precluding the perception of the represented depths or slants? Should these not be seen merely as patterns of pigment on paper, which is what they are? Although Gibson has worked at several solutions to this problem and made significant contributions to our understanding of the nature of picture perception in the process, and although Gibsonian accounts of picture perception have been attempted (Hagen, 1974; Kennedy, 1974), I find the fit of picture perception with his theory an uneasy one, and the essential problem remains unresolved. In any case, if special learning should turn out to be needed in a Gibsonian explanation of picture perception, it will be in terms of paying attention to those aspects of information that pictures share with the world, not in terms of an arbitrary association of perceptual habits.

Unlike Gestalt theorists, neither Gibson nor the Helmholtzians would be disturbed to find that pictorial perception is a learned ability. The fact is that the facts are by no means clear-cut, but at least the theoretically important features of picture perception appear not to require special learning. Specific training to learn what line drawings mean is not necessary in order to perceive them (Hochberg & Brooks, 1962a; Kennedy, 1977), and it is clear that pictorial perception is not an arbitrary conventional skill, like reading: If

---

* Despite the many books for artists that introduce the Gestalt philosophy and demonstrations, a cookbook on their application to pictorial intelligibility remains at once possible, desirable, and unwritten. The possible effects of ground (the space *between* the shapes) as a factor in composition has long been raised in connection with the theory of design (cf. Taylor, 1964) and should theoretically be quantifiable in that regard, but research on this has not been done.

its elements are learned at all, they are learned by commerce with the real world. We will return to this point later. It should be noted that unlearned perception of line drawings means that some minimum of what Gestalt psychologists call figure–ground differentiation is unlearned. Increasing sophistication in "reading" outline objects appears to reflect improvements in the older child's ability to perceive a line as belonging to more than one shape (Ghent, 1956), and in the child's ability to perceive an object for which only partial outlines are given, with less of the line actually present (Gollin, 1960). Whatever causes viewers to take outlines as equivalent to objects' edges is not "symbol learning."

This does not mean that pictorial education does not contribute to the ability of viewers to interpret distance and size relations in pictures (Olson, 1975; Yonas & Hagen, 1973), particularly in highly impoverished pictures: There is some indication that, as their pictorial experience increases, native Africans are better able to perceive spatial arrangements in pictures that contain sparse and somewhat ambiguous linear perspective (Hudson, 1960, 1962, 1967; Kilbride & Robbins, 1968; Mundy-Castle, 1966), although those results can be questioned on various theoretical and empirical grounds (Deregowski, 1968; Hagen, 1974; Hochberg, 1972b, p. 501; Kennedy, 1977; Omari & Cook, 1972). Also, as we have seen, there is improvement with age in the ability to complete and to see alternative objects in outline drawings. One thing that the untutored ability to respond to outline pictures of objects and scenes does tell us is that definitions of pictorial representation solely in terms of the fidelity of the surrogate simply will not do. As we have seen, such a definition is insufficient. The fact that pictures drawn in outlines, i.e., in ribbons of pigment on paper (Gibson, 1951), are recognized naturally, shows that fidelity in the array is not *necessary*, either: If a line on paper is taken by a viewer as equivalent to the abrupt change in texture–density gradient that occurs at an object's edge, that phenomenon *reflects an attribute of the viewer, not of the light at the eye.*

Two other major pictorial phenomena also show, in quite different ways, that projective fidelity is neither sufficient nor necessary for the production of recognizable representations.

If a picture is defined in terms of a surrogate object that must be viewed from the mathematically correct station point [and in fact, a picture that is viewed from its proper station point may be mistaken for a real scene, even when it is not very faithful in other ways, as long as its geometry is preserved (Gibson, 1951; Smith & Smith, 1961)], then the picture must change the scene it represents with each change in the viewer's position. In fact, movement of the viewer should specify that the picture is not a scene, but only a dappled plane surface. What actually happens when pictures are viewed from incorrect station points?

Pirenne (1970) points out two major departures from this psychophysical or geometrical explanation of picture perception. The first is that pictures are of course viewed at all angles, and from various distances, but do not appear to be noticeably distorted. He argues that this is because we are aware of the picture as a flat patterned surface (because of its frame, its texture, our binocular parallax, etc.), and therefore can compensate for the slant of the picture in responding to the pattern that lies upon it. The second is that artists present certain objects (especially familiar ones) as though their main surfaces were always parallel to the picture plane, regardless of the object's depicted orientation. This is done, he suggests, because in that way the viewer needs only to compensate for the slant of the picture plane in order to have compensated as well for the slant of the represented objects' surfaces. Both of these issues are important for art theory and for perceptual and cognitive psychology. We consider them separately because they really have quite different implications.

Compensation for differences in distance or slant of the picture, or both, puts the entire process of the perception of pictorial space, and of space in the real world, into a Helmholtzian framework, necessarily implying the operation of *mental structure* (i.e., the viewer's use of unconscious knowledge about the geometrical couplings of the physical world). This would mean that we must replace the transparent psychophysics of Leonardo's window and Gibson's direct theory of perception with a postulated system of mediating cognitive structures, messy though that would be. It is not a matter only for museum directors and gallery owners, therefore, to know about the effects of compensation in picture perception. The issue has theoretical weight. Is there unequivocal evidence for such compensation? The issue is still open. As Farber and Rosinski have shown (1978), increases and decreases in viewing distance produce magnification and compressed depth, and minification and increased depth, respectively, and changes in viewing angle produce shear (e.g., a cube becomes a nonretangular parallelopiped). With respect to viewing distances, the familiar compression effect in telephoto pictures and movies provides anecdotal evidence that the change in viewpoint has some effect. This is supported by laboratory measurements of changes in perceived *distance* in photographs as a function of the difference between the viewing distance of subject and camera (Smith & Gruber, 1958). Perceived *size* of represented objects was not, however, affected by such a change in viewpoint (Smith, 1958), as it should have been by the geometry. With respect to viewing angle changes (that is, looking at the picture from some slant to its surface), it is clear from the example of anamorphic pictures [that is, pictures in which the viewers can only see the desired scene if they respond to the pattern of proximal stimulation presented to their eye, and not to the distorted pattern on the painting that is designed to be viewed from an extreme angle (Clerici, 1954)] that there is some point beyond which the picture's slant is *not* taken into account. Furthermore, there is also anecdotal evidence (Gombrich, 1972b) that as the viewer moves there is apparent movement *within* the represented view, as the represented scene changes in accordance with what we would expect from the changing viewpoint if no compensation occurred. Laboratory studies show, however, that viewing angle has no effect on objects' apparent sizes (Hagen, 1976), on apparent slant (Rosinski *et al.*, 1977), or on objects' apparent forms (i.e., their rectangularity or nonrectangularity: Perkins, 1973) except at extreme viewing angles. Most of these workers conclude that some degree of compensation for picture plane must occur. That may be true, but we should note that it remains to be shown conclusively.

It may be (Hochberg, 1971) that the compensation that Pirenne proposes is an unmediated response to the ratios of textural units subtended by the different parts of any surface shape at a slant to the line of sight, as Gibson in fact proposed in 1950. Because both kinds of distortion that result from viewpoint changes are affine transformations (Farber & Rosinski, 1977), such ratios would remain invariant along any dimension considered separately, regardless of the change in viewpoint. Compensation is thus not established, nor is the implication of mental structure that it carries obligatory.

There is another possibility (Hochberg, 1971) that opens up an even wider issue: It may be that the distortions are perceived, but are merely not attended. Let us see what this might mean, by turning to the second kind of departure from projective fidelity that Pirenne noted: Inconsistencies must often be introduced into pictorial perspective if the picture is to look right. This is not merely due to painters' foibles; subjects judge objects that are presented in parallel perspective (which would, of course, be correct only when viewed from infinity) to be both more realistic and more accurate than those drawn in the converging perspective correct for their viewing position (Hagen & Elliott, 1976). This has implications that go far beyond the matter of spatial representations. When an artist paints an object as a circle even though the perspective of the rest of the picture calls for an ellipse, he has introduced an inconsistency that is only a mild example of what our eye will tolerate. The pictures of Escher (and some of Pirenesi's) and Albers, and the laboratory figures of Penrose and Penrose (1958) and Hochberg (1968), show that pictures of objects can be constructed, using lines, and even shading, that are blatantly impossible: For example, a three-dimensional object whose corners face in opposite directions yet are connected by unbroken lines, nevertheless looks perfectly three-dimensional, and the inconsistency is not evident unless either the viewer searches it out or the inconsistent features are brought into close proximity (Hochberg, 1968).

I believe that these pictorial phenomena are extremely important for an understanding of psychology in general, and that they will do a great deal to bring the psychology of art into sharper focus, while widening its subject matter to include more that is of concern to the artist and aesthetician. What appears to be happening in these pictures is that the viewer can only detect the depth arrangement represented by each corner when he looks directly at it, and what he sees in his peripheral vision while he does so is not sufficient to establish more than general masses of color and form. The viewer must look at any object, scene or picture by a succession of just such restricted glances, and unless he makes a deliberate effort to extrapolate what the spatial implications of one glance hold for the next (i.e., to *attend* their mutual spatial relationship by formulating and testing specific expectations about it), he does not encode or store all of the aspects of the object nor all of the spatial information that is given (Hochberg, 1968, 1970, 1972a, 1974b). Let us consider those issues first, and then their relationship to the nonrepresentational functions of visual and nonvisual art.

D. Perception as Purposive Behavior: Schemas, Canonical Forms, and Caricature

Unless we restrict our definition of visual art to the case of the high-fidelity surrogate or trompe l'oeil, I cannot see how our psychophysical knowledge concerning color mixing and the geometry of distal–proximal projection can be of more than technical and parochial interest. With the examination of the impossible figures and their implications, our scope increases considerably. Let me briefly outline the case, which is presented in greater depth in the papers previously referenced.

The impossible figures remind us that we move our eyes in ballistic saccades that bring some point, first seen only in vague peripheral vision, to the central, detailed vision of the fovea. When we look at a picture, we do not (and cannot) direct our eyes everywhere. The eyes are first directed to those parts of the picture that are most likely to be informative [by subjects' ratings or by experimenters' definitions (Antes, 1974; Brooks, 1961; Hochberg & Brooks, 1962; Loftus, 1976; Mackworth & Morandi, 1967; Pollack & Spence, 1968)] and touch on the main features of the composition (Bouleau, 1963; Buswell, 1935; Molnar, 1964, 1968) as it would be described from a design standpoint. We move our eyes with a purpose, and with some expectation of where we will be able to fulfill this purpose. This movement is guided by what we make out vaguely in peripheral vision, aided by the redundancy of normal scenes and pictures [a particular object can be located faster when it is in a normal, appropriate scene than when it is in a jumbled or inappropriate one (Biederman, 1972)].

We look at pictures (and at the world) piecemeal, obtaining successive glances to which we must fit our perceptions (Gombrich, 1963; Hochberg, 1968). This is true for the normal picture, but some reflection about how we perceive anamorphic pictures will make the point more dramatically and tell us more about how we normally perceive the world, as well. An anamorphic picture, it will be remembered, is one in which the painting must be viewed from an extreme angle in order to make the represented scene recognizable. In order to see such a picture, we must combine the foveal information about points that are at different distances (since the picture plane is inclined) into a single scene, and in that case the regions that fall outside of our foveas in any glance are poorly visible not only because they lie in peripheral vision; they are, additionally, out of focus, since they lie nearer or farther than the point at which our eye is momentarily directed. Nevertheless, what we perceive, assembled from these highly restricted glances, is an apparently complete picture, free and independent of the surface of the plane that carries the information. That picture exists only as a mathematical abstraction in space and a construction in the mind's eye of the viewer.

As I have argued elsewhere (1968, 1974), these facts are sufficient to force us to discard the Gestalt explanation of how we see (and, in particular, of how we see pictures). Only two viable alternatives remain. We may restrict ourselves to an explanation based on mathematical abstraction (this, as I see it, is Gibson's position), or we may posit acquired mental structure— schematic maps (Hochberg, 1968) or hypothesized objects (Gregory, 1970)—that serve several important perceptual functions. Such structures would have to motivate successive glances by posing the questions for perceptual inquiry (*Is this a car or a cat?*), guiding the sampling behavior by which the questions are answered (*If this is a car, I must look over there to see if it has a headlight*), serving as the criterion to terminate the inquiry (*It has a hubcap and a headlight, so it is a car and not a cat, and there is no need to look further*), and storing the results of the inquiry (*It was a car*).

To such a theoretical viewpoint—which is really a development of the Helmholtz–Brunswik (1954)–Hebb (1949) position, and which is essentially also that of Neisser, 1967, 1976—the nature of the mental structure by which we integrate our successive glances, and the conditions for motivating the perceptual inquiry that drives them, must be questions of the highest priority. And they are questions that quite naturally turn to research about the arts for their answers.

First, as to the nature of the mental structure. The inconsistent pictures of Escher, Albers, and Penrose—of which Pierenne's observations about the violations of perspective remind us may be more the rule than the exception—tell us that *we do not store physical objects in our perceptual repertory. Whatever consistency there is in the world is imposed by the world, not by our nervous systems.* Figure–ground is merely a name for our expectations of where we will find objects' edges when we look to one region or another (Hochberg, 1962, 1974b). Outlines will serve as surrogates for objects' edges because they share the same receptor mechanisms that are sensitive to luminance differences, and because most objects' edges and corners are marked by an abrupt luminance change that remains detectable in peripheral vision where other information, more powerful but more dependent on detail, fails. The Gestalt laws are themselves cues as to which side of an edge is part of the object, and which parts of the visual field will move together as a unit when we move our heads or eyes.*

Some object cues are less ambiguous than others [e.g., intersections and corners (Guzman, 1968; Hochberg, 1968; cf. Ratoosh, 1949)],† and some are more characteristic of a particular object than others [e.g., viewed from above, a glass tumbler or a pyramid will appear as a set of concentric circles and a square with crossing diagonals, respectively—surely not the most distinctive aspects by which to identify those objects (cf. Gibson, 1969)]. In the accidental concatenation of features that is provided by a photograph, or by any other high-fidelity surrogate, it is unlikely that the most informative features and characteristic shapes will be presented in a form as economical and uncluttered as that which an artist can choose to create.

We can now understand what was surely the most difficult of facts to assimilate to any surrogate theory of pictures , that is, the fact that cartoons or caricatures, with their inherent loss of information and fidelity, are often better at representing the world and clarifying visual relationships (Arnheim, 1969) than more representational pictures are. Thus, Ryan and Schwarz (1956) showed that when the same objects were represented by photographs, shaded drawings, outline drawings, and cartoons that had been prepared by an artist keeping the previously mentioned principles in mind, cartoons were perceived at a briefer tachistoscopic exposure than were the high-fidelity photographs. How can fidelity decrease and recognizability increase?

A good cartoon, as any other good work of representational art, combines the object's least ambiguous and most characteristic feature, even though in reality they could not all be simultaneously visible. Presenting an object in what we may call its *canonical form* (Hochberg, 1972a) (i.e., the form that best displays its characteristic features) provides the viewer with a prototype that will help him encode and store similar objects in the future (cf. Attneave, 1957). In this sense, by providing us with sharper schemas than we can form from direct experience with the world itself, art may affect our perceptions (Gombrich, 1956)—as is suggested by the widespread reliance on stylized diagrams in training manuals and political cartoons in partisan newspapers.

Research on the procedures that make representation more effective with fewer features, and on its effects in encoding and storing, would certainly be desirable for both theoretical and paractical reasons, and such research

---

* For example, the law of good continuation is a case of *interposition,* in the sense that it is extremely unlikely that two different objects, at different distances, will line up within the tolerances of our excellent ability to distinguish misalignments (Hochberg, 1972b); the law of proximity reflects the fact that things that are close together are more likely to be part of one object (Brunswik & Kamiya, 1953).

† Although an ingenious experiment can always find some set of overlapping shapes that will employ the same set of lines differently (Chapanis & McCleary, 1953; Dinnerstein & Wertheimer, 1957), and so can an ingenious perceiver.

should not be inordinately difficult to undertake, given the pioneering work of Ryan and Schwarz, and given what we know about local depth cues. The fact is, however, that most people who are interested in art, or even in cartoons and caricatures, are not particularly concerned with their representational function. That function has been emphasized in perception texts because there are reasonable criteria for the goodness with which a picture communicates spatial layout, and because understanding something about the mechanics of how a representational piece of art works probably helps us to appreciate it (especially when there is so little else that the novice can find out about art that is that definite). But there are the other functions to consider: Caricatures communicate more than the spatial forms they represent, and both visual and nonvisual art in general do more than represent objects, scenes, and people. Let us turn to the two major nonrepresentational perceptual functions that the arts can serve.

III. NONREPRESENTATIONAL FUNCTIONS
OF ARTISTIC PRESENTATIONS:
EXPRESSIVE AND AESTHETIC

Once the artist is freed from the constraints of projective fidelity, other goals can be maximized in addition to, or even superceding, representation. The expressive and the aesthetic are often considered as a single function, but as I treat them here, they are separate and not, in fact, coordinate. *Expressive* refers to feelings, emotions and attitudes, and the self-expression of the artist; *aesthetic* refers (originally) to beauty and the pleasure of beholding it, and to whatever factors, including those arising from the other two functions, engage the disinterested evaluative attention of the audience [disinterested in the sense that no extrinsic or *exogenous* motive (Kruglanski, 1975) can be assigned as the source of the evaluative attention].

A. Expression and Feeling

The caricaturist may choose to use a broad, jagged line to draw the blunt, harsh person; he may use a thin, tremulous line and an unbalanced, tense composition to express his anxiety about an event that he depicts. The represented demeanors and facial expressions of the persons he portrays express their feelings, whereas the proper use of the medium expresses the feelings of the artist. When "Rembrandt depicts *unflinchingly* the gradual decline and decay of his body [Zucker, 1963]," it is not Rembrandt, the subject of the self-portrait, but Rembrandt, the painter, who expresses this unflinching firmness (Sircello, 1965). The artist may communicate the expression that depicts the feelings of the person portrayed, he may use the medium to express his feelings in a way that the audience can share, or, in still another sense of the word, he may express *himself* as an identifiable and unique individual. He can employ a personal style that both establishes his identity and carries connotative meaning (e.g., that of being whimsical or brooding, or perhaps some nonverbalizable flavor, flourish, or mood). Goya, Feiffer, Steinberg, and Gropper (to continue with the example of caricaturists) all use the elements of the medium not only as signatures (i.e., to identify themselves), but also as signals of their attitudes toward their subject matter (and to some degree, as constraints upon their subject matter) as well.

We have a great deal of testimony to the effect that color and composition in the visual arts (Ball, 1965; Kepes, 1964; Poore, 1903; Taylor, 1964); melodic structure, scale, and rhythm in music (Gutheil, 1948; Meyer, 1956); words and sounds in poetry and prose (Belknap, 1934; Pope, 1711; Wilson, 1931); and movements in dance (Davis, 1972; Kreitler & Kreitler, 1972; Martin, 1939; Sorell, 1966) all carry specific expressive meaning. There is also a large but scattered body of experimental evidence to this point. The experiments have usually been directed to show that expressive, or *physiognomic* (Werner, 1948) judgments can be obtained from subjects who are shown such elements in isolation. Reviews of early research of this kind can be found in Hammond (1933) and in Chandler and Barnhart (1938); a large body of later research is referenced in Pickford (1972).

Lest this sound accidental and inconsequential, consider one field of applied art (out of many) to which such analyses are critical: advertising. In advertising (and propaganda) it is a matter of very careful consideration that the connotations of words, of visual elements, of layout composition, of mood music, etc., relate appropriately and contribute to the image that the audience will form of the product or the person being represented, and the relevant research (and more that has reputedly been performed in-house and kept as trade secrets) is carefully weighed (albeit with almost completely unknown validity). If the psychology of expressive art languishes today, it is not for want of belief in its potential economic payoff.

What is missing is a well-developed psychological theory in terms of which such research can be ordered. It is not the case that no general explanations have been offered: At least three classes of theory appear in various guises. The empiricist approach (e.g., associations to the physical properties shared by the elements, the melodic aspects of the language that are associated with different classes of message, and the abstraction of a form or category to deal with experience) has been represented by a range of theories, such as those of Osgood (1976) and Langer (1958). The empathy theory (as in Lipps' attempt in 1900 to explain aesthetics, as well as the geometrical illusions (1897) in terms of the emotional or reactive response of the observer when he looks at even relatively simple stimuli) is represented more or less directly by Gombrich (1972a) in his hypotheses about portrait perception, by Schillinger on music (1948), and (via identification with what he terms modal–vectorial bodily functions and rates) by Gardner (1973). Words, shapes, colors, and feelings may all share a single isomorphic internal response—a position represented by the Gestalt theorists (see Koffka, 1935), by Arnheim in 1954 and, in a complex way, by Smets (1973). Smets has proposed that an aesthetic stimulus elicits those emotional and synesthetic connotations that also evoke the same degree of arousal (measuring arousal in terms of the desynchronization of alpha-waves activity), and has demonstrated such equivalences with colors, shapes, and connotative descriptions.*

These classes of explanation are not strongly exclusive, nor do they seem to me to be what is needed in the way of a theory at this point. We do not know whether or by what means the effects of a work of art can be expressed in terms of the effects of its parts. This is, of course, the problem on which Structuralism foundered (Hochberg, 1972a), and despite the fact that a work of art is often didactically analyzed in terms of the effects aroused by its component elements, I know of no theory that provides combining rules, and without them these studies of the components are neither theoretically nor practically useful.

In the example with which we started the discussion of artistic expression, the expressive features of a medium communicated something *about* a represented object or scene, but that is obviously not necessary. *If the elements of the artist's medium are themselves expressive, the artistic presentation may be expressive without representing anything at all, as in music:* We therefore say that the music *is* joyous, not that the music is *about* a joyous event (cf. Beardsley, 1958, 1965; Zinc, 1960).

It seems clear enough that such statements can be made about artistic presentations (especially those, like music and dancing, that are the normal means of celebrating such feelings); there has been far less research directed to this point than there has been for the study of the elements mentioned previously. We know that subjects will refer to the emotional impact of abstract pictures (Hussain, 1968) and that mood responses are made with some reliability to musical selections (Berger, 1970). Pickford (1972) and Child (1972) have done general reviews, and Berlyne and Ogilvie (1974) and Pickford (1955) have done factor-analytic studies of subjects' responses to works of art, but all such work shares a dependence on some kind of analytic response from the subject, and there is a real question of whether words or rating scales can adequately translate the effect of an artistic presentation (cf. Gardner, 1973), especially with naïve subjects. Consequently, I see as more promising the methods that ask subjects to perform more objective

---

* More physiological arousal had previously been found in response to red than to blue (Gerard, 1958; Wilson, 1966), and Smets reports that subjects matched colors, shapes, and verbal expressive concepts to each other in the same way that their arousal patterns were related (using the duration of desynchronization of alpha waves as the measure of arousal). What the meaning of alpha-wave desynchronization is, is of course another question.

tasks that, by their design, depend on reliable sensitivity to nonrepresentational qualities of the art. For example, subjects will reliably match titles (not necessarily those given by the artist) with abstract paintings, will correctly assign tops and bottoms to them (Lindauer, 1970), and are able to match paintings by Klee with the music that presumably inspired them (Minnigerode, Cianco, & Sbarboro, 1976; Peretti, 1972; Wehner, 1966).

Similar measurement procedures can be applied to artists' styles, which are also nonrepresentational and which may be expressive in both senses of the word. As with the individual work of art itself, it seems possible, in principle, to describe what is common across a group of works in terms of the physical variables of shape, color, movement, etc., that compose their common characteristics. The complexity of a real work of art, however, as opposed to laboratory stimuli, is such that for precise characterization of a style, whether of artist or of period, even trained art historians must compare examples directly to each other, or to a standard work (Schapiro, 1961). There is no reason to expect that naïve subjects' verbal descriptions or ratings of actual artworks, therefore, will prove particularly informative, but the method of work-to-work comparison is readily adapted to perceptual inquiry. For example, a similar procedure has been used to measure aesthetic sensitivity, namely, the ability to judge whether works of art are or are not by the same artist, using literary selections (Westland, 1968), musical selections (Gardner, 1972), and paintings (Smets & Knops, 1976). One purpose motivating the use of this procedure is to avoid some of the problems inherent in standard tests of aesthetic judgment (Child, 1964). Since Smets and Knopf obtained split-half reliabilities of .91 in differentiating subjects from each other, the method must also provide a research tool for the measurement of artists and periods, as well.

Why be concerned with artistic style? It may be the most important aspect of the expressive function of art. Style, or recognizable individual differences in artistic production (what is usually meant by "expressing one's personality," by those who use the term), has since the Renaissance been an ever-increasing component of the art market and, therefore, of aesthetic development (cf. Grosser, 1971). It may in fact be expressive, in the sense that it involves differences in mood, emotion, or attitude; or it may merely involve differences in the ways in which problems of composition and aesthetic value are solved. In any case, however, without a distinctive and memorable style, no pure artist (and few applied artists, such as cartoonists, singers, or dress designers) can have a viable career.

To some, the expressive function of art is its most important.* We must

---

* For example, Tolstoy, 1899; Croce, 1915; Collingwood, 1938; and some to whom the major function of art education is to teach children to express themselves (Read, 1943; Gardner, 1973). From that viewpoint, the fact that the clearly recognizable individuality of children's drawings declines as they mature is necessarily evidence that a decline in artistic ability has occurred, but we should notice that that judgment rests on which definition of artistic function is emphasized.

note, however, that just as it is possible to find many examples of recognized art that have little or no representational intent, and are not to be evaluated in terms of how good they are as likenesses, there are also many works of art that are devoid of expression in any reasonable sense of that word. The traditional subject matter of experimental aesthetics comes closest to being applicable to those enterprises. We consider that field next.

B. Art as Pleasurable or Engaging: Experimental Aesthetics and Preference

Experimental aesthetics was founded by Fechner in 1876 (Fechner was also, of course, the founder of psychophysics). Woodworth (1938) has presented an admirable discussion of the field to his time, and early bibliographies were published by Hammond (1933) and by Chandler and Barnhart (1938). Reviews or collections of papers are found in Berlyne (1971, 1972a,b, 1973, 1974), Child (1972; this volume), and Pickford (1972). I will raise some of the points made in Woodworth's discussion and then, adding some of my own will consider the state of knowledge in the field and discuss why perception psychologists who subscribe to a schema-testing or constructivist approach should be concerned with it. Much of this introductory statement is by way of saying that most of the research really has nothing to do with the perception of beauty or the arousal of an aesthetic emotion, and that preference judgments will not support a simple interpretation. *For those very reasons,* however, I believe that the research that has been done in this area is applicable to the appreciation of art (particularly, pure art), and that although the criticisms that have been raised in this regard are probably valid, the area of research remains important both for art and for psychology.

Woodworth pointed out that in experimental aesthetics the object of study is the response to the beautiful, the sublime, the tragic, the comic, or the pathetic. The response should depend on the subject's feeling, rather than on his intellectual perceptions or judgments. In the laboratory, however, the subject usually takes the questions to mean not "how much feeling is aroused in you?" but "is this object pleasing or displeasing?" so that the results belong under the heading of judgment rather than feeling. Most of the methods employed in research in this area have involved asking the subject to make rankings or choices according to preference, and Woodworth noted that the very fact that nearly everyone was able to select a most pleasing rectangle when Fechner solicited such judgments in the process of testing claims that had been made about the "golden section" (to which we will return in a moment) was itself an important psychological result: "A mere rectangle, we might suppose, could have no esthetic effect one way or the other [Woodworth, 1938, p. 385]."

To these comments, I would add the following. We have known for decades that introspection will not serve to discern the inner workings of our minds. Helmholtz taught us that we make our judgments by fitting the most probable explanation to the information we receive, and the James–Lange theory of emotions and the attribution theory of social psychology have both underscored the applicability of this dictum to our judgments about our feelings and attitudes (cf. Bem, 1967; Nisbett & Wilson, 1977; Schachter & Singer, 1962). Subjects have to figure out what their preferences are, deducing them from their other observable responses and their knowledge about what they are being shown. That is to say, preferences are not directly observable entities (cf. Valins, 1966), and even if subjects did have access to their preferences, we know that they seem to do more of what the situation demands than what they are told to (Orne, 1962). One might think that the last point can be disregarded precisely because the stimuli that are usually used to study experimental aesthetics are simple rectangles, random polygons, or other relatively neutral patterns. I do not believe, however, that such is the case. The aesthetic-preference task is not a neutral one: It asks subjects to expose their taste and their sensibilities, to make themselves vulnerable with regard to a dimension of preference having the strongest social and class connotations. (In fact preference tests are indeed also used as personality tests: cf. Barron & Welsh, 1952.) Nonsense patterns though they may be, the stimuli are not alone in the subject's field of judgment. First, they imply the entire class of stimuli from which he can infer them to have been generated, and that affects his judgment of their goodness (Garner, 1966; Garner & Clement, 1963), which must surely interact with what he knows of the canons of the culture. Second, we note that the stimuli used are, by and large, random shapes of a sort that no reasonable person would spend a glance on outside of the experiment, and surely not worth either arousal or preference. Yet arousal and preference there are, which must, it seems to me, derive from the challenge of grasping the principles that should guide the choices. We will return to this point after surveying the research area.

Complaints about the narrowness of the research and proposals to move out of the laboratory have been made, and some steps have been taken in remedial directions (cf. Lindauer, 1970, 1973; Wallach, 1959). Also, as we have noted, some factor analyses of similarity judgments or rating scales of various selections of pictures have been reviewed by Berlyne (1974) and Pickford (1972). The bulk of the research remains with work on color preference (summarized in Pickford, 1972), and on how the complexity of visual and auditory nonsense patterns affects subjects' interest in them and judgments of preference or pleasingness about them (a great deal of the work with adults is summarized in Berlyne, 1974, some work with children is summarized in Gardner, 1971, 1973, and Pickford, 1972, and work with differential habituation of infants' looking at various kinds of stimuli is summarized in Cohen, 1976, and Olson, 1976). With the exception of the study by Smets (1973), which I have mentioned above, the color work does not seem to me to be of theoretical interest at this time. I believe that the work on the effects of complexity is.

Perhaps the three most famous prescriptions for beauty in visual art are those of the "golden section" (that is, the most pleasing proportion), which since antiquity was claimed to be one in which the whole is to the larger part as the larger is to the smaller: $1/x = x/1 - x$), or $x = .618$ (in a rectangle, that would require one side to be .618 times the length of the other); Hogarth's Line of Beauty (an ogive, or S-curve), which has been used as the main line of myriad works of painting, sculpture, ornamentation, and pottery; and Polyclitus's Doryphoros, a statue embodying the canon for early Greek statuary. Of these, the first has been subject to the most research (reviewed by Woodworth, 1938, and Valentine, 1962). Rectangles with that proportion are, by and large, the central tendency of preference judgments. Why?

Witmer (1894) ascribed its preferred status to a pleasing unity of diverse parts; Weber (1931) proposed (in the *Journal of Applied Psychology,* we should note, in which a fair amount of such work was published) that any figure sets its viewer the problem of seeing it as a unit and, if it is too easy to do so, interest is quickly lost, whereas too much difficulty spoils the aesthetic effect.

These formulations reflect an age-old conviction that beauty or pleasingness is some function of complexity. What function will predict subjects' preference judgments (i.e., the so-called hedonic tone of the stimuli) from measures of the objects they are judging? Birkhoff (1933) proposed that, within a class of objects, the aesthetic value $M = O/C$, where O is some measure of order and C is a measure of complexity. Means of subjects' preferences for polygons he had constructed gave the same order as his measure of M. There have been several failures to corroborate this model (Davis, 1936; Eysenck, 1968; Eysenck & Castle, 1970). Other quantitative models have been proposed. Adding a "pleasure center" to his nerve-net model for the detection of lines and angles, Rashevsky (1940) provided a good fit to Davis' data. A remarkable effort to provide the basis for a technology for manufacturing music according to his own mathematical principles was published by Schillinger in 1948—with what effect, I do not know. Information-theory variations of Birkhoff's formula (Gunzenhäuser, 1968) provide for $M = R/H$, where $H =$ statistical information in its conventional meaning, but R is *subjective* redundancy, which should vary with learning and motivation (cf. Moles, 1958; Smets, 1973, measured subjective redundancy in her research by a version of Attneave's 1954 guessing technique). Eysenck proposed an inverted-U-shaped function relating preference and complexity (Eysenck, 1968; Eysenck & Castle, 1970). So does Berlyne (1967), on the grounds that arousal (of the activation of a cortical reward system) increases linearly with complexity, whereas hedonic tone is greatest at an intermediate level of arousal (Hebb, 1955; Lindsley, 1957).

According to Berlyne's proposal, the arousal potential of a stimulus pattern depends on a number of factors, including the pattern's intensity, its association with significant events, and its *collative properties*. These last are formal characteristics such as the pattern's variation along such dimensions as familiar–novel, simple–complex, expected–surprising, etc. Since arousal presumably increases with complexity (among other things), and hedonic tone is greatest at intermediate arousal levels, the graph of hedonic tone plotted against complexity should be an inverted-U function. Judgments of interest versus disinterest, however, and of complexity versus simplicity (and other verbal measures of arousal) should increase with the complexity of the stimulus (often measured in informational terms, or uncertainty).

In many cases (Bragg & Crozier, 1974; Crozier, 1974; Dorfman & McKenna, 1966; Normore, 1974; Vitz, 1966; Walker, 1970; Wohlwill, 1968), the expected relationship between hedonic tone and complexity is found; in others, pleasantness or preference ratings increase monotonically with complexity (Hare, 1974a; Jones, 1964; Reich & Moody, 1970; Vitz, 1964). There are even cases in which pleasantness declines with complexity, in agreement with Birkhoff's proposal, as Reich and Moody found (1970) when they used stimuli to which subjects had been habituated. As Smets (1973) pointed out, however, and demonstrated (using two-element matrix patterns that varied in redundancy as well as in number of elements; cf. also Snodgrass, 1971), with a nonmonotonic function the part of the curve that one obtains depends on the range tested. Since the effective order, structure, or redundancy that a subject can discern will depend on his familiarity with the stimulus pattern (cf. Goldstein, 1961; Harrison & Zajonc, 1970) and perhaps on the artistic training he has received (Smets, 1973; Hare, 1974b). Whether this is because of a larger available "vocabulary," a greater readiness to expend perceptual effort to detect structure, or a preference for greater complexity, we can expect that even if hedonic tone is a single-peaked function of complexity, interexperimental variation will occur. It seems safe to conclude that pleasingness and preference judgments are a function of complexity in such experiments, and that the function is nonmonotonic.

There are alternative models that can be fitted to these facts, such as the proposal of McClelland *et al.* (1953) that a stimulus at adaptation level (Helson, 1964) to which we are habituated is neither pleasing nor displeasing, and as it departs from adaptation level it passes through a maximum of pleasingness and finally becomes unpleasant and noxious. An application to stimulus complexity is reasonably straightforward (Terwilliger, 1963). We would not expect the "butterfly curve" of this proposal to be manifested unless the range of stimuli used within a given experiment straddled the indifference point as it is set by experience with stimuli within and outside the experiment, but it has been found in some experimental situations (Day, 1967; Haber, 1958; Munsinger & Kessen, 1964), and the cycle of unpopularity, popularity, and neutrality through which popular songs and other fashions swing grant it considerable anecdotal plausibility (see also Wohlwill, 1966). We would expect, in fact, that small departures from some familiar and well-formed schema would be important to the initiation and maintainance of perceptual inquiry, and it is interesting to note that both the golden section (Fischer, 1969; Lalo, 1908) and Polyclitus's canon (Ruesch, 1977) may be cultural rather than mathematical norms (in fact, Ruesch makes a good case that Polyclitus's canon is an embodiment of the central tendencies of actual early anthropometric measurements from which, once established, subsequent sculptors departed for specific effects).

A plausible parallel can thus be drawn between the body of laboratory work, and at least some features of the less simplistic real world of art. What is missing from the accounts of both, as I see it, is the question of motivation. In the tasks of experimental aesthetics, the subject has agreed to try to grasp the relative merits of the members of the stimulus set with which he has been presented. That effort, and the challenge to display his aesthetic expertise, and not the inherent beauty or interest of the stimuli (as Normore's subjects asked spontaneously in one experiment, "How can a dot be beautiful?" 1974, p. 119) is what maintains his interest. Note that all of the collative variables are such that as they increase so should the time and effort that is required to grasp the structure of the stimulus pattern, if there is something to grasp. Because of that, we would expect that looking and listening time increases with the complexity of the stimulus patterns, as in fact it does (Berlyne, 1974; Crozier, 1974; Faw & Nunnally, 1967; Hochberg & Brooks, in press), as do subjects' ratings of *interestingness* as well (reviewed by Berlyne, 1974). The latter, in fact, increase *monotonically* with complexity, reflecting, I suggest, the subjects' continued search to find some order or principle in the pattern that will account for the occurrence and placement of most (or at least some) of the elements.

What about the hedonic tone associated with such schema-testing activities? Weber's explanation (p. 248) will do nicely: If a pattern is so simple that there is no principle to generate and test, or if it is so complex that (given the subject's background and motivation) the subject cannot find some schema that, with relative economy, makes the pattern "right," it is not pleasing, as no perceptual achievement has rewarded his efforts. Note that this makes the grasping and testing of the schema, not the complexity or the arousal per se, the basis of the hedonic tone, and that a motive to undertake the task is needed: *The hedonic tone is not inherent in the stimuli.*

There is much that such a schema-testing account must leave out,* but

---

* For example, Christine and Fred Attneave's response to an earlier version of this proposal was: "What about the pleasure of first seeing an intensely blue lake?" I think it is likely that such questions can be handled, but this is not the place to try to do so. Another troublesome class of problem is concerned with how much a member of the audience expects to be able to fit into a given schema. Some amount of any work of art (particularly one in which the elements are

there is also much that seems to me to be close to the actual operation of the aesthetic function of art. In many lines of art, *sophistication brings simplification* (e.g., minimal art). A great deal of education in the artist's premises and purposes, and the nonverbalizable concepts that are furnished by the tradition against which the artist makes his "statement," is necessary before the member of the audience will be capable of perceiving aesthetic order. Without that education, or without the intention to perceive how the parts fit each other and fit the schema provided by the tradition in which the work is being executed (and to which it inescapably refers), there is nothing for the viewer to achieve. If he does not know anything about art, he cannot know what he likes.

To the psychologist who views the process of perception as being a purposive activity of fitting schemas to the samples of the world that are produced by perceptual inquiry, the nature of art (and in particular those features that initiate and sustain perceptual inquiry) is not merely another area of research, with interesting cultural and humanistic overtones, for it raises most of the problems, in an immediate way, with which he must eventually be able to deal in an explicit and testable fashion.

References

Angier, R. P. The aesthetics of unequal division. *Psychology Review, Monograph Supplement,* 1903, **4**, 541–561.

Antes, J. R. The time course of picture viewing. *Journal of Experimental Psychology,* 1974, **103**, 162–170.

Arnheim, R. Gestalt and art. *Journal of Aesthetics and Art Criticism,* 1943, **2**, 71–75.

Arnheim, R. *Art and visual perception.* Berkeley, California: Univ. of California Press, 1954.

Arnheim, R. *Toward a psychology of art.* Berkeley: Univ. of California Press, 1966. P. 200.

Arnheim, R. *Visual thinking.* Berkeley: Univ. of California Press, 1969.

Attneave, F. Some informational aspects of visual perception. *Psychological Review,* 1954, **61**, 183–193.

Attneave, F. Physical determinants of the judged complexity of shapes. *Journal of Experimental Psychology,* 1957, **53**, 221–227.

Attneave, F., & Frost, R. The discrimination of perceived tridimensional orientation by minimum criteria. *Perception & Psychophysics,* 1969, **6**, 391–396.

Ball, U. K. The aesthetics of color: A review of fifty years of experimentation. *Journal of Aesthetics and Art Criticism,* 1965, **23**, 441–452.

Barron, F., & Welsh, G. S. Artistic perception as a factor in personality style: Its measurement by a picture-preference test. *American Journal of Psychology,* 1952, **33**, 199–203.

Beardsley, M. *Aesthetics: Problems in the philosophy of criticism.* New York: Harcourt Brace, 1958.

---

presented over time under the artist's control, like music, dance, literature, or motion pictures) is *texture*, and is needed merely for verisimilitude. Some artwork will have *outcome* and be important to the final structure. In assessing how economical a work of art is, we probably should be attending not to the total complexity, but to that portion that the viewer or listener takes as part of the structure (i.e., his *subjective outcome structure*). In painting and in drawing, one does not count the brush strokes and the cross-hatches as elements, yet some of them, in each case, do serve special functions in the design.

Beardsley, M. On the creation of art. *Journal of Aesthetics and Art Criticism,* 1965, **23,** 291–304.

Belknap, G. N. *Guide to reading in aesthetics and theory of poetry,* Eugene: Univ. Oregon Publ. 1934, **4,** 9.

Bem, D. J. Self-perception: An alternative interpretation of cognitive dissonance phenomena. *Psychological Review,* 1967, **74,** 188–200.

Berlyne, D. Arousal and reinforcement. In D. Levine (Ed.), *Nebraska Symposium on motivation,* 1967, Lincoln, Nebraska: Univ. of Nebraska Press, 1967.

Berlyne, D. E., McDonnell, P., Nicky, R. M., & Parham, L. C. Effects of auditory pitch and complexity on E.E.G. desynchronization and on verbally expressed judgments. *Canadian Journal of Psychology,* 1967, **21,** 346–367.

Berlyne, D. E. *Aesthetics and psychobiology.* New York: Appleton, 1971.

Berlyne, D. E. Ends and means of experimental aesthetics. *Canadian Journal of Psychology,* 1972, **26,** 303–325. (a)

Berlyne, D. E. Reinforcement values of visual patterns compared through concurrent performances. *Journal of the Experimental Analysis of Behavior,* 1972, **18,** 281–285. (b)

Berlyne, D. E. The vicissitudes of aplopathematic and thelematoscopic pneumatology (*or* The hydrography of hedonism. In D. E. Berlyne & K. B. Madsen (Eds.), *Pleasure, reward, preference.* New York: Academic Press, 1973.

Berlyne, D. E., & Ogilvie, J. C. Dimensions of perception of paintings. In D. E. Berlyne (Ed.), *Studies in the new experimental aesthetics.* Wash., D.C.: Hemisphere, 1974.

Biederman, J. Perceiving real-world scenes. *Science,* 1972, 77–80.

Birkhoff, G. *Aesthetic measure.* Cambridge: Harvard Univ. Press, 1933.

Bouleau, C. The painter's secret geometry: A study of composition in art. New York: Thames, Hudson & Harcourt, 1963.

Bragg, B. W. E., & Crozier, J. B. The development with age of verbal and exploratory responses to sound sequences varying in uncertainty level. In D. E. Berlyne, 1974.

Breger, I. Affective response to meaningful sound stimuli. *Perceptual and Motor Skill,* 1970, **30,** P. 842.

Brooks, V. An exploratory comparison of some measures of attention. M. A. Thesis, Cornell Univ., 1961.

Brunswik, E., & Kamiya, J. Ecological cue-validity of "proximity" and other Gestalt factors. *American Journal of Psychology,* 1953, **66,** 20–32.

Brunswik, E. *Perception and the representative design of psychological experiments* (2nd ed.). Berkeley: Univ. of California Press, 1956.

Buswell, G. T. *How people look at pictures.* Chicago: Univ. of Chicago Press, 1935.

Chandler, A., & Barnhart, E. *A bibliography of physiological and experimental esthetics.* Berkeley: Univ. of California Press, 1938.

Chapanis, A., & McCleary, R. A. Interposition as a cue for the perception of relative distance. *Journal of General Psychology,* 1953, **48,** 113–132.

Child, I. Esthetics. In G. Lindzey & E. Aronson, *Handbook of Social Psychology* (Vol. 3). Reading, Massachusetts: Addison-Wesley, 1969. Pp. 853–916.

Child, I. Esthetics. *Annual Review of Psychology,* 1972, **23,** 669–694.

Child, I. Observations on the meaning of some measures of esthetic sensitivity. *Journal of Psychology,* 1964, **57,** 49–64.

Clerici, F. The grand illusion. *Art News Annual,* 1954, **23,** 98–180.

Cohen, L. B. Habituation of infant visual attention. In T. J. Tighe & R. N. Leaton (Eds.), *Habituation.* Hillsdale, New Jersey: Erlbaum, 1976.

Collingwood, R. G. *The principles of art.* Oxford: Clarendon, 1938.

Croce, B. *Breviary of aesthetic.* Houston: Rice Institute Pamphlet, Vol. 2, 1915. Pp. 223–310.

Crozier, J. B. Verbal and exploratory responses to sound sequences varying in uncertainty level. In D. E. Berlyne (Ed.), *Studies in the new experimental aesthetics.* Washington, D.C.: Hemisphere, 1974.

Davis, M., (Ed.), *Research approaches to movement and personality*. New York: Arno, 1972.

Davis, R. C. An evaluation and test of Birkhoff's aesthetic measure formula. *Journal of General Psychology*, 1936, **15**, 231–240.

Day, H. Evaluations of subjective complexity, pleasingness and interestingness for a series of random polygons varying in complexity. *Perception & Psychophysics*, 1967, **2**, 281–286.

Deregowski, J. B. Difficulties in pictorial depth perception in Africa. *British Journal of Psychology*, 1968, **59**, 195–204.

Dinnerstein, D., & Wertheimer, M. Some determinants of phenomenal overlapping. *American Journal of Psychology*, 1957, **70**, 21–37.

Dorfman, D., & McKenna, H. Pattern Preference as a function of pattern uncertainty. *Canadian Journal of Psychology*, 1966, **20**, 143–153.

Eysenck, H. J. An experimental study of aesthetic preference for polygonal figures. *Journal of General Psychology*, 1968, **79**, 3–17.

Eysenck, H., & Castle, M. Training in art as a factor in the determination of preference judgments for polygons. *British Journal of Psychology*, 1970, **61**, 65–81.

Farber, J., & Rosinski, R. R. Geometric transformations of pictured space. *Perception*, 1978, **7**, 269–282.

Faw, T. T., & Nunnally, J. C. The effects on eye movements of complexity, novelty and affective tone. *Perception & Psychophysics*, 1967, **2**, 263–267.

Fechner, G. *Vorschule der Aesthetik*. Leipzig: Breitkopf & Hartel, 1876.

Fischer, R. Out on a (phantom) limb. Variations on a theme: Stability of body image and the Golden Section. *Perspectives in Biology & Medicine*, 1969, **12**, 259–273.

Gardner, H. The development of sensitivity to artistic styles. *Journal of Aesthetics and Art Criticism*, 1971, **29**, 515–527.

Gardner, H. Style sensitivity in children. *Human Development*, 1972, **15**, 325–338.

Gardner, H. *The arts and human development*. New York: Wiley, 1973.

Garner, W. R. To perceive is to know. *American Psychology*, 1966, **21**, 11–19.

Garner, W. R., & Clement, D. E. Goodness of pattern and pattern uncertainty. *Journal of Verbal Learning and Verbal Behavior*, 1963, **2**, 446–452.

Gerard, R. M. *Differential effects of colored lights on psychophysiological functions* Ph.D. dissertation, Univ. of California, 1958.

Ghent, L. Perception of overlapping and embedded figures by children of different age. *American Journal of Psychology*, 1956, **69**, 575–587.

Gibson, E. J. *Principles of perceptual learning and development*. Englewood Cliffs, New Jersey: Prentice-Hall, 1969.

Gibson, J. J. A theory of pictorial perception. *Audio-Visual Communications Review*, 1954, **1**, 3–23.

Gibson, J. J. *The visual world*. Boston: Houghton Mifflin, 1950.

Gibson, J. J. What is a form? *Psychology Review*, 1951, **58**, 403–412.

Gibson, J. J. *The senses considered as perceptual systems*. Boston: Houghton Mifflin, 1966.

Gibson, J. J. The information available in pictures. *Leonardo*, 1971, **4**, 27–35.

Goldstein, A. G. Familiarity and apparent complexity of random shapes, *Journal of Experimental Psychology*, 1961, **62**, 594–597.

Gollin, E. S. Developmental studies of visual recognition of incomplete objects. *Perceptual and Motor Skills*, 1960, **11**, 289–298.

Gombrich, E. H. *Art and illusion*. New York: Pantheon, 1956.

Gombrich, E. H. *Meditations on a hobby-horse*. London: Phaidon, 1963.

Gombrich, E. H. The mask and the face: The perception of physiognomic likeness in life and art. In E. H. Gombrich, J. Hochberg, & M. Black, *Art, perception and reality*. Baltimore: The Johns Hopkins Univ. Press, 1972. (a)

Gombrich, E. H. The "What" and the "How": Perspective representation and the phenomenal world. In R. Rudner & Israel Sckeffler (Eds.), *Logic and art, essays in honor of Nelson Goodman*. Indianapolis, Indiana: Bobbs-Merrill, 1972. (b)

Goodman, N. *Languages of art: An approach to a theory of symbols*. Indianapolis, Indiana: Bobbs-Merrill, 1968.

Gregory, R. L. *The intelligent eye*. New York: McGraw-Hill, 1970.

Grice, H. Utterer's meaning, sentence-meaning and word-meaning. *Foundations of Language*, 1968, **4**, 225–242.

Grosser, M. *Painter's progress*. New York: Potter, 1971.

Gunzenhäuser, R. Das ästhetische Mass Birkhoffs in Informations ästhetischer Sicht. In H. Ronge (Ed.), Kunst and Kybernetik, Köln: DuMont, 1968.

Gutheil, E. *Music and your emotions*. New York: Liveright, 1948.

Guzmán, A. Computer recognition of three-dimensional objects in a visual scene. *MIT Artificial Intelligence Laboratory Project MAC-TR-59*, 1968.

Haber, R. N. Discrepancy from adaptation level as a source of affect. *Journal of Experimental Psychology*, 1958, **56**, 370–375.

Hagen, M. A. Picture perception: Toward a theoretical model. *Psychological Bulletin*, 1974, **81**, 471–497.

Hagen, M. A. Influence of picture surface and station point on the ability to compensate for oblique view in pictorial perception. *Developmental Psychology*, 1976, **12**, 57–63.

Hagen, M. A., & Elliott, H. B. An investigation of the relationship between viewing condition and preference for true and modified linear perspective. *Journal of Experimental Psychology: Human Perception and Performance*, 1976, **2**, 479–490.

Hammond, W. A. A bibliography of aesthetics and of the philosophy of the fine arts from 1900 to 1932. New York: Longmans, Green, 1933.

Hare, F. G. Verbal responses to visual patterns varying in distributional redundancy and in variety. In D. E. Berlyne (Ed.), *Studies in the new experimental aesthetics*. Washington, D.C.: Hemisphere, 1974. (a)

Hare, F. G. Artistic training and responses to visual and auditory patterns varying in uncertainty. In D. E. Berlyne (Ed.), *Studies in the new experimental aesthetics*. Washington, D.C.: Hemisphere, 1974. (b)

Harrison, A. A., & Zajonc, R. B. The effects of frequency and duration of exposure on response competition and affective ratings. *Journal of Psychology*, 1970, **75**, 163–169.

Hebb, D. *The organization of behavior*. New York: Wiley, 1949.

Hebb, D. Drives and the C.N.S. *Psychology Review*, 1955, **62**, 243–254.

Helson, H. *Adaptation level theory*. New York: Harper & Row, 1964.

Hevner, K. Experimental studies of the affective values of colors and lines. *Journal of Applied Psychology*, 1935, **19**, 385–398.

Hochberg, J. The psychophysics of pictorial perception. *Audio-Visual Communications Review*, 1962, **10**, 22–54.

Hochberg, J. In the mind's eye. In R. N. Haber (Ed.), *Contemporary theory and research in visual perception*. New York: Holt, Rinehart & Winston, 1968.

Hochberg, J. Attention, organization and consciousness. In D. I. Mostofsky (Ed.), *Attention: Contemporary theory and analysis*. New York: Appleton-Century-Crofts, 1970.

Hochberg, J. Pirenne's Optics, painting and photography. *Science*, 1971, **172**, 685–686.

Hochberg, J. The representation of things and people. In E. H. Gombrich, J. Hochberg, and M. Black, *Art, perception and reality*. Baltimore: The Johns Hopkins Univ. Press, 1972. (a)

Hochberg, J. Perception II. Space and movement. In J. W. Kling and L. A. Riggs (Eds.), *Woodworth & Schlosberg's Experimental Psychology*. New York: Holt, Rinehart & Winston, 1972. (b)

Hochberg, J. Higher-order stimuli and interresponse coupling in the perception of the visual world. In R. B. Macleod and H. L. Picks (Eds.), *Perception: Essays in honor of James J. Gibson*. Ithaca: Cornell Univ. Press, 1974, 17–39. (a)

Hochberg, J. Organization and the Gestalt tradition. In E. C. Carterette and M. Friedman (Eds.), *Handbook of Perception*. Vol. I. New York: Academic Press, 1974. (b)

Hochberg, J., and Brooks, V. The psychophysics of form: Reversible-perspective drawings of spatial objects. *American Journal of Psychology,* 1960, **73**, 337–354.

Hochberg, J., & Brooks, V. Pictorial recognition as an unlearned ability: A study of one child's performance. *American Journal of Psychology,* 1962a, **75**, 624–628.

Hochberg, J., & Brooks, V. The prediction of visual attention to designs and paintings. *American Psychologist,* 1962b, **17**. (Abstract)

Hochberg, J., & Brooks, V. Film cutting and visual momentum. In R. Monty & J. Senders (Eds.), *Eye movements and psychological processes, II.* Hillsdale, New Jersey: Erlbaum. (In press)

Hudson, W. Pictorial depth perception in sub-cultural groups in Africa. *Journal of Social Psychology,* 1960, **52**, 183–208.

Hudson, W. Pictorial perception and educational adaptation in Africa. *Psychologia Africana,* 1962, **9**, 226–239.

Hudson, W. The study of the problem of pictorial perception among unacculturated groups. *International Journal of Psychology,* 1967, **2**, 89–107.

Hussain, F. Une approche psychologique de l'art abstrait. *Proceedings of Fifth International Congress of Aesthetics.* Amsterdam: Mouton, 1964.

Jameson, D., and Hurvich, L. M. From contrast to assimilation: In art and in the eye. *Leonardo,* 1975, **8**, 125–131.

Jones, A. Drive and the incentive variables associated with the statistical properties of sequences of stimuli. *Journal of Experimental Psychology,* 1964, **67**, 423–431.

Kennedy, J. M. *A psychology of picture perception.* San Francisco: Jossey-Bass, 1974.

Kennedy, J. M. Ancient and modern picture-perception abilities in Africa. *Journal of Aesthetics and Art Criticism,* 1977, **35**, 293–300.

Kennick, W. Does traditional esthetics rest on a mistake? *Mind,* 1958, **68**.

Kepes, G. *Language of vision.* Chicago: Theobald, 1944.

Kilbride, P. L., & Robbins, M. C. Linear perspective, pictorial depth perception and education among the Baganda. *Perceptual and Motor Skills,* 1968, **27**, 601–602.

Koffka, K. *Principles of Gestalt Psychology.* New York: Harcourt Brace, 1935.

Krietler, H., & Krietler, S. *Psychology of the arts.* Durham: Duke Univ. Press, 1972.

Kruglanski, A. W. The endogenous-exogenous partition in attribution theory. *Psychology Review,* 1975, **82**, 387–406.

Lalo, C. *L'Esthétique expérimentale contemporaine.* Paris: Alcan, 1908.

Langer, S. K. *Philosophy in a new key.* New York: Mentor, 1958.

Lindauer, M. S. Psychological aspects of form perception in abstract art. *Scientific Aesthetics,* 1970, **7**, 19–24.

Lindauer, M. S. Toward a liberalization of experimental aesthetics. *Journal of Aesthetics and Art Criticism,* 1973, **31**, 459–465.

Lindsley, D. Psychophysiology and motivation. In M. Jones (Ed.), *Nebraska symposium on motivation,* 1957. Lincoln: Univ. of Nebraska Press, 1957.

Lipps, T. *Raumaesthetik und Geometrisch-Optische Tauschungen.* Leipzig, 1897.

Lipps, T. Aesthetische Einfühlung. *Zeitschrift fur Psychologie und Physiologie der Sinnesorgane,* 1900, **22**, 415–450.

Loftus, G. R. A framework for a theory of picture recognition. In R. A. Monty and J. W. Senders (Eds.), *Eye movements and psychological processes.* Hillsdale, New Jersey: Erlbaum, 1976.

Mackworth, N. H., & Morandi, A. J. The gaze selects informative details within pictures. *Perception & Psychophysics,* 1967, **2**, 547–552.

Martin, J. *Introduction to the dance.* New York: Norton, 1939.

McClelland, D., Atkinson, J., Clark, R., & Lowell, E. *The achievement motive.* New York: Appleton-Century-Crofts, 1953.

Meyer, L. B. *Emotion and meaning in music.* Chicago: Univ. of Chicago Press, 1956.

Minnigerode, F. A., Ciancio, D. W., & Sbarboro, L. A. Matching music with paintings by Klee. *Perceptual and Motor Skills*, 1976, **42**, 269–270.

Moles, A. *Information theory and esthetic perception*. Urbana, Illinois: Univ. of Illinois Press, 1966.

Molnar, F. Les mouvements exploratoires des yeux dans la composition picturale. *Sciences de l'Art*, 1964, **1**, 135–50.

Molnar, F. Recherche experimentale sur le role des mouvements oculaires dans l'appreciation de la composition picturale. *Proceedings Fifth International Congress Aesthetics*, 1968.

Mundy-Castle, A. C. Pictorial depth perception in Ghanaian children. *International Journal of Psychology*, 1966, **1**, 288–300.

Munsinger, H., & Kessen, W. Uncertainty, structure and preference. *Psychological Monographs*, 1964, **78**, 586.

Munsinger, H., & Weir, M. Infants' and young children's preferences for complexity. *Journal of Child Psychology*, 1967, **5**, 69–73.

Neisser, U. *Cognitive psychology*. New York: Appleton, 1967.

Neisser, U. *Cognition and reality*. San Francisco: Freeman, 1976.

Nisbett, R. E., & Wilson, T. D. Telling more than we can know: Verbal reports on mental processes. *Psychological Review*, 1977, **84**, 231–259.

Normore, L. F. Verbal responses to visual sequences varying in uncertainty level. In D. E. Berlyne (Ed.), *Studies in the new experimental aesthetics*. Washington, D.C.: Hemisphere, 1974.

Olds, J., & Olds, M. E. Drives and the brain. In F. Barron *et al.*, *New Directions in Psychology (II)* New York: Holt, 1965.

Olson, G. M. An information processing analysis of visual memory and habituation in infants. In T. J. Tighe and R. N. Leaton (Eds.), *Habituation*. Hillsdale, New Jersey: Erlbaum, 1976.

Olson, R. K. Children's sensitivity to pictorial depth information. *Perception & Psychophysics*, 1975, **71**, 59–64.

Omari, I. M., & Cook, H. Differential cognitive cues in pictorial depth perception. *Journal of Cross-Cultural Psychology*, 1972, **3**, 321–325.

Orne, M. T. On the social psychology of the psychological experiment: With particular reference to demand characteristics and their implications. *American Psychologist*, 1962, **17**, 776–783.

Osgood, C. E. *Focus on meaning*. The Hague: Mouton, 1976.

Penrose, L., & Penrose, P. Impossible objects: A special type of visual illusion. *British Journal of Psychology*, 1958, **49**, 31–33.

Peretti, P. A study of student correlations between music and six paintings by Klee. *Journal of Research in Music Education*, 1972, **20**, 501–504.

Perkins, D. N. Compensating for distortion in viewing pictures obliquely. *Perception & Psychophysics*, 1973, **14**, 13–18.

Pickford, R. W. Factorial studies of aesthetic judgments. In A. A. Roback (Ed.), *Present-day Psychology*. New York: Philosophical Library, 1955.

Pickford, R. W. Psychology and visual aesthetics. London: Hutchinson, 1972.

Pillsbury, W., & Schaefer, B. A note on advancing-retreating colors. *American Journal of Psychology*, 1937, **49**, 126–130.

Pirenne, M. *Optics, painting and photography*. Cambridge, England: Cambridge Univ. Press, 1970.

Polanyi, M. Introduction. In M. Pirenne (Ed.), *Optics, painting and photography*. Cambridge, England: Cambridge Univ. Press, 1970.

Pollack, I., & Spence, D. Subjective pictorial information and visual search. *Perception & Psychophysics*, 1968, **3**, 41–44.

Poore, H. R. *Pictorial composition and the critical judgment of pictures*. New York: Baker & Taylor, 1903.

Pope, A. *The language of drawing and painting.* Cambridge, Massachusetts: Harvard Univ. Press, 1949.

Pressey, C. L. The influence of color upon mental and motor efficiency. *American Journal of Psychology,* 1921, **32,** 326–356.

Rank, O. *Art and artist.* New York: Knopf, 1932.

Rashevsky, N. *Advances and applications of mathematical biology.* Chicago: Univ. of Chicago Press, 1940.

Ratoosh, P. On interposition as a cue for the perception of distance. *Proceedings of the National Academy of Science,* 1949, **35,** 257–259.

Read, H. *Education though art.* London: Faber & Faber, 1943.

Reich, J., & Moody, C. Stimulus properties, frequency of exposure, and affective responding. *Perceptual and Motor Skills,* 1970, **30,** 27–35.

Rosinski, R. R., Mulholland, T., Degelman, D., & Farber, J. Pictorial space perception: An analysis of visual compensation. *Perception & Psychophysics,* 1977. (In press)

Ruesch, J. *Greek statuary of the fifth and fourth centuries B.C.* Ph.D. Dissertation, Columbia Univ., 1977.

Ryan, T. A., & Schwartz, C. Speed of perception as a function of mode of representation. *American Journal of Psychology,* 1956, **69,** 60–69.

Schachter, S., & Singer, J. E. Cognitive, social, and physiological determinants of emotional state. *Psychological Review,* 1962, **69,** 379–399.

Schaie, K. W. Scaling the association between colors and moodtones. *American Journal of Psychology,* 1961, **74,** 266–273.

Schapiro, M. Style. In M. Philipson (Ed.), *Aesthetics today.* New York: Meridian, 1961.

Schillinger, J. *The mathematical basis of the arts.* New York: Philosophical Library, 1948.

Schmidt, C. F. Understanding human actions. In *Theoretical issues in natural language processing,* Report of an Interdisciplinary Workship in Computational Linguistics, Psychology Linguistics and Artificial Intelligence. Cambridge, Massachusetts: B. L. Nash Webber, Bolt Beranek and Newman, 1975.

Searle, J. R. Speech arts: an essay in the philosophy of language. Cambridge, England: Cambridge Univ. Press, 1969.

Sircello, G. Perceptual acts and pictorial art: A defense of expression theory. *Journal of Philosophy,* 1965, **62,** 669–677.

Smets, G. *Aesthetic judgment and arousal.* Louvain, Belgium: Leuven Univ. Press, 1973.

Smets, G., & Knops, L. Measuring visual esthetic sensitivity: An alternative procedure. *Perceptual and Motor Skills,* 1976, **42,** 867–874.

Smith, O. W. Judgments of size and distance in photographs. *American Journal of Psychology,* 1958, **71,** 529–538.

Smith, O. W., & Gruber, H. Perception of depth in photographs. *Perceptual and Motor Skills,* 1958, **8,** 307–313.

Smith, P. C., & Smith, O. W. Ball-throwing responses to photographically portrayed targets. *Journal of Experimental Psychology,* 1961, **62,** 223–233.

Snodgrass, J. G. Objective and subjective complexity measures for a new population of patterns. *Perception & Psychophysics,* 1971, **10,** 217–224.

Sorrell, W. (Ed.) *The dance has many faces.* New York: Columbia Univ. Press, 1966.

Szarkowski, J. *From the picture press.* New York: Museum of Modern Art, 1973.

Taylor, J. *Design and expression in the visual arts.* New York: Dover, 1964.

Terwilliger, R. F. Pattern complexity and affective arousal. *Perceptual and Motor Skills,* 1963, **17,** 387–395.

Thomas, H. Preferences for random shapes: Ages six through nineteen years. *Child Development,* 1966, **37,** 843–859.

Tolstoy, L. *What is art?* A. Maude (trans.) London: Oxford Univ. Press, 1899.

Valentine, C. W. *The experimental psychology of beauty.* London: Methuen, 1962.

Valins, S. Cognitive effects of false heart-rate feedback. *Journal of Personality and Social Psychology,* 1966, **4,** 400–408.

Vitz, P. Preferences for rates of information presented by sequences of tones. *Journal of Experimental Psychology,* 1964, **68,** 176–183.

Vitz, P. Preferences for different amounts of visual complexity. *Behavioral Science,* 1966, **11,** 105–114.

Walker, E. L. Psychological complexity and preference: A hedgehog theory of behavior. In D. E. Berlyne & K. B. Madsen (Eds.), *Pleasure, reward, preference.* New York: Academic Press, 1973. Pp. 65–97.

Wallach, M. A. Art, science and representation: Toward an experimental psychology of aesthetics. *Journal of Aesthetics and Art Criticism,* 1959, **18,** 159–173.

Weber, C. O. Esthetics of rectangles and theories of affect. *Journal of Applied Psychology,* 1931, **15,** 310–318.

Wehner, W. L. The relation between six paintings by Klee and selected musical compositions. *Journal of Research in Music Education,* 1966, **14,** 220–224.

Weitz, M. The role of theory in esthetics. *Journal of Aesthetics and Art Criticism,* 1956, **15.**

Weitz, M. The role of theory in esthetics. In. M. Rader (Ed.), *A modern book of esthetics.* New York: Holt, 1960.

Werner, H. Comparative psychology of mental development. Chicago: Follett, 1948.

Westland, G. The construction of objective tests of a form of aesthetic judgment. *British Journal of Aesthetics,* 1968, **8,** 387–393.

Wilson, E. Axel's castle: A study in the imaginative literature of 1870–1930. New York: Scribner's, 1931.

Wilson, G. Arousal properties of red vs. green. *Perceptual and Motor Skills,* 1966, **26,** 947–949.

Witmer, L. Zur experimentellen Aesthetik einfacher räumlicher Formverhältnisse. *Philosophische Studien,* 1893, **9,** 96–144, 209–263; Leipzig: Englemann, 1894.

Wohlwill, J. F. The physical environment: a problem for a psychology of stimulation. *Journal of Social Issues,* 1966, **4,** 29–38.

Wohlwill, J. F. Amount of stimulus exploration and preference as differential functions of stimulus complexity. *Perception & Psychophysics,* 1968, **4,** 307–312.

Woodworth, R. S. *Experimental psychology.* New York: Holt, Rinehart and Winston, 1938.

Wollheim, R. Art and illusion. *British Journal of Aesthetics,* 1963, **3,** 15–37.

Yonas, A., & Hagen, M. A. Effects of static and kinetic depth information on the perception of size in children and adults. *Journal of Experimental Child Psychology,* 1973, **15,** 254–265.

Zink, S. Is music really sad? *Journal of Aesthetics and Art Criticism,* 1960, **2,** 197–207.

Zucker, P. *Styles in a painting: A comparative study.* New York: Dover, 1963.

Chapter 11

THE PERCEPTION OF MOTION PICTURES*

JULIAN HOCHBERG AND VIRGINIA BROOKS

I. INTRODUCTION

Motion pictures and television provide an arena in which most of the results of perceptual inquiry find immediate application or challenge. Still pictures, and Leonardo's analysis of the pictorial means for portraying space (the *depth cues*), were the starting point for the major classical problems of perceptual research and theory. The investigation of the rules of motion picture perception promises to be at least as important to psychologists, by providing both the tool and the occasion for examining the transient characteristics of the normal perceptual process that are so often lost in the steady state of protracted presentation, or masked by the sustained response to a tachistoscopic exposure. An understanding of the processes that initiate and sustain the succession of glimpses by which we sample the world, and of the

* The preparation of this chapter was partially supported by NICHHD 1RO1-HD-06768-01A2.

mechanisms by which we integrate the informative content of such sequences, is fundamental to any general theory of perceptual organization and attention (Hochberg, 1968, 1970), and motion pictures provide a major route to such understanding.

Cinema (a term that we will use to include both motion-picture and television displays) can do at least five things that still pictures cannot that are of theoretical interest as well as of practical value:

1. They can provide movement-dependent information about tridimensional spatial arrangement (motion depth cues) that are unavailable in still pictures and that contradict by their absence whatever depth is otherwise portrayed in stills.
2. Scenes that are very much larger than the size of the motion picture screen (or television tube) can be represented by successive views, calling upon a storage capacity for visual information that we must use in normal perceptual integration, as well.
3. The motion picture characteristically permits—in fact, depends on— change per se, making possible a level of interest-maintenance that cannot be sustained in an equivalent still picture.
4. Motion pictures permit scenes and events to be represented piecemeal, by juxtaposing views of objects that were not in the same place when they were photographed.
5. Redundant sections of actions, periods of time, or extents of space can be elided, and series of events can thereby be reduced to their minimal communicative features.

We first discuss briefly the nature of the medium, and then consider the relevant sensory and perceptual issues.

The enormous effectiveness of cinema as a pastime, especially in the form of television, is widely accepted (cf. Lyle & Hoffman, 1971; Rutstein, 1974; Winn, 1977). A great deal has been written about the perception of these displays that is portentous but difficult to phrase in testable form (most notably, McLuhan, 1964, 1969). There has also been a steady stream of research directed to a much less ambitious point, namely, testing variations in the presentation of educational motion pictures (cf. Grover, 1975; Minter, Albert, & Powers, 1961; Salomon, 1972; VanderMeer, 1954) to determine the effects of such changes on the educational impact of the films—a literature that we cannot begin to review here (Findahl, 1971; Guba, Wolf, de Groot, Knemeyer, Van Atta, & Light, 1964). There is also an extensive body of research on various tasks that have been presumed to be more or less closely related to the cinema situation, for educational purposes (cf. Grover, 1975).

On the other hand, relatively little research has been addressed to the fundamental perceptual aspects of moving pictures (i.e., to the general theoretical issues that cut across the two disciplines of film theory and perceptual theory), or to the practical ways in which one can assist the other. And that is odd, because the implications are both evident and important.

A. The Nature of the Medium:
What Is a Motion Picture?

1. Viewing the Display as a Surrogate:
Distance, Size, and Resolution

First, of course, cinema consists of moving *pictures*. It is in some sense a *surrogate* of the scene or event being portrayed, and one way in which it can operate is by presenting to the eye an optic array, a field of patterned light, that is in its essential features similar to that which would be produced by the scene or event itself. That would seem to permit a reasonably straightforward definition of *fidelity*, at least in principle (Gibson, 1947, 1954a) and an application of equally straightforward questions of visual acuity: It would be possible to decide the optimal seating distances, audience volumes (McVey, 1970), and resolution limits as these are imposed by the grain of the scanning raster in TV displays, etc. A small amount of research has indeed been directed to some of these points (cf. Enoch, 1959; Meister, 1966; Wadsworth, 1969), and an attempt at a synthesis of these has been made by McVey (1970). We should note, however, that the matter of resolution and screen size cannot be so simply settled.

The degrading effects that are due to the width of the scanning raster are surely greater in foveal vision than they are in peripheral vision; in fact, poor peripheral acuity may act as a low-pass filter to restore details that cannot be discerned foveally (cf. Harmon & Julesz, 1973). A reduction in the viewing angle subtended by the screen necessarily decreases the share that is contributed by the viewer's peripheral vision. This, in turn, may well decrease the viewer's state of readiness for the next view that will be presented. It may also impair the effectiveness of the display as a framework (cf. Hochberg & Brooks, 1973; Wist, Dienes, Dichganz, & Brandt, 1975). Without further research, therefore, one cannot simply trade off image resolution for viewing distance, given a constant screen size.

Nor can we simply apply another obvious criterion for viewing distance, namely, that the viewing angle for the screen should be the same as that for the camera in order to bring the pattern of light at the eye from the surrogate as close as possible to that from the original scene. This criterion follows directly from any definition of a picture as surrogate stimulus display. The fact is however that not only can the viewer tolerate differences in viewing angle and in distance that result in substantial retinal distortions of shape and perspective (Pirenne, 1970), but, in addition, there actually seems to be a preference for the kinds of canonical presentations (Gombrich, 1960; Hochberg, 1972) that are provided by telephoto lenses [i.e., in which the degree of convergence for an object of a given size is far less than that which the correct viewing distance would produce (Hagen & Elliott, 1976)].

These are questions about pictorial perception in general that are particularly important in motion pictures only because they interact with the characteristics of the medium: For example, cinema and TV, in different proportions, rely heavily on changes in the effective distance between the scene and the camera (closeup, longshot, etc.), and we will consider some perceptual consequences of the changes on pp. 280f.

We consider next how motion pictures "move."

2. STROBOSCOPIC MOVEMENT AND THE RELATED PERCEPTUAL PROBLEMS

Motion pictures consist, as everybody knows, of a succession of static pictures, usually at a rate of 24 views each second for sound motion pictures, and always at a rate of 30 views each second for American TV. In the first case, the frequency of view change is barely within the range of detectable flicker, but an episcotister additionally interrupts each view to provide an actual interruption rate of from 72 to 120 Hz. In the second case, the image is produced by a rapidly moving electron beam that lays out alternate lines of the raster (the modulated bright lines traced out on the phosphor of the cathode-ray tube) at 30 Hz, so that the overall picture is actually refreshed, by alternate lines, at 60 Hz.*

Thus, motion pictures and television images are constructed in very different ways. The difference in the underlying display process has been considered to be relevant to the message and its aesthetics (McLuhan, 1964; Zettl, 1973), but since in both cases the processes are well within the temporal resolving power of the visual system, the difference due to the method of production (as distinct from differences in contour stability, resolution, contrast, luminance, etc.) is surely irrelevant as an aesthetic issue (Layer, 1974).

What is important to both procedures is that a small displacement from one view to the next is perceived not as a succession of static views, but as a movement from one place to the next. This is the heart of the process, and it is often misinterpreted both in popular and in professional film and TV texts.

If small progressive changes are made from one view to the next, the perceptual system responds as though smoothly moving stimuli had confronted it (although not in every way, of course—probes can be used to demonstrate that the retina has not actually received a moving stimulus in such cases; cf. Kolers, 1963). This phenomenon is usually called *strobo-scopic* (or *beta*) *movement*. It is still sometimes wrongly attributed to "persis-

---

* In addition, we should note that the detection of a pattern probably has a lower contrast threshold once the frequency approaches 30 Hz (Keesey, 1972), a point that will become relevant to us again when we consider the effects of an abrupt change in views (i.e., a *cut*).

tence of vision," that is, to what is now frequently called an *icon* in the information-processing literature (Neisser, 1967). It is, of course, nothing of the sort, since visual persistence alone would merely cause successive frames to be superimposed in the resultant field of view.

In fact, either some kind of successive masking, or an "off" signal, must probably be invoked to explain why visual persistence does not preserve all of the static intermediate views through which a moving object passes in cinematic presentation.* But in any case, persistence does not equal movement.

a. THE BASIC FACTS AND PROBLEMS OF STROBOSCOPIC MOTION. Very little research on stroboscopic motion has used the kinds of rich, complicated, and articulated stimuli that are used in motion pictures. We have a body of research with simple stimuli that probably explicates some but not all of the relevant processes.

If two spots of light or other simple identical patterns are shown at locations separated by a distance s, and by an interstimulus interval of time t during which neither is presented, there is some domain of s and t in which the viewer will see spatial movement occur. The physical variables seem simple and straightforward. The responses (cf. Kenkel, 1913; Wertheimer, 1912) vary over a range from pure phi movement (in which no objects are seen, but a strong and independent sensation of movement is reported), through beta movement (in which one object is perceived to move from one location to the other), to discrete succession. Under appropriate conditions, beta movement is indistinguishable from real movement (DeSilva, 1929; Dimmick & Scahill, 1925; Stratton, 1911; Wertheimer, 1925). With an "obstacle" placed between a and b, or if the two patterns are mirror images of each other that could only move through s on the retina if they swing through the third dimension, as in Figs. 1(b) and 1(c), we see the appropriate movement in depth. In general, the perceptual system treats a succession of static views, taken with a fine enough temporal grain, as being equivalent to the continuous movement that would normally produce those views as a temporal sample.

This is, of course, what makes motion pictures possible: The cameraman normally needs only to point the camera at the scene, and the apparent motion that results when the film is projected will be essentially what it would be if the camera had somehow produced a continuous (instead of a saltatory) record of the event.

Normal stroboscopic recording thus rarely makes any demands on our

---

* For research on the question of masking, see Matin, 1975. Research on an off-signal can be found in the work on successive integration in which two stimulus fields, each containing only a random field of dots, would produce a clearly recognizable pattern (such as a word, which the subject was to read out, or a complete matrix from which only one dot was missing and whose location the subject was to recognize), only if the two patterns fused over time (Eriksen & Collins, 1967; Cohene & Bechtoldt, 1975; Hogben & Di Lollo, 1974).

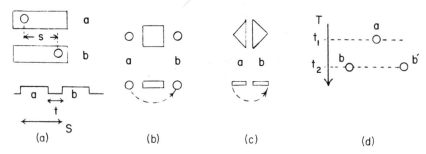

FIG. 1. Stroboscopic movement. (a): With appropriate values of distance *s* and of interval *t* (or Stimulus Onset Asynchrony, *S*), Points *a* and *b* are perceived as being a single point moving through space. The two successive views are shown sbove; their succession in time is shown below. (b, c): Presented in succession, *a* and *b* are perceived as a single object moving through the third dimension. The two successive views are shown above; in the lower section of each figure, they are represented as they would look if viewed from above, moving along paths shown by the dotted arrows. (d): Because *a* can be followed equally well by either *b* or *b'*, it is clear that the direction of apparent motion during the interval $t_2 - t_1$ cannot be decided until after the interval is over (i.e., the movement is fitted to the stimulus sequence retrospectively).

knowledge of the determinants of perceived motion. It is only in the cases of interruptions of normal stroboscopic recording, as in the *cuts* that we discuss on pp. 281–286, that a knowledge of the determinants of apparent motion becomes important.*

b. KORTE'S LAWS AND TERNUS'S PHENOMENA: THE PROBLEM OF IDENTITY. With *a* and *b* as simple identical patterns of measurable luminance, and *s* and *t* as independent variables, and beta movement as the dependent response variable, the issue seems straightforward enough to permit psychophysical research [Korte (1915); Neuhaus (1930; Sgro (1963); cf. summaries by Hochberg (1971) and by Kaufman (1974)]. In general, the findings are consistent with Helmholtz's "rule" that we perceive just that state of affairs that would be most likely to produce a given set of sensory events: That is, for a longer time *t* (and a constant velocity), *a*, and *b* need to be more widely separated, and vice versa. In normal continuous motion picture presentation, *t* is very small, either ranging from 8 to 21 msec, or from 33 to 42 msec, depending on whether it is the interstimulus interval (ISI) or the stimulus-onset asynchrony (SOA), as indicated by *S* in Fig. 1(a), that is taken as the relevant variable (the latter is probably the appropriate one). In either case, the displacements that will generate smooth movement are also quite small, which is about what one would expect to find in motion pictures.

There are four points to note about this kind of inquiry that make it

---

* Other causes arise occasionally, of course, like the classic interaction in which the stroboscopic samples of the real motion produces an apparent backward rotation of a carriage wheel or an airplane propeller, and similar concerns probably apply to other cases, such as expanded or contracted time.

considerably less simple, and more important to perceptual and cognitive psychology, than it first appears to be.

First, note that whatever process underlies the motion perception in such situations, it cannot occur *on line:* Inasmuch as the direction of the motion in Fig. 1(d) is not determined until *either b* or *b'* is presented, the attribution of motion must occur *after* the sequence is completed. This is a minor matter where the case of a single pair of views is concerned, spanning 67–83 msec (two views of video or motion pictures, respectively). It becomes important when movements of greater duration (of about 1500 msec or more) are presented. Surely there must be some interval t greater than 1500 msec, approximately, past which the movement perceived is not a single response to the entire sequence, including the *earliest* views. The perceived event must be partly a fitting of a schema to the earliest part of the total sequence, and partly a testing of what that schema predicts. We have no research directly to this point, but we will have some phenomena to consider under the topic of bad cuts that are indirectly related to it.

Second, a "phenomenal identity" must be considered that transcends the physically identifiable stimulus variables: In Fig. 2, the sequence is ambiguous, in that the motion of either Fig. 2(b) or Fig. 2(c) can be perceived, or they may alternate in a ratio that depends on stimulus conditions (Petersik & Pantle, 1976). By making $t = .0$ for the two center dots b and c, the apparent motion is decided in favor of alternative 2(c) (Ternus, 1938). This presumably depends on whether dots b and c are perceived as being identical across the two presentations, making a and d identical, or whether a, b, and c are identical to b, c, and d, respectively. Here, incidentally, is one case in which it is the interstimulus interval (ISI) rather than the SOA that is important, presumably because the ISI presents an off-signal (cf. Eriksen & Collins, 1967, 1968). Whether phenomenal identity can, in fact, be thought of as an *independent* variable here, or whether it is merely a dependent variable affected by the same factors that determine the perceived motion path, has not been established. We will see in a moment, however, that there are cases

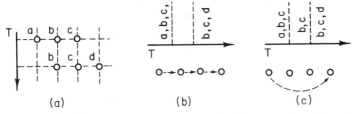

(a)   (b)   (c)

FIG. 2. Phenomenal identity. (a): The basic setup (Ternus, 1938) consists of three lights (a, b, c) followed by another set of three lights (b, c, d). (b): If a dark period intervenes between the two sets (as shown at the top), a is perceived as moving to b, b to c, and c to d, as shown below. (c): If lights b and c remain continuously on (as shown at the top), a appears to move to d, moving through the third dimension, as shown below.

in which it seems reasonable to think of something like such *phenomenal causation.*

Third, lest the notion of phenomenal identity be taken more strongly than the facts justify, note that apparent motion can occur between quite dissimilar patterns: Not only will the pattern be seen as moving from one place to the other, but it will change shape or color in the process (Pomerantz, 1971; Kolers & von Grünau, 1976; Navon, 1976; Orlansky, 1940). The finding is analogous to the impossible pictures designed by Penrose and Penrose (1958). If indeed the Helmholtzian rule—that we see what is most likely to fit the sensory pattern—is to be applied, what is "most likely" is not immediately evident to the theorist in advance of the data (Hochberg, 1968, 1974a,b). Moreover, response to the sensory pattern occurs at different levels, and the cognitive explanations (e.g., about what is "most likely") surely do not apply to all domains (Hochberg, 1968). For example, at critical rates, the stimulus situation at (b) in Fig. 2 becomes ambiguous, alternating between the percepts represented at (b) and (c) (Petersik, 1975), which can be separately adapted, which are differently affected by light adaptation. (Light adaptation favors the "group" movement of (b), whereas dark adaptation favors the "element" movement of (c); Petersik & Pantle, 1976).

Finally, we have not specified the way in which s and t are t o be measured. If the viewer is at a fixed distance from the screen on which the objects are presented, measurement appears straightforward; but in that case, we cannot tell whether it is distance in the retinal image (or optic array) that is important, or the distance in physical space that is important. That is, we must ask what the medium is in which s and t are measured.

c. THE "MEDIUM" IN WHICH STROBOSCOPIC MOVEMENT OCCURS. Suppose we hold the visual angle subtended by the distance s constant, but vary the distance between the viewer and the screen on which objects a and b in Fig. 1(a) appear (i.e., the retinal value of s is constant, but the physical separation between a and b increases as the viewing distance increases). If stroboscopic motion were merely a simple peripherally determined and primitive phenomenon, we would expect that the value of t needed to yield good beta movement would depend on retinal size alone. On the other hand, if apparent movement occurred between apparent positions in phenomenal space, and if phenomenal separation were close to the physical separation (i.e., size constancy prevailed), then the t required for good beta movement would depend on the physical separation between a and b.

There is, in fact, a growing body of work that seems to fit this kind of interpretation (Attneave & Block, 1973; Corbin, 1942; Rock & Ebenholtz, 1962; Shepard & Judd, 1976). In the latest of these studies, for example, Shepard and Judd determined the minimum cycle duration that was required in order for the alternation between two perspective views of the same three-dimensional object to give rise to a clear perception of rigid rotation. They found that the interval varied linearly with the difference in orientation of the two shapes, and that the slope of the function that relates orientation difference to minimum cycle time was the same, regardless of whether the alternation was one of rotation between two orientations in the picture plane or between two positions in three-dimensional space. There is some reason to believe (see p. 283) that something like this applies as well to the speed with which a movie cut is grasped.

We should not overinterpret these data, however. There are probably several quite different kinds of responses, potentially separable from each other, that are involved in the perception of stroboscopic movement. Some of these processes surely depend strictly on the parameters of the retinal image, and we shall see that these are clearly important in understanding motion-picture cutting (and that, conversely, the study of motion-picture cutting will help us to understand those processes).

d. Multiple processes of apparent motion: transients, "blobs," and identifying details. When different shapes fall successively on the same place, one is seen as transforming into another (Berliner, 1948); when different shapes are presented at different locations, apparent movement will occur between them (Hochberg & Brooks, 1974; Kolers & Pomerantz, 1971; Navon, 1976; Orlansky, 1940). Shape preservation thus does not appear to be an essential feature in stroboscopic motion. We have also seen however that "decisions" about apparent identity determine at least certain kinds of perceived movement, and that some movement occurs according to parameters of *apparent tridimensional space,* which must itself be a product of considerable processing and rest on shape information. There may be a problem here, but it need not be a paradox; there are several quite different components to stroboscopic movement.*

We should distinguish at least two types of determinants. A model that appears consistent with both the body of laboratory research and with our observations of cinematic cutting (cf. p. 283) is this: After an abrupt change of view, there is a rapid and transient response of apparent movement between regions of the same luminance that occupy nearby locations in the successive views. The precise nature of the stimulus conditions that elicit this transient response is not presently known. The idea of an early response to general "blobs" in the field of view, that is, to aspects of *low spatial*

---

* For example, we can make gross distinctions between absolute- and relative-movement responses that are mediated by very different mechanisms. Absolute retinal movement, if sufficiently rapid, can be detected and will generate aftereffects, and it is easy to assign such response to *movement detectors.* Relative movement can be detected at much slower rates; where the two objects whose separation is changing are close together in the retinal image, we can imagine relatively peripheral mechanisms that operate as *shear detectors* (for a recent review, see Sekuler, 1975); where they are far apart in the retinal image, more central machinery must be invoked. The point to be made here is that, with multiple components, some may be retinal and fixed to the characteristics of the optic array, whereas others may be mediated by judgments that involve tridimensional or *phenomenal* space, like those described in the previous section.

frequency of the stimulus is consistent with present data (Saucer, 1954; Breitmeyer & Ganz, 1976; Breitmeyer & Julesz,1975; Breitmeyer, Love, & Wepman, 1974). Thus, reaction times for the detection of patterns having different spatial frequencies range from about 200 msec for patterns of .5 c deg⁻¹, to 350 msec for patterns of 10 c deg⁻¹ (Breitmeyer, 1975). That the reaction-time differences reflect differences in the speed of sensory processing, rather than in decision or execution time, is shown both by the fact that the same curve fits the latency of responses in the visual cortex (Williamson, Kaufman, & Brenner, 1977) and by the fact that the apparent movement elicited by a sequence of views that is too rapid to permit either decisions or overt responses to be executed to the individual frames can be made to be opposite to the actual direction of displacement between views by suitably arranging different objects in successively adjacent positions (p. 283). We do not yet know whether "low spatial frequencies" constitute a precise description (e.g., the same phenomenon of form independence in apparent movement might be due to a piecemeal local relationship between successive bits of contour), but it is at least a useful metaphor at this point.

Whatever the precise stimulus conditions may be that are needed to elicit the transient response, the response itself is a momentary but quite compelling sensation of movement.

In addition to the transient, form-independent response, there are also, of course, slower responses to the displacement of objects between views. It seems plausible that these are initiated in parallel with the fast transient responses. These do take into account the overall shape of objects and the small details that identify them. Such form-dependent responses appear to take a considerably longer time—on the order of upwards of 500 msec (Hochberg & Brooks, 1974). It seems most likely that the phenomena of apparent movement that seem to take place in phenomenal space are in this class of slow responses.

It is probably safe to summarize the facts with a rough rule that the components of low spatial frequency dominate the integration of successive views at high temporal frequencies of cutting, and that information of high spatial frequency prevails at low cutting rates.

With small movements of the eyes, and with camera movements that are small with respect to the distance between the major contours of the scene being recorded, both processes occur in the same direction, and no conflict arises. With larger saccades, or with greater movements of the camera, the two no longer must coincide and, as we will see when we discuss overlapping cuts, the conflict may make the transitions difficult to comprehend.

e. THE PARTITIONING OF RELATIVE MOVEMENT: INDUCED MOVEMENT, "SEPARATION OF SYSTEMS," AND THE PERCEPTION OF INVARIANTS UNDER TRANSFORMATION. The threshold for relative movement is lower than that for absolute movement (Aubert, 1886; Brown & Conklin, 1954). This

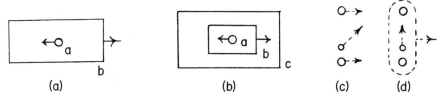

FIG. 3. The partitioning of perceived movement. (a): Induced movement. If *b* moves and *a* is stationary in an otherwise empty field, *a* appears to move and *b* appears to be stationary. (b): "Separation of systems" (see text). (c, d): The Johansson effect. If three spots of light in an otherwise dark room move as shown by the dotted arrows in (c), the observer sees instead the movements shown at (d).

suggests (but does not imply) that there is a range of events under which the viewer will be certain that movement has occurred, but not certain of which of two objects has moved and, consequently, of what the direction of movement is.*

If we present a stationary dot *a* surrounded by a moving frame *b* in an otherwise dark or featureless space, the frame appears stationary and the dot appears to move (Dunker, 1929). See Fig. 3(a). In general, the smaller of two objects will usually appear to move, particularly if the larger encloses it.

Objects that we would expect to be mobile (cars, airplanes, people) are more prone to be perceived as moving (Brosgole & Whalen, 1967; Comalli, Werner, & Wapner, 1957; Duncker, 1929; Jensen, 1960), but the difference can be eradicated if the stationary member of the pair is enclosed in a moving frame (Brosgole & Whalen, 1967).

If a stationary object lies within a stationary frame, and a textured field or background moves continuously behind the object, the latter is perceived as moving in the direction opposite to that of the background. Because the object is motionless with respect to the outer frame, but appears to be moving, the logical (and, to some extent, the perceptual) implication is that the frame is keeping pace with the moving object. This apparently paradoxical phenomenon is absolutely essential to the cinematic representation of movements that continue for any appreciable duration (since an object that actually moves relative to the screen will soon run off it). How does it fit the rule of induced movement that we stated above?

* Note that the only visual test that will distinguish these is to change our gaze in a known direction (e.g., to determine whether we have to move our eyes to keep one or the other foveally centered). Although we do know with some assurance the direction in which saccades have been initiated, our knowledge of the extent and even the direction of pursuit movements is more in doubt (Festinger & Easton, 1974; Mack & Herman, 1973; Stoper, 1973), and, of course, the precision with which we can identify the effects of changes in our bodily position, or even of the support on which we rest (witness the moving train illusion, etc.) are notoriously worse. We need other bases, then, for attributing the relative motion to one or to both objects in the field in Fig. 3(a). These uncertainties probably help make possible the most characteristic feature of cinema (that is, the expansion of space beyond the screen), but may also create incomprehensibilities unintended by the filmmaker (cf. Vorkapich, 1972).

There are four possible bases for this important cinematic effect. First, the fact that the object is immediately adjacent to its moving background may provide a purely local relative movement and may override the effects of the frame, which lies at a greater distance from the object (cf. Gogel, 1977).* Second, the movement of the surround in the peripheral portions of the retinal image may misinform the viewer that his direction of gaze is changing (see p. 276).† Most traditionally, one may argue that the viewer accepts the moving background within the frame as being the implied surrounding (just as the scene framed by a train window is part of the general, stationary surround; cf. Koffka, 1935). Finally, Wallach's (1959) proposal is that the general rule is one of a *separation of systems,* in which apparent movement is always determined by the immediately enclosing frame: Thus, in Fig. 3(b) (which is a version of a demonstration described by Wallach), the objective movement of the inner rectangle, b, induces Point a to appear to move in the opposite direction, even though a is stationary with respect to c.

Any or all of these explanations may be true. Research is sparse, but not difficult *in principle,* in that the various explanations have different cinematic implications. For example, according to the first explanation, the effect would decrease as the visual angle subtended by the screen decreased, whereas the last two explanations do not lead to this prediction. In fact, there is a question of whether the effect illustrated in Fig. 3(b) is reliable enough to explain the cinematic phenomenon (Farber & McConkie, 1977), which may be related to a general issue that arises with respect to the phenomena in this and in the next section: These are all ambiguous: The situation of Fig. 3(b) may be viewed as two stationary objects (a and c) and one moving one (b), two moving objects and one stationary one (a and c moving to the left, with b stationary, or a moving to the left on b, which is moving to the right behind a stationary aperture c), or other fractional partitionings of the relative movements. As is common in connection with research on ambiguous stimulus situations, it is difficult in these experiments to be sure of the criterion that the subject uses to decide which object is moving, and in what direction. The conditions under which viewers respond ambiguously to stimuli like those in Fig. 3(b) and Fig. 3(c) (which we discuss at a later point) must obviously be determined before we can be confident that these situations tap the same mechanisms that are responsible for the more robust-appearing motion-picture phenomena.

In the context of his search for a unified perceptual theory, Gibson has argued that our perceptual apparatus extracts the invariant structure from

---

* Like the impossible figures (Hochberg, 1968), the partition of motion may be primarily a local matter, and the effects of the ground on the object may not interact with the more distant frame.

   † This would be consistent both with the findings by Held *et al.* (1975) and Wist *et al.* (1975) that rotation of stripes, etc., in the visual periphery changes the observer's perceived orientation in space and his apparent direction, respectively, and with the known differential sensitivity of peripheral vision for moving and stationary targets (i.e., the peripheral vision of the viewer may be more sensitive to the fact that the contents of the frame are moving than that the frame itself is stationary).

the transformations it undergoes in the optic array (1954b, 1957, 1966). More specifically, Johansson (1950, 1974) has proposed that the visual system extracts a motion that is common to all of the moving parts of the field of view and that this motion itself becomes the framework against which the residual movement is seen. In Fig. 3(c), if the points of light move as indicated by the dotted arrows in an otherwise dark room, what subjects will see is shown by the dotted arrows in Fig. 3(d). This principle will be important to us when we discuss the problem of how we comprehend overlapping successive views.

3. THE MOTION PICTURE AS A SURROGATE FOR EVENTS IN SPACE AND TIME

The phenomena that we have been discussing above have been studied to some extent independently of the motion picture. Let us discuss the application of the principles that those studies tap, and then outline the points at which the motion pictures have gone beyond psychologists' explorations of the underlying processes.

a. PICTURES THAT MOVE: THEIR HISTORY. The attempt to make pictures that move is an ancient one (cf. Cook, 1963; Pratt, 1973). Recent devices abound: the Zöotrope, the Praxinoscope, and Muybridge's line of cameras, each of which took a picture as the moving subject tripped a wire. These devices have been replaced, of course, by the linear sequence of photographs on successive frames of film (and by the magnetic storage of an electrical signal that modulates the intensity of the flying video spot).

Motion-picture technology was developed for scientific and technical reasons as well as for entertainment. One of these reasons, particularly important to its development, is the way in which motion pictures free the viewer from his own perceptual limitations in space and time.

b. THE EXPANSION AND CONTRACTION OF TIME. Muybridge (1882) first set up his string of cameras and recorded the successive images of a fast-moving horse to enable him to determine the sequence in which a galloping horse moves its legs—a question that unaided vision cannot resolve. Conversely, by taking pictures at slow rates (for example, 1 per day) and projecting them at normal rates, events that are normally too slow to perceive, like the growth of plants, are made perceptible. These changes of time scale have many functions, but there is another method that is in even wider use: The filmmaker may simply run the camera in normal speed to record an event or part of an event (say, the planting of a seed in a flower pot) and then stop the camera, returning to resume filming, still at normal speed, only later (say, after the plant has sprouted). Given a little time to recover from the abrupt change in view, the viewer is perfectly capable of picking up the thread and of accepting the elision of the (redundant) intervening time: The filmmaker is thus able to select only those features he wants to out of the flow of time. As we will now see, film permits the filmmaker to exert complete control of space and time, departing so drastically from any plausible meaning of the term *surrogate fidelity* as to make it essentially useless.

c. THE CONSTRUCTION OF SPACE AND TIME: PARALLEL, REPEATED, AND MULTIPLE IMAGES. The filmmaker can, as we noted, elide stretches of time that are as long as he likes simply by not photographing them (or by cutting them from the film record). He can also juxtapose two events that are separated in space without actually traversing the intervening distance (e.g., a scene in New York and a scene in Paris, the one immediately after the other), and in so doing, he can make clear that the events that are being projected successively in fact occur at the same time. Unlike a theatrical drama, which *must* present at least some of the events in real time because the actors portraying those events are themselves constrained to act in real time, the motion picture is capable of retaining only those features that are of interest—a matter of economy that is the essence of an art form, and that imposes its own requirements in a medium that the viewer knows to be a record of past events.*

By assembling a sequence of views that did not actually come from a single place or event, the filmmaker can represent what would have been received by straightforward camera sampling of a place (or happening) existing only in his imagination and in the perceptions of his audience. In fact, he can do this by the most minimal snatches of view, using fragments of scenes that no one before Porter's epoch-making construction of *The Life of an American Fireman* in 1903 would have believed (Pratt, 1973) to be comprehensible. Since then, time and space are routinely contracted, constructed, and even expanded: When the filmmaker alternately shows two events that are both presented as occurring simultaneously [some cue is needed to inform the audience of this, as the viewer's assumption otherwise is that time moves inexorably forward (Arnheim, 1960, p. 21)], the viewer is perfectly capable of keeping track of them, just as he can keep track of the alternating chapters in the novels of Edgar Rice Burroughs. In cinematic montage, as in reading a story, prior context determines the effect that each new image will have and how it will be integrated into the apprehended meaning of the sequence. The increasing use of multiple-image presentations, especially for educational purposes (Allen & Cooney, 1964; Perrin, 1969; Goldstein, 1975) offers the viewer an opportunity for more dense, simultaneous comparison; but it is not clear that any new theoretical issues are raised in such procedures.

The major features of motion-picture communication that are unique to

---

* The live TV presentation of an event may be viewed with a tolerance that a work of man's hand, such as a rebroadcast of the same event or, of course, any edited motion-picture film, would not receive. The "rhythmic requirements of the re-created event are quite different from those of the live event. The condensing of the event to its 'highlights' is often a necessary reenergizing procedure when it is replayed at a later date [Zettl, 1973, p. 265]."

cinema and also of importance to perceptual psychology are not associated with the possibilities of using flashbacks and parallel action: Those devices are used in literature, too. The perceptually unique features of motion pictures arise from the fact that the camera moves in relation to the scene, whereas the viewer is stationary with respect to the projection screen, and from the massive use of discontinuous cuts between places that are separated in space, time, or both. We discuss these in turn.

II. THE MOVING CAMERA AND THE REPRESENTATION OF SPACE

There are, as we have noted, four consequences of the fact that the camera is free to move and change its viewpoint abruptly: movement information about depth, the construction of a "mind's-eye" space that is many times bigger than the screen on which the momentary image is projected, the problem of determining relative direction for a stationary viewer, and the ease of maintenance of visual interest. We consider first the main classes of camera movement and their informativeness about depth.

A. The Varieties of Continuous Changes of View and Their Differences in Spatial Informativeness: Movement Perspective, Dynamic Occlusion, and Transformational Invariants

As Leonardo da Vinci pointed out in his original analysis of pictorial depth cues, the static picture cannot provide movement cues to distance. In the perception of still pictures, consequently, there is a degree of ambiguity, as well as a tolerance of distortion that is presumably absent in the motion picture. We know that viewers are sensitive to some of the information about the visual world that can be reflected in the transformations of moving patterns on a screen (cf. Green, 1961; Braunstein, 1966, 1968). In the transformational theories, like Gibson's, there is no reason to believe that any of the static Gestalt laws, which can govern the concealment or disclosure of hidden figures or camouflage, will work with motion pictures. There are frequent statements, like "the animal has only to move and its camouflage fails," that suggest that the traditional pictorial factors are parochial. The matter is not so clear-cut, however, especially for short shots.

For one thing, the very fact that animation is used (where feasible) to reduce objects to their simplest forms and arrangements (Caldwell, 1973) suggests that clarity is not automatically achieved simply through motion parallax. Protective coloration and camouflage would be useless if the stationary bird were immediately perceived as an identifiable object by the moving hunter. More directly, there are laboratory demonstrations that show that static factors can overcome the information about distance that is given by movement. A Necker cube, when set on glass plates and arranged so that its pieces (which, under normal conditions, seem to belong with each other by reason of good continuation, forming the familiar tridimensional appearance of the cube) actually lie at different distances, unrelated to each other, is reported to continue to look like a cube, even when the observer moves his head (Kopfermann, 1930). A three-dimensional model of a house, set in a frame so that it looks like a picture, is indistinguishable from a flat picture of the house when both are presented in a film that incorporates motion (Hochberg, 1962). Most spectacular, perhaps, is the Ames Window, in which static linear perspective prevails over actual shape and movement to result in an incorrect perception of the former and a wildly incorrect perception of the latter (Ittelson, 1952). Finally, Hershberger and Starzec (1974) have shown that the information that is potentially available to the eye from the geometry of movement parallax and motion perspective can be broken down into its components and that viewers do not use these compo-nents equally well. It is clear by now that no amount of purely mathematical analysis of the information that is potentially available in the motion-picture array (or in the stimulus array that confronts the eye of the moving observer) can replace the research that is needed to determine what information is actually used by the viewer, and under what circumstances.

1. DOLLY, TRACK, PAN, AND ZOOM:
   POTENTIAL MOVEMENT INFORMATION
   ABOUT THREE-DIMENSIONAL SPACE

We can dissect camera movements into two classes: those that produce lateral movements of the scene on the screen—*pan* and *tracking*, or *truck-ing*, shots, shown in Figs. 4(a) and 4(b), respectively—and those that change size on the screen—*zoom* and *dolly* shots, shown in Figs. 4(c) and 4(d), respectively. Within these two classes, one member of each pair provides motion information about the depth relations within the scene, and the other

---

FIG. 4. The effects of camera motion. (a): The pan. The camera swivels on its tripod from left to right. Note that no relative movements occur within the scene and that what is occluded in one view remains occluded in the next. (b): The tracking shot. The camera travels along a path parallel to the stairs (perpendicular to the direction in which the lens is pointed) from left to right. Compare this sequence to the pan in (a); there is a gradient of motion perspective within the scene and objects that are occluded in one view are revealed in the others. (c): The zoom. The focal length of the camera lens is increased from wide angle to telephoto, and the views range in consequence from long shot to closeup. Again, only magnification occurs, and no relative movement, from one view to the next. (d): The dolly shot. We use the term here for the case in which the camera moves into or out of the scene, along the direction in which the lens is pointed. Compare this sequence to the zoom in (c); here, as in (b), there is relative movement within the scene from one view to the next.

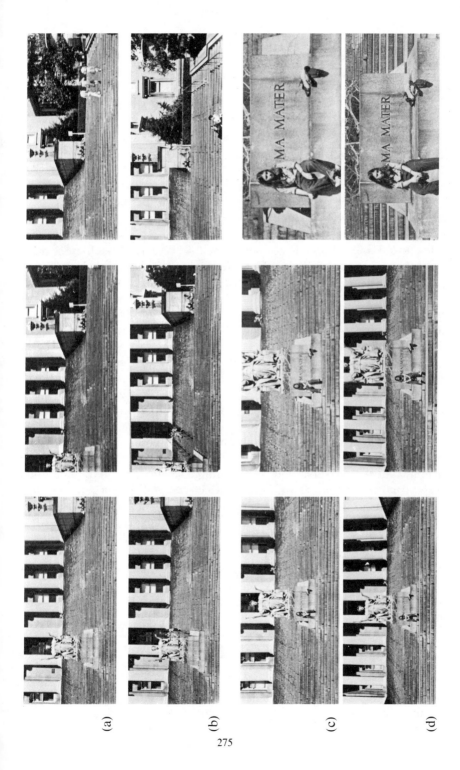

(a)

(b)

(c)

(d)

275

does not. (We are using these terms in a slightly specialized way, but they should nonetheless remain comprehensible to filmmakers.)

The camera may sweep laterally across a scene by moving on a track at right angles to the camera direction—the *tracking shot* in Fig. 4(b)—or it may merely sweep across the scene by swiveling around in a stationary center—for example, the *pan* in Fig. 4(a). As an inspection of the two series of photographs will show, both methods include the same elements of the scene, but the pan contains no motion parallax: Objects' distances have no effect on their relative positions in the successive frames of the pan. Similarly, motion information about distance abounds in the dolly shot in Fig. 4(d), in which the camera is moved on a track *into* the picture, whereas the successive frames of a zoom only change the degree of magnification of the image in Fig. 4(c).

Track and dolly shots, then, contain the full panoply of depth information concerning the position of the objects in the scene. They provide the viewer with all of the information (with the exception of vestibular and other proprioceptive information) that he would get were he actually to traverse the course followed by the camera. In fact, if the field of view is very wide (as it is in Cinerama, or when one sits close to a widescreen picture) the viewer's peripheral vision of the motion will interact with his vestibular motion sense (as we would expect from the work of Held, Ditchgans, and Bower, 1975, and Wist *et al.*, 1975), and the viewer *feels* himself move.

In order to produce track shots and dolly shots, however, the filmmaker must provide a smooth course for the camera to run on, and must arrange for sets that permit such movement to occur. This is often impossible, and always very expensive. Accordingly, in order to produce the same flow of information about the whole scene (i.e., to include overall view and closeup, or to include widely separated views within a single continuous shot) and to keep visual movement on the screen (which we will see on pp. 293–295 is perceptually desirable for its own reasons), the filmmaker will use the pan instead of the track shot and the zoom (which is now accomplished simply by changing the focal length of the lens in a stationary camera) instead of the dolly. These expedients must be worse than providing no information at all, from Gibson's standpoint, as the very absence of motion parallax, is itself information that the parts of the scene all lie in the same plane, information that should make the pan or zoom look flatter than the equivalent still picture or shot.

Nevertheless, pan and zoom shots are widely used, and surely are more widely used than track and dolly shots. What their bad effects are, if any, and how those effects may be minimized, is a question for research. Such research would not only be informative to filmmakers, it would be of considerable interest to the perception psychologist, as well. As Brunswik pointed out to little avail (Brunswik, 1956), to start with impoverished stimuli, like dots on a cathode-ray tube, and gradually build up to more representative displays, is to make the research captive to one's theory of what information (or cues) are effective. The use of motion pictures of real scenes provides for some minimum degree of ecological representativeness. The fact that pan and zoom shots are so often treated by filmmakers as though they were interchangeable with track and dolly shots is itself an omen of theoretical upsets in the offing.

There are reasons other than the desire to represent depth that lead filmmakers to use these procedures, of course, and these other reasons may be so important that the loss of depth information is trivial in comparison. Two of these purposes will concern us here: first, the construction of space by successive presentation, and second, the motivation of visual attention.

B. Space beyond the Screen and the Simulation of a Moving Observer

Evident in both pan and tracking shots (and somewhat less obvious, but true as well with zoom and dolly shots) is the ability of the motion picture to provide the visual information for a scene or layout that is many times larger than the screen (cf. Burch, 1973). By successive piecemeal presentations of portions of a scene or object, visual information about the spatial whole is given to the viewer over a period of time.

What makes this practice of particular interest to the perception psychologist is that it mimics a task that we must perform many times in each minute of each day, and it is very likely that an understanding of the nature and limits of what we may call the *space beyond the screen* will prove helpful in understanding how we perform that common task. Our foveas, with which we receive clear and detailed vision, occupy only a very small part of our field of view, and the use of the foveas in sampling the visual world, as the eye moves in the head and the head moves in space, requires us to combine the visual input from successive partial glimpses in order to construct our perceptions of the world.

What principles govern the way in which we combine our successive glances?

1. THE CLASSIC PROBLEM OF COMPENSATION AND REAFFERENCE

One class of explanation, debated since Helmholtz and James, is that either the efferent signals that have directed the muscles whose contractions cause the gaze to change, or the afferent signals from the muscles themselves are taken into account in interpreting the changing visual information. Relatively specific forms of these "compensations for visual direction," have been proposed (Festinger, Ono, Burnham, & Bamber, 1967; Held, 1961; Holst, 1954). There is a considerable body of research on this point, but we do not yet have a clear answer concerning how such nonvisual information about the eye movements is used.

In any case, the fact that we can comprehend the visual information that is provided by the changing camera when it is presented on a stationary screen or TV tube, is clear evidence that nonvisual information about the movements and directions of the eye are not necessary to solve the perceptual problem. Although the camera has virtually unlimited freedom to move around and change its viewpoint, the projection is normally restricted to a small region of space: the projection screen or the TV tube. This both provides the filmmaker (and the perception psychologist) with great opportunities and great difficulties. Whether the camera is elevated to face an approach down a mountain slope or up one, from left, right, or straight ahead, the viewer is in all cases confronted by a head-on approach. The camera may change its focal length, and fill the field with a small object viewed from closeup or with a large one viewed from far away (or, by changing focal lengths, with a small object from far away), but the viewer's distance from the screen is fixed, and none of his usual use of spatial information will tell him otherwise. Or, of most immediate concern to us, the camera may point in different directions at different times, but the scenes are still all viewed only from straight ahead.

At the very most, the most precise nonvisual information about where our gaze is directed could tell us only that all of the successive views in a motion picture are appearing at the same place in space. We need something more to explain the integration of successive visual information in motion pictures, and it seems reasonable that when we know what that is, it will help us to understand how we integrate the successive glimpses that we obtain of the world in normal circumstances as well.

There are two classes of alternative explanations. One of them is capable of reasonably precise formulation, whereas the other is still in a more incoherent and formative stage. We will consider them in that order.

2. OPTICAL KINESTHESIS AS AN ALTERNATIVE TO NONVISUAL PROPRIOCEPTION

Gibson (1954b) proposed that we respond to our views of the world, which change over time, by extracting the invariant structure (which mirrors the structure of the stationary surfaces in the world) as it undergoes the continuous transformation in the optic array that confronts the eye. We have noted this before in connection with the perception of movement; we are now concerned with it as far as it will provide for an alternative to nonvisual information about the direction of the gaze.

There are really three questions here:

1. Can we find any direct or indirect evidence to support this proposition?
2. Is the process one of *direct perception,* an autonomous discrimination

of the informative higher-order variables of stimulation that provide potentially direct information about the movement and about the underlying structure, as Gibson proposes?

3. Will it suffice to account for the way in which we construct the space beyond the screen—the space in the mind's eye (Hochberg, 1968)—which is the primary domain in which motion pictures (at least) run their course?

We will return to the first question, the viability of the model, after we have considered the gamut of what has to be explained. We should note here that in some (modified) form it remains a serious contender. With respect to the second question, whether the process is to be viewed as "automatic pickup" of information or whether the viewer's intentions (and what mental structure he can bring to bear) must enter into the explanation, let us note that there is little basis for choice as long as we consider only motion-picture sequences in which all changes are *continuous*.* We will consider the third question, that is, whether this kind of analysis will in principle allow us to understand the space in the mind's eye.

Gibson has proposed that we learn to differentiate those features of any environment that lead from one place to another—the sequences of visual transformation as four-dimensional invariants. It is hard to see, however, how this formulation really explains how we extract a space that can be manipulated, *and through which we can take shortcuts*. It is easy to demonstrate such shortcutting: If a picture of a cross is presented piecemeal, by filling the screen with only one angle at a time in closeup and panning continuously around the perimeter of the figure, and if the camera simply shortcuts one of the arms before returning to its starting point after having circumnavigated the perimeter, the viewer will identify the shortcut immediately for what it is (especially if the sequence has been preceded by a long shot [Hochberg, 1968]; cf. p. 286). It is hard to talk about this kind of phenomenon, however, without including some kind of *cognitive map* in the discussion. That map may be envisioned as something spatial and formlike, or as a specified feature list (Pylyshyn, 1973), or as a set of contingent expectations or "sensorimotor plans"—what the viewer would see if he looked at this or that point on the object or in the scene (Hochberg, 1968, 1970).

We will return to this point, the nature of mental content (and how it is achieved), after we consider the motion-picture technique that best raises the issue, that is, the motion-picture *cut*.

* A severe limitation to this model is that its "mathematical" formulation ignores the differences between periphery and fovea. These differences are extremely important as regards the eye's ability to use just that spatial information that Gibson (1957, 1966) proposed as being offered by the stimulus. Fovea and periphery differ also in their ability to induce the viewer to perceive himself as moving (Wist *et al.*, 1975; Held *et al.*, 1975)—the very point to which this analysis of visual proprioception was addressed.

III. DISCONTINUOUS CUTS AND THEIR CONTRIBUTION TO MENTAL STRUCTURE AND VISUAL MOMENTUM

A. The Varieties of Discontinuous Transitions (Cuts) and Their Cinematic Uses

A *cut* is the transition between the end of one shot and the beginning of the next. Before we discuss the perception of cuts, we will first classify the shots between which cuts are made, in order to describe something of their usage and to provide a terminology.

1. CLASSIFICATION AND TERMINOLOGY

A *shot* is a single run of the camera, and the film resulting from it. As a unit of film construction in this sense, we can distinguish the major ways in which shots can differ.

a. THE PROPORTION OF THE FRAME AREA THAT IS OCCUPIED BY THE SUBJECT. This is a central variable; the three usual terms are *long shot, medium shot* and *closeup* (see Fig. 4). This is usually determined by the focal length of the lens and the various "distortions of perspective," well known in still pictures, appear here and are accompanied by corresponding "distortions of velocity."*

b. ANGLE OF SHOT. An event may persist over several shots, as when the camera viewpoint cuts from one angle to another during a continuing action. This is an *angle shot*. When the camera angle changes by almost 180°—see Fig. 5(a)—that is a *reverse angle shot* (changes of more than 180° are known as "crossing the camera axis"; they tend to produce confusion for reasons given on p. 283).

c. USES OF CUTTING. Cuts between shots are made for various purposes: to represent a scene that is longer than can be projected on the screen at one time (or that really does not exist in one place), to convey some sequential message, to obtain a rhythm of change, and to maintain visual interest. Cuts are also made for technical and adventitious reasons that have nothing to do with our present concerns.

We will introduce the topic of how cuts are used in representing events within a larger scene, and provide some terminology for further discussion.

---

* A movement in depth or movement laterally on the screen makes less of a size change and covers less of the screen in long focal length (long shot, telephoto) and in medium than in closeup (wide-angle). That is, the movement on the screen is slowed down in long shot and speeded up in closeup. These effects are not merely theoretical possibilities, but affect viewers' judgments of a person's speed of movement (Brooks). If such effects are not intended and the filmmaker does not take them into account, they can most surely be bewildering or ludicrous.

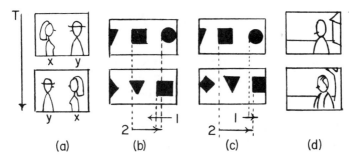

FIG. 5. Discontinuous transitions (cuts). In each case, the temporal sequence runs from above to below. (See text).

Because the viewer has not himself generated the sequence of views, an *establishing shot* is often used to orient him as to the overall layout, place, time, etc. A *long shot* establishes the relationship between objects that will be shown in more detail in later shots. A cut to a *medium shot* and then a cut to a *closeup* serves to channel the viewer's attention and permit the display of detail that could not be discerned in a long shot (especially in TV, with its relatively small screen and poor resolution). *Reestablishing shots* (again, usually a long shot) may be needed after the sequence has gone on for a while, and especially after a *cut-away shot* has been used to show other events going on elsewhere (usually *parallel action*). A sequence of short shots, often having a definite rhythm and accelerating or decelerating pace, is called a *montage*.

B. The Integration of Discontinuous Successive Views

1. THE RELATIONSHIP TO SACCADIC VIEWING

In many cases, the change in camera viewpoint is small and there is substantial overlap between successive views (see Fig. 6). This will also be true for small saccades (i.e., saccadic, or jumping, eye movements), so that we can apply those explanations of saccadic integration that rely only on visual information to the comprehension of overlapping cuts.

As we noted, Gibson and Johansson proposed that the perceptual system can respond directly to the invariant undergoing transformation, a proposal

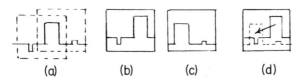

FIG. 6. Two overlapping views of the same scene. (a): The fields covered by two directions of the camera. (b, c): The two views successively presented on the screen. (d): The displacement vector shared by all points within the frame as the view in (c) succeeds the view in (b).

that was designed originally to apply to phenomena of continuous transformation. In a saccade, the transformation is a rigid translation—for example, the arrow in Fig. 6(d). If that is detected and discounted the apparent position in space of the shared portion of the two views remains unchanged by the translation; moreover, if the rigid translation is applied to the nonoverlapping portions, they will automatically be assigned to their appropriate relative locations in the overall layout. In Johansson's formulation, the perceptual system extracts the common vector shared by all elements in the field, which becomes the framework (i.e., the translational movement of the gaze). If there are no residual vectors, the scene appears stationary despite its shift in the retinal image (Johansson, 1950, 1974). This is not an ad hoc proposal devised to deal specifically with transitions such as those shown in Fig. 6: Something at least roughly like this is clearly also needed to explain the phenomena with which Johansson began, such as that shown in Fig. 3(d). Before we could take these proposals seriously, we would have to be sure that the defining phenomena themselves really fit those formulations, and are not purely peripheral products of eye movements [e.g., uncompensated pursuit movements in the direction of the horizontal arrow in Fig. 3(d), as Stoper has suggested (1973)]. We now have proof that these phenomena are not peripheral (Hochberg & Fallon, 1976). We also need some evidence that these phenomena are not only the results of continuous movement, but can also be obtained with a succession of discrete views (which is what both saccadic glances and discontinuous cuts amount to); in fact, the Johansson phenomenon can be obtained as well with saltatory displays of static views at the rate of about six views per second (Hochberg, Fallon, & Brooks, 1977). It is not unreasonable, therefore, to accept the suggestion that we combine overlapping successive shots by recognizing the invariant under transformation, but we shall see that the formulation is incomplete in major ways. It is incomplete because, as we noted before, it really tells us nothing about characteristics of the space in the mind's eye. Furthermore, it sets no limits on the nature of the stimulus information, or on the perceptual task of the viewer. If the proposal about transformational analysis were correct as it stands, all overlapping cuts would be equally good, which we shall see is not the case.

2. What Are Bad Cuts? The Limits of a Transformational Analysis

There is a considerable lore, of course, on what a film editor must do in order to make cuts comprehensible. Let us note some of the major injunctions (cf. Reisz & Millar, 1968; Vorkapich, 1972), discuss what research is available, and then consider what model will fit these observations.

Prescriptions fall into four categories.

1. The viewer should expect to be shown what the transition brings (Reisz & Millar, 1968).
2. The cut should not come in the midst of a movement, but should be made at its inception or terminus (Reisz & Millar, 1968).
3. A shift from one focal length to another (e.g., longshot to medium shot) should be substantial, and not merely a slight change (Reisz & Millar, 1968).
4. Reverse angle shots (see Section III, A, 1) are difficult to comprehend (Reisz & Millar, 1968; Vorkapich, 1972).

The first prescription is a cognitive matter, and we will return to it later, and to a discussion of why it should be necessary. The remaining prescriptions are mechanical ones, and they are regarded not as inviolable prohibitions but as precautions about what will, without special efforts, be jarring or incomprehensible to the viewer.

We believe that most or all bad cuts share a single feature: They entail an initial misidentification of one object with another, and an apparent movement from one view to the next that is different from the change in the camera's direction. Other factors may of course also be involved: For example, the work by Shepard and his colleagues (Cooper & Shepard, 1973, 1976; Shepard & Judd, 1976; Shepard & Metzler, 1971), showing that "mental rotation" takes time, suggests that (other things being equal) the time taken to grasp a cut between two views will be proportional to the angle that the camera has moved. The false-identity issue is stronger and faster, however, and seems to us to be the most important one to tease out first.

a. FALSE IDENTITY AND APPARENT MOVEMENT ACROSS CUTS. As we noted in our discussion of stroboscopic movement, on p. 268, there are probably fast and relatively shape-blind responses that will cause apparent movement to occur between objects that fall near each other in successive views, regardless of their specific shapes. A momentary apparent movement in the direction dictated by two objects falling next to each other in successive views that is different from that of the direction of movement of the camera will cause a momentary disorientation (cf. Vorkapich, 1972). Let us note how it applies to a given case. Consider a cut between a shot and a reverse angle shot, as in Fig. 5(a). To a leisurely inspection, it is clear that the camera's viewpoint has been reversed, but the momentary identification is between man x and woman y in the first view, with woman y and man x in the second, respectively, instead of a change in camera angle.

The same factor can also explain why other cuts are bad: In the case of a too-small change in focal length, apparent movement, outward or inward, will occur between the contours of the two successive views of the same object.*

* The movement, if any, going on in the two shots between which a cut is made also seems to

There is more than anecdotal evidence to support this model. In successions of views like those in Fig. 5(b), viewers report movements to the left
at fast rates (333 msec per view) and displacement to the right, at slow rates
(Hochberg & Brooks, 1974). The prescriptions for the filmmaker are relatively easy to formulate.

If the same person or object appears in both views, the displacement (1)
should be opposite in direction (2) to the movement of the camera,Fig. 5(c).
In cuts in which the main object in the second view is different from that in
the first, they should lie far apart from each other, and some other indication
of the direction of the cut should be made. Filmmakers often avoid the
"jump" that is inherent in such a discontinuity by framing the new object (or
the same object or person in a new scene) so that its contours remain as
undisturbed by the cut as possible as illustrated in Fig. 5(d). This eliminates
the jump, but it probably also increases the time that it takes the viewer to
grasp that a change has occurred. It would seem better to follow the principle in Fig. 5(c), so that the viewer at least has correct information about the
direction, if not the extent, of the camera movement. In any case, where the
principle shown in Fig. 5(c) cannot be followed, the filmmaker should allow
a longer dwell time on each shot (i.e., employ a lower cutting rate). (We say
more to this point on pp. 286f.)

The implications for the filmmaker are not spectacular ones, although they
may prove helpful in codifying a lot of otherwise unrelated observations and
rules of thumb (some of them seemingly counterintuitive). The implications
for a perception psychologist (and particularly for one with high hopes for
transformational analysis of the integration of successive views) are, in
contrast, very serious.

b. THE LIMITED UTILITY OF FULL TRANSFORMATIONAL INFORMATION:
CUTS WITHOUT LANDMARKS, AND THE IMPORTANCE OF SCHEMAS. In a cut
between two views in which the fast (undetailed) determinants elicit an
erroneous initial perceived movement, as in Fig. 5(b), we might say that the
momentary response is an aberration somehow specific to the artificial
situations we are using, and we could try to save the transformational
analysis by pointing out that when slower cutting rates are used, the transients are swamped and, as we have seen, the veridical transformation
prevails.

That will not do: If the succession of views is a random array of elements,
like the visual maze shown in Fig. 7(a), or a random-dot matrix, viewers can
recognize the direction of a small displacement (about 3.5°), which brings
most contours in the second view near their location in the first view, so that

affect comprehensibility. Thus, when a cut is made between two shots containing motion, and
these motions are adjacent but not colinear and equal in velocity in two-dimensional projection,
that inequality is probably a rapid and strong determinant of the perception of still another
motion (i.e., the acceleration that will convert one into the other). This assertion is at present
supported only by personal observations in the course of watching movies.

(a)   (b)

FIG. 7. Two overlapping views of the same maze.

the fast and local factors can operate. With a larger displacement, the viewer has no way of identifying any part of the maze, and his recognition of the direction of movement drops to chance(Hochberg, Brooks, & Roule, 1977). Thus, although the mathematical transformation is every bit as specified for a maze as it is for some more simple and common pattern in which the viewer has some noticeable landmark on which he can focus his attention, the mathematical information about the transformation alone, once it exceeds the field of operation of what we might think of as low-level movement detectors (p. 267n) is insufficient: The viewer must have some discernible feature that anchors the transformation and allows him to test expectations about it.

In short, neither the momentary transient effects nor the more protracted effects fit a transformational model. What alternative do we have?

At present, our only alternative is a much more vaguely formulated explanation in terms of schematic maps or sensorimotor expectations —expectations of what one would see if one looked at this place or at that one. This argument will be more convincing, we believe, when we consider the cognitive abilities that must contribute to the perception of *non*overlapping successive glances: Most cuts do *not* contain appreciable overlap. If we can explain how they are fitted together, that explanation might apply as well to the cases in which successive glimpses of the world overlap each other.

3. NONOVERLAPPING SUCCESSIVE VIEWS

Most cuts do not bridge overlapping shots. In fact, what many film theorists (Colpi, 1966; Eisenstein, 1942; Godard, 1966; Pudovkin, 1958; Spottiswoode, 1933) appear to regard as the most characteristically cinematic device, the montage (see Section III, A, 1), provides sequences of views that are not related to each other by overlap or common background. The transformational proposal can do no better, in this situation, than the reafference proposal that we rejected much earlier. Consider the sequence in Fig. 8. It is a sequential view of a cross, circumnavigating its perimeter by means of static, nonoverlapping segments. Given only Views 2 through 12, the viewer sees either the hands of a clock jumping erratically to different locations or an equally erratic set of views of a square. Given an establishing long shot of a cross—that is, if the sequence begins as in View 1—the sequence is perceived very much as it was in the case of continuous move-

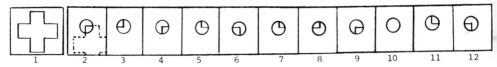

FIG. 8. Nonoverlapping views of a cross.

ment (p. 279): When the sequence comes to View 10 in Fig. 8, the viewer reports a shortcut *across* the right arm of the cross.

Here is a clear case of *mental* structure: There is simply no information in the stimulus, as such, that relates one view to another without reference to the schematic map that the viewer is testing. Although we have no definitive research addressed to the question, incidental observations suggest that the process is a relatively slow one (at least 200 msec per view). Here our earlier discussion of the components of stroboscopic movement becomes relevant. Let us sketch as much of an alternative to the transformational model as we can at this time.

4. The Components of Motion-picture Perception

We may identify three classes of process that contribute to the perception of motion-picture sequences and make at least rough estimates of the kinds of factors that govern them and of the time scales on which they operate.

a. Type I: fast stimulus factors. Apparent motion, clearly related to beta and phi motion, occurs between the nearest objects that occupy adjacent regions at successive times. These factors act rapidly, providing a momentary transient pulse (p. 267). In a succession of views in which cutting rate is not too large in relation to the durations of these transients—with an SOA (Stimulus Onset Asynchrony) of the order of 33–350 msec—these factors determine the apparent movement. With longer SOAs, the viewer will respond to the slower determinants (Types II and III), perhaps because he has time to recover from the fast transients. Because the fast factors are locally determined (i.e., appear to operate only on contours that are no more than about 4° apart) and may also be insensitive to small detail, they will often occur between objects that are only very grossly similar to each other.

b. Type II: slow stimulus factors. Objects' specific shapes become important in determining the direction of an apparent change in location only with relatively long viewing times (about 350–500 msec per view). It is possible that something like Gibson's transformational model (p. 278) can be applied to these relatively slow processes, but serious modifications would be needed: Mathematical identity between views (or parts of views) will not be sufficient to define the perceptual invariant undergoing transformation. The views must also offer some landmarks that the viewer can identify from one to the next. When there is *no* readily recognizable feature by which the viewer can identify the same part in a scene from one view to the next, his ability to determine the direction of displacement falls to chance if the displacement between successive views exceeds the distance over which corresponding parts in those views fall closer to each other than they do to noncorresponding parts (Fig. 7). If there is a landmark that the viewer can identify, the SOA needed is, very roughly, of the order of 500 msec per view, but it depends on how salient the landmark is—that is, on how long it takes the viewer to discover it, and on whether it is gross enough and different enough from its surroundings to provide a fast (Type I) basis for apparent movement*—so it is not possible to specify the viewing times with any greater precision or confidence.

c. TYPE III: SLOW NONSTIMULUS (COGNITIVE) FACTORS. When, as in nonoverlapping cutting, successive glances do not contain any object or landmarks in common, the relative location of successive views must be established by other means. First, of course, the viewer must be ready to assume that any view belongs to the same spatial domain that is being represented by the previous view(s) and is not a cut to a different scene.† Given the assumption that the next shot is part of the same event, the viewer must have some overall expectation either of where it is with respect to the previous shot (e.g., when one shot contains a closeup of an actor looking to the right, the subsequent shot is usually interpreted as showing the region at which he was looking), or he must have some overall expectation about the contents of the scene (as established by a long shot, as in Fig. 8).

These are clearly longer-lasting determinants (i.e., one establishing shot may have effects that bridge a long series of subsequent shots, as in Fig. 8); the time required to assimilate each shot in a sequence seems to be about the same as those needed for the slow stimulus (Type II) factors. But the processes we are considering here are not necessarily visual in nature. Thus, in Fig. 8, one could presumably use a verbal label to identify the cross, if the viewer were also given information about where the first view lay on the cross, and given time to mobilize an image of the cross (about 500 msec) again (Posner, Boises, Eichelman, & Taylor, 1969), or to activate a feature list (Pylyshyn, 1973) or a schematic map (Hochberg, 1968). In short, we have

---

* In order to operate as a landmark, a feature must be recognizable at a distance—that is, even when the viewer is looking in a different direction and the landmark therefore falls in the field of peripheral vision (Hochberg & Gellman, 1977). The landmark must therefore meet physical criteria of size and contrast, and if the landmark is thereby made very different from the rest of the field of view, it may be subject to the fast factors, though we do not know the distances over which these will operate.

† That assumption may in part be mediated by visual dissimilarity (e.g., when the gross character of the landscape, or the time of day, abruptly changes); it may be signaled by a convention (e.g., by a fade or a dissolve); or it may arise simply by the presentation of information that is inappropriate to everything that the viewer has learned about the event he was watching.

left the purely perceptual line of inquiry and entered the more general realm of narrative meaning.

C. Nonrepresentation (Noniconic) Effects of Sequence: Syntax, Affect, and Momentum

We have proposed that the perception of sequential pictures draws on three sets of determinants: (a) fast sensory factors, that are local and/or specific to the low-frequency features of the stimulus display; (b) slow, pattern- or object-responsive processes, which use information available over extended areas of the display and require identifiable features (landmarks) in order to be used; and (c) slow, nonstimulus determinants (mental maps, schemas, etc.), such as knowledge that the World Trade Center is south of the Empire State Building, or memory of where the establishing shots showed the Earp brothers and the Clantons to be deployed in the OK Corral. The time scale in the last set must be quite variable: If the viewer has a reasonably specific schematic map in mind and is presented with the successive features in an order and at a rate that he has been led to expect, a very brief set of glimpses should suffice, *as long as the fast (Type I) factors are arranged so as not to interfere* (cf. p. 284).

Somewhere between Type II and III, we leave the realm of purely perceptual processes. To the degree that we can substitute verbally communicated information for the visual sequence and obtain the same perceptual interpretation of the subsequent sequence, then the information is not specifically visual or even sensory, and the process is therefore not perceptual in the usual sense of the term. This distinction offers us an operational definition of what is visual–perceptual and specifically cinematic, and what is more general, conceptual, and shared with other means of narration.

Unfortunately, we know of no research that has used a criterion of this kind to determine what, in motion pictures, is specific to the medium. In fact, despite much writing to the grander aspects of this question, we know of no research of any kind, with any criterion. In what follows, we can only guess what the outcome would be if we did have experimental bases for applying this criterion to various questions of cinematic usage.

1. THE DIRECTION OF IDEATION AND THE QUESTION OF A GRAMMAR OF MOTION PICTURES

We noted previously that cutting could be used to direct the viewer's thought to something by cutting to a closeup of it. This is an approach to the study of thinking and problem solving that remains virtually unexplored. The two classical Russian theorists, Eisenstein (1942, 1949) and Pudovkin (1958), offered conflicting and only tentative prescriptions about how film sequences affected the thought processes of the viewers. To Pudovkin, ideas are to be assembled by the sequential presentation of their elements; to Eisenstein, new ideas emerge out of the conflict within the montage of views that are actually presented.

In practice, it is not clear that these filmmakers really differed in the way in which they worked: To advance a narrative, Eisenstein had no choice but to follow Pudovkin's thesis, and detailed study of Pudovkin's work shows his heavy reliance on a dialectic of ideas, if only to provide comment by contrast. In either case, although there is some reason to believe that we can find at least rough rules that determine how ideas will be combined by the viewer, there is a serious question as to whether those rules are in any way specific to cinema.

Most of the research actually directed to this point has been concerned only with cuts between a few shots; these have recently been reviewed by Isenhour (1975). The most famous experiment was probably one by Kuleshov and Pudovkin (Pudovkin, 1958), in which similar closeups of an actor, posed to express no feeling at all, were juxtaposed with a bowl of soup, a dead woman in a coffin, and a child playing. Audience judgments of the actor's expression differed appropriately with context. In an armchair experiment, Pudovkin also pointed out that the meaning of a shot depended on the order of the sequence: a three-shot sequence of a man smiling, a pistol pointing, and the man looking frightened will surely say different things about the man than will the reverse order. Subsequent demonstrations that the judged expression of an actor can be varied by changing the preceding context (Goldberg, 1951; Kuiper, 1958) or by changing both preceding and succeeding context and order (Foley, 1966) corroborate Pudovkin's assertion. Using abstract shapes (e.g., circles and triangles), Worth (1968) reported that the order of a sequence affects its meaning as measured by a modified semantic differential, and that the more similar the members of a sequence, the greater the effect of sequence order on the meaning. In Worth's (1968) terms, Foley's experiments (and Pudovkin's armchair experiment) showed that $(AB \neq BA)$, where A and B are individual shots.

Despite Eisenstein's assertion (1949) that two pieces of film of any kind, when placed together, inevitably combine into a new concept or quality, arising out of their juxtaposition, there is no reason to believe that the processes are automatic: Unless the viewer is actively trying to put the two together, and unless he assumes (formally or informally) that the purpose with which the filmmaker assembled those pieces will be understandable to him if he makes that effort, there is no reason to believe that he will perceive anything other than a meaningless flight of visual fragments, relieved by an occasional meaning that chunks the montage into a memorable unit.*

* As in verbal communication, the viewer who responds to such sequences of shots must see them as being connected in some way. There is, of course, the inescapable fact that any viewer who thinks about it at all knows that the images that are presented to him have been assembled in the order, with the characteristics that they have, by a purposive filmmaker who intends to

Granted that the viewer makes the effort, sequences of shots must be grouped, must be perceived as providing their mutual context. If we follow the man–pistol–man sequence in the Pudovkin experiment with a mother–child sequence, there must be some basis on which the viewer knows that he should place a boundary between the two sequences. Again, in Worth's terms, given a sequence of shots A,B,C, what are the conditions in which the sequence is seen as (A,B) (C) as opposed to (A) (B,C)? The problem is, of course, similar to the one that linguists face in seeking the mechanisms that define word, clause, and phrase boundaries. What forms such bonds?

Gregory (1961), assuming with Osgood, Suci, and Tannenbaum (1957) that the meaning of two signs (shots, in this case) will affect each other only when they are coupled by some "assertion," proposes that associative cues (like the tools on the wall that identify two shots as both occurring in a workshop, or the knowledge about the activities that people usually engage in that permits us to recognize the shot of a man hammering as being connected to the closeup of the hammerhead on the nail in the next shot) provide the basis for the coupling or assertion. Isenhour argues that the spatial, tonal, and movement contents that relate one shot to another is enough to connect two shots, and proposes that Osgood's *principle of congruity* applies to any set of connected shots: The meaning of each shot shifts toward that of the other, and the amount each changes is inversely proportional to the intensity of its original meaning.

There are other ways in which sequence affects meaning: If too fast, the representation fails. There are several possible reasons for this, some of which we have outlined in Section III, B, 2. Once the durations of the shots are sufficient to permit clear recognition of each, and once the rhythm is established, any departure from that rhythm, such as an especially long presentation of one shot, is a signal that it is important. Similarly, once a level of detail is established, presenting information in more detail is a signal that it is important. An example of both of these is the glass of milk in Hitchcock's *Suspicion* (Truffaut, 1967, p. 103), into which a lamp was set to increase its luminance and attract the viewer's attention; this effect signaled the viewer to think about the glass and all of the possibilities (poison, intentions to murder, etc.) that might lead the filmmaker to emphasize it.

It is clear that there is something approaching a language here.* Is it cinematic? Is it even perceptual?

---

communicate something to him (cf. Metz, 1974, p. 47). Even viewers who do not think about it (any more than they think about the fact that a soap opera or a comic book has been assembled for some purpose and is not merely a window on the world) have learned that things will be represented and events will occur if they attend to the flickering images, paying attention to their sequences by attempting to fit them into some schematic map or schematic event sequence (Hochberg, 1968, 1970).

* With context, order, and emphasis all shown to be important to the meaning of a sequence of shots, we have met most of the requirements for a language, and one can discuss whether or not there is evidence for a systematic grammar (Pryluck & Snow, 1967). Whether or not there is

There are some aspects of such communication that depend on vision—for example, the similarity of lighting in a particular sequence which, when it changes abruptly, is a signal that a new sequence has begun. It seems to us however that this is merely a *device*, like a paragraph: The syntax is not clearly specific to cinema. The very example with which we started—the man–pistol–man armchair experiment—was not a truly *visual* experiment. It was in fact a *verbal* demonstration that the determinants are verbal, or even amodal, but not visual. Even the effects of clearly deliberate emphasis achieved by an overlong shot, overbright lighting (as exemplified by the milk-glass shot), and by unnecessary detail is not specific to either motion pictures or to visual, pictorial communication. Precisely the same kinds of emphasis phenomena are to be found in speech, in ways that have only recently been brought under inquiry in the study of speech acts (Grice, 1968; Searle, 1969), namely, the ubiquitous kinds of communication that we can understand "not just because we share common knowledge about the syntactic and semantic conventions for the use of words, but also because we share common knowledge about the forms of life or social reality with which we live and act [Schmidt, 1975]." That is not to say that this aspect of communication is not worth studying; quite the contrary. (For a sample of what a dictionary of motifs might look like, cf. Durgnat, 1971, pp. 229–235.) However, until it is demonstrated that the sequence of ideas that is produced by cinematic cutting is essentially different in a significant way from that which would be produced by conveying the same information in, say, verbal narrative (which is what was actually done after all, in the man–pistol–man experiment), there is no reason to consider the processes to be perceptual.

There are other features of cutting that are related neither to the representation of things and events, nor to the narrative flow of ideas. We consider them next.

2. Affective and Connotative Effects of Cutting Rate

Whether or not they really agreed on the cognitive effects of cutting, Eisenstein and Pudovkin did agree (as have many of their successors) about the emotional effects of cutting. Because each cut produces a momentary state of arousal, the pace and rhythm of the cutting will presumably be reflected in the physiological state of the viewer. Although there has been very little experimental research directed to this issue, what little there is is encouraging. There is some evidence that a film appears to be more *active* at higher cutting rates (Gregory, 1961; Malpass, Dolan, & Coles, 1976). Penn

currently a set of rules that would meet the criterion set by the psycholinguist, there is every reason to believe that one will emerge with the increasing sophistication and evolution of film devices (Pryluck, 1968; Worth, 1968, 1969). The emergence of a film language would surely be of value in that a hard record (most of the films themselves) exists as a fossil history, but we can question whether its language-like aspects are specifically dependent on visual perception.

(1971) has shown that the connotative meaning of a film (as measured by ratings on a semantic differential) and its meaningfulness—as measured by Noble's (1952) measure—can be changed as a function of the film's subject matter, its cutting rate, and the constancy of its cutting rate. Although the results cannot be summarized simply,* the procedure did show that effects could be obtained.

What would seem to be needed now are simplifying yet specific theoretical models, and measures that have more known consequence than do the scales of connotative meaning on the semantic differential.

One reasonably powerful and simple model would appear to flow from attribution theory in social psychology. The proposal by Schachter and his colleagues (Schachter & Singer, 1962) that our perceptions of our emotions are the results of attempting to account for whatever cues we have concerning our internal states. In terms of the cognitive situation, this would seem to have a fairly direct application to understanding the effects of the cutting rate. By simulating the pattern of responses that would occur in some emotion, the momentary transients of arousal that occur with each change in view should simulate the pattern of internal cues that would be offered the viewer by that emotional situation. This should lead the viewer to perceive himself as experiencing that emotion if the supporting cognitive content in the film permitted the attribution. Thus, by filming a scene in a ragged and accelerating rhythm, similar to hearing one's heartbeat during fear, or by suddenly interrupting an expected and strong rhythm, the viewer will presumably be led to the same emotion. Although there is no actual study of such procedures that we know of, they do suggest reasonably specific testing procedure, and an experiment by Valins (1966), in which the subjects' evaluations of the attractiveness of pinup pictures were manipulated by changes in the rate of what they were told were amplifications of their own heartbeats, is an exceedingly indirect but encouraging finding relevant to this point.

Figure 9(a) represents a proposal made by Spottiswoode, in 1962, based only on his careful observation of the effects of cutting rate on his experience of montage. The graph shows the *affective tone* (his judgment of the quantity of emotional effect) produced by each new shot as a function of the time, in

---

* Penn constructed films in which objects were either stationary, moved toward each other slowly, or moved toward each other rapidly. The subject matter was either two automobiles, two people, or two rectangles. Cutting rates were either constant (at 8, 2 and .5 sec c^{-1}) or nonconstant (accelerating and decelerating, from .25 to 5 sec c^{-1}, or vice versa). Cars moved at two rates of speed, actors walked or ran, and rectangles were set into induced movement by a moving background (see Section II, A,2,e). Subjects rated concepts drawn from each film (e.g., white car, black car, the pair, the scene as a whole) on a semantic differential, and wrote down as many words as they could about each concept in 60 sec to provide a measure of meaningfulness (Noble, 1952). Motion and subject matter interacted significantly in their effects on the potency and activity scales in the films using cars and people, and a smattering of other specific comparisons were significant.

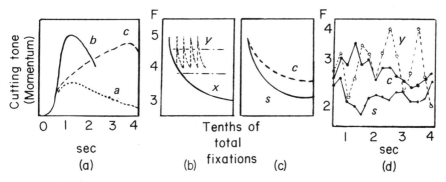

FIG. 9. The time course of cutting tone and visual momentum. (a): Spottiswoode's graph of cutting tone as a function of content. (b, c): The ordinate is the number of glances per second (saccadic frequency, F); the abscissa is the course of looking, as scaled in tenths of total fixations. The curve marked x in (b) is the time course of looking at a still picture, as measured by Antes (1974). Curve y in (b) is what we would expect to happen with a repeated change in view; Curves s and c in (c) are the expected course of looking with sequences of simple and of attentionally complex views, respectively. (d): The ordinate is saccadic frequency, and the abscissa is in seconds of viewing time. Curves s and c show the time course of 4-second views of picture sequences that are attentionally simple and complex, respectively; y is a sequence of four 1-second views of simple pictures.

seconds, after a cut has been made. Affective tone varies with two independent factors, cutting rate and substantive content: Curve a shows the time course of affect after a simple and striking shot has been presented; Curve b, the effect of a more complex, intrinsically beautiful, or meaningful shot. Although the model appears to be both valuable and specific, no research has been directed to test it. This is probably due, in part, to the absence of any acceptable measure of momentary affective tone, but the curves may also reasonably be expected to reflect the time course of another response as well, namely, the visual interest or *visual momentum* that is aroused by each cut, and that dependent variable can be made quite specific and testable.

3. VISUAL MOMENTUM AND THE MAINTENANCE OF LOOKING

Although the gathering of visual information usually appears to be as effortless as breathing, like breathing it depends on a set of well developed, purposeful actions. When first confronted by a still picture or scene, the viewer executes a number of rapid glances to establish the nature of the optic array that confronts him, and his subsequent rate of looking then subsides, as in Curve x of Fig. 9(b) (Antes, 1974). The initial glances are directed toward parts of the field that are likely to be informative, or that subjects rate as being prominent (Antes, 1974; Brooks, 1961; Hochberg & Brooks, 1962; Loftus, 1976; Mackworth & Morandi, 1967; Pollack & Spence, 1968).

How may we sustain a high rate of looking for a longer period? For one thing, we can give the viewer more to look at. A page of dense text can keep the viewer busy for a much longer period than a simple picture, and Berlyne (as part of a long tradition relating complexity and novelty to esthetic value—cf. Berlyne, 1971; Birkhoff, 1933; Rashevsky, 1960; Vitz, 1966; etc.) has shown that viewers look longer at more novel and more complex stimulus patterns (Berlyne, 1958; Faw & Nunally, 1967). Another tactic would be to change the display before the viewer has quite finished his initial rapid exploratory search. Pictorial change is the heart of moving pictures. Let us return to Spottiswoode's model with these facts in mind.

Replace Spottiswoode's abscissa with one that stands for the impetus to visual exploratory activity; that is, for what we have called *visual momentum* (Brooks & Hochberg, 1976; Hochberg & Brooks, in press). Visual momentum depends on two independent factors, cutting rate and substantive content, each factor having some effect in the absence of the other (even at a cutting rate of zero, content can sustain looking behavior as the eye continues to find more to search out; with zero substantive interest, there is some cutting rate at which change per se will maintain visual exploration).

Cutting rate presumably affects momentum in this way: Each change in view is arousing, or "surprising." The content of a given shot may be grasped very rapidly, and the information quickly incorporated into a growing schema if it is simple, familiar, or expected. The curve marked *a* in Fig. 9(a) is our application of Spottiswoode's model to the case in which content contributes nothing to momentum. Spottiswoode assumes this to represent the minimum effect that content can exert. Such a very simple shot may be presented for only a very brief period (say, 500 msec), and it should not be shown much longer, as arousal will again diminish as habituation to the view, or boredom, sets in. More meaningful, more unexpected, or more complex shots both require longer presentations, and can sustain lower cutting rates: Curves *b* and *c* in Fig. 9(a) represent responses to sequences of simple and complex views, respectively.

More subtle and complex possibilities inhere in this model,* and it is clearly capable of further specification and amendment. Before we consider such possibilities we must ask whether there is any quantitative, empirical support for the general features of the model.

In a sense, Antes' curve in Fig. 9(b) is a test of one combination of content and rate. Suppose that the frequency with which eye movements are

---

* Because Spottiswoode believes that the shortest shot that can be registered is 200 msec, he assumed that much of each presentation is without effect, but that then the arousal rises rapidly and probably falls more slowly than it rises. If the next cut is made just after the increment produced by the first one has returned to zero, no overall increase in momentum occurs. With longer shots, there is a net drop in arousal; with shorter shots, there is a net accrual, and momentum continues to increase. (Momentum, of course, must have an upper limit, since saccades cannot be executed faster than four or five every second, whereas Spottiswoode's *cutting tone* need not be limited.) After the first few cuts, however, the viewer comes to expect them, they become less surprising, increments in arousal become smaller, and in order to maintain an increasing momentum, a progressively accelerated cutting rate would be required.

made is (with some reservations about what will happen at the extemes: cf. Potter & Levy, 1969) a good measure of visual momentum. Curve x in Fig. 9(b) is the time course of the frequency of eye movements that we would expect to get with a single view. Replacing that view with another before the curve falls far (y) should keep the average glance rate higher. With cutting rate constant, content will presumably affect momentum too; for example, with a picture that has more centers of attention (i.e., more places to look at), the curve should fall more slowly, as in Fig. 9(c).

These expectations are reasonably well fulfilled (Brooks & Hochberg, 1976; Hochberg & Brooks, in press). Abstract views were composed having one, two, or four centers of attention, and film sequences made up of these views were presented at rates of from 1 view per sec to 1 view per 4 sec while viewers' eye movements were recorded. The course of looking activity with the simplest (s) and most complex (c) view sequences are shown by the solid curves in Fig. 9(d). The same figure shows the effect of cutting rate: Compare one cut per second (dotted line y) with the corresponding sequence presented at one cut per four sec (the solid line s). Very similar results have obtained with sequences of meaningful views. The frequencies with which eye movements are recruited by sequences of abstract patterns and of meaningful pictures are therefore reasonably well fitted by the simple models in Figs. 9(b) and 9(c) as a first, semiquantitative prediction of the time course of the response to cinematic cutting. The conception of visual momentum is not, however, simply another name for eye-movement frequency. A sequence of shots that is expected to have higher momentum should also be expected to keep the viewer looking at it longer, which in fact is the case when two sequences are projected next to each other and the viewer is free to look at either or neither (Hochberg & Brooks, in press).

At least one of the nonrepresentational consequences of cinematic cutting (namely, visual momentum) thus seems to be reasonably lawful, robust, and amenable to quantitative study. Spottiswoode's introspective semiquantitative analysis of affective cutting tone implies a number of relationships that would be important for the filmmaker to know, and these should be pursued using the visual-momentum measures. For the psychologist, these relationships may offer an "online" measure of processing time (and thereby of complexity, comprehensibility, and expectation or preparation), and an opportunity to manipulate and study the course of purposive looking behavior, which is an activity of increasing theoretical importance.

IV. SUMMARY AND CONCLUSIONS

We have surveyed several problems, of theoretical importance to perceptual psychologists that are advantageously studied by means of motion pictures and that are of practical importance to filmmakers. Four of the research areas that are identified in this paper arise out of filmmakers' characteristically heavy use of changes in camera viewpoint. Because the consequent changes on the screen do not result from the viewer's own perceptuomotor actions, his comprehension of such sequences cannot be based on his efferent records or proprioceptions, and a theory that will explain motion-picture perception, beyond the level of stroboscopic movement with which such analyses usually stop, is therefore needed.

Two general explanations are considered. The first, which can be made quite specific, is that viewers respond directly to the visual information about the invariant scene that is mathematically specifiable as undergoing the transformations on the screen (Gibson, 1966; Johansson, 1974). The second, much less specific, explanation is that when a viewer attends to a sequences of sensory patterns (like a succession of views), he formulates and tests schematic maps or schematic events, that is, structures of perceptuomotor expectations. Of the four areas we consider to be particularly important, the second seems to provide the best opportunity to display the virtues of the transformational theory, whereas the third and fourth seem naturally suited to study the manner in which viewers develop and test their visual schemas.

Transient response to pictures (or patterns) can be separated from more sustained responses and studied by varying the rate at which sequences of views are presented. When such transients are not taken into account by the filmmaker, they result in unintended perceptions of movement, mistaken assumptions of identity, and in momentarily incomprehensible cuts. With an understanding of the phenomena, the filmmaker can minimize these effects. Because the transients are unaffected by the detailed information in the stimulus patterns, the effects that they produce are not those called for by the transformational theory.

Some kinds of camera movement provide optical information about three-dimensional space, if the viewer is capable of using the information about the three-dimensional layout that is invariant under transformation. Other camera movements do not, and even provide movement-parallax information about the scene's flatness that contradicts whatever static pictorial depth cues are present. The freedom with which filmmakers use these uninformative camera movements challenges the transformational theory, but we do not as yet have any experimental data about how much is lost by using such procedures.

Motion pictures characteristically use successive overlapping (continuous or discontinuous) views to present scenes that are larger than the screen. It is easy to apply the transformational explanation to such presentations, but the facts do not fit that explanation. Fast sequences are dominated by the transients and are as likely as not to be incorrectly perceived; in order for slow sequences to be perceived correctly, the views must share landmarks that the viewer can identify. Mathematical invariance alone, therefore, does not suffice to explain how we perceive scenes revealed by successive overlapping views, but even if it did, most cinematic sequences are made up of nonoverlapping views, and therefore provide no information that specifies any invariant scene. In such sequences, the filmmaker relies on the viewer's knowledge about the world, or on establishing shots. This cinematic practice must tap abilities that we employ in the real world to guide our purposeful perceptual inquiries: The actions by which we obtain the perceptual information (e.g., ballistic saccades) to guide our larger actions (like locomotion) must themselves be guided by some expectations about what the eye will see. Film editors say, in fact, that good, rapidly comprehended cuts are those that provide the viewer with the answer to the visual question he would normally be free to answer for himself.

In his normal visual sampling of scenes and events, the sampling is under the viewer's control, and the processes are too rapid and covert to study moment by moment. With motion pictures, we can intervene in, and thereby study, the course of active looking. One method of doing so is by the use of cinematic montage.

When static pictures are first presented, the viewer looks first at the most informative regions, with a glance rate that is initially high and that declines rapidly. In our terms, the viewer quickly develops and tests a schematic map of the scene. After this, his impetus to perform sensory tests, his momentary visual momentum, wanes.

Visual momentum (as measured by the time course of saccadic eye movements, and by the viewer's tendency to keep looking at one sequence when he is free to look at another) should therefore (and does) vary with the rate at which one view replaces another, and with the attentional complexity of each view (and of course with the viewer's task or intention). The functions that relate momentum to these stimulus variables are consistent with Spottiswoode's semiquantitative but introspective theory about what he called *affective cutting tone* in cinematic montage. To the filmmaker, visual momentum is (if we are right) what sustains and motivates moment-by-moment visual attention and keeps the picture cinematically "alive." To the psychologist, it reflects the course of attentive looking in ways that, hopefully, will permit that process to be modeled and studied and that provide an independent measure of the attentional complexity of the views in a stimulus sequence.

For the filmmaker, such perceptual research promises to provide assistance like that provided the painter by the principles of geometrical perspective and color mixture. That is, research can provide a compact set of principles (sometimes counterintuitive—see Section III,B) to replace a larger number of ad hoc rules and tricks. They cannot, of course, substitute for creativity, experience, or imagination.

For the psychologist, motion pictures are particularly suited to the study of the dynamic and purposeful aspects of perception. Beyond the purely perceptual aspects of cinema, to which we have limited ourselves in this paper, motion pictures offer a visual approach to the nature of narration and discourse that is important to pursue in parallel to the present almost exclusively verbal line of inquiry.

References

Allen, W. H., & Cooney, S. M. Nonlinearity in filmic presentation. *AV Communication Review,* 1964, **12,** 164–176.

Antes, J. R. The time course of picture viewing. *Journal of Experimental Psychology,* 1974, **103,** 62–70.

Arnheim, R. *Film as art,* Berkeley, California: Univ. of California Press, 1960.

Arnheim, R. *Visual thinking.* Berkeley, California: Univ. of California Press, 1970.

Attneave, F., & Block, G. Apparent movement in tridimensional space. *Perception & Psychophysics,* 1973, **13,** 301–307.

Aubert, H. Die Bewegungsempfindung. *Archive für die Gesamte Physiologie,* 1886, **39,** 347–370.

Bazin, A. *What is cinema?* (Vol. 1). Berkeley, California: Univ. of California Press, 1967.

Berliner, A. *Lectures on visual psychology.* Chicago: Professional Press, 1948.

Bazin, A. What is cinema? (Vol. 2). Berkeley, California: Univ. of California Press, 1972.

Berlyne, D. E. The influence of complexity and novelty in visual figures on orienting responses. *Journal of Experimental Pyschology,* 1958, **55,** 289–296.

Berlyne, D. E. *Aesthetics and psychobiology.* New York: Appleton, 1971.

Birkhoff, G. D. *Aesthetic measure.* Cambridge, Massachusetts: Harvard Univ. Press, 1933.

Braunstein, M. L. Sensitivity of the observer to transformations of the visual field. *Journal of Experimental Psychology,* 1966, **72,** 683–689.

Braunstein, M. L. Motion and texture as sources of slant information. *Journal of Experimental Psychology,* 1968, **78,** 247–253.

Breitmeyer, B. G. Simple reaction time as a measure of the temporal response properties of transient and sustained channels. *Vision Research,* 1975, **15,** 1411–1412.

Breitmeyer, B. G., & Ganz, L. Implications of sustained and transient channels for theories of visual pattern masking, saccadic suppression, and information processing. *Psychological Review,* 1976, **83,** 1–36.

Breitmeyer, B. G., & Julesz, B. The role of on and off transients in determining the psychophysical spatial frequency response. *Vision Research,* 1975, **15,** 411–415.

Breitmeyer, B. G., Love, R., & Wepman, B. Contour suppression during stroboscopic motion and metacontrast. *Vision Research,* 1974, **14,** 1451–1455.

Brooks, V. *An exploratory comparison of some measures of attention.* Masters thesis, Cornell Univ., 1961.

Brooks, V. The perceptual factors involved in filming dance: I. The effect of frame area on perceived velocity. Columbia Univ., 1977. (Research report)

Brooks, V., & Hochberg, J. Control of active looking by motion picture cutting rate. *Proceedings of the Eastern Psychological Association,* 1976, **49.** (Abstract)

Brosgole, L., & Whalen, P. M. The effect of meaning on the allocation of visually induced movement. *Perception & Psychophysics,* 1967, **2,** 275–277.

Brown, R. H., & Conklin, J. E. The lower threshold of visible movement as a function of exposure time. *American Journal of Psychology,* 1954, **67,** 104–110.

Brunswik, E. *Perception and the representative design of psychological experiments* (2nd ed.). Berkeley: Univ. of California Press, 1956.

Burch, N. *Theory of film practice.* New York: Praeger, 1973.

Caldwell, K. S. *Guidelines and principles for the utilization of animation in instructional films and videotapes.* Univ. of Southern California, 1973.

Cohene, L. S., & Bechtoldt, H. P. Visual recognition of dot-pattern bigrams: An extension and replication. *American Journal of Psychology,* 1975, **88,** 187–199.

Colpi, H. Debasement of the art of montage. *Cahiers du Cinema in English*, 1966, **3**, 44–45.

Comalli, P. E., Jr., Werner, H., & Wapner, S. Studies in physiognomic perception: III. Effect of directional dynamics and meaning-induced sets on autokinetic motions. *Journal of Psychology*, 1957, **43**, 289–299.

Cook, O. *Movement in two dimensions*. London: Hutchinson, 1963.

Cooper, L. A., & Shepard, R. N. The time to prepare for a rotated stimulus. *Memory & Cognition*, 1973, **1**, 246–250.

Cooper, L. A., & Shepard, R. N. Transformations of objects in space. *Technical Report No. 59, Center for Human Information Processing, Univ. of California, San Diego*, 1976.

Corbin, H. H. The perception of grouping and apparent movement in visual depth. *Archives of Psychology*, 1942, **27**(3).

DeSilva, H. R. An analysis of the visual perception of movement. *British Journal of Psychology*, 1929, **19**, 268–305

Dimmick, F. L., & Scahill, H. G. Visual perception of movement. *American Journal of Psychology*, 1925, **36**, 412–417.

Duncker, K. Über induzierte Bewegung. *Psychologishe Forschung*, 1929, **12**, 180–259.

Durgnat, R. *Films and feelings*. Cambridge, Massachusetts: MIT Press, 1971.

Enoch, J. M. Effect of the size of a complex display upon visual search. *Journal of the Optical Society of America*, 1959, **49**, 280–286.

Eriksen, C. W., & Collins, J. F. Sensory traces versus the psychological moment in the temporal organization of form. *Journal of Experimental Psychology*, 1968, **77**, 376–382.

Eisenstein, S. M. *Film sense*. New York: Harcourt, 1942.

Eisenstein, S. M. *Film form*. New York: Harcourt, 1949.

Eriksen, C. W., & Collins, J. F. Some temporal characteristics of visual pattern perception, *Journal of Experimental Psychology*, 1967, **74**, 476–484.

Farber, J., & McConkie, A. Linkages between apparent depth and motion in linear flow fields. *Bulletin of the Psychonomic Society*, 1977, **10**, 250 (Abstract).

Faw, T. T., & Nunnally, J. C. The effects on eye movements of complexity, novelty and affective tone. *Perception and Psychophysics*, 1967, **2**, 263–267.

Festinger, L., & Easton, A. M. Inferences about the efferent system based on a perceptual illusion produced by eye movements. *Psychological Review*, 1974, **81**(1), 44–58.

Festinger, L., Ono, H., Burnham, C. A., & Bamber, D. Efference and the conscious experience of perception. *Journal of Experimental Psychology Monograph*, 1967, Whole No. 637.

Findahl, O. *The effect of visual illustrations upon perception and retention of news programmes*. Stockholm: Swedish Broadcasting Corp., 1971 (ERIC ED 054631).

Foley, J. M. *The bilateral effect of film context*. Unpublished masters thesis, Univ. of Iowa, 1966.

Gibson, J. J. *The perception of the visual world*. Boston: Houghton Mifflin, 1950.

Gibson, J. J. A theory of pictorial perception. *Audio-Visual Communication Review*, 1954, **1**, 3–23. (a)

Gibson, J. J. The visual perception of objective motion and subjective movement. *Psychological Review*, 1954, **61**, 304–314. (b)

Gibson, J. J. Optical motions and transformations as stimuli for visual perception. *Psychological Review*, 1957, **64**, 288–295.

Gibson, J. J. *The senses considered as perceptual systems*. Boston: Houghton Mifflin, 1966.

Gibson, J. J. Motion picture testing and research. *Army Air Forces Aviation Psychology Program Research Reports*, 1947, No. 7. Chapter 8: Pictures as substitutes for visual realities.

Godard, J. L. Montage, mon beau souci. *Cahiers du Cinema in English*, 1966, **3**, 45–46.

Gogel, W. C. The metric of visual space. In W. Epstein (Ed.), *Stability and constancy in visual perception*. New York: Wiley, 1977.

Goldberg, H. D. The role of "cutting" in the perception of the motion picture. *Journal of Applied Psychology*, 1951, **35**, 70–71.

Goldstein, B. The perception of multiple images. *AV Communication Review*, Spring 1975, **23**(1), 34–68.

Gombrich, E. H. *Art and illusion: A study in the psychology of pictorial perception*. New York: Pantheon, 1960.

Green, B. F., Jr. Figure coherence in the kinetic depth effect. *Journal of Experimental Psychology*, 1961, **62**, 272–282.

Gregory, J. R. *Some psychological aspects of motion picture montage*. Unpublished doctoral dissertation. Univ. of Illinois, 1961.

Grice, H. P. Utterer's meaning, sentence-meaning and word-meaning. *Foundations of language*, 1968, **4**, 225–242.

Grover, P. L., Jr. Effect of varied stimulus complexity and duration upon immediate recall of visual material in a serial learning task. *Audio-Visual Communications Review*, 1975, **22**, 439–452.

Guba, E., Wolf, W., de Groot, S., Knemeyer, M., Van Atta, R., & Light, L. Eye-movements and TV viewing in children. *Audio-Visual Communications Review*, 1964, **12**, 386–401.

Hagen, M. A., & Elliott, H. B. An investigation of the relationship between viewing condition and preference for true and modified linear perspective with adults. *Journal of Experimental Psychology: Human Perception and Performance*, 1976, **2**, 479–490.

Harmon, L. D., & Julesz, B. Masking in visual recognition: Effects of two-dimensional filtered noise. *Science*, 1973, **180**, 1194–1197.

Held, R. Exposure-history as a factor in maintaining stability of perception and coordination. *Journal of Nervous and Mental Disorders*, 1961, **132**, 26–32.

Held, R., Ditchgans, J., & Bauer, J. Characteristics of moving visual scenes influencing spatial orientation. *Vision Research*, 1975, **15**, 357–365.

Hershberger, W. A., & Starzec, J. J. Motion-parallax cues in one-dimensional polar and parallel projections: Differential velocity and acceleration/displacement change. *Journal of Experimental Psychology*, 1974, **103**, 717–723.

Hochberg, J. The psychophysics of pictorial perception. *Audio-Visual Communications Review*, 1962, **10**, 22–54.

Hochberg, J. In the mind's eye. In R. N. Haber (Ed.), *Contemporary theory and research in visual perception*. New York: Holt, 1968.

Hochberg, J. Attention, organization and consciousness. In D. I. Mostofsky (Ed.), *Attention: contemporary theory and analysis*. New York: Appleton, 1970.

Hochberg, J. Perception; II. Space and movement. In J. W. Kling & L. A. Riggs, (Eds.), *Woodworth and Schlosberg's experimental psychology* (3rd ed.). New York: Holt, 1971.

Hochberg, J. The representation of things and people. In E. H. Gombrich, J. Hochberg, & M. Black (Eds.), *Art, perception & reality*. Baltimore: Johns Hopkins Univ. Press, 1972.

Hochberg, J. Organization and the Gestalt tradition. In E. C. Carterette & M. P. Friedman (Eds.), *Handbook of perception*. Vol. I. New York: Academic Press, 1974. (a)

Hochberg, J. Higher order stimuli and inter-response coupling in the perception of the visual world. In R. B. MacLeod & H. L. Pick (Eds.), *Perception: Essays in Honor of James J. Gibson*. Ithaca, New York: Cornell Univ. Press, 1974. (b)

Hochberg, J., & Brooks, V. The prediction of visual attention to designs and paintings. *American Psychologist*, 1962, **17**, 437. (Abstract)

Hochberg, J., & Brooks, V. *The perception of television displays*. New York: The Experimental Television Laboratory of the Education Broadcasting System, 1973.

Hochberg, J., & Brooks, V. The integration of successive cinematic views of simple scenes. *Bulletin of the Psychonomic Society*, 1974, **4**, 263. (Abstract)

Hochberg, J., & Brooks, V. The prediction of visual attention to designs and paintings. (Eds.), *Eye movements and psychological processes, II*. Hillsdale, New Jersey: Erlbaum. (In press)

Hochberg, J., Brooks, V., & Roule, P. Movies of mazes and wallpaper. *Proceedings of the Eastern Psychological Association*, April, 1977, p. 179. (Abstract)

Hochberg, J., & Fallon, P. Perceptual analysis of moving patterns. *Science,* 1976, **194,** 1081–1083.

Hochberg, J., Fallon, P., & Brooks, V. Motion organization in "stop action" sequences. *Scandinavian Journal of Psychology,* 1977, **18,** 187–191.

Hochberg, J., & Gellman, L. Feature saliency, "mental rotation" times and the integration of successive views. *Memory & Cognition,* 1977, **5,** 23–26.

Hogben, J., & Di Lollo, V. Effects of duration of masking stimulus and dark interval on the detection of a test disk. *Journal of Experimental Psychology,* 1972, **95,** 245–250.

Holst, E. von Relations between the central nervous system and the peripheral organs. *British Journal of Animal Behavior,* 1954, **2,** 89–94.

Isenhour, J. P. The effects of context and order in film editing. *Audio-Visual Communications Review,* 1975, **23**(1), 69–80.

Ittelson, W. W. H. *The Ames demonstrations in perception.* Princeton, New Jersey: Princeton Univ. Press, 1952.

Jensen, G. D. Effect of past experience upon induced movement. *Perceptual and Motor Skills,* 1960, **11,** 281–288.

Johansson, G. *Configurations in event perception.* Uppsala: Almquist and Wiksells, 1950.

Johansson, G. *Spatio-temporal differentiation and integration in visual motion perception.* (Report No. 160). Department of Psychology, Uppsala Univ., Sweden, 1974.

Kaufman, L. *Sight and mind.* New York: Oxford Univ. Press, 1974.

Kaufman, L., Cyrulnick, I., Kaplowitz, J., Melnick, G., & Stof, D. The complementarity of apparent and real motion. *Psychologische Forschung,* 1971, **34,** 343–348.

Keesey, U. T. Flicker and pattern detection: A comparison of thresholds. *Journal of the Optical Society of America,* 1972, **62,** 446–448.

Kenkel, F. Untersuchungen über den Zusammenhang Zurschen Erscheinungsgrösse und Erscheinungsbewegung bei einigen sogen annten optischen Täuschungen. *Zeitschrift für Psychologie,* 1913, **67,** 358–447.

Knowlton, J. Q. *A socio- and psycho-linguistic theory of pictorial communication.* Bloomington, Indiana: Division of Educational Media and Audio-Visual Center, Indiana Univ., 1964 (NDEA Title VII, Project No. B-297).

Koffka, K. *Principles of Gestalt psychology.* New York: Harcourt, 1935.

Kolers, P. Some differences between real and apparent movement. *Vision Research,* 1963, **3,** 191–206.

Kolers, P. A., & Pomerantz, J. R. Figural change in apparent motion. *Journal of Experimental Psychology,* 1971, **87,** 99–108.

Kolers, P. A., & von Grünau, M. Shape and color in apparent motion. *Vision Research,* 1976, **16,** 329–335.

Kopfermann, H. Psychologische Untersuchungen über die Wirkung Zweidimensionälar Darstellungen körperlicher Gebilde. *Psychologische Forschung,* 1930, **13,** 293–364.

Korte, A. Kinematoskopische Untersuchungen. *Zeitschrift für Psychologie,* 1915, **72,** 193–296.

Kuiper, J. B. The relationship between context and the meaning of a single shot in a motion picture sequence. Unpublished paper, Univ. of Iowa, Department of Speech and Dramatic Art, Division of TV–Radio–Film, 1958.

Layer, H. A. The aesthetic basis for media design. *Audio-Visual Communications Review,* 1974, **22,** 328–330.

Loftus, G. R. A framework for a theory of picture recognition. In R. A. Monty & J. W. Senders (Eds.), *Eye movements and psychological processes.* Hillsdale, New Jersey: Erlbaum, 1976.

Lyle, J., & Hoffman, H. R. Explorations in patterns of television viewing by preschoolage children. In *Television and social behavior: A technical report to the surgeon general's scientific advisory committee on television and social behavior* (Vol. IV). Washington, D.C.: U.S. Government Printing Office, 1971.

Mack, A., & Herman, E. Position constancy during pursuit eye movement: An investigation of the Filehne illusion. *Quarterly Journal of Experimental Psychology*, 1973, **25**, 71–84.

Mackworth, N., & Morandi, A. J. The gaze selects informative details within pictures. *Perception & Psychophysics*, 1967, **2**, 547–552.

Malpass, R. S., Dolan, J. A., & Coles, M. Effects of film content and technique on observer's arousal. Mimeograph communication, 1976, SUNY College of Arts and Science, Plattsburgh, New York.

Matin, E. The two-transient (masking) paradigm. *Psychological Review*, 1975, **82**, 451–461.

McLuhan, M. *Understanding media: The extensions of man*. New York: McGraw-Hill, 1964.

McLuhan, M. *Counterblast*. New York: Harcourt, 1969.

McVey, G. F. Television: Some viewer-display considerations. *Audio-Visual Communication Review*, 1970, **18**, 277–290.

Meister, R. The iso-deformation of images and the criterion for delineation of the usable areas in cine-auditoriums. *Journal of the Society of Motion Picture and Television Engineers*, 1966, **75**, 179–182.

Metz, C. *Film language*. New York: Oxford Univ. Press, 1974.

Minter, P. C., Albert, F. A., & Powers, R. D. Does method influence film learning. *Audio-Visual Communications Review*, 1961, **9**(4), 195–200.

Muybridge, E. *The attitudes of animals in motion*. Paper read before the Society of Arts, London, April 4, 1882. *The Scientific American Supplement*, 1882, **14**(343), 5469–5470.

Navon, D. Irrelevance of figural identity for resolving ambiguities in apparent motion. *Journal of Experimental Psychology; Human Perception and Performance*, 1976, **2**, 130–138.

Neuhaus, W. Experimentelle Untersuchung der Scheinbewegung. *Archiv für gesamte Psychologie*, 1930, **75**, 315–458.

Noble, C. E. An analysis of meaning. *Psychological Review*, 1952, **59**, 421–430.

Orlansky, J. The Effect of Similarity and Difference in Form on Apparent Visual Movement. *Archives of Psychology*, 1940, **246**, 85.

Osgood, C., Suci, G. J., & Tannenbaum, P. H. *The measurement of meaning*. Urbana: Univ. of Illinois Press, 1957.

Penn, R. Effects of motion and cutting rate in motion pictures. *Audio-Visual Communication Review*, 1971, **19**, 29–50.

Penrose, L., & Penrose, R. Impossible objects: A special type of visual illusion. *British Journal of Psychology*, 1958, **49**, 31–33.

Perrin, D. G. A theory of multiple-image communication. *Audio-Visual Communication Review*, 1969, **17**, 368–382.

Petersik, J. T. Two types of stroboscopic movement in the same visual display. *Bulletin of the Psychonomic Society*, 1975, **6**(4b), 433. (Abstract)

Petersik, J. T., & Pantle, A. J. Contrast response of antagonistic movement-analysing mechanisms. *Bulletin of the Psychonomic Society*, 1976, **8**(4), 240. (Abstract)

Pirenne, M. *Optics, painting and photography*. Cambridge, England: Cambridge Univ. Press, 1970.

Pollack, I., & Spence, D. Subjective pictorial information and visual search. *Perception & Psychophysics*, 1968, **3**(1-B), 41–44.

Posner, M. I., Boies, S. J., Eichelman, W. H., & Taylor, L. Retention of visual and name codes of single letters. *Journal of Experimental Psychology*, 1969, **7**(1), Part 2, 1–16.

Potter, M. C., & Levy, E. I. Recognition memory for a rapid sequence of pictures. *Journal of Experimental Psychology*, 1969, **81**, 10–15.

Pratt, G. *Spellbound in darkness*. Greenwich, Connecticut: New York Graphics Society, 1973.

Pryluck, C., & Snow, R. E. Toward a psycholinguistics of cinema. *Audio-Visual Communication Review*, 1967, **15**, 54–75.

Pryluck, C. Structural analysis of motion pictures as a symbol system. *Audio-Visual Communication Review*, 1968, **16**, 372–402.

Pudovkin, V. I. *Film technique and film acting*. London: Vision Press, 1958.

Pylyshyn, Z. W. What the mind's eye tells the mind's brain: A critique of mental imagery. *Psychological Bulletin*, 1973, **80**, 1–24.

Rashevsky, N. *Mathematical biophysics* (Vol. 2). New York: Dover, 1960.

Reisz, K., & Millar, G. *The technique of film editing*. New York: Hastings House, 1968.

Rock, I., & Ebenholtz, S. Stroboscopic movement based on change of phenomenal rather than retinal location. *American Journal of Psychology*, 1962, **75**, 193–207.

Rutstein, N. *Go watch TV*, New York: Sheed & Ward, 1974.

Salomon, G. Can we affect cognitive skills through visual media? An hypothesis and initial findings. *Audio-Visual Communication Review*, 1972, **20**, 401–422.

Samuels, S. J. Attentional processes in reading: The effect of pictures on the acquisition of reading responses. *Journal of Educational Psychology*, 1967, **58**, 337–342.

Saucer, R. T. Processes of motion perception. *Science*, 1954, **120**, 806–807.

Schachter, S., & Singer, J. Cognitive, social and psychological determinants of emotional state. *Psychological Review*, 1962, **69**, 379–399.

Schmidt, C. F. Understanding human action. In *Theoretical issues in natural language processing*. Report of an Interdisciplinary Workshop in Computational Linguistics, Psychology Linguistics and Artificial Intelligence. Cambridge, Massachusetts: B. L. Nash Webber, Bolt Baranek and Newman, Inc., 1975.

Searle, J. R. *Speech acts: An essay in the philosophy of language*. New York: Cambridge Univ. Press, 1969.

Sekuler, R. Visual motion perception. In E. C. Carterette & M. P. Freidman (Eds.), *Handbook of perception*. Vol. V. New York: Academic Press, 1975.

Sekuler, R., & Levinson, E. The perception of moving targets. *Scientific American*, 1977, **236**(1), 60–73.

Sgro, R. J. Beta motion thresholds. *Journal of Experimental Psychology*, 1963, **66**, 281–285.

Shepard, R. N., & Judd, S. A. Perceptual illusion of rotation of three-dimensional objects. *Science*, 1976, **191**, 952–954.

Shepard, R. N., & Metzler, J. Mental rotation of three-dimensional objects. *Science*, 1971, **171**, 701–703.

Spottiswoode, R. *A grammar of the film*. Berkeley: Univ. of California Press, 1962. (Originally published, 1933.)

Stoper, A. E. Apparent motion of stimuli presented stroboscopically during pursuit movement of the eye. *Perception and Psychophysics*, 1973, **13**, 201–211.

Stratton, G. M. The psychology of change: How is the perception of movement related to that of succession? *Psychological Review*, 1911, **18**, 262–293.

Tannenbaum, P. H. The indexing process in communication. *Public Opinion Quarterly*, 1955, **19**, 292–302.

Tannenbaum, P. H., & Fosdick, J. A. The effect of lighting angle on the judgment of photographed subjects. *Audio-Visual Communication Review*, 1960, **8**(6), 253–262.

Ternus, J. The problem of phenomenal identity. In W. D. Ellis (trans. & editor) *A sourcebook of Gestalt psychology*. London: Routledge & Kegan Paul, 1938.

Truffaut, F. *Hitchcock*. New York: Simon & Schuster, 1967.

Ulrich, R. E. A behavioral view of Sesame Street. *Educational Broadcasting Review*, 1970, **4**, 17–22.

Valins, S. Cognitive effects of false heart-rate feed-back. *Journal of Personality and Social Psychology*, 1966, **4**, 400–408.

VanderMeer, M. A. Color versus black and white in instructional films. *Audio-Visual Communication Review*, 1954, **2**, 121–134.

Vitz, P. C. Preference for different amounts of visual complexity. *Behavioral Science*, 1966, **11**, 105–114.

Vorkapich, S. A fresh look at the dynamics of film-making. *American Cinematographer*, 1972, **53**, 182–195.

Wadsworth, R. H. THe practical considerations in designing audio-visual facilities. *Architectural Record,* 1968, **144,** 149–160.

Wallach, H. The perception of motion. *Scientific American,* 1959, **201,** 56–60.

Wertheimer, M. Experimentelle Studien über das Sehen von Bewegung. *Zeitschrift für Psychologie,* 1912, **61,** 161–265.

Wertheimer, M. Drei Abhandlungen zur Gestalttheorie. Erlangen: *Philosophischen Akademie,* 1925.

Williamson, S. J., Kaufman, L., & Brenner, D. Biomagnetism. In B. Schwartz & S. Foner (Eds.), *Superconductor applications: Squids and machines.* New York: Plenum, 1977.

Winn, M. *The plug-in drug.* New York: Viking, 1977.

Wist, E., Dienes, H., Dichganz, J., & Brandt, T. Perceived distance and the perceived speed of self-motion: Linear versus angular velocity? *Perception and Psychophysics,* 1975, **17,** 549–554.

Worth, S. Cognitive aspects of sequence in visual communication. *Audio-Visual Communication Review,* 1968, **16,** 121–145.

Worth, S. The development of a semiotic film. *Semiotica,* 1969, **1,** 282–321.

Zettl, H. *Sight-sound-motion: Applied media aesthetics.* Belmont, California: Wadsworth, 1973.

Part V

Odor and Taste

Chapter 12

ODORS IN THE ENVIRONMENT: HEDONICS, PERFUMERY, AND ODOR ABATEMENT

HOWARD R. MOSKOWITZ

I. INTRODUCTION

This review concerns two primary areas in which olfactory hedonics plays an important role: perfumery and the abatement of noxious odors. Perfumery is the art (for it cannot yet be considered a science) of blending together combinations of chemicals in order to obtain a pleasing combina-

HANDBOOK OF PERCEPTION, VOL. X

tion. In contrast, the assessment and abatement of noxious odors is a technology in which the engineer or scientist attempts to assess the degree to which an environmental odor annoys individuals and then attempts to eliminate the odor, by destroying it physically or by masking it with a more pleasing odor.

During the past three decades, substantial information has appeared concerning both of these subjects. Information pertaining to perfumery can usually be found in any of several different technical and trade journals devoted to perfumery and cosmetics. Information pertaining to odor abatement is often found in engineering journals, especially those devoted to environmental sciences. There are no specific journals at this time that deal specifically with the abatement of noxious odors. Typically, odor problems are treated by engineers in tandem with other problems created by noxious chemicals.

II. ODOR HEDONICS

Odor hedonics, the liking or disliking of an odorant, is an important aspect of both perfumery and odor abatement. Much of our knowledge of odor hedonics derives from a series of studies that have been reported over the last half century. These concern:

1. How we measure the hedonic tone of odors.
2. How the hedonic tone of an odor varies with age and stage of development.
3. How the hedonic tone varies with the nature of the stimulus and the situation in which the odor is evaluated.

A. Measurement of Odor Hedonics

A variety of procedures have been used to measure the hedonic tone of odors. These are summarized in the portion of the text that follows.

1. SIMPLE CLASSIFICATION

In this procedure, observers are instructed to state whether they like or dislike an odor. Substantial numbers of early reports on hedonics in general, and on odor hedonics in particular, used simple classification (Beebe-Center, 1932). The classification method is still used for situations in which it is difficult or impossible to obtain a graded measure of hedonics (such as assessment of infant response, or evaluation of the hedonic tone of noxious air pollution emitted from a chimney, where the measure is the number of phone calls received).

2. Rank Order Scaling

This method instructs observers to rank stimuli in order of the hedonic tone. Moncrieff (1966) used the ranking method extensively in assessing many different odorants. Ranking provides an order of different odorants, but does not indicate the degree of difference in hedonic tone between one odorant and another, nor does it specify whether an odorant is liked or disliked.

3. Category Scaling

In category scaling, observers are instructed to assign category-scale values (e.g., 1–5 or 1–9) to stimuli, with the proviso that the category scale be used as an equal interval scale. Category scaling is a popular scaling procedure today for hedonics assessment and is widely used in the food industry to assess food preferences (Peryam & Pilgrim, 1957). Category scaling is easily understood by the typical untrained observer, and can be rapidly implemented in field situations to evaluate an individual's responses to environmental odors. Although category scaling is supposed to produce a scale that has equal-interval properties, it does not. The psychological differences in hedonic tone between adjacent scale values are not equal at different parts of the scale. To change scale value by one point requires a smaller hedonic shift in the middle range than at the top (e.g., from 8 to 9), where a substantial increase in hedonic level must be made.

4. Thurstonian Scaling

In this method, used by Engen (1974), observers are instructed to choose which odorant of a pair they prefer. The matrix of preferences can be converted into a matrix of scale values (Thurstone, 1927), with the property that higher scale values correspond to those odor stimuli preferred more often. Problems with the procedure are that it (a) takes a long time (since for n stimuli there are $n(n-1)/2$ comparisons); (b) requires that the panelist compare two odorants, and thus potentiates systematic contrast effects; and (c) requires care on the experimenter's part that the first stimulus be sufficiently cleared from the panelist's nose before the next stimulus is smelled [this is an especially important problem for odorants such as eucalyptol and guaiacol, which are retained in the nose after the stimulus has disappeared (Dravnieks & Prokop, 1973)]. The advantages of paired comparison over the other scaling methods are (a) it provides a simple response (preference of one odor or the other) and thus can be used with children and with adults (as well as with individuals from different cultures); and (b) it can be used in connection with an underlying theoretical system (Thurstonian analysis) to generate metric-scale values from simple choice information.

5. Magnitude Estimation

This method requires that the observer assign numbers to stimuli to reflect relative liking. Magnitude estimation was originally used by Engen and McBurney (1964) to assess relative liking of many different odorants, and by Henion (1971) to assess the relative liking of different concentrations of amyl acetate. In those versions of magnitude estimation the observer was permitted to use only positive numbers, with low numbers reflecting disliking, and high numbers reflecting liking. One of the difficulties that ensued from the early version of magnitude estimation for hedonics was the inability to distinguish between stimuli that were classified as being liked and those that were classified as being disliked. No neutral point was used, nor could one be determined from the magnitude estimates alone. The existence of two hedonic continua (liking versus disliking) could not be established. Later experiments (Doty, 1975; Moskowitz, Dravnieks, & Gerbers, 1974; Moskowitz, Dravnieks, & Klarman, 1976) used a dual scaling arrangement for magnitude estimation. Positive numbers with ratio properties were used to indicate increasing degrees of liking, and negative numbers with ratio properties were used to indicate increasing degrees of disliking. Zero was used to indicate neutrality. The method has proved an easily implemented one, and is currently being used commercially in the assessment of fragrances and perfumes (Moskowitz, 1976).

6. Reaction Time

This method of assessment is an old one used extensively by nineteenth-century European investigators to assess hedonic tone (Beebe-Center, 1932). Reaction time does not appear to have been used for olfactory hedonic measurement, with the exception of a study by Wells (1929), who placed odorous substances in a stoppered bottle. Five of the odors were perfumes, and five were unpleasant stimuli (hydrogen sulfide, putrid meat, oleic acid, capryl alcohol, and butyric acid). It took observers longer to react to the smell per se than to react to the hedonic impact (liking–disliking of the smell), suggesting that hedonics and sensory information are different. However, Wells did not use the relative reaction time as a metric for relative preference.

One of the major problems associated with reaction time is the physical stimulus itself. The nature of the olfactory stimulus is that it diffuses into the ambient air from its container. The diffusion rate depends upon the stimulus and upon the solvent in which it is dissolved. Once the stimulus has diffused, it must be inhaled, and may find substantial affinity with the inner linings of the nares. This complicates matters once again, since the odorant will be selectively retarded in its passage toward the olfactory mucosa simply by the nature of its physico-chemical properties.

7. Multidimensional Scaling

The traditional use of multidimensional scaling is to obtain an idea of what the basic attributes of stimuli are. Observers provide estimates of how qualitatively different two stimuli appear to be (in a set of 10 stimuli this generates a matrix of $10 \times 9 \div 2$, or 45 pairs of stimuli to be evaluated). The matrix of difference or dissimilarity (or even similarity) judgments is treated as a matrix of interstimulus distances. The matrix can then be used to generate a configuration of stimuli in a geometrical space of low dimensionality, with the property that the interstimulus distances computed for all of the stimulus pairs best accord with the empirical estimates. There are numerous methods for determining such an empirical space (see Green & Rao, 1972 for a detailed approach). When applied to odors, often only two or three primary dimensions emerge, with the first dimension usually being hedonics. This has been reported by many different investigators (e.g., Berglund, Berglund, Engen, & Ekman, 1973; Moskowitz & Gerbers, 1974; Schiffman, 1974; Woskow, 1968; Yoshida, 1964). The relative positions of odorants on the dimension or axis that corresponds to hedonics become measures of relative liking or disliking. The measures have only interval level properties (i.e., only the distances between stimuli on the hedonics coordinate convey information, and not the ratios of coordinate values).

The method of multidimensional scaling is an inefficient one to discover valid hedonic tones for stimuli, since it relies upon the selection of an appropriate axis and upon the nature of the other stimuli in the experiment. The locations of stimuli in the multidimensional space will vary if the experimenter introduces other stimuli into the experiment. In addition, the conclusion that one of the axes (or even an oblique axis) is the appropriate hedonic axis may be incorrect, and the interpretation is left too much to the experimenter's intuition. In defense of the procedure, however, is the possibility of discovering different hedonic dimensions that might be impossible to discover by any other scaling method. Were the experimenter to instruct observers to estimate differences in hedonic tone and then process all of the data, what might be obtained is a two-dimensional hedonic space. This procedure (of directly setting up a "scenario," or basis, as to the attribute to be used for dissimilarity estimates) does not seem to have been used for hedonics, but was used by Green and Rao (1972) for evaluation of the dissimilarity of pairs of breakfast items.

B. Development of Hedonics

Affective responses to odor depend upon the child's age. Studies by Steiner (1974) using neonates and presenting the odorants to them by means of a cotton swab held in front of the nostrils suggest that neonates exhibit hedonic responses. The dependent variable in Steiner's studies was the *gustofacial reflex,* a stereotyped response in which the neonate may purse the lips and appear to withdraw (for unpleasant stimuli) or may relax and appear to smile (for pleasant stimuli). Steiner reported that for unpleasant smells, such as that provoked by asafetida, the neonate exhibited a response suggesting disliking, whereas for more pleasant smells, such as those elicited by milk or cream, the neonate exhibited a response suggesting liking.

As the child grows, the hedonic responses change in type and character. For example, Stein, Ottenberg, and Roulet (1958) found that the hedonic responses to amyl acetate (which smells like banana oil at low concentrations) remain constant over a period of 3–30 years. Approximately 50–75% of their observers stated that they liked the smell. In contrast, the majority of 3-year-old children reported that the odors of synthetic sweat and synthetic feces were agreeable, whereas at the age of 5–6 the children no longer found the smells to be pleasing. According to Stein *et al.*, the change in hedonic tone for feces and sweat is not connected with the toilet-training period (which occurs between 2 and 3 years), but may be linked with the oedipal phase.

In another series of investigations, Peo (1936) used smells corresponding to Henning's (1915) odor primaries (e.g., spicy = anise, fragrant = various perfumes, resinous = camphor and pine tar, putrid = asafetida, etc.). Peo selected young children who knew the experimenter (to eliminate fear) and presented the stimuli to them. For the younger children, a withdrawal signaled disliking, whereas for older children (8 years or more) the responses were obtained verbally. The results from examinations of 293 children showed the following:

1. For the 92 children under 5 (1 month–5 years), 89 showed no response that could be considered one of disgust.
2. For the 39 children of ages 5–6, 11 showed no hedonic reaction; 19 showed disgust.
3. For the remaining children older than 6 years, the majority showed clear-cut hedonic reactions.

In other studies with children by Engen and his colleagues, the principal set of findings and trends reported were:

1. Children (especially around 4–5 years) preferred butyric acid, whereas adults did not (Engen & Corbit, 1970).
2. Preference scales (by Thurstonian analysis) for children (4–7 years) and for adults appeared similar in many respects when the following five stimuli were evaluated: rapeseed oil (odor like castor oil), butyric acid (odor of rancid butter), neroli, safrole, and diethyl phthalate. However, the differences between odorants on the scale were smaller for the younger children (Engen & Corbit, 1970).

3. In another study using other odorants, Engen (1974) evaluated relative preferences of safrole, neroli (both pleasant), heptanal, 70% unscented alcohol, and aromatic spirits of ammonia by means of paired comparisons. All pairs of the five odorants (except the identical ones) were presented. By Thurstonian analysis of the variability of preferences, Engen found that the children exhibited a smaller scale than did adults. For adults the range of hedonic values was -1.20 to $+.84$, for 7-year-old children it was smaller ($-.59$ to $-.35$), and for 4-year-old children it was virtually 0. In contrast, for taste materials inserted in the mouth (cinnamon, cherry, peppermint, horehound) children showed a much larger range of hedonic values.

Other studies, using adolescents and adults, have shown another set of results (although no contradictory ones). Foster (1950a,b) selected a large number of observers from four age groups (nursery school, third grade, seventh grade, and college) as well as a group of old adults. Observers evaluated the hedonic tone of odorants by assigning a plus ($+$) for liking, and a negative ($-$) for disliking. Table I shows the ratings in terms of the percentage of observers who stated each odorant as pleasing. In general, an odorant that an adult finds unpleasant, a child will find unpleasant as well (for 8 of 10 odorants). Early adolescents (ages 12–14) appear to be less tolerant of odors than other groups, and the youngest group seems to be the most tolerant of odors. Some of the differences between groups, in terms of hedonics, could be correlated with flavors and aromas experienced in daily life. For example, many nursery-school children rejected spearmint (which is highly acceptable to older children), perhaps because in the 1940s spearmint was used to flavor children's medicine.

C. Why Are Odorants Liked or Disliked?

Odor hedonics may be highly personalized. Some individuals may strongly prefer a specific smell (e.g., the smoky smell of guaiacol), whereas others will just as strongly abhor it. Why? Although there are no clear answers as yet, a number of different experiments have shown that olfactory hedonic responses either vary randomly, or can be varied. Some of the factors are discussed in the following text.

1. INDIVIDUAL MENTAL REACTIONS OR ASSOCIATIONS MAY NOT BE INFLUENTIAL

A study by Kenneth (1924) concerned associations with a variety of different chemicals representing known pleasant and unpleasant stimuli (e.g., oil of rose, amyl acetate, and oil of lavender, for pleasant odors, and asafetida and carbon bisulfide for unpleasant odors). Otto (or oil) of rose provoked almost universally pleasant hedonic reactions, whereas carbon

TABLE I
HEDONIC RESPONSES TO ODORS

Stimulus	Percentages Positive Responses to Odors by Four Age Groups			
	3–5	8–9	12–14	Adults
Aldehyde perfume	57	67	79	95
Patchouli oil	39	33	0	37
Alpha-Ionone	38	40	9	36
Di-p-cresyl carbonate	36	38	24	32
Cottonseed oil	47	39	38	24
Diethyl sebacate	28	37	24	20
Benzyl benzoate	42	44	37	58
Lauryl mercaptan	31	36	0	2
Musk xylol	45	34	23	78
Amyl phenyl acetate	34	22	16	9
Mean	40.7	39	25.0	39.1

Stimulus	Percentages Positive Responses to Odors by Five Age Groups				
	3–5	8–9	12–14	18–30	Over 50
Spearmint	55	96	91	90	86
Amyl acetate	42	53	70	73	68
Musk xylol	45	34	23	78	59
Cottonseed oil	47	39	38	24	45
Benzyl benzoate	42	44	37	58	32
Alpha-Ionone	38	40	9	36	63
Patchouli oil	39	33	0	37	59
Phenylethyl alcohol	15	36	14	77	60
Diethyl sebacate	28	37	24	20	41
Amyl phenyl acetate	34	22	16	9	45
Acetic acid	31	33	8	17	57
Mean	37.8	42.4	30	47.2	56.1

Stimulus	Percentages Positive Responses to Odors by Three Age Groups		
	3–5	8–9	12–14
Spearmint	55	96	91
Phenylethyl alcohol	15	36	14
Amyl acetate	42	53	70
Acetic acid	31	33	8
Mean	35.8	54.5	45.8

SOURCE: [Foster (1950 a,b).]

bisulphide evoked almost universally unpleasant hedonic reactions. Some individuals thought menthol to be pleasant, with a slight tinge of unpleasantness. The associations made to the positive odor of otto of rose were those of the garden, roses, lilacs, soap, sweetness, honey, etc. The associations to musk (which ranged in hedonic tone from entirely pleasant to entirely unpleasant) were much more vivid, and referred to sex, the smell of cows, etc. From Kenneth's initial study it was not clear whether the associations determined the hedonic tone, or vice versa, or whether the two were entirely independent.

In a subsequent study, Kenneth (1928) categorized the kinds of individual associations. The associations could be classified as:

1. Type of association; for example, synesthetic ones (colors, tastes, sounds, tactual, and thermal impressions)
2. Contracted (associations identical to other odors); for example, menthol associated with a bottle of smelling salts
3. Expanded (not limited to identical stimuli); for example, rose oil evoking an image of home
4. Indirect through a mediating memory; for example, clove oil elicited a memory of the city of Ekaterinberg via a memory of a toothache during the observer's stay in Ekaterinberg
5. Egocentric (personal valuation); for example, musk = immoral

Kenneth's experimental work suggested that odor preferences remain constant over a 4–5 year period. When considered closely, a specific odor could be judged pleasant and yet recall both pleasant and unpleasant memories (for example, cedarwood oil).

2. INTENSITY OF ODORANTS IS IMPORTANT

A comparison of odor intensity and odor hedonics often reveals that hedonics may depend upon perceived odor strength. An intensity–hedonics comparison was done in an early study by Engen and McBurney (1964), who evaluated a large set of odorants at one fixed set of concentrations and found an approximately 1–125 range for hedonics (using positive magnitude estimates only), but only a 1–2 range in perceived odor intensities.

Later studies systematically varied the concentration of one or several chemicals and obtained estimates of intensity and hedonics from the same observers. These studies suggested a set of much more definitive relations. Henion (1971) reported that ratio scales of the odor intensity of amyl acetate (dissolved in a liquid) gave power functions for intensity with an exponent ranging from +.144 to +.245. The same observers gave magnitude estimates of liking with exponents ranging between −.235 and −.355 for amyl acetate (reminiscent of banana oil). Henion suggested that odor unpleasantness and intensity were effectively the same continuum, but based his conclusion upon only one chemical from the many thousands that provoke odor impressions.

Later studies by Doty (1975) and Moskowitz *et al.* (1974, 1976) have suggested that:

1. At the group level (average data) *unpleasant stimuli* (e.g., butanol, thiophene, pyridine) exhibit parallel unpleasantness and intensity functions.
2. At the individual level there is little or no correlation between pleasantness (or unpleasantness) and sensory intensity (for butanol, evaluated by both magnitude estimation and category scaling).
3. For odorants that are pleasant (e.g., benzaldehyde, which provokes the odor of almonds, or vanillin, which smells like vanilla) the relation between hedonics and sensory intensity may be either linear, flat (no change in hedonics with sensory intensity) or may show an inverted U-shaped function, with pleasantness reaching a maximum at an intermediate sensory intensity.
4. For pleasant food odorants (Moskowitz, 1976) there is no systematic change in rated liking (on a 10-point category scale) versus odorant concentration or odorant intensity. Examples of these pleasant food odorants are the oils of the orange, lemon, and grapefruit. For unpleasant food odorants (e.g., pork odor or cheese odor) unpleasantness grows monotonically with odor intensity.

3. Odor Mixtures Are Pleasing

Most of the naturally occurring aroma stimuli in foods are mixtures comprising many volatiles. In the typical laboratory study of odor hedonics the experimenter often chooses chemically pure single substances. At low concentrations some of these chemicals are reminiscent of natural aromas (e.g., amyl acetate and or iso-pentyl acetate are reminiscent of oil of banana), but at higher concentrations the same chemical provokes a harsh and unpleasant smell.

Moncrieff (1966) instructed observers to arrange many stimuli in order of preference. The rankings showed that the natural food odors were almost always more preferred to the pure chemicals that were qualitatively similar. The essence of expert flavoring and perfuming is to construct a composition of chemicals that will produce the required smell, but that will be sufficiently complex to be acceptable. For example, in producing a rose scent, the chemical geraniol is predominant, but the use of geraniol alone, or even in combination with another roselike chemical, phenyl ethanol, in no way produces an acceptable rose scent. Other chemicals must be added (Genders, 1972).

Spence and Guilford (1933) evaluated the nature of hedonic mixture by presenting one odor to one nostril and another to the second nostril. By using a nine-point category scale, and using six pleasing odors and seven displeasing ones (e.g., orange oil, anise, carbon bisulfide, etc.), they were able to estimate the hedonic tones of components and mixtures. The range of the hedonic tones of the mixtures was smaller than that of the components and could be predicted by the following equation:

$$\text{Hedonics (Mixtures)} = .54 \begin{bmatrix} \text{Pleasant} \\ \text{Component} \end{bmatrix} + .69 \begin{bmatrix} \text{Unpleasant} \\ \text{Component} \end{bmatrix} - .21$$

The equation means that there is a slight asymmetry in the hedonic-mixture equations, with the unpleasant odorant contributing slightly more toward the overall hedonics of the mixture. For cases in which one odorant was reported to dominate the mixture, the dominating odor contributed four times more than did the unpleasant one (i.e., hedonics of the mixture = k [hedonics of the less dominant component] + $4k$ [hedonics of the more dominant] + c).

4. INDIVIDUALS EXHIBIT DIFFERENCES

Perhaps in no other sense are there so many individual differences when observers evaluate hedonic tone than in olfaction. A number of studies have shown this repeatedly. Young (1937) asked observers to classify 16 odorants into liked or disliked groups. Individuals differed in their classification of the same odorant and in their strategy of assigning liked versus disliked. The odorants that were most consistently rated were those that had the most intense hedonic tones (e.g., methyl salicylate [oil of wintergreen] and vanillin for liked stimuli, versus heptyl aldehyde and n-caproic acid for disliked stimuli).

Young (1923) presented odor substances to four observers three times per week for 5 weeks, with instructions to report hedonic tone (from +3 to −3). As noted earlier, the subjects agreed about the extremes (most pleasant and most unpleasant), but were most variable in ratings in the middle range, toward neutrality.

Part of the reason for individual differences may be that odors may smell qualitatively different to some individuals. Amoore (1969) has reported that individuals exhibit specific anosmias to some chemicals. These anosmias are revealed quantitatively as an elevated threshold. Such anosmias can also show up as a quality shift. Little systematic work appears to have been reported on the shift in hedonic tone with specific anosmia. Another factor influencing quality perception and hedonics is culture. Harper (Personal communication, 1974) has noted that in the United States individuals describe methyl salicylate as a sweet scented odor (it smells like the oil of wintergreen). In Britain individuals characterize it as umistakably carbolic, and individuals in Wales and Scotland note even other differences. Such idiosyncrasies in quality description may play an important role in altering odor preferences.

III. PERFUMERY

Perfumery is an ancient art, stretching back thousands of years into prehistory. Each civilization adorned itself with different types of smells, chosen by the dictates of fashion and by the ability of chemists or practitioners to isolate the different odiferous materials from animals and plants in the environment. Today, with the advent of synthetic organic chemistry, perfumery has grown more scientific. Perfumers are often trained chemists who opt to specialize in perfumery. Their knowledge of chemistry and of the nature of thousands of potentially useful compounds, in concert with their creative talents, allow these perfumers to produce for the consumer many new types of fragrances each year.

A. Perfume Development

Perfumes are not developed randomly. In the development cycle of a fragrance, a number of steps must occur, beginning with the evaluation of different chemicals in the technical section of the fragrance house and the development of a concept of the perfume in the marketing or creative section of the same fragrance house. With ensuing refinements, the perfumers mix chemicals together until they find the appropriate mixture that accords with creative and marketing aims.

1. THE FRAGRANCE LIBRARY

In the standard perfume and fragrance houses there are usually many thousands of chemicals available to the perfumer. These chemicals are usually maintained in a specific room (called the odor library) in small vials at high concentration. The odor library comprises chemicals that have been screened, and the chemicals are available to the perfumer at all times. Arranged in the library may be three- or four-dozen chemicals that smell similar to each other, but yet have slight nuances that distinguish them from each other. Every effort is made to ensure that the components in the library are as chemically pure as possible (when the aim is to have available simple chemicals). This requirement necessitates changing the contents of the bottle periodically, since many pure chemicals are not stable on the shelf for long periods of time. The fragrance chemicals can alter in character, darken, or change chemically in reaction with the air entrapped in the bottle, thus ceasing to be good references.

Modules or "subs" are also available to the perfumer in this library. Modules are combinations of chemicals in specific proportions that produce known fragrances. They are building blocks for more complex fragrances. For example, a perfume house may possess 20–30 (or more) different modules for woody or for rose fragrances. Each module smells slightly different from the other and is potentially useful for a specific type of perfume. The importance of modules is that they save the perfumer a substantial amount of time when preparing a new fragrance. Instead of blending together a dozen or more chemicals to achieve one section of a much more complex fragrance (e.g., a woody "note" or smell, which would be only one constituent), the perfumer may pull a woody module from the shelf and use the module in its entirety. Modules developed by perfumers are used in their creations, as well as donated to the odor library. Sometimes one fragrance house will sell a module to another fragrance house. If a specific module has just the right characteristics for a specific end use in the perfume, it is substantially simpler to purchase the module rather than reproduce it laboriously by the combination of pure chemicals.

Many essential oils, extracts, and concentrates of natural aromas are also included in the odor library. There are hundreds of different essential oils that a perfumer can use. These essential oils vary in quality and composition from one batch to another as a result of location of the source, as some locations produce fruits and flowers with different profiles of chemical concentrations than other locations do. The essential oils are always less stable than pure chemicals because they contain many chemicals that react with each other to produce new chemical by-products, each with its own unique smell. Nonetheless, the essential oils and other natural ingredients form a basic segment of the fragrances available to the perfumer. Prior to the development and expansion of organic chemistry, these natural ingredients provided the sole contents of the perfumer's odor library.

Table II presents a compilation of the classes of materials that are often used by perfumers to produce rose, jasmine, and floral–woody perfumes. Many of the chemicals are synthetics: In fact, were the perfumer to use only natural materials he would lose approximately 95% of the chemicals available to him, and his range of perfumes would be commensurately smaller (Shiftan, 1967).

2. FRAGRANCE EVALUATION

During a typical fragrance evaluation the perfumers gather together to determine which of any new chemicals that have been recently developed or synthesized in the chemical laboratories have potential use. The method for evaluation at these meetings is fairly rigorous. The *odor board* (as it is called in some companies) meets during specified periods of the year and comprises the senior and junior perfumers. The evaluation group is usually led by the master perfumer. Chemicals are brought in, and the perfumers dip a perfumer's blotter into the chemical, lift it out, and evaluate it. The perfumer's blotter is a long, narrow piece of paper that is thick and porous. It is manufactured commercially, and may be 2–3 in. long in some cases. For spray chemicals the perfumer's blotter is a wider rectangle.

After dipping the blotter into the chemical and removing it (and shaking off any excess chemical back into the bottle), the perfumer smells the initial

TABLE II
Composition of Some Commercial Fragrance Formulations

Ingredients	Parts by weight		
	Perfume	Cream	Soap
Formulas for rose bases			
Rhodinol	50	15	
Geraniol coeur (perfume grade)	5	15	15
Citronellol coeur	10	30	15
Phenylethyl alcohol coeur	10	15	20
Phenylethyl alcohol white extra			
Nerol coeur	5	5	
Geranyl acetate	2	2	5
Aldehyde C-8, 10%	4	4	5
Aldehyde C-9, 10%	4	4	5
Benzophenone	3.5	1.5	6
Rose oxide, 1%	1	1	
Rosalva	0.5	0.5	1
Geranium bourbon, natural or artificial		5	15
Essence of styrax	3	2	3
Guaiacwood oil	2		10
Total	100	100	100
Formulas for jasmin base			
Benzyl acetate	20	20	30
Benzyl alcohol	10	14	10
Linalyl acetate	15	15	15
Linalool	5	8	10
Jasmone or isojasmone	1	1	1
Peach aldehyde C-14 (undecalactone), 25%	1	1	1
Hexylcinnamic aldehyde	8	10	10
Indole, 10%	8		1.5
Methyl anthranilate	1		
Ylang-ylang oil extra	10	10	
Ylang-ylang oil artificial for soaps			10
Phenylethyl alcohol coeur	20	20	
Phenylethyl alcohol white extra			10
Jasmine absolute	1		
Methyl β-naphthyl ketone		1	1.5
Total	100	100	100
Composition of a floral, woody, oriental perfume concentrate			
Base O.T.	40		
Base O.T. for creams		40	
Base O.T. for soaps			40
Aldehyde C-10 (decyl aldehyde), 1%	5	5	5
Aldehyde C-11 (undecylenic aldehyde), 1%	3	3	3
Methylnonylacetaldehyde, 10%	1	1	1

TABLE II (Continued)

Ingredients	Parts by weight		
	Perfume	Cream	Soap
Oil of tangerine	2		
Oil of bergamot natural	6		
Oil of bergamot artificial or soap			6
Linalyl acetate		5	
Linalool	2	3	2
Oil of neroli bigarade petals	1		
Oil of neroli artificial for creams and soaps		1	1
Dimethyl anthranilate, 10%		2	2
Oil of ylang-ylang extra	5		
Oil of ylang-ylang 2nd quality		5	
Oil of ylang-ylang for soaps			5
Methylionone coeur	10		
Methylionone -A		10	10
Synthetic rose	12	12	12
Synthetic jasmin	5	7	7
Oil of patchouli	1	1	1
Tincture of natural musk (4 oz/gal)	10		
Tincture of civet (4 oz/gal)	5		
Galaxolide (IFF), 50%		5	5
Jasmin absolute	1		
Rose absolute	1		
Total	100	100	100

Source: [Shiftan (1967).]

fragrance and evaluates the *top note*. This is the initial-impact fragrance. If the chemical is pure, then the top note should be the only smell that can be perceived, unless the chemical changes in fragrance character upon dilution, as some chemicals do (e.g., benzaldehyde, which smells like almond, also smells harsh at high concentrations, as does alpha ionone, which smells like violets at low levels). If the chemical is not pure, or if the evaluation is made of an essential oil, then the perfumer looks for the *middle* and *dry down* notes, which are the odors that occur after the initial top note and the strong impression have faded. Quite often the balance of chemicals remaining on the blotter after 1 hr is quite different than after 30 sec, and a blotter may change in smell continuously over an hour or even over a day. The perfumer notes the types of changes that occur, the intensities of the different smells, and the potential usefulness of the chemicals, and submits these to the evaluation group for discussion.

Because several dozen different chemicals may be evaluated at a single sitting, a requirement for the perfumer is that he have a good memory at these odor boards and be able to discern subtle differences between the chemicals presented. In addition, at these boards the perfumers must evaluate the importance of each chemical for perfumery, and thus the perfumer must be able to imagine the chemical acting in concert (in a mixture) with other chemicals that are normally used.

3. THE DEVELOPMENT OF A PERFUMER

Perfumery has not always been a chemical art. The ancient Egyptians were among the first to use perfumes. The Bible recounts the anointing of individuals with different spices in order to enhance their religious spirit, to purify them, and to make them attractive (especially women). At that time the perfumer's only task was to imitate nature or to improve upon it. Perfumery was an art, and the perfumer needed to know the range of available materials. The modern perfumer, in contrast, not only creates fragrances that must have a more interesting character than before, but must also maintain the exciting richness of the classical perfumes and be concerned with color and stability, as well as with the compatibility of the perfume chemicals with the solvents and bases in which they are embedded. The safety of the perfume components is also important. Hence, the perfumer has increasingly been drawn from the ranks of professionally trained chemists, who are familiar with changing chemical characteristics, chemical purity, and the effects of mixing chemicals together. This trend has followed the increasing use of pure chemicals in perfumery. In the nineteenth century chemical research first began in France, then in Switzerland, Germany, and England. The early chemists had just a few chemicals to choose from, and did not need an advanced knowledge of chemistry to work with such simple chemicals as amyl salicylate and methyl nonyl acetaldehyde (which were used in the creation of the famous perfumes *Trefle Incarnat* and *Rêve d'Or*). Today, the perfumer must be familiar with more than 5000 different chemicals, and new ones are being discovered or synthesized every day (Shiftan, 1973).

For practical purposes in using his art, the perfume creator must be able to discern among 500–2000 different raw materials. The perfumer should be able to recognize all or most of them in a mixture. To this end, the perfumer is aided by the chemical procedure of gas–liquid chromatography (GLC). The GLC can separate the mélange of chemicals into several purer sets, and with its aid the perfumer can separate a perfume into a set of components (although knowledge of those components and their concentrations in the perfume may not be sufficient to reconstruct the perfume).

Studies on the information-transmittal capacity of the perfumer suggest that as far as basic classification ability is concerned, the perfumer does not score substantially better than the normal individual (Jones, 1968). However, because of his familiarity with the different perfume chemicals, a perfumer can distinguish various odor notes in chemicals that would typically elude the scrutiny of the novice. The "nose" of the perfumer is trained, not for greater sensitivity, but rather for a better utilization of sensory cues that the chemical provides.

In addition to a knowledge of the available materials for blending, a good perfumer must possess an instinct for odor harmony and the intelligence to achieve that harmony. The perfume must be tried on the skin and blend with skin odor, which requires that in evaluating different materials for blending the perfumer be able to judge which chemicals will be most compatible with skin odor. The ultimate success of the perfumer depends critically on how well he can introduce into his creation a quality of "true beauty [Shiftan, 1967]" infused by a suggestive theme. The goal of the perfumer is to create a fragrance that arouses emotion in the individual who will wear it or be attracted by it.

4. CREATION OF A PERFUME

Usually the perfumer is inspired by a natural product that he has smelled, or perhaps by a synthetic product presented to him. The perfumer may be guided by an inspiration to create an artificial essence that will become a beautiful perfume or by the necessity of developing a fragrance to be used in a mass-produced toiletry. The creative aspect is no different for the two tasks. The perfumer first makes a prototype mixture of four to five components. Left alone, and operating randomly, the perfumer could make millions of such mixtures, of which only one or a few would fulfill the requirements for the new fragrance. Here the perfumer's instincts and knowledge help him. Once he finds a mixture that brings out the smell to the best advantage, the perfumer uses his knowledge of mixtures to build up this new base so that it will possess desired characteristics. The perfume may be designed to evoke a refreshing or brilliant top note (initial impression when the perfume is just applied), followed by a characteristic middle note that trails into a specific end (base) note (which stays for a long period of time after the top and middle notes have evaporated). Table III provides a set of chemicals corresponding to the top, middle, and end notes.

In his search for the optimum fragrance the perfumer must build upon materials already available. For example, a perfumer might have chemicals that produce a conventional end note and then conceive of a perfume that possesses a radically new top note. The art of perfumery is to compound these two smells together, so that one blends gently and continuously into the other as the perfume remains and evaporates on the skin.

The elements of creating a perfume are both flashes of creation and solid marketing-research work. Quite often the perfumer works together with a market-research group. The group determines the type of perfume the population of consumers desires or, in the case of a personal toiletry product, determines whether a current product needs a new scent (e.g., soap or deodorant). The market-research group may do a number of concept tests in

TABLE III
PERFUMER'S NOTES AND COMPONENTS

Top notes	Representatives
Aldehyde	Aliphatic aldehyde; C-8, C-9, C-10, C-11, C-12, + ylang-ylang, bergamot, lime.
Citrus	Mixtures of citrus oils (e.g., bergamot, lemon, lime, sweet orange, mandarin, grapefruit).
Fruity	Mixtures of fruity-smelling esters and lactones (e.g., undecalactone, nonalactone). This mixture is half mixed with refreshing notes (e.g., bergamot, linalyl acetate).
Green	Aromatics having an odor of leaves or green bark (phenyl acetaldehyde, hydrotropic aldehyde, extract of violet leaves, galbanum oil).
Light floral	Muguet (lily of the valley), cyclamen, ylang-ylang, cyclamen aldehyde.
Heavy floral	Orange flower, tuberose, hyacinth, lilac, heavy rose (e.g., jasome, isojasmone, methyl anthranilate, p cresyl acetate).
Linalool–lavender	Linalool-linalyl acetate, lavender oil, lavandin, bergamot oil.

Middle notes (modifiers)	Representatives
Floral bases	Carnation, jasmine, lily of the valley, lilac, neroli, orange flower, violet.
Floral base and aromatics	Including cinnamic alcohol, phenylethanol, methyl ionones, rhodinol, ylang-ylang, attar-of-rose.

End notes (basic notes)	Representatives
Mixture of resins	
Heavy essential oils	Ambrette seed, patchouli, vetiver, Sandalwood.
Chemicals with heavy smell	Ionones, musk (ambrette, ketone, xylene), Celestolide, Galaxolide, Exaltolide.
Long lasting chemicals	Isoeugenol, eugenol, coumarin, heliotropin, vanillin.
Animal tinctures	Artificial musks, civet.

SOURCE: [Shiftan (1967).]

order to determine the type of perfume that people feel is appropriate. The population's responses are usually obtained in nontechnical language, which the perfumer takes and translates into a combination of chemicals that will provide the odor impression desired by the consumer.

If the product being developed is a fine perfume, the perfumer quite often follows a different approach. A fine perfume is an entity in itself, not connected with a particular functional product, such as a toiletry. The appeal of the perfume must derive from its odor, its packaging, its advertising, and its pricing, and not from its function as a toiletry. The initial stage may be the development of a concept around which the perfume will be built (e.g., developing a perfume that is sensuous and reminds one of Paris). This idea must be followed by a number of tests of potential names, for in perfumery, the name conveys a strong impression of the perfume. Names must be tested for appropriateness (usually by market researchers, but sometimes the name may be suggested by the perfumer himself). The next step in development is the combination of the appropriate set of odor notes so that (*a*) the fragrance is aesthetically beautiful; (*b*) the fragrance follows a time course of sensations that allows the perfume to slowly change character as it is worn without dramatically altering its character at any particular moment; and (*c*) the fragrance excites the particular emotion that the perfumer seeks to convey (e.g., sensuousness, in a perfume to be worn in the evening). Finally, the search is undertaken for an appropriate container (including color, shape, and designs on the glass). The form of the container also conveys a message about the type of perfume that is contained inside. If the container is inappropriate for the underlying concept, the product may not be successful.

5. THE CHEMICALS AND NOTES OF PERFUMES

Because the perfumer must create a fragrance that does not dramatically change over time, he searches for two things. One of these is an eutectic mixture, which is a mixture in which the components (or at least most of the components) evaporate at the same rate when the perfume is applied on the skin. This eutectic mixture should be long-lasting and behave (physically) as if it were a single component when evaporating. Fixatives are often used to slow the rate of evaporation. Some chemical fixatives include diethyl phthalate and benzyl benzoate. These are artificial materials, but natural fixatives have been used over the past several thousand years. Such fixatives are civet, musk, ambergris, and castoreum, all of which possess their own odors. These natural fixatives often penetrate the perfume compound, and although they may or may not modify the original character, the fixatives bring the fragrance to life, enhance its diffusion, and improve its long-lasting qualities.

Stability of perfumes is another consideration. Organic chemistry has indicated that a mixture of chemicals will show new compounds not originally present. Gas–liquid chromatography is especially useful in determining the presence of such new *reaction products,* which develop as the perfume stands and ages. Some perfumes will improve as they age, whereas others turn bad. There comes a time when all perfumes tend to go bad. Quite often, however, 6 months must pass after a perfume is placed on the shelf before the perfume becomes optimally acceptable. This aging then may continue up to a year or two as the reaction products in the perfume build up. After 3 years or so, all reactions are complete, and the product fragrance begins to deteriorate.

6. SUBJECTIVE ASPECTS OF PERFUMES

No matter what type of perfume he creates, the perfumer strives for several things. One is long lastingness: The perfume should not "come on" suddenly and then evaporate quickly. Rather, the perfume must sustain itself for several hours. Another is the proper top notes that give the fragrance the appropriate character. If the perfume is designed for young individuals, then the perfumer will try to give it a citrus note, or perhaps bergamot. More sophisticated perfumes often use such esoteric substances as Ylang-ylang, Clary Sage, fatty aldehydes (octaldehyde, nonaldehyde, decaldehyde, unde-caldehyde, the C_8–C_{11} aldehydes). These aromatic and floral smelling compounds are put into the perfume mixture in small concentrations and blended in until the proper balance is obtained (Chaleyer, 1948).

A study of naïve panelists' perceptions of perfume suggests that they may be unaware of the relative cheapness of perfume. Jewett (1945) evaluated preferences for pairs of perfumes, in which one member of the pair was expensive and the other was qualitatively similar, but cheaper. The major finding of that study was that a perfume that could last 8 hr was found to be satisfactory by all of the panelists. Hence, to some degree, naïve individuals are satisfied by some criteria, but not by all criteria, that the perfumer uses.

Unfortunately, there is only a tiny literature pertaining to the perception of perfumes by the consumer herself or himself. Rarely does experimentation pertain, in olfaction, to the perception of actual perfumes themselves. Thus, the principal information pertaining to the psychology of perfumery (and especially the perception of perfumes) derives from the writings of experts in the area, and not from experimentation.

IV. EVALUATION AND CONTROL OF MALODORS

A. Scope of the Problem

Odor pollution is a form of annoyance in which noxious odorants escape from a source (e.g., a paper mill, rendering plant, a pig farm) and linger in the atmosphere. Although pollution is widespread, it is not presently possible to place a monetary figure on its degree, except in extreme cases, or to assess the impact of the odor pollution upon the values of property and the discomfort to life (Flesh, 1974). The most direct procedure, typically used by air pollution control groups, is the survey. Table IV shows a typical survey of air pollution sources (Flesh, Burns, & Turk, 1974).

Sociologically, noxious odors do more than simply annoy. According to Sullivan (1969) noxious odors ruin personal and community pride, interfere with human relations, lower the community's economic status, damage its reputation, and stifle its growth. Both industry and labor tend to resettle in a desirable area, without odor pollution. Thus property values will decline and the tax base will shrink in polluted areas. Odor pollution can affect an individual in more measureable ways. For example, an individual exposed to odors in an unventilated room for 4–7 hr daily will consume approximately

TABLE IV

ODOR COMPLAINTS AGAINST SOURCES SUSPECTED BY AGENCIES OF CAUSING ODOR PROBLEMS
IN TEST AREAS (JANUARY–SEPTEMBER 1972)[a]

Public attitude survey set number	Source(s) of odor	Number of odor complaints against source(s)	
		From all persons	From residents of test area
	City of Houston Department of Public Health		
1	Sanitary landfill manufacturer	2	2
2	Asphalt & pesticide manufacturer	3	2
3	Refineries & rubber manufacturer	88	35
4(a)[b]	Pesticides & general chemical manufacturer	NA	NA
5	Refineries & rubber manufacturer	88	35
6(c)	Rubber manufacturer	88	32
7(b)	Pesticides & general chemical manufacturer	NA	NA
8(d)	Rubber manufacturer	88	32
	Hillsborough County Environmental Protection Commission		
1	Sewage treatment plant	3	1
2	Fertilizer manufacturer	9	5
3	Barbecue restaurant	1	1
4	Citrus processing plants	NA	NA
5	Natural organic decomposition (Hillsborough Bay)	1	0
6	Asphalt manufacturer	NA	NA
7	Natural organic decomposition (Hillsborough Bay)	1	0
8	Natural organic decomposition (Hillsborough Bay)	1	0
	Columbia-Willamette Air Pollution Authority		
1	Pulp mill	5	0
2(a)	Pulp mill	5	1
3	Animal rendering plant	4	0
4	Wood preserving plant	0	0
5(b)	Pulp mill	5	1
6	Pulp mill	5	1
	State of Maryland Bureau of Air Quality Control[c]		
1(a)	Distillery	2	0
2	Sewage treatment plant	3	1
3	Asphalt manufacturer	2	2
4	Coffee manufacturer	9	0
5	Sewage treatment plant	0	0
6(b)	Distillery	2	0

SOURCE: [Flesh et al. (1974).]

[a] Approximately the period during which the field activities were performed.

[b] Letters shown in parentheses after the survey set numbers refer to the initial and replicate sets of public attitude surveys conducted in the same test and control areas. For each of three agencies, set (b) is replicate of set (a) and for one agency, set (d) is a replicate of set (c).

[c] The number of odor complaints shown for the State of Maryland include some complaints received by the Baltimore County and Prince George County Health Departments.

5% less food, implying that a stale, odorous environment will reduce food consumption. (Winslow & Palmer, 1915, cited by Sullivan, 1969). Other effects include insomnia and mental perturbation. Individuals report that they have trouble sleeping, and can be aroused by a particularly strong whiff of a noxious odor. The odors can cause headaches, nausea, and other discomfort. Eventually, upon repeated exposures, even pleasing odors can be responsible for these effects.

Reactions to noxious odors do not come equally spaced in time; there are patterns. Huey (1960) studies the frequency of complaints, in terms of which day of the week, what time of day, the ambient temperature and pressure, and humidity and wind velocity, from individuals living near a rendering plant. The number of complaints increased on weekends, increased during the day, increased with rising temperatures, increased when the air pressure exceeded 28.84 millibars, increased with decreasing humidity, and was highest in summer months.

B. Measurement: Ambient Situations

In the traditional measurement of air pollution, experimenters have been forced to evaluate pollution that may be episodic, that may be punctate (so that one region is polluted for a short period of time, whereas other regions are free from the odorant), or that may be correlated with a stimulus whose source cannot be easily identified and whose concentrations may not be adequately measured.

Studies on odorants emitted by stacks are particularly subject to the inherent variations forced on the emissions by the prevailing atmospheric conditions. The noxious odorant is usually emitted in a plume, from the top of the stack. This plume is carried by the prevailing winds and is diluted during its journey. The effective concentration of the noxious odorant varies at every point along the stream, and occasionally an area close to the stack will be exposed to a lower concentration of the odorant than will an area farther away. As a result of the physics of the situation, and of the temporal interruptions in the emission of the odorants (which are caused by shifts in the production schedule of the factory), experimenters have resorted to other measurements that are more instrumentally oriented and hopefully more reliable.

C. Instrumental Measures of Concentration
of Pollutants

A variety of instrumental methods have been devised for assessing odor pollution. Most of these methods attempt to capture the ambient odorant in a container (or sample the odorant currently in the environment). Others attempt to present to the panelist a set of prearranged odors that will match, as closely as possible, odorants in the environment.

1. Devices That Capture the Ambient Odorant Dynamically and Present the Odorant to the Panelist at the Test Site

The principal device in this category is the Barneby–Cheney *Scentometer*, which is a Plexiglas box from which a nosepiece protrudes. The panelist inhales through the nosepiece. This inhalation provides an input stream of air directly from the odor source to the nose. Concurrently, the panelist has available to him three holes, which also admit the odorant. These holes are of various sizes. The air that is pulled in by the inhalation from these holes is passed over activated charcoal and then sent to the nosepiece. This second stream joins the odorous stream as clean, purified, and odorless air. By covering one, two, or all three holes the panelist can produce one of three different dilutions of the ambient odor. The device is used in Colorado as the standard testing device (Prokop, 1974), and odor nuisance regulations are built around admissible Barneby–Cheney *Scentometer* readings. However, the device is not sensitive at lower concentrations (Leonardos, 1974).

The dynamic-dilution olfactometer proposed by Lindvall at the Karolinska Institute in Stockholm is another device. The olfactometer is housed in a bus, which can be driven to the odor site. Panelists sit in a special hood in the bus and smell the odor of the external environment. During the session they are presented with various dilutions of other noxious odorants from source tanks in the bus and asked to find a match. The concentration of the noxious odorants can be experimentally controlled by the experimenter or by the observer. The result of this procedure is an equal-unpleasantness match. In a study of the method, Lindvall and Svensson (1971) used five different odorants. The odorants were produced by the combustion of animal manure through three different electrical combustion units, one gas-fed furnace, and one oil-fed furnace. The observers varied the concentration of hydrogen sulfide to equal the unpleasantness of the different samples, at varying concentrations of the malodor. The results yielded power functions relating the concentration of the test malodors to the concentration of hydrogen sulfide. Substantively, the experiment showed that the rate of increase of unpleasantness of the test manure odor did not change with changes in combustion type. Experimentally, the studies showed the feasibility of using the dynamic-dilution system in situations where ambient odorants are present.

2. Devices That Capture the Malodor, Store It, and Then Are Used as Presentation Devices to the Panelist

The most important of these devices, at least historically, is the American Society of Testing Materials (ASTM) Syringe Dilution Technique. A set of standard test methods has been developed, based upon this method (ASTM, 1967). Briefly, the malodor to be rated is captured inside a wide-barreled glass syringe. The contents of the syringe are diluted with additional air, at various volumes, so that the experimenter can produce varying odor dilutions in 100-cc syringes. Panelists smell (rather momentarily) a rapidly expelled pulse of odorous air from the syringe when the tip is directed toward the nostrils and report the presence or absence of odor. The method lacks a defined procedure for presentation, since odor dilutions are randomly presented to the panel by mixing the odors of strong and weak dilutions. The rate of expulsion, the precise amount of expelled air, and the location of the tip of the syringe relative to the nostril all vary, producing variations in the actual concentration presented to the nose.

A later device constructed on the basis of much sounder physical and psychophysical principles is the dynamic-dilution, forced-choice olfactometer. Developed by the Illinois Institute of Technology Research Institute (IITRI), under the direction of Dr. A. Dravnieks, the device has the following specifications: (a) the odor is trapped, at the site, in large bags; (b) at the test laboratory the odor is delivered to the main entry port of an olfactometer; (c) the odor is split into several streams; (d) each stream is diluted, to different amounts with clean, odorless air; (e) each odorized stream, at its own concentration of odorant, is sent to a smelling or sniffing port; (f) each sniffing port comprises three outlet streams, two of which present pure, odorless air and the third presents the odorized stream (all at the same flow rate). The observer's job is to judge, for each sniff station, which stream contains the odorized air. The concentration at which the observers just detect the odor is defined as the threshold, and can be used as a measure of the odor level in the environment (Dravnieks & Prokop, Personal communication, 1973).

Finally, other refinements exist. The odorant can be captured in heavy, tedlar (nonabsorbing) bags, each holding 10 or more liters. The odorant can be forced into a high-volume flow system, at which threshold is tested (Schuetzie, Prater, & Ruddell, 1975). By appropriate flow control of pure air versus odorized air, the experimenter can determine threshold. Both this high-volume procedure and the IITRI lower-volume procedure are dynamic, and during the test the source odorant should not vary in composition or concentration, or be affected by a background odor.

3. TRAPPING AND STORING TECHNIQUES

Occasionally, experimenters may wish to store an odorant for a longer period of time than a day or two. In such cases a bag would not be adequate, since all bags tend to leak. Sullivan and Leonardos (1974) have reported the successful use of a method in which 500 liters of odorous air are passed from a source to absorbent traps (technically, Chromosorb 102). The trap is later heated electrically and then, in the laboratory, odorless pentane (a moderate-weight hydrocarbon) is used to elute the absorbed odorant from the Chromosorb 102 trap to a sniffing port. The malodor is diluted, and a panel of four trained panelists is used to determine the character and intensity of the trapped components. The dilutions used range from 1 part in 165 to 1 part in 1,280,000. The odorant is injected into an olfactorium (a room specifically designed for such tests) and panelists evaluate the odor for approximately 15 min, using a specific descriptive technique developed by the Arthur D. Little Co., Inc., in Cambridge, Massachusetts. The average odor intensities and the probability of detection are computed, and dose–response relations obtained.

4. USE OF MATCHING STANDARDS

Turk (1967) developed a series of reference standards for the quality and intensity evaluation of diesel-exhaust odor. The Turk kit, adopted by the Environmental Protection Agency, comprises 29 squeeze bottles, each partially filled with a different intensity of a specific odor. The kit comprises an overall diesel odor (D) in 12 sets of increasing concentration, with each subsequent concentration twice as strong (in concentration) as the previous one. Diesel odor is a mixture of four qualities: burnt–smoky, oily, aromatic, and pungent, each of which is also presented in a separate concentration series of four levels. The diesel bus to be evaluated operates on a chassis dynamometer in order to simulate road conditions, and the bus is run to mimic steady-state vehicular cruising and idling, as well as transients (such as acceleration and deceleration). The observers try to find the matching samples in the kit. Table V shows a comparison of the odor ratings for two different types of diesel fuels, evaluted on the four attributes, with the engine operating at different rates (Springer & Shahman, 1974).

In a validation study for the Turk descriptive method, Springer and Shahman (1974) polled 3000 individuals in five cities to determine the noxiousness of three odorants (D2, D4, and D6 concentrations in the Turk kit). Figure 1 illustrates the relation between the percentage of individuals finding an odor in the D system noxious and the D rating.

D. Polling the Population: Studies with Naïve Observers

In the typical laboratory-controlled survey the experimenter can present to the observer stimuli of known concentration (or at least of known dilution). This includes the studies mentioned above, in which the experimenters presented observers with external odorants in a laboratory setting, and obtained ratings from them. In the more realistic situation, faced by governmental agencies concerned with odor control, the situation is much different. For one thing, the method is a passive collection of data, rather than an active one. The population may respond in a variety of ways to indicate the presence of malodor, as shown in Table VI.

These reactions of affected individuals can include interference with

TABLE V
COMPARISON OF ODOR RATINGS USING THE TURK SCALE FOR LOCALLY AVAILABLE DF-1 AND CHICAGO AREA DF-2 FUELS

Running condition	Fuel	Composite	Burnt	Oily	Aromatic	Pungent
24 mph	EM-165-F (DF-1)	2.7	1.0	.8	.8	.4
900 rpm	EM-166-F (DF-2)	4.4	1.4	1.1	1.0	.8
half load [a]	Net change	+1.7	+.4	+.3	+.2	+.4
	U_s statistic	0	0	0	+[b]	.5
32 mph	EM-165-F (DF-1)	2.3	.9	.7	.6	.1
1200 rpm	EM-166-F (DF-2)	4.4	1.3	1.1	1.0	.9
half load	Net change	+2.1	+.4	+.4	+.4	+.8
	U_s statistic	0	.5	0	.5	0
40 mph	EM-165-F (DF-1)	3.1	1.0	1.0	.8	.5
1500 rpm	EM-166-F (DF-2)	3.9	1.2	1.0	1.0	.8
half load	Net change	+.8	+.2	0	+.2	+.3
	U_s statistic	1	+	+	.5	+
Idle	EM-165-F (DF-1)	3.2	1.0	.9	.7	.5
	EM-166-F (DF-2)	4.4	1.3	1.1	.9	1.0
	Net change	+1.2	+.3	+.2	+.2	+.5
	U^s statistic	0	0	2	+	0
Idle–Acceleration	EM-165-F (DF-1)	3.9	1.2	1.0	1.0	.8
	EM-166-F (DF-2)	4.3	1.3	1.0	1.0	.9
	Net change	+.4	+.1	0	0	+.1
	U_s statistic	+	+	+	+	+
Deceleration	EM-165-F (DF-1)	2.9	1.0	.9	.7	.4
	EM-166-F (DF-2)	2.7	1.0	.8	.5	.3
	Net change	−.2	0	−.1	−.2	−.1
	U_s statistic	+	+	+	+	+

SOURCE: [Adapted from Springer & Shahman (1974).]
[a] Engine operated at a fuel rate midway between maximum and no-load fuel rate.
[b] U_s greater than 2; no statistical difference apparent.

everyday activities, physiological symptoms, feelings of annoyance, and actual complaints to authority. The nature of the environmental stimulus is also more complex than the controlled stimulus presented in the laboratory. Several short episodes of malodor, in one or two days, can easily be transformed (by a respondent telephoning in) into an entire previous week characterized by the presence of a noxious odor (Dravnieks, 1971).

For the effective assessment of community air-pollution problems the experimenters (or the odor-control experts) must familiarize themselves with the topography of an area, especially when the odor disturbance is intermittent. Sullivan and Leonardos (1974) suggested that control agencies obtain topographic as well as local maps of an area in order to familiarize themselves properly. During an actual survey, the odor analyst drives

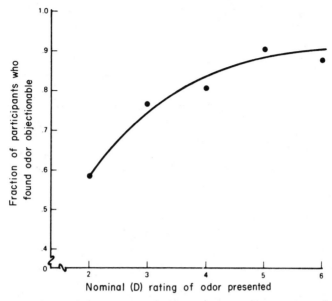

FIG. 1. Diesel value of an odor (from the Turk system) versus the percentage of responses to the odor. [From Springer & Shahman (1974), reprinted with permission.]

TABLE VI

CONSEQUENCES OF ODOR POLLUTION

Interference with the everyday activities
    Forms   Interference with relaxation, rest, sleep
                Interference with entertainment of friends or relatives

Physical symptoms or physiological changes

Feelings of annoyance
    Forms   Willingness to visit an official
                Assist in forming a community action group
                Write or phone an official
                Attend a meeting (to discuss odor problem)
                Sign a petition

Actual complaints to an authority

Other individual actions
    Forms   Install air conditioning
                Use masking odors (fragrances)
                Move out of area
                Shut windows
                Increase drug consumption

SOURCE: [Dravnieks (1971).]

around a route, usually fairly slowly, and takes account of the prevailing wind direction. With the car window open, the expert remains alert for odor, and when an odor is perceived, the expert stops the car, walks around to determine the type, intensity, and width of the odor path. Figure 2 shows a typical odor map obtained by evaluating a region near a coffee-processing plant.

Among the problems that research organizations usually face in this ecologically valid method of assessing odor is the variations among the expected odor intensity in a region. Sometimes odor measurements made in a stack (or chimney) cannot be easily correlated with the odor farther downstream, even when the experimenter has a fairly good idea of the volume dilution that the concentrated emission will encounter as it is carried downstream.

Among the other problems that occur in the environmental assessment of odors are the motivating factors behind annoyance complaints and the influence that expectation plays on community response to odor pollution. According to a symposium of experts (Lindvall, 1970), complaints, voluntarily given, do not appear to be an adequate way to measure annoyance reactions. Rather, the committee felt that a community survey would be better. In a survey, respondents are polled, rather than permitted to call when they sense a malodor. The surveyor must always keep in mind that when an individual responds that an odor is present, the individual may be

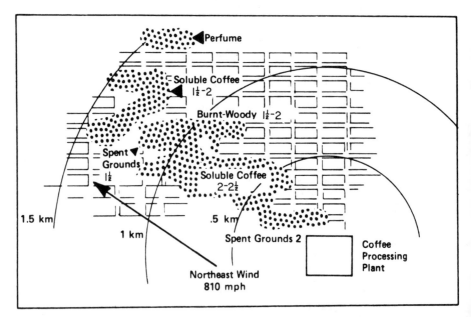

FIG. 2. Odor map of a coffee plant, showing location and sensory intensity (as well as quality) of malodors. [From Sullivan & Leonardos (1974), reprinted with permission.]

reflecting social concerns, rather than personal annoyance. As for the role of expectations, Dravnieks (Personal communication, 1975) has suggested that odors are often assigned to the category of annoyers on the basis of preconceived notions. For example, when individuals are polled who live near a dump, they may not find a specific odor unpleasant, because they associate that odor with the dump and have grown used to it. If, on the contrary, the same odor is presented in a different area, individuals may complain about precisely the same smell.

E. Regulations Concerning Odor

Despite the difficulties encountered in odor evaluation for control purposes, a number of states, counties, and cities in the United States have passed regulations that define a community annoyance. For example, the state of Alabama requires that "No person shall cause air pollution . . . presence in the outdoor atmosphere of one or more contaminants (including odors) in such quantities and duration as are . . . injurious to humans . . . or would interfere with the enjoyment of life or property." The state of Iowa more succinctly defines an objectionable odor as one that is judged to be objectionable by 30% or more of a panel of 30 people, or 75% of the panel, if the panel comprises fewer than 30 individuals. The state of Wisconsin leaves the definition of an objectionable odor to the discretion of the inspecting office (Prokop, 1974).

More quantitative methods for defining an annoying odor exist. The most restrictive definition is that an odor is defined to be obnoxious if it can be smelled at all. However, the presence of an odor is usually not the sole operative factor. Rather, the intensity, the quality, the frequency, and the duration of the odor are important as determinants, and several regulatory agencies are recognizing them as such.

The state of odor regulations in the United States is a patchwork of standards. Occasionally, the regulations specify specific instruments, as for example, the Scentometer (Colorado). Other states specify syringe dilution techniques based on that of the ASTM. In still other instances, odor regulations are couched in terms of units of odor emission or units of odor concentration. These are defined as the number of standard cubic feet of odor-free air needed to dilute each cubic foot of contaminated air so that the odor is reduced below threshold. Sometimes the regulations specify that the stack emission must be no more intense than 120 odor units for every cubic foot of air sampled (Illinois): An odor more intense than this would be defined as noxious.

In summary, therefore, the scope of odor evaluation and abatement in the environment is large and diffuse. The procedures have as much variety as the number of investigators. Active assessment of odors in the environment is hindered by two things. First, it is difficult to assess the concentration of a stimulus that varies over time as a function of manufacturing conditions and ambient weather conditions. Second, the methods used to assess subjective reactions are all somewhat crude. Perhaps the best that can be said at present is that attempts to bring the environment into the laboratory (e.g., as is done by the IITRI forced-choice dynamic olfactometer) represent the best approach. The state of the art in odor regulation represents a branch of applied psychophysics that has at its disposal the experimental designs, instruments, and analytical capabilities developed by decades of research in odor science. Within the next decade it is quite likely that some of the advanced methods used in laboratory experimentation today to assess odor perception (intensity, quality) and hedonic response may appear in the regulations set forth by responsible governmental agencies.

V. ODOR COUNTERACTION

A variety of methods have been proposed for eliminating noxious odors. Two of the most effective methods are destruction of the odors by heat or their adsorbtion into activated charcoal. Another method is to mix two odorants together and hope that one odorant will either chemically destroy the other (i.e., through chemical reaction, if they are both in solution) or will neutralize the smell of the other and itself leave little or no residual odor.

A. Chemical–Physical Elimination

These methods, such as chemical reaction (e.g., with potassium permanganate) or *through heating* (i.e., passing the odorant through an extremely hot chamber, where the odorant is converted to carbon dioxide and water by combustion) represent physical modifications of odor. They are of little interest to psychologists, since they do not reflect procedures that take into account the process of odor perception.

Among the other methods of counteraction are the use of activated charcoal (which adsorbs odorants at its surface, holding them there), the use of ozone as a deodorizer, and antibacterial chemicals for odors that arise from bacterial decomposition (Moncrieff, 1955; Kulka, 1965).

B. Odor Mixtures

If two odorants are mixed together, a number of perceptual changes can occur. These can be classified as follows (Cain & Drexler, 1974):

1. The odor intensity of the mixture exceeds the expected total intensity

of the components, which would be obtained by adding the component intensities together arithmetically (hyperaddition, synergism).
2. The odor intensity of the mixture equals the odor intensities of the components (additivity).
3. The odor intensity of the mixture exceeds both component odor intensities, but does not equal their sum (partial additivity).
4. The odor intensity of the mixture equals the odor intensity of the higher component.
5. The odor intensity of the mixture lies intermediate to the odor intensity of the components (compromise).
6. The odor intensity of the mixture equals the odor intensity of the lower component.
7. The odor intensity of the mixture is lower than either component (compensation).

In addition to the shifts in odor intensity, there can be shifts in the quality and the hedonics of the odor. The smell of the mixture may change, and two or more smells may alternate with each other (rivalry) rather than blend. The mixture may smell more pleasant, equally pleasant, or less pleasant than the components. In some cases the mixture may so change in intensity and quality that a residual smell is left, but is so weak and unidentifiable that it blends into the background.

For purposes of odor counteraction, mixtures of odors have the greatest use. In commercial establishments it is possible to cover up noxious odors by the addition of sweet, perfume-like smells. Bathroom sprays use this principle. The addition of sweet yet potent-smelling citrus and other aromatic chemicals to an aerosol delivery system effectively disperses the odorant into the atmosphere in small particles. The evaporation of these particles provides a masking cloud of odorant that literally covers the malodor. In toiletries, soap is often unpleasant. Soap may be perfumed with any of a large number of chemicals that are chemically stable. These perfumes simply cover up the malodor associated with soap. Moncrieff (1955) reports that sulfur dioxide is used for temporary odor masking in confined space. Incense and other strong yet pleasing odors may be used to overcome the stale and musty odors in retail stores. In a kitchen pervaded by the noxious smell of onions or cabbage, Moncrieff reported that burning twine provides a good odor mask. In laboratories, paradichlorobenzene and naphthalene are used as odor counteractants, especially against odorants emitted by bacteria and fungi.

There have been a number of systematic studies of odor counteraction by mixture that have attempted to define the limits of masking and the perceptual changes that occur as its result. The most important studies have been those of Zwaardemaker, Moncrieff, Berglund et al., and Cain.

C. Zwaardemaker's Studies

In his studies performed almost three-quarters of a century ago using the original olfactometer, Zwaardemaker reported that certain pairs of odors counteracted each other. These antagonistic odors were: (*a*) iodoform–Peru balsam; (*b*) musk–bitter almond; (*c*) ammonia–acetic acid; (*d*) cedarwood–rubber; (*e*) beeswax–Tolu balsam; (*f*) benzoin–rubber; and (*g*) camphor–eau de cologne.

In Zwaardemaker's (1959) experiments the odors were presented dichorhinically. One odor was presented to the right nostril and the other odor to the left nostril, a regimen that would prevent any chemical combination. One of the important findings from this set of studies was that the number of *olfacties* (Zwaardemaker's measure of intensity, using his olfactometer) need not be the same for two components that neutralized each other. In spite of the odor counteraction, the odors rarely disappeared. Rather, there usually remained an undefinable olfactory sensation, in which the individual smells could not be recognized.

In evaluating Zwaardemaker's results, it is not clear what he actually meant by odor counteraction. Is it the total disappearance of both odors, so that the resultant sensation is equivalent to that provoked by blank, odorless air? Or is odor counteraction the removal of noticeable aroma, with a residual still present, but of undefinable quality?

D. Moncrieff's Studies

A half century later the odor scientist R. W. Moncrieff reported an interesting series of experiments on odor counteraction, dealing in part with commercial air fresheners and in part with pure chemicals. In one experiment, Moncrieff (1958) presented butyric acid and oil of juniper together. These mixtures produced a diminished smell sensation, although observers reported that there remained an indefinable "something" whose quality could not be clearly discerned. In an evaluation of concentration effects Moncrieff reported a 500-fold increase in the malodorous butyric acid could be counteracted by only a 20-fold increase in oil of juniper. Unbeknownst to Moncrieff at that time, such an asymmetry is expected when odorants are governed by different power functions. A 10-fold change in one odorant may be matched by a 100-fold change (or greater) in another (Cain, 1969, Moskowitz et al., 1974).

In another study, Moncrieff (1955) evaluated malodors at threshold, presented alone, with air freshener, and with a masking agent. The action of the air freshener was to reduce the detectability of mercaptan (a foul-smelling, sulfur-containing malodor, often used to odorize gas lines). The threshold of mercaptan was doubled in the presence of the air freshener. Two masking agents, para-dichlorobenzene and phenyl acetic acid, also increased the threshold of mercaptan.

Moncrieff's conception of the mechanism underlying odor counteraction comprises two parts. Masking of an odor is effected when the masking agent produces a more compelling sensation, and this compelling sensation interferes with all others (including pleasing, delicate odors, such as those emitted by flowers and herbs). An odor counteractant can be developed that eliminates unpleasant odors but by itself has only an unobtrusive smell. In Moncrieff's study, the antiodorant air freshener did permit the observer to smell some of the more pleasant fragrances, such as mimosa flower, caraway seeds, and dried thyme. In contrast, two known odor maskers, amyl butyrate and benzyl acetate, produced fairly strong smells, and in the presence of amyl butyrate and benzyl acetate observers failed to detect the mimosa smell.

E. The Berglund–Lindvall Studies

According to Berglund *et al.* (1971, 1973b) and Berglund (1974), the appropriate method of studying odor mixtures is to develop models of how odors add (or subtract) in intensity when mixed with each other. An early set of studies with pairs of malodors (dimethyl sulfide and dimethyl disulfide) revealed two things about mixtures:

1. The component odor intensities conformed to power functions, with exponents of approximately .5. This exponent value is similar to exponents reported by other investigators who also used air dilution olfactometers (Cain, 1969).
2. When mixed together, the odor intensity of the components did not add arithmetically (which the Cain and Cain & Drexler studies confirmed). Rather, the odors added as if they were vectors, separated by a constant angle.

The rule for vector addition is

$$AB = [A^2 + B^2 + 2AB(\cos \alpha)]^{.5}$$

If alpha, the angle separating the vectors, is 0, then the odor intensities should add arithmetically. For mixtures of dimethyl disulfide and methyl disulfide, alpha turned out to be between 100° and 105°.

If the model for odor mixture requires an angle of 180°, then the odorants can be conceptualized as lying diametrically opposite to each other. The vector sum would be 0, and the odors could be said to counteract each other. Were the odorants to have equal intensities (i.e., equal vector lengths), then the mixture would have no intensity at all. Intermediate levels of counteraction, in the vector model, would occur under the following conditions:

1. The odorants were separated by an angle of 180°, but were not equally intense, in which case the resultant odor would be diminished by subtraction, but not equal 0.
2. The odorants were separated by an angle varying between 180°–90°, in which case the mixture would be less intense than the sum.

Additivity, in the vector model, would occur if:

1. The odorants were separated by an angle of 0° (in which case the mixture intensity would equal the arithmetic sum of the components).
2. The odorants were separated by an angle varying between 0–90° (in which case the mixture intensity would be less intense than the sum of the components).

Applications of the vector model of odor additivity to multicomponent mixtures, with especial relevance to environmental pollution, appear possible. Berglund (1974) reported that in the evaluation of mixtures comprising up to five components, the total odor intensity only slightly exceeded the odor intensity of one component alone. The additive process of odor mixture predicts the intensity of two- or three-component mixtures, whereas an interactive, suppressive model predicts the intensity of four- and five-component mixtures. Both additivity and interaction–suppression are natural outcomes of the simple vector model of summation, generalized to two to five vectors separated by different angles. Table VII presents the results of a study in which five odor sources were characterized in terms of varying components (e.g., hydrogen sulfide, etc.), the absolute thresholds of those components, and the relative odor intensities of the components. The vector model was used to predict the overall mixture intensity, which could then be compared to the odor intensity stated by the observers in the experiment, who evaluated the mixtures directly. The model does not fit perfectly. However, as Berglund (1974) states, one should know all of the components of the effluent in order to have a perfectly fitting model. Here, at least, is presented an experimental approach that may eventually lead to such a model.

In a later set of experiments, Berglund (1974) utilized a three-component mixture, again with the components of the model being (a) the psychophysical function relating concentration of components to sensory intensities; and (b) the sensory intensity of a mixture predicted from the vector sum of the sensory intensities of the components. Three component mixtures (comprising hydrogen sulfide, dimethyl disulfide, and pyridine) produced an alpha value of around 102–115°, similar to the value for binary mixtures.

Although the vector model does not strictly address the question of odor counteraction, it sheds light on the mixture process in olfaction, which lies at the heart of odor counteraction.

TABLE VII

CONCENTRATIONS (S) AND PERCEIVED ODOR-STRENGTH (R) VALUES OF KNOWN SUBSTANCES FROM FIVE SOURCES TABULATED TOGETHER WITH THE ABSOLUTE ODOR THRESHOLDS (AT) AND PERCEIVED ODOR-STRENGTH VALUES OF THE EFFLUENTS

Source	Hydrogen sulfide		Methyl mercaptan		Dimethyl disulfide		Dimethyl monosulfide		Effluent		Calculated odor strength (R) of known odors[c]
	S^a	R^b	S^a	R^b	S^a	R^b	S^a	R^b	AT	R^b	
Main stack	4.69	2.6	—	—	—	—	—	—	3.62	56.2	2.6
Lime kiln	7.92	3.2	—	—	—	—	—	—	4.92	83.2	3.2
Solving tank	5.79	2.8	7.72	26.3	—	—	—	—	4.66	67.6	25.9
Washery	—	—	6.56	25.1	13.33	20.0	10.76	26.3	4.25	72.4	32.9
Oxidation scrubber	—	—	10.36	27.5	20.58	21.9	14.27	27.5	5.30	190.5	34.4

SOURCE: [From Berglund (1975) with permission.]

[a] S is expressed in 10^{-6} mg liter^{-1} (at 20° C).

[b] R is expressed in perceptual units relative to the perceived odor strength of 2.29 mg liter^{-1} acetone in air.

[c] According to the vector model (see Section V,E).

F. Cain and Drexler's Studies

Cain (1975) and Cain and Drexler (1974) have approached the problem of odor counteraction and mixture from the point of view of the new psychophysics (Marks, 1974; Stevens, 1975). In their experiments, comprising the evaluation of binary mixtures, they asked observers to rate two aspects of each mixture: the malodor itself and the total odor intensity of the mixture. This joint-evaluation task is possible if observers can (a) separate the components in an odor mixture (which they appear to do quite reproducibly); and (b) attend to the components separately and scale them according to the same scale unit (modulus).

In all of their studies, using pyridine and propanol as the malodors and linalyl acetate, linalool, lavandin, and amyl butyrate as the masking agents, they found that

1. In no case was the total odor of the mixture ever equal to the expected sum of odor intensities of components. This failure to add was very noticeable at high concentrations.
2. In cases of low levels of components the mixture smelled weaker than the stronger component, and stronger than the weaker. Thus, there is compromise.
3. The mixture effect depended upon concentration. For example, if the malodor was intense to begin with and a moderate concentration of the masking agent was added, then the overall perceived magnitude of the mixture was diminished. If the malodor was weak and a strong masking agent was added, the overall odor intensity was slightly enhanced. The rule that appeared to emerge was that strong odors suppressed each other, but a weak odor added to a strong odor lost its identity and increased the total intensity slightly.

Cain (1975) has reported data that supports the vector model of additivity, from an experiment in which he mixed together amyl butyrate (a masking agent) and propanol. Figure 3 shows the relation between the perceived magnitude of mixtures (ordinate), the expected total odor intensity obtained by summing together the perceived intensities of propanol and amyl butyrate (top panel), and the expected total intensity of propanol alone. The angle in the vector model for these studies was 108°, suggesting counteraction (or at least suppression).

G. The Problem of Shifts in Odor Quality

In odor masking, the effect of adding another odorant can be a shift of the mixture quality. The principle of altering odors by mixture, which applies so well in perfumery, also applies when a masking agent is added to a noxious odor. To some degree, this quality shift can be effectively used if the

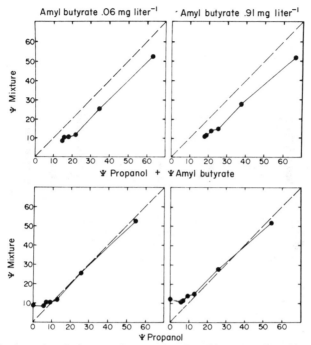

FIG. 3. Odor intensity of mixtures of propanol and amyl butyrate, plotted in two ways. The top panel represents the empirically obtained sum versus the expected sum versus the perceived level of propanol. [Reprinted from *Food Technology, Journal of Food Science*, Vol. 1, 1975, p. 343. Copyright © by Institute of Food Technologists.]

malodor is constant (such as that emanating form a rendering plant). The odor counteractant can be a fragrance with the specific property that when its quality combines with the quality of the malodor, a more acceptable fragrance (or a much less noxious odor) emerges. That is, the odor counteractant can be considered as one component of a "perfume" and the malodor to be another component (Kulka, 1965).

One of the problems in predicting the effectiveness of an odor masker is the inability, at present, to predict the quality of a mixture of two or more odorants, knowing the qualities of the individual components (Moskowitz, 1976). Figure 4 shows a profile of odor qualities obtained by magnitude estimation. The odorants were the pleasing odor of benzaldehyde and the displeasing odor of cycloheptanol. Observers rated the perceived intensity, the pleasantness–unpleasantness, and some specific quality attributes of the odorants, all by magnitude estimation. Both the odor intensity of the mixture and its pleasantness diminished. The specific quality attributes of the mixture in general cannot be predicted from the quality attributes of the components. Thus, in odor counteraction by masking, the best that can be predicted is the change in intensity and occasionally the change in hedonic tone of the malodor–odor-counteractant mixture.

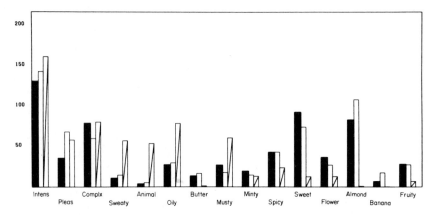

FIG. 4. Odor intensity, hedonics, and quality of a two-component mixture comprising benzaldehyde (reminiscent of almonds) and cycloheptanol (chemical-like), □ = benzaldehyde; ▨ = cycloheptanol; ■ = mixture). The method of magnitude estimation was used, and the figure shows the intensity–quality profile for both components, and for their mixture in air.

VI. AN OVERVIEW

The foregoing division of odors by the subject areas of hedonics, perfume, and malodor control represents a portion of the growing science of odor. Many scientific and technological disciplines contribute to this field. These disciplines bring to bear approaches and philosophies that quite often diverge from each other. Perhaps more important is the striking dichotomy between the relaxed, data-intensive approach espoused by scientific workers interested in the mechanisms of odor hedonics and odor mixtures, and the real-world requirements of perfumers and odor-abatement engineers, who must produce or reduce smells according to specified criteria.

The prospects for a continued intertwining of the scientific and technological areas appear bright. Every decade, since 1954, the New York Academy of Sciences has sponsored a conference on odors, which brings together biologists, physicists, psychologists, food scientists, chemists, odor-abatement engineers, and other workers in odor from diverse disciplines. The conferences have fostered a sense of unity in the pursuit of fact and theory in odor research. Since 1966 the Gordon Research conferences have also met, every 3 years, in order to bring together workers in the chemical senses (usually odor scientists and odor engineers). Finally, with the continuing interest of environmental-regulation agencies in odor and odor annoyances, engineers and scientists have been forced to consult with each other in order to develop better ways of assessing and combatting environmental odors. Each of these interfaces provides the scientist with the impetus to attack real-world problems with rigorous techniques, and provides the engineer and technologist with the impetus to refine his methods of measurement and learn something about the human organism that perceives what he is creating or abating.

References

American Society for Testing and Materials (ASTM) Standard method for evaluating odor in atmospheres. 1967, Standard No. 1391–1457.

Amoore, J. E. A plan to identify most of the primary odors. In C. Pfaffmann (Ed.), *Olfaction and Taste III.* New York: Rockefeller Univ. Press, 1969. Pp. 158–171.

Beebe-Center, J. G. *The psychology of pleasantness and unpleasantness.* New York: Van Nostrand, 1932.

Berglund, B. Quantitative and qualitative analysis of industrial odors with human observers. *Annals of the New York Academy of Sciences,* 1974, **237,** 35–51.

Berglund, B., Berglund, U., Engen, T., & Ekman, G. Multi-dimensional analysis of twenty-one odors. *Scandinavian Journal of Psychology,* 1973, **14,** 131–137. (a)

Berglund, B., Berglund, U., & Lindvall, T. On the principle of odor interaction. *Acta Psychologica,* 1971, **35,** 255–268.

Berglund, B., Berglund, U., Lindvall, T., & Svensson, L. T. A quantitative principle of perceived intensity summation in odor mixtures. *Journal of Experimental Psychology,* 1973, **100,** 29–38. (b)

Cain, W. S. Odor intensity: Differences in the exponent of the psychophysical function. *Perception & Psychophysics,* 1969, **6,** 349–354.

Cain, W. S. Odor intensity: Mixtures and masking. *Chemical Senses and Flavor,* 1975, **1,** 339–352.

Cain, W. S., & Drexler, M. Scope and evaluation of odor counteraction and masking. *Annals of the New York Academy of Sciences,* 1974, **237,** 427–439.

Chaleyer, P. H. Basic principles of perfumery. *Drug and Cosmetic Industry,* 1948, **62,** 131–133.

Doty, R. L. An examination of the relationship between the pleasantness, intensity, and concentration of 10 odorous stimuli. *Perception & Psychophysics,* 1975, **17,** 492–496.

Dravnieks, A. L. Fundamentals of odor perception - Their applicability to air pollution control programs. National Council of the Paper Industry for Air and Stream Improvement, Inc., *Bulletin* No. **54,** 1971.

Engen, T. Method and theory in the study of odor preferences. In A. Turk, J. W. Johnston, Jr., & D. G. Moulton (Eds.), *Human responses to environmental odors.* New York: Academic Press, 1974. Pp. 121–141.

Engen, T., & Corbit, T. E. Feasibility of olfactory coding of noxious substances to assure aversive responses in young children. *Research Report ICRL-RR-69-6,* Injury Control Research Laboratory, U.S. Dept. of Health, Education and Welfare, 1970.

Engen, T., & McBurney, D. H. Magnitude and category scales of the pleasantness of odors. *Journal of Experimental Psychology,* 1964, **68,** 435–440.

Flesh, R. D. Social and economic criteria for odor control effectiveness. *Annals of the New York Academy of Sciences,* 1974, **237,** 320–327.

Flesh, R. D., Burns, J. C., & Turk, A. An evaluation of community problems caused by industrial odors. In A. Turk, J. W. Johnston, Jr., & D. G. Moulton (Eds.), *Human responses to environmental odors.* New York: Academic Press, 1974. Pp. 33–44.

Foster, D. The development of olfactory preference. *Perfumery and Essential Oil Record,* 1950, **248,** 244–246. (a)

Foster, D. Olfactory preference. *Drug and Cosmetic Industry*, 1950, **67**, 46–47, 134–137. (b)

Genders, R. *Perfume through the ages*. New York: Putnam, 1972.

Green, P., & Rao, V. *Applied multidimensional scaling*. New York: Holt, 1972.

Henion, K. E. Odor pleasantness and intensity: A single dimension? *Journal of Experimental Psychology*, 1971, **80**, 275–279.

Henning, H. Der Geruch. I, II, III, IV. *Zeitschrift für Psychologie*, 1915–1916, **73**, 161–257; **74**, 305–434; **75**, 177–230; **76**, 1–127.

Huey, N. A. Objective odor pollution control investigation. *Journal of the Air Pollution Control Association*, 1960, **10**, 441.

Jewett, G. M. A note on the relation between subjective estimates of the desirability and the long lasting quality of certain perfumes and their costs. *Journal of General Psychology*, 1945, **33**, 285–290.

Jones, F. N. Information content of olfactory quality. In N. Tanyolac (Ed.), *Theories of odor and odor measurement*. Robert College, Istanbul, 1968.

Kenneth, J. H. Some experiments on mental reactions to odors. *The Perfumery and Essential Oil Record*, 1924, 85–87.

Kenneth, J. H. A few odor preferences and their constancy. *Journal of Experimental Psychology*, 1928, **11**, 56–61.

Kulka, K. Odor control by modification. *Annals of the New York Academy of Sciences*, 1965, **116**, 676–681.

Leonardos, G. A critical review of regulations for the control of odorous pollutants. In H. M. Englund & W. T. Beery (Eds.), *Air Pollution Control Association Critical Reviews*, 1974.

Lindvall, T. On sensory evaluation of odorous air pollutant intensities. *Nord Hygiensik Tidskrift*, Supplementum **2**, 1970, 1–180.

Lindvall, T., & Svensson, T. Unpleasantness matching in olfaction. Psychological Laboratories, Univ. of Stockholm, Sweden, Report No. **341**, 1971.

Marks, L. E. *Sensory processes: The new psychophysics*. New York: Academic Press, 1974.

Moncrieff, R. W. How air fresheners work. *Perfumery and Essential Oil Record*, 1955, **46**, 189–196, 227–231.

Moncrieff, R. W. Odour counteraction. *Perfumery and Essential Oil Record*, 1958, **49**, 808–811.

Moncrieff, R. W. *Odour preferences*. New York: Wiley, 1966.

Moskowitz, H. R. Multidimensional scaling of odorants and their mixtures. *Lebensmittel Wissenschaft und Technologie*, 1976, **9**, 232–238.

Moskowitz, H. R., Dravnieks, A. L., & Gerbers, C. Odor intensity and pleasantness of butanol. *Journal of Experimental Psychology*, 1974, **103**, 216–223.

Moskowitz, H. R., Dravnieks, A. L., & Klarman, L. Odor intensity and pleasantness for a diverse set of odorants. *Perception & Psychophysics*, 1976, **19**, 122–128.

Moskowitz, H. R., & Gerbers, C. Dimensional salience of odors. *Annals of the New York Academy of Sciences*, 1974, **237**, 3–16.

Peo, E. Contributions to the development of smell feeling. *British Journal of Medical Psychology*, 1936, **15**, 314–320.

Peryam, D. R., & Pilgrim, F. J. Hedonic scale method of measuring food preferences. *Food Technology*, 1957, **11**, 9–14.

Prokop, W. J. Status of regulations for source emission and ambient odors. *Annals of the New York Academy of Sciences*, 1974, **237**, 288–308.

Scheuetzie, D., Prater, R. J., & Ruddell, S. R. sampling and analysis of emissions from stationary sources. 1. Odor and total hydrocarbons. *Journal of the Air Pollution Control Association*, 1975, **25**, 925–932.

Schiffman, S. S. Contributions to the physicochemical dimensions of odor: A psychophysical approach. *Annals of the New York Academy of Sciences*, 1974, **237**, 164–183.

Shiftan, E. Perfumes. In *Encyclopedia of chemical technology*. Volume 14. New York: Wiley, 1967.

Shiftan, E. Review of the history of perfumes. Paper presented at the Second Joint Perfumery Symposium, British Society of Perfumes and Society of Cosmetic Chemists of Great Britain, 1973.

Spence, W., & Guilford, J. P. The affective value of combinations of odors. *American Journal of Psychology,* 1933, **45,** 495–501.

Springer, K. J., & Shahman, R. C. Control of diesel exhaust odors. *Annals of the New York Academy of Sciences,* 1974, **237,** 409–426.

Stein, M., Ottenberg, P., & Roulet, N. A study of the development of olfactory preferences. *American Medical Association Archives of Neurological Psychiatry,* 1958, **80,** 264–266.

Steiner, J. E. Discriminative human facial expressions to taste and smell stimulation. *Annals of the New York Academy of Sciences,* 1974, **237,** 229–233.

Stevens, S. S. *Psychophysics: Introduction to its perceptual, neural and social prospects.* New York: Wiley, 1975.

Sullivan, F., & Leonardos, G. Determination of odor sources for control. *Annals of the New York Academy of Sciences,* 1974, **237,** 339–349.

Sullivan, R. J. *Preliminary air pollution survey of odorous compounds. A literature review.* Washington, D.C.: U.S. Department of Health, Education and Welfare, 1969.

Thurstone, L. L. A law of comparative judgment. *Psychological Review,* 1927, **34,** 273–286.

Turk, A. Selection and training of judges for sensory evaluation of intensity and character of diesel exhaust odors. U.S. Dept. of Health, Education and Welfare, Public Health Service, 1967.

Wells, F. L.. Reaction times to affects accompanying smell stimuli. *American Journal of Psychology,* 1929, **41,** 83–86.

Winslow, C. E. A., & Palmer, G. T. Proceedings of the Society of Experimental Biology & Medicine, 1915. 21, 141. (Cited by R. J. Sullivan, Preliminary Air Pollution Survey of Odorus Compounds, U.S. Dept. of Health, Education and Welfare, 1969).

Woskow, M. H. Multidimensional scaling of odors. In N. Tanyolac (Ed.), *Theories of odor and odor measurement.* Robert College, Istanbul, 1968. Pp. 147–188.

Yoshida, M. Studies in psychometric classification of odors. *Japanese Psychological Research,* 1964, **14,** 70–86.

Young, P. T. Constancy of affective judgments to odors. *Journal of Experimental Psychology,* 1923, **6,** 182–191.

Young, P. T. A group experiment upon the affective reaction to odors. *American Journal of Psychology,* 1937, **49,** 227–286.

Zwaardemaker, H. C. Smell compensation. *Perfumery & Essential Oil Record,* 1959, **50,** 217–221.

Chapter 13

FOOD AND FOOD TECHNOLOGY: FOOD HABITS, GASTRONOMY, FLAVORS, AND SENSORY EVALUATION

HOWARD R. MOSKOWITZ

I. INTRODUCTION

This chapter concerns several topics that relate to food. They are:

1. Food habits, acceptance, and rejection
2. Gastronomy, the art of eating and appreciating food

HANDBOOK OF PERCEPTION, VOL. X

3. The analysis of flavors and foods by chemical means to determine the components that together yield flavor
4. The methods used presently to test the sensory and acceptance properties of foods.

II. FOOD ACCEPTANCE AND FOOD REJECTION

People show remarkably strong and persistent preferences and aversions to foods. These attitudes may arise during childhood as a result of parental influence, or they may arise because the individual has experienced the food during a pleasant or unpleasant period. Preferences and aversions to food may be so strong in some situations that individuals might prefer to die or go hungry rather than eat a certain food. The preferences and aversions might be so weak, however, that just a bit more familiarization with the food would suffice to reverse the attitude.

To some degree, food habits and preferences are coextensive with man's history. Staple items, such as corn, wheat, and potatoes, usually have been accepted by individuals in most cultures. The seeds and remnants of these staples are often found in archaeological diggings (Lowenberg, 1974). In prehistory, when new foods were introduced via agriculture, food preferences no doubt shifted to accommodate these new foods, since at that time there was no luxury of choice.

The discovery of fire played an important role in shaping food likes. Fire generates heat, which denatures proteins in fish and meat, altering the composition of amino acids (nonvolatile flavor components) and volatiles, which contribute to fish and meat flavor. This change becomes a change in the flavor. Today we appreciate cooked foods, and it is the unusual, ethnic (usually nonWestern) cuisine that calls for meats, fish, or eggs served raw. The Japanese raw fish dishes (e.g., sushi) or raw chopped beef with egg and spices (steak tartare) are unusual to the Western palate and are not usually eaten as staple foods today. The change of bread with culture is a good index of changes in food habits. As man became more used to agriculture and less of a nomad his use of bread increased. Originally, bread was a small unleavened loaf, with little art attached to its production. Today, with agricultural society having had the time to develop, bread has taken on a role as an important staple food, and abundant varieties of bread types exist, some of which require substantially longer and more intricate preparation than the early unleavened loaf.

A survey of the cuisines that have appeared and disappeared during history would take an entire volume. However, some generalities that bear upon food habits in general, and gastronomy in particular, can be stated.

First, food habits change during migration and dispersal. Each population develops its own cuisines, with specialty dishes, based upon the interaction of foods available in the new location with the historical likes and dislikes of foods previously enjoyed, and with the foods available to their new neighbors. Historically, dispersions occurred over periods lasting generations, and the change in cuisine was gradual. Today jets traverse the world in less than 24 hr, and multiply the cultural shifts by several orders of magnitude. Cuisines from all over the world can be found in New York City, and the affluent (and not-so-affluent) cuisines from foreign cultures are often easily available.

Second, food habits develop from the religious taboos of people. In antiquity, writers described the various foods and beverages that were used in festivals, as well as those foods that were to be scrupulously avoided. Several hypotheses have originated to account for the development of these taboos.

1. Divine ordinance: Dietary codes in the Old Testament were the word of God, and scientific explanation was unnecessary.
2. Literary or allegorical: The codes reflect allegorical parallels that support economic or religious beliefs. The avoidance of pork may symbolize the distaste for Rome (of which pigs were a symbol). Animals that chew the cud may reflect the ideal of meditation and contemplation.
3. Aesthetic: The behavior of certain animals is revolting to man, or their habits are polluting, and hence these animals should be avoided.
4. Moral restraint: Foods were originally eaten with relish, but were later avoided to instill moral discipline.
5. Health and sanitation: The ingestion of certain foods in the old days triggered diseases because of sanitary problems. Swine carried trichina worms, which cause trichinosis, and may have been avoided because of the disease.
6. Ethnic identity: Some foods were chosen in order to forge an identity by setting its consumers apart. In numerous places in the Old Testament the prohibition against unkosher food is combined with statements about the desire to set apart the Jews.
7. Ecology: Some foods were favored because of the interrelations between man and animal, whereas others were excluded because of economic necessity (Grivetti & Pangborn, 1974).

Of the foregoing food habits, the best known are the aversions of orthodox Jews and Moslems to pork and pork products, as well as the aversion of Jews to a variety of other foods (e.g., shellfish, animals that do not chew their cud, animals with cloven hoofs). The Moslems abstain from alcohol (Sakr, 1971), and according to Moslem tradition, when slaughtering an animal one should mention the name of Allah, in order to signify the importance of food and the holiness of the act.

A. Local Food Habits

Local food customs are usually tenacious, and symbolize an individual's culture. Our knowledge of these customs is usually obtained from the reports of anthropologists, who study the entire cultures. In each of these cultures, food is a component, often with many symbolic functions. Jelliffe (1966) developed food classifications in order to distinguish the roles that food plays in different cultures. These classifications are discussed in the following text.

1. CULTURAL SUPERFOODS

In all communities one or more items occupies this dominant role. The food is usually a dominant staple and a major source of calories for the individual. Its production requires considerable community effort, both domestically and agriculturally, to raise and process the food for consumption. Cultural superfoods have emotional value and are often woven closely into the community's cultural, religious, mythological, and historical roots. For example, in northwestern Europe, wheat bread is the cultural superfood and is associated both with the "staff of life" and the Lord's Prayer. In India, rice is the staple, and the Hindus prescribe a rice-eating ceremony for infants. In Buganda, East Africa, steamed plantain plays this role. Legend has it that Kintu, the founder of the Bugandan people, introduced plantain to their ancestors. In Central America (e.g., Guatamala) corn (in the form of maize) is the superfood, and corn was worshipped in preconquistador days, when the people were culturally isolated.

2. PRESTIGE FOODS

These foods are reserved for important occasions and are consumed by the important members of the community. In northwestern Europe pheasant and venison (game foods) occupy this role. In India a special milk dessert, *schreekand,* is served to vegetarians to show esteem, whereas in the Arab world camel stuffed successively with goat, guinea fowl, chicken, and dove is served. In ancient Hawaii the poi dog occupied the role of the prestige food. Such foods are usually of animal origin (except where cultural mores forbid meat) and are highly proteinaceous. The prestige food is usually difficult to obtain and expensive to prepare, and its use can be often traced back historically.

3. BODY IMAGE FOODS

These are foods that reflect how the culture perceives the working of the body. In India, there is the difference betwen hot and cold foods. In China, dishes are selected that balance the two universal principles, Yin and Yang (the concept of dualism in the universe). In England, milk is considered unsuitable for young men because it is choleric, whereas spleen is inedible because it is assumed to lead to melancholia.

4. Sympathetic, Magic Foods

These foods are usually thought to possess magic or curative properties, either traditionally or because the food resembles some physical object thought to be related to the disease. In Bengal, pomegranate juice is believed to cure hemorrhage, whereas in India (Gumerat) walnuts are believed to improve intellectual functioning. In the United States, fish is occasionally regarded as "brain food," and thought to be a stimulant to intellectual growth. Underdone steak in England was fed to athletes because it was presumed to improve their performance.

5. Physiologically Important Foods

These are foods that are often reserved for, or forbidden to, certain groups, based upon presumed physiological needs or weaknesses. Elderly individuals, women (especially when pregnant or lactating), and infants often are members of this group, for whom numerous restrictions apply. In East Africa, eggs, chicken, mutton, and fish are often restricted for women. In ancient Hawaii, pork was restricted for women, whereas in Malaya, fish was restricted for children up to 2 years old (Olivella, 1966).

B. Roles Played by Foods in the Diet of the United States

In the U.S. diet, foods are usually considered as components of meals, and the traditional concept of what a meal actually is has become a fluid entity during cultural changes of the past 50 years. Guth and Mead (1943) suggested that the following sets of expectations about foods may apply, and gave some roles that today, three decades later, may still apply.

1. Meat

Meat is considered to be a dinner food, whether or not it is thought of as filling, tasty, healthful, or economically affordable. Traditionally, meat was served to the husband and is often considered a luxury item that is eliminated from the diet during times of economic privation. Meat is not usually perceived as being a breakfast item, although there are some specific meat items (e.g., bacon and sausages) that can be eaten for breakfast. Typically, meat is perceived as a food that one prepares for a group of individuals (or at least for oneself and someone else) and not as an item that one prepares for oneself. This last point is quite important, since it leads to the speculation that foods that are perceived as being difficult to prepare (or at least that require substantial preparation before eating) may also be perceived as foods that should be eaten in a group, rather than by oneself.

2. MILK

Milk ranks next to vegetables as an essential food. During periods of economic hardship the consumption of milk is usually maintained at previous levels. Milk is often perceived to be a breakfast or a lunch food, but rarely a dinner food. Milk is not usually served on those occasions that demand the special preparation of foods, such as formal dinners. Although milk is a commonly drunk beverage, its appeal does not usually lie with its flavor, which is very mild.

3. POTATOES

Potatoes are considered to be a dinner food. They are filling and are often considered to be essential for a meal to be acceptable. Their importance can be differentiated according to the economic class of the user: Whereas high income groups do not fuss over potatoes, but rather use them to accompany the main dish, poor groups tend to use a great deal of imagination in embellishing the potato dish so that it becomes a "fuss food [Joffe, 1943]."

4. SALADS

Salads are almost always considered to be a lunch or supper food, and almost never to be a breakfast food. Salads are usually prepared to appeal to taste and are considered to be appropriate for a component of an important, formal dinner. The salad dish plays a role in the meal structure of upper-income individuals, but salads are not considered to be an essential health food important for nutrition. Seldom is salad mentioned specifically for one group of consumers in the family (i.e., husband, wife, or children). Today salads have become important as appropriate foods for dieters interested in reducing weight or maintaining a low level of blood cholesterol.

C. Cognitive Structure and Food

What we consider to be food is based upon what we have been told and taught. Many naturally occurring products can be used as foods but are never culturally perceived as being foods, although for some groups of individuals these same items are prized as delicacies. The range of these edible items is large compared to the small range of common foods. Live grasshoppers, for example, are food for some Africans, and rattlesnake meat appropriately brined is a delicacy to some in the United States. Within cultures, socioeconomic class may dictate that some foods (e.g., kidney and viscera) be perceived as being foods (e.g., for Southern blacks), whereas for a different class living in the same region these same food items would be perceived as waste products that remain after the edible portions are removed.

A variety of factors influence how individuals perceive items as being foods besides the physical characteristics of the food.

1. SOCIAL ORGANIZATION

In almost every culture only part of the available food supply is used, and within these food groups various items can be differentiated. Some foods are perceived as being rarer or finer than others, and perhaps more delicate and more desirable. These distinctions are usually implicit and well known. Inexpensive foods are often perceived as appropriate for consumers of low social status, and more affluent groups may actively reject such foods. Attempts to alter food habits in order to improve nutrition may fail when the nutrition program selects foods that are perceived as being socially inappropriate for the consumer's class.

2. SPECIFIC OCCASIONS

Foods are often used to mark celebrations (e.g., rites of passage, weddings, and funerals). Resistance to changes of food by members of a culture is often linked to the fear of losing one's identity, and the repeated serving of festival foods during specific occasions during the year allays that fear and maintains the outward appearance of the culture. Feast dishes often symbolize either specific historical events (e.g., the Paschal lamb eaten during the Jewish Passover seder commemorates the sacrifice to God), or else the composition of the feast dishes might symbolize the familiar diet itself. Foods may be considered appropriate only when guests are to be fed (e.g., prime ribs of beef in the United States) and would never be considered for dining alone or dining with one's nuclear family. In mass feeding, the inclusion of a valued dish can often remove the consumer's objections to a great number of other changes in the diet.

3. FOOD ETIQUETTE

During the course of learning about foods, other things pertinent to the eating situation are instilled. Food habits involve etiquette, such as one's manner and physical actions when eating the food. With developing cultures and rising social status as much emphasis may be placed on the rituals of etiquette as upon the food itself. Care may be lavished on the containers in which food is presented, and the perception of foods becomes as tied to the decor, dinner company, and minor accompaniment of the meal as to the food itself.

4. FOOD FADS

Novel perceptions of food may arise out of either spiritual reasons (e.g., vegetarians, who believe in the soul-enhancing properties of a flesh-free diet) or out of the desire to achieve some physical objective by altering the pattern of consumption (e.g., looking slim or achieving a better complexion). Some foods (e.g., bread and grapefruit) may come to take on importance far beyond their ordinary aspects. Other foods, such as milk, may signal negative properties of food, and be rejected, even though such rejection is unwarranted (e.g., the fear of too much blood cholesterol). Numerous fad diets work because foods are assigned the property of removing excess fat, and are perceived as being able to work physiological miracles.

5. PREVIOUS-USE HISTORY

Individuals often classify foods into groups based upon previous usage. Some foods (e.g., milk, gruel, and sweetened cereals) are considered to be breakfast foods for children. A biscuit would be first served to the father in a family and is considered only secondarily as a child's food. Yet cereal, made from the same ingredients, is often first fed to the child, and oftentimes is never even considered as a parent's food (Eppright, 1950).

D. Ethnic Food Habits

Each subculture in the United States brings with it traditional cuisines from the country of its origin. Such cuisines often reflect the taste preferences of the individuals, as well as the adaptation of the cuisine to the local foods available. Today, as assimilation of these subgroups continues rapidly in the United States, such local food customs, once the standard way of preparing foods for consumption, are often relegated to restaurants that maintain the tradition. The foods and the cuisine change subtly over time, and many dishes fade out of consumption (Bavly, 1966).

1. ITALIAN CUISINE

Imported cheese, olive oil, and vegetables are widely served in the Italian cuisine. To the Italian, bread (and pasta dishes) is important ("bread makes blood"). Italian food is often red because of widespread use of tomato and tomato extracts, although efforts are made to achieve a blend of soft colors. The sequence of meals in an Italian home follows a specific course, with fish served on Fridays, pasta (as a main dish) served on Thursdays, and a fancy veal dish served for Sunday lunch.

2. EASTERN EUROPEANS: POLES, SLOVAKS, HUNGARIANS

In Poland the farmers were accustomed to rich vegetable soups, bean soups, sour cream, and cottage-cheese dishes. As the Polish immigrants adopted American customs these dishes were abandoned in home cooking, but are maintained in Polish restaurants. Hungarian cuisine comprises four or five meals per day in Hungary. Traditionally, much of their breakfast food was bread and smoked fat (or cheese). In the United States, this has given way to preferences for sweet buns. The traditionally heavy noon meal has given way to sandwich lunches. The traditional dinner, comprising vegetables, eggs, sausage and cheese has been displaced by a typically heavy U.S. meal that includes meat, and in which the raw vegetables no longer predominate. The traditional Czech diet comprises rye bread, pork, sauerkraut, pastry, and beer. This cuisine was maintained for quite a long time by Czech immigrants during their ritualized Sunday dinner.

BLACKS

The Black cuisine cannot be truly identified as being one single cuisine, since the choice of foods depends upon the region. In the northern United States, the diet is similar to that of the white. In the rural South, however, the traditional diet comprises meat, meal, molasses, collard and turnip greens, and fish. Quite often the insides of the alimentary canal (namely, chitterlings) are eaten, after a considerable amount of cooking by boiling (Joffe, 1943).

E. The Development of Food Likes and Dislikes

Very young children do not usually exhibit well-founded likes and dislikes of particular food. Instead, these preferences (and aversions) may change from month to month. A child's perception of a food is intimately tied up with the situation in which the food is presented. In addition, both children and adults prefer foods that they know, in contrast to foods that they do not know. Guth and Mead (1945) referred to this process as *canalization*. Objects that first provide satisfaction for the individual are preferred to other objects, even though the later ones would eventually provide even greater satisfaction were they to be accepted. People like what they eat, rather than eat what they like.

Experiments have been done to ascertain the lability of children's food preferences. For example, Gauger (1929) studied nursery school children in a standardized situation lasting 35 days. The children were given distasteful solutions of strong salt solution (salty), vinegar (sour), weak salt solution, and raw egg white. In each case the aversive stimulus was followed by a very small piece of milk chocolate. The greatest modification of the children's reactions to the distasteful stimuli (as judged by adult raters) were with regard to the strong salt solution, which originally had been the most disliked stimulus. With repeated presentations of all the stimuli, including the slice of milk chocolate, the intensity of the hedonic reactions decreased, implying that taste preferences can be modified by experience. The experiment suggested that in order to change a child's food dislike, one may have to eliminate the child's emotional reaction to the food.

In other experiments with children that were designed to test the lability of preferences, Duncker (1938) permitted nursery school children to choose which one of six foods they liked most. Later each child was given an opportunity to repeat the choice, this time after having observed the choice made by another child. Choice was often socially determined. When age was varied systematically, the very young child (less than 2 years, 8 months old) did not imitate other children and chose on the basis of his own likes and dislikes. For the older children, imitation became important, and younger children above the critical age imitated older children when choosing. In a further study of this behavior, Marinho (1942) investigated the choice behavior of children, 4–6 years old, in kindergarten. Each child was first tested for preference, with fruit paste as the food. Then, each child was told either to choose a fruit paste that the other children had been avoiding (if there was a definite aversion), or else, if the other children did not show a definite preference, to select one of the fruit pastes. Marinho attempted to change an indefinite preference to a definite one, and controlled for imitation by instructing the children to do the opposite of what the other children were doing. It appeared easier to set up definite preferences in children who had not originally shown a preference for any specific fruit paste. These children showed the greatest change in the preference, and that change was observed for a year or more.

Although very young children usually do not have any well founded likes and dislikes (these may change from month to month), nevertheless, by the time the child reaches the age of 5 or 6 the food likes and dislikes are fairly well established. Breckenridge (1959) reported the results of a food-preference study with children, aged 5–12 years, conducted in a summer camp. The experiment was designed to ascertain what effects social experience might play on food preference. One important finding was that children exhibit wide variation in food likes and dislikes. One child mentioned disliking no foods, whereas another child stated a dislike for 21 out of 25 items surveyed. Table I shows a list of likes and dislikes from the Breckenridge study. Children preferred meats prepared alone, rather than meats in stew or in a casserole, and among their favorite foods were ice cream, potatoes, bread, milk, and cake. Children disliked cooked vegetables and soft-cooked eggs. Finally, the social experience gain in camp also played a role: 14 of the children liked more foods at the end of the summer compared to their likings at the start, whereas 11 liked fewer foods.

Other methods are useful to ascertain what foods children like and dislike. One of the most useful tools is the dietitian's 24-hr recall procedure, in which the interviewee (whether adult or child) is asked to list as many items as he or she can recall, as well as the approximate amount that had been consumed in the 24-hr period prior to the session. Emmons and Hayes (1973) reported that elementary-school children can recall the items that they eat, and that

TABLE I
NUMBER[a] AND PERCENTAGE OF CHILDREN LIKING FOOD ITEMS

Item	Number	Percentage
Meat	50	98
Meat prepared alone	50	98
Ice cream	50	98
Potatoes	49	97
Bread, crackers	49	97
Milk	48	94
Lean meat	47	92
Fruit, raw	47	92
Cereals	46	90
Cake	46	90
Vegetables, raw	45	88
Candy	45	88
Sweets	44	86
Fruit juices	43	84
Butter and substitutes	43	84
Pastry	42	83
Fruit, cooked or canned	40	78
Yellow cheese	35	69
Eggs	33	65
Meat prepared with other foods	32	63
Cheese	31	61
Cottage cheese	31	61
Vegetables, cooked	30	59
Fish	28	55
Fat meat	12	24

Response	Mean	Range
Like	19.9	10–24
Dislike	3.0	1–13
Indifferent	1.6	0–11

SOURCE: [Breckenridge, (1959).]
[a] $N = 51$.

school records substantiated this recall (as did mothers' reports of what the children ate at home). Children recalled primary items (e.g., spaghetti and meatballs, or frankfurters) more easily and accurately than they recalled secondary items (e.g., buttered bread), which do not usually play an important role in the meal. In addition, the children recalled some primary foods more easily than others. Among the most difficult to recall were foods such as pork-pie wheels, chili con carne, and veal cutlets. The reason for such difficulty is not clear, although the difficulty might be either in coding the information about the food while eating (novel input) or recalling such novel food during the recall session.

Children do not develop food preferences strictly from their idiosyncratic taste experiences. Parental attitudes influence children, oftentimes quite dramatically. The child probably learns much about food preferences from his day-to-day experiences with his parents, even if the parents do not go out of their way to instill those biases. Bryan and Lowenberg (1958) evaluated the father's influence on the food preferences of his young children. Both children and their fathers were asked to state which of 36 common foods they liked and which they disliked. Table II shows the relation between the two sets of judgments. The two groups agreed primarily on their preferences for vegetables. The other food classes exhibited poor agreement. One of the interesting things from the Bryan and Lowenberg study is that fathers often stated that they would accept and consume some foods even if they disliked those foods, whereas children who disliked a food stated that they would refuse entirely to eat that food.

There are several reasons for the dislikes uncovered by this study. These reasons varied according to the individual, and according to the position in the family. Mothers often mentioned the attributes of foods: Lima beans have skin on them, cooked cereal may be too mushy to eat, some fish dishes have a too-white color, and liver and oranges are difficult to eat. The father's responses for disliking foods were more general. Fathers mentioned texture, taste, and odor, but they gave fewer details about the attributes of the foods. Both fathers and mothers often stated that they disliked specific items (e.g., spinach, broccoli, and fish) because they had disliked the items as children and that the dislike had been carried over to adulthood. Other dislikes arose because the parents had been served the foods overly often as children (e.g., cottage cheese, prepared cereals, etc.).

Studies of young adults (especially those in college and in military service) also show a consistent pattern of food likes and dislikes (Knickrehm, Cotner, & Kendrick, 1969). Meiselman, Van Horne, Hasenzahl, and Wehrly (1972) surveyed 378 food items, requesting that the respondent rate both the liking of the item (using the 9 Point Hedonic Scale, 9 would indicate extreme liking, 5 would indicate neither like nor dislike, and 1 would indicate extreme dislike; Peryam & Pilgrim, 1959), as well as how often they would like to have the items served (in times per month). Table III shows a list of foods, divided into groups, based upon the results of that survey. The military respondents exhibited the traditional preferences for meat and potato items and disliked vegetables, a pattern that may have developed in childhood. Such preferences for frequency of serving indicates that the respondents wished to be served vegetables less often than they were currently being served in the military dining hall.

Food preferences such as the one developed by Meiselman *et al.* are both

TABLE II
LIKE RATINGS OF CHILDREN AND FATHERS[a]

Food groups	Children			Fathers		
	Number of food ratings	Number of "like" ratings	Percentage of "like" ratings	Number of food ratings	Number of "like" ratings	Percentage of "like" ratings
All foods	2129	1307	61	2330	1695	73
Vegetables	714	292	41	777	502	65
Fruits	463	355	77	506	433	86
Meats, chicken, fish, cheese	604	371	61	656	485	74
Milk as beverage	63	55	87	60	51	85
Fats	100	97	97	119	91	76
Bread and cereals	187	139	74	206	133	65

SOURCE: [Bryan & Lowenberg (1958).]

[a] Correlation coefficient: all foods, .09; vegetables, .28 (significant at the 5% level); fruits, .06; protein foods (exclusive of milk), .0.

TABLE III

Relationship between Preference Scales for Main Dinner Dishes

Frequency Scale	Hedonic Scale		
	Low	Moderate	High
Low	(A) Sardines (C) Beef liver	(A) Fried oysters (D) Liverwurst	
Moderate		(A) Fish Shrimp creole Breaded shrimp Tuna salad Seafood platter Baked tuna and noodles Lobster Lobster newberg Salmon (B) Baked macaroni and cheese Lasagna Ravioli Chili macaroni (C) Veal roast Spareribs/Sauerkraut Corned beef BBQ beef cubes Veal parmesan Veal burger Breaded veal steaks Baked stuffed pork slices Swedish meat balls Pepper steak Lamb roast Italian sausage Chili con carne Chili con carne/Beans Polish sausage Lamb chops (D) Bologna Frankfurter Sloppy joe Salami, ham Turkey club sandwich Submarine sandwich Luncheon meat Chicken club sandwich Meatball submarine Cervelot Fish sandwich Tacos/Hot tamales Western sandwich	(B) Pizza Spaghetti (C) Roast beef Canned ham Sliced roast pork Roast pork Pot roast Barbecued spare ribs Salisbury steak Meat loaf Turkey slices (D) Grilled cheese sandwich Swiss steak Turkey Ham
High		(C) Grilled steak Chicken Fried chicken	(D) Hamburger Cheeseburger Grilled cheese and ham Hot roast beef sandwich Hot turkey sandwich

indicators of current likes and dislikes of one segment of the population (and thus can be used to compare different groups of respondents), and are tools that menu planners can use when attempting to develop optimally acceptable menus, with optimal serving frequency of various items.

F. Sex Differences and Food Preferences

Men and women like different foods. Kennedy (1958) evaluated the food likes and dislikes of 45 college women who were 17–19 years old (an age range similar to that of the military population). Their data were similar to that of the military population. Women wanted fruit, fruit juices, and breadstuffs quite often for breakfast, but in contrast to male respondents relatively few desired cereal. For lunch and supper women also preferred to eat salads, rather than potatoes and meat items.

According to Kennedy, the menu that would be optimum for this group (i.e., comprising food items desired by more than 33% of the respondents) would be

Breakfast: Milk (or coffee), orange juice, toast with butter, scrambled eggs, bacon, jam (or jelly)
Lunch: Milk, apple or cookies, vegetable salad, cheese (or ham) sandwich, vegetable soup
Supper: Milk, beef steak, ice cream (or pie), pear, carrot, tossed green salad, baked (or mashed) potatoes, rolls and butter

G. Types of Food-Preference Measures

Many procedures have been used to assess the likes and dislikes of a population, and to some extent the methods used influence the results and can distort the picture of what foods are preferred. In addition, some measures must be taken at face value, for there do not exist validating operations.

1. CATEGORY SCALING OF PREFERENCE

Here the respondent is instructed to rate the degree of liking (or disliking) using a category scale that comprises categories for items liked and items disliked. The most widely used one is the Hedonic Scale (Peryam & Pilgrim, 1959), in which the scale permits the respondent to use nine ordered categories of liking and disliking. The method is used extensively by the U.S. Army to evaluate foods for procurement, as well as to evaluate (by survey) the soldier's preferences for food items. Modifications of the scale have been made for specific applications, so that the original set of nine categories is reduced to fewer (as low as three; Meiselman, 1978), but the logic of the scaling is maintained.

2. FREQUENCY MEASURES OF PREFERENCE

The respondent may be asked one of two things: How often he would like to eat a food during a specified period (e.g., 1 month), or else how many days should separate servings of the same item (e.g., Schuh, Moore, & Tuthill, 1967). These two questions require two entirely different response sets. Both allow for immediate validation of the questionnaire by serving the food items at the preferred frequency and then determining (for other serving frequencies) whether or not the food was served too often, not often enough, etc.

Schuh *et al.* (1967) instructed hospital patients to indicate how often they would like to be served a variety of vegetables, entrees, salads, and desserts. The response scale comprised six categories (varying from once a week to never). Since the respondents were hospital patients, they could be served the foods at any frequency they wished (or desired by the experimenter). The respondents were served the items more often than the median frequency. Were the questionnaire information to portray the desired frequency accurately, then one would expect the respondents to notice that the items were being overserved, and that the food was becoming monotonous. To see whether this was the case they measured plate waste, which should increase if preferences for the items diminish and if preference correlates with intake. Plate waste did not correlate with serving frequency. Items may be served as frequently or even more frequently than the median value stated on questionnaires. For example, items stated as being desired once a week could be served twice a week without any loss of acceptability.

More recent studies by Balintfy and his colleagues (Balintfy, Duffy, & Sinha, 1974) concern the relative frequency with which individuals would like to be served foods and the development of optimally acceptable menus based upon scheduling these items. According to Balintfy, preferences for items increase in a specifiable manner as a function of time elapsed since the last serving (the function is basically an exponential one, which accounts for increases in preference toward a maximal asymptote). The exponential equation allows menu planners to schedule different foods items during a long-term, cyclic menu period (e.g., 3 months or more), with the property that each item is served sufficiently often to maximize its preference at each serving, as well as to maximize the total preference for all items, summed across all servings during the menu cycle. Serving the item more often than the optimal frequency reduces the over-all preference of the menu cycle, since other items must be served less often than their optimal frequency.

Balintfy's work, and its utilization for computer-based menu planning (Balintfy, 1969), is a fine example of the consolidation of computer-based menu development with both psychometric scaling of food preference and mathematical programming for optimal solutions. It can be expanded (and has been) to include nutritional and cost constraints as well.

III. FOOD QUALITY AND GASTRONOMY

In addition to the routine preparation of foods as staples for life, food is a stimulus whose consumption itself can be pleasurable, and with the right surroundings can become a source of exquisite joy. Great care is taken to prepare foods in order to produce acceptable menu items, whether in the home, or in a restaurant, or by gourmets interested in maximizing their sensory pleasures during eating.

A. What Makes Food Acceptable to the Consumer?

Food quality is often mentioned as one of the prime determiners of food acceptability. We have seen that individuals in various cultures ascribe to food different properties, and that foods may be cultural superfoods, foods served only on ceremonial occasions, or else foods relegated to lower-class consumers. To the U.S. consuming public a variety of attributes make food acceptable.

To some, the appearance of food is important, and much of the acceptability of a food is determined by the appearance on the plate. Appearance may be a variable factor, different for each individual. Criteria differ, depending upon idiosyncratic factors. To one person a food might look tempting if it had been cooked for 2 hr, because this was the way the individual remembers having seen the food at home as a child, whereas to someone else, cooking the same food for 10 min is the limit, again because this was the accepted home preparation. Another sensory attribute is the food's taste, which more often than not is the flavor (determined principally by the food's aroma). McCune (1962) noted, however, that the overall flavor of a food is not, by itself, a critical determinant of acceptability. Rather, the milieu in which that food is eaten plays a crucial role, and even modifies an individual's judgment about flavor acceptability. Aged steak, with its characteristic flavor, is acceptable and desirable at a steak restaurant, where it is expected and becomes a premium item. In a hospital setting, aged meat is not at all acceptable. Texture is a third sensory attribute that contributes to acceptability, but the criteria governing good texture are nebulous.

The individual's background is also important. For example, Midwesterners accept fried cornmeal mush as a breakfast item, whereas the Southerner might prefer hominy grits, and Easterners (especially in Philadelphia) might prefer corn in the form of scrapple. Americans of non-German descent like pancakes, but American–German cuisine specializes in the traditional combination of applesauce and potato pancakes.

The individual's experience (an idiosyncratic factor) plays an additional role. Our judgment of how acceptable a bowl of chili is depends as much upon our previous experiences with chili (and our expectations) as upon the taste properties themselves. Were we to be raised with chili containing a lot of kidney beans and little meat, we would probably find that chili is more acceptable with many kidney beans than a bowl with much meat and few beans.

Emotional state at the time of eating may make the food "taste different." When we are angry and upset we feel differently about a cup of coffee than on the day when all goes well, even though the cup of coffee may be physically identical in the two situations. Obese individuals often eat in order to gratify themselves, and food may seem to them to be unusually attractive during a depressed period, even though the individual may not be particularly hungry at that moment. Food may also be associated with love, and the parent who feeds the child and associates that feeding with praise and reinforcement will attach extraneous meaning to the food beyond its capacity to satisfy hunger. Schachter's experiments (1971) suggest that obese individuals eat foods because the food is available, not because of their hunger and internal state.

As an individual develops socially and educationally, he is exposed to a host of new situations, including new cuisines. New foods are presented, and the individual may well develop new likes and dislikes during this period. Adventurous eaters may be shaped from nonadventurous eaters through this socialization process.

B. Gastronomy

Gastronomy is the art of enjoying foods. Gastronomy refers to both the actual process of eating and appreciating foods, as well as to the appreciation that is directed toward the ambiance of the meal (the decor, the settings, etc.). We do not eat in a vacuum. All individuals are continually confronted with the appearance of the food, the coordination of the table and its accoutrements, the selection of foods (to optimize compatibility), the type of preparation (which should optimally bring out the specific characteristics of the food), and the drinks that accompany the foods (e.g., aperitifs, dinner and after-dinner wines, liqueurs, etc.).

Gastronomy did not begin with the French, nor was Jean Anthelme Brillat-Savarin (the author of the famous text on gastronomy *The Physiology of Taste*) the first to write of the pleasures of the table. The Romans were notorious for their Lucullan feasts, during which they dined on such esoteric delicacies as peacock's tongue and drank wines (often to excess). Appreciation of food was so important to the Roman upper class that they often prolonged their sensory pleasure by regurgitating the already eaten foods in specially constructed rooms, the *vomitoria*. Having emptied their stomachs (an act not particularly antisocial in that context) the Romans were then able to continue enjoying the sensory impact of still further culinary delights.

Care was taken to ensure tasty food in abundance, and every effort was made to please and excite the senses (Brillat-Savarin, 1948).

During the Middle Ages, the art of cuisine fell into a decline paralleling the decline of other aspects of culture. Eating became less adventurous, and individuals remained committed to consuming common fare. The nobility consumed ordinary meat and wines (or mead, a drink made from fermented honey). Trade with spice-producing countries was limited, so that the introduction of new spices to accentuate the flavor of food was stifled. The Renaissance opened up trade, and with it gastronomy grew again. The Italians played an important role, because it was there that gastronomy first reawakened. During the course of the next two or three centuries gastronomy spread, and the nobility again began to cultivate the joy of eating fine foods. During the reigns of Louis XIV and Louis XV the feasts became magnificent and rivaled the feasts of the Romans and the Athenians. Restaurants came into existence, and it was there that middle-class folks were able to sample foods that they could not prepare in their own kitchens.

A beginning gastronomer is trained to appreciate the sensations and perceptions involved in eating. Visual attractiveness of the food is of utmost importance, for foods that do not go well together visually will not be acceptable for consumption. (This rule of gastronomy continues to recur in both the commercial application of dietetic principles to food service, where foods must look attractive to be sold, and in the scientific analysis of what aspects of food lead to their acceptance by the consumer.) The appropriate selection of colors is as important to the consumer as it is to the restauranteur or institutional feeder, although the former consumes exquisitely prepared meals, whereas the latter must consider cost, nutrition, and ease of preparation. The cardinal rule of lighting for the gastronomer is that it should be soft, so that the individual may concentrate his attention upon the characteristics of the food with a pleasing background. Typically, the food should present a soft, pleasing aroma that is not too strong. Smell at a distance provides only a fleeting impression, and should be an invitation to consume the food and relish its full flavor. A too-strong aroma at a distance is a sign that the flavor of the food will be overwhelming and might destroy the gastronomer's ability to appreciate other foods and the accompanying wines.

When the gastronomer eats the food he makes sure to savor it, looking for its various tastes (their time course of appearance and disappearance), as well as the nuances of texture. The overall impression of the food, which is the integration of taste, aroma, texture, and appearance, is the important thing. The flavor of the food is richer when it is sampled by mouth, since the gastronomer can savor and chew the food. The crushing action and the rolling of the food around the mouth release further volatiles that stimulate the olfactory mucosa (via the back of the mouth). Quite often, the flavor that is obtained from eating the food differs from the flavor that is obtained when the consumer simply smells the food (the flavor is much higher and more full-bodied). Von Sydow, Moskowitz, Jacobs, and Meiselman (1974) reported that the appreciation of the flavor of fruit juices sweetened with varying amounts of sucrose improved when their observers sipped the juice, rather than when they simply sampled the aroma that was concentrated at the top of the glass.

Spices, when correctly selected and used, are also important in gastronomy. Food aromas are correlated with sulfur- and nitrogen-containing compounds (with the exception of fruits, which contain numerous esters, the products from reactions of organic acids with alcohols). These aromas are usually meat-like or vegetable-like. Spices add to the basic aroma quality a heavy, sweet, character, which entirely alters the sensory characteristics of the aroma. The taste and smell senses synthesize the mixture of underlying aroma and spice aroma to develop an entirely new, qualitatively distinct, and highly acceptable mixture. The judicious addition of spices produces a mixture in which neither the spice aroma nor the underlying aroma remains unchanged. Rather, an entirely new blend of aromas appears. The taste and smell senses, when confronted with these complex stimuli evoking many qualities, blend the components. It is this richer impression of the blend that the gastronomer seeks and that renders a dish memorable. Similar findings (about the greater preference for complex mixtures of aromas) was reported for simpler systems by Moncrieff (1966). Other components add to flavor, but are not volatile. Salt produces no odor at all, but does modify the overall taste of the food by suppressing some taste qualities and enhancing others. Salt also produces a taste impression that, by its quality, blends quite well with meat and vegetable flavor.

Other nonvolatiles play an important role in enhancing flavor perception. Monosodium glutamate (MSG) is often used to enhance the flavor of meats and soups (Cairncross & Sjostrom, 1948). It does not alter one's ability to perceive tastes (i.e., it does not sensitize the taste sense), but MSG does produce an additional taste and texture impression, which has been called *Vollmundigkeit* (mouth fullness). It is often used in foods to create a blended impression, so that the various attributes of the flavor can be more readily appreciated (especially in meats and in vegetables, as well as in soups) (Monosodium Glutamate Symposium, 1948). Other flavor enhancers, such as the 5′ nucleotides (Kuninaka, 1960) have also been used in the same way.

The appreciation of fine wines is also the mark of the gastronomer. Wine tastes must be developed. Because many wines produce sensations of bitterness and dryness (as well as earthiness and astringency), the innate taste qualities may not be enjoyed by young children, who show marked preferences for sweetness. As a wine taster becomes experienced, he switches from sweeter to dryer wines. Whether the actual dryness (and slight bitterness) itself comes to be pleasant or whether the taste is pleasant because it is associated with a growing appreciation of the aromatic qualities of wine is not clear. Nonetheless, gastronomers are famous for their appreciation of wine qualities and their selection of wines to accompany a meal.

Traditionally, white wines accompany fish and fowl, because the aroma and taste of white wine are sufficiently light and delicate so as not to cover up or mask the aroma of the food. Red wines accompany meat, whose volatiles are usually more concentrated and intense, and so are not overshadowed by the volatiles from the wine. Rosé wines, which are somewhat sweeter, can accompany either type of dish. One of the interesting things about the selection of wines is the rigidity with which this custom of white wine for fowl and fish and red wine for meat is observed among individuals who are not even aware of the reason for it. The social prestige gained by being considered somewhat of a gourmet often leads to such imitative behavior without understanding.

There exists a controversy (more in the public realm than in the scientific one) about whether individuals can distinguish the differences among wines of the same type. Wines of different vintages, but of the same class, command different prices and have different prestige values. Each type of wine comprises its own unique set of volatile constitutents that provide it with a "signature" or a unique aroma. This aroma can be distinguished even in wines of the same class. Some wine fanciers claim that they can distinguish wines from different regions in the same valley (for example, different clarets). This claim is difficult to justify. Blind tests in which the individual must classify the wines from several regions and correctly identify each wine occasionally show the expected identification, but just as often they show that the taster's ability falls far short of his expectation. Wine scandals bear out this point. Wine producers often can adulterate wine without the knowledge or suspicion of most wine drinkers.

One of the cardinal rules of gastronomy is to maintain one's sensory organs in perfect working order. It is well known that food appreciation declines markedly during a cold, when one's nose is occluded and smell perceptivity is diminished. However, relatively few individuals are aware of the deleterious effects of alcohol before a meal. Alcoholic drinks (e.g., martinis) prior to eating often reduce the individual's capacity to enjoy the subtle nuances of food flavor. The experienced gastronomer will refuse the highball before dinner, although he might indulge himself in a bitter tasting aperitif (e.g., campari) to improve the appreciation of food. During the meal the gastronomer avoids smoking in order to maintain his sensory acuity, as smoke interferes with the appreciation of food flavors, although experimentally it is not clear what effect smoking plays on taste or smell acuity (Joyner, 1964; Krut, Perrin, & Bronte-Stewart, 1961). The meal itself is arranged so that the sweet portion is last, because of the belief that sweetness dulls the appreciation of foods that follow it.

In sum, gastronomy represents man's attempt to achieve a sensory nirvana, even if only for a short period of time, by surrounding himself with tempting food and grandiose surroundings. To the gastronomer, quantity does not determine fine eating, nor does the well-prepared food alone suffice. Rather, it is the artistic creation of the chef, the memorable interaction of taste, flavor texture, and appearance, and the ambiance in which the food is consumed that produces the art of gastronomy (Brillat-Savarin, 1948; Conil 1961; Dumas, 1958).

IV. FLAVORS, FLAVOR DEVELOPMENT, AND FOOD CHEMISTRY

No study of foods would be complete without a study of flavors. Traditionally, flavors were derived from natural ingredients: sweetness from honey, salt from mines or salt water, spices from plants, etc. Organic chemistry provides the flavorist with thousands of additional aromatic compounds, some of which are safe and can be used to flavor food. As a consequence, the flavor chemist has available to him a "library" of different starting ingredients (pure chemicals, natural flavors, modules, or combinations of chemicals that are used as if they were simple chemicals). By appropriate mixtures of these ingredients, and through his art, experience, and training the expert flavor chemist can duplicate many natural essences. Other tasks may be to enhance a naturally occurring flavor by adding some natural or chemical components. Half-and-half mixtures (or other fractional compositions) are often used: Half of the flavor is contributed through the painstaking refinement and concentration of natural ingredients, whereas the other half is the addition of a variety of chemicals that broaden, enhance, and improve the overall flavor.

Many simple chemicals are reminiscent of natural flavors. Amyl acetate and isoamyl acetate each smell like banana oil in low concentrations (although they have a harsh smell like nail polish remover at higher levels). Both compounds can be used to simulate banana essence, although by themselves neither is an acceptable banana substitute (Moncrieff, 1966). The consumer would not accept a banana flavor that comprised primarily amyl acetate because the flavor would be too chemical-like and would not be the same as the more complex flavor produced by the real banana (with its several dozen other components that stimulate olfactory impressions). In many foods where banana flavor is a contributory note but not the sole characteristic, the chemical note is often masked, and amyl acetate can supplement or replace banana oil (e.g., in a pudding or in a cake).

In order to create aromas, flavorists must have ideas about what chemical constituents are present in naturally occurring flavors. Ordinarily, a natural flavor comprises several dozen constituents, all present at varying concentrations. The aroma of coffee may contain several hundred such constituents (Reichstein & Staudinger, 1955), and different varieties of coffee contain these constituents in varying amounts. Some of these components alone can evoke the aroma, almost in its entirety. These are called *character-impact* compounds, and are relatively rare, being most common for fruits. For the banana, the impact is from amyl and isoamyl acetate, whereas for grapefruit the impact is from nookatone.

Until the 1950s chemists could do little to truly break apart a natural flavor into its constituents. The amounts with which researchers worked were microscopic, since relatively little gas (from volatiles) was needed to excite the sense of smell during the appreciation of an aroma. Thus, the gases needed to be concentrated, and extensive chemical apparatus was needed to produce measurable amounts of liquid concentrates. In addition, chemists relied upon chemical reactions with known reagents, and these slow reactions often produced side-components unbeknownst to the chemist. With increasing sophistication, it was found that many of the flavor components were so volatile, or occurred at concentrations so low, that even the most tedious and lengthy concentration phase would not suffice to yield measurable amounts of these components. The flavor chemist was left with only a partial list of flavor components, many of which were common to all flavors and appeared from one study to another because these were the components most amenable to concentration and chemical analysis.

More recent work has used two new analytical methods, gas chromatography and mass spectrometry, to break apart a flavor into its constituents so that the flavor chemist is provided with the chemical signature.

The principle of gas chromatography is to separate out the components of the aromas by selective retention and then to determine the concentration of each component, after separation, by burning the component in a hydrogen flame (the *detector*) and registering the degree of ionization produced. The principal section of a typical gas chromatograph is a long metal (or glass) tube that contains solid material (e.g., crushed brick). On this solid material is adsorbed a liquid, which forms a thin layer around each particle of the solid. These are the solid and liquid phases, respectively. The actual retention takes place on the liquid surface as molecules of the aroma components selectively enter the liquid phase, remain there for a while, and then leave. The chemist injects the aroma (oftentimes this is done by taking a syringe full of the vapor concentrated above a food, which is called the *headspace* of the food) into the gas chromatograph by inserting it, in the form of a vapor slug, into an ongoing stream of carrier gas (e.g., nitrogen or helium) that continually flows through the long metal tube (the *column*). Since this column has been packed with a specific type of liquid phase that has differential affinities for some kinds of molecules, but not for others, the vapor mixture soon becomes less mixed. Those molecules that have no affinity with the liquid phase pass quickly to the end of the column, where they are burned in the flame. Molecules with increasing degrees of affinity are selectively retained, with increasing retention time for the molecules with the most affinity. The output is a series of separated slugs of vapor, with the slugs varying in their affinity. With the appropriate kinds of columns, and a sufficient column length, the analytical chemist can determine how many different components are in a vapor. Also, if he knows ahead of time what components are present, he can then calibrate the detector to determine concentration. This is done by injecting known amounts of each component and determining the amount of ionization (this is done by recording the amount of ionization on a moving X–Y chart recorder, which shows up as a series of peaks—the area under the peak being a measure of concentration). The calibration allows the experimenter to compare the area under the peak for a stimulus as a known quantity with the area for the same stimulus after it has been separated out from the aroma (Issenberg, Kobayashi, & Mysliwy, 1969; Wick, 1968).

In addition to the recordings, many experimenters have employed splitting devices, so that 50% of the effluent odor from the column goes to the flame, where it produces a chart with different peak area (corresponding to intensity), and 50% goes to a nose port, where a technician can smell it coming out at the same time and jot down the aroma qualities (and perhaps scale them as well). Figure 1 shows just such a tracing, along with the written descriptions of what the components might be.

The second device that is commonly used is the mass spectrometer, which is used more as an identification device (for what components are present) than as a separating one. The machine bombards the chemical vapor with a stream of electrons, breaking down many of the molecules. The resulting mass and composition of the elements and particles present a spectrum of

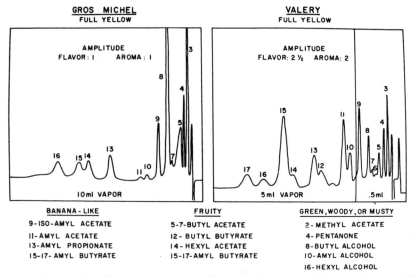

FIG. 1. Correlation of banana components (from gas-chromatographic separation) and their sensory contribution to the aroma of banana for two different varieties of banana. Each peak represents the recorder tracing when the component is ionized in a flame and the degree of such ionization is measured. [Data from Issenberg et al. (1969), reprinted with permission.]

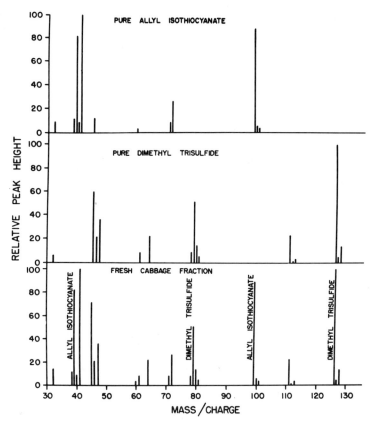

FIG. 2. Mass spectrogram of the odor components of fresh cabbage. The reference mass spectra are shown for two components (allyl isothiocyanate and dimethyl trisulfide) as well as the spectra for the mixture. Reference spectra are used as means for identifying unknown aromas in the food vapor. [Data from Bailey, Bazinet, Driscoll, & McCarthy (1961), reprinted with permission.]

peaks (see Fig. 2). Each set of elements and particles presents a unique spectrum of peaks, and there exist reference libraries of mass spectrometric patterns available to the experimenter. The experimenter can compare the set of peaks experimentally obtained against those in the library in order to identify what chemicals are in the aroma. This is usually done by a small computer, so that at the end of a run the experimenter can press a button, initiating the search, and quickly learn many of the components that were present.

Mass spectrometry and gas chromatography are commonly used together by flavor researchers interested in the components of a flavor (Heins, Maarse, Ten Noeyer, De Brauu, & Weurman, 1966). What is unknown, however, is how we perceive the mixture to be a particular aroma, knowing what the components are. Relatively few flavors are fortunate enough to be determined by their character-impact compounds. The addition together of an aroma's chemicals to reproduce the original aroma is not necessarily successful in reproducing the correct flavor (Alabran, Moskowitz & Mabrouk, 1975). Nor do the chemicals that are highest in concentration in the actual flavor play the most important roles. Some chemicals that are present at high levels (such as alcohol) may produce only small sensory effects, whereas others, present as only a few parts per million or billion, may be much more important. Guadagni and his colleagues (Guadagni, Okano, Buttery, & Burr, 1966) have suggested that for flavor evaluation with gas chromatography, each peak (and therefore every component) should be identified by three things:

1. The chemical itself
2. The actual concentration in the vapor
3. The concentration designated in terms of multiples of thresholds

With these threshold values being sensorially determined, Guadagni's proposal would designate chemical composition of food aroma in terms of both physical concentrations and relative subjective intensities.

Work by Dravnieks and his colleagues (Dravnieks, Reilich, & Whitfield, 1973) has focused on the use of statistical analysis of gas-chromatographic measures in order to understand flavor perception and predict flavor quality. Dravnieks's approach is to consider the recorder tracings from the chromatographic separation as a series of different, undetermined chemicals whose actual determination must await the hand of the adept chemist. However, if all conditions are maintained during separate chromatographic analyses of different aromas, then these tracings themselves can be statistically analyzed to determine a variety of things.

For example, the method of multiple-discriminant analysis can be used if a food aroma is classified into one of several groups (good quality, average quality, poor quality, etc.). For each sample there also exists the series of components separated out by the gas chromatograph and quantified by the ionization of the vapor. With discriminant analysis the experimenter can determine which are the most important peaks to study further, and which are present but irrelevant.

Other work by Bednarczyk and Kramer (1975) utilizes the method of multiple linear regression. Using gas chromatography, they investigated the chemicals that produced the flavor of ginger. From the analyses, they obtained four principal peaks, of which three were pure chemicals and one was a mixture. By instructing their observers to rate overall ginger flavor for known concentrations of the four components, they arrived at a predictor regression equation:

$$\text{Ginger flavor} = 13.96 + .52\,A + 1.35\,B + .99\,C + .97\,D$$

where A = mixture of citral and terpineol, B = sesquiphellandrene, C = arcurcumene, and D = nerolidol.

Attractive as these procedures appear to be at first glance, the reader should bear in mind that in all such studies the analysis of the component chemicals does not always provide the necessary stimuli that in concert reproduce the flavor. Small concentrations of trace chemicals provide the aromatic nuances that distinguish one variety of product from another. For the same general aroma, the important components may be present in different ratios, but yet the varieties may smell quite similar to each other.

Wick (1968) and Issenberg and Wick (1966) discussed the analysis of chemicals present in banana oil. Some of these clearly smelled like banana oil itself (e.g., the amyl and isoamyl acetates mentioned previously, as well as amyl propionate and amyl butyrate, which are also esters that have sweet, flowery, fruity smells). The combination of all of these components varies from one variety of banana to another (McCarthy, Palmer, Shaw, & Anderson, 1963), as shown by the gas chromatography of two different banana oils, one from *gros michel* and one from *valery*. What the human being does to integrate this information and extract from signals of varying types a common recognition remains as much of a problem for the psychologist interested in odor perception as for the chemist interested in the chemical components of the "ideal banana."

V. APPLIED TASTE TESTING OF FOODS

Our last topic concerns the applications of psychometric and psychophysical test procedures to foods in order to produce new foods in the development laboratory or else to ensure that foods that the consumer purchases are optimally acceptable. In no other applied area of research has so much work been done to develop testing procedures as in the evaluation of foods by the food industry (cf. Amerine, Pangborn, & Roessler, 1965).

There are three principal classes of taste tests commonly used today:

1. Discrimination tests, which determine whether the observer can discriminate two or more foods from each other
2. Affective tests, which determine the degree of liking or disliking for the products
3. Descriptive tests, which require that the observer generate a description of the sensory characteristics of the product

A. Discrimination Tests

Discrimination tests are useful when the product developer wishes to substitute one variant of a food for another. For example, the component of a food (such as a spice, a sweetener, a flavor) may be varied, but the marketer would not wish to have the consumer perceive a difference, for that might lead to rejection. The product developer usually tries to minimize the qualitative dissimilarity between the variant product just developed and the product to which the consumer has become accustomed (were the difference to be large, the consumer might reject the variant as possessing an off-taste or off-flavor). Discrimination tests are also used when the quality-control manager is required to maintain a standard of identity. Food products vary in the composition of their starting components, especially when these components are obtained from natural sources that themselves vary in quality. Ideally, the finished product should exhibit as little batch-to-batch variation as possible, despite the initial component variations. Quality-control managers in a production plant use panelists and discrimination tests to ascertain that their tests do not discriminate between a reference batch (the product ideal) and the current batch being evaluated.

The usual types of discrimination tests are either paired comparisons (determining if two substances are the same or different) or the triangle test (determining which substance is different from the other two). Statistical criteria exist, for given numbers of testers, that allow the tester to determine whether there exists a statistically significant difference between the reference and the test batch (Amerine, Pangborn, & Roessler, 1965).

B. Affective Tests

Affective tests find use when the product developer wishes to measure the degree to which the population likes a new product. They are often used to estimate liking for products that are ready to be marketed. Affective tests are used at all stages in product development and testing, from the informal lab-bench evaluation of candidate foods to the development laboratory's assessment of different finished products, and even beyond this to market-research tests using central location (e.g., taste testing in a supermarket) or actual home use (where the product is placed in the home for a trial period, and liking assessed at the end of that period).

Several types of affective tests have been used. The simplest is categorization by like or dislike. This *yes–no* answer provides less information than the evaluation of degree of liking. The 9-Point Hedonic Scale (Peryam & Pilgrim, 1959), which we have seen used for food preference surveys, is widely used to obtain such gradations.

Although the categories are supposed to be equally spaced psychologically, in practice most individuals shy away from using the endpoints of the scale. This occurs because the panelists are afraid of ''running out of numbers'' in order to express their extremes of liking and disliking and is known as the *category-end effect* (Stevens & Galanter, 1957). Other variants of the affective scale exist in which the panelist rates the samples of three numbers, five, etc. Oftentimes the panelist is not permitted to use the neutral category and must be content with liking or disliking. Recently, magnitude estimation has come into use for sensory testing, so that ratios of liking or disliking can be estimated (Moskowitz & Sidel, 1971).

Usually the experiments present the panelist with several varieties of a product. These may be varying formulations (e.g., for a sausage, formulations for a cookie product, etc.). The experimenter instructs the panelist to rate the overall integrated acceptability of each sample, or, if specific attributes are of interest, he may instruct the panelist to rate each of several attributes, both for intensity and for liking. This information provides the data that the product developer can analyze by statistical means (e.g., analysis of variance) to determine whether there exist statistical differences in acceptability between samples. Occasionally, refinements in the approach are made, so that within each set of samples there is provided an internal reference sample against which all other samples are compared (or a blind internal reference, which is used as a standard only in the postexperimental comparisons). That reference provides an anchoring point, and data treated with reference to the internal standard exhibit less variation than data treated "as is," without comparison to a standard. The reference sample may be the market leader or a reference that the product developer believes does not change from one experiment to another.

C. Descriptive Tests

Descriptive tests are most often used in the early and middle stages of product development. A group of panelists is trained with a common vocabulary and taught to describe qualitative nuances of a food product. The Flavor-Profile method (Caul, 1957) typifies this descriptive approach. Panelists are presented with a variety of descriptive terms, and are encouraged to develop their own terms as well. Efforts are made to assure that the terms used are common to all panelists, and that general agreement has been obtained about what physical referents correspond to those terms. The rating system for the Flavor Profile system is a pseudocategory scale, with categories for threshold, weak, moderate, and strong. Panelists' responses are not averaged, however, in the Flavor Profile System.

A variety of other descriptive systems have been proposed. For texture, Szczesniak and her colleagues (Szczesniak, Brandt, & Friedman, 1963) proposed the Texture Profile System. This system comprises a series of initial textural attributes (hardness, viscosity, and brittleness) masticatory attributes (gumming, chewiness, and adhesiveness), and other attributes (rate of breakdown, type of breakdown, moisture absorption, and mouthcoating). Each attribute can be scaled by means of a category scale comprising a fixed number of categories. What is important about the Texture Profile is that for each category scale Szczesniak has designated a series of reference foods, so that the observer is able to refer back to the foods, and know, unambiguously, what each category means.

The method of qualitative descriptive analysis (QDA) proposed by Stone and his colleagues (Stone, Sidel, Oliver, Woolsey, & Singleton, 1974) represents a refinement of the standard flavor-profile procedure. The QDA procedure requires that the observer rate a food on a series of attributes specified at the start of the experiment. Like the Flavor-Profile method, QDA takes care to instruct the observer carefully so that he is aware of the attributes and knows what to look for when sampling a food. Each food is rated by means of a marker placed along some position on a line (from one extreme, meaning none at all, to the other extreme, meaning extremely strong on that attribute). The average positions on the line, for each attribute, define a signature of the food product in terms of its sensory attributes. A product developer can compare the signatures or the profiles of two foods by comparing their component profile ratings. Qualitative descriptive analysis is a refinement of the Flavor-Profile method because it permits the observer to use a continuum of numbers (actually line position on a bounded interval). Neither procedure produces ratio-scale values of perceived attribute strength, so that a rating of 7 and a rating of 3.5 for the QDA mean only that one food has 3.5 units more of an attribute (e.g., spiciness) than another.

D. The Taste-Test Laboratory

Sensory-evaluation laboratories are constructed to ensure that several rigid criteria are met. Among these are the following:

1. Temperature must be controlled, both for the food and for the serving situation. Quite often equipment such as a *bain-marie* (a water bath capable of holding food in containers) is necessary, especially when the food is a beverage that must be served at 40°F or, on the other hand, a meat that must be kept hot. For cold storage, the bain-marie is filled with ice, and heat may be selectively applied to raise the food temperature to 40°F. If the food must be served hot to the panelist, then it must be served quickly from the preparation site (usually part of a kitchen associated with the laboratory), or its temperature must be maintained in a thermally insulated container or in a hot-water bain-marie.

2. Lighting must be controlled in order for the tester to attend to the taste (or flavor) of the product and not be distracted by the product appearance. Appearance often plays a critical role in acceptance judgments, and its effect can be neutralized by serving all foods in a booth whose lighting is pure red. This diminishes the effect due to surface variations in color, especially for meats, whose colors vary from pink to red to brown. For other experiments, the booth may be illuminated by a variety of different white lights to simulate either daylight, kitchen light, or supermarket neon lights. These lighting

conditions often are used to determine how the individual will respond to the food under the lighting conditions that are to be expected.

3. Odors other than those of the food being tested must be eliminated. If odors waft through the laboratory while an individual is testing, the results of the test may be seriously affected, even if the individual does not consciously attend to the extraneous odor. To ensure that odors are eliminated, the laboratory is usually ventilated and is maintained at a slight positive pressure relative to the outside, so that air tends to escape from the laboratory, rather than enter it.

4. Isolation between the experimenter and the panelist must be maintained to avoid the transmission of cues that could influence the individual's sensory judgments of the food. This isolation of the tester is accomplished in several ways. The simplest is to erect a small board between the tester and the experimenter, and have one individual sit on one side and pass the food to the other. More elaborate schemes include placing the tester in a booth (with appropriately colored lights providing illumination) and passing the food through a door (much like a revolving door). All contact with the tester is through that door, and the experiment is run without the panelist or the experimenter knowing each other.

5. Timed intervals between tests must be maintained, so that the tester does not become overloaded with samples and lose his sensitivity. Usually at least 30 sec are allowed to elapse between successive tastings. When the panelist tastes spicy foods, the interval must be lengthened, because spices tend to linger on the tongue and the palate for longer periods of time.

E. Panel Training and Food Evaluation

Workers in the food industry distinguish between two types of panelists: trained and untrained. Trained panelists are individuals who have been instructed to search for specific taste and aroma qualities in foods, often formally through training sessions. Occasionally, these panelists may be instructed to evaluate foods for quality control; the panelist is often introduced to the expected types of off-flavors that might arise during the course of food preparation. Knowledge of these off-notes allows the panelist to search through his sensory experience while evaluating the food, in order to see whether the food evokes one or more of the undesirable sensory characteristics.

Untrained panelists, or consumer panelists, are individuals whose opinions are sought, usually for the acceptance or rejection of a product. Usually, their judgments are more variable than those of trained panelists doing the same task, since the untrained individual attends to substantially more extraneous information when making judgments. One rule of thumb has been to use larger groups (25–50 individuals, or even more) of untrained panelists, whereas fewer (about 12 or fewer) will suffice for trained panelists.

However, that rule of thumb varies according to the type of product being evaluated. It should be borne in mind that a panelist considered trained for one food (e.g., milk evaluation) may not be trained for others (e.g., meat evaluation), even though there is some generalization from one food-evaluation task to the other.

VI. AN OVERVIEW

The study of food behavior is not a discipline limited to psychologists. As can be seen from the preceding review, more often than not the important contributions have been made by a variety of experimenters (and connoisseurs) interested in one or another aspect of food. Since food is of prime importance as a staple of civilization, it should come as no surprise that many of the bases of our knowledge derive from practical problems requiring practical solutions (e.g., developing flavor optimization). These problems have spurred on considerable research, much of which has developed into the corpus of scientific knowledge falling under the rubric of *food behavior*. The role of psychology heretofore has been as a resource science with available tools for measurement, rather than as a discipline whose workers actually gathered information on food and food behavior. Hopefully, future researchers will utilize the newly developing procedures in psychometrics and in food intake and appetite control (as well as in psychophysics) to investigate the responses of people toward the foods that they consume.

References

Alabran, D. M., Moskowitz, H. R., & Mabrouk, A. F. Carrot-root oil components and their dimensional characterization of aroma. *Agricultural and Food Chemistry,* 1975, **23,** 229–232.
Amerine, M. A., Pangborn, R. M., & Roessler, E. B. *Principles of sensory evaluation of food.* New York: Academic Press, 1965.
Bailey, S. D., Bazinet, M. L., Driscoll, J. L., & McCarthy, A. I. The volatile sulfur components of cabbage. *Journal of Food Science,* 1961, **23,** 163–170.
Balintfy, J. L. System/360 computer assisted menu planning. Contributed Program Library 360D-15.2.013 IBM Corporation, Hawthorne, New York, 1969.
Balintfy, J. L., Duffy, W. J., & Sinha, P. Modeling food preferences over time. *Operations Research,* 1974, **22,** 711–727.
Bavly, S. Changes in food habits in Israel. *Journal of the American Dietetic Association,* 1966, **48,** 488–495.
Bednarcyzk, A. A., & Kramer, A. Identification and evaluation of the flavor-significant components of ginger essential oil. *Chemical Senses and Flavor,* 1975, **1,** 377–386.
Breckenridge, M. E. Food attitudes of five-to-twelve-year-old children. *Journal of the American Dietetic Association,* 1959, **35,** 704–709.
Brillat-Savarin, J. A. *The physiology of taste.* New York: Liveright, 1948.
Bryan, M. E., & Lowenberg, M. S. The father's influence on young children's food preferences. *Journal of the American Dietetic Association,* 1958, **34,** 30–35.

Cairncross, S. E., & Sjostrom, L. B. What glutamate does in food. *Food Industries*, 1948, **20**, 982.

Caul, J. F. The profile method of flavor analysis. *Advances in Food Research*, 1957, **7**, 1–40.

Committee on Food Habits. The problem of changing food habits. *Bulletin of the National Research Council*, 1943, **108**, 1–177.

Conil, J. *Haute cuisine*. London: Faber and Faber, 1961.

Crocker, E. C. *Flavor*. New York: McGraw-Hill, 1945.

Dravnieks, A. L., Reilich, H. G., & Whitfield, J. Classification of corn odor by statistical analysis of gas chromatarraphic patterns of headspace volatiles. *Journal of Food Science*, 1973, **38**, 34–39.

Dumas, A. *Dictionary of cuisine*. New York: Simon & Schuster, 1958.

Duncker, K. Experimental modification of childrens' food preferences through social suggestion. *Journal of Abnormal & Social Psychology*, 1938, **33**, 489–507.

Emmons, L., & Hayes, M. Accuracy of 24 hr. recalls of young children. *Journal of the American Dietetic Association*, 1973, **62**, 409–416.

Eppright, E. S. Food habits and preferences: A study of Iowa people of two age groups. *Research Bulletin* **376**, Agricultural Experiment Station, Iowa State College, Ames, Iowa, 1950.

Gauger, M. E. The modifiability of response to taste stimuli in the preschool child. *Teachers College Report* #**348**, 1929.

Grivetti, L., & Pangborn, R. M. Dietary prohibitions of the Old Testament. *Journal of the American Dietetic Association*, 1974, **65**, 634–638.

Guadagni, D. G., Okano, S., Buttery, R. G., & Burr, H. K. Correlation of sensory and gas-liquid chromatographic measurement of apple volatiles. *Food Technology*, 1966, **20**, 518–521.

Guth, C. E., & Mead, M. The problem of changing food habits. *Report of the Committee on Food Habits*, National Research Council, 1943, 108.

Guth, C. E., & Mead, M. Manual for the study of food habits. National Research Council, 1945, Bulletin 111.

Heins, J. R., Maarse, H., Ten Noeyer, DeBrauw, H., & Weurman, C. Direct food vapor analysis and component identification by coupled capillary GLC-MS arrangement. *Journal of Gas Chromatography*, 1966, **6**, 395–397.

Issenberg, P., Kobayashi, A., & Mysliwy, T. J. Combined gas chromatography mass spectrometry in flavor research. *Agricultural and Food Chemistry*, 1969, **17**, 1377–1386.

Issenberg, P., & Wick, E. L. Volatile banana components. American Chemical Society, Abstract No. **12**, 152 Meeting, September, 1966.

Jelliffe, D. B. Parallel food classification in developing and industrialized countries. In *Proceedings of the Seventh International Congress of Nutrition*. Elmsford, New York: Pergamon, 1966. Pp. 147–149.

Joffe, N. F. Food habits of selected subcultures in the United States. In *The problem of changing food habits*. Bulletin 108, National Research Council, 1943. Pp. 97–103.

Joyner, R. E. Effect of cigarette smoking on olfactory acuity. *Archives of Otolaryngology*, 1964, **80**, 576–579.

Kennedy, B. M. Food preferences of college women. *Journal of the American Dietetic Association*, 1958, **34**, 501–506.

Knickrehm, M. E., Cotner, C. G., & Kendrick, J. G. Acceptance of menu items by college students. *Journal of the American Dietetic Association*, 1969, **55**, 117–120.

Krut, L. H., Perrin, J., & Bronte-Stewart, B. Taste perception in smokers and non-smokers. *British Medical Journal*, 1961, **522**, 384–387.

Kuninaka, A. Studies on the taste of ribonucleic acid derivatives. *Journal of the Agricultural Chemistry Society of Japan*, 1960, **34**, 489–492.

Lewin, K. Forces behind food habits and methods of change. *Report of the Committee on Food Habits*, Bulletin 108. National Research Council, 1943. Pp. 55–64.

Lowenberg, M. S. The development of food patterns. *Journal of the American Dietetic Association,* 1974, **65,** 263–268.

McCarthy, A. I., Palmer, J. K., Shaw, C. P., & Anderson, E. E. Correlation of gas chromatographic data with flavor profiles of fresh banana fruit. *Journal of Food Science,* 1963, **28,** 327.

McCune, E. Patients' and dietitians' ideas about 'Quality' food. *Journal of the American Dietetic Association,* 1962, **10,** 321–324.

Marinho, H. Social influence in the formation of enduring preferences. *Journal of Abnormal and Social Psychology,* 1942, **37,** 448–468.

Mead, M. The problems of changing food habits. *Report of the Committee on Food Habits,* Bulletin **108.** National Research Council, 1943. P. 21.

Mieselman, H. L. Scales for measuring food preference. In M. Peterson & A. H. Johnson (Eds.), *Encyclopedia of Food Science,* Wesport, Connecticut: AVI Press, 1978. Pp. 675–677.

Meiselman, H. L., Van Horne, W., Hasenzahl, B., & Wehrly, T. The 1971 Fort Lewis food preference survey. United States Army Natick Laboratories, 1972.

Moncrieff, R. W. *Odour preferences.* London: Leonard Hill, 1966.

Monosodium Glutamate—A symposium, Chicago. Quatermaster Food and Container Institute, 1948.

Moskowitz, H. R., & Sidel, J. L. Magnitude and hedonic scales of food acceptability. *Journal of Food Science,* 1971, **36,** 677–680.

Olivella, J. Z. The fear of food. In *Proceedings of the Seventh International Congress of Nutrition.* Elmsford, New York: Pergamon, 1966. Pp. 172–174.

Peryam, D. R., & Pilgrim, F. J. Hedonic scale method for measuring food preferences. *Food Technology,* 1959, **11,** 9–14.

Reichstein, T., & Staudinger, H. The aroma of coffee. *Perfumery and Essential Oil Record,* 1955, 86–88.

Sakr, A. H. Dietary regulations and food habits of Muslims. *Journal of the American Dietetic Association,* 1971, **58,** 123–126.

Schachter, S. Some extraordinary facts about obese humans and rats. *American Psychologist,* 1971, **26,** 129–144.

Schuh, D. D., Moore, A. N., & Tuthill, B. H. Measuring food acceptability by frequency ratings. *Journal of the American Dietetic Association,* 1967, **51,** 340–343.

Schutz, H. G. A food action rating scale for measuring food acceptance. *Journal of Food Science,* 1965, **30,** 365–374.

Stevens, S. S., & Galanter, E. Ratio scales and category scales for a dozen perceptual continua. *Journal of Experimental Psychology,* 1957, **54,** 377–411.

Stone, H., Sidel, J. L., Oliver, S., Woolsey, A., & Singleton, R. C. Sensory evaluation by quantitative descriptive analysis. *Food Technology,* 1974, **28,** 24, 26, 28–29, 32, 34.

Szczesniak, A. S., Brandt, M. A., & Friedman, H. H. Development of standard rating scales for mechanical parameters of texture and correlation between the objective and the sensory methods of texture evaluation. *Journal of Food Science,* 1963, **28,** 397–403.

Von Sydow, E., Moskowitz, H. R., Jacobs, H. L., & Meiselman, H. L. Odor-taste interaction in fruit juices. *Lebensmittel-Wissenchaft und Technologie,* 1974, **7,** 18–24.

Wick, E. L. Some chemical and sensory aspects of flavor research. *World Review of Nutrition and Dietetics,* 1968, 161–180.

Part VI

Parapsychology

Chapter 14

PARAPSYCHOLOGY*

EDWARD GIRDEN

I. INTRODUCTION

The topic of psychic phenomena has been subject to controversy for more than 100 years, and discussed by American psychologists for more than 50 years. Some attention will be given to purported qualitative reports, but the

* Special assistance from the Penrose Fund of the American Philosophical Society is gratefully acknowledged.

emphasis in this chapter will be upon the experimental evidence, in order to assess the status of parapsychology and to determine why this paradox (being "outside of accepted opinion," in the words of Augustus De Morgan, 1872) has not been accepted by the community of orthodox sciences. In addition, an attempt will be made to pinpoint some recurrent themes in its history.

The beginnings of purported psychical phenomena were perhaps the unrecorded thoughts of the caveman, and the alleged phenomena can be traced to antiquity, with biblical references to be noted. There exists a potpourri from poltergeists to reincarnation, and for each variety true believers can be found.

A. Transition to the Modern Period

There is some value to be derived from beginning with a brief consideration of the qualitative phenomena. In modern times, the interest in spiritualism began in 1848, with the spirit rappings of two young daughters of the Fox family, 6.5 and 8 years of age, on their farm in New York State. Soon, everywhere, séances were given by mediums who communicated with the dead by means of rappings and there developed a religious movement with thousands of adherents. Margaret, the older daughter, publicly confessed 40 years later that the rappings were made with the joints of the fingers and later by means of the joint in the big toe. In the 1920s, ouija boards became a fad and were used by mediums to receive spirit messages. Murphy and Dale (1961) refer to their present use to receive purported messages from the dead. In addition to sections on psychic photography and reincarnation, Pratt (1973) also devotes a chapter to poltergeists that includes a study of the Seaford family in Long Island. The family consisted of the parents and two children, ages 12 and 13. It is to be noted that such episodes generally occur when there are youngsters about.

If one proceeds to the mediums per se, the material becomes voluminous indeed. The London Society for Psychical Research (SPR) report on Palladino, a physical medium, was massive. A famous mental medium was Mrs. Piper. Some of the authoritative "para" authors cite one or the other or both of these mediums as conclusive evidence of psychical phenomena. The division between the "paras" and the skeptics is sharp; for opposite views, cf. Murphy and Dale (1961), Thouless (1972), and West (1954); Christopher (1975), Hansel (1966), and Houdini (1924). Some believers continued to accept the validity of some mediums as truly psychical, notwithstanding the exposure of fraud. See Nicol (1977) and for a different view, Hansel (1966). In each generation there were outstanding figures who were firm believers. A. Conan Doyle could never be convinced that Houdini was not psychic, even by Houdini himself.

It was this period, the latter half of the nineteenth and the first quarter of the twentieth century, that could well be described as the golden age of the mediums. At one time in this country, mediums "were said to constitute the second-highest-paid profession open to women [Hansel, 1966, p. 235]."* It is not astonishing that their most serious difficulties came from the professional magicians who rose in wrath against this fraudulent economic competition. Magicians still continue to be the bane of the mediums' existence with the revival of physical "operators," such as Uri Geller (Randi, 1975). The wheel comes a full turn, and one should heed Houdini (1924) who cautioned, "It is not for us to prove that the mediums are dishonest, it is for them to prove that they are honest [p. 270]."

Spiritualism continued with studies of mediums by the SPR. In the latter part of the nineteenth century, interest in psychic phenomena was manifested by American universities, and Richet in France introduced card-guessing tests. Early in the twentieth century, the American Society for Psychical Research (ASPR) was developed, groups met in Boston and New York, and other organizations soon developed in this country and in Europe. The first university endowment was the Hodgson Fund for psychical research in 1912 at Harvard University. Stanford University was the first to establish a psychical-research division within a psychology department, fully equipped with library and laboratory.

B. Beginning of the Modern Period

The beginning of the modern period is usually associated with the formation of the SPR in 1882. Popular interest was markedly increased in the United States with the first publications from the Duke University laboratory in the early 1930s, many remaining unaware of the activities of SPR. By the middle of the twentieth century, Great Britain, Holland, and the United States were the main centers for these efforts. At one time the USSR officially disapproved of such activities, although it apparently has made a turnabout. At present, laboratories are to be found in a number of countries.

C. Subject Matter

The experimental areas of concern are telepathy, clairvoyance, precognition, and psychokinesis (PK). The term *general extrasensory perception* (GESP) was introduced to cover telepathy and clairvoyance when the test was incapable of distinguishing between the two purported phenomena. At present, the neutral term *psi* is in common usage to encompass ESP and PK.

Telepathy represents mind-to-mind communication. In a "pure" test of

---

* Professor David E. Clement, of the University of South Florida, has commented that even then physical labor was more remunerative; cf. university professors' salaries with that of San Francisco garbagemen.

telepathy, one person thinks of a random order of the five ESP symbols, and the percipient tries to determine the order on which the agent is concentrating. Clairvoyance can be considered as knowledge of information or events obtained independently of known communication channels of perceiving or reasoning. In one test, the subject attempts to determine the order of a shuffled deck of cards. If, however, the experimenter looks at each card and the subject then guesses, it is a GESP test because it could be mind-to-mind or mind-to-cards. In precognition, knowledge of future events is obtained by paranormal channels: Thus, the subject calls card-order before deck is shuffled. When the card following the target card is called correctly, it is recorded as a precognitive +1 score. If the card before the target card is consistently called correctly, it would be scored −1. This *displacement* effect will be noted with Mrs. Stewart Shackelton (Soal & Bateman, 1954). In PK, the subject wishes or wills that dice or other objects, hand- or machine-cast, come up with specified faces, or that cast objects fall in specified areas of the casting surface. Richet used ordinary playing cards, as did Coover (1917). The Duke laboratory introduced the Zener cards composed of five copies of five different figures: wavy lines, square, circle, star, and cross. Soal, in England, used five animal figures: elephant, lion, giraffe, zebra, and pelican.

In psychology, most of the controversy concerning purported psychic phenomena has been concentrated on the experimental quantitative reports, (e.g., card guessing and dice throwing). However, in recent years, the areas of study have become quite diversified (e.g., the relationship between dreaming and ESP). The qualitative reports are of some concern, if only for the fact that these data are the basis of belief for some believers who discount the experimental data entirely. There also appears to be increased interest in areas that for years were of relatively little concern during the height of the popularity of the card tests (e.g., poltergeists, physical mediums, and the like). It will be of interest to note that some common characteristics occur in all phases of this controversy. The first consideration will be the work carried out at the Duke laboratory, which was the main source of the controversy in the United States.

II. THE MODERN PERIOD

A. The Early Days at Duke University

The dispute over the initial ESP reports was triggered with Rhine's publications, *Extra-sensory perception* in 1934 (ESP-34) and *The new frontiers of the mind* in 1937. The latter was a Book-of-the-Month Club selection that year, and card-guessing became a popular fad. The reviews by psychologists started in 1935, with major critiques by Wolfle (1938) and Kennedy (1939) bracketing the ESP symposium at the meetings of the American Psychological Association (ESP symposium at the A.P.A., 1938). The reactions were vehement, not only from the American professional psychologists, but also the British paramutual interests. Rhine's books were woefully limited in source material, and there were serious contradictions between them.

Wolfle called attention to the potential danger of paid subjects (it was during the Great Depression), because continued employment was a function of continuing success in guessing. He also noted that Rhine reported the procedure to be simple and particularly suitable for student research because the techniques were not difficult, and added that "Only when psychologists trained in experimental methods fail to confirm Rhine's results is the technique called difficult [Wolfle, 1938, p. 945]." Fraud was not an issue at the time, although apparently Wolfle has recently modified his position. Commenting upon the *affiliation* of the Parapsychological Association with the AAAS in 1970 (not membership) Wolfle stated that "You can't know whether it is real or a fraud [Marrocco, 1974, p. 16]."

Kennedy's review (1939) pinpointed a still-persisting issue when he noted that if

> the mathematics of chance expectancy does not indicate a functional relationship between variables . . . [the causes] must be sought in the experimental conditions and controls, not in the mathematics of chance. This inductive leap from extra-chance scores to extra-sensory perception has been one of the underlying reasons for the controversy [p. 96].

Years later he commented, "Still unproven" (Kennedy, 1952).

Members of the SPR were as disturbed as the American psychologists at being unable to replicate the Duke findings. Soal noted that, although there were at Duke a surprising number of high scorers, 9 to 10 in all, finding a "sensitive" in Britain was a rare phenomenon. Soal in 1948 commented: "Positive results in card guessing and dice throwing have been reported in America on a scale for which there is no parallel [in England]. If the American claims are genuine we should be forced to assume that the psychic faculty is extremely rare in England compared to America [EG, p. 382]."*

B. The Psychokinesis (PK) Controversy

The PK data were first published by Rhine in 1943, but properly belong with the early ESP data because they were carried out 6–9 years (1934–1937) earlier. Publication had been delayed because it was considered desirable to

---

* In order to confine the list of references within reasonable limits, where possible, citations will be taken from the review (Girden, 1962), from which the original sources can be obtained. The review will be identified in text as (EG, p. 00) with the appropriate page reference within the parenthesis.

postpone their appearance until the storm over the original ESP work had subsided. There is an extended review by Girden (1962), which was reprinted with a discussion by a number of parapsychologists (Discussion of PK, 1964).

For Rhine, in 1947, "The most revealing fact about PK is its close tie-up with ESP . . . PK implies ESP, and ESP implies PK [EG, p. 353f]." The test for PK was an extrachance score in wished-for target faces. Later, a second criterion was added, namely, an extrachance decline in the rate of hits for the specified target faces. The extrachance score is considered psychically significant whether it is above or below expected chance level, and the direction is never specified. The decline in scoring was developed as an additional criterion of PK as a consequence of an analysis of the early dice tests. Some 76 published PK studies were examined, as well as additional unpublished data by Girden (1962), from which the following topics will be treated here: The dice tests, the decline effect, and placement wishing.

C. Dice Tests

The 19 positive studies in the early dice tests reported highly significant critical ratios ranging from 2.56 to over 40, but upon analysis revealed serious experimental weaknesses. Little or no effort had been made to ensure the accuracy of recordings. The studies by Kennedy and Uphoff (1939) with card-guessing and Kaufman and Shefield with dice (PK experiment, 1952) both found that believers tend to make recording errors in favor of psi and disbelievers make errors in the opposite direction, indicating the need for two independent recorders of different biases, or objective records. This requirement constitutes an additional ground for precluding solo performances. There were also inadequate control tests, and in only few cases did all die faces serve as targets. Most studies used subjects' target preferences (i.e., high die faces). Pitted dice are "loaded" for excesses of fives and sixes, as reported for Weldon by Pearson (1900), long before the study was quoted in Fisher (also cf. Scarne, 1956). Under these circumstances, and lacking a control group, use of the theoretical-probability model is inappropriate.

It was generally recognized that the early dice tests were poorly designed and that the execution left much to be desired. As with the first ESP reports, the British SPR and the American professional psychologists were largely skeptical of the number of reported high PK scorers—because of their inability to replicate the results. For Soal, it was an "alleged effect" and Flew (1953) had to "confess to almost invincible incredulity [EG, p. 354]." Soal's 1948 conclusion appears justified that these "Duke experiments seem to have fallen into pitfalls that an intelligent school boy should have avoided [EG, p. 382]."

The later dice tests, some 30 reports by various investigators, were improved in design and execution. Unwitnessed tests were few and most studies included targets from one to six or high–low. Tests carried out in England by Hyde (1945), and Parsons (1945) and two unpublished studies by Scott and West were all uniformly negative with respect both to hit scores and declines. The Dale (1946) and McConnell, Snowdon, and Powell (1955) studies, as well as those by Forwald, have been defended by Murphy in his critique (1962) as evidence of PK. Also compare the views with respect to Binski and Blundun (Discussion of PK, 1964; EG, 1962; and Hansel, 1966). In passing, Dr. Blundun suggests pertinent sources of error in one of the rare introspective reports of a card-guessing subject.*

D. Decline Effect

The concern with the decline effect, specifically the *quarterly decline* (QD), in scoring is important because, contrary to popular opinion, the QD is considered the main evidence for PK by Rhine (PK experiment at Yale, 1952). Yet the evidence from the better reports is scarce. None of the British tests nor most of the later dice tests supported the hypothesis. An examination of 10 studies in which all dice faces were represented as targets indicated "no sound evidence that a Quarterly Decline in scoring occurs on all six faces [Personal communication, Denys Parsons, 1961]." Support for the hypothesis comes from the small significant decline reported by McConnell *et al.* (1955) and the Dale (1946) study, both of which lacked confirmation in the subsequent Dale and Woodruff studies (1947); the latter three were uniformly negative. Murphy and Dale (1961) ignore the replication of that study with the same apparatus by Dale and Woodruff in 1951–1952 (Murphy, 1952), in which the results were insignificant, both for hits and declines. McConnell *et al.* considered their 1955 article to be a preliminary statement to be followed by a more extensive report (McConnell, 1959, personal communication).

Extremely interesting was Oram's experiment of the random selection of numbers from the Kendall and Smith tables, which, according to Nicol, in 1955, provided "*the most singificant single QD in the annals of psychical research* [EG, p. 382; italics in original]." The most probable interpretation of the decline effect is that it is an attribute of high-face dice bias. With careful selection of true dice, and their regularly spaced replacement, Scarne (1956) threw a pair of dice for 6,000,000 throws over a period of 15 years. Recording for highs and lows, with sevens as targets, the scores for the three categories were a textbook fit to theoretical expectations.†

* It is with considerable pleasure that I am afforded this opportunity of apologizing to Dr. Blundun, of whom I have no personal knowledge, for a completely unconscious error of consistently misspelling her name in the review (EG, 1962).

† Concerning Scarne, the number 250,000,000 is in error, with an excess of two zeroes (EG, p. 365). The correct number, as used here, is 2,500,000. The final tabulation was 2,499,998 Lows, 2,500,001 Highs, with the remainder turning up as 7s.

E. Placement Tests

The placement tests were concerned with dropping objects to fall in the specified left or right half of a surface, usually measured as lateral displacement from the midline. Of the 17 reports, four tests were positive. The two tests by Knowles and Cox suffered design weaknesses and were unacceptable by the criteria of "counter hypotheses" of "ESP-60" (Pratt, Rhine, Smith, Stuart, & Greenwood, 1940). Of the 9 reports by Forwald, two tests were the remaining positive studies, and on six tests he worked solo. The criterion of scoring for specified areas was later replaced by a criterion of mean scores (cf. EG, p. 375). In the only study that involved as many as six subjects (Pratt & Forwald, 1958), there was optional stopping and lack of adequate supervision. And there was insufficient formality to provide safeguards against the possibility of errors. Forwald's work is the longest performance (1951–1961) in all the history of the parapsychology movement, excelling that of any of Rhine's or Soal's previous subjects. The Duke laboratory awarded Forwald the $1000 McDougall Award.

In a paper almost a decade later, McConnell and Forwald (1967a) reported that in the final series (Pratt & Forwald, 1958) the situation was "not under the same calm psychological conditions as had prevailed [in the penultimate series] because we knew we had to finish within a comparatively short time and we were expected to get good results [p. 56]." In addition, the original data sheets could not be located and there was a change in the cubes that had not been reported in the 1958 paper. The latter report was prepared by Pratt and published at once, to Forwald's surprise. A final experiment was then carried out by McConnell with Forwald, two series at Pittsburgh and six series by Forwald, solo, when he returned to Sweden and used his own apparatus. The first two series with McConnell were negative and the six in Sweden were positive. The difference was attributed to the psychological factors of relaxing at home (McConnell & Forwald, 1967b).

Murphy (1962) is "sure there is a *'psychological'* difference between the first and subsequent calls [in the Forward studies] [p. 257, italics in original]," and finally, "what is featured is the fact that initially Forwald worked alone. What bearing this has on the situation in PK research today is not clear to me [p. 256]." By the standards of ESP-60, every one of Forwald's studies would have been unacceptable. And with clear reference to Forwald, Nicol, a respected parapsychologist of long standing, commented in 1954, "At what stage in the difficult history of psychical research it became permissible for sensitives to report their own results and expect them to be accepted as serious evidence in psychical research, I do not know. The number of such reports has grown disturbingly in recent years [EG, p. 377]." One of the most telling criticisms of PK arising from many sources was formulated by Soal, who charged that "Unlike any other force of which we have any experience it [PK] is more successful in influencing 96 dice thrown together than a single die . . . yet it is incapable of moving a delicately suspended needle [EG, p. 384]." This suggestion was repeatedly proposed at Duke (Flew, 1953). No such report was made from there, but British tests, both published and unpublished, were uniformly negative. Recent claims of such psychic ability (e.g., those of Uri Geller) will be considered later.

Contrary to Forwald's assumption of a psychic force is a physicalistic interpretation by Gregory (cited in Hansel, 1966). Gregory's hypothesis, that the lateral displacement is a component of a random scatter of the cubes in all directions, can be readily settled by blind measurements of the final positions of the dropped cubes both in the lateral and medial distances from the center of the platform. According to Stanford (1977), there was a clear decrease in the 1960s of the number of PK studies.

F. British Sensitives

Paralleling the activities at the Duke laboratory were the efforts carried out in Great Britain. After reports of Rhine's successes reached Britain, Soal undertook the search in 1934, testing 160 subjects who made more than 128,000 guesses with uniformly chance results. This was at a time when the reports of many good subjects came from the Duke laboratory, and the annoyance of the British was understandable. A few years later, it was suggested that Soal recheck his results, looking for displacement hits before and after the respective target cards. From the group he uncovered two very good sets of results, those of Shackelton and Mrs. Stewart. Neither subject then or subsequently could score well with clairvoyance. Shackelton was retested during the war, 1941–1943, by Soal and Goldney, and Mrs. Stewart was retested in 1945 by Soal.

In the later tests, Shackelton scored well on +1, and Mrs. Stewart, demonstrating no displacement, was successful with the target card. On the earlier test, they both had done well on −1 and +1. The later test with Shackelton was precognitive telepathy or, in today's terms, precognitive GESP. For the considerable period of time over which the tests were run, Shackelton's average, on the order of 7.5 (out of a 25-card run), was extraordinarily good by statistical criteria. From a qualitative point of view such as reports of physical and mental mediums and communication with the dead, one might consider such data disappointing (cf. Boring, 1955). In these experiments, with an agent (as distinct from the recorder who saw the stimuli) serving as the "transmitter" to the subject, Mrs. Stewart scored well with 15 out of 20 agents, but Shackelton was successful with only 3 out of 10 agents. The conditions for Mrs. Stewart's retest were not as strict as those with Shackelton because the experimenters were attempting to disclose something about the scoring process (Soal & Bateman, 1954). These two studies will be considered in a later section.

In his final contribution, Soal tested two young Welsh boys, cousins, with whom fantastic scores were obtained. Many of the tests were poorly controlled and, in one situation, good scores were obtained only when the door was open between the boys' rooms. On some of the tests, the boys were actually caught cheating (Soal & Bowden, 1959). For critiques, cf. Birge (1960), Hansel (1966), and Nicol (1961).

III. EXAMINATION OF OUTSTANDING STUDIES

A. Purportedly Conclusive Reports

It appears evident that among believers there is a lack of unanimity over the years as to the conclusive experimental evidence for psi. As Nicol noted at the Ciba Symposium (Wolstenholme & Millar, 1956), there is little agreement between ESP-60 and Soal and Bateman (1954). A more recent and detailed examination of the reported evidence was made by Hansel (1966). The differences increase as more publications are added, but there tends to be some agreement about a few reports, which will merit some consideration. A sample of purported outstanding studies is summarized in Table I. A few, necessarily limited, remarks are pertinent, because a thorough analysis requires an extended discussion of the original literature.

TABLE I

Successive Comparison of Experts' Judgments of "Best Studies"

	Authority					
Study	ESP-60 (1940)	Soal & Bateman (1954)	Rhine & Pratt (1957)	McConnell (1956)[a]	Schmeidler & McConnell (1958)	Thouless (1972)
Pearce–Pratt	A	A	A	A	A	A
Pratt–Woodruff	A	(fair)	A		A	
Lucien–Warner	A					A
Turner–Ownbey	A	A?				
Reiss	A	NA		A	A	
Murphy–Taves	A					
Soal–Goldney		A	A		A	A
Soal–Bateman		A	A			
Brugman et al.					A	
Ryzl–Otani						A
Schmidt						A

Note: A = Acceptable; A? = Acceptable, with some doubt; NA = Not acceptable; Blank indicates no comment made about study.

[a] Data from Wolstenholme and Millar (1966).

Selected for first consideration are those studies about which there is less agreement, the references for which are in Table I. Warner, with the assistance of Raible, tested a single subject alone in a separate room who averaged 9.3 hits per run (25 trials) on a limited series of 250 trials. As Kennedy (1939) emphasized, the duration of the signal light was not fixed, and variability in duration could serve as a cue. In addition, there was a nonrandom distribution of frequencies of card symbols: Two of them occurred much more frequently than the other three cards. No further tests were made with this subject.

The Turner–Ownbey tests and those with Zirkle were carried out in 1933 and first reported in ESP-60 as a single experiment. Both Turner and Zirkle, in different locations, were the subjects in this distance test, well beyond 100 miles from Ownbey, the experimenter, at the Duke laboratory. According to the plan, both experimenter and subjects were to transmit their score sheets directly to J. B. Rhine. The tests, first with Turner and then with Zirkle, were extremely good. If, however, the first three runs with Turner are separated, the score with Zirkle alone is within the limits of chance expectancy. Unlike Zirkle, who followed the planned procedure, Turner mailed her scores directly to Ownbey, Mrs. Zirkle, who then transmitted them with the target lists to Rhine. The experiment was obviously faulted.

Possibly one of the more intriguing reports is that of Riess's test with one subject who scored consistently high, day after day, attaining scores of 17 to 21 correct per run on the last 10 days. The total score constitutes one of the most remarkable reports in ESP history. The tests were made from the respective homes, separating experimenter and subject by about 1 mile. There was independent recording, but no witnesses to check for recording errors (Kennedy, 1939). Some doubts were raised about the quality of security conditions and whether the data were "suggestive" or definitive (cf. Hansel, 1966). All attempts to induce the subject to continue further testing were fruitless, followed "by the sudden vanishing of Dr. Riess's phantom percipient into the blue of the Middle West [Soal, 1947, p. 26]."

The Murphy–Taves report, listed in ESP-60, is entirely ignored by Murphy and Dale (1961). The test was carefully executed and involved a considerable number of subjects. The ESP test-scores were statistically insignificant, but there were significant correlations between several of the tests that might be suggestive of stable attitudes in the subjects. No follow-up study was made to test this "post hoc" finding, which had not been part of the original experimental design.

The report by Brugman in 1919 is rarely quoted these days. The subject scored correctly in 60 out of 187 trials, much better than chance expectancy. Its design was not foolproof, and evidence has been offered to indicate how secondary, unconscious cues ("Clever Hans") could have played an important role. Such factors could be rigorously controlled today simply by closed-circuit TV (cf. Hansel, 1966). The results with Stepaneck, by Ryzl and Otani, were not confirmed by Beloff, who used his own test-cards. Schmidt's results, as Thouless (1972) acknowledged, were not subsequently confirmed when the same automated equipment was used by others.

It can be noted in Table I that in the opinion of some experts, three studies offer clear evidence for psi. These are those of Pearce–Pratt, Pratt–Woodruff, and that of Shackelton by Soal–Goldney. The argument, in the "legal" sense, is long, and the trail in the literature covers more than two decades. Even if a definitive decision may not be forthcoming, it is necessary, first, to face the issue of fraud.

B. Price Challenge for Fraud-Proof Test

One issue in the recent modern period was triggered by Price's (1955) critique that, in the absence of a foolproof experiment, the most likely explanation is that of fraud. His argument rested partly on logical grounds, the contradiction between the main body of established scientific data and the purported findings. If, with appropriate controls and in the absence of the usual experimental errors, statistically significant results are obtained, rather than discarding the main body of scientific data, the only logical alternative is fraud. Price's analysis of the Shackelton tests purported to demonstrate how fraud could have been contrived in at least six ways. The immediate replies to Price are to be found in the same issue as Bridgman's comments (1956). The response to the challenge was violent and, for those familiar with the murky history of this controversy, would appear to be overreactive; since antiquity, fraud has been a besetting problem.

Assuming the problem is not an artifact, a basic difficulty is that psi is not "on call," or evocable on demand; it is not replicable under specified conditions as in the normal scientific practice. Hence, believers defend most strenuously those studies considered to be proof of psi. Some critics accepting this ground rule have concentrated their efforts on post-mortem dissections of proffered proofs. This could include the study of design, data, and target and score frequencies, consulting where possible with subjects, agents, and experimenters. The goals were to determine whether the design was without blemish, whether the statistical analysis uncovered any suspicious aspects, and whether conditions permitted fraud (and if so, how it could have been effected).

As noted in the discussion of Table I, there appeared to be some consensus among the sampled, as well as unquoted, authorities that three studies constituted the best experimental proof of psi: those of Pearce–Pratt, Pratt–Woodruff, and Soal–Goldney in their retest of Shackelton. The first postmortem criticism was an analysis of the Pearce–Pratt and Pratt–Woodruff studies by Hansel (1961a, b), to which a reply was made in the same issue by Rhine and Pratt. After an extensive examination of the data, including a trip to the old Duke laboratory, Hansel had concluded that neither of the two "conclusive" Duke studies were fraud-proof, a conclusion to which he also came with respect to the retest of Shackelton (Hansel, 1966). The most recent report from which one can review the American work is by Medhurst and Scott (1974); for the British work, there is the report by Scott and Haskell (1974) with an associated discussion in the same issue. An overall source of much of the material as well as considerable coverage of the entire field is the controversial book by Hansel (1966).

It is not possible to briefly summarize the basic material. As illustrative, consider one aspect of the Shackelton retest by Soal and Goldney (Soal & Bateman, 1954). Shackelton was successful with only three agents, Soal acting as recorder: Soal's barber, Mrs. Albert, and Rita Elliot, later Mrs. Soal. Mrs. Albert was dropped from the study after reporting to Mrs. Goldney that "she had seen Soal 'altering the figures' several times [Scott & Haskell, 1974, p. 43]"—a matter repressed for 17 years. There was a detailed analysis of target sequences by computer search to determine whether the charge that ones were changed to fours and fives—these numbers being used in identifying the respective animal test cards.* An entire issue of the *Proceedings* was required for the paper by Scott and Haskell (1974) and the associated discussion. This was equally true of the other critiques noted. The material is voluminous.

For the critics, the four papers (Hansel, 1961a,b; Medhurst & Scott, 1974; Scott & Haskell, 1974) unequivocally establish that fraud occurred in the three cited studies. However, this part of the present discussion belongs in the following section, which deals specifically with the problems of fraud, but this is a matter of minor moment. In the absence of a detailed consideration of the evidence, a judgment of fraud would be inappropriate here. The sources are available and noted for interested parties. Of greater significance is the fact that the residual of almost 74 years of work are three possible, questioned "proofs." In the case of the Jones boys (Soal & Bowden, 1959), the Welsh cousins who were caught cheating, under ordinary circumstances the report would be ignored, and it is omitted from Table I. It is noteworthy, however, that a technique was proposed (the use of a supersonic whistle) to explain one way in which the boys could have perpetrated fraud. It was tested with, and mystified, Slavin, the elderly magician who had supervised a number of tests with the Jones boys (Scott & Goldney, 1960).

That the reassessments of studies completed decades earlier were not wasted efforts says much for the astuteness and tenacity of those who executed these "archaeological reconstructions." At least the charges and countercharges are in the record for scholarly examination. Pessimistically,

---

* In one of a series of interviews in this country before going to Great Britain, during 1958–1959, the discussion turned to the loss of the original protocols by Soal during World War II. One very knowledgeable believer remarked that a study of the original data sheets should have readily exposed any tampering with the numbers. Not many alterations would have been necessary to reduce Shackelton's scores to chance level.

however, the outcome is unpredictable; even the Jones boys may be redis-
covered in the future, while the discrediting evidence remains ignored and
lost in the dusty archives.

But tracing parties involved in these studies for their testimony is of
dubious value. A letter from Pearce, now a man of the cloth, was published
some four decades after the Pearce–Pratt tests. Similarly, much effort was
expended in locating Soal's barber, now past the age of 70. Of what worth is
testimony colored with belief and age? Of what scientific value would the
comments be, so many, many years after the fact? One does not have to be a
psychologist or psychiatrist to be familiar with the common experience that
at all ages, and especially with the elderly, retrospective falsification is not
uncommon. In any case, it would ultimately make no difference whether
they confessed or maintained their innocence. Examine the cases of
Blackburn, the rapping Fox girls, and Serios. Some confessed, and others
confessed and retracted; the believers continued to believe (Christopher,
1975; Hansel, 1966; Houdini, 1924; Murchison, 1927; Rinn, 1950).

In London, all this was brewing in 1959 and the hottest thing going was the
scandal of the Welsh boys' fraud. And when some of us were chatting about
cheating and about tracking down some of the participants in the questioned
studies, I commented, "What an awful waste of time and such skilled
efforts; why not do another experiment?" We grinned and I looked around
to see if the smile of the Cheshire cat was about.

IV. THE MORAL OF FRAUD

A. Sensitives

The issue of fraud in psychic research was a perennial problem during the
period of the great mediums, 1880–1925. The story is long, and the counterar-
guments were profuse and sometimes bordered on the profane. The question
was faced at the very beginning of the London SPR in 1882. Professor Henry
Sidgwick, the first president, commented that "though it would be a mistake
to lay down a hard and fast rule [i.e., not to use paid performers or paid
mediums], still we shall, as much as possible, direct our investigations to
phenomena where no ordinary motives to fraud—at any rate I may say no
pecuniary motives—can come in [Sidgwick, 1882, p. 11]." And in her
presidential address, Mrs. H. Sidgwick (1908) said that "I should like to urge
strongly that fraud should be more seriously discouraged than it is at present. . . . And the reason there is so much fraud is that it pays so well [p. 10]."
It is unfortunate that this sound advice was not followed. The same situation
today again faces the professional magician, the interested psychic investigator, and the nonprofessional citizenry.

There has been recent interest in "sightless vision." One instance was a report about a blindfolded Soviet girl who could see [i.e., read] printed matter and distinguish colors with her fingertips. A similar occurrence was reported in the United States that received considerable publicity. In the first case, psychic interpretations were suggested. In the latter case, a heat mechanism in the fingertips was hypothesized. In an assessment of the purported phenomena, it was pointed out that "nose peeking" with a blindfold was an old magician's trick and that, instead of a blindfold, the head should be enclosed in a box fitting tightly around the neck (cf. Gardner, 1966). Whatever the outcome of the Soviet example, with tighter controls (although lacking the head box) negative results were obtained with the American woman. Likewise, working with a professional magician, James Randi, Zubin obtained negative findings with an adolescent after the blindfolds had been secured around the edges with adhesive tape (For details, cf. Gardner, 1966; Randi, 1975). Earlier and more recent material on sightless vision is also analyzed by Christopher (1975).

One of the recent publicity-attracting phenomena is Uri Geller. He was reported as being capable of bending metal without touching it, naming the contents of closed boxes, and demonstrating purportedly psychic phenomena. Geller, temperamental and moody, would demonstrate under his stipulations, sometimes performing, sometimes refusing to do so. He was discovered in Israel by Puharich and brought to the United States. Through TV, national magazines, and the lecture route, Geller received world-wide publicity. A study of his performances was made at the Stanford Research Institute (SRI) (not related to Stanford University) by Targ and Puthoff (1974), laser physicists who had joined SRI to do psychic research.

Geller agreed to appear, but later reneged on his written commitment to be tested by a select committee in London under the auspices of the *New Scientist*. Puharich indicated that Geller would probably have refused a total X-ray examination. Among Puharich's inventions is a miniaturized radio capable of insertion into a "live" tooth. In addition, there are available radio devices that can transmit into shielded rooms—one of the conditions under which Geller was tested at SRI (Hanlon, 1974). According to Tobias (1973), Puharich confirmed that he and Geller were on a flying saucer together, and Mrs. Skutch, who says that "flying saucers to me make sense [p. 40]," is President of the Foundation of ParaSensory Investigation, which gave SRI $60,000 for the further study of Geller. In a double-blind experiment, a die was contained in an opaque box, which was shaken vigorously between trials and presumably remained untouched by the blindfolded Geller. He called the hidden die face correctly on eight trials in a row. With Tobias's own metal file box containing a die, Geller's score was zero in eight trials. Hanlon (1974) has reported that there are available in London, for about 27 British pounds, dice that will transmit radio signals indicating which face is up. For an alternate interpretation of this trick, cf. Randi (1975). A Geller demonstration for *Time* magazine editors was replicated, trick for trick, after

Geller's departure by the magician Randi, who had been secretly present throughout. Geller will not perform with magicians present (Tobias, 1973).

There are important implications here, both for people and scientists. Themes are found to repeat themselves in time and those familiar with the history of physical mediums should be experiencing a déjà vu (cf. Houdini, 1924). The physical mediums have returned in spite of their decline after infrared light was introduced to check on fraud. It is Randi's view that scientists are the easiest people to fool because they think logically. What magicians seem to resent most about so-called psychics is the easy life they lead. If they cannot make anything happen, they say they are not feeling right. If they can, they attribute it to the supernatural. Randi holds "that Geller is a fraud and a liar, and 'a very dangerous man.' . . . [For he is] living off the money of people who believe in what he says, [and] he also may lead people looking for something to believe in to change their views of the world and the way they lead their lives, based on false information [Tobias, 1973, p. 42]." Rather complete treatments of the Geller phenomenon are now available (cf. Gardner, 1976b, 1977; Marks & Kammann, 1977; Randi, 1975). For insightful contrasts, cf. Christopher (1975), Hanlon (1974), and Targ and Puthoff (1974).

Another phenomenal person of the last decade was Serios, who was presumed to demonstrate *thought photography* when film and camera were apparently not under his control. Eisenbud became convinced of the reality of this phenomenon, reported about it before a meeting of parapsychologists, and a follow-up study was made by Pratt and Stevenson. Pratt attributed the subsequent eclipse in Serios's ability in *psychic photography* to the latter's reaction to criticisms made by two photographers, Eisendrath and Reynolds (cf. Pratt, 1973). A postscript was the report that Randi appeared with Serios on *Today,* the NBC TV show, and duplicated Serios's performance. After the demonstration, when Serios told Eisenbud that his method had been exposed, the latter remained a convinced believer in Serios's psychic abilities (Tobias, 1973). Eysenck, also a believer, warned in 1974 that it was mandatory for psychic researchers to know all the tricks of a skilled magician. Enough of psychic photography; For comparisons, contrast Christopher (1975) with Pratt (1973).

B. The Laboratory

Attention has already been drawn to the charges of fradulent practices in the purportedly conclusive studies, as well as that of the Jones boys, who had been caught cheating (Soal & Bowden, 1959). In 1974, Levy, whom Rhine had selected as the new director of his laboratory, was doing work with animals involving implanted electrodes in a PK test. Initially significant results had fallen to chance level, when Levy was caught tampering with the random generator so as to score hits (Rhine, 1974b). A most surprising coincidence is a previous consideration by Rhine (1974a) of the problem of deception, describing a dozen or more cases of fraud by ESP experimenters. Notwithstanding, Rhine maintained that this instance of experimenter fraud by Levy was an isolated one, and that all of Levy's work until then was authentic; nevertheless, judgment would be withheld until it all could be independently replicated.

During the same year, 1974, two cases of fraud in the orthodox sciences were publicized. In the spring, a researcher confessed to having painted black patches on laboratory animals and passing them off as successful skin transplants between genetically incompatible animals. In the fall, an honors student who had played an important role in a series of immunological researches was discovered to have doctored his own letters of recommendation to medical schools, as well as those for a scholarship. Having admitted to these acts, he was forced to resign from the institution but remained adamant that his research data were genuine. The early series looked so promising that the work had been reported to the National Academy of Sciences. Because it was not possible subsequently to confirm these data, the project director felt compelled to write to the academy that there was no assurance that the early results could be replicated.

C. The Moral for Psi and Science

The considerations here are not trivial. To begin with, fraudulent practices are not necessarily motivated by financial gain, although this may occur in some spheres of life. For some mediums, the dominant theme may not be direct financial benefit, and fraud is probably rare in the scientific domain. In the cases just described, recognition, honor and fame might have been the compelling motives. One would be hard put to pin down the primary drives for fraud in some of the cases considered. In his analysis of the possibility of fraud in the psychical realm, Hansel (1966) examined a number of specific cases for possible motivational bases.

The problem of paid subjects is viewed differently by parapsychological supporters and the orthodox of the scientific community. The first generations of the British Society warned repeatedly of the dangers of paying mediums. Wolfle (1938) pointed out that, although paying a subject was a legitimate motivation, a danger lay in the fact that continued employment was a function of high-score guessing. The Duke subjects were paid regularly; Stewart was paid by Soal, until she quit after becoming financially independent; the financial consideration was the sole interest of the Jones boys, who collected handsome sums; and the modern "sensitives" such as Geller did (or may still be doing) well.

Considering the issue of paid subjects, the orthodox scientist has a built-in protection in the form of experimental "ground rules." Depending upon the design, the subjects usually are not aware of the experimental objectives. If

the experimenter is involved in observing or recording, double-blind experiments are available. Also, under penalty of contaminated data, one must not
forget the "Clever Hans" effect (cf. Rosenthal, 1966).

The approach to the problem of fraud at present must necessarily be
different in the areas of psychic investigations and scientific research. The
history of the former is permeated with fraud, which has continued with the
development of automated equipment. Before the Levy episode, Rhine
noted that apparatus can be used to conceal trickery. Because replication is
rare and confirmation lacking in psychic studies, Price (1955) issued the
challenge for a foolproof, or fraud-proof, experiment. Of course, trickery
can be replicated, time and again—magicians legitimately do this as part of
their honorable profession. However, for the establishment of the reality of a
given phenomenon in the scientific endeavor, the built-in protection, the sine
qua non, is repeated independent *confirmation* under specified conditions. In
this fashion, the immorality of the issue of fraud is minimized. The experimenter knows that the report will have to face a jury of his peers in the
scientific community and that the verdict will depend upon the independent
confirmation of the experimental findings, and many are well aware of
studies which have properly descended into oblivion in the absence of
confirmation.

V. RECENT RESEARCH TRENDS

As an early step in the preparation of this chapter, an attempt was made to
determine recent publication trends with respect to the quantitative reports.
Plotting chronologically all the data studies published in the *Journal of
Parapsychology* since its inception in 1937, it is clear that the greatest
number of publications occurred in 1938 and 1972–1973. The first peak
represents the backlog that was the rationale for founding the journal. The
peak in the latter 2 years is related to the introduction of automated equipment in Rhine's new laboratory, with the first papers appearing in 1969.
Compared to an average of 110 data reports per decade, 1940–1960 inclusive, 80 studies were then printed in the first half of the decade of 1970, by far
the largest half-decade total in the history of the journal. In the first issue of
1975, there was a single report. What will happen to the publication rate in
the immediate future remains to be seen. Some of the events in the recent
past are readily apparent. Rhine's laboratory at Duke was terminated in the
early 1960s, and he established the Foundation for Research on the Nature
of Man in Durham, North Carolina. Also located in Durham is a splinter
group of the "old school"—the Psychical Research Foundation. Among
other new centers is the Institute of Noetic Sciences, set up by E. D.
Mitchell, a former astronaut. The future of some of the many new groups is
problematical in this period of economic difficulties.

The introduction of automated equipment should be noted. In the early

1960s, with the use of Veritag, scores of 37 subjects on 55,000 trials for clairvoyance, precognition, and GESP were completely within chance expectancy, as was a test for "sheep" and goats" (i.e., believers and disbelievers) (cited in Hansel, 1966; Gardner, 1975). Recently, a test for clairvoyance, with more sophisticated equipment, was made by Targ, Cole, and Puthoff (1974) at the SRI. Supported with a grant of $80,000 from the National Aeronautics and Space Administration (NASA), the scores were insignificant for all 145 subjects on the screening test and for the most promising 12 subjects subsequently tested; nor did any of the latter manifest evidence of learning (i.e., improvement in scores during the test). An important critique of this study was made by Gardner (1975). Perhaps of more importance is the report by Gardner (1976a) of an offer made the previous October of an inspection of the original tapes by a statistician acceptable to all parties, to be funded by the *Scientific American*. At the present time, the offer remains unanswered (Gardner, personal communication). Disregarding the basic scientific ground rule of the availability of original protocols for independent inspection, there is a double jeopardy in the violation of the spirit of federal funding of a study not dealing in the domain of national security. For those interested, a more recent publication by Targ and Puthoff (1976), supported by psychic groups and NASA, might be consulted. One should not belittle the potentialities of automated equipment because of the Levy affair or any other scientific misbehavior. Perhaps the biggest weakness will be the tendency for such instrumentation to be taken as an end in itself, instead of a potential aid in research.

A printout obtained from the National Clearinghouse of Mental Health in 1975 contained about 25% of the data reports out of a total of over 260 titles in psi. Although the printout covered articles from over 1000 relevant journals and additional sources of material, the sample is probably not representative because a number of publications in which psi articles may be found are not in the category of mental health. Nonetheless, the sample is useful in several ways, suggesting areas of study and outlets not covered in the JP.

In the late 1960s and early 1970s, considerable work was done with groups (e.g., classrooms). Also, during this time, efforts were extended into a number of areas, such as searching for relationships with dreaming, using a number of physiological indices: drugs, hypnosis, analytic and psychiatric areas, brain waves, and feedback. Here too, the perennial criticisms appeared: For example, the inability to obtain replication in another laboratory with the best subject in the tests carried out during the Maimonides experiments (cf. Hall, 1975). A complicating condition, not unlike the orthodox situation, is that a number of variables, such as emotional attitudes and introversion–extraversion, still resist precise measurement. With the acknowledged elusiveness of psi, this only magnifies the difficulties. With the beginning of the 1970s, there was a noticeable trend in Rhine's laboratory toward the use of automated equipment with animals. Following the study of the effect of PK on a fungus culture in the late 1960s, from 1970 through 1974 there were at least 10 studies published in the *Journal of Parapsychology* alone using infrahuman subjects: among others were larva, jirds, gerbils, mice, and hamsters. These studies were concerned largely with precognition and PK.

A noticeable change was a widening of the publication outlets in which psi papers appeared. In addition to a number of analytic magazines there are to be noted the *International Journal of Neuropsychiatry, Gifted Child Quarterly, Journal of the American Society of Psychosomatic Dentistry and Medicine, Journal of Humanistic Society, Experimental Surgery and Medicine, Perceptual and Motor Skills,* and *Psychology Today.* There also appears to be increased publication in a number of countries and languages formerly not interested in this area. The meaning of an apparent reversal in Soviet policy, permitting research in psi, is not at all clear. It may be an important new dimension for Soviet psychologists or, as some professional psychologists have suggested, it may simply represent a power play between psychologists and other scientists in the USSR. The *Journal of Parapsychology* probably has been the major outlet in the field. It would be of some interest to determine if the noted trends are reflected in other English and foreign-language outlets.

As to the quality of the efforts, if past experience is of any value, their worth will not be assessed satisfactorily for at least another decade. For example, the Shackelton data remain in a disputed state as the whole controversy over the retroactive analyses of the purportedly conclusive studies continues. Finally, as noted earlier, there appears to be considerable increased interest throughout the entire psychical spectrum: mediumship, postmortem survival, reincarnation, hauntings, poltergeists, and apparitions. Here, too, the wheel has come to a full turn.

VI. THEORETICAL BASIS OF THE PSYCHICAL CONTROVERSY

A. Conceptual Hazards

There are serious theoretical difficulties about psi at whatever level these problems are examined. Consider the following problem areas: dualism, conservation of energy, distance effect of psi, the inverse-square law, precognition, and telepathy–clairvoyance. The range is from the dualistic views of Rhine and Broad (1962) to the "compatibility of science and ESP [Meehl & Scriven, 1956]." The monistic physicalist, of which Boring is an example, sees the issue as one of simplicity, a parsimonious elegance in attempting accurate descriptions of natural processes.

A difficulty for many scientists is the lack of evidential tie-up with the factual scientific structures. For many physicists and others, PK represents a violation of the laws of conservation of physical energy. The effect of PK apparently is the same whether one wishes with one die or 50 dice and this seems to make no sense with respect to energy outputs. Yet no authenticated success has been obtained in willing the motion of a delicately balanced pointer. Distance tests with ESP and PK, in which the scoring remains equally good, appear to contradict the physical phenomena that attenuate with increasing distance. Usually, the criticism is expressed as a violation of the inverse-square law. It is not as simple as all that: for magnetism, it is an inverse-cube law; from magnet to magnet, it is an inverse law to the fourth power.*

Precognition cannot be accounted for by any presently known scientific field, whatever the discipline. If all psi verbalisms were eliminated, as Flew recommended, and behavioristic terminology was adopted, as Soal suggested, precognition would still not constitute a form of knowledge. Furthermore, cognition, or knowing, is not operative in any of the four basic experimental areas in psi. Operationally, the experiments remain a matter of guessing at a statistically significant level. The psychological attributes, as compared to the statistical ones, appear, if anywhere, in dealing with apparitions and other spontaneous phenomena, as Broad has pointed out (Physicality and psi, 1961).

The difficulty in distinguishing between telepathy and clairvoyance is now generally recognized. Thouless and Rhine abandoned the distinction because there was no foolproof way of testing for "pure" telepathy without its potential "contamination" by possibly precognitive clairvoyance. Furthermore, because, for some believers, the distance tests demonstrate no reduction in psychic power, there is no way to preclude the possibility of any person's thoughts impacting on the subject in any given experiment in progress; shielded rooms, for some, are presumed to be no barrier. Consider the lengths to which the views may be extended. In line with the views of McConnell (EG, p. 380) and Pratt (EG, p. 384), Rhine (1975) has stated that "it actually *can be questioned whether any PK experiment has ever been reported in which, if an experimenter or other person was involved, his influence on the results was adequately ruled out by the test design* [p. 46, original italics]." This would also appear to be applicable to ESP card-guessing tests, and if one adds precognition to the situation, matters become unbearably sticky. Whatever the views of the possible role of the experimenter in psi tests, they are pure speculation. There has been no experimental evidence that an experimenter has ever had such an effect in PK tests or, for that matter, in any ESP tests. Such speculations are in contrast with the

---

* The illustrations are not variants of the same function, although the only index used here is the power level. As with all aspects of psi, the believers themselves hold different positions. For some, the distance effect is rejected; for others, a shielded room is no barrier, as reported by the SRI of its tests with Geller.

established experimental phenomena in psychological research (Rosenthal, 1966).

B. Experimental Difficulties

One aspect of the conflict between parapsychology and the orthodox establishment is the difference in the application of the experimental method and related statistics. Operationally, psi *is a statistic,* and to all intents and purposes the humans, animals, paramecia, larva, and fungi used in psi experiments constitute guessing machines. If one assumes that in some situations communication between individuals is only by means of unknown (unknowable?) mechanisms, then necessarily all known communication systems should be neutralized in the test situation. If the unknown is found to be the result of a normal phenomenon, it is then incorporated as part of the main body of scientific knowledge. In this sense parapsychology is in the business of putting itself out of business.

The crux of the controversy in this area lies in the absence of an independent variable in psi. In such a situation, the observed differences in performances face a court of statistical assessment in which they are measured against the theoretical expectancies. The end product of dice throwing or card tests is a statistic suggesting whether the guess-response score for the specified number of trials was better than the usually accepted limits of chance expectancy. The *para* assumes all was under control and that no knowable communication took place; significant results must therefore be psychic. The establishment disagrees and, from a number of different facets, comes to the conclusion that the statistic is inapplicable, and that the end result is simply "ignorance" of probably knowable but *at the moment unknown* operating conditions.

Fisher, repeatedly quoted in regard to the psychic controversy, stated that "Perhaps, I may say, with respect to the use of statements of very long odds that . . . they are much less relevant to the establishment of the facts of nature than would be a demonstration of the reliable reproducibility of the phenomena [ESP–APA Symposium, 1938, p. 267]." Bridgman, the physicist, noted that "It does not seem to be generally recognized that the application of probability analysis to ESP is not of the first, positive kind which has been amply justified in practice, but it is of the quite different second, negative kind which *attempts to justify a failure* [Bridgman, 1959, 126f; italics added]."

For Boring, ESP was a negative concept, and a universal negative cannot be proven. "Statistical facts are never scientifically ideal because they resist further analysis. You would like to know *why* a particular event occurs when it occurs, not merely how often . . . . What, moreover, is even a subscientist doing with this loose superstition called 'chance,' meaning that in the face of human ignorance nature sees to it that positive and negative deviations are equally frequent—'equal distribution of ignorance' as Boole called it more than 100 years ago? [Boring, 1962, p. 357].'' The implications for behavioral investigators in general were emphasized by Stevens (1960) who stated "the working rule:When in doubt, try to run another experiment .... My quarrel is simply that the fashion of processing each table of data by a meaningless ordeal of pedantic computations has the unhappy consequence that the elaborate analysis of past observations becomes the excuse for not running new experiments [p. 276]." Here, the issue is *not* between the out-group and the establishment, but cuts across all of the behavioral sciences. This issue may be one of the roots in the present-day crisis in psychology.

The obsession with the statistic has progressed to the point that any significant deviation from theoretical expectancy suggests at once to the believer the possibility of psi. In noting that one player at Las Vegas had held the dice for 1 hr and 20 min as an example of a run of luck (EG, p. 529), Rush had no hesitancy in suggesting that such a performance might be well worth investigating for possible psi (Discussion of PK, 1964). Murphy likewise defended *one* subject out of 117 reported by Binski, even though later tests with the subject were not worth reporting. In this reasoning, there are two fallacies: selected samples and optional stopping. These apply equally, for example, to my going to the horse races and, with some friends, winning all six races and the daily double, never to return again. All professional gambling houses survive economically, because they recognize that runs of luck vary from one extreme to the other. The statisticians work out the theoretical probabilities, adding a percentage so that the transactions should show a financial gain. Most appropriate illustrations of this sampling fallacy have been available for almost 20 years in Gardner (1957, pp. 303, 307). Any unusual phenomenon may be searched for possible psi. Boring, in reading Rosenthal's account of Clever Hans, noted that with the proper attitude it could be very easily read *parascientifically*. In 1972, a study was reported of the possibility of a telepathic *experimental effect* (Rosenthal, 1966) in animal research.

There is a problem here that has a direct bearing on the approach to experimental attitudes, which may or may not belong to the area of theoretical considerations. The believer's attitude or mode of reasoning is that if one cannot find or think of any normal (known) process underlying or related to a phenomenon, then, by inference, it is based on psi. This is a jump from "we can't think of" to "there can't be" a scientific, rational description (i.e., unknowable). This inferential sequence is of course untenable as a criterion for the existence of psi, and it would appear as if there would have to be an appropriate climate for the early development of attitudes sympathetic or amenable to this kind of rationalization, an example of primitive magical thinking.

More often than not, paranormal or otherwise, the statistics per se appear to be the cause of nothing except, perhaps, a debate. Consider the furor over the respective roles of environmental and genetic contributors to the complex performance of intelligence (cf. Cronbach, 1975). Given a statistically significant difference, of what worth is it in the absence of an independent variable? Any attempt to formulate a precise definition of ESP, clairvoyance, or (especially) precognition will invariably end up with a statistic. An operational definition has of course its limitations, but even a first approximation of definition here is completely elusive. The lack of substantial, replicable data and the absence of appropriate concepts suggest that studies in parapsychology are a statistic in search of a theory.

VII. THE FUTURE

For the foreseeable future, it is pertinent to consider the dynamics of a twentieth century in disarray as the result of an explosive Renaissance. One of the end-products is manifested in individual uncertainties and stresses that may be manifested in a variety of behaviors, including an increased need for magic. Sir James Frazer (1922) described an order of hypotheses in the progression from magic, to religion, to rational descriptions of man's world. Throughout history, both the irrational, magical and the rational, scientific strains can be detected, with each in ascendancy at different times. Magic would appear to be increasing at a faster rate than at any other time in this century. In comparatively stable times, magic and reality remain separate in logic-tight compartments; in this respect, we all are multiple personalities. If, however, reality outstrips magic and the two come into conflict, then it is reality, not magic, that must suffer; for man as yet cannot forego magic.

There appears to be a marked increase in the lunatic-fringe interests. How shall one draw a line between fact, fad, fallacy, and fraud? Consider "Silva Mind Control," the "neural efficiency analyzer," wishing with plants, effects of thought on the growth of a fungus culture, and precognition in larva: How does one distinguish between valid scientific efforts and pseudoscience? No accurate criteria are available, although an occasional suggestion has appeared. Gruenberger (1964) has suggested some 13 criteria and reported a comparison of three groups: physicists, ESPers, and dowsers. Gardner (1957) has suggested 5 criteria to identify the pseudoscientists' paranoia. For one approach to personality assessment of believers of extraordinary phenomena, cf. Windholtz and Diamont (1974). This is an area that might prove to be a subject of useful study.

The main body of observed facts and principles still constitutes the bulwark of the edifice of science. Of course, if the structure is cemented with a political glue, then particulars may be written in or out simply by rewriting the history. This happened with Lysenko and, apparently, with psi in the USSR. As it has been said that bad money drives out good money, it would appear that bad science drives out good science. Perhaps it is time that the establishment stop leaning over backward in attempting to demonstrate fairness; additional bends, and the cost to science and society, may be enormous before necessary correctives are introduced.

If one of the fundamental human motivations is the wish for survival, of life after death, there would appear to be no relationship between such wishes and a person averaging 7.7 out of 25 cards guessed correctly—even for a period of months. For those who are unimpressed with statistics, it is the qualitative aspects of parapsychological phenomena that are important. It was noted that there was increased interest during the mid-1960s in the nonquantitative aspects of the psychical controversy (Girden, 1966). It would appear that this trend is continuing, as noted by the consideration of the physical mediums, poltergeists, and life after death (cf. Murphy & Dale, 1961; Pratt, 1973; Thouless, 1972).

Psi will not go quietly away. It is not irrelevant that the popular books often bear little resemblance to the published reports. The believers believe, and they are selling their merchandise. Max Planck has been repeatedly quoted to the effect that controversy is never resolved; it ends only when the last defender dies. There are several examples that support this depressing thought. From one view of this complexity, a modified Planck dictum might apply to ESP: The controversy will cease only when the last of mankind dies, for we are dealing with a deep motivational need for magic.

> [The] belief in the sympathetic influence exerted on each other by persons or things at a distance is of the essence of magic. Whatever doubts science may entertain as to the possibility of action at a distance, magic has none; faith in telepathy is one of its first principles. A modern advocate of the influence of mind upon mind at a distance would have no difficulty in convincing a savage; the savage believed in it long ago, and what is more, he acted on his belief with a logical consistency such as his civilised brother in the faith has not yet, so far as I am aware, exhibited in his conduct [Frazer, 1922, p. 25f].

From another viewpoint, one that is more fruitful and optimistic for those still immune or resistant to the sirens of magic, the value of a rational construct is ever so more potentially challenging and rewarding. It is this characteristic that is an essential requisite for the civilized man. When dealing with magic, there is no better scientific maxim than the words of Coover (1927); "Reliance upon the scientific method is the price of admissible evidence."

References

Birge, R. T. Telepathic experiments in Wales. (Review of *The Mind Readers* by S. G. Soal & H. T. Bowden). *International Journal of Parapsychology*, 1960, **2**, 5–20.

Boring, E. G. The present status of parapsychology. *American Scientist*, 1955, **43**, 108–117.

Boring, E. G. Parascience. *Contemporary Psychology*, 1962, **7**, 356–357.

Bridgman, P. W. Probability, logic, and ESP. *Science*, 1956, **123**, 15–17.

Bridgman, P. W. *The way things are*. Cambridge, Massachusetts: Harvard Univ. Press, 1959.

Broad, C. D. *Lectures on psychical research*. New York: Humanities Press, 1962.

Christopher, M. *Mediums, mystics and the occult*. New York: Crowell, 1975.

Coover, J. E. *Experiments in psychical research*. Stanford, California: Stanford Univ. Press, 1917.

Coover, J. E. Metaphysics and the incredulity of psychologists. In C. Murchison (Ed.), *The case for and against psychical belief*. Worcester, Massachusetts. Clark Univ., 1927.

Cronbach, L. J. Five decades of public controversy over mental testing. *American Psychologist*, 1975, **30**, 1–14.

Dale, L. A. The psychokinetic effect. The first A.S.P.R. experiment. *Journal of American Society for Psychical Research*, 1946, **40**, 123–151.

Dale, L. A., & Woodruff, J. L. The psychokinetic effect: Further A.S.P.R. experiments. *Journal of American Society for Psychical Research*, 1947, **41**, 65–82.

de Morgan, A. *A budget of paradoxes* (2nd ed.). Freeport, New York: Book for Libraries Press, 1969. (Originally published, 1872.)

Discussion of psychokinesis, *International Journal of Parapsychology*, 1964, **6**, 26–138.

ESP symposium at the A.P.A. *Journal of Parapsychology*, 1938, **2**, 247–272.

Eysenck, H. J. Parapsychological phenomena, theories of. *Encyclopaedia Britannica*, 1974, 1002–1004.

Flew, A. *A new approach to psychical research*. London: Watts, 1953.

Frazer, James G. *The golden bough*. New York: Macmillan, 1922.

Gardner, M. *Fads and fallacies in the name of science*. New York: Dover Publications, 1957.

Gardner, M. Dermo-optical perception: A peek down the nose. *Science*, 1966, **151**, 654–657.

Gardner, M. Concerning an effort to demonstrate extrasensory perception by machine. *Scientific American*, 1975, **233**(4), No. 4, 114–118.

Gardner, M. Letters. *Scientific American*, 1976, **234**(8). (a)

Gardner, M. Magic and paraphysics. *Technology Review*, 1976, **78**, 42–51. (b)

Gardner, M. A sceptic's view of parapsychology. *The Humanist*, 1977, **37**, 45–46.

Girden, E. A review of psychokinesis (PK). *Psychological Bulletin*, 1962, **59**, 353–388, 529–531.

Girden, E. Parapsychology. *Encyclopaedia Britannica*, 1966, 320–323.

Gruenberger, F. J. A measure for crackpots. *Science*, 1964, **145**, 1413–1415.

Hall, C. S. Psi after dark. (Review of dream telepathy: Experiments in nocturnal ESP by M. Ullman, S. Krippner, & A. Vaughn.) *Contemporary Psychology*, 1975, **20**, 566–567.

Hanlon, J. Uri Geller and science. *New Scientist*, Oct. 17, 1974, **64**, 170–185.

Hansel, C. E. M. A critical analysis of the Pearce–Pratt experiment. *Journal of Parapsychology*, 1961, **25**, 87–91. (a)

Hansel, C. E. M. A critical analysis of the Pratt–Woodruff experiment. *Journal of Parapsychology*, 1961, **25**, 99–113. (b)

Hansel, C. E. M. *E.S.P. A scientific evaluation*. Introduction by E. G. Boring. New York: Scribners, 1966.

Houdini, H. *Houdini: A magician among the spirits*. New York: Harper, 1924. [Reprinted by Arno Press, 1972.]

Hyde, D. H. A report on some English PK trials. *Proceedings of the Society for Psychical Research*, 1945, **47**, 293–296.

Kennedy, J. L. A methodological review of extra-sensory perception. *Psychological Bulletin*, 1939, **36**, 59–103.

Kennedy, J. L. An evaluation of extra-sensory perception. *Proceedings of American Philosophical Society*, 1952, **96**, 513–518.

Kennedy, J. L., & Uphoff, H. F. Experiments on the nature of extrasensory perception. III. The recording error criticism of extra-chance scores. *Journal of Parapsychology*, 1939, **3**, 226–245.

Marks, D., & Kammann, R. The nonpsychic powers of Uri Geller. *The Zetetic*, 1977, **1**, No. 1, 9–17.

Marrocco, M. Special report. *AAAS Bulletin,* June 1974, **19,** No. 2, 16.

McConnell, R. A., & Forwald, H. Psychokinetic placement. I. A re-examination of the Forwald Durham experiment. *Journal of Parapsychology,* 1967, **31,** 51–69. (a)

McConnell, R. A., & Forwald, H. Psychokinetic placement. II. Factorial analysis of successful and unsuccessful series. *Journal of Parapsychology,* 1967, **31,** 198–213. (b)

McConnell, R. A., Snowdon, R. J., & Powell, K. F. Wishing with dice. *Journal of Experimental Psychology,* 1955, **50,** 269–275.

Medhurst, R. G., & Scott, C. A re-examination of C. E. M. Hansel's criticism of the Pratt–Woodruff experiment. *Journal of Parapsychology,* 1974, **38,** 163–184.

Meehl, P. E., & Scriven, M. Compatibility of science and ESP. *Science,* 1956, **123,** 14–15.

Murchison, C. (Ed.). *The case for and against psychical belief.* Worcester, Massachusetts: Clark Univ., 1927.

Murphy, G. Report of the research committee. *Journal of American Society for Psychical Research,* 1952, **46,** 71–72.

Murphy, G. Report on paper by Edward Girden on psychokinesis. *Psychological Bulletin,* 1962, **59,** 520–528.

Murphy, G., & Dale, L. A. *Challenge of psychical research.* New York: Harper, 1961.

Nicol, J. F. Keeping up with the Joneses. (Review of *The mind readers* by S. G. Soal & H. T. Bowden.) *Tomorrow Magazine,* 1961, **1,** 58–66.

Nicol, J. F. Historical background. In B. B. Wolman (Ed.), *Handbook of parapsychology,* New York: Van Nostrand Reinhold, 1977.

Parsons, D. Experiments on PK with inclined plane and rotating cage. *Proceedings of the Society for Psychical Research,* 1945, **47,** 296–300.

Pearson, K. Deviations from the probable in a correlated system of variables. *Philosophical Magazine,* 1900, **50,** 157–175.

Physicality and psi. A symposium and forum discussion. *Journal of Parapsychology,* 1961, **25,** 13–31.

A PK experiment at Yale starts a controversy. *Journal of American Society for Psychical Research,* 1952, **46,** 111–117.

Pratt, J. G. *Research today: A study of developments in parapsychology since 1960.* Metuchen, New Jersey: Scarecrow Press, 1973.

Pratt, J. G., & Forwald, H. Confirmation of the PK placement effect. *Journal of Parapsychology,* 1958, **22,** 1–19.

Pratt, J. G., Rhine, J. B., Smith, B. M., Stuart, C. E., & Greenwood, J. A. *Extra-sensory perception after sixty years.* New York: Holt, 1940.

Price, G. R. Science and the supernatural. *Science,* 1955, **122,** 359–367.

Randi, The Amazing. *The magic of Uri Geller.* New York: Ballantine Books, 1975.

Rhine, J. B. *Extra-sensory perception.* Boston: Bruce Humphreys, 1934.

Rhine, J. B. *New frontiers of the mind.* New York: Farrar and Rinehart, 1937.

Rhine, J. B. Security versus deception in parapsychology. *Journal of Parapsychology,* 1974, **38,** 99–121. (a)

Rhine, J. B. A new case of experimenter unreliability. *Journal of Parapsychology,* 1974, **38,** 215–225. (b)

Rhine, J. B. Psi methods reexamined. *Journal of Parapsychology,* 1975, **39,** 38–58.

Rhine, J. B., & Pratt, J. G. *Parapsychology: Frontier science of the mind.* Springfield, Illinois: Thomas, 1957.

Rinn, J. F. *Sixty years of psychical research.* New York: The Truth Seeker Co., 1950.

Rosenthal, R. *Experimenter effects in behavioral research.* New York: Appleton, 1966.

Scarne, J. *Amazing world of John Scarne.* New York: Crown, 1956.

Schmeidler, G. R., & McConnell, R. A. *ESP and personality patterns.* New Haven: Yale Univ. Press, 1958.

Scott, C., & Goldney, K. M. The Jones boys and the ultrasonic whistle. *Journal of the Society for Psychical Research,* 1960, **40,** 249–260.

Scott, C., & Haskell, P. Fresh light on the Shackelton experiments? *Proceedings of the Society for Psychical Research,* 1974, **56,** 43–72.

Sidgwick, H. President's address. *Proceedings of Society for Psychical Research,* 1882, **1,** 7–12.

Sidgwick, H. Mrs. President's Address. *Proceedings of Society for Psychical Research,* 1908, **22,** 1–18.

Soal, S. G. *The experimental situation in psychical research.* London: Society for Psychical Research, 1947.

Soal, S. G., & Bateman, F. *Modern experiments in telepathy.* (2nd ed.) New Haven: Yale Univ. Press, 1954.

Soal, S. G., & Bowden, H. T. *The mind readers.* London: Faber and Faber, 1959.

Stanford, Rex G. Experimental psychokinesis: a review from diverse perspectives. In B. B. Wolman (Ed.), *Handbook of parapsychology,* New York: Van Nostrand Reinhold, 1977.

Stevens, S. S. The predicament in design and significance. (Review of *Statistical theory* by L. Hogben.) *Contemporary Psychology,* 1960, **5,** 273–276.

Targ, R., Cole, P., & Puthoff, H. *Development of techniques to enhance man/machine communication.* Menlo Park, California: Stanford Research Institute, 1974.

Targ, R., & Puthoff, H. Information under conditions of sensory shielding. *Nature,* 1974, **251,** 602–607.

Targ, R., & Puthoff, H. A perceptual channel for information transfer over kilometer distances: Historical perspective and recent research. *Proceedings of the Institute of Electrical and Electronic Engineers,* 1976, **64,** 329–354.

Thouless, R. H. *From anecdote to experiment in psychical research.* London: Routledge & Kegan Paul, 1972.

Tobias, A. Okay, he averted World War III, but can he bend a nail? *New York,* September 10, 1973, **6,** 39–43.

West, D. J. *Psychical research today.* London: Duckworth, 1954.

Windholtz, G., & Diamant, L. Some personality traits of believers in extraordinary phenomena. *Bulletin Psychonomic Society,* 1974, **3,** 125–126.

Wolfle, D. L. A review of the work on extrasensory perception. *American Journal of Psychiatry,* 1938, **94,** 943–955.

Wolstenholme, G. E. W., & Millar, E. C. P. (Eds.) *Ciba Foundation symposium on extrasensory perception.* Boston: Little, Brown, 1956.

AUTHOR INDEX

Numbers in italics refer to the pages on which the complete references are listed.

Doehring, D. G., 52, 53, *60*
Dolan, J. A., 291, *302*
Dolezal, H., 100, *105*
Doob, A. N., 215, *221*
Dorfman, D., 249, *253*
Doty, R. L., 310, 316, *345*
Dowling, W. J., 193, 196, 198, 199, 202, 203, 206, *220*
Down, R. M., 171, *188*
Dravnieks, A. L., 310, 316, 330, 333, 338, 343, *345,* 374, *381*
Dressler, F. B., 100, *105*
Drexler, M., 336, 342, *345*
Driscoll, J. L., 373, *380*
Drobisch, M. W., 193, *220*
Duffy, W. J., 364, *380*
Dumas, A., 370, *381*
Duncan, H. F., 24, *37*
Duncker, K., 269, *299,* 358, *381*
DuPlessis, C. F., 24, *37*
Duran, P., 70, *87*
Durgant, R., 291, *299*
Dutoit, B. M., 21, *37*
Dyk, R. B., 32, *39*
Dytell, R. S., 46, 52, *63*

E

Easton, A. M., 269, *299*
Eaves, L., 75, *87*
Ebenholtz, S., 266, *303*
Ebert, P. C., 27, *37*
Efron, R., 217, *220*
Eichelman, W. H., 287, *302*
Eisenstein, S. M., 285, 288, 289, *299*
Ekman, G., 311, *345*
Elkind, D., 45, *60*
Ellenberger, R. L., 56, *61*
Elliott, H. B., 238, *254,* 262, 300
Emmons, L., 358, *381*
Emond, T., 146, *151*
Engelman, S., 55, *60*
Engen, T., 309, 310, 311, 312, 313, 315, *345*
Enoch, J. M., 261, *299*
Eppright, E. S., 356, *381*
Erber, N. P., 55, 58, 59, *60, 61*
Erickson, R., 203, *220*
Erikson, C. W., 263, 265, *299*
Evans, E. F., 193, *220*
Ewart, A. G., 75, *87*
Ewing, A. W. G., 94, *105*
Ewing, I. R., 94, *105*

Eysenck, H. J., 117, 118, 120, *129, 130,* 147, *151,* 248, *253,* 400, 410

F

Fairbairn, W. R. D., 127, *129*
Fallon, P., 282, *301*
Farber, J., 237, 238, *253, 257*
Farmer, R. M., 204, *224*
Farnsworth, P. R., 116, *129,* 214, *220*
Faterson, H. F., 32, *39*
Faw, T. T., 250, *253,* 294, *299*
Fechner, G. T., 112, 118, 129, 246, *253*
Feinstein, S. H., 68, *89,* 101, *106*
Feroe, J., 209, 210, *220*
Festinger, L., 100, *105, 269, 277*
Findahl, O., 260, *299*
Fischer, R., 250, *253*
Fish, R. M., 80, *87*
Fisher, B., 95, *105*
Fisher, G. H., 67, 79, *87*
Fisher, J. D., 113, *129*
Fiske, D. W., 123, *129*
Fitch, J. L., 47, *61*
Flesh, R. D., 326, 327, *345*
Flew, A., 390, 393, *410*
Florian, V. A., 45, 56, 59, *61, 62*
Foard, C. F., 214, *219*
Foley, J. E., 99, *105*
Forwald, H., 392, *411*
Fosdick, J. A., *303*
Foster, D., 313, 314, *345, 346*
Foulke, E., 70, 71, 72, 73, *87, 88*
Fox, N., 98, *106*
Fraisse, P., 204, *220*
Francès, R., 112, 120, 121, 124, *129,* 195, 211, *220*
Franklin, S., *188*
Frankmann, J. P., 95, 96, *106*
Fransson, F., 212, *220*
Frazer, James, G., 408, 409, *410*
Freeman, R. B., Jr., 22, *38*
Freides, D., 53, *61*
Friedman, F., 66, 75, 77, *90*
Friedman, H. H., 377, *382*
Friedman, L. A., 57, *61*
Friedman, M. P., 209, *219*
Frost, R., 235, *251*
Fucks, W., 203, *220*
Fujitani, D. S., 196, *220*
Furth, H. G., 47, *61*
Futer, D. S., 216, *221*

SUBJECT INDEX

HANDBOOK OF PERCEPTION

EDITORS: *Edward C. Carterette and Morton P. Friedman*

Department of Psychology
University of California, Los Angeles
Los Angeles, California

Volume I: Historical and Philosophical Roots of Perception. 1974

Volume II: Psychophysical Judgment and Measurement. 1974

Volume III: Biology of Perceptual Systems. 1973

Volume IV: Hearing. 1978

Volume V: Seeing. 1975

Volume VIA: Tasting and Smelling. 1978

Volume VIB: Feeling and Hurting. 1978

Volume VII: Language and Speech. 1976

Volume VIII: Perceptual Coding. 1978

Volume IX: Perceptual Processing. 1978

Volume X: Perceptual Ecology. 1978

· · · · ·

CONTENTS OF OTHER VOLUMES